THE PREPARE CURRICULUM

Teaching Prosocial Competencies

Arnold P. Goldstein

Research Press · 2612 North Mattis Avenue · Champaign, Illinois 61821

Advisory Editor, Frederick H. Kanfer

To Lenore,

Whose gentle footprints multiply
as the years roll by

Contents

Figures and Tables

Figures

Tables

Acknowledgments

I view The Prepare Curriculum as the culmination of research on prosocial training that I first became involved with in the late 1960s. How does one adequately acknowledge the contributions from a wealth of students and colleagues to 20 years of work? *Wealth* is the correct term, for in these efforts I have been most fortunate to have a rich variety of bright, energetic, and committed co-workers. I cannot name them all because I speak here of literally dozens of thesis and dissertation advisees and many colleagues within my university, from other universities, and in the schools and clinical settings in which our program development and evaluation efforts took place. All I can do is say thank you, acknowledge how much one learns from one's students, and point out how much inspiration one can gather from the front-line people who daily seek to enhance the lives of troubled adolescents and children. Indeed, I thank you all.

But my most special acknowledgment, my most appreciative thank you, is for my wife Lenore, now deceased. Besides her great love and companionship, she brought to our marriage a deep sense of concern for others, an unshakable fairness in her own human relations, and an acuteness of sensitivity to the feelings and needs of those around her that daily served as both inspiration and guidance to me in the prosocial journey of my work life. She was a most remarkable woman. My name appears alone as the writer of this book, but she most thoroughly was its spiritual co-author.

A. P. G.

Chapter 1

Introduction

The Prepare Curriculum is a series of coordinated psychoeducational courses explicitly designed to teach an array of prosocial, psychological competencies to adolescents and younger children who are demonstrably deficient in such competencies. It seeks to teach interpersonal skills to aggressive, antisocial youth as well as to those who are withdrawn and socially isolated. It seeks to teach empathy to the insensitive, cooperativeness to the uncooperative, problem solving to the inadequate, negotiating skill to the acting-out, anger control to the impulsive, allocentrism to the egocentric, group processes to the isolated, stress management to the anxious, social perceptiveness to the socially confused, and more. It is an ambitious curriculum yet one that already rests on at least a beginning foundation of demonstrated effectiveness. We wish in this introductory chapter to specify in greater depth the types of youngsters for whom the Prepare Curriculum is designed, share a sense of its underlying history, and introduce both the courses themselves as well as considerations associated with their delivery.

The Prepare Curriculum Trainee

Prepare is designed for youth who are deficient in prosocial competencies. They may be described by what they rarely do (e.g., show interpersonal skills, anger control, high levels of moral reasoning, empathy, and so forth). Or, more usefully, they may be described by the behaviors they do regularly display. The adolescent or younger child for whom Prepare is appropriate is, first of all, a youngster demonstrating prosocial deficiencies that fall toward either end of a continuum defined at one extreme by chronic aggressiveness, antisocial behavior, and even juvenile delinquency and at the other extreme by chronic withdrawal, asocial behavior, and social isolation. More modal youth, showing only moderate—not chronic—aggressiveness or withdrawal, are also viable candidates for Prepare. In the sense of secondary prevention, Prepare participation for such trainees holds potential for thwarting the development of more extreme levels of antisocial or asocial behavior. Finally, the Prepare Curriculum may also be used with youth displaying neither type of difficulty as tertiary prevention to facilitate the development of their personal competence. We will focus this discussion on the extremes of our potential continuum of trainees because it is mostly the aggressive or withdrawn youngster on whom our curriculum development and evaluation efforts have focused thus far.

The Aggressive Trainee

It has been convincingly demonstrated during the past decade that aggressive behavior is *learned* behavior. Though the belief in instinct, not learning, as the primary source of human aggression dies hard, evidence to the contrary is overwhelming (Bandura, 1973; Goldstein, 1983). Not only is aggression primarily learned, but the manner in which such acquisition occurs has been shown in an extended series of social learning investigations to be no different from how all other behaviors—both antisocial and prosocial—are also learned. Thus manipulativeness, cheating, teasing, and bullying, as well as altruism, cooperation, sharing and empathy—and aggression—appear to be learned largely by means of either observational, vicarious experiences (e.g., seeing others perform the behavior and receive reward for doing so) or direct experiences (e.g., enacting the behavior oneself and receiving reward for doing so).

Chronically aggressive youngsters are characteristically individuals with a life history in which, from their early years on, aggression was frequently used, and used successfully, by family, peers, media figures, and others constituting the youth's real-world environment. Such aggression by others, increasingly learned and used by the youth, is very often richly, reliably, and immediately rewarded. It works; it pays off; it is reinforced—thus making it behavior that is quite difficult to change. The fact that such youth are often markedly deficient in alternative prosocial behaviors (i.e., in achieving life satisfactions and effectiveness via prosocial rather than antisocial routes) makes their chronic aggressiveness all the more difficult to change.

And prosocially deficient they are. A substantial body of literature has directly demonstrated that chronically aggressive youngsters display widespread interpersonal, planning, aggression management, and other prosocial skill deficiencies. Freedman, Rosenthal, Donahoe, Schlundt, and McFall (1978) examined the comparative skill competence levels of a group of such adolescents and a matched group (age, IQ, social background) of nonaggressive youth in response to a series of standardized role-play situations. The aggressive adolescent sample responded in a consistently less skillful manner. Spence (1981) constituted comparable adolescent offender and nonoffender samples and videotaped their individual interviews with a previously unknown adult. The offender group evidenced significantly fewer instances of eye contact, appropriate head movements, and speech, as well as significantly more fiddling and gross body movement. Conger, Miller, and Walsmith (1975) added further to this picture of skill deficiency. They concluded from their evidence that juvenile delinquents, as compared to nondelinquent cohorts,

> had more difficulty in getting along with peers, both in individual one-to-one contacts and in group situations, and were less willing or able to treat others courteously and tactfully, and less able to be fair in dealing with them. In return, they were less well liked and accepted by their peers. (p. 442)

Patterson, Reid, Jones, and Conger (1975), also studying chronically aggressive youngsters, observed the following:

> The socialization process appears to be severely impeded for many aggressive youngsters. Their behavioral adjustments are often immature and they do not seem to have learned the key social skills necessary for initiating and maintaining positive social relationships with others. Peer groups often reject, avoid, and/or punish aggressive children, thereby excluding them from positive learning experiences with others. (p. 4)

As Patterson et al. (1975) appear to be proposing, the discrepancy in social competence between aggressive youngsters and their nonaggressive peers has early childhood roots. This suggestion has found support in evidence provided by Mussen, Conger, Kagan, and Gerwitz (1979). Boys in their longitudinal study who later became delinquent were appraised by their teachers as less well adjusted socially than their classmates as early as third grade. Those who would become delinquent appeared less friendly, responsible, or fair in dealing with others and more impulsive and antagonistic toward authority. Poor peer relations (being less friendly toward classmates and less well liked by peers) were further developmental predictors of later delinquency. Thus it may be safely concluded that prosocial skill deficiencies of diverse—especially interpersonal—types characterize both the early development and adolescent behavior of delinquent and aggressive youngsters to a degree that significantly differentiates them from their nondelinquent, nonaggressive peers.

The Withdrawn Trainee

Prosocially deficient youth may manifest their lack of competence in ways quite opposite to those employed by the aggressive youngster. Such children or adolescents—often described as withdrawn, isolated, rejected, unpopular, or shy—are the youngsters who play alone, who are selected last if at all in games, whom no one wishes to sit next to on the schoolbus, who appear to be overinvolved in fantasy activities, and who frequently are ignored or forgotten by harried teachers forced to be responsive in their classes to the noisier, more overtly demanding youth whose prosocial deficiencies are manifest in the aggressive, acting-out behaviors described earlier. Withdrawn social behaviors may feed on themselves, as it were, and spiral to longer term prosocial deficiencies (Roff, Sell, & Golden, 1972; Whitman, Mercurio, & Caponigri, 1970). Oden (1980) observes in this regard that

> it is often believed that a child will "outgrow" isolation or rejection from peers . . . Meanwhile, compared to other children, these children are likely to become increasingly excluded from positive or friendly interactions and relationships with peers and, thereby, they are excluded from important social learning. Ultimately, due to reputational factors and limitation in social ability, the child's experiences with peers may be constrained to a cyclical pattern of peer rejection or isolation. A few longitudinal studies have found that social isolation or problematic peer relationships in childhood are predictors of social and emotional adjustment problems in young adulthood. (p. 180)

Although the majority of our curriculum implementation and evaluation efforts have been directed toward the aggressive end of the continuum of potential trainees, we wish to underscore the relevance of prosocial competency training for the equally needy withdrawn and rejected youngster.

History of the Prepare Curriculum

Until the early 1970s, there existed primarily three major clusters of psychological and psychotherapeutic interventions designed to alter the behavior of aggressive, withdrawn, ineffective, or disturbed individuals: psychodynamic/psychoanalytic, humanistic/client-centered, and behavior modification. Each of these diverse orientations found concrete expression in individual and group approaches targeted to aggressive and, to a lesser extent, withdrawn adolescents and younger children. The psychodynamic approach involved psychoanalytically oriented individual psychotherapy (Guttman, 1970), activity group therapy

(Slavson, 1964), and the varied array of treatment procedures developed by Redl and Wineman (1957). The humanistic/client-centered approach found expression in applications with juvenile delinquents (e.g., Truax, Wargo, & Silber, 1966) of the client-centered psychotherapy of Carl Rogers (1957), the therapeutic community applications of Jones (1953), Guided Group Interaction (McCorkle, Elias, & Bixby, 1958) the Positive Peer Culture (Vorrath & Brendtro, 1974), and the school discipline approach of Dreikurs, Grunwald, and Pepper (1971). Behavior modification involved a wide variety of interventions reflecting the systematic use of contingency management, contracting, and the training of teachers and parents as behavior change managers (O'Leary, O'Leary, & Becker, 1967; Reid & Patterson, 1976; Walker, 1979). Though each of these intervention philosophies differed from the others in several major respects, a significant commonality was the shared assumption that the youngster had somewhere within, as yet unexpressed, the effective, satisfying, nonaggressive, or prosocial behaviors whose expression was among the goals of the intervention. Such latent potentials, in all three approaches, would be realized by the client if the change agent were sufficiently skilled in reducing or removing obstacles to such realization. The psychodynamicist sought to do so in discussion or play activities by calling forth and interpreting unconscious material blocking progress-relevant awareness. The humanistic/client-centered change agent, who in particular believed that the potential for change resides within the client, sought to free this potential by providing a warm, empathic, maximally accepting helping environment. And the behavior modifier, by means of one or more contingency management procedures, attempted to see to it that when the latent desirable behaviors or approximations thereto did occur, the client received appropriate contingent reinforcement, thus increasing the probability that these behaviors would reoccur. Therefore, whether sought by means of interpretation or therapeutic climate, or by offering contingent reward, all three approaches assumed that somewhere within the individual's repertoire resided the desired, effective, sought-after goal behaviors.

In the early 1970s, an important new intervention approach began to emerge, an approach resting upon rather different assumptions: psychological skills training. Viewing the helpee more in educational, pedogogic terms than as a client in need of counseling or psychotherapy, the psychological skills trainer assumed that the individual was lacking, deficient, or at best weak in the skills necessary for effective and satisfying personal and interpersonal functioning. The task of the skills trainer became, therefore, not interpretation, reflection, or reinforcement, but the active and deliberate teaching of desirable behaviors. Rather than an intervention called *psychotherapy,* between a patient and a psychotherapist, or *counseling,* between a client and a counselor, what emerged was *training,* between a trainee and a psychological skills trainer.

The roots of the psychological skills training movement lay within both education and psychology. The notion of seeking to teach desirable behaviors has often, if sporadically, been a significant goal of the American educational establishment. The Character Education Movement of the 1920s and more contemporary moral education and values clarification programs are but a few possible examples. In addition to the interest in skills training exhibited in the schools, numerous interpersonal and planning skills courses are taught in America's over 2,000 community colleges, and hundreds of self-help books focusing on similar skill-enhancement goals are available. Clearly, the formal and informal educational establishment in America has provided the fertile soil and the stimulation necessary for the psychological skills training movement to grow.

Much the same can be said for American psychology, as it too has laid the groundwork in its prevailing philosophy and specific interests for the development of this new movement. The learning process has, above all else, been the central theoretical and investigative concern of American psychology since the late nineteenth century. This focal interest also assumed major therapeutic form in the 1950s, as psychotherapy practitioners and researchers alike came to view psychotherapeutic treatment more and more in learning terms. The very healthy and still-expanding field of behavior modification grew from this joint learning-clinical focus and may be appropriately viewed as the immediately preceding context in which psychological skills training came to be developed. In companion with the growth of behavior modification, psychological thinking increasingly shifted from a strict emphasis on remediation to one that was equally concerned with prevention, and the bases for this shift included movement away from a medical model concept toward what may most aptly be called a psychoeducational theoretical stance. Both of these thrusts—heightened concern with prevention and a psychoeducational perspective—gave strong added impetus to the viability of the psychological skills training movement.

Perhaps psychology's most direct contribution to psychological skills training came from social learning theory, and in particular from the work conducted and stimulated by Albert Bandura. Basing his remarks upon the same broad array of modeling, behavioral rehearsal, and social reinforcement investigations that helped stimulate and direct the development of our own approach to skill training, Bandura (1973) comments as follows:

> The method that has yielded the most impressive results with diverse problems contains three major components. First, alternative modes of response are repeatedly modeled, preferably by several people who demonstrate how the new style of behavior can be used in dealing with a variety of... situations. Second, learners are provided with necessary guidance and ample opportunities to practice the modeled behavior under favorable conditions until they perform it skillfully and spontaneously. The latter procedures are ideally suited for developing new social skills, but they are unlikely to be adopted unless they produce rewarding consequences. Arrangement of success experiences particularly for initial efforts at behaving differently, constitute the third component in this powerful composite method.... Given adequate demonstration, guided practice, and success experiences, this method is almost certain to produce favorable results. (p. 253)

Other events of the 1970s provided still further stimulation for the growth of the skills training movement. The inadequacy of prompting, shaping, and related operant procedures for adding *new* behaviors to individuals' behavioral repertoires was increasingly apparent. The widespread reliance upon deinstitutionalization that lay at the heart of the community mental health movement resulted in the discharge from America's public mental hospitals of approximately 400,000 persons, the majority of whom were substantially deficient in important daily functioning skills. And, especially to us, it had grown particularly clear that what the American mental health movement had available to offer clients from lower socioeconomic levels was grossly inadequate in meeting their psychotherapeutic needs. These factors (i.e., relevant supportive research, the incompleteness of operant approaches, large populations of grossly skill-deficient individuals, and the paucity of useful interventions for large segments of American society), all in the context of historically supportive roots in both education and psychology, came together in the thinking of several researchers and practitioners as demanding a new intervention, something prescriptively responsive to these needs. Psychological skills training was the answer, and a movement was launched.

Our involvement in this movement, a psychological skill training approach we initially termed *Structured Learning,* began in the early

1970s, (Goldstein, 1973; Goldstein, Sprafkin, & Gershaw, 1976). At that time, and for several years thereafter, our studies were conducted in public mental hospitals with long-term, highly skill-deficient, chronic patients, especially those preparing for deinstitutionalization into the community. As our research program progressed and demonstrated with regularity successful skill enhancement effects (Goldstein, 1981), we shifted in our focus from teaching a broad array of interpersonal and daily living skills to adult psychiatric inpatients to a more explicit concern with skills training for aggressive individuals. Our trainee groups included spouses engaged in family disputes violent enough to warrant police intervention (Goldstein, Monti, Sardino, & Green, 1979; Goldstein & Rosenbaum, 1982), child-abusing parents (Goldstein, Keller, & Erne, 1985; Solomon, 1977; Sturm, 1980), and, most especially, overtly aggressive adolescents (Goldstein, Sherman, Gershaw, Sprafkin, & Glick, 1978; Goldstein, Sprafkin, Gershaw, & Klein, 1980). As our implementation and evaluation of psychological skills training with adolescents continued (Goldstein & Pentz, 1984) and was extended to younger children (Keller, Goldstein, & Wynn, 1987; McGinnis & Goldstein, 1984), we renamed our approach, calling it *Skillstreaming*, and, encouraged by our outcome results, began considering its broad extension to other domains of prosocial competency enhancement. Chapter 3 of this book, which presents the Prepare course on Interpersonal Skills Training, describes the current extension of our earlier Skillstreaming work. Several of the other course chapters are our extension of this work to new areas of prosocial competency.

The 10 course-length interventions that constitute the Prepare Curriculum derived in both content and their diverse format from four broad sources. The first is our own experiences as trainers, investigators, and citizens concerned with youth and their life satisfaction and effectiveness. The second is the perceptions, impressions, and speculations of the many trainers and graduate students who have been the creative workers in our efforts during the past two decades. The third is the relevant theoretical, research, and experiential literature, in both psychology and education, and, fourth and finally, the youth themselves. We have tried to listen carefully and openly to what these, our "consumers," have had to say and learn when we could from their wisdom.

The Plan of This Book

We present first the 10 Prepare Curriculum courses. Their use in any given setting and with any particular youngster will necessarily be responsive to demand qualities of the setting and prescriptive qualities of the trainees. Thus we recommend no fixed course sequence but instead suggest a variable arrangement to be determined largely by the prosocial deficiencies of the participating trainees. This recommendation notwithstanding, we still wish to suggest certain sequences and subgroupings of courses. Problem-solving Training (chapter 2) is presented first for its value not only as a skill per se but also for its usefulness as an organizer of decisions about which of the other course contents to select from and employ. Interpersonal Skills Training (chapter 3) is next, presented at this early point both for its demonstrated usefulness in a great variety of life settings and for its relationship to the course we subsequently consider. Situational Perception Training (chapter 4) is an important companion of Interpersonal Skills Training and must, we feel, accompany or closely follow it. Interpersonal skill deficiencies occur because the youth does not know the skill and thus must be taught it (chapter 3), or does know it but is not competent in diagnosing when, where, and with whom to use it. Situational Perception Training teaches such diagnostic skills. Thus one useful sequence or subgrouping of Prepare courses is Problem-solving Training, Interpersonal Skills Training, and Situational Perception Training.

Anger Control Training (chapter 5) and Moral Reasoning Training (chapter 6) follow next. These two courses, in combination with Interpersonal Skills Training, were employed by our research group in a series of programs designed to alter the behavior of incarcerated and paroled juvenile delinquents. Evaluations of these programs revealed outcomes including enhanced interpersonal skillfulness, diminished aggression, and improved community functioning (Goldstein & Glick, 1987). We therefore recommend that this triad of courses be offered together.

Stress Management Training (chapter 7) and Empathy Training (chapter 8) seek to provide the Prepare trainee with vital skills relevant to, respectively, the trainee's own emotional world and that of others. These two courses seem to us to be especially valuable in their own right, to bear importantly on facilitation of all other Prepare courses, and to be prerequisite to the final three components of the curriculum.

Recruiting Supportive Models (chapter 9) offers a means of teaching youth how to identify, seek out, and establish and maintain relationships with prosocially oriented adult or peer models. It is a course explicitly responsive to the research finding that having at least one such model differentiates youth from very difficult environments who survive and thrive as they develop from those who, in a sense, succumb and turn toward disturbed, antisocial, or asocial lives. It is also a course, it should be noted, whose contents rely heavily on the lessons of Interpersonal Skills Training. Cooperation Training (chapter 10) and Understanding and Using Groups (chapter 11) complete the Prepare Curriculum. Both courses rely heavily for their enactment on games, simulations, and group activities, all of which often have special motivational appeal to the action-oriented youth who constitute a significant portion of the Prepare Curriculum's target trainees.

We have briefly introduced the 10 Prepare courses and have offered beginning suggestions for their grouping and sequencing. But curriculum delivery consists of much more than course coordination. In chapter 12, we present an extended series of techniques designed to maximize the likelihood that the prosocial lessons learned in the Prepare courses will be used by the trainee in new settings (transfer) and enduringly over time (maintenance).

Effective delivery of the Prepare Curriculum is more than a matter of interesting course contents and attempts to enhance transfer and maintenance of performance. It also requires competent trainers, who are not only interested in youth development and curricular contents but who also have effective skills in managing what at times (perhaps oftentimes) will be a difficult classroom environment. Prepare does focus on moderately to severely aggressive and withdrawn youth, whose disturbing and disturbed behaviors will, with varying frequency, manifest themselves during course delivery. Thus the Prepare trainer must be readily able to reduce disruption and maintain on-task trainee behavior. Chapter 13 offers a detailed presentation of behavioral techniques of demonstrated value for classroom management.

In the book's final chapter, which suggests future directions that may be profitably followed by those interested in the further development of the Prepare Curriculum, we address several issues: the enhancement of trainee motivation; curriculum evaluation and the assessment of competence; curriculum utilization for both remedial and preventive purposes; curriculum enhancement in the context of the broader family, school, and community system in which Prepare training goes forward; and curriculum expansion, in which we consider additional prosocial course domains that might be added to the current Prepare Curriculum.

Chapter 2

Problem-solving Training

The development of high levels of competence in problem solving is an especially central goal of the Prepare Curriculum. Problem-solving ability is, first of all, an immensely important set of skills in its own right. Youngsters are faced daily with conflict, confusion, difficult choices, and a wide variety of other problematic situations. To have an operational means or scheme in place to apply to such diverse challenges will often prove to be of great value in problem resolution. But problem solving also appears early in the proposed sequence of interventions that constitutes this curriculum because of its considerable relevance to the successful application of all other Prepare courses.

As will be described in detail, problem-solving ability typically is defined as a stepwise sequence of problem definition, identification of alternative solutions, choice of one solution as probably optimal, implementation of this chosen resolution, and evaluation of the solution's effectiveness. This sequence of problem-solving steps, as the remainder of this book makes clear, may be advantageously employed in making judicious decisions about the use of all other Prepare courses—for example, in deciding which skills to use in Interpersonal Skills Training (chapter 3); in choosing appropriate contexts in Situational Perception Training (chapter 4); in matching arousal reduction techniques to particular provocations in Anger Control Training (chapter 5); in evaluating alternative solutions to dilemmas posed in Moral Reasoning Training (chapter 6); in determining which stress reduction techniques to employ and where, when, and how long to employ them in Stress Management Training (chapter 7); in solving the many problems of leadership, clique formation, peer pressure, and power tactics described in Understanding and Using Groups (chapter 11); and so on for the other components of the Prepare Curriculum. In short, problem solving should be viewed in the context of this curriculum as both skill and meta-skill. Its importance in both regards is especially substantial.

Theory and Research

This chapter will examine two general types of problem-solving training. The first focuses explicitly upon *interpersonal problem solving*. Our concern will be how individuals faced with problematic events involving a peer, parent, sibling, teacher, boss, or other person may be effectively trained to engage in competent problem solving. Our second major focus will be upon a body of applied literature best described as *impersonal problem solving*. Here the concern is not avoiding or resolving person-to-person hostilities or learning means for working through other problematic interpersonal events. Instead, impersonal problem solving is more concerned with cognitive events, with solving rational—usually nonemotional—problems, and with fostering creativity and originality. Whereas interpersonal problem solving is largely the concern of the mental health specialist, counselor, or special educator, impersonal problem solving has traditionally been the domain of the academician, the industrial consultant, and the experimental psychologist. As is illustrated in detail later in this chapter, our own training and research philosophy is in part extrapolatory. In other words, we will propose that the procedures, techniques, and materials at the core of impersonal problem solving have, by extrapolation, real and substantial implications for improving the effectiveness of interpersonal problem solving. We now turn, however, to our first concern: direct training in interpersonal problem solving.

Interpersonal Problem Solving

The notion that problem-solving ability might be among the factors that contribute to the quality of an individual's psychological adjustment and use of prosocial versus antisocial behavior is both relatively recent and not frequently advanced. Jahoda (1953, 1958) was an early advocate of this view, and we see a similar position in Weinstein's (1969) focus on the development of interpersonal competence and in the delineation of stages in the problem-solving process described by D'Zurilla and Goldfried (1971). In the context of the Prepare Curriculum, the general stance is that inadequate problem-solving skills in the interpersonal and personal spheres of functioning result in too frequent reliance on socially unacceptable and nonenduring solutions to real-life difficulties, especially solutions of an "acting-out" nature. This viewpoint directly parallels our position regarding Interpersonal Skills Training (chapter 3), in which it is assumed that skilled interpersonal behaviors can successfully be taught as viable substitutes for aggression, even in situations in which aggression—at least on a short-term basis—pays off. With regard to problem-solving skills, in lieu of hitting, grabbing, insulting, pushing, threatening, or other aggressive behavioral solutions to provocative interpersonal problems, individuals can learn the cognitive, reasoning, and delaying skills necessary to reach satisfying, constructive, nonaggressive solutions. The remainder of this section will examine the specific attempts made thus far to train people in such problem-solving skills. In doing so, we describe a number of modest preliminary attempts at such training and offer an in-depth examination of the one effort in this domain that has already yielded a comprehensive training program. The chapter concludes with a description of our own recent attempt to create a systematic problem-solving training sequence that builds upon and goes beyond this earlier approach.

Pilot Training Programs

Early training efforts aimed at enhancing problem-solving skills were initiated by Holzworth (1964) and Giebink, Stover, and Fahl (1968). By using game-like and other instructional materials, these investigators sought to teach impulsive children adaptive means for handling frustrating situations. Despite the small sample sizes in these studies, each investigation produced suggestively positive results. Tentatively positive findings were also observed in beginning research efforts to teach problem-solving skills to alcoholic patients (Intagliata, 1976) and to hospitalized psychiatric patients (Coche & Flick, 1975). Branca, D'Augelli, and Evans (1975) provided similarly encouraging early results for their training program in decision-making skills for preadolescents. As is the case for most of the programs examined in this chapter, the focus is upon teaching the *process* of decision making or problem solving and not upon the rightness or wrongness of any particular decision or problem solution. As is also true of several other programs, the decision-making process is segmented and viewed as a phased process involving problem definition, identification of alternative solutions, and evaluation of a trial solution. In a similar program named Thresholds (Burglass & Duffy, 1974), trainers sought to teach a problem-solving process whose sequential steps involved (1) defining the situation, (2) expanding possibilities, (3) evaluating possibilities, (4) establishing decisional criteria, (5) making a decision, (6) acting on the decision, and (7) ratifying the decision.

Whereas Branca et al. (1975) and Burglass and Duffy (1974) have implemented their training efforts via an array of didactic, discussional, and simulation activities, Blechman (1974) has taught problem-solving skills in the context of a game format. Her Family Contract Game is designed for use by family units experiencing marked conflict and inability to deal successfully with the interpersonal problems that involve them. The game is structured to circumvent or minimize the conflicting behaviors that usually characterize the interaction patterns of the participating families: complaining, criticizing, interrupting, being unresponsive, and so forth. Again following a stage model, game participation seeks to teach (1) definition of the problem, (2) collection of relevant information, (3) examination of alternatives, (4) selection of a course of action, and (5) evaluation of consequences.

In a seminal article, D'Zurilla and Goldfried (1971) explored the manner in which an array of behavior modification approaches, especially those concerned with self-control, might constitute an effective clinical reflection of experimental psychology's efforts in the problem-solving arena. They describe separate behavior therapy procedures for teaching what they view as the essential stages of effective problem solving: (1) general orientation, (2) problem definition, (3) generation of alternatives, (4) decision making, and (5) verification. Goldfried and Davison (1976) have described actual clinical applications of these suggested problem-solving methods, and a few investigators have begun to conduct the evaluation research necessary to test the actual efficacy of these applications (Asarnow & Callan, 1985; Elardo & Caldwell, 1979; Marsh, 1982; Ross & Ross, 1973; Stone, Hinds, & Schmidt, 1975; Wagner, Breitmeyer, & Bottum, 1975; Weissberg et al., 1981).

Impulsive youngsters have been the target of the problem-solving training effort put forth in the Think Aloud Program (Bash & Camp, 1985a, 1985b; Camp & Bash, 1981, 1985). By use of an extended series of didactic lessons, games, and other activities, trainees are taught a variety of self-instructional procedures aimed at increasing their reflectiveness, as well as at improving such specific problem-solving skills as the ability to develop alternative solutions to interpersonal problems, to consider possible consequences, and to create a plan of action based upon this formulation. These and related problem-solving interventions have recently been reviewed and critically evaluated by Durlak (1983), Kirschenbaum and Ordman (1984), and Rubin and Krasnor (1986).

The Interpersonal Cognitive Problem-solving Program

The pioneering work on problem-solving training was conducted over a 15-year period by George Spivack, Myrna B. Shure, Jerome J. Platt, and their co-workers. The fruits of their efforts appear in three volumes: *Social Adjustment of Young Children* (Spivack & Shure, 1974), *The Problem-solving Approach to Adjustment* (Spivack, Platt, & Shure, 1976), and *Problem-solving Techniques in Childrearing* (Shure & Spivack, 1978). While we will seek to do justice to this seminal research and materials development program, the reader is strongly encouraged to examine these primary references directly.

In its earliest phase, training in Interpersonal Cognitive Problem Solving (ICPS) was oriented primarily toward young children. The following comment by Spivack and Shure (1974) communicates a sense of why, in the context of aggressive behavior, they view problem-solving skills as worth teaching:

> What might an adult say to a preschool child who hits another or grabs a toy or cries? One possible response is, "Kevin, I know you feel angry at Paul, but I can't let you hit him." Another is, "Paul doesn't like to be hit." Sean snatches a truck from Robert and the adult asks him why he has taken the truck. "I want it!" is the answer. "Wait until Robert is finished and then you can play with it," says the adult. . . .
>
> In handling such behaviors as hitting and grabbing, many teachers and parents of young children demand that the behavior stop "because I said so." They often explain why the behavior is unacceptable. ("You can't hit Paul because you might hurt him.") If the hitting persists in school, the child might be isolated from the other children until he calms down or is judged to be ready to play without hitting.
>
> We believe that such techniques have serious limitations if one's goal is to help children develop effective ways of handling personal and interpersonal problems. First, the adult is too often doing the thinking for the child. The child is told he should wait his turn or stay away from another child or not hit. . . . The child neither solves his problem nor is helped to discover a solution of his own. Second, the adult in attempting to help a child often assumes that the child has a real understanding of the language of emotions ("I know you feel angry") or of negation ("but I can't let you hit him") or of causal relationships ("because you might hurt him"). Many young children do not have mastery of the language concepts necessary to solve interpersonal problems. . . . Finally, solving a problem for a child does little to help him feel good about himself. He is simply told what he

can or cannot do, even though the reasons may be explained and the solution may work in that particular instance. He does not experience mastery that emerges when one has solved a problem. He may feel protected, but not competent. (pp. ix–x)

It is from this rationale that the ICPS program emerged. ICPS training was designed to teach children (and later, adolescents and adults) how to think, not what to think—the problem-solving process, not problem solutions. In the case of young children, prerequisite language and conceptual skills must also be taught. More generally, from the viewpoint articulated above, there emerged a series of principles or guidelines from which the specific content and procedures of the ICPS program would follow.

Principles underlying ICPS

The first principle underlying ICPS training for young children concerns prerequisite language and conceptual skills. To help children learn to construe alternative solutions, games and other activities are first used to teach the meaning of words such as "or," "and," and "not." To aid in later understanding of individual preferences and interpersonal differences, words such as "some," "same," and "different" must be understood. And in the affective realm, of relevance to interpersonal sensitivity and empathy, notions of "happy," "sad," "mad," and the like are provided.

The second principle is that it is easier to teach new concepts with words already familiar to the child. Thus a major effort is made to utilize previously learned content to teach new materials. The third principle is that program content and situations should center on interpersonal themes, not impersonal problems.

An emphasis on conceptual learning and understanding, rather than on the use of specific words or sentences, reflects the fourth principle. (For example, emphasis is on the *idea* of negation rather than on its accurate grammatical representation in any given sentence.) The fifth principle, one lying at the heart of ICPS training, emphasizes teaching the child the habit of seeking alternative solutions and evaluating them on the basis of their potential consequences. Spivack and Shure (1974) observe with regard to this principle that no emphasis is placed in training upon the absolute merits of any given solution. If a child states "hit him" as a solution for getting a toy from another child, the teacher-trainer says, just as she would if a more socially acceptable solution were offered, "That's one idea. Can you think of a different idea?" (if the trainer is teaching the seeking of alternatives). Or the trainer might comment, "That's one idea. What might happen next if you hit him?" (if the trainer is teaching the seeking of consequences). To buttress the subsequent implementation of this principle, and thus aid trainee ability to evaluate alternative solutions, additional prerequisite skill words and concepts are taught (e.g., "maybe," "might," "why-because," "if-then").

The sixth guiding principle underlying ICPS training stresses that the child think of and evaluate her own ideas and be encouraged to offer them in the context of problem situations. This principle, Spivack and Shure note, rests on the belief that a child is more likely to act on a conclusion she views as her own than upon problem solutions provided by others.

Finally, ICPS training grows from the principle that the prerequisite language and cognitive problem-solving skills, which together constitute the training goals of the program, are not ends in themselves but instead should be conceptualized as antecedent, mediating skills necessary to enhance behavioral adjustment and reduce such maladaptive behaviors as impulsiveness, aggressiveness, and overinhibition.

ICPS Skills

A number of specific problem-solving skills constitute the focal training targets of the ICPS program. The following discussion provides a comprehensive consideration of the methods and materials utilized in teaching these target skills. This presentation focuses upon the several ICPS programs across age samples, which include not only young children but also preadolescents, adolescents, and adults. The six target skills are as follows:

1. Alternative solution thinking

A person's ability to generate different options or solutions that could potentially be utilized to solve a problem defines his capacity for alternative solution thinking. ICPS training for this skill has typically centered upon problems in trainee interpersonal relationships with a variety of types of persons but has focused especially on peers and authority figures. Spivack et al. (1976) observe, in partial explanation of their interest in promoting this skill, that if someone has only one or two solutions available to him in any given problematic situation, his chances of success are less than is the case for an individual who can turn to alternative solutions when the first option attempted fails to resolve the problem. The following example illustrates this idea:

> Among four- and five-year-olds, for instance, a girl may want her sister to let her play with her doll. She may ask her, and her sister may say

no. Of interest is whether the child who wants the toy would conceive of an alternative way to get her sister to let her play with the doll. . . . If the girl's sister consistently says no every time she is asked for something, and no other options are available to the girl, she would soon become frustrated with her sister. She might react aggressively and exhibit impulsive behavior (for example, she might grab the toy) or she might avoid the problem entirely by withdrawing. (Spivack et al., 1976, p. 19)

2. Consequential thinking

This second ICPS skill is defined as an ability to consider how one's actions may affect both other people and oneself, as well as the subsequent reactions these behaviors may engender. The process of consequential thinking includes a consideration of pros and cons associated with an interpersonal act that goes beyond the simple enumeration of alternative events that might ensue. As will be seen in our subsequent examination of ICPS training procedures and materials, consequential thinking is stimulated by having the trainer follow the offering of problem solutions with such questions as "What might happen next?" "How will this make Mary feel?" "What will happen in the short run?" and "What will happen in the long run?"

3. Causal thinking

Causal, or cause-and-effect, thinking associated with interpersonal problem situations is the ability to relate one event to another over time with regard to the "why" that might have precipitated any given act. At the simplest level, to continue the example described earlier, if the girl wishing to obtain the doll from her sister hits her sister, accurate cause-and-effect thinking would make the girl aware she hit her sister because the sister would not let her play with the doll (or, stated another way, because of the girl's anger at not being given the doll). If her sister hits her back as a result of having been hit, accurate causal thinking should lead the child to be aware that her sister hit her because she herself hit first.

The inclusion of causal thinking as a skill-training goal in the ICPS program was initially based, in part, on the position of Muuss (1960). His concern was social causal thinking across developmental levels. Muuss viewed causal thinking, at its optimal level, as

an understanding and appreciation of the dynamic, complex and interacting nature of the forces that operate in human behavior. It involves an attitude of flexibility, of seeing things from the point of view of others as well as an awareness of the probabalistic nature of knowledge. A causally oriented person is capable of suspending judgment until sufficient factual information is available. (p. 122)

Relevant to our present purposes, in Muuss's view, is a low level of causal thinking and its companion, poor insight into the dynamics of behavior. These factors make it difficult to react logically and appropriately to the behavior of others and, hence, "behavior of others may be misunderstood and perceived as threatening, and such misunderstanding could lead to heightened conflict between the parties involved" (Spivack et al., 1976, p. 75).

4. Interpersonal sensitivity

This problem-solving skill concerns an individual's awareness that an interpersonal problem in fact exists. It is the ability to perceive such problems combined with skill in focusing upon the problems' interpersonal components. As Spivack et al. (1976) comment,

> To carry our example of the girl who wanted her sister's doll one step further, it seems reasonable to assume that if she were aware that [an interpersonal] problem or potential problem could develop once she decides to ask for a doll, her behavior and/or problem-solving strategies may differ from what might ensue in the absence of such sensitivity. (pp. 33–34)

However, as subsequent discussion makes clear, empirical evidence examining the degree to which the several ICPS skills discriminate between well-adjusted and poorly adjusted individuals, or between aggressive and impulsive versus nonaggressive and more reflective persons, does not support interpersonal sensitivity as being among the highly potent ICPS skills.

5. Means-ends thinking

Means-ends thinking is careful, step-by-step planning in order to reach a given goal. Such planning, Spivack et al. (1976) observe, includes insight and forethought to forestall or circumvent potential obstacles and, in addition, having available alternative means when needed to deal with realistic obstacles in the way of reaching one's goals. Means-ends thinking also involves awareness that goals are not always reached immediately and that the timing of one's behavior is also often relevant to goal attainment. Spivack et al. (1976) comment illustratively that

> a child adept at means-ends thinking may consider, I can go visit the boy next door (means) but he won't know me and won't let me in

(obstacle). If I call first and tell him I just moved in and ask if I can come over (means), he'll say okay. But I better not go at dinnertime or his mother will be mad (time and obstacle) and he won't like me. (p. 64)

6. Perspective taking

This interpersonal problem-solving skill is reflected by the extent to which an individual recognizes and can integrate the fact that different people may have different motives and viewpoints, and thus may respond differently in any given situation. Perspective taking closely resembles aspects of what others have termed *role taking* or *empathy* (see chapter 8). A fuller sense of the meaning of this ICPS skill can be obtained from an understanding of its measurement. In ICPS research on perspective taking, use was made of Feffer and Jahelka's (1968) Thematic Apperception Test (TAT) procedure. After following standard TAT instructions to create stories for four TAT cards, the trainee is presented with the same cards again and asked to retell the initial story from the viewpoint of each of its characters. Among other qualities of taking the perspective of others, scoring reflects the degree of coordination among the various versions.

Competence in these six problem-solving skills is the overall training goal of the ICPS program. The program's success in achieving this goal and its impact on the overt aggressive and impulsive behavior of ICPS trainees—as well as on their more general adjustment—are described next.

ICPS Research

A substantial number of evaluative studies of the ICPS program have been conducted. Many have been comparisons, on each ICPS skill, of trainees who are high versus low in adjustment, aggressiveness, impulsiveness, or inhibition. Others, seeking to provide complementary information, have examined the degree of correlation among the skills and these same criterion measures. Table 1 summarizes the major results of these experimental and correlational studies. It presents, for each of the major ICPS trainee age groups, an indication of the presence or absence of a significant impact of each skill upon the criteria studied.

Before turning to specific results—especially those relevant to aggression and its reduction—with particular trainee samples, it is important to reiterate that the developers of ICPS set forth as their final guiding principle in undertaking this work the notion that the problem-

Table 1

ICPS Skills Relevant to Training Criteria: Adjustment, Aggression, Impulsivity, Inhibition

Trainee age group	Alternatives	Consequences	Causality	Interpersonal sensitivity	Means-ends thinking	Perspective taking
				Skill		
Early childhood (Age 4–5)	yes	yes	no	no	——	——
Middle childhood (Age 9–12)	yes	no	yes	——	yes	——
Adolescence (Age 13–17)	yes	yes	no	no	yes	yes
Adulthood	yes	yes	yes	no	yes	yes

21

solving skills are not taught as ends in themselves but as antecedent, mediating skills necessary to enhance behavior adjustment and reduce aggressiveness, impulsivity, and overinhibition. Table 1 illustrates that, although not all the skills have had an impact in all the samples, Spivack, Shure, and Platt have essentially succeeded in their goal.

With regard to specific findings, let us examine alternative thinking first. Shure, Spivack, and Powell (1972) found that youngsters whose behavior ratings indicated a predominance of either acting-out behaviors or inhibition conceptualized significantly fewer solutions to problem situations than did children rated as well-adjusted. Elardo and Caldwell (cited in Spivack et al., 1976) found that, as alternative thinking improved, disrespect, defiance, inattentiveness, withdrawal, and overreliance on others all decreased. Two studies demonstrated that increased levels of alternative thinking on posttraining test situations are also paralleled by analogously high levels in real-life contexts (Larcen, Chinsky, Allen, Lochman, & Selinger, 1974; McClure, 1975). As was true for children, poor levels of adjustment correlate with deficient alternative thinking in both adolescents (Shure & Spivack, 1970) and adults (Platt & Spivack, 1973).

Consequential thinking was examined by Shure, Newman, and Silver (1973) and Spivack and Shure (1975). These studies indicated that 4-year-olds rated as behaviorally adjusted conceptualized a greater number of different, relevant consequences for such aggressive acts as grabbing toys and taking objects belonging to others without permission than did children rated as impulsive or inhibited. Shure and Spivack (1972) found that the number of consequences given by a youngster increased as a function of ICPS training. Comparisons of normal versus impulsive adolescents (Spivack & Levine, 1973) and normal adults versus adult psychiatric patients (Platt & Spivack, 1973) revealed that the normal sample in each instance provided significantly more consequences.

Platt and Spivack (1973) have reported similar differential results favoring the normal adult sample on causal thinking. These individuals were significantly more likely to think in terms of prior causes and the relationship between past and present events than were psychiatric patients, and this quality of thinking was unrelated to IQ. Larcen, Spivack, and Shure (1972) found a significant relationship between causal thinking and measures of both impulsivity and inhibition in 9- to 12-year-olds, with well-adjusted youngsters identifying causal statements significantly more often than did those displaying behavioral deviance. No such result emerged in other examinations of this relationship involving 4- to 5-year-olds or adolescents.

Level of interpersonal sensitivity in the sense defined earlier (i.e., degree of awareness that an interpersonal problem exists) did not differentiate between adjusted and more deviant child (Spivack & Shure, 1975), adolescent (Platt, Spivack, Altman, Altman, & Peizer, 1974), or adult (Platt & Spivack, 1973) samples. Perspective taking, a separate skill reflecting a different type of interpersonal sensitivity (e.g., role taking), has found greater success in ICPS evaluative research. Platt et al. (1974) found significantly greater ability on this skill in normal adolescents as compared with disturbed youngsters. Platt and Spivack (1973) and Suchotliff (1970) found parallel results at the adult level.

Finally, with regard to research on means-ends thinking, Larcen et al. (1972), in a sample of 9- to 12-year-old children, found a significant inverse relationship between the level of means-ends thinking skill and such behaviors as social aggression, inability to delay, and emotionality. Working with the same age level, Shure and Spivack (1972) obtained evidence that normal, as compared with disturbed, youngsters conceptualized more means (steps) to reach a goal and more obstacles that might be met on the way to that goal. They also gave more consideration to the importance of time. In addition to mentioning fewer means, obstacles, and time considerations in reaching a goal, less well-adjusted youngsters expressed stories more often limited to impulsive and aggressive means. As noted in Table 1, means-ends thinking is an equally significant problem-solving skill at the adolescent (Platt, Scura, & Hannon, 1973; Spivack & Levine, 1973) and adult (Platt & Spivack, 1975) levels.

This brief overview of ICPS outcome research confirms the conclusion we drew earlier in our summary of Table 1. The skills examined, with few exceptions, appear meaningfully and significantly to relate to and differentiate among samples varying in levels of adjustment, aggression, impulsivity, and inhibition. Their importance seems well-established.

Although the strengths of this program have been emphasized, the approach is not without its difficulties. As Maher and Zins (1987) comment,

> Spivack and Shure's intervention efforts have had an enormously positive impact on the field, but have attracted criticism as well. Contributions include: (a) establishment of a place in the school curriculum for social competence promotion, (b) development and

dissemination of detailed practical training manuals and materials, (c) cost-effective benefits to thousands of children, and finally, (d) the many extensions and alternative models this work has spawned. Critics of Spivack and Shure and related [social problem-solving] interventions cite: (a) the absence of attention-placebo control groups in many studies, (b) the heavy reliance on potentially biased teacher behavior ratings, (c) the use of training packages that include an amalgamation of procedures (e.g., modeling, role-playing, etc.) that make it difficult to identify the active ingredients (Gresham, 1985) and (d) the fact that some, but not all replications have been successful (Durlak, 1983). (p. 124)

ICPS Training

Discussion to this point has concerned the underlying rationale and guiding principles of the ICPS program, its skill targets, and its supporting research. The final aspect of ICPS we will address is training. This section will briefly consider, separately for young child and adult trainees, the specific materials and procedures utilized to teach the ICPS skills.

The ICPS training program for young children (ages 4 to 5) makes use of a variety of age-relevant materials: games, cut-out dolls, face puppets, picture sets, and the like. The program, according to its developers, is optimally implemented for 20 minutes per day over a 3-month period. The trainer may be a teacher and/or aide working in a classroom setting (Spivack & Shure, 1974) or a parent teaching his own child or children in the home setting (Shure & Spivack, 1978). In content, the program consists of 24 games or lessons devoted to prerequisite language and conceptual skills (phase 1) and 12 aimed directly at ICPS skills (phase 2). As mentioned earlier in this chapter, the prerequisite skills include focus on such language concepts as "is," "not," "all," "same," "or," "same-different," and "if-then," as well as on more general ideas associated with emotional awareness, identifying feelings and preferences in others, what might happen next (consequences), and fairness.

The following excerpt will provide a sense of how a parent or teacher in the second phase of the program seeks to teach one of the ICPS skills—in this instance, alternative thinking:

> The goal is to stimulate the child to think of as many different solutions as possible to the everyday interpersonal problems presented to him. The emphasis here is on "What else can I do?" when confronted with such a problem.

To elicit solutions, use the following techniques. Show the child a picture, puppets, or other visual materials and state the problem.... Say: "The idea of this game is to think of lots of different ways (or ideas) for [repeat the problem]. I'm going to write all your ideas on the board." Despite the fact that the child cannot read, this has been a very useful motivating technique.

After the first idea is given, say: "That's one way. Now the idea of the game is to think of lots of different ways. Can you think of a different (new, another) way? What else can this child [point to picture, puppet, etc.] do to [repeat problem]?" ... After a few ideas are given, count on your fingers: "Way number one [repeat solution], way number two" and so on. Then ask: "Can you think of way number three?" If the child has been proposing things for the child character to do, switch the question to: "What can he say?" If the youngster jumps the gun and offers a consequence to a solution, recognize it, do not discourage it, then continue asking for a solution.

An enumeration is a variation of the same solution but not a different solution. The most common enumerations are giving something (give him candy, give him ice cream, give him potato chips), telling someone (tell his daddy, tell his mommy, tell his sister), and hurting someone (hit him, kick him, bite him). Let the child enumerate for a while, then classify, using the following words: "Giving ice cream and candy and potato chips are all giving something to eat. Can you think of an idea that's different from giving something to eat?"

If an idea is relevant to the problem as stated, it is acceptable, and value judgments are not communicated to the child. "Hit him" is just as relevant as "please." The general dialogue is: "That's one way. Can you think of a different idea? Remember the idea of the game is to think of lots of ways." (Shure & Spivack, 1978, pp. 86–87; bracketed material appears in the original)

Shure and Spivack (1978) report that, beyond the formal ICPS training program outlined and illustrated here, mothers who consistently applied the ICPS skills when actual problems arose involving their children had children who most improved in the ICPS skills and subsequent behavioral adjustment. They term this trainer problem-solving style *interpersonal problem-solving dialoguing*. The following example of such supplementary training-by-dialoguing illustrates how the mother's statements pointedly encourage, respectively, (1) perspective taking, (2) causality, (3) alternative thinking, and (4) consequences:

Four-year-old Ralph let a friend play with his racing car, but the friend has played with it a long time and Ralph has just grabbed it back.

Mother:	How do you think your friend feels when you grab toys? [Encourages perspective taking]
Ralph:	Mad, but I don't care, it's mine!
Mother:	What did your friend do when you grabbed the toy? [Encourages cause and effect thinking]
Ralph:	He hit me but I want my toy!
Mother:	How did that make you feel? [Encourages emotional awareness]
Ralph:	Mad.
Mother:	You're mad and your friend is mad, and he hit you. Can you think of a different way to get your toy back so you both won't be mad and so John won't hit you? [Encourages alternative thinking]
Ralph:	I could ask him.
Mother:	And what might happen then? [Encourages consequential thinking]
Ralph:	He'll say no.
Mother:	He might say no. What else can you think of doing so your friend will give you back your racing car? [Encourages alternative thinking]
Ralph:	I could let him have my match-box cars.
Mother:	You thought of two different ways. (pp. 36–37; bracketed material appears in the original)

These materials, procedures, and illustrative dialogues, although geared toward young children, serve to show how ICPS skills may be optimally taught. One final example will conclude our description of the ICPS programs. Siegel and Spivack (1973) also developed an ICPS training program designed to teach the basic problem-solving skills to adults and older adolescents. It consists of 12 game-like exercises, each of which takes 20 to 45 minutes. These exercises can be used on an individual or small-group basis. At the outset of their program participation, trainees are provided with the following structuring statement:

The purpose of this program is to help people learn to solve problems that have caused them trouble. Many people do not know how to go about thinking of the ways to solve problems. There are a number of useful steps in the solving of problems. This program is intended to teach you these steps and to give you practice in mastering each of the steps. The steps are:

1. *Recognition of problems.* Problems are a part of real life. Everybody has them. Some people are just better at solving them than others. The first step in successful problem solving is to learn how to recognize problems. In this first step, you will be given a

number of exercises to give you practice to be better at recognizing problems.

2. *Definition of problems.* After you learn how to better recognize problems, you will be given practice in how to define problems clearly by learning how to find out about problems and their solutions.

3. *Alternative ways of solving problems.* The third and possibly most important step in problem solving is looking at alternate ways of solving problems. There may be more ways of solving a problem than one. Some of the ways may be clearly better than other ways. To learn this step you will practice thinking about alternate ways to solve problems.

4. *Deciding which solution is the best way to solve the problem.* The final step you learn is how to evaluate different solutions to a problem, and try to make a decision. In this step you will get practice at looking at the pros and cons of various solutions to problems, and trying to decide which one is best. (pp. 229–230)

The first step in this program, termed *problem recognition,* appears to be designed to teach the ICPS skill, interpersonal sensitivity. That is, the adult trainee is helped to see problems where they exist and to conceptualize them interpersonally. For example, one exercise in this phase of the program, Magazine Faces, requires the trainee to respond to magazine pictures of people experiencing some emotion by describing the emotion and constructing a story explaining what might have led up to the feeling depicted. A second exercise, Finding Problems, involves showing the trainee photographs of people in real-life interpersonal problem situations (e.g., a fight at a party, a drunken spouse) and asking the trainee to identify the problem.

The activities of the second step of this ICPS program, *problem definition,* seem oriented toward teaching perspective taking and, to a lesser extent, cause-and-effect thinking. One exercise in this phase, for example, is Finding Out about People. In it, the trainee listens to a series of taped "playlets" illustrating an array of means for learning about the feelings and thoughts of others. These means include (1) asking direct questions of a third party, (2) indirectly bringing up the subject in conversation, and (3) interacting with the person directly.

Training in *alternative thinking* is the target of the third step. One exercise in this phase is a picture-card sorting task, Finding Alternatives. In a manner not unrelated to training in means-ends thinking, the trainee is presented with a problem (a card with a picture of a lonely, dejected person) and an outcome (a card with the same person at a party). A number of other cards depict the person in other situations and activities, some of which could reasonably lead (if ordered correctly) from the problem to the outcome. The trainee's task is to select and order the alternative solutions. In this step, the trainee is taught not only to recognize alternatives, but also to generate them. In the exercise Creating Alternatives, the trainee is presented with interpersonal problem situations (e.g., getting along with one's boss, changing the annoying behavior of a friend) and encouraged by the trainer to come up with as many solutions as possible.

The final stage, *deciding which solution is best,* is oriented toward consequential thinking—that is, toward evaluation of the relative strengths and weaknesses of the available alternatives. The exercise Impulsivity-Reflection Slide in this step seeks to accomplish this goal by a series of demonstrations to the trainee that the initial, frequently impulsively chosen, solution to an interpersonal problem is often not the best one and that it is often better to wait and reflect on alternative solutions before taking action. In Decision Faces, the trainee is given practice in enumerating the pros and cons of each alternative. In the final program exercise, Plays, the trainee is asked to bring together and sequentially enact all four steps of the problem-solving process as defined by this ICPS program.

This consideration of ICPS program procedures and materials concludes our consideration of the work of Spivack, Platt, and Shure. Their contribution to this domain is substantial and continuing, and has formed an excellent foundation for the Prepare Curriculum course on Problem-solving Training. Before presenting this course, however, we will focus discussion on its second basis, at least in spirit: impersonal problem solving.

Impersonal Problem Solving

In the following section, methods will be described for the enhancement of the ability to solve intellectual and cognitive problems, to function more creatively, and to respond with higher levels of problem-solving originality. We embark on this consideration of the impersonal to understand the personal better because we have long believed that such an effort might be profitable. We are guided, in effect, by an extrapolatory strategy. A host of problem-solving and creativity-enhancing methods have been actively used for a number of years in industrial, educational, and laboratory contexts. Their use has not been oriented toward the building of prosocial skills or the resolution of personal deficiencies. Instead, these methods have been employed in order to enhance organizational effectiveness; to develop new products; to resolve cognitive dilemmas; to improve the on-the-job functioning of managers, teachers, scientists, and other applied problem solvers; and to further the experimental goal of better understanding the intellectual and cognitive processes involved in effective problem solving and creativity.

Whether this vast, and only partially research-based, literature does in fact have significant implications for the enhancement of prosocial behavior remains a matter for substantive research scrutiny. We have been implementing an extrapolatory research philosophy in another context for many years by drawing on social-psychological laboratory research for testable hypotheses relevant to enhancing the effectiveness of psychotherapy (Goldstein, Heller, & Sechrest, 1966; Goldstein & Simonson, 1971). During the course of this extended research program, it has become clear that some change-enhancing methods developed in laboratory contexts can find direct, applied usefulness in an interpersonal framework; some can also find such usefulness but must first be altered or adapted; and others have essentially no import for applied concerns. We suspect much the same outcome will in the long run prove true for the extrapolation of impersonal problem-solving methods to the personal problem-solving domain: Which impersonal methods will prove valuable, which will have to be adapted, and which will prove useless for these purposes is a matter for future formal and informal research. It is to stimulate just such inquiry, as well as to provide an additional foundation for our Prepare Curriculum course in Problem-solving Training, that the following sections are included. Specifically, we will examine brainstorming, synectics, morphological analysis, attribute listing, and a number of other techniques purporting to enhance impersonal problem-solving skill and to stimulate creativity. Consistent with the extrapolatory viewpoint we champion here, it is important to note that, unlike such personal problem-solving methods as ICPS, none of the impersonal methods considered has been concerned in any substantial way with the enhancement of prosocial behavior, aggression reduction, anger control, or the like. We urge upon the interested reader the challenge of just such extrapolatory translation and experimental examination.

Brainstorming
Brainstorming is an idea-generating, problem-solving technique developed by Osborn in 1938 and first explicated in detail in his book

Applied Imagination (Osborn, 1953). It is a widely used technique, particularly in industrial and educational settings. Osborn differentiated between the idea-finding and solution-finding phases of the creative problem-solving process, identifying the goal of brainstorming to be the production of a substantial quantity of high-quality, problem-relevant ideas. The second phase, not relevant to brainstorming, is evaluative. Here the ideas of the first phase are judged, considered, evaluated, winnowed, and eventually adopted.

To promote the overriding idea-generating purpose of brainstorming, two guiding principles have been put forth. The first, *deferment of judgment,* requires participants to verbalize or write down their ideas during the brainstorming session without concern for their value, feasibility, or significance. Within the stipulation that the ideas be problem-relevant—that is, not "free association"—the brainstormer is asked to suspend what Osborn (1953) calls the "judicial mind," which analyzes, compares, and chooses. Instead, Osborn urges that the "creative mind"—which visualizes, foresees, and generates ideas—be encouraged. The second basic brainstorming principle is that *quantity breeds quality.* This principle rests on notions beyond the simple idea of "the more the better." As Stein (1974) observes,

> The rationale for this dictum originates in associationistic psychology, which assumes that our thoughts or associations are structured hierarchically. The most dominant thoughts in this hierarchy are those which are most habitual, common, or usual, and are therefore likely to be, from other points of view, the "safest" and most acceptable to others. It is necessary to "get through" these conventional ideas if we are to arrive at original ones. (p. 29)

Four operational rules that grow from these two principles guide the actual conduct of the brainstorming session:

1. *Criticism is ruled out.* This rule is the operational underpinning for the deferment-of-judgment principle. In group brainstorming, for example, criticism of another's or of one's own ideas and apologizing are actively discouraged. Evaluation, adverse judgments, and the like are kept strictly off limits.

2. *Freewheeling is welcomed.* As Davis (1973) notes, "The wilder the idea, the better; it is easier to tame down than to think up.... The brainstormer—as any other creative thinker—must be consciously set to be imaginative, to try different and unusual strategies, and to view the problem from novel perspectives—in a word, to suggest anything" (p. 93).

3. *Quantity is wanted.* This rule directly reflects the second basic principle of brainstorming. In all possible ways, sheer quantity of ideas is to be encouraged.

4. *Combination and improvement are sought.* Participants are urged to build on the ideas of others, especially by showing how previously offered ideas can be improved, combined, or otherwise transformed for the better.

Brainstorming can be conducted on an individual or group basis. If conducted in a group, it is customary for 10 to 12 persons to participate. Ideally, participants are heterogeneous in training, experience vis-à-vis the focal problem, sex, and similar characteristics—except rank or status within the organization, dimensions on which similarity is considered best.

Osborn is among the many writers on creativity, problem solving, and originality who believe strongly in *incubation effects*—that is, the preconscious progress made by individuals toward idea generation when they seem, to themselves and others, otherwise occupied. To provide systematic opportunity for incubation to occur, it is recommended that participants in a brainstorming group be advised of the problem to be dealt with 2 days in advance of the actual session. The session itself, usually 30 to 45 minutes in length, usually involves the participants, a leader, an associate leader, and a recording secretary. Sessions typically open with warm-up activities, a presentation of the four rules, and a call for ideas and suggestions from the group. Osborn comments that

> [the leader] quickly recognizes those who raise their hands to signify they have ideas to offer. Sometimes so many hands are raised that he simply goes around the table and lets each person present one idea in turn. Participants should never be allowed to read off lists of ideas which they may have brought to the meeting. . . . Only one idea at a time should be offered by any brainstormer. Otherwise the pace would be badly impeded because the opportunity for "hitch-hikes" (one idea stimulating a related idea) would be precluded. (p. 176)

Various techniques—such as use of Osborn's (1953) idea-spurring questions; stop-and-go brainstorming, in which freewheeling periods and evaluative ones are alternated; and ideas put forth by the leaders—are used for stimulation when the group seems to be "running dry."

Since brainstorming procedures specifically preclude the type of idea evaluation and analysis necessary for problem solution, the total problem-solving process involves submitting the ideas generated by the brainstorming group to an idea evaluation group. This latter panel may or may not contain some of the members of the original brainstorming group. Regardless of whether or not they were involved in the brainstorming, members should be people with direct future responsibility for the focal problem. It is their task to evaluate the raw or edited brainstormed ideas for simplicity, timeliness, cost, feasibility, and other factors involved in organizational implementation.

These descriptive comments complete our consideration of brainstorming. How the individual, group, or organization may optimally use these procedures for the purposes at the heart of the Prepare Curriculum is an as yet untested empirical question, the answer to which requires substantial doses of the very creativity that procedures such as brainstorming are designed to elicit.

Synectics

Synectics is a problem-solving approach initially developed by Gordon in 1944 and comprehensively described in *Synectics* (Gordon, 1961), *The Metaphorical Way* (Gordon, 1971), and *The Practice of Creativity* (Prince, 1970). Synectics, not unlike brainstorming and many other creative problem-solving techniques, rests on a rationale and procedures that seek to help the user both "break free" and move beyond evaluative analytical and conventional thinking. "Naturally" creative problem solving allows this approach; synectics seeks consciously to institute such a cognitive state (e.g., detachment, unconventionality, metaphorical wordplay, apparent irrelevance, empathy). It is, as we will see, a system based largely on the use of metaphor and analogy.

A synectics group typically consists of five to seven members, one of whom is the designated leader and one of whom is the group's client-expert, a resource person included largely for her factual understanding of the focal problem. Meetings typically last an hour. Synectics programs vary in length, but all reflect a three-phase problem-solving process. The steps constituting the first phase of synectics are devoted to defining, elaborating, analyzing, and understanding the problem. This initial phase is followed by one in which the basic operating mechanisms of synectics, metaphors and analogies, are utilized. Finally, in the "force fit" steps of the last phase, the effort is made to use the fruits of the metaphorical and analogical phase to move toward problem solution. The flow of a synectics effort from problem to solution may be clarified by the following presentation of the specific steps involved in synectic problem solving.

1. *Problem as given.* A statement of the focal problem is presented to the synectics group. As Gordon (1961) notes, this statement may prove to be an accurate statement of the problem, or, as initially given, it may in part hide or confuse the question to be addressed.

2. *Analysis.* To clarify the nature and substance of the problem and to reduce ambiguities associated with the problem as given, the group's client-expert is called upon to present an analysis of it.

3. *Purge.* A number of problem solutions typically emerge spontaneously from group members during the initial steps of the synectics process. Such solutions, much like the earliest expressed ideas in a brainstorming session, tend to be superficial and generally obvious. Their verbalization at this time permits the group's expert to explain their inadequacy, thus simultaneously "purging" the inadequate solutions and further clarifying the focal problem.

4. *Problem as understood.* Prince (1970) suggests that at this step each participant be called upon to come up with his own view of the problem and his fantasy solution. This process enables each participant to begin "owning" the problem personally, takes advantage of the group's diversity, and helps break the problem into manageable sub-problems when needed. In addition, the use of fantasy or wishful thinking at this point begins the transition to the level of thinking required at the next (analogical) step of the synectics process. This step ends when the leader, after checking with the expert, selects one of the group's problems as given to be the groupwide problem goal to resolve.

5. *Excursion.* During this step in the synectics process, the different operational mechanisms that lie at the creative core of the program are utilized. These mechanisms involve the use by group members of different types of analogies to help move away from the problem into a speculative mode, in order to return later with a very different perspective. In fact, in this step, the participants are directly asked to forget the problem per se, to take a mental excursion from it. This step is an effort to evoke, as in all creative problem-solving programs, nonevaluative, nonanalytical thinking of a metaphorical nature. It is, as Gordon terms it, an effort to "make the familiar strange" and thus view the familiar problem later from brand new perspectives. He observes further that

> analogies are developed which are relative to (and evoked by) the problem as understood. This phase pushes and pulls the problem as understood out of its rigid form of impregnable regularity into a form

that offers some conceptual finger holds. These finger holds open up the problem as understood. (Gordon, 1961, p. 157)

The analogical mechanisms thus utilized are of three types. In the first, *personal analogy,* the individual seeks to engage in what Gordon calls "an extensive loss of self" and images himself to be the object involved in the problem as understood. As Stein (1974) observes, "he 'becomes' the spring in the apparatus and feels its tension, or he 'becomes' the pane of glass and allows himself to 'feel' like the molecules in it as they push and pull against each other" (p. 187). Gordon (1961) stresses that the operative process here is empathic identification and not an identity-losing role playing. Four levels of increasingly deep empathic identification, as a result of use of personal analogy, are described in *Making It Strange—Teacher's Manual* (Synectics, 1968):

1. *First-person description of facts.* Someone asked to imagine she is a fiddler crab states she would have a hard outside, soft inside, and so on.

2. *First-person description of emotions.* In the example above, the person responds that she was busily involved in gathering food for herself and had to be on guard for fear she herself might become food for a bigger fish.

3. *Identification with a living thing.*[1] This level is viewed as genuine personal analogy, involving both kinesthetic and emotional identification with the object. In the fiddler crab example, the person might state that her big claw is a useless burden because it is heavy and frightens no one when she waves it.

4. *Identification with a nonliving object.* This level is viewed as the deepest and most difficult to achieve personal analogy. It apparently requires, in practice, the greatest analogical effort by participants.

---

[1] A problem-solving approach closely resembling this aspect of personal analogy is Bionics (Papanek, 1969). Using "the infinite storehouse of ideas in nature itself," Bionics is the study of the structure, function, and mechanisms of plants and animals to gain design information for analogous systems created by humans. As Davis (1973) observes, the bionicist's strategy is "to examine closely the motor, circulatory, neural, and especially sensory capabilities of organisms from . . . the animal kingdom—mammals, birds, reptiles, amphibians, fish, and insects. The ambition of each bionicist . . . is to achieve an occasional breakthrough in such engineering goals as increasing reliability, sensitivity, strength, maneuverability, or speed, while reducing size, weight, or power requirements. On all counts, the bionicist can easily point to biological systems which overwhelmingly outstrip any man-made analog" (p. 129).

A second type of excursion from the problem as understood involves the use of *direct analogy*. For inexperienced participants, direct analogy is the easiest analogical method to master, and thus is often the first introduced. Unlike personal analogy, in which the individual is asked to "become" an aspect of the problem, direct analogy requires turning outward. Facts, knowledge, and technology from one domain are utilized analogically to view the problem domain more clearly. As Gordon (1961) comments,

> Brunel solved the problem of underwater construction by watching a shipworm tunneling into a timber. The worm constructed a tube for itself as it moved forward, and the classical notion of caissons came to Brunel by direct analogy. . . . Alexander Graham Bell recalled, "It struck me that the bones of the human ear were very massive, indeed, as compared with the delicate thin membrane that operated them, and the thought occurred that if a membrane so delicate could move bones relatively so massive, why should not a thicker and stouter piece of membrane move my piece of steel." And the telephone was conceived. (p. 42)

A variety of fields have been drawn upon for direct analogical purposes in synectics groups, but it is clear that biology has been most frequently used in this manner. Whatever the field drawn upon, Prince (1970) claims that the greater the logical distance between the problem object and the analogy—the less the apparent relevance of the latter to the former—the more likely it will be helpful in the problem-solving process.

The third analogical mechanism used during the excursion step is *symbolic analogy,* also variously called Book Title, Essential Paradox, and Compressed Conflict. This type of analogy is frequently used to suggest other, direct analogies. Prince (1970) comments that

> the Book Title . . . helps take a more interesting and therefore better vacation from the problem. In form, a Book Title is a two-word phrase that captures both an essence of and a paradox involved in a particular thing or set of feelings. The combination of an adjective and a noun is the most workable form. The usual purpose of a Book Title is to generalize about a particular and then use it to suggest another example (i.e., Direct Analogy). This procedure also helps hardcase, stay-on-the-problem types get away from the problem. (p. 95)

5. *Force fit.* The goal of the next step in the synectics process is to return to the problem from the analogical excursion and try to come up with a practical application of the analogy to the problem. The

analogical material has been developed, and in spite of its apparent irrelevance, the group must now force it to fit the problem in a useful manner. Gordon (1961) reports the force fit activities of a synectics group dealing with the problem of inventing a better mousetrap. In its analogical excursion, the group came up with the Book Title "Trojan Horse," reflecting the idea of leaving something around that mice will covet so much that they will pull it into their nests. The force fit interactions led to the notion that lint, which could be used by mice in this manner, be left around; the lint would be treated so that when warmed by the mice in the nest it would give off a painless but lethal gas.

  6. *Viewpoint.* The return to the real problem, seeking workable solutions, continues in this next and final stage of the synectics process. This stage in a sense involves the evaluation of the analogically derived force fit. Is the fit viable? Has the solution been reached? If answered affirmatively, the synectics problem-solving process is completed.

Creative Problem Solving

Creative Problem Solving is a comprehensive series of training programs developed by Parnes and described in detail in *Creative Behavior Guidebook* (Parnes, 1967a) and *Creative Behavior Workbook* (Parnes, 1967b). Numerous articles in the *Journal of Creative Behavior,* a publication founded by Parnes, further describe and evaluate this approach. Parnes' methods rely heavily on fostering the cognitive aspects of the creative process, placing considerably less emphasis than brainstorming and synectics on promoting the intuitive or preconscious components of this process. The approach uses a wide variety of techniques and materials rather didactically to teach individuals how to apply "deliberate creative effort." In this view, to be handled effectively problems must be refined, clarified, and worked on through stages of (1) fact finding, (2) problem finding, (3) idea finding, (4) solution finding, and (5) acceptance finding.

  The Creative Problem Solving training program can be implemented by persons working alone (using the two program texts cited) or in classes of as many as 25 members. The total program consists of 16 sessions, designed as a group to train participants in how to be effective in the five-step problem-solving process just enumerated and to give them increasingly autonomous practice in doing so. A better overall sense of this program can be obtained by a brief look at the substance of each session, as described in Parnes 1967a and 1967b:

Session 1: Training in problem sensitivity, or how to become aware of problems that can be worked on creatively.

Session 2: Training in problem definition, to arrive at a clearer and more manipulable statement of the problem.

Session 3: Training in brainstorming rationale and technique.

Session 4: Training in "forced relationship" techniques designed to help the trainee overcome fixed ways of thinking by learning how to force a relationship between, or to combine, two quite unrelated ideas or objects.

Session 5: Training in the development and use of evaluation criteria. The criteria developed are actually applied to the ideas generated in preceding sessions.

Session 6: Training in how to gain acceptance of one's solutions. Use is made here of an implementation checklist that raises questions regarding possible advantages, objections, anticipated responses to criticism of one's solution, and the optimal time and place for solution implementation.

Session 7: A demonstration by the Creative Problem Solving instructor of the total problem-solving process as taught in the preceding sessions. This is the first of four "experience cycle" sessions in which the participants, with increasing autonomy, have an opportunity to experience the complete problem-solving process.

Session 8: Additional training in fact finding, with particular emphasis on the use of descriptive categories.

Session 9: The second experience cycle session focusing on the entire problem-solving process. Rather than having the process modeled by the instructor (as in Session 7), the trainee works with a small group of other trainees.

Session 10: Additional training in idea finding, with particular emphasis on the use of manipulative categories.

Session 11: Additional training in solution finding. Part of this session deals with the utilization of strange, unusual, and even seemingly silly potential solutions. The remainder focuses on how evaluation criteria may be used to stimulate enhanced creativity.

Session 12: The third experience cycle session. In this instance, the trainee works in two-person teams, as well as alone.

Session 13: Additional training in acceptance finding. Using a "who, what, where, why, and how" checklist, trainees are taught to "sell" their obtained problem solutions.

Session 14: The final experience cycle session, in which the trainee works alone through all steps of the problem-solving process on a problem of her own choosing.

Session 15: Training in the use of the Creative Problem Solving procedures to make rapid, on-the-spot decisions.

Session 16: Review of the program.

Restructuring Techniques

A group of problem-solving techniques share the common goal of producing novel idea combinations and the common methodology of part or characteristic change. These include attribute listing, morphological analysis, and checklists. We consider these as a group and, following Rickards (1974), term them *restructuring techniques.*

Attribute listing

Crawford is the developer of attribute listing, a problem-solving approach he explores in his books *How to Get Ideas* (Crawford, 1950) and *Techniques of Creative Thinking* (Crawford, 1954). According to this approach, any idea, object, or product may potentially be improved by isolating and modifying any of its individual attributes or qualities. Attribute listing involves the literal listing of ideas or object attributes to aid in consideration of their subsequent possible modification. As Davis (1973) comments, "In designing clothes, attribute listing is almost the modus operandi. . . . Consider the creation of a shirt or blouse: the cuffs, sleeves, collar, 'cut,' colors and color patterns, material and closure device are separately considered attributes that may be modified or perhaps removed" (p. 104). Stein (1974) provides a second example of attribute listing and modification:

> During the course of time each of the attributes of the screwdriver has undergone some kind of modification. The former round shank now has a hexagonal cross section, which is easier to grip with a wrench to gain more torque. For longer use, the handle is now made of plastic rather than wood. The traditional flat wedge-shaped end has been modified for use with many different types of screws. Electric motors now provide power and there are screwdrivers that develop torque by being pushed rather than twisted. (pp. 214–215)

Crawford (1954) captures the essence of his view of attribute listing with his suggestion that "being original is simply reaching over and shifting attributes in what is before you" (p. 17). The method we consider next provides a systematic basis for the attribute-shifting process.

Morphological analysis

This problem-solving approach, a logical extension of attribute listing, was developed by Zwicky and elaborated in *Morphological Astronomy* (Zwicky, 1957) and *Discovery, Invention, Research: Through the Morphological Approach* (Zwicky, 1969). In morphological analysis, one first identifies two or more major dimensions or attributes of the problem. In the shirt design problem alluded to earlier, relevant dimensions were cuffs, sleeves, collar, cut, colors and color patterns, material, and closure device. Next, one lists alternative ideas or implementations for each dimension. For example, for cuffs, one could readily list one-button, two-button, French, and none. Davis (1973) notes that 43,200 different shirts are possible by means of enumerating attributes and then systematically grouping these attributes into all possible combinations. In a simpler example, Davis (1973) also reports a morphological analysis done by a sixth-grade class in which the dimensions of flavors and extras were examined in an effort to develop new ice creams. Fifty-six flavors were systematically paired with 36 extras (nuts, fruits, vegetables, etc.) to yield 2,016 ice creams. A number of variations of this approach have been described, usually under the category of forced relationship techniques. Three of the more frequently mentioned are the catalog technique, the listing technique, and the focused object technique. (See Whiting, 1958, for more detailed information on the character of these variants.)

Checklists

Two broad types of checklists have been used for problem-solving purposes: specialized and generalized (Whiting, 1958). The specialized lists, as used in business and industry, are reminders and guidelines for such purposes as introducing a new product or making a sale. Their general purpose is to remind the user of the essential steps that ideally constitute a given process. The generalized checklist, as its name implies, can be applied to a variety of situations. One frequently used list of this type is Osborn's (1953) checklist of nine basic categories of "idea-spurring questions" for altering an existing idea, object, or product:

1. Put to other uses? New ways to use as is? Other uses if modified?
2. Adapt? What else is like this? What other idea does this suggest? Does past offer parallel? What could I copy? Whom could I emulate?
3. Modify? New twist? Change meaning, color, motion, odor, form, shape? Other changes?

4. Magnify? What to add? More time? Greater frequency? Stronger? Larger? Thicker? Extra value? Plus ingredients? Duplicate? Multiply? Exaggerate?

5. Minify? What to substitute? Smaller? Condensed? Miniature? Lower? Shorter? Lighter? Omit? Streamline? Split up? Understate?

6. Substitute? Who else instead? What else instead? Other ingredients? Other material? Other process? Other place? Other approach? Other tone of voice?

7. Rearrange? Interchange components? Other pattern? Other layout? Other sequence? Transpose cause and effect? Change pace? Change schedule?

8. Reverse? Transpose positive and negative? How about opposites? Turn it backward? Turn it upside down? Reverse roles? Change shoes? Turn tables? Turn other cheek?

9. Combine? How about a blend, an alloy, an assortment, an ensemble? Combine units? Combine purposes? Combine appeals? Combine ideas? (pp. 30–31)

In addition to attribute listing, morphological analysis, and the use of idea-stimulating checklists, other lesser known restructuring techniques for problem solving have been described. These techniques, which the interested reader may wish to pursue further, include the Vice-Versa Approach (Goldner, 1962), the Input-Output Technique (Whiting, 1958), Use of the Ridiculous (Von Fange, 1959), the Fresh Eye (Whiting, 1958), and Relevance Systems (Rickards, 1974).

Other Sources for Extrapolation
The present discussion has described the more widely known approaches to impersonal problem solving and has simultaneously urged an extrapolatory frame of reference. This frame of reference seeks to encourage attempts to view techniques designed to enhance problem-solving effectiveness in industry, education, and the experimental laboratory as being of potential value for frustration reduction and problem solving in the interpersonal realm. Experimental psychology has long been seriously involved in providing yet another important domain for such possible extrapolation. Investigators have devoted substantial amounts of effort seeking in laboratory contexts to clarify the problem-solving process. These efforts have generally sought to identify and describe task variables influencing problem difficulty, problem-solving styles and strategies, and personality characteristics that aid or hinder problem-solving effectiveness. Three theoretical viewpoints have emerged: The Gestalt view of problem solving sees

this activity as involving directed learning, including conscious and purposive processes. A mentalistic theory, this orientation assumes a situation in which the problem solver actively hypothesizes, reasons, follows leads, encodes, deduces, makes and tests predictions, and, especially, gains insight. The associationistic view, by contrast, seeks to explain learning in conditioning (stimulus-response) terms. In this view, trial-and-error learning, rather than insight, is the dominant process. Responses are organized in response hierarchies, and problem solving is looked on as a process of rearrangement of responses in such a hierarchy. The third theoretical view, information processing, has been closely tied to computer simulation methodology and technology. Computers can be programmed to simulate significant cognitive processes: forming associations, hypothesis testing, comparison of information, remembering, and so forth. The fact that such complex formulation and evaluation processes can be simulated has enabled information-processing investigators to examine increasingly complex problems and the means by which they may be resolved.

Although these theories and the companion research they have stimulated are quite substantial, it must be stressed again that one is faced here with questions of extrapolatory appropriateness. Laboratory investigators of impersonal problem solving study anagrams, maze tests, perceptual problems, logic, chess, checkers, abstract concept development, and a host of problems seemingly far removed from the interpersonal domains at the heart of the Prepare Curriculum. Making use of such laboratory-based findings will require open-mindedness, as well as both formal and informal research.

Much the same point can be made regarding the substantial theoretical and research literature on creativity and its enhancement. A great many creativity enhancement programs exist and are prime extrapolatory targets. These include Torrance's (1975) seminal, long-term program for enhancing creativity in schoolchildren; Maltzman's (1960) training for originality; Mearns' (1958) procedures for the reinforcement of original behavior; the Williams Total Creativity Program (Williams, 1972); the Purdue Creativity Program (Covington, Crutchfield, & Davies, 1966); the Myers and Torrance (1965) ideabooks; the Productive Thinking Program (Crutchfield & Covington, 1964); Inquiry Training (Suchman, 1961); and the Inductive Teaching Program (Karlins & Schroder, 1967). Together, these approaches constitute a mass of exciting procedures and insights of potential viability for the interpersonal problem-solving domain.

Beyond the formulation and evaluation of creativity-enhancing programs, procedures, and materials, creativity research has yielded two additional bodies of information of potential value for interpersonal problem solving. One concerns the identification of characteristics of creative individuals. Of course, our concern here is for the development and accentuation of these characteristics, which appear to include open-mindedness, nonconformity, assertiveness, independence, perseverance, willingness to consider the irrational, tolerance of ambiguity, and flexibility. The second grows from studies on blocks to or inhibitors of creativity, and here, of course, our concern is for their diminution or elimination. Such blocks include excessive reliance on logic; over-commitment to a single approach; unwillingness to speculate; excessive deference to experts; stereotyping; a belief that fantasy and playfulness are inappropriate for adults; and other perceptual, cultural, emotional, intellectual, and expressive impediments. These domains, too, might well be explored for their interpersonal problem-solving implications.

Training Procedures

The first part of this chapter described a number of early attempts to train interpersonal problem-solving skills and examined one viable program, Interpersonal Cognitive Problem Solving (ICPS), in considerable depth.* Several approaches to dealing with impersonal problem domains were also considered for both their substance and possible relevance, by extension, to the Prepare Curriculum. We now wish to turn to the Prepare approach for Problem-solving Training. It is an approach that reflects both the spirit and general thrust of ICPS, though little of its contents and much of the spirit of the array of impersonal problem-solving techniques considered. While targeting the goals of problem identification, information gathering, the generation of alternative solutions, and so forth, we have in the methods and contents of this course developed a problem-solving training sequence that can be integrated with the methods and contents of a number of other Prepare courses. In this way, development of the present course contributes to our overarching goal of creating an integrated, coordinated curriculum. Specifically, Prepare Problem-solving Training methodology involves the

---

*The training procedures presented in this section are from *Problem Solving Interventions for Adolescent Males: A Preliminary Investigation* (pp. 116-163), by J. E. Grant, 1987, Syracuse, NY: Unpublished doctoral dissertation, Syracuse University. Adapted by permission.

chaining of a sequence of incremental responses (as in Anger Control Training, chapter 5) and uses interpersonal skills (as in Interpersonal Skills Training, chapter 3) that are situation-relevant (as in Situational Perception Training, chapter 4) and empathic skill (as in Empathy Training, chapter 8) as components of problem resolution. As a further departure from ICPS and most other existing interpersonal problem-solving training efforts, the approach incorporates in a substantial way the impersonal problem-solving method of brainstorming as a means for generating alternative problem solutions.

Prepare Problem-solving Training was systematically evaluated in a pilot research examination conducted by Grant (1987). Her subjects were 60 incarcerated delinquent male adolescents. Twenty-four received an 8-week version of Problem-solving Training; 24 were assigned to a motivation-control condition; and 12 youths were no-training controls. Clear trends emerged in this pilot investigation pointing to increases in desirable, appropriate behavioral solutions to real-life problems, and decreases in undesirable, inappropriate solutions as a function of Problem-solving Training. Only this brief (8-week) version of the course was implemented, and not all study hypotheses were confirmed. But as a pilot project, encouraging of further utilization and evaluation of Problem-solving Training, Grant's (1987) findings are affirmative.

A session-by-session outline of problem-solving activities is presented in Table 2. Although presented as an eight-session sequence, the course will often take several meetings longer. As in the Prepare Interpersonal Skills Training and Anger Control Training courses (see chapters 3 and 5, respectively), every participant should have the opportunity via role playing to practice and receive feedback on each course segment. To do so may take two or three sessions for any given segment or segments, thus resulting in a program considerably stretched out beyond the eight sessions now described.

Session 1: Introduction

Rationale
"Sell" the program to adolescents and obtain commitment from the group and/or make the following points in the discussion:

1. We make decisions every day (e.g., getting up or deciding what to eat). Many of these decisions are automatic.

Table 2
Outline of Problem-solving Training Sessions

Session 1: Introduction

Rationale
Rules and procedures
Overview of problem-solving steps
Problem Log
Review Session 1

Session 2: Stop and Think

Rationale
Review Session 1
Stop and think
Be a detective
Role play: Stop and think
Review Session 2

Session 3: Problem Identification

Rationale
Review Session 2
Learn to define (What's the problem?)
Ways to define a problem
Role play: Stop and think + problem identification
Review Session 3

Session 4: Gathering Information/Own Perspective

Rationale
Review Session 3
Fact or opinion (What do I see? What are the facts?)
Information (What do I see? What do I need to know?)
Role play: Stop and think + problem identification + gathering information/
   own perspective
Review Session 4

Session 5: Gathering Information/Others' Perspectives

Rationale
Review Session 4
Others' views (What do others see? What do others think?)
Others' emotions (What do others feel?)
Role play: Stop and think + problem identification + gathering information/
   own and others' perspectives
Review Session 5

Table 2 *(continued)*

Session 6: Alternatives

Rationale
Review Session 5
Options (What can I do or say?)
Brainstorming (What are my choices?)
Role play: Stop and think + problem identification + gathering information/
    own and others' perspectives + alternatives
Review Session 6

Session 7: Evaluating Consequences and Outcomes

Rationale
Review Session 6
Consequences (What will happen if I do or say that?)
Choices (How do I decide what to do?)
Role play: Stop and think + problem identification + gathering information/
    own and others' perspectives + evaluating consequences and outcomes
Review Session 7

Session 8: Practice

Rationale
Review Session 7
Role play: Stop and think + problem identification + gathering information/
    own and others' perspectives + evaluating consequences and outcomes
Reinforcement

---

2. Decisions are harder to make when they are in more complicated problem situations. Problems are difficult situations that we don't
know exactly what to do about.

3. Problems can be solved. The reason for training is that it
teaches a way to solve them. A person doesn't have to do the first thing
that comes to mind or give up and do nothing. *Examples:* Fighting to
solve a problem or letting others make your decisions for you.

4. Problems have two characteristics in common: goals and
obstacles. Problems are difficult situations because we have a goal or
something we want and there is an obstacle or something that gets in
the way of what we want. (Imagine that we want to go down a particular
road and a tree has fallen in the path.) *Examples:* Losing weight or
getting along with friends.

5. Common types of problems include
    - Control problems (getting someone to do what we want)
    - Differences between people's personal goals
    - A search for something or someone
    - Problems caused by uncertainty or unclear expectations

6. By learning how to approach decision making more slowly and carefully, we have more control over what happens to us. *Example:* By thinking about how friends think or feel, we can say things that will make them like us.

7. After discussing these points with the group, encourage commitment to try the program.

Rules and procedures

If the group needs structure, rules and procedures may be explained at the beginning of the session. In any case, the following points should be covered:

1. Meeting times will be determined by trainers.

2. Each group member is expected to participate actively and cooperatively, and to respect other group members (e.g., not interrupting or making fun of others' comments).

3. Group members will be expected to keep track of their problems outside the group in a Problem Log (see Figure 1). (Redefine a problem as a difficult situation in which we have a goal or objective that we cannot reach easily.)

4. Over the next few sessions, a way of thinking about problems and making decisions will be described and demonstrated by the trainer and role played and practiced by each group member. Problems from Problem Logs will be used in the role play so that group members can think about and choose how they will act next time.

Overview of problem-solving steps

During each session, display a poster that shows the steps of the problem-solving process being covered in that session. In addition, leave on display the posters from any previous sessions for that problem-solving training group, thus gradually posting the sequence of responses that constitute the complete problem-solving chain. Points to be covered in the overview include the following:

1. You will learn to stop and think.

Figure 1
Problem Log

Date _____

What is the problem? Describe it (who is involved, where did it happen, and what happened?).

What do you *want* to happen?

What did you do or say to solve the problem?

Did your choice solve the problem?

How well did it work?

1	2	3	4	5
Poorly	Not so well	Okay	Good	Great

Homework:

2. You will be able to ask yourself the following questions:
- What is my problem?
- What are the facts? What do I need to know?
- What can I do or say? What are my choices?
- What will happen if I do this or if I do that?
- How can I make a choice and check out what happened?

3. After making these points, give an example of a problem and demonstrate each of the steps, in detail, modeling the questions as inner thoughts. *Example:* Deciding whether or not to buy a car.

4. Pass out folders for group members to keep materials in.

Problem Log

1. Explain the importance of the Problem Log:
- On a weekly basis, gives an accurate report of problems or things you don't know exactly what to do about.
- Helps you figure out what your problem situations are and begin thinking about how you can handle problems.
- Provides material for the role play of problem-solving techniques.

2. Show an example of a Problem Log already filled out. (See Figure 2 for an example concerning an adolescent presented with peer pressure to run away from an institutional facility.) Depending on the group's academic abilities, ask different members to read different items or have a trainer read.

3. Pass out Problem Log forms to put in folders. Tell group members to fill them out as soon after the problem situation as possible.

Review Session 1

1. Review reasons for careful problem solving (to increase control over and manage one's life more effectively and to better meet one's needs).

2. Review rules and procedures, particularly the importance of the Problem Log.

Session 2: Stop and Think

Rationale

State at the start of the session that successful problem solving depends on (1) thinking before you act and (2) knowing you have a problem.

Figure 2
Example Problem Log

Date _____

What is the problem? Describe what happened (who is involved, where did it happen, and what happened?).

Three residents have just asked me to go AWOL with them. I really don't like it in the facility, but I want to do well. I don't want them to not like me if I don't go either.

What do you *want* to happen?

I'd really like to leave the facility but I'd rather leave by going through the program. If you run away, you just get caught.

What did you do or say to solve the problem?

I said, "No, I can't run away. I don't want to get set back in the program when they catch me."

Did your choice solve the problem?

I didn't get set back in the program. My friends went anyway and got brought back.

How well did it work?

1	2	3	4	5
Poorly	Not so well	Okay	Good	Great

Homework:

Review Session 1

1. Review rules and procedures set up in Session 1.

2. Reiterate that problems are part of life and that with practice you can learn to make decisions about them rather than acting too quickly or letting someone else decide for you.

3. Briefly review the problem example used in the first session and model *all* previously described steps in the problem-solving training chain. *Example:* Deciding whether or not to buy a car.

Stop and think

The important point to stress here is that, if we have a problem, we have to stop and think or we may decide too quickly. We want to be able to think of alternate ways to handle the problem. Specifically, the trainer should

1. Explain that people can have a lot of different reactions to problems and that you need to learn to recognize that you have a problem by how you think and feel.
   - Describe different thoughts: "Most of the time you just won't know what to do. You'll have questions, doubts, and you're not sure what is best. You may know what you want, but you can't figure out how to get it."
   - Describe different feelings: "Many times you'll have uncomfortable feelings that let you know you have a problem. You may feel frustrated, tense, restless, or confused about your choices."

2. Ask adolescents to describe their own reactions to problems and to write them on an easel or blackboard.

3. Compare their list to the list of common reactions to problems given in Table 3. Add those they have not suggested.

4. Explain how taking several slow deep breaths and saying to yourself, "stop and think" will give you time to decide what you want to do.

5. Model the sequence by using a problem situation offered by a group member or the example following. *Example:* Deciding whether or not to go "AWOL" from the institutional facility. (See Figure 2.)
   - Model what thoughts and feelings you yourself would use to tell that you have a problem.
   - Model how to take several deep breaths and say, "stop and think."
   - Model how this gives you time to think of ways to handle the situation. (Make sure you model only stop and think.)

6. Role play a problem with the group through stop and think, being sure to give every group member a chance to participate. Elicit from the group members their thoughts and feelings after they experience the role-played problem. *Example:* A group member has to talk to a staff person to discuss an incident in which he has been disrespectful and cursed at her.

Table 3
Stop and Think: Common Reactions to Problems

Discouraged
Feel like you can't make the best decision anyway
Confused
Uncertain
Uptight
Tense
Doubtful
Feel like giving up
Worried
Inadequate
Angry
Annoyed
Unhappy
Uncomfortable
Put down
Questioning
Restless
Want to escape
Avoid by doing something else
Frustrated
Sad
Do anything just to get it done
Sleep

Be a detective

Explain that a good problem solver has to be a good detective and *notice all the clues* in a situation.

    1. Stress that, to know what your problem is, you must first observe exactly what is happening.

- Give part of the group an unfamiliar but relevant problem situation to enact. *Example:* A group member has a confrontation with a counselor about the youth's bad behavior, which is affecting team performance.

- Ask other members to observe and tell exactly what happened in the role play. Elicit as many details about the interaction as possible and point out how different group members notice different things.

2. Using picture stimuli (magazine pictures that show detailed interactions among several people), ask group members to tell what they see.

- Point out that not everyone sees the same thing.
- Define the problem in the picture differently by using different details from two group members to show how different observations affect the definition of the problem.

3. Have group members describe in detail another member of the group without looking at him. (Do this only if the group will not use the exercise to ridicule the group member chosen.)

Role play
Stop and think
Have group members role play either the example below or one from their Problem Logs. Encourage them to include the main actor's thoughts in role play. Each group member should role play the main actor. Assist role play and give feedback on and reinforcement for performance. *Example:* Another resident in your team has lost his home visit. He says that you started a fight with him that made this happen, and he's very angry with you.

Review Session 2

1. Review the use of the Problem Log and stress the importance of having each member complete the logs as assigned.

2. Review each group member's thoughts and feelings associated with problems.

3. Review taking slow, deep breaths and saying, "stop and think" to yourself.

4. Review the importance of observing situations.

5. Assign homework: Try to identify problem signs and practice stop and think.

Session 3: Problem Identification

Rationale
State at the beginning of the session that, once we feel the signs of a problem and have stopped to think, we have to state the problem clearly and specifically.

Review Session 2

1. By going over the Problem Logs, review how to tell you have a problem and how to use stop and think.

- Ask each group member to use his completed Problem Log and tell others in the group what he thought or felt when he had a problem.
- Ask whether the group tried stop and think, and, using the Problem Logs, discuss their answers. Provide reinforcement for successful use and, at the same time, check Problem Logs to see that they are filled in correctly.

2. Review the *whole* decision-making process, using the same training example first introduced in Session 1. Refer to the posters detailing the problem-solving steps and model the questions as internal thoughts. *Example from Session 1:* Deciding whether or not to buy a car.

Learn to define
(What's the problem?)
The most important part of this step is learning to say what the problem is as clearly and as specifically as you can.

1. Explain that you can't solve a problem that is too big and too confused or so small that information is left out.

- Give an example of a problem that has been too broadly defined. *Example:* You can say that getting along with teachers is your problem, but this really tells very little about what it is that teachers do that bothers you.
- Give an example of a problem too narrowly defined. *Example:* You can say that your problem is Mr. Jones' yelling, but this gives too little information about the type of problem as a whole.

2. Show several magazine pictures that illustrate a problem situation. (These should show people that youth can identify with or funny, unexpected situations that create interest.)

- Ask different group members to state the problem.
- Ask questions to elicit more specific responses and reinforce statements that note specific details related to specific behavior.

Ways to define a problem
Explain that, in order to make good decisions, you have to ask yourself questions to get at exactly what your problem is. If you experience bad feelings, these can be a signal that you have a problem.

    1. What questions can you then ask yourself?
       • What do you really want? What is your *goal*?
       • What *don't you like*?
       • What is getting in the way of what you want? What is the *obstacle*?
       • What *change* is needed?

    2. Model the use of these questions in a specific situation. *Example:* You have to call your mother this afternoon and tell her that because you got into a fight your home visit will be delayed for 2 weeks.
       • The *goal* is to do well in the program and leave the facility.
       • You *don't like* having to call your mother and not being able to go on a home visit.
       • The *obstacle* is fighting.
       • The *change* needed involves learning ways to control anger and fighting.

    3. Tell the group about the importance of "I" statements in problem definition. (In other words, the goals must be yours, and the only behavior you can change for certain is your own.)
    4. Role play the example: Have two of the group members discuss the cancelled home visit. Have one of them ask the necessary questions and the other provide the answers. (Write the words that are italicized on an easel or blackboard: *goal, don't like, obstacle, change.*)

Role play
Stop and think + problem identification
Assist role play and give feedback on the sequence learned. Have group members use problems from their Problem Logs. Emphasize problem statement, "I" statements, and asking questions of self.

Review Session 3

    1. Review the problem-solving sequence learned so far, including thoughts and feelings that let us know we have a problem, stop and think, and finding out what the problem is.

2. Remind group members about Problem Logs and assign home-work: Practice writing problems in the logs clearly and notice exactly what was happening in the situation.

Session 4: Gathering Information/Own Perspective

Rationale
Explain that, in order to figure out what to do or say when we have a problem, we have to have information about (1) how we see the situation and (2) how others see the problem. Emphasize that this session will look at what *we* see—the next session will concentrate on others' perceptions.

Review Session 3

1. Review problem identification by using the Problem Logs. Use one problem each from one or two members and help each of them state the problem specifically and elicit observations about the situation.

2. Model the *whole* decision-making sequence by going over the questions for each step as listed on the posters. Use the same training example as presented earlier. *Example from Session 1:* Deciding whether or not to buy a car.

Fact or opinion
(What do I see? What are the facts?)
Provide the following explanation to the group: "We have already learned to be good detectives and notice all the clues. We also have to learn the difference between fact and opinion. Acting quickly on the wrong information can make the situation much worse." *Example:* You think your girlfriend wants to break up, so you break up first. Later, you find you were wrong about her feelings.

1. Explain that, to be a good problem solver, you have to know the difference between what *is* true and what you *think* may be true.

2. Using pictures that are ambiguous or that have been cut in half so not all the information is available, have the group practice finding evidence. Help them understand the difference between this process and making inferences without enough information.

3. Role play several situations from the Problem Logs. Ask group members to decide what the facts of the problem are and what inferences could be made about the situation. Alternatively, set up a

false accusation situation in which a main actor emphasizes an accuser's different interpretation of the other's behavior.

Information
(What do I see? What do I need to know?)
Point out that, if we can't figure out what is happening or we don't have enough information, we have to ask. *Example:* You break up with your girlfriend because you haven't heard from her in over a week. Later, you find out she has been ill.

Role play
Stop and think + problem identification +
gathering information/own perspective
Role play one of the situations from a group member's Problem Log and have the main actor identify problem signs, stop and think, identify the problem, and gather facts about the situation. Assist role play and provide feedback on the sequence learned. *Example:* Team staff have delayed your home visit. You think you should be able to go home because you haven't broken any rules.

Review Session 4

    1. Summarize the use of the problem-solving chain described so far and indicate how thinking about a situation before acting can increase a sense of control and make things turn out better.
    2. Assign homework: Ask group members to identify a problem for which more information is needed and to practice asking questions to get it.

Session 5: Gathering Information/
Others' Perspectives

Rationale
Express the following ideas to the group: "Now that we have learned to look at the situation more carefully ourselves, we must learn to look at situations from other people's points of view. Doing so gives more information on which to make a choice. *Example:* Your girlfriend may appear to want to break up but may actually be concerned about something else. Thinking about her point of view might stop you from breaking up before you ask her what she really feels.

Review Session 4

1. Using the Problem Logs, review the difference between fact and opinion and the need to ask for information
- Ask a member to report a situation as he saw it and tell the group what he *knows* and what he *thinks he knows.*
- Also ask whether anyone asked a question to get more information. Discuss, provide feedback, and give reinforcement.

2. Model the *whole* decision-making process by going over the steps presented on the posters, using the same training example presented earlier. *Example from Session 1:* Deciding whether or not to buy a car.

Others' views
(What do others see? What do others think?)
Point out that we need to recognize that others may see a problem differently from the way we do and that anticipating how others see our behavior gives us more understanding of a problem and more control over what happens. *Example:* You are accused by a store owner of shoplifting a pair of pants. How would knowing how the store owner feels about shoplifting change the way you act in the situation?

1. Model the role-taking response by
- Using two common objects and pointing out that what a person sees depends on where he is sitting.
- Having group members stand in various parts of the room and describe the room from different angles.

2. Using pictures, ask each group member to say how each person in the picture sees the situation.

3. Role play the situation in which the main actor is accused by a store owner of shoplifting a pair of pants. Build into the role play the fact that the youth had behaved in a way that the store owner might have perceived as suspicious.

4. Have each member of the group take other roles in the situation. Provide feedback and reinforce efforts to respond differently in different parts.

Others' emotions
(What do others feel?)[2]

Tell the group that, if we know how others feel in a problem situation, we can better anticipate how that person is going to act. *Example:* You ask permission for something from a person who is already angry.

1. Using pictures of faces, have the group practice identifying different emotions and describing different facial expressions.

2. Teach one of the following:

Interpersonal Skill 17: Understanding the Feelings of Others (See chapter 3, p. 109)

- Watch the other person.
- Listen to what the other person is saying.
- Figure out what the other person might be feeling.
- Think about ways to show you understand what he/she is feeling.
- Decide on the best way and do it.

Model, role play, and give feedback on skill steps. *Example:* A resident you know in another team is upset because his parents, who promised to visit him for 3 weeks running, have not shown up.

Interpersonal Skill 18: Dealing with Someone Else's Anger (See chapter 3, p. 110)

- Listen to the person who is angry.
- Try to understand what the angry person is saying and feeling.
- Decide if you can say or do something to deal with the situation.
- If you can, deal with the other person's anger (assertiveness, ignoring, listening, empathic response, corrective action).

Model, role play, and provide feedback on skill steps. *Example:* Your counselor is angry because your team has come in last on the Team-of-the-Week competition for the last 5 weeks.

---

[2]Skills derived from Prepare Empathy Training (see chapter 8) may be employed as part of this training segment.

Role play
Stop and think + problem identification + gathering information/
own and others' perspectives
Role play situations from the Problem Logs. Make sure that the main actor identifies problem signs, stops and thinks, defines the problem, and gathers information from self and others. Emphasize understanding of others' perspectives. Provide reinforcement and feedback on role play. Have as many members participate as time allows.

Review Session 5

1. Summarize the problem-solving chain so far. Review that people have different perspectives and can think differently about a problem. Emphasize that understanding others' feelings will help us solve problems and get more of what we want.
2. Assign homework: Ask the group to write down what they think others see in a problem situation drawn from their Problem Logs.

Session 6: Alternatives

Rationale
Stress that, to make a good choice in any situation, we have to think of more than one way to act. Point out that, if you have a difference of opinion with someone, knowing how to negotiate, stand up for your rights, and avoid trouble are all choices in the situation. *Example:* You're accused by a store owner of shoplifting a pair of pants.

Review Session 5

1. Review the importance of different points of view in determining what each person does in a situation. Ask a group member to tell of a problem in which there were two clear points of view and to explain how these two points of view came about. Provide feedback and reinforcement.
2. Review and model the *whole* decision-making sequence by going over the steps and questions on the posters, using the same training example presented earlier. *Example:* Deciding whether or not to buy a car.

Options
(What can I do or say?)
Present the following explanation: "Every problem has a number of solutions. The more solutions you can think of, the better your chance of getting what you want and getting around things that are in the way. For example, what choices do you have for dealing with other people's anger? How can negotiating, ignoring the situation, self-control, or assertiveness make you feel more in charge of your life? *Example:* Your friend yells at you because he believes you have gotten him into trouble with his counselor.

1. Teach one of the following skills:

Interpersonal Skill 25: Negotiating (See chapter 3, p. 117.)
- Decide if you and the other person are having a difference of opinion.
- Tell the other person what you think about the problem.
- Ask the other person what he/she thinks about the problem.
- Listen openly to his/her answer.
- Think about why the other person might feel this way.
- Suggest a compromise.

Model, role play, and give feedback on skill steps, emphasizing compromise and role taking. *Example:* Negotiating with a friend about which recreational activity to do.

Interpersonal Skill 27: Standing Up for Your Rights (See chapter 3, p. 119.)
- Pay attention to what is going on in your body. That helps you know that you are dissatisfied and would like to stand up for your rights.
- Decide what happened to make you feel dissatisfied.
- Think about ways in which you might stand up for yourself and choose one.
- Stand up for yourself in a direct and reasonable way.
- Model, role play, and give feedback on the skill. *Example:* Approaching staff about what you feel is an unfair decision: not being allowed a home visit when you've followed the rules.

Interpersonal Skill 29: Avoiding Trouble with Others (See chapter 3, p. 121.)
- Decide if you are in a situation that might get you into trouble.

- Decide if you want to get out of the situation.
- Tell other people what you decided and why.
- Suggest other things you might do.
- Do what you think is best for you.

Model, role play, and give feedback on the skill. *Example:* Three friends pull over in a car you think might be stolen. They ask you to get in and go for a ride.

2. Role play a situation from a Problem Log concerning dealing with another's anger, having each member enact the aggression alternative skill that was taught.

Brainstorming
(What are my choices?)
Emphasize that, for each problem situation, we must come up with as many choices as we can. One way to do this is *brainstorming*. Brainstorming increases the chance that we are successful problem solvers.

1. Introduce the idea of brainstorming. Tell the group about the rules (as many ideas as possible with no evaluation).
2. Ask the group to develop as many alternative behaviors as they can think of to deal with common problems they will face. List these behaviors on an easel or blackboard and add any given in Table 4 that the group does not mention.
3. Use a problem situation from a Problem Log for the group to brainstorm alternatives. At your discretion, have one person keep a record. Remind the group of brainstorming rules if necessary.

Role play
Stop and think + problem identification + gathering information/ own and others' perspectives + alternatives
Assist role play based on one of the problems from a Problem Log. (It is especially good to choose a problem that provides an opportunity to practice the aggression alternative skill learned: avoiding trouble with others, negotiating, or standing up for your rights.) Make sure that the main actor identifies his problem signs, stops and thinks, identifies the problem, gathers information from self and others, and thinks of possible choices. Provide reinforcement and feedback.

Table 4
Alternatives for Dealing with Problem Situations

Assertiveness
Ignoring the situation
Calm, non-hostile response
Negotiating another alternative
Rational, logical arguments
Clear, direct answers
Pleasant, firm tone of voice
Accepting responsibility for behavior
Apologizing
Asking for a chance to discuss problem
Humorous answer
Inviting others to join your group
Asking for help
Asking for information
Understanding your own feelings
Thinking about how others think
Thinking about how others feel

Review Session 6

1. Summarize the problem-solving chain so far. Emphasize the importance of thinking of a number of different choices or alternatives to solve a particular problem: A greater number of choices increases your control over the outcome of your decisions.

2. Assign homework: Ask the group to write in their Problem Logs as many alternatives as they can think of to each of their problems.

Session 7: Evaluating Consequences and Outcomes

Rationale
Summarize the content of the following statement: "We have learned how to think about a number of choices, but now we have to think about what will happen if we choose one alternative over another. In this session we will (1) evaluate the consequences of choices and (2) make a choice and learn to look at what happens."

Review Session 6

1. Review thinking of alternatives. Go over the Problem Logs, using a problem from a member who has written out alternatives. Provide feedback and reinforcement.

2. Review the *whole* decision-making sequence by going over the question for each step, using the same training example presented earlier. *Example:* Deciding whether or not to buy a car.

Consequences
(What will happen if I do or say that?)

Stress that learning how to figure out what will happen when we choose to do something gives us power over what happens to us. For example, there are different consequences for different behaviors when dealing with an authority figure such as a police officer.

1. Discuss with the group the consequences of two behaviors, one positive and one negative. *Example:* When a cop stops you, you are wise and flip or you are calm and cooperative.

2. Have group members brainstorm alternatives for one of the problem situations in the Problem Logs or for one of the following examples:

- Your team members tell you that they're going to steal cigarettes from a resident who is a member of another team and they want you to be the lookout.
- You're walking down the street and a cop stops you and accuses you of burglarizing a house.

3. Encourage the group to evaluate consequences of each alternative. Use the concept of the worst and best consequences or pros and cons of each alternative. Model the evaluation process with inner thoughts and questions: "If I do this, what is the worst that can happen? What is likely to happen?"

4. Role play the consequences of one positive and one negative alternative suggested by the group.

Choices
(How do I decide what to do?)

Now that group members can evaluate the consequences of their choices, point out that deciding which choice is best is the next step. Introduce the idea of evaluating what happens *after* you make a particular decision and emphasize how looking at the effects of your choice helps you in future decisions.

1. Give an example of a decision that you made that you later regretted, particularly one in which you did not evaluate consequences adequately.

2. Ask the group to make a choice between the positive and negative alternatives they just role played (being wise and flip or calm and cooperative when stopped by a policeman).

Role play
Stop and think + problem identification + gathering information/ own and others' perspectives + alternatives + evaluating consequences and outcomes
Assist role play by using one of the problems from the Problem Logs. Have the main actor stop and think, identify the problem, get information from self and others, think of alternatives, think of what will happen if he chooses from among different alternatives, and make a decision. Have the actor consider evaluating the decision. Provide feedback and reinforcement for efforts.

Review Session 7

1. Summarize the decision-making chain and emphasize the importance of evaluating consequences in deciding what to do.
2. Assign homework: Ask the group to write down pros and cons of different alternatives to a problem, make a decision, and act. (At the next session, have participants tell the group how their problem came out and talk about what they could have done differently.)

Session 8: Practice

Rationale
Introduce the session by explaining the following: "We have learned the problem-solving process. Today, we are going to practice the steps using problems from the Problem Logs."

Review Session 7

1. Review homework assignment. Ask group members to give examples from their Problem Logs about decisions that they made and to explain how the decisions came out. Emphasize the importance of looking at the outcome of decisions.
2. Review the *whole* decision-making sequence by going over the questions for each step shown on the posters, using the same training example presented earlier. *Example from Session 1:* Deciding whether or not to buy a car.

Role play
*Stop and think + problem identification + gathering information/
own and others' perspectives + alternatives + evaluating
consequences and outcomes*

1. Recap each step of the process.
2. Role play the complete problem-solving chain by using several problems from Problem Logs. Role play with as many group members as possible.

Reinforcement
Provide encouragement and reinforcement for the group to continue to try these problem-solving methods.

Chapter 3

Interpersonal Skills Training

In the early 1970s, an important new intervention approach began to emerge in the interface between psychology and education.* The aggressive, withdrawn, or otherwise interpersonally skill deficient youngster came to be viewed more in educational, pedagogic terms than as a client in need of counseling or psychotherapy, and the mental health professional assumed she was dealing with an individual lacking, or at best weak in, the abilities necessary for effective and satisfying personal and interpersonal functioning rather than suffering from mental disorder or emotional disturbance. The task of the professional became, therefore, not interpretation, reflection, or reinforcement—as, respectively, in psychodynamic, client-centered, and behavior modification interventions with such youth—but the active and deliberate teaching of desirable behaviors. Rather than an intervention called *psychotherapy,* between patient and psychotherapist, or *counseling,* between client and counselor, what emerged was an intervention called *training,* between trainee and interpersonal skills trainer.

Theory and Research

Our interpersonal skills training approach, originally called *Structured Learning,* began in the early 1970s (Goldstein, 1973; Goldstein, Sprafkin, & Gershaw, 1976). At that time, and for several years thereafter, our training and research efforts were conducted in public mental hospitals with long-term, highly skill deficient, chronic patients, especially those preparing for return to the community as a result of deinstitutionalization. As our program progressed and demonstrated with regularity successful skill enhancement effects (Goldstein, 1981), we shifted our focus from teaching a broad array of interpersonal skills to adult psychiatric inpatients to a more explicit concern for such skill training

---

*Portions of this chapter first appeared in *Skillstreaming the Adolescent: A Structured Learning Approach to Teaching Prosocial Skills,* by A. P. Goldstein, R. P. Sprafkin, N. J. Gershaw, and P. Klein, 1980, and *Skillstreaming the Elementary School Child: A Guide for Teaching Prosocial Skills,* by E. McGinnis and A. P. Goldstein, 1984, Champaign, IL: Research Press.

for aggressive individuals. Our trainee groups included spouses engaged in family disputes violent enough to warrant police intervention (Goldstein, Monti, Sardino, & Green, 1977; Goldstein & Rosenbaum, 1982), child-abusing parents (Goldstein, Keller, & Erne, 1985; Solomon, 1977; Sturm, 1980), and, most especially, both overtly aggressive adolescents (Goldstein, Sherman, Gershaw, Sprafkin, & Glick, 1978; Goldstein, Sprafkin, Gershaw, & Klein, 1980) and younger children (Keller, Goldstein, & Wynn, 1987; McGinnis & Goldstein, 1984).

Our research group has conducted a systematic program oriented toward evaluating and improving the effectiveness of our Interpersonal Skills Training approach. Approximately 60 investigations involving a wide variety of trainee populations and trainers have been conducted. These populations include chronic adult schizophrenics (Goldstein, 1973; Goldstein et al., 1976; Liberman, 1970; Orenstein, 1973; Sutton-Simon, 1973), geriatric patients (Lopez, 1977; Lopez, Hoyer, Goldstein, Gershaw, & Sprafkin, 1982), child-abusing parents (Fischman, 1984, 1985; Goldstein et al., 1985; Solomon, 1977; Sturm, 1980), young children (Hummel, 1980; Keller et al., 1987; McGinnis & Goldstein, 1984; Spatz-Norton, 1985; Swanstrom, 1974), such change-agent trainees as mental hospital staff (Berlin, 1976; Goldstein & Goedhart, 1973; Lack, 1975; Robinson, 1973; Schneiman, 1972), police (Goldstein et al., 1977), persons employed in industrial contexts (Goldstein & Sorcher, 1973, 1974), and, in recent years, aggressive and other interpersonally skill deficient adolescents (Goldstein & Glick, 1987).

With regard to adolescent trainees, Interpersonal Skills Training has been successful in enhancing such prosocial skills as empathy, negotiation, assertiveness, instruction following, self-control, conflict resolution, and perspective taking. Beyond these demonstrations that Interpersonal Skills Training enhances prosocial skill competencies, our adolescent studies have also highlighted other aspects of the teaching of prosocial behaviors. Fleming (1976), in an effort to capitalize upon adolescent responsiveness to peer influence, demonstrated that gains in negotiating skill are as great when the Interpersonal Skills Training group leader is a respected peer as when the leader is an adult. Litwack (1976), more concerned with the skill-enhancing effects of an adolescent's anticipating that he will later serve as a peer leader, showed that such helper role expectation increases the degree of skill acquired. Apparently, when the adolescent expects to teach others a skill, his own level of skill acquisition increases, a finding clearly relevant to Reissman's (1965) helper therapy principle. Trief (1976) demonstrated that successful use of Interpersonal Skills Training to increase the perspective-taking skill (i.e., seeing matters from other people's viewpoints) also leads to consequent increases in cooperative behavior. The significant transfer effects both in this study and in the Golden (1975), Litwack (1976), and Raleigh (1977) investigations have been important sign-posts in planning further research on transfer enhancement.

As in earlier efforts with adult trainees, the value of teaching certain skill combinations has begun to be examined. Aggression-prone adolescents often get into difficulty when they respond with overt aggression to authority figures with whom they disagree. Golden (1975), responding to this type of event, successfully used Interpersonal Skills Training to teach such adolescents resistance-reducing behavior, defined as a combination of reflection of feeling (the authority figure's) and assertiveness (forthright but nonaggressive statement of one's own position). Jennings (1975) was able to use Interpersonal Skills Training successfully to instruct adolescents in several of the verbal skills necessary for satisfactory participation in more traditional, insight-oriented psychotherapy. Guzzetta (1974) was successful in providing means to help close the gap between adolescents and their parents by using Interpersonal Skills Training to teach empathic skills to parents. But the major findings of our adolescent studies for our present purposes pertain to skill-enhancement effectiveness. The overall conclusions that may justifiably be drawn from these several empirical evaluations (conclusions identical to those one may draw for adult Interpersonal Skills Training studies) concern *skill acquisition* and *skill transfer.*

Across diverse trainee populations (clearly including aggressive adolescents in urban secondary schools and juvenile detention centers) and target skills, skill acquisition is a reliable training outcome, occurring in well over 90 percent of participants in Interpersonal Skills Training. Although pleased with this outcome, we are acutely aware that gains demonstrable in the training context are rather easily accomplished—given the potency, support, encouragement, and low threat value of trainers—but that the more consequential outcome question by far pertains to trainee skill performance in real-world contexts (i.e., skill transfer).

Across diverse trainee populations, target skills, and applied (real-world) settings, skill transfer occurs with approximately 45 to 50 percent of participants in Interpersonal Skills Training sessions. Goldstein and Kanfer (1979), as well as Karoly and Steffen (1980), have indicated that, across several dozen types of psychotherapy involving many different types of psychopathology, the average transfer rate on follow-up is between 15 and 20 percent of patients seen. The near 50 percent rate consequent to Interpersonal Skills Training is a significant improvement upon this collective base rate, although it must immediately be underscored that this cumulative average transfer finding also means that the gains shown by half of our trainees were limited to in-session acquisition. Of special consequence, however, is the consistently clear manner in which skill transfer in our studies was a function of the explicit implementation of laboratory derived transfer-enhancing techniques, such as those described in chapter 12.

Concurrent with or following our development of Interpersonal Skills Training, a number of similar programmatic attempts to enhance social competency emerged. Those that focused in large part on aggressive youngsters and their prosocial training include Life Skills Education (Adkins, 1970), Social Skills Training (Argyle, Trower, & Bryant, 1974), AWARE: Activities for Social Development (Elardo & Cooper, 1977), Relationship Enhancement (Guerney, 1977), Teaching Conflict Resolution (Hare, 1976), Developing Human Potential (Hawley & Hawley, 1975), ASSET (Hazel, Schumaker, Sherman, & Sheldon-Wildgen, 1981), Interpersonal Communication (Heiman, 1973), and Directive Teaching (Stephens, 1976). The instructional techniques that constitute each of these skills-training efforts derive from social learning theory and typically consist of instructions, modeling, role playing, and performance feedback—with ancillary use in some instances of contingent reinforcement, prompting, shaping, or related behavioral techniques. Developing in part out of the empirical tradition of behavior modification, interpersonal skills training efforts not surprisingly came under early and continuing research scrutiny.

Our recent examination of research by other investigators concerned with interpersonal skills training involving aggressive adolescent and preadolescent subjects identified 30 relevant evaluation studies (Goldstein & Glick, 1987). Two-thirds of these studies are of multiple-group design; the remainder are single-subject studies. As noted earlier, interpersonal skills training is operationally defined in an almost identical manner across all of these investigations, usually as a combination of modeling, role playing, and performance feedback. In some instances, one or more transfer enhancement procedures are added. Study subjects are adjudicated juvenile delinquents, status offenders, or chronically aggressive youngsters studied in secondary or elementary school settings. Although target skills have varied across investigations, for the most part these skills have concerned interpersonal, prosocial alternatives to aggression and aggression management or aggression inhibition behaviors. As Spence (1981) notes, the single-case studies have tended toward microskill training targets (eye contact, head nods, and the like), and the multiple-group studies have sought to teach more macroskill competencies (e.g., coping with criticism, negotiation, problem solving). Results for skill acquisition have been quite consistently positive. Aggressive adolescents are able to learn a broad array of previously unavailable interpersonal, aggression management, affect-relevant, and related psychological competencies via the training methods examined here. Evaluation for maintenance and transfer of acquired skills yields a rather different outcome. Many studies test for neither. Those that do evaluate long-term acquisition and generalization provide an inconsistent picture. As noted earlier, our own investigative efforts in this regard (Goldstein, 1981) point to the not surprising conclusion that generalization of skill competency across settings (transfer) and time (maintenance) is very much a direct function of the degree to which the investigator/trainer has implemented as a part of the training effort procedures explicitly designed to enhance transfer and/or maintenance.

To summarize our view of empirical efforts to date, Interpersonal Skills Training with aggressive and other skill deficient youngsters rests on a firm investigative foundation. A variety of investigators, designs, subjects, settings, and target skills are providing a healthy examination of the effectiveness of such training. Skill acquisition is a reliable outcome, but the social validity of this consistent result is tempered substantially by the frequent failure—or at least indeterminacy—of transfer and maintenance.

Training Procedures

We have placed Interpersonal Skills Training early in the Prepare Curriculum's constituent courses to underscore its central role. Not only is interpersonal competence crucial in its own right, but such prosocial abilities are important prerequisites or corequisites to other Prepare domains. Both Problem-solving Training (chapter 2) and Recruiting Supportive Models (chapter 9), for example, require as part of their successful enactment the ability to draw upon subsets of this course's interpersonal skills repertoire. Situational Perception Training (chapter 4) essentially teaches trainees the diagnostic skills necessary to know where, when, and with whom to employ previously learned interpersonal skills. And, in similar fashion, Interpersonal Skills Training has been used with demonstrated effectiveness in tandem with Anger Control Training (chapter 5) and Moral Reasoning Training (chapter 6) in a combined intervention we have called *Aggression Replacement Training* (Goldstein & Glick, 1987). Clearly, Interpersonal Skills Training plays a key role in Prepare. The remainder of this chapter is a detailed presentation of the specific training procedures that constitute this course and the interpersonal skills that are its lessons.

The selection, preparation, and instruction of adolescent and younger child trainees will be our major focus. We will attend to such organizational decisions as the optimal number, length, timing, spacing, and location of the Interpersonal Skills Training sessions themselves; describe how to implement the Interpersonal Skills Training procedures (modeling, role playing, performance feedback, and transfer training) in opening and later sessions; and offer a full curriculum of skills for adolescent and for younger child trainees.

Preparing for Interpersonal Skills Training

Selecting Trainers
A wide variety of individuals have served successfully as trainers. Their educational backgrounds have been especially varied, ranging from high school degree only through various graduate degrees. Although formal training as an educator or in one of the helping professions is both useful and relevant to becoming a competent Interpersonal Skills Training trainer, we have found characteristics such as sensitivity, flexibility, and instructional talent to be considerably more important than formal education. We have also made frequent and successful use of trainers best described as paraprofessionals, particularly with trainees from lower socioeconomic levels. In general, we select trainers based upon the nature and demands of the Interpersonal Skills Training group. Two types of trainer skills appear crucial for successfully conducting an Interpersonal Skills Training group. The first might be described as general trainer skills—that is, those skills requisite for success in almost any training or teaching effort. These include

1. Oral communication and teaching ability,
2. Flexibility and resourcefulness,
3. Enthusiasm,
4. Ability to work under pressure,
5. Interpersonal sensitivity,
6. Listening skills,
7. Knowledge of the subject (adolescent development, aggression management, peer pressures on adolescents, etc.).

The second type of skills necessary includes specific trainer skills—that is, those skills relevant to Interpersonal Skills Training in particular. These include

1. Knowledge of Interpersonal Skills Training—its background, procedures, and goals;
2. Ability to orient both trainees and supporting staff to Interpersonal Skills Training;
3. Ability to plan and present live modeling displays;
4. Ability to initiate and sustain role playing;
5. Ability to present material in concrete, behavioral form;
6. Ability to deal with group management problems effectively;
7. Accuracy and sensitivity in providing corrective feedback.

How can we tell if potential trainers are skilled enough to become effective group leaders? We use behavioral observation, actually seeing how competently potential trainers lead mock and then actual Interpersonal Skills Training groups during our trainer preparation phase.

Preparing Trainers

We strongly believe in learning by doing. Our chief means of preparing trainers for Interpersonal Skills Training group leadership is, first, to have them participate in an intensive, 2-day workshop designed to provide the knowledge and experience needed for beginning competence. In the workshop, we use Interpersonal Skills Training to teach trainer competency. Initially, we assign relevant reading materials for background information. Next, trainees observe skilled and experienced Interpersonal Skills Training group leaders model the central modeling display presentation, role playing, performance feedback, and transfer training procedures that constitute the core elements of the Interpersonal Skills Training session. Then workshop participants role play in pairs these group leadership behaviors and receive detailed feedback from the workshop leaders and others in the training group regarding the degree to which their group leadership behaviors match or depart from those modeled by the workshop leaders. To assist workshop learning in transferring smoothly and fully to the actual training setting, regular and continuing supervisory sessions are held after the workshop with the newly created Interpersonal Skills Training group leaders. These booster/monitoring/supervision meetings, when added to the several opportunities available for trainer performance evaluation during the workshop itself, provide a large sample of behaviors upon which to base a fair and appropriate trainer selection decision.

Selecting Trainees

Who belongs in the Interpersonal Skills Training group? We have long held that no therapy or training approach is optimal for all clients and that our effectiveness as helpers or trainers will grow to the degree that we become prescriptive in our helping efforts (Goldstein, 1978; Goldstein & Stein, 1976). As noted earlier, Interpersonal Skills Training grew originally from a behavior-deficit view of the asocial and antisocial behavior displayed by youth for whom the Prepare Curriculum is designed. If such behavior is due in substantial part to a lack of ability in a variety of alternative, prosocial skills of an interpersonal, personal, aggression management, or related nature, our selection goal is defined for us. The Interpersonal Skills Training group should consist of youngsters weak or deficient in one or more clusters of skills that constitute the Interpersonal Skills Training curriculum. Optimally, this selection process will involve the use of interview, direct observation, behavioral testing procedures, and appropriate skill checklists (Goldstein et al., 1980). In chapter 14, we elaborate further on selection procedures of value both for this, as well as other, segments of Prepare. Largely or entirely irrelevant to the selection decision are most of the usual bases for training selection decisions. If the clients are skill deficient and possess a few very basic group participation skills, we are largely unconcerned with their age, sex, race, social class, or, within very broad limits, even their mental health. At times, we have had to exclude persons who were severely emotionally disturbed, too hyperactive for a 30-minute session, or so developmentally disabled that they lacked the rudimentary memory and imaginative abilities necessary for adequate group participation. But such persons have been relatively few and far between. Thus, although Interpersonal Skills Training is not a prescription designed for all aggressive, withdrawn, or otherwise skill-deficient youth, its range of appropriate use is nevertheless quite broad.

Group Organization

The preparation phase of the Interpersonal Skills Training group is completed by attention to those organizational details necessary for a smoothly initiated, appropriately paced, and highly instructional group to begin. Factors to be considered in organizing the group are number of trainees, number of trainers, number of sessions, and spacing of sessions.

Number of trainees

Since trainee behavior in an Interpersonal Skills Training group may vary greatly from person to person and group to group, it is not appropriate that we recommend a single, specific number of trainees as optimal. Ideally, the number of trainees will permit all to role play, will lead to optimal levels of group interaction, and will provide a diverse source of performance feedback opportunities. In our experience with aggressive youngsters, these goals have usually been met when the group's size was from five to seven trainees.

Number of trainers

The role playing and feedback that make up most of each Interpersonal Skills Training session are a series of "action-reaction" sequences in which effective skill behaviors are first rehearsed (role play) and then critiqued (feedback). Thus the trainer must both lead and observe. We have found that one trainer is hard pressed to do both of these tasks well at the same time, and we strongly recommend that each session be led by a team of two trainers. One trainer can usually pay special attention to the main actor, helping the actor "set the stage" and enact the skill's behavioral steps. While this is occurring, the other trainer can attend to the remainder of the group and help them as they observe and evaluate the unfolding role play. The two trainers can then exchange these responsibilities on the next role play.

Number of sessions

Interpersonal Skills Training groups typically seek to cover one skill in one or two sessions. The central task is to make certain that every trainee in the group role plays the given skill correctly at least once— and preferably more than once. Most Interpersonal Skills Training groups have met this curriculum requirement by holding sessions once or twice per week. Groups have varied greatly in the total number of meetings they have held.

Spacing of sessions

The goal of Interpersonal Skills Training is not merely skill learning or acquisition; much more important is skill transfer. Performance of the skill in the training setting is desired, but performance of it in the school, institutional facility, or community is crucial. Several aspects of Interpersonal Skills Training, discussed later in this chapter, are designed to enhance the likelihood of such skill transfer. Session spacing is one such factor. As will be described, after the trainee role plays successfully in the group and receives thorough performance feedback, she is assigned homework—that is, the task of carrying out in the real world the skill she just performed correctly in the group. In order to ensure ample time and opportunity to carry out this very important task, Interpersonal Skills Training sessions must be scheduled at least a few days apart.

Length and location of sessions

One-hour sessions are the typical Interpersonal Skills Training format, though both somewhat briefer and somewhat longer sessions have been successful. In general, the session goal that must be met is successful role playing and clarifying feedback for all participants, be it in 45 minutes, 1 hour, or 1 1/2 hours.

In most schools or agencies, a reasonably quiet and comfortable office, classroom, or similar setting can be found or created for the use of Interpersonal Skills Training groups. We suggest no special requirements for the meeting place beyond those that make sense for any kind of group instruction: that it be free of distraction and at least minimally equipped with chairs, chalkboard, and adequate lighting. How shall the room be arranged? Again, no single, fixed pattern is required, but one functional and comfortable layout is the horseshoe or U-shaped arrangement, which we have often employed—sometimes with and sometimes without tables. Figure 3 depicts this room arrangement. Note how in this group arrangement all observing trainees and the main actor can watch the trainer point to the given skill's behavioral steps written on the chalkboard while the role play is taking place. In this manner, any necessary prompting is provided immediately and at the same time that the role play is serving as an additional modeling display for observing trainees.

It should be noted that these several recommendations regarding optimal numbers of trainees, trainers, sessions, and spacing are offered with regard to Interpersonal Skills Training only and are not necessarily optimal for all Prepare courses. In later chapters, we will seek to prescriptively describe differential teaching parameters as they fit the diverse Prepare offerings.

Meeting with the Trainees before the First Session

A final step that must be taken before holding the first session of a new Interpersonal Skills Training group is preparing the trainees who have

Figure 3
A Functional Room Arrangement for Interpersonal Skills Training

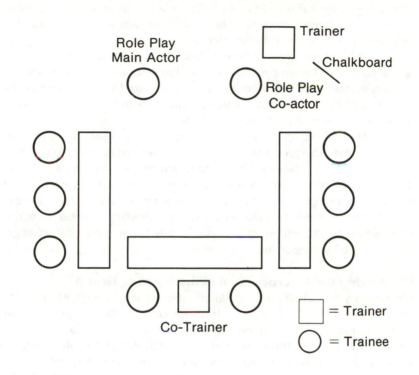

been selected for what they ought to expect and what will be expected of them. What this premeeting might include follows:

1. *Describing what the purposes of the group will be as they relate to the trainee's specific skill deficits.* For example, the trainer might say, "Remember when you lost privileges because you thought Henry had insulted you and you got in a shoving match with him? Well, in Interpersonal Skills Training, you'll be able to learn what to do in a situation like that so you can handle it without fighting and still settle calmly whatever is going on."

2. *Describing briefly the procedure that will be used.* Although we believe that trainees typically will not have a full understanding of what Interpersonal Skills Training is and what it can accomplish until after the group has begun and they have experienced it, verbal, pregroup structuring of procedures is a useful beginning. It conveys at least a part of the information necessary to help trainees know what to expect.

The trainer might say, "In order to learn to handle these problem situations better, we're going to see and hear some examples of how different people handle them well. Then you will actually take turns trying some of these ways right here. We'll let you know how you did, and you'll have a chance to practice on your own."

3. *Describing some of the hoped-for benefits of active trainee participation in the group.* If the trainer has relevant information about a trainee, the possible benefits described might appropriately be improved proficiency in the particular interpersonal skills in which the trainee rates himself as especially deficient.

4. *Describing group rules.* These rules include whatever the trainer believes the group members must adhere to in order to function smoothly and effectively with regard to attendance, punctuality, confidentiality, completion of homework assignments, and so forth. At this premeeting stage, rule structuring should be brief and tentative. Reserve a fuller discussion of this matter for the group's first session, in which all members can be encouraged to participate and in which rule changes can be made by consensus.

Conducting the Interpersonal Skills Training Group

We now wish to turn to a detailed, step-by-step description of the procedures that constitute the Interpersonal Skills Training session. The opening session will be considered first. The elements of this session that get the Interpersonal Skills Training group off to a good start will be emphasized, and an outline will be given. The section will subsequently describe the procedures that constitute the bulk of most Interpersonal Skills Training sessions: modeling, role playing, performance feedback, and transfer training. Then an outline that can be followed for sessions after the first will be presented.

The opening session is designed to create a safe, nurturing, nonthreatening environment for trainees; to stimulate their interest in the group; and to give more detailed information to them than was provided in their individual orientations. The trainers open the session with a brief warm-up period to help participants become comfortable when interacting with the group leaders and with one another. Content for this initial phase should be interesting and nonthreatening to the trainees. Next, trainers introduce the Interpersonal Skills Training program by providing trainees with a brief description of what skills training is about. Typically, this introduction covers such topics as the importance of interpersonal skills for effective and satisfying living, examples of skills that will be taught, and how these skills can be useful to trainees in their everyday lives. It is often helpful to expand this discussion of everyday skill use to emphasize the importance of the undertaking and the personal relevance to the participants of learning the skill. The specific training procedures (modeling, role playing, performance feedback, and transfer training) are then described at a level that the group can easily understand. We recommend that trainers describe procedures briefly, with the expectation that trainees will understand them more fully once they have actually participated in their use. A detailed outline of the procedures that ideally make up this opening session follows.

Outline of Opening Session Procedures

A. Introductions
  1. Trainers introduce themselves.
  2. Trainers invite trainees to introduce themselves. As a way of relaxing trainees and beginning to familiarize them with one another, the trainer can elicit from each trainee some nonprivate information such as neighborhood of residence, school background, special interests or hobbies, and so forth.
B. Overview of Interpersonal Skills Training
  Although some or all of this material may have been discussed in earlier individual meetings with trainees, a portion of the opening session should be devoted to a presentation and group discussion of the purposes, procedures, and potential benefits of Interpersonal Skills Training. The discussion of the group's purposes should stress the probable remediation of those skill deficits that trainees in the group are aware of, concerned about, and eager to change. The procedures that make up the typical Interpersonal Skills Training session should be explained again and discussed with give and take from the group. The language used to explain the procedures should be geared to the trainees' level of understanding—that is, the terms *show, try, discuss,* and *practice* should be respectively used for the words *modeling, role playing, performance feedback,* and *transfer training.* Heaviest stress at this point should perhaps be placed on presenting and examining the potential benefits to trainees of their participation in Interpersonal Skills Training. Concrete examples of the diverse ways that skill proficiencies could, and probably will, have a positive effect on the lives of trainees should be the focus of this effort.
C. Discussion of group rules
  The rules that will govern participation in the Interpersonal Skills Training group should be presented by the trainers during the

opening session. If appropriate, this presentation should permit and encourage group discussion designed to give members a sense of participation in the group's decision making. That is, members should be encouraged to accept and live by those rules they agree with and seek to alter those they wish to change. Group rules may be necessary and appropriate concerning attendance, lateness, size of the group, and time and place of the meetings. This is also a good time to provide reassurance to group members about concerns they may have, such as confidentiality, embarrassment, and fear of performing.

D. Introduction of the first interpersonal skill

Following introductions, the overview of Interpersonal Skills Training, and the presentation of group rules, the trainers should proceed to introducing and modeling the group's first skill, conducting role plays on that skill, giving performance feedback, and encouraging transfer training. These activities make up all subsequent Interpersonal Skills Training sessions.

The following training procedures, illustrated in the opening session as they relate to the group's first skill performance, are also vital in the core procedures of later sessions.

Modeling

The modeling display presented to trainees should depict the behavioral steps that constitute the skill being taught in a clear and unambiguous manner. All of the steps making up the skill should be modeled in the correct sequence. Generally, the modeling will consist of live vignettes enacted by the two trainers, although trainees may be involved in the modeling display in some instances. (If available, an audio or audiovisual modeling display, instead of live modeling, may be presented.) When two trainers are not available, a reasonably skillful trainee may serve as a model along with the trainer. In all instances, it is especially important that the trainers rehearse the vignettes carefully prior to the group meeting, making sure that all of the skill's steps are enacted correctly and in the proper sequence.

Trainers should plan their modeling display carefully. Content should be selected that is relevant to the immediate life situations of the trainees in the group. At least two examples should be modeled for each skill so that trainees are exposed to skill use in different situations. Thus two or more different content areas are depicted. We have found that trainers usually do not have to write out scripts for the modeling display but can instead plan their roles and likely responses in outline form and rehearse them in their preclass preparations. These modeling display outlines should incorporate the guidelines that follow:

1. At least two examples of different situations for each demonstration of a skill should be used. If a given skill is taught in more than one group meeting, two more new modeling displays should be developed.
2. Situations that are relevant to the trainees' real-life circumstances should be selected.
3. The main actor—that is, the person enacting the behavioral steps of the skill—should be portrayed as a person reasonably similar to the people in the Interpersonal Skills Training group in age, socioeconomic background, verbal ability, and other salient characteristics.
4. Modeling displays should depict only one skill at a time. All extraneous content should be eliminated.
5. All modeling displays should depict all the behavioral steps of the skill being modeled in the correct sequence.
6. All displays should depict positive outcomes. Displays should always end with reinforcement to the model.

In order to help trainees attend to the skill enactments, Skill Cards, which contain the name of the skill being taught and its behavioral steps, are distributed prior to the modeling display. Trainees are told to watch and listen closely as the models portray the skill. Particular care should be given to helping trainees identify the behavioral steps as they are presented in the context of the modeling vignettes. Trainers should also remind the trainees that, in order to depict some of the behavioral steps in certain skills, the actors will occasionally be "thinking out loud" statements that would ordinarily be thought silently and that this process is done to facilitate learning.

Role playing

Following the modeling display, discussion should focus on relating the modeled skill to the lives of trainees. Trainers should invite comments on the behavioral steps and how these steps might be useful in real-life situations that trainees encounter. It is most helpful to focus on current and future skill use rather than only on past events or general issues involving the skill. Role playing in Interpersonal Skills Training is intended to serve as behavioral rehearsal or practice for future use of the skill. Role playing of past events that have little relevance to future situations is of limited value to trainees. However, discussion of past events involving skill use can be relevant in stimulating trainees to think of times when a similar situation might occur in the future. The hypothetical future situation, rather than a reenactment of the past event, would therefore be selected for role playing.

Once a trainee has described a situation in her own life in which the skill might be helpful, that trainee is designated the main actor. She chooses a second trainee (the co-actor) to play the role of the other person (mother, peer, staff member, etc.) in her life who is relevant to the situation. The trainee should be urged to pick as a co-actor someone who resembles the real-life person in as many ways as possible—physically, expressively, etc. The trainers then elicit from the main actor any additional information needed to set the stage for role playing. To make role playing as realistic as possible, the trainers should obtain a description of the physical setting, of the events immediately preceding the role play, and the manner the co-actor should display, as well as any other information that would increase realism.

It is crucial that the main actor use the behavioral steps that have been modeled. This is the main purpose of the role playing. Before beginning the actual role playing, the trainer should go over each step as it applies to the particular role-play situation, thus preparing the main actor to make a successful effort. The main actor is told to refer to the Skill Card on which the behavioral steps are printed. As noted previously, the behavioral steps are written on a chalkboard visible to the main actor as well as the rest of the group during the role playing. Before the role playing begins, trainers should remind all of the participants of their roles and responsibilities: The main actor is told to follow the behavioral steps; the co-actor, to stay in the role of the other person; and the observers, to watch carefully for the enactment of the behavioral steps. At times, feedback from other trainees is facilitated by assigning each one a single behavioral step to focus and provide feedback on after the role play. For the first several role plays, the observers also can be coached on kinds of cues to observe (posture, tone of voice, content of speech, etc.).

During the role play, it is the responsibility of one of the trainers to provide the main actor with whatever help, coaching, and encouragement he needs to keep the role playing going according to the behavioral steps. Trainees who "break role" and begin to explain their behavior or make observer-like comments should be urged to get back into the role and explain later. If the role play is clearly going astray from the behavioral steps, the scene can be stopped, needed instruction can be provided, and then the role play can be restarted. One trainer should be positioned near the chalkboard in order to point to each of the behavioral steps in turn as the role play unfolds, thus helping the main actor (as well as the other trainees) to follow each of the steps in order. The second trainer should sit with the observing trainees to be available as needed to keep them on task.

The role playing should be continued until all trainees have had an opportunity to participate in the role of main actor. Sometimes this will require two or three sessions for a given skill. As we suggested before, each session should begin with two new modeling vignettes for the chosen skill, even if the skill is not new to the group. It is important to note once again that, although the framework (behavioral steps) of each role play in the series remains the same, the actual content can and should change from role play to role play. It is the problem as it actually occurs, or could occur, in each trainee's real-life environment that should be the content of the given role play.

There are a few more ways to increase the effectiveness of role playing. Role reversal is often a useful role-play procedure. A trainee role playing a skill may on occasion have a difficult time perceiving her co-actor's viewpoint and vice versa. Having the actors exchange roles and resume the role play can be most helpful in this regard. At times, the trainer can also assume the co-actor role in an effort to give the trainee the opportunity to handle types of reactions not otherwise role played during the session. For example, it may be crucial to have a difficult co-actor realistically portrayed. The trainer as co-actor may also be particularly helpful when dealing with less verbal or more hesitant trainees.

Performance feedback

A brief feedback period follows each role play. This helps the main actor find out how well he followed or departed from the behavioral steps. It also examines the psychological impact of the enactment on the co-actor and provides the main actor with encouragement to try out the role-played behaviors in real life. The trainer should ask the main actor to wait until he has heard everyone's comments before responding to any of them.

The co-actor is asked about his reactions first. Next, the observers comment on how well the behavioral steps were followed and other relevant aspects of the role play. Then the trainers comment in particular on how well the behavioral steps were followed and provide social reinforcement (praise, approval, encouragement) for close following. To be most effective in their use of reinforcement, trainers should follow these guidelines:

1. Provide reinforcement only after role plays that follow the behavioral steps;
2. Provide reinforcement at the earliest appropriate opportunity after role plays that follow the behavioral steps;

3. Vary the specific content of the reinforcements offered—for example, praise particular aspects of the performance, such as tone of voice, posture, phrasing, etc.;
4. Provide enough role-playing activity for each group member to have sufficient opportunity to be reinforced;
5. Provide reinforcement in an amount consistent with the quality of the given role play;
6. Provide no reinforcement when the role play departs significantly from the behavioral steps (except for "trying" in the first session or two);
7. Provide reinforcement for an individual trainee's improvement over previous performances;
8. Always provide reinforcement to the co-actor for being helpful, cooperative, etc.

In all aspects of feedback, it is crucial that the trainer maintain the behavioral focus of Interpersonal Skills Training. Both trainer and trainee comments should point to the presence or absence of specific, concrete behaviors and not take the form of global evaluations or broad generalities. Feedback, of course, may be positive or negative in content. Negative comments should always be followed by a constructive comment as to how a particular fault might be improved. At minimum, a "poor" performance can be praised as "a good try" at the same time that it is being criticized for its real faults. If at all possible, trainees failing to follow the relevant behavioral steps in their role play should be given the opportunity to role play these same behavioral steps again after receiving corrective feedback. At times, as a further feedback procedure, we have audio- or videotaped entire role plays. Giving trainees opportunities following role play to observe themselves on tape can be an effective aid, enabling them to reflect on their own verbal and nonverbal behavior and its impact upon others.

Since a primary goal of Interpersonal Skills Training is skill flexibility, role plays that depart somewhat from the behavioral steps may not be "wrong." That is, a different approach to the skill may in fact work in some situations. Trainers should stress that they are trying to teach effective alternatives and that the trainees would do well to have the behavioral steps being taught, or as collaboratively modified, in their respective repertoires of skill behaviors, available to use when appropriate.

Transfer training
Several aspects of the training sessions already described have been designed primarily to make it likely that learning in the training setting

will transfer to the trainees' real-life environments. These and related transfer- and maintenance-enhancing procedures are presented in detail in chapter 12. How they are employed in Interpersonal Skills Training is examined below.

Provision of general principles. It has been demonstrated that transfer of training is facilitated by providing trainees with general mediating principles governing successful or competent performance in both the training and real-world settings. This idea has been operationalized in laboratory contexts by providing subjects with the organizing concepts, principles, strategies, or rationales that explain the stimulus-response relationships operating in both the training and application settings. General principles of skill selection and utilization are provided to trainees verbally, visually, and in written form.

Overlearning. Overlearning involves training in a skill beyond what is necessary to produce initial changes in behavior. The overlearning, or repetition of successful skill enhancement, in the typical Interpersonal Skills Training session is quite substantial. Each skill is taught, and its behavioral steps are

1. Modeled several times,
2. Role played one or more times by the trainee,
3. Observed live by the trainee as every other group member role plays,
4. Read by the trainee from a chalkboard and a Skill Card,
5. Practiced in real-life settings one or more times by the trainee as part of a formal homework assignment.

Identical elements. The greater the similarity of physical and interpersonal stimuli in the Interpersonal Skills Training setting and the home, community, or other setting in which the skill is to be applied, the greater the likelihood of transfer. Interpersonal Skills Training is made similar to real life in several ways. These include

1. Designing the live modeling displays to be highly similar to what trainees face in their daily lives through the representative, relevant, and realistic portrayal of the models, protagonists, and situations;
2. Designing the role plays to be similar to real-life situations through the use of props, the physical arrangement of the setting, and the choice of realistic co-actors;
3. Conducting the role plays to be as responsive as possible to the real-life interpersonal stimuli to which the trainees must actually respond later with the given skill;

4. Rehearsing of each skill in role plays as the trainees actually plan to use it;
5. Assigning of homework.

Stimulus variability. Positive transfer is greater when a variety of relevant training stimuli are employed (Callantine & Warren, 1955; Duncan, 1958; Shore & Sechrest, 1961). Stimulus variability may be implemented in Interpersonal Skills Training sessions by use of

1. Rotation of group leaders across groups,
2. Rotation of trainees across groups,
3. Role playing of a given skill by trainees with several different co-actors,
4. Role playing of a given skill by trainees across several relevant settings,
5. Completion of multiple homework assignments for each given skill.

Real-life reinforcement. Given successful implementation of both appropriate Interpersonal Skills Training procedures and transfer enhancement procedures, skill maintenance may still fail to occur. As Agras (1967), Gruber (1971), Patterson and Anderson (1964), Tharp and Wetzel (1969), and dozens of other investigators have shown, stable and enduring performance of newly learned skills in application settings is very much at the mercy of real-life reinforcement contingencies. We have found it useful to implement several supplemental programs outside of the Interpersonal Skills Training setting that can help to provide the rewards trainees need to maintain new behaviors. These programs include provision for both external social rewards (provided by people in the trainees' real-life environments) and self-rewards (provided by the trainees themselves).

A particularly useful tool for transfer enhancement—a tool combining the possibilities of identical elements, stimulus variability, and real-life reinforcement—is the skill homework assignment. When possible, we urge the use of this homework technique, which we have found to be successful with most groups. In this procedure, trainees are instructed to try in their own real-life settings the behaviors they have practiced during the session. The name of the person(s) with whom they will try the behaviors, the day, the place, etc. are all discussed. The trainee is urged to take notes on her attempt to use the skill on the Homework Report form (Figure 4). This form requests detailed information about what happened when the trainee attempted the homework assignment, how well she followed the relevant behavioral steps, the

Figure 4
Homework Report

Name _____ Date _____

Group leaders _____

Fill in during this class

1. Homework assignment:

   a. Skill:

   b. Use with whom:

   c. Use when:

   d. Use where:

2. Steps to be followed:

Fill in before next class

3. Describe what happened when you did the homework assignment:

4. Steps you actually followed:

5. Rate yourself on how well you used the skill (check one):

   Excellent ____   Good ____   Fair ____   Poor ____

6. Describe what you feel should be your *next* homework assignment:

trainee's evaluation of her performance, and thoughts about what the next assignment might appropriately be.

It has often proven useful to start with relatively simple homework behaviors and, as mastery is achieved, work up to more complex and demanding assignments. This provides both the trainer and the people who are the targets of the homework with an opportunity to reinforce each approximation of the more complex target behavior. Successful experiences at beginning homework attempts are crucial in encouraging the trainee to make further attempts at real-life use of the skill.

The first part of each Interpersonal Skills Training session is devoted to presenting and discussing these homework reports. When trainees have made an effort to complete their homework assignments, trainers should provide social reinforcement. Failure to do homework should be met with some expressed disappointment, followed by support and encouragement to complete the assignment. It cannot be stressed too strongly that, without these or similar attempts to maximize transfer, the value of the entire training effort is in severe jeopardy.

Much of the foregoing procedural material may be conveniently summarized for purposes of review by the following outline.

Outline of Later Session Procedures

A. Trainer and trainees review homework.
B. Trainer presents overview of the skill.
  1. Introduces skill briefly prior to showing modeling display.
  2. Asks questions that will help trainees define the skill in their own language.
     Examples: "Who knows what _____ is?"
     "What does _____ mean to you?"
     "Who can define _____?"
  3. Postpones lengthier discussion until after trainees view the modeling display. If trainees want to engage in further discussion, the trainer might say, "Let's wait until after we've seen some examples of people using the skill before we talk about it in more detail."
  4. Makes a statement about what will follow the modeling display.
     Example: "After we see the examples, we will talk about times when you've had to use _____ and times when you may have to use that skill in the future."
  5. Distributes Skill Cards, asking a trainee to read the behavioral steps aloud.
  6. Asks trainees to follow each step in the modeling display as the step is depicted.

C. Trainer presents modeling display of two relevant examples of the skill in use, following its behavioral steps.

D. Trainer invites discussion of skill that has been modeled.

    1. Invites comments on how the situation modeled may remind trainees of situations involving skill usage in their own lives.

    Example: "Did any of the situations you just saw remind you of times when you have had to _____?"

    2. Asks questions that encourage trainees to talk about skill usage and problems involving skill usage.

    Examples: "What do you do in situations where you have to _____?"

    "Have you ever had to _____ ?"

    "Have you ever had difficulty _____ ?"

E. Trainer organizes role play.

    1. Asks a trainee who has volunteered a situation to elaborate on his remarks, obtaining details on where, when, and with whom the skill might be useful in the future.

    2. Designates this trainee as a main actor and asks the trainee to choose a co-actor (someone who reminds the main actor of the person with whom the skill will be used in the real-life situation).

    Examples: "What does _____ look like?"

    "Who in the group reminds you of _____ in some way?"

    3. Gets additional information from the main actor, if necessary, and sets the stage for the role playing (including props, furniture arrangement, etc.).

    Examples: "Where might you be talking to _____?"

    "How is the room furnished?"

    "Would you be standing or sitting?"

    "What time of day will it be?"

    4. Rehearses with the main actor what he will say and do during the role play.

    Examples: "What will you say for the first step of the skill?"

    "What will you do if the co-actor does _____?"

    5. Gives group members some final instructions as to their parts just prior to role playing.

    Examples: To the main actor: "Try to follow all of the steps as best you can."

    To the co-actor: "Try to play the part of _____ as best you can. Say and do what you think _____ would do when _____ follows the skill's steps."

To the other trainees in the group: "Watch how well
_____ follows the steps so that we can talk about it after the
role play."

F. Trainer instructs the role players to begin.

1. One trainer stands at the chalkboard and points to each step as it is enacted and provides whatever coaching or prompting is needed by the main actor or co-actor.

2. The other trainer sits with the observing trainees to help keep them attending to the unfolding role play.

3. In the event that the role play strays markedly from the behavioral steps, the trainers stop the scene, provide needed instruction, and begin again.

G. Trainer invites feedback following role play.

1. Asks the main actor to wait until he has heard everyone's comments before talking.

2. Asks the co-actor, "In the role of _____, how did _____ make you feel? What were your reactions to him?"

3. Asks observing trainees, "How well were the behavioral steps followed?" "What specific things did you like or dislike?" "In what ways did the co-actor do a good job?"

4. Comments on how the behavioral steps were followed, provides social reward, points out what was done well, and comments on what else might be done to make the enactment even better.

5. Asks the main actor, "Now that you have heard everyone's comments, how do you feel about the job you did?" "How do you think that following the steps worked out?"

H. Trainer helps role player to plan homework.

1. Asks the main actor how, when, and with whom he might attempt the behavioral steps prior to the next class meeting.

2. As appropriate, assigns the Homework Report to get a written commitment from the main actor to try out his new skill and report back to the group at the next meeting.

3. Assigns homework to trainees who have not had a chance to role play during a particular class in the form of looking for situations relevant to the skill that they might role play during the next class meeting.

Skills for Adolescents

Our presentation thus far has sought to make clear how Interpersonal Skills Training groups are planned, organized, and conducted. We now turn away from concern with how skills are taught and focus instead on the Interpersonal Skills Training curriculum (i.e., the specific skills taught in the Interpersonal Skills Training group). These 50 skills come from a number of sources. Some derive from our extensive examination of relevant research (i.e., diverse educational and psychological studies yielding information on which behaviors constitute successful adolescent functioning in school, at home, with peers, and so forth). Our own direct observation of youngsters in various classroom and other real-life settings is a second source. Many Interpersonal Skills Training groups have been conducted—by us, by school and residential center personnel, and by others. Trainers and trainees in these groups have also provided a particularly valuable fund of skill-relevant information.

This section includes a description of the behavioral steps that constitute each skill, trainer notes and suggested content for effective modeling displays, and further comments. The skill steps are the framework for the vignettes or stories that are modeled by trainers and then role played by trainees, and they are central to the portrayal. Following the presentation of the skills, a complete, verbatim script for two modeling vignettes (Skill 42: Dealing with Group Pressure) is presented.

The 50 skills are listed here in the order they will be considered. Note that they are divided into six groups: Beginning Social Skills, Advanced Social Skills, Skills for Dealing with Feelings, Skill Alternatives to Aggression, Skills for Dealing with Stress, and Planning Skills.

Group I: BEGINNING SOCIAL SKILLS

1. Listening
2. Starting a Conversation
3. Having a Conversation
4. Asking a Question
5. Saying Thank You
6. Introducing Yourself
7. Introducing Other People
8. Giving a Compliment

Group II: ADVANCED SOCIAL SKILLS

9. Asking for Help
10. Joining In
11. Giving Instructions
12. Following Instructions
13. Apologizing
14. Convincing Others

Group III: SKILLS FOR DEALING WITH FEELINGS
15. Knowing Your Feelings
16. Expressing Your Feelings
17. Understanding the Feelings of Others
18. Dealing with Someone Else's Anger
19. Expressing Affection
20. Dealing with Fear
21. Rewarding Yourself

Group IV: SKILL ALTERNATIVES TO AGGRESSION
22. Asking Permission
23. Sharing Something
24. Helping Others
25. Negotiating
26. Using Self-control
27. Standing Up for Your Rights
28. Responding to Teasing
29. Avoiding Trouble with Others
30. Keeping Out of Fights

Group V: SKILLS FOR DEALING WITH STRESS
31. Making a Complaint
32. Answering a Complaint
33. Sportsmanship after the Game
34. Dealing with Embarrassment
35. Dealing with Being Left Out
36. Standing Up for a Friend
37. Responding to Persuasion
38. Responding to Failure
39. Dealing with Contradictory Messages
40. Dealing with an Accusation
41. Getting Ready for a Difficult Conversation
42. Dealing with Group Pressure

Group VI: PLANNING SKILLS
43. Deciding on Something to Do
44. Deciding What Caused a Problem
45. Setting a Goal
46. Deciding on Your Abilities
47. Gathering Information
48. Arranging Problems by Importance
49. Making a Decision
50. Concentrating on a Task

GROUP I: BEGINNING SOCIAL SKILLS
Skill 1: Listening

STEPS	TRAINER NOTES
1. Look at the person who is talking.	Face the person; establish eye contact.
2. Think about what is being said.	Show this by nodding your head, saying, "mm-hmm."
3. Wait your turn to talk.	Don't fidget; don't shuffle your feet.
4. Say what you want to say.	Ask questions; express feelings; express your ideas.

SUGGESTED CONTENT FOR MODELING DISPLAYS

A. *School or neighborhood:* Teacher explains classroom assignment to main actor.

B. *Home:* Mother feels sad, and main actor listens.

C. *Peer group:* Friend describes interesting movie to main actor.

COMMENTS

All of the beginning social skills are basic to the functioning of the group. In starting an Interpersonal Skills Training group, it is useful for trainees to have a reasonable grasp of these skills before proceeding to other skills.

Like Step 2 above, many of the behavioral steps that make up the skills described in this chapter are thinking steps. That is, in actual, real-world use of many skills, certain steps are private and occur only in the thinking of the skill user. When modeling or role playing such thinking steps in Interpersonal Skills Training, however, it is crucial that the enactment be out loud. Such public display of thinking steps is a significant aid to rapid and lasting learning.

GROUP I: BEGINNING SOCIAL SKILLS
Skill 2: Starting a Conversation

STEPS	TRAINER NOTES
1. Greet the other person.	Say "hi"; shake hands; choose the right time and place.
2. Make small talk.	
3. Decide if the other person is listening.	Check if the other person is listening; looking at you, nodding, saying "mm-hmm."
4. Bring up the main topic.	

SUGGESTED CONTENT FOR MODELING DISPLAYS

A. *School or neighborhood:* Main actor starts conversation with secretary in school office.

B. *Home:* Main actor discusses allowance and/or privileges with parent.

C. *Peer group:* Main actor suggests weekend plans to a friend.

COMMENTS

We have found that this is frequently one of the best skills to teach in the first Interpersonal Skills Training session with a new group of trainees.

GROUP I: BEGINNING SOCIAL SKILLS
SKILL 3: Having a Conversation

STEPS	TRAINER NOTES
1. Say what you want to say.	
2. Ask the other person what he/she thinks.	
3. Listen to what the other person says.	
4. Say what you think.	Respond to the other person; add new information; ask questions.
5. Make a closing remark.	Steps 1–4 can be repeated many times before Step 5 is done.

SUGGESTED CONTENT FOR MODELING DISPLAYS

A. *School or neighborhood:* Main actor talks with coach about upcoming game.

B. *Home:* Main actor talks with brother or sister about school experiences.

C. *Peer group:* Main actor discusses vacation plans with friend.

COMMENTS

This skill starts where Skill 2 leaves off. After practicing each skill separately, trainers may want to give trainees practice in using these skills successively.

GROUP I: BEGINNING SOCIAL SKILLS
Skill 4: Asking a Question

STEPS	TRAINER NOTES
1. Decide what you'd like to know more about.	Ask about something you don't understand, something you didn't hear, or something confusing.
2. Decide whom to ask.	Think about who has the best information on a topic; consider asking several people.
3. Think about different ways to ask your question and pick one way.	Think about wording; raise your hand; ask nonchallengingly.
4. Pick the right time and place to ask your question.	Wait for a pause; wait for privacy.
5. Ask your question.	

SUGGESTED CONTENT FOR MODELING DISPLAYS

A. *School or neighborhood:* Main actor asks teacher to explain something he/she finds unclear.

B. *Home:* Main actor asks mother to explain new curfew decision.

C. *Peer group:* Main actor asks classmate about missed schoolwork.

COMMENTS

Trainers are advised to model only single, answerable questions. In role play, trainees should be instructed to do likewise.

GROUP I: BEGINNING SOCIAL SKILLS
SKILL 5: Saying Thank You

STEPS	TRAINER NOTES
1. Decide if the other person said or did something that you want to thank him/her for.	It may be a compliment, favor, or gift.
2. Choose a good time and place to thank the other person.	
3. Thank the other person in a friendly way.	Express thanks with words, a gift, a letter, or do a return favor.
4. Tell the other person why you are thanking him/her.	

SUGGESTED CONTENT FOR MODELING DISPLAYS

A. *School or neighborhood:* Main actor thanks teacher for help on a project.

B. *Home:* Main actor thanks mother for fixing shirt.

C. *Peer group:* Main actor thanks friend for advice.

GROUP I: BEGINNING SOCIAL SKILLS
SKILL 6: Introducing Yourself

STEPS	TRAINER NOTES
1. Choose the right time and place to introduce yourself.	
2. Greet the other person and tell your name.	Shake hands, if appropriate.
3. Ask the other person his/her name if you need to.	
4. Tell or ask the other person something to help start your conversation.	Tell something about yourself; comment on something you both have in common; ask a question.

SUGGESTED CONTENT FOR MODELING DISPLAYS

A. *School or neighborhood:* Main actor introduces self to new neighbor.

B. *Home:* Main actor introduces self to friend of parents.

C. *Peer group:* Main actor introduces self to several classmates at start of school year.

COMMENTS

This skill and Skill 7 (Introducing Other People) are extremely important in a youngster's efforts to establish social contacts. They are not intended as lessons in "etiquette." Trainers should be attuned to choosing language appropriate to the particular situation.

GROUP I: BEGINNING SOCIAL SKILLS
SKILL 7: Introducing Other People

STEPS	TRAINER NOTES
1. Name the first person and tell him/her the name of the second person.	Speak clearly and loudly enough so that the names are heard by both people.
2. Name the second person and tell him/her the name of the first person.	
3. Say something that helps the two people get to know each other.	Mention something they have in common; invite them to talk or do something with you; say how you know each of them.

SUGGESTED CONTENT FOR MODELING DISPLAYS

A. *School or neighborhood:* Main actor introduces parent to guidance counselor or teacher.

B. *Home:* Main actor introduces new friend to parent.

C. *Peer group:* Main actor introduces new neighbor to friends.

GROUP I: BEGINNING SOCIAL SKILLS
SKILL 8: Giving a Compliment

STEPS	TRAINER NOTES
1. Decide what you want to compliment about the other person.	It may be the person's appearance, behavior, or an accomplishment.
2. Decide how to give the compliment.	Consider the wording and ways to keep the other person and yourself from feeling embarrassed.
3. Choose the right time and place to say it.	It may be a private place, or a time when the other person is unoccupied.
4. Give the compliment.	Be friendly and sincere.

SUGGESTED CONTENT FOR MODELING DISPLAYS

A. *School or neighborhood:* Main actor compliments neighbor on new car.

B. *Home:* Main actor compliments parents on good dinner.

C. *Peer group:* Main actor compliments friend for avoiding fight.

GROUP II: ADVANCED SOCIAL SKILLS
SKILL 9: Asking for Help

STEPS	TRAINER NOTES
1. Decide what the problem is.	Be specific; who and what are contributing to the problem; what is its effect on you.
2. Decide if you want help for the problem.	Figure out if you can solve the problem alone.
3. Think about different people who might help you and pick one.	Consider all possible helpers and choose the best one.
4. Tell the person about the problem and ask that person to help you.	

SUGGESTED CONTENT FOR MODELING DISPLAYS

A. *School or neighborhood:* Main actor asks teacher for help with difficult homework problem.

B. *Home:* Main actor asks parent for help with personal problem.

C. *Peer group:* Main actor asks friend for advice with dating.

COMMENTS

The definition of *problem,* as used in this skill, is anything one needs help with, varying from problems with other people to school and other informational problems.

GROUP II: ADVANCED SOCIAL SKILLS
SKILL 10: Joining In

STEPS	TRAINER NOTES
1. Decide if you want to join in an activity others are doing.	Check the advantages and disadvantages. Be sure you want to participate in and not disrupt what others are doing.
2. Decide the best way to join in.	You might ask, apply, start a conversation, or introduce yourself.
3. Choose the best time to join in.	Good times are usually during a break in the activity or before the activity gets started.
4. Join in the activity.	

SUGGESTED CONTENT FOR MODELING DISPLAYS

A. *School or neighborhood:* Main actor signs up for neighborhood sports team.

B. *Home:* Main actor joins family in recreational activity.

C. *Peer group:* Main actor joins peers in ongoing pickup game, recreational activity, or conversation.

GROUP II. ADVANCED SOCIAL SKILLS
SKILL 11: Giving Instructions

STEPS	TRAINER NOTES
1. Decide what needs to be done.	It might be a chore or a favor.
2. Think about the different people who could do it and choose one.	
3. Ask that person to do what you want done.	Tell the person how to do the task when it is complex.
4. Ask the other person if he/she understands what to do.	
5. Change or repeat your instructions if you need to.	This step is optional.

SUGGESTED CONTENT FOR MODELING DISPLAYS

A. *School or neighborhood:* Main actor divides chores for decorating gym for school party.

B. *Home:* Main actor tells little sister how to put records away correctly.

C. *Peer group:* Main actor instructs friends on how to care for pets.

COMMENTS

This skill refers to the enlistment of others to carry out a task and thus requires youngsters to think about division of responsibility.

GROUP II: ADVANCED SOCIAL SKILLS
SKILL 12: Following Instructions

STEPS	TRAINER NOTES
1. Listen carefully while you are being told what to do.	Take notes if necessary; nod your head; say, "mm-hmm."
2. Ask questions about anything you don't understand.	The goal is making instructions more specific, more clear.
3. Decide if you want to follow the instructions and let the other person know your decision.	
4. Repeat the instructions to yourself.	Do this in your own words.
5. Do what you have been asked to do.	

SUGGESTED CONTENT FOR MODELING DISPLAYS

A. *School or neighborhood:* Main actor follows classroom instruction given by teacher.

B. *Home:* Main actor follows parent's instructions on operating home appliance.

C. *Peer group:* Main actor follows friend's instructions on fixing bicycle.

COMMENTS

This skill concerns complying with the requests of another person. If the task seems unreasonable, it may be an instance in which another skill is needed (e.g., Skill 25: Negotiating, Skill 31: Making a Complaint, etc.).

GROUP II: ADVANCED SOCIAL SKILLS
SKILL 13: Apologizing

STEPS	TRAINER NOTES
1. Decide if it would be best for you to apologize for something you did.	You might apologize for breaking something, making an error, or interrupting someone.
2. Think of the different ways you could apologize.	Say something; do something; write something.
3. Choose the best time and place to apologize.	Do it privately and as quickly as possible after creating the problem.
4. Make your apology.	This might include an offer to make up for what happened.

SUGGESTED CONTENT FOR MODELING DISPLAYS

A. *School or neighborhood:* Main actor apologizes to neighbor for broken window.

B. *Home:* Main actor apologizes to younger brother for picking on him.

C. *Peer group:* Main actor apologizes to friend for betraying a confidence.

GROUP II: ADVANCED SOCIAL SKILLS
Skill 14: Convincing Others

STEPS	TRAINER NOTES
1. Decide if you want to convince someone about something.	It might be doing something your way, going someplace, interpreting events, or evaluating ideas.
2. Tell the other person your ideas.	Focus on both content of ideas and feelings about point of view.
3. Ask the other person what he/she thinks about it.	This requires use of listening skill.
4. Tell why you think your idea is a good one.	
5. Ask the other person to think about what you said before making up his/her mind.	Check on the other person's decision at a later point in time.

SUGGESTED CONTENT FOR MODELING DISPLAYS

A. *School or neighborhood:* Main actor convinces storekeeper that he/she deserves a job.

B. *Home:* Main actor convinces parent that he/she is responsible enough to stay out late.

C. *Peer group:* Main actor convinces friend to include new person in game.

COMMENTS

In persuading someone of something, a person needs to understand both sides of the argument. Use of this skill assumes that, if the other person is asked about his/her position and there is no difference of opinion, the role play should end at Step 3.

GROUP III: SKILLS FOR DEALING WITH FEELINGS
SKILL 15: Knowing Your Feelings

STEPS	TRAINER NOTES
1. Tune in to what is going on in your body that helps you know what you are feeling.	Some cues are blushing, butterflies in your stomach, tight muscles, etc.
2. Decide what happened to make you feel that way.	Focus on outside events such as a fight, a surprise, etc.
3. Decide what you could call the feeling.	Possibilities are anger, fear, embarrassment, joy, happiness, sadness, disappointment, frustration, excitement, anxiety, etc. Trainer should place a list of feelings on the board and encourage trainees to contribute additional suggestions.

SUGGESTED CONTENT FOR MODELING DISPLAYS

A. *School or neighborhood:* Main actor feels embarrassed when caught unprepared in class.

B. *Home:* Main actor is angry when unjustly accused at home.

C. *Peer group:* Main actor is happy when friend pays compliment.

COMMENTS

This has been included as a separate skill for adolescents to learn prior to practicing the expression of feelings to another person. Frequently, feelings can be confused with one another, resulting in rather vague, but strong, emotions. Once the feeling can be labeled accurately, the trainee can go on to the next skill, which involves prosocial modes of expressing the feeling.

Step 1, involving "tuning in" to body feelings, is often a new experience for many people. Spend as much time as needed in discussing, giving examples, and practicing this step before going on to subsequent steps.

GROUP III: SKILLS FOR DEALING WITH FEELINGS
SKILL 16: Expressing Your Feelings

STEPS	TRAINER NOTES
1. Tune in to what is going on in your body.	
2. Decide what happened to make you feel that way.	
3. Decide what you are feeling.	Possibilities are happy, sad, in a bad mood, nervous, worried, scared, embarrassed, disappointed, frustrated, etc. Trainer should place a list of feelings on the board.
4. Think about the different ways to express your feeling and pick one.	Consider prosocial alternatives such as talking about a feeling, doing a physical activity to blow off steam, telling the object of the feeling about the feeling, walking away from emotional situations, or delaying action. Consider how, when, where, and to whom the feeling could be expressed.
5. Express your feeling.	

SUGGESTED CONTENT FOR MODELING DISPLAYS

A. *School or neighborhood:* Main actor tells teacher about feeling nervous before test.

B. *Home:* Main actor tells parent about feeling embarrassed when treated like a child.

C. *Peer group:* Main actor hugs friend when learning of friend's success.

GROUP III: SKILLS FOR DEALING WITH FEELINGS
Skill 17: Understanding the Feelings of Others

STEPS	TRAINER NOTES
1. Watch the other person.	Notice tone of voice, posture, and facial expression.
2. Listen to what the person is saying.	Try to understand the content.
3. Figure out what the person might be feeling.	He/she may be angry, sad, anxious, etc.
4. Think about ways to show you understand what he/she is feeling.	You might tell him/her, touch him/her, or leave the person alone.
5. Decide on the best way and do it.	

SUGGESTED CONTENT FOR MODELING DISPLAYS

A. *School or neighborhood:* Main actor brings gift to neighbor whose spouse has been ill.

B. *Home:* Main actor recognizes parent is preoccupied with financial concerns and decides to leave parent alone.

C. *Peer group:* Main actor lets friend know he/she understands friend's discomfort on meeting new people.

COMMENTS

This skill is closely related to empathy, described and operationalized for training purposes in chapter 8.

GROUP III: SKILLS FOR DEALING WITH FEELINGS
Skill 18: Dealing with Someone Else's Anger

STEPS	TRAINER NOTES
1. Listen to the person who is angry.	Don't interrupt; stay calm.
2. Try to understand what the angry person is saying and feeling.	Ask questions to get explanations of what you don't understand; restate them to yourself.
3. Decide if you can say or do something to deal with the situation.	Think about ways of dealing with the problem. This may include just listening, being empathic, doing something to correct the problem, ignoring it, or being assertive.
4. If you can, deal with the other person's anger.	

SUGGESTED CONTENT FOR MODELING DISPLAYS

A. *School or neighborhood:* Main actor responds to teacher who is angry about disruptive behavior in class by agreeing to cooperate by paying attention.

B. *Home:* Main actor responds to parent who is angry about messy house by agreeing to do a fair share of work.

C. *Peer group:* Main actor responds to friend's anger about name-calling by denying that he/she took part in it.

COMMENTS

This skill refers to anger being directed at the trainee. As such, it usually requires some action on the part of the trainee to deal with the situation. Trainer should have trainee make use of the steps for Skill 1 (Listening) when enacting the first step of this skill.

GROUP III: SKILLS FOR DEALING WITH FEELINGS
SKILL 19: Expressing Affection

STEPS	TRAINER NOTES
1. Decide if you have good feelings about the other person.	
2. Decide if the other person would like to know about your feelings.	Consider the possible consequences (e.g., happiness, misinterpretation, embarrassment, encouragement of friendship, etc.).
3. Choose the best way to express your feelings.	Do something; say something.
4. Choose the best time and place to express your feelings.	
5. Express your feelings in a friendly way.	

SUGGESTED CONTENT FOR MODELING DISPLAYS

A. *School or neighborhood:* Main actor expresses positive feelings toward guidance counselor after unburdening personal problem.

B. *Home:* Main actor brings small gift to parent as token of affection.

C. *Peer group:* Main actor expresses friendly feelings toward new friend.

COMMENTS

Although trainees initially will associate this skill with romantic relationships, they will soon grasp the notion that affection and caring can be expressed toward a wide variety of persons.

GROUP III: SKILLS FOR DEALING WITH FEELINGS
SKILL 20: Dealing with Fear

STEPS	TRAINER NOTES
1. Decide if you are feeling afraid.	Use Skill 15: Knowing Your Feelings.
2. Think about what you might be afraid of.	Think about alternative possibilities and choose the most likely one.
3. Figure out if the fear is realistic.	Is the feared object really a threat? You may need to check this out with another person or may need more information.
4. Take steps to reduce your fear.	You might talk with someone, leave the scene, or gradually approach the fearful situation.

SUGGESTED CONTENT FOR MODELING DISPLAYS

A. *School or neighborhood:* Main actor is fearful of repercussions after breaking neighbor's window and discusses fear with parent.

B. *Home:* Main actor is afraid of being home alone and arranges to have friend visit.

C. *Peer group:* After being teased by older neighborhood youth, main actor is fearful of being beaten up and takes steps to avoid confrontation.

COMMENTS

Group discussion can be quite useful in examining how realistic particular fears are. Trainers should be sensitive to the fact that trainees may be reluctant to reveal their fears to peers. Modeling of fearful situations may help them to overcome this reluctance.

GROUP III: SKILLS FOR DEALING WITH FEELINGS
Skill 21: Rewarding Yourself

STEPS	TRAINER NOTES
1. Decide if you have done something that deserves a reward.	It might be something you have succeeded at or some area of progress.
2. Decide what you could say to reward yourself.	Use praise, approval, or encouragement.
3. Decide what you could do to reward yourself.	You might buy something, go someplace, or increase or decrease an activity.
4. Reward yourself.	Say and do it.

SUGGESTED CONTENT FOR MODELING DISPLAYS

A. *School or neighborhood:* Main actor rewards self after studying hard and doing well on exam by going to movie after school.

B. *Home:* Main actor rewards self with positive self-statement after avoiding fight with older sibling.

C. *Peer group:* Main actor rewards self by buying soda after convincing peers to join neighborhood club.

COMMENTS

Be sure trainee tries to apply the following rules, all of which increase the effectiveness of self-reward:
1. Reward yourself as soon as possible after successful performance.
2. Reward yourself only after successful performance, not before.
3. The better your performance, the better your self-reward.
See chapter 12 for further discussion of self-reward.

GROUP IV: SKILL ALTERNATIVES TO AGGRESSION
Skill 22: Asking Permission

STEPS	TRAINER NOTES
1. Decide what you would like to do for which you need permission.	Ask if you want to borrow something or request a special privilege.
2. Decide whom you have to ask for permission.	Ask the owner, manager, or teacher.
3. Decide how to ask for permission.	Ask out loud; ask privately; ask in writing.
4. Pick the right time and place.	
5. Ask for permission.	

SUGGESTED CONTENT FOR MODELING DISPLAYS

A. *School or neighborhood:* Main actor asks shop teacher for permission to use new power tool.

B. *Home:* Main actor asks parent for permission to stay out past curfew.

C. *Peer group:* Main actor asks friend for permission to borrow sporting equipment.

COMMENTS

Prior to practicing this skill, it is frequently useful to discuss situations that require permission. Some youngsters may tend to ask permission for things that could be done independently (without permission), while others neglect to ask permission in situations that require doing so.

GROUP IV: SKILL ALTERNATIVES TO AGGRESSION
Skill 23: Sharing Something

STEPS	TRAINER NOTES
1. Decide if you might like to share some of what you have.	You could divide the item between yourself and others or allow others to use the item.
2. Think about how the other person might feel about your sharing.	He/she might feel pleased, indifferent, suspicious, or insulted.
3. Offer to share in a direct and friendly way.	Make the offer sincere, allowing the other to decline if he/she wishes.

SUGGESTED CONTENT FOR MODELING DISPLAYS

A. *School or neighborhood:* Main actor offers to share book with classmate who has forgotten own book.

B. *Home:* Main actor offers to share candy with sibling.

C. *Peer group:* Main actor invites friend to try his/her new bicycle.

the other person; observe.

2. Think of the ways you could be helpful.	You could be doing something, giving encouragement, or getting help from someone else.
3. Ask the other person if he/she needs and wants your help.	Make the offer sincere, allowing the other to decline if he/she wishes.
4. Help the other person.	

SUGGESTED CONTENT FOR MODELING DISPLAYS

A. *School or neighborhood:* Main actor offers to help teacher arrange chairs in classroom.

B. *Home:* Main actor offers to prepare dinner.

C. *Peer group:* Main actor offers to bring class assignments home for sick friend.

GROUP IV: SKILL ALTERNATIVES TO AGGRESSION
SKILL 25: Negotiating

STEPS	TRAINER NOTES
1. Decide if you and the other person are having a difference of opinion.	Are you getting tense or arguing?
2. Tell the other person what you think about the problem.	State your own position and your perception of the other's position.
3. Ask the other person what he/she thinks about the problem.	
4. Listen openly to his/her answer.	
5. Think about why the other person might feel this way.	
6. Suggest a compromise.	Be sure the proposed compromise takes into account the opinions and feelings of both persons.

SUGGESTED CONTENT FOR MODELING DISPLAYS

A. *School or neighborhood:* Main actor negotiates with neighbor a fee for after-school chores.

B. *Home:* Main actor negotiates with parent about curfew.

C. *Peer group:* Main actor negotiates with friend about what recreational activity to participate in.

COMMENTS

Negotiating is a skill that presupposes an ability to understand the feelings of others (Skill 17). We suggest that Skill 17 be reviewed prior to teaching Negotiating. Negotiating is also similar in some respects to Skill 14 (Convincing Others). Negotiating, however, introduces the concept of compromise, a concept that is often worth discussing before role playing this skill.

GROUP IV: SKILL ALTERNATIVES TO AGGRESSION
16. Using Self-control

TRAINER NOTES

1. Tune in to what is going on in your body that helps you know that you are about to lose control of yourself.

   Are you getting tense, angry, hot, fidgety?

2. Decide what happened to make you feel this way.

   Consider outside events or "internal" events (thoughts).

3. Think about ways in which you might control yourself.

   Slow down; count to 10; assert yourself; leave; do something else.

4. Choose the best way to control yourself and do it.

SUGGESTED CONTENT FOR MODELING DISPLAYS

A. *School or neighborhood:* Main actor controls yelling at teacher when teacher criticizes harshly.

B. *Home:* Main actor controls self when parent forbids desired activity.

C. *Peer group:* Main actor controls self when friend takes something without asking permission.

COMMENTS

It is often helpful to discuss various ways of controlling oneself before role playing the skill. The list of self-control techniques can be written on the board and used to generate alternative tactics youngsters can use in a variety of situations.

GROUP IV: SKILL ALTERNATIVES TO AGGRESSION
Skill 27: Standing Up for Your Rights

STEPS	TRAINER NOTES
1. Pay attention to what is going on in your body that helps you know that you are dissatisfied and would like to stand up for yourself.	Cues are tight muscles, butterflies in your stomach, etc.
2. Decide what happened to make you feel dissatisfied.	Are you being taken advantage of, ignored, mistreated, or teased?
3. Think about ways in which you might stand up for yourself and choose one.	Seek help; say what is on your mind; get a majority opinion; choose the right time and place.
4. Stand up for yourself in a direct and reasonable way.	

SUGGESTED CONTENT FOR MODELING DISPLAYS

A. *School or neighborhood:* Main actor approaches teacher after being disciplined unfairly.

B. *Home:* Main actor talks with parent about need for privacy.

C. *Peer group:* Main actor talks with peer after not being chosen for the club (team).

COMMENTS

Also known as *assertiveness,* this skill is particularly important for withdrawn or shy trainees, as well as for trainees whose typical responses are inappropriately aggressive.

GROUP IV: SKILL ALTERNATIVES TO AGGRESSION
SKILL 28: Responding to Teasing

STEPS	TRAINER NOTES
1. Decide if you are being teased.	Are others making jokes or whispering?
2. Think about ways to deal with the teasing.	Gracefully accept it; make a joke of it; ignore it.
3. Choose the best way and do it.	When possible, avoid alternatives that foster aggression, malicious counterteasing, and withdrawal.

SUGGESTED CONTENT FOR MODELING DISPLAYS

A. *School or neighborhood:* Main actor ignores classmate's comments when volunteering to help teacher after class.

B. *Home:* Main actor tells sibling to stop teasing about new haircut.

C. *Peer group:* Main actor deals with peer's teasing about a girlfriend or boyfriend by making a joke of it.

GROUP IV: SKILL ALTERNATIVES TO AGGRESSION
Skill 29: Avoiding Trouble with Others

STEPS	TRAINER NOTES
1. Decide if you are in a situation that might get you into trouble.	Examine immediate and long-range consequences.
2. Decide if you want to get out of the situation.	Consider risks versus gains.
3. Tell the other people what you decided and why.	
4. Suggest other things you might do.	Consider prosocial alternatives.
5. Do what you think is best for you.	

SUGGESTED CONTENT FOR MODELING DISPLAYS

A. *School or neighborhood:* Main actor tells classmates he/she will not cut class with them.

B. *Home:* Main actor refuses to go for ride in family car without permission.

C. *Peer group:* Main actor decides not to join peers in petty shoplifting.

COMMENTS

In Step 3, the reasons for decisions may vary according to the trainee's level of moral reasoning (e.g., fear of punishment, social conformity, or concern for others).

GROUP IV: SKILL ALTERNATIVES TO AGGRESSION
Skill 30: Keeping Out of Fights

STEPS	TRAINER NOTES
1. Stop and think about why you want to fight.	
2. Decide what you want to happen in the long run.	What is the long-range outcome?
3. Think about other ways to handle the situation besides fighting.	You might negotiate, stand up for your rights, ask for help, or pacify him/her.
4. Decide on the best way to handle the situation and do it.	

SUGGESTED CONTENT FOR MODELING DISPLAYS

A. *School or neighborhood:* Main actor tells classmate that he/she wants to talk out their differences instead of being pressured to fight.

B. *Home:* Main actor resolves potential fight with older sibling by asking parent to intervene.

C. *Peer group:* Main actor goes for help when he/she sees peers fighting on school steps.

COMMENTS

Prior to teaching this skill, it is often useful to review Skill 26 (Using Self-control).

GROUP V: SKILLS FOR DEALING WITH STRESS
SKILL 31: Making a Complaint

STEPS	TRAINER NOTES
1. Decide what your complaint is.	What is the problem?
2. Decide whom to complain to.	Who can resolve it?
3. Tell that person your complaint.	Consider alternative ways to complain (e.g., politely, assertively, privately).
4. Tell that person what you would like done about the problem.	Offer a helpful suggestion about resolving the problem.
5. Ask how he/she feels about what you've said.	

SUGGESTED CONTENT FOR MODELING DISPLAYS

A. *School or neighborhood:* Main actor complains to guidance counselor about being assigned to class that is too difficult.

B. *Home:* Main actor complains to sibling about unfair division of chores.

C. *Peer group:* Main actor complains to friend about spreading a rumor.

GROUP V: SKILLS FOR DEALING WITH STRESS
SKILL 32: Answering a Complaint

STEPS	TRAINER NOTES
1. Listen to the complaint.	Listen openly.
2. Ask the person to explain anything you don't understand.	
3. Tell the person that you understand the complaint.	Rephrase; acknowledge the content and feeling.
4. State your ideas about the complaint, accepting the blame if appropriate.	
5. Suggest what each of you could do about the complaint.	You might compromise, defend your position, or apologize.

SUGGESTED CONTENT FOR MODELING DISPLAYS

A. *School or neighborhood:* Main actor responds to neighbor's complaint about noisy party.

B. *Home:* Main actor responds to parent's complaint about selection of friends.

C. *Peer group:* Main actor responds to friend's complaint about returning sporting equipment in poor condition.

GROUP V: SKILLS FOR DEALING WITH STRESS
SKILL 33: Sportsmanship after the Game

STEPS	TRAINER NOTES
1. Think about how you did and how the other person did in the game you played.	
2. Think of a true compliment you could give the other person about his/her game.	Say "good try," "congratulations," or "getting better."
3. Think about his/her reactions to what you might say.	The reaction might be pleasure, anger, or embarrassment.
4. Choose the compliment you think is best and say it.	

SUGGESTED CONTENT FOR MODELING DISPLAYS

A. *School or neighborhood:* Main actor talks to classmate who has made starting team.

B. *Home:* Main actor wins Monopoly game against younger sibling.

C. *Peer group:* New acquaintance does well in pickup game.

GROUP V: SKILLS FOR DEALING WITH STRESS
Skill 34: Dealing with Embarrassment

STEPS	TRAINER NOTES
1. Decide if you are feeling embarrassed.	
2. Decide what happened to make you feel embarrassed.	
3. Decide on what will help you feel less embarrassed and do it.	Correct the cause; minimize it; ignore it; distract others; use humor; reassure yourself.

SUGGESTED CONTENT FOR MODELING DISPLAYS

A. *School or neighborhood:* Main actor deals with embarrassment of going to school wearing glasses for first time.

B. *Home:* Mother catches main actor necking with boyfriend/girlfriend.

C. *Peer group:* Main actor is embarrassed by being overheard when discussing private matter.

COMMENTS

Prior to teaching this skill, it is often useful to review Skill 15 (Knowing Your Feelings).

GROUP V: SKILLS FOR DEALING WITH STRESS
SKILL 35: Dealing with Being Left Out

STEPS	TRAINER NOTES
1. Decide if you are being left out.	Are you being ignored or rejected?
2. Think about why the other people might be leaving you out of something.	
3. Decide how you could deal with the problem.	You might wait, leave, tell the other people how their behavior affects you, or ask to be included.
4. Choose the best way and do it.	

SUGGESTED CONTENT FOR MODELING DISPLAYS

A. *School or neighborhood:* Main actor tells teacher of disappointment after not being picked for committee.

B. *Home:* Main actor asks sibling to include him/her in planned activity with other friends.

C. *Peer group:* Main actor is left out of plans for party.

GROUP V: SKILLS FOR DEALING WITH STRESS
SKILL 36: **Standing Up for a Friend**

STEPS	TRAINER NOTES
1. Decide if your friend has not been treated fairly by others.	Has your friend been criticized, teased, or taken advantage of?
2. Decide if your friend wants you to stand up for him/her.	
3. Decide how to stand up for your friend.	You might assert his/her rights, explain, or apologize.
4. Stand up for your friend.	

SUGGESTED CONTENT FOR MODELING DISPLAYS

A. *School or neighborhood:* Main actor explains to teacher that friend has been accused unjustly.

B. *Home:* Main actor defends friend's reputation when parent is critical.

C. *Peer group:* Main actor defends friend when peers are teasing.

GROUP V: SKILLS FOR DEALING WITH STRESS
SKILL 37: Responding to Persuasion

STEPS	TRAINER NOTES
1. Listen to the other person's ideas on the topic.	
2. Decide what you think about the topic.	Distinguish your own ideas from the ideas of others.
3. Compare what he/she said with what you think.	
4. Decide which idea you like better and tell the other person about it.	Agree; disagree; modify; postpone a decision.

SUGGESTED CONTENT FOR MODELING DISPLAYS

A. *School or neighborhood:* Main actor deals with high-pressure sales pitch.

B. *Home:* Main actor deals with parental pressure to dress in a particular way for job interview.

C. *Peer group:* Main actor deals with friend's persuasive argument to try drugs.

GROUP V: SKILLS FOR DEALING WITH STRESS
SKILL 38: Responding to Failure

STEPS	TRAINER NOTES
1. Decide if you have failed at something.	The failure may be interpersonal, academic, or athletic.
2. Think about why you failed.	It could be due to skill, motivation, or luck. Include personal reasons and circumstances.
3. Think about what you could do to keep from failing another time.	Evaluate what is under your control to change; if a skill problem—practice; if motivation—increase effort; if circumstances—think of ways to change them.
4. Decide if you want to try again.	
5. Try again using your new idea.	

SUGGESTED CONTENT FOR MODELING DISPLAYS

A. *School or neighborhood:* Main actor deals with failing grade on exam.

B. *Home:* Main actor fails at attempt to help younger sibling with a project.

C. *Peer group:* Main actor deals with being turned down for date.

GROUP V: SKILLS FOR DEALING WITH STRESS
SKILL 39: Dealing with Contradictory Messages

STEPS	TRAINER NOTES
1. Decide if someone is telling you two opposite things at the same time.	This could be in words, in nonverbal behavior, or in saying one thing and doing another.
2. Think of ways to tell the other person that you don't understand what he/she means.	Confront him/her; ask.
3. Choose the best way to tell the person and do it.	

SUGGESTED CONTENT FOR MODELING DISPLAYS

A. *School or neighborhood:* Main actor deals with teacher who verbalizes approval but scowls at same time.

B. *Home:* Main actor confronts parent who verbalizes trust but refuses to grant privileges.

C. *Peer group:* Main actor deals with friend who makes general invitation but never really includes main actor in plans.

COMMENTS

In teaching this skill, it is important to encourage youngsters to observe closely the behaviors of others around them. See if they can think about a person who says "yes" but at the same time shakes his/her head to mean no. See if they can think about a person who says "take your time" but at the same time makes them hurry up. That is, be sure to include situations in which the person is told two conflicting things, as well as those involving a person saying one thing and doing the opposite. In Step 1, this deciphering of the message is essential; otherwise, the trainee will be unable to proceed to Steps 2 and 3.

GROUP V: SKILLS FOR DEALING WITH STRESS
Skill 40: Dealing with an Accusation

STEPS	TRAINER NOTES
1. Think about what the other person has accused you of.	Is the accusation accurate or inaccurate? Was it said in a mean way or a constructive way?
2. Think about why the person might have accused you.	Have you infringed on his/her rights or property? Has a rumor been started by someone else?
3. Think about ways to answer the person's accusation.	Deny it; explain your own behavior; correct the other person's perceptions; assert yourself; apologize; offer to make up for what happened.
4. Choose the best way and do it.	

SUGGESTED CONTENT FOR MODELING DISPLAYS

A. *School or neighborhood:* Main actor is accused of breaking neighbor's window.

B. *Home:* Parent accuses main actor of hurting sibling's feelings.

C. *Peer group:* Friend accuses main actor of lying.

GROUP V: SKILLS FOR DEALING WITH STRESS
SKILL 41: Getting Ready for a Difficult Conversation

STEPS	TRAINER NOTES
1. Think about how you will feel during the conversation.	You might be tense, anxious, or impatient.
2. Think about how the other person will feel.	He/she may feel anxious, bored, or angry.
3. Think about different ways you could say what you want to say.	
4. Think about what the other person might say back to you.	
5. Think about any other things that might happen during the conversation.	Repeat Steps 1–5 at least twice, using different approaches to the situation.
6. Choose the best approach you can think of and try it.	

SUGGESTED CONTENT FOR MODELING DISPLAYS

A. *School or neighborhood:* Main actor prepares to talk with teacher about dropping subject.

B. *Home:* Main actor prepares to tell parent about school failure.

C. *Peer group:* Main actor prepares to ask for first date.

COMMENTS

In preparing for difficult or stressful conversations, it is useful for youngsters to see that the way they approach the situation can influence the final outcome. This skill involves rehearsing a variety of approaches and then reflecting upon which approach produces the best results. Feedback from group members on the effectiveness of each approach can be particularly useful in this regard.

GROUP V: SKILLS FOR DEALING WITH STRESS
Skill 42: Dealing with Group Pressure

STEPS	TRAINER NOTES
1. Think about what the group wants you to do and why.	Listen to other people; decide what the real meaning is; try to understand what is being said.
2. Decide what you want to do.	Yield; resist; delay; negotiate.
3. Decide how to tell the group what you want to do.	Give reasons; talk to one person only; delay; assert yourself.
4. Tell the group what you have decided.	

SUGGESTED CONTENT FOR MODELING DISPLAYS

A. *School or neighborhood:* Main actor deals with group pressure to vandalize neighborhood.

B. *Home:* Main actor deals with family pressure to break up friendship.

C. *Peer group:* Main actor deals with pressure to fight.

GROUP VI: PLANNING SKILLS
SKILL 43: Deciding on Something to Do

STEPS	TRAINER NOTES
1. Decide whether you are feeling bored or dissatisfied with what you are doing.	Are you not concentrating, getting fidgety, or disrupting others who are involved in an activity?
2. Think of things you have enjoyed doing in the past.	
3. Decide which one you might be able to do now.	Focus on prosocial alternatives; include others if appropriate.
4. Start the activity.	

SUGGESTED CONTENT FOR MODELING DISPLAYS

A. *School or neighborhood:* Main actor chooses after-school activity in which to participate.

B. *Home:* Main actor thinks up activity that will earn him/her money.

C. *Peer group:* Main actor suggests that friends play basketball instead of hanging around.

GROUP VI: PLANNING SKILLS
SKILL 44: Deciding What Caused a Problem

STEPS	TRAINER NOTES
1. Define what the problem is.	
2. Think about possible causes of the problem.	Was it yourself, others, or events?
3. Decide which are the most likely causes of the problem.	
4. Check out what really caused the problem.	Ask others; observe the situation again.

SUGGESTED CONTENT FOR MODELING DISPLAYS

A. *School or neighborhood:* Main actor evaluates reasons for teacher's abruptness.

B. *Home:* Main actor evaluates likely causes of parents having an argument.

C. *Peer group:* Main actor evaluates why he/she feels nervous with particular friend.

COMMENTS

This skill is intended to help youngsters determine the degree to which they are responsible for a particular problem and the degree to which the causes of the problem are outside of their control.

GROUP VI: PLANNING SKILLS
SKILL 45: Setting a Goal

STEPS	TRAINER NOTES
1. Figure out what goal you want to reach.	
2. Find out all the information you can about how to reach your goal.	Talk with friends; read; ask authorities.
3. Think about the steps you will need to take to reach your goal.	Consider the order of steps, materials, help from others, and skills needed.
4. Take the first step toward your goal.	

SUGGESTED CONTENT FOR MODELING DISPLAYS

A. *School or neighborhood:* Main actor decides to find a job.

B. *Home:* Main actor decides to improve appearance.

C. *Peer group:* Main actor decides to have a party.

GROUP VI: PLANNING SKILLS
SKILL 46: Deciding on Your Abilities

STEPS	TRAINER NOTES
1. Decide which abilities you might want to use.	Take the setting, circumstances, and goal into account.
2. Think about how you have done in the past when you have tried to use these abilities.	
3. Get other people's opinions about your abilities.	Ask others; take test; check records.
4. Think about what you found out and decide how well you use these abilities.	Consider the evidence from both Steps 2 and 3

SUGGESTED CONTENT FOR MODELING DISPLAYS

A. *School or neighborhood:* Main actor decides type of school curriculum to pursue.

B. *Home:* Main actor evaluates ability to repair broken bicycle (appliance).

C. *Peer group:* Main actor decides whether to try out for team (play).

COMMENTS

This skill is intended to help youngsters evaluate their capabilities realistically in view of available evidence. This skill is often tied to Skill 45 (Setting a Goal).

GROUP VI: PLANNING SKILLS
SKILL 47: Gathering Information

STEPS	TRAINER NOTES
1. Decide what information you need.	
2. Decide how you can get the information	Can get information from people, books, etc.
3. Do things to get the information.	Ask questions; make telephone calls; look in books.

SUGGESTED CONTENT FOR MODELING DISPLAYS

A. *School or neighborhood:* Main actor gathers information on available jobs.

B. *Home:* Main actor gathers information on where to shop for particular item.

C. *Peer group:* Main actor finds out what kinds of things date likes to do.

COMMENTS

This skill often precedes Skill 49 (Making a Decision). Although each constitutes a separate skill, when taken together, they comprise an effective approach to problem solving.

GROUP VI: PLANNING SKILLS
SKILL 48: Arranging Problems by Importance

STEPS	TRAINER NOTES
1. Think about the problems that are bothering you.	Make a list; be inclusive.
2. List these problems from most to least important.	
3. Do what you can to hold off on your less important problems.	Delegate them; postpone them; avoid them.
4. Go to work on your most important problems.	Plan first steps in dealing with the most important problem; rehearse these steps in your imagination.

SUGGESTED CONTENT FOR MODELING DISPLAYS

A. *School or neighborhood:* Main actor is worried about large number of school assignments.

B. *Home:* Parent tells main actor to take care of a number of chores before going out.

C. *Peer group:* Main actor has difficulty balancing school responsibilities, chores, and time with friends.

COMMENTS

This skill is intended to help the youngster who feels overwhelmed by a number of difficulties. The youngster is instructed how to evaluate the relative urgency of the various problems and to deal with each according to its priority of importance.

GROUP VI: PLANNING SKILLS
SKILL 49: Making a Decision

STEPS	TRAINER NOTES
1. Think about the problem that requires you to make a decision.	
2. Think about possible decisions you could make.	Generate a number of possible alternatives; avoid premature closure.
3. Gather accurate information about these possible decisions.	Ask others; read; observe.
4. Reconsider your possible decisions using the information you have gathered.	
5. Make the best decision.	

SUGGESTED CONTENT FOR MODELING DISPLAYS

A. *School or neighborhood:* Main actor decides what job to apply for.

B. *Home:* Main actor decides how to spend money he/she has earned.

C. *Peer group:* Main actor decides whether to participate with friends in a weekend activity.

COMMENTS

This skill generally follows Skill 47 (Gathering Information) to constitute the general skill of problem solving.

GROUP VI: PLANNING SKILLS
Skill 50: Concentrating on a Task

STEPS	TRAINER NOTES
1. Decide what your task is.	
2. Decide on a time to work on this task.	Consider when and how long to work.
3. Gather the materials you need.	
4. Decide on a place to work.	Consider where; minimize distractions.
5. Decide if you are ready to concentrate.	

SUGGESTED CONTENT FOR MODELING DISPLAYS

A. *School or neighborhood:* Main actor prepares to research and write a report.

B. *Home:* Main actor prepares to repair bicycle (appliance).

C. *Peer group:* Main actor gathers material necessary for trip with friends.

COMMENTS

This skill helps youngsters overcome problems with distractions by focusing on relevant planning prior to undertaking a task. Planning, in this sense, involves scheduling and arranging materials and the work environment.

Sample Modeling Displays

The following is a script of an introductory narration and two modeling vignettes for Skill 42 (Dealing with Group Pressure).

Introduction to Dealing with Group Pressure

Dealing with group pressure means deciding what you want to do when other people are trying to get you to do something that they want you to do. Sometimes you will want to go along with them, and sometimes you will want to do something else. All of the time you will feel best about your decision if you give yourself a chance to stop and think about your choices before deciding whether or not to go along with the group.

What you will see and hear next are some examples of young people dealing with different kinds of group pressure. In each example, they make a decision that is right for them by thinking about what to do before making up their minds.

They do this by going through a series of steps for dealing with group pressure. These steps are as follows:

1. Think about what the group wants you to do and why,
2. Decide what you want to do,
3. Decide how to tell the group what you want to do,
4. Tell the group what you have decided.

By learning to use these steps in your life, you can learn how to make up your own mind and deal with group pressure from your friends, from your family, and from others.

Once you have seen and heard the examples, you will then have a chance to try out this new way of dealing with group pressure.

Vignette 1

In this vignette, group pressure is put upon the main actor to fight someone. By thinking clearly about the situation and what he wants to do, the main actor avoids fighting without angering the group.

Scene:	Several young people converge upon Jeff, who is standing on the steps outside of school.
Main Actor:	Jeff
Co-actors:	A, B, C (all males), Louie

A: (*Out of breath*) Hey, Jeff, wait till you hear what Louie said about you!

B: Yeah, he said he'd beat you up any time—no problem!

C: You gonna let him get away with that?

A: C'mon, Jeff, grab him when he comes outside.

B: You ain't gonna back out, are you?

Step 1:   Think about what the group wants you to do and why.

Jeff: (*To self*) What are these guys trying to push me into? These guys are really coming on strong. I hope they tell me what this hassle with Louie is about. I'd like to understand what they are pushing me to fight for.

Jeff: What's going on guys? Why is he going around telling people that?

A: You're going to have to straighten him out. He's telling everyone he's going to take care of you later today.

Step 2:   Decide what you want to do.

Jeff: (*To self*) I don't like what they're saying Louie said about me. These guys want to see me fight. What should I do? I could give in and wait for Louie to come out, but then they would definitely push for the fight.
I could resist their pushing by just brushing it off and walking away. But they would hassle me about it later. You know, these guys could be just trying to get up a fight. Louie's working in the cafeteria now. If I talked to him alone, I think I could straighten this out without a hassle. Yeah, I've got to see him alone.

A: Hey, c'mon, man—you gonna fight him or not?

B: I'll go in and get him out here!

Jeff: Hold on a minute!

Step 3:   Decide how to tell the group what you want to do.

Jeff: (*To self*) How can I tell them what I want to do? I could call their bluff, but that would only rile them up more.
I could try to get inside alone and then find Louie, and they'll let me if I tell them I'm going in to straighten it out by myself.
Yeah! That's what I'll do! I'll tell them I'm going in alone.

A, B, C:	He's a chicken!!
Step 4:	**Tell the group what you have decided.**
Jeff:	Listen, you guys wait here; I'm going to handle this my way. I'm going inside alone to get some things worked out with Louie.
A, B, C:	We'll go with you!
Jeff:	No, you said he's been talking about me. I know the guy. If the problem is with me, he'll tell me.
B:	You gonna fight him?
Jeff:	You guys let me deal with this my way. If there is a misunderstanding, I think he and I can work it out. You wait here, OK?
A, B, C:	OK, but call us if you need help!

(Jeff leaves—goes into school—sees Louie in the cafeteria.)

Jeff:	(*To self*) There he is now—he sees me; he waved to me—doesn't look mad at all ... I'm glad I decided to straighten this out myself.
Jeff:	Hey, Louie!
Louie:	How's it going, man! Saw your buddies running through here before, talking up a storm. What kind of trouble are they stirring up?
Jeff:	Oh, you know the guys. I think they're always trying to stir up a fight or cause some trouble!

Vignette 2

The second vignette shows group pressure being put upon the main actor to vandalize an old school building. For several reasons, the main actor decides that he'd rather not join his friends in defacing the school, and he finds the courage to tell them so.

Scene:	Several young people are standing outside a store talking to each other. One of them, Mike, has a paper bag full of spray paint cans. Joe comes walking up and hears them talking.
Main Actor:	Joe
Co-actors:	Eddie, Curtis, Mike, Lisa

Group:	Hi, Joe!
Joe:	What's goin' on tonight?
Eddie:	Wait till you hear this. Mike just got all this great spray paint. Show him, Mike.
Mike:	(*Holding can of paint*) We're going to go up to the old school and "decorate."
Lisa:	Let's spray paint names on the wall.
Curtis:	Great! Hey, Joe, we brought some extra cans. We knew you were coming. Ha! Ha!
Step 1:	**Think about what the group wants you to do and why.**
Joe:	(*To self*) Looks like this group is all set to go over and mess up the old school, and now they want me to go along with them. Seems like they're getting ready to leave right away.
Eddie:	What color paint you want, Joe? Blue . . . green . . . red? Hey, look here, silver!
Mike:	There's no one around there now, just a couple of old houses and garages.
Step 2:	**Decide what you want to do.**
Joe:	(*To self*) What am I gonna do? I never did like that old school, that's for sure. But they're gonna really do a job on it.
	They're sure they're not going to get caught—if they do, I could be in big trouble. No, I just don't feel right about it. That old school is still in someone's neighborhood, and I think they have plans to work on it. If these guys go and paint the walls, the city's going to have to hire someone to clean up their mess. And how are the people going to feel who live in that neighborhood? I wouldn't like it if someone came and painted up the buildings where I live.
	No, I'm not going along with it. No way!
Lisa:	Oh! Look at this! I'm taking the silver paint. When we get there I'll spray the windows.
Step 3:	**Decide how to tell the group what you want to do.**
Joe:	(*To self*) How do I tell them to count me out? They're all excited about it, and they're not going to listen to a

lot of talking either—though I wish I could change their minds. But there are too many of them to deal with.

The best thing I could do is tell them I don't want to do it and leave. I just hope they change their minds. OK! I'll tell them I don't want to do it because it's unfair to mess up a building like that and make problems for someone else to take care of—that's what I'll tell them!

Curtis: OK, Lisa, you get the silver paint. Eddie's got the red, Mike, the green. I want the yellow. Joe, that leaves you with . . .

Step 4: **Tell the group what you have decided.**

Joe: Forget it, Curtis. Count me out. You guys may be convinced that you'll get away with it, but even if you do, I don't feel right about it. Marking up a building that someone else has to clean up doesn't make me feel right! I wouldn't want anyone to make a mess like that where I live. I'd have more fun going to a movie tonight. I saw a few fellas walking down there before I came here. I'm going to catch up with them. Are you coming?

Curtis: Who wants to see some dumb ol' movie?

Eddie: Yeah!

Lisa: I'll go along, Joe. You reminded me of something my parents said the other day about the old school being used for a youth center if this city raises enough money, and I'd rather see the movie.

Eddie: Hey, you guys want to paint or not?

Mike: If that place could become our "rec" center, let's lay off. What about you, Curtis?

Curtis: Oh, man! Nobody's gonna build any youth center. You believe that? Let's hit the supermarket windows instead!

Mike: Forget it! I'm gonna try to make it to the movie. Joe, you know what time it starts?

Joe: At seven, I think. Let's hurry!

Joe: (*To self*) I didn't expect to change anyone's mind. I'm glad Mike and Lisa decided to come. It sure came out better than I thought it would!

Skills for Elementary-age Children

The 60 prosocial skills that follow are divided into the following five skill groups: Classroom Survival Skills, Friendship-making Skills, Skills for Dealing with Feelings, Skill Alternatives to Aggression, and Skills for Dealing with Stress. The skills presented are those believed to be related to a child's social competence (Spivack & Shure, 1974); those suggested by research to be related to peer acceptance (Mesibov & LaGreca, 1981), positive teacher attention, and academic success (Cartledge & Milburn, 1980); and those likely to provide effective interpersonal performance and personal satisfaction in the student's natural environment (Goldstein et al., 1980). This skills curriculum is by no means all-inclusive. As students express concerns and difficulties they are experiencing, and as the teacher observes problems the students encounter, new skills can and should be developed for instruction. Furthermore, in individual instances—depending on the child and her real-life circumstances—it may be appropriate to retain and teach a given skill but alter one or more of its behavioral steps. It will often be the case that both teacher and student together will effectively engage in this skill development or skill alteration process.

It will also often be necessary to simplify many behavioral skill steps for effective instruction of children in the primary grades. Pictorial cues that illustrate these steps will further clarify the steps for such younger children and other nonreaders. In addition to simplifying the wording of skill steps and providing pictorial cues to accompany them, it will often prove helpful with younger students to simplify the names of the skills to be taught. Examples include the following:

Skill 6:   Completing Assignments—change to Finishing Work

Skill 11: Making Corrections—change to Fixing Mistakes

Skill 15: Apologizing—change to Saying Sorry

Skill 27: Expressing Your Feelings—change to Saying What You Feel

Skill 30: Expressing Concern for Another—change to Caring

Skill 32: Dealing with Another's Anger—change to When Somebody is Angry with You

Group I: Classroom Survival Skills

1. Listening
2. Asking for Help
3. Saying Thank You
4. Bringing Materials to Class

5. Following Instructions
6. Completing Assignments
7. Contributing to Discussions
8. Offering Help to an Adult
9. Asking a Question
10. Ignoring Distractions
11. Making Corrections
12. Deciding on Something to Do
13. Setting a Goal

Group II: Friendship-making Skills

14. Introducing Yourself
15. Beginning a Conversation
16. Ending a Conversation
17. Joining In
18. Playing a Game
19. Asking a Favor
20. Offering Help to a Classmate
21. Giving a Compliment
22. Accepting a Compliment
23. Suggesting an Activity
24. Sharing
25. Apologizing

Group III: Skills for Dealing with Feelings

26. Knowing Your Feelings
27. Expressing Your Feelings
28. Recognizing Another's Feelings
29. Showing Understanding of Another's Feelings
30. Expressing Concern for Another
31. Dealing with Your Anger
32. Dealing with Another's Anger
33. Expressing Affection
34. Dealing with Fear
35. Rewarding Yourself

Group IV: Skill Alternatives to Aggression

36. Using Self-control
37. Asking Permission
38. Responding to Teasing
39. Avoiding Trouble
40. Staying Out of Fights

GROUP I: CLASSROOM SURVIVAL SKILLS
Skill 1: Listening

STEPS	TRAINER NOTES
1. Look at the person who is talking.	Point out to students that sometimes others may think someone isn't listening, even though he/she really is. These steps are to show someone that you are really listening.
2. Remember to sit quietly.	Tell students to face the person and remember not to laugh, fidget, play with something, etc.
3. Think about what is being said.	
4. Say yes or nod your head.	
5. Ask a question about the topic to find out more.	Discuss relevant questions (i.e., ones that do not change the topic).

SUGGESTED CONTENT FOR MODELING DISPLAYS

A. *School or neighborhood:* Your teacher explains an assignment.

B. *Home:* Your parents are talking with you about a problem.

C. *Peer group:* Another student tells of a television program he/she watched or what he/she did over the weekend.

COMMENTS

This is an excellent skill with which to begin your Interpersonal Skills Training group. Once the skill of Listening is learned by students, it is useful to incorporate it into group or classroom rules. It is important to emphasize showing someone the behaviors that indicate that the student is listening. When a student is talking with the teacher, it is useful for the teacher to model these listening behaviors.

GROUP I: CLASSROOM SURVIVAL SKILLS
Skill 2: Asking for Help

STEPS	TRAINER NOTES
1. Ask yourself, "Can I do this alone?"	Students should be sure to read directions and try the assignment on their own (at least one problem or question).
2. If not, raise your hand.	Discuss that this is appropriate in class, not at home or with friends.
3. Wait. Say to yourself, "I know I can wait without talking."	Instruct the students to say this to themselves until the desired help is given.
4. Ask for help in a friendly way.	Discuss what constitutes a friendly manner (e.g., tone of voice, facial expression, content).

SUGGESTED CONTENT FOR MODELING DISPLAYS

A. *School:* You want help with an assignment or you don't understand what you are supposed to do.

B. *Home:* You can't find your skates and ask your mom to help look for them.

C. *Peer group:* You want your friend to teach you a new dance that everyone is doing at birthday parties.

COMMENTS

It is very important to discuss body language, or "body talk," with the students throughout Interpersonal Skills Training. When first introducing terminology such as "in a friendly way," spending time discussing and modeling friendly behaviors and nonverbal communicators is essential.

GROUP I: CLASSROOM SURVIVAL SKILLS
SKILL 3: Saying Thank You

STEPS	TRAINER NOTES
1. Decide if you want to thank someone.	Discuss the purpose of saying thank you (i.e., it's a way of telling someone that you appreciate what he/she did). Emphasize that this must be sincere. You thank someone when you want to or feel it is deserved, such as for a favor, help given, or a compliment.
2. Choose a good time and place.	Discuss how to choose a good time: when the person is not busy with something or someone else.
3. Thank the person in a friendly way.	Let students know that it is okay to tell why you are thanking the person (i.e., that they really needed the help or that something the person did made them feel good).

SUGGESTED CONTENT FOR MODELING DISPLAYS

A. *School:* Someone helps you with your schoolwork.

B. *Home:* Your parents help you with your chores or your homework, or let you do something you have asked to do.

C. *Peer group:* Someone lends you a pencil or compliments you.

COMMENTS

The use of this skill may appear very mechanical in the beginning. The students may also begin to use this skill frequently following initial instruction. This is quite natural, and should not be interpreted as insincere use of the skill. It may be useful to discuss and practice different ways of saying thank you (e.g., "It made me feel good when you . . ."; doing something nice for the person).

GROUP I: CLASSROOM SURVIVAL SKILLS
SKILL 4: Bringing Materials to Class

STEPS	TRAINER NOTES
1. Ask yourself, "What materials do I need for this class?"	Students may have to make a list of needed items, such as a pencil, crayons, paper, or notebook.
2. Gather the materials together.	Students should remember not to take something that isn't needed (e.g., toys).
3. Ask yourself, "Do I have everything I need?"	
4. Recheck your materials and pack them up.	

SUGGESTED CONTENT FOR MODELING DISPLAYS

A. *School:* You are going to a special area class (e.g., art, music, physical education) or attending a class in another classroom.

B. *Home:* You are going to attend outside club events or activities (e.g., Boy Scouts, Girl Scouts, church activities).

C. *Peer group:* You will be staying overnight at a friend's house.

COMMENTS

This skill assists the students in becoming more organized. For some students, providing a written list of what is needed may be necessary initially. Also, providing a notebook or folder where the materials can be kept may assist students in performing this skill. Posting a "cue card" (the list of the skill steps) near the doorway or on the classroom door may help students to remember to check for materials they will need before they leave the classroom.

GROUP I: CLASSROOM SURVIVAL SKILLS
SKILL 5: Following Instructions

STEPS	TRAINER NOTES
1. Listen carefully to the instructions.	Remind students that they should think about what is being said.
2. Ask questions about anything you don't understand.	Students should be taught Skill 2 (Asking for Help) or Skill 9 (Asking a Question).
3. Repeat the instructions to the person (or to yourself).	This step is necessary to be sure that the directions are clearly understood.
4. Follow the instructions.	

SUGGESTED CONTENT FOR MODELING DISPLAYS

A. *School:* A teacher explains an assignment.

B. *Home:* Your mom or dad gives you instructions on how to cook.

C. *Peer group:* A friend gives you directions for getting to his/her house.

COMMENTS

It is crucial that the students be able to complete the task requested of them independently. The skill will only serve to frustrate students if they follow the steps to Following Instructions and then find the task is far too difficult for them.

GROUP I: CLASSROOM SURVIVAL SKILLS
SKILL 6: **Completing Assignments**

STEPS	TRAINER NOTES
1. Ask yourself, "Is my work finished?"	Have students practice reviewing each item to be certain that all questions are answered.
2. Look over each question to be sure.	Remind students to fill in the missing answers if items aren't complete.
3. When you are sure your work is finished, hand it in.	Specific classroom rules for handing in completed work can be included in this step.
4. Say to yourself, "Good for me! I finished it!"	Discuss ways of rewarding oneself.

SUGGESTED CONTENT FOR MODELING DISPLAYS

A. *School:* Complete academic assignments given by the teacher or activities at a learning center.

B. *Home:* Finish a project or activity you started at home (making a toy spaceship from a kit or cleaning your room).

C. *Peer group:* Complete a project you promised to do for a friend.

COMENTS

This skill facilitates organizational ability and is particularly useful for the learning-disabled student or others who have specific difficulties in task completion. It should be noted that this skill ideally should be practiced in the setting where the skill is needed. For example, if practice in seatwork completion is needed, the students should practice this skill at their desks. Again, it is most important that students have the skills, knowledge, and motor responses needed to complete the assignment successfully. Therefore, the teacher must be certain that the task requested is one students can, in fact, complete independently. Self-reward (Step 4) is a skill (Skill 35) that may provide the student with necessary reinforcement until the skill can be reinforced by the teacher or parent.

GROUP I: CLASSROOM SURVIVAL SKILLS
SKILL 7: Contributing to Discussions

STEPS	TRAINER NOTES
1. Decide if you have something you want to say.	
2. Ask yourself, "Is this related to the discussion?"	Discuss that the comments must be relevant to the discussion. Give examples of relevant comments.
3. Decide exactly what you want to say.	Students may need the additional step of deciding how to say it.
4. Raise your hand.	Steps 4 and 5 should be in accordance with your classroom rules. Students should be told to eliminate these steps for use at home and with friends.
5. When you are called on, say what you want to say.	

SUGGESTED CONTENT FOR MODELING DISPLAYS

A. *School:* Say something in a class discussion when you have something you want to say.

B. *Home:* Say something in a family meeting or during dinner.

C. *Peer group:* Say something in a discussion with friends after school.

COMMENTS

Emphasis can be placed on when this skill is appropriate to use. For example, some teachers may not want a class discussion of a particular topic. The students must learn the cues communicated by a given teacher that indicate that contributing is not acceptable. Additionally, the students should be able to discriminate among the persons with whom the skill is used. For example, contributing to a discussion among friends would be carried out differently in manner and content than contributing to a discussion in class. When providing the opportunities to practice this skill, the teacher should choose topics for discussion that the students have knowledge of and an interest in.

GROUP I: CLASSROOM SURVIVAL SKILLS
SKILL 8: Offering Help to an Adult

STEPS	TRAINER NOTES
1. Decide if the adult needs your help.	Discuss how the student can tell if the adult could use the help.
2. Think of what you may do to help.	
3. Decide how to ask if you can help.	Discuss different ways of asking (e.g., "May I help you do that?").
4. Ask yourself, "Is this a good time to offer help?"	Remind students to be sure that their work is completed and there isn't something else they are supposed to do. If this is not a good time, they should wait until it is a good time.
5. Ask the adult if you may help.	
6. Help the adult.	Discuss the importance of following through with help.

SUGGESTED CONTENT FOR MODELING DISPLAYS

A. *School:* The teacher is making a bulletin board or rearranging the classroom.

B. *Home:* Your mom or dad is fixing dinner.

COMMENTS

With some students, it is especially important to emphasize Step 1, deciding if the teacher or parent needs the help. A student who frequently requests to help may be using this as a method of gaining attention or a way to avoid academic tasks. However, in such cases, this skill can be useful in teaching the student when it is appropriate to offer assistance.

GROUP I: CLASSROOM SURVIVAL SKILLS
SKILL 9: Asking a Question

STEPS	TRAINER NOTES
1. Decide what you need to ask.	Discuss how students can decide whether they really need to ask this question.
2. Decide whom you will ask.	Discuss how to decide whether to ask the teacher, an aide, a classmate, or someone else.
3. Decide how you will ask.	Stress asking in a friendly way—that it is not only what is said, but how it is said (e.g., you will have a better chance of getting an answer if you ask with a friendly look and tone of voice).
4. Choose a good time and place.	Discuss how to choose a good time (when the other person isn't busy or talking with someone) and when to follow classroom rules.
5. Ask your question.	
6. Thank the person for giving you the answer.	Students should be taught Skill 3 (Saying Thank You).

SUGGESTED CONTENT FOR MODELING DISPLAYS

A. *School:* Ask the teacher about something you don't understand.

B. *Home:* Ask your mom and dad about their work or hobbies.

C. *Peer group:* Ask another student how to play a game.

COMMENTS

It will be appropriate to discuss the times when asking a question is needed. Students should be encouraged to use this skill only when a legitimate question needs to be asked. The discussion, therefore, can include other ways of finding needed information (e.g., consulting a dictionary or encyclopedia).

GROUP I: CLASSROOM SURVIVAL SKILLS
SKILL 10: Ignoring Distractions

STEPS	TRAINER NOTES
1. Count to five.	Discuss that counting to five will give the student the time needed to recall the remainder of the steps to the skill.
2. Say to yourself, "I won't look. I'll keep on working."	These statements should be spoken out loud during modeling and role playing.
3. Continue to work.	
4. Say to yourself, "Good for me. I did it!"	Discuss ways of rewarding oneself.

SUGGESTED CONTENT FOR MODELING DISPLAYS

A. *School:* Another teacher comes into the room to talk with your teacher.

B. *Home:* Your brother or sister tries to distract you from your chores or homework.

C. *Peer group:* A classmate tries to get your attention in class or to distract you from a game at recess.

COMMENTS

It may help if the student gives himself/herself a checkmark on a card for each time he/she ignores a distraction. This self-recording card can then be shown to the teacher for additional praise or other reinforcement if needed. Self-reward (Step 4) is a skill (Skill 35) that may provide the student with necessary reinforcement until the skill can be reinforced by the teacher or parent.

GROUP I: CLASSROOM SURVIVAL SKILLS
SKILL 11: Making Corrections

STEPS	TRAINER NOTES
1. Look at the first correction.	Discuss dealing with one correction at a time, rather than looking at them all. This will help lessen the frustration of having to do a task over again.
2. Try to answer the question (or do the task) again.	
3. If you don't understand the question, ask someone.	Students should be taught Skill 2 (Asking for Help).
4. Write in your new answer (or do the activity over).	Discuss the feeling of frustration when tasks must be done again.
5. Say to yourself, "Good. That one is done."	
6. Go on to the next correction.	

SUGGESTED CONTENT FOR MODELING DISPLAYS

A. *School:* A math assignment is given back to you to correct.

B. *Home:* You must do a chore over again.

C. *Peer group:* You made something for a friend, but it didn't turn out right.

COMMENTS

Redoing tasks or academic assignments can be extremely frustrating for young children. This skill should assist with dealing with this type of frustration. It is crucial that the task be within the skills of the student. If many errors are made on an assignment, it is most important that the teacher analyze these errors and reteach the necessary skills. The skill of Making Corrections is most useful following such a reteaching effort or for assignments that are completed carelessly.

GROUP I: CLASSROOM SURVIVAL SKILLS
SKILL 12: Deciding on Something to Do

STEPS	TRAINER NOTES
1. Check to be sure you have finished all of your work.	For many young students, an assignment sheet where the student can check off work as it is completed will assist with this first step.
2. Think of the activities you would like to do.	Generate a list of acceptable activities. Students should be sure these activities are within the rules.
3. Choose one.	Students should be sure the activity chosen will not disrupt classmates who have not yet completed their schoolwork (or brothers or sisters, if the students are at home).

SUGGESTED CONTENT FOR MODELING DISPLAYS

A. *School:* Decide on an activity during free time in the classroom or when you have a few minutes after finishing your work.

B. *Home:* Choose something to do after you have finished your homework and chores.

COMMENTS

It would be helpful if the students generated a list of quiet activities (those in which they could engage when other students are still working on their academic tasks) and less quiet ones (those activities in which they can participate during a free activity period for the entire class). These, along with the behavioral steps needed to achieve the skill, could then be displayed in the classroom for easy student reference. Skill 45 (Dealing with Boredom) is a similar skill geared for use outside of the academic learning setting.

GROUP I: CLASSROOM SURVIVAL SKILLS
SKILL 13: Setting a Goal

STEPS	TRAINER NOTES
1. Decide on a goal you want to reach.	Discuss choosing a realistic goal (i.e., content, time frame).
2. Decide on the steps you will need to take to get there.	It may be helpful to list the steps and post the list on a bulletin board or include it in a student folder.
3. Take the first step.	
4. Take all other steps, one at a time.	Have the students mark off each step as it is achieved or place a sticker on the list of steps.
5. Reward yourself when your goal is reached.	Discuss ways of rewarding oneself.

SUGGESTED CONTENT FOR MODELING DISPLAYS

A. *School:* Set and reach an academic goal.

B. *Home:* Clean your room or the garage.

C. *Peer group:* Make a new friend.

COMMENTS

Many elementary-age students enjoy setting academic goals (e.g., learning addition facts, reading a given number of books). It is important that these goals be within their reach within a relatively short period of time. Setting small goals that can be easily achieved (e.g., learning the addition facts to sums of 10) is more beneficial than setting goals that will take students a long time. Goal setting is also useful for nonacademic areas, such as prosocial skills development. Examples of such goals might include practicing a given skill a certain number of times or using it in home or peer group settings. Self-reward (Step 5) is a skill (Skill 35) that may provide the student with necessary reinforcement until the skill can be reinforced by the teacher or parent.

GROUP II: FRIENDSHIP-MAKING SKILLS
Skill 14: Introducing Yourself

STEPS	TRAINER NOTES
1. Decide if you want to meet the person.	Discuss why students might want to meet a person (the person looks friendly, the person is new to the school, etc.).
2. Decide if it is a good time.	Discuss how to choose a good time (when the person is not busy with something or someone else).
3. Walk up to the person.	Watch for appropriate distance.
4. Introduce yourself.	Discuss ways to introduce yourself (e.g., say, "Hi, my name is _____.").
5. Wait for the person to tell you his/her name. If he/she doesn't tell you, ask.	Discuss appropriate ways to ask a person's name.

SUGGESTED CONTENT FOR MODELING DISPLAYS

A. *School:* There is a new student in your classroom.

B. *Home:* A friend of your parents is visiting your home.

C. *Peer group:* A new boy or girl moves into your neighborhood.

COMMENTS

Practicing this skill will also assist a child in knowing what to do when someone introduces himself/herself. When this skill is learned, have the students go on to Skill 15 (Beginning a Conversation).

GROUP II: FRIENDSHIP-MAKING SKILLS
SKILL 15: Beginning a Conversation

STEPS	TRAINER NOTES
1. Choose whom you want to talk with.	Remind students to consider whether their talking is going to bother someone else (for example, someone who is trying to work).
2. Decide what you want to say.	Suggest as topics something the students did during the weekend or something that is bothering them.
3. Choose a good time and place.	Discuss how to choose a good time (when the other person isn't busy or when the student isn't supposed to be doing something else).
4. Start talking in a friendly way.	Discuss the body language and nonverbal communicators that show a friendly attitude and suggest watching the person to see if he/she seems interested and not talking too long without giving the other person a chance to talk.

SUGGESTED CONTENT FOR MODELING DISPLAYS

A. *School:* Tell a classmate about an art project you did.

B. *Home:* Tell your parents what happened at school.

C. *Peer group:* Tell a friend what you did during the weekend.

COMMENTS

It is recommended that this skill be taught directly following Skill 14 (Introducing Yourself). Skill 16 (Ending a Conversation) is suggested as a follow-up skill.

GROUP II: FRIENDSHIP-MAKING SKILLS
SKILL 16: Ending a Conversation

STEPS	TRAINER NOTES
1. Decide if you need to finish the conversation.	
2. Decide the reason you need to end the conversation.	Tell students to ask themselves, "What is the reason?" (I'm late, I'm supposed to do something else, etc.).
3. Decide what to say.	Give students examples: "I have to go now, but I'll talk with you later." "I have to get back to my work." Students may want to suggest another time to continue the conversation.
4. Wait until the other person stops talking.	Discuss the importance of not interrupting and of thinking whether or not this is a good time to end the conversation.
5. Say it in a friendly way.	Remind students of the body language and nonverbal communicators that show a friendly attitude.

SUGGESTED CONTENT FOR MODELING DISPLAYS

A. *School:* Recess or free time in the classroom is over.

B. *Home:* You are talking with your parents and a friend is waiting for you.

C. *Peer group:* Your mother tells you to come inside or stop talking on the telephone.

COMMENTS

This skill begins where Skill 15 (Beginning a Conversation) leaves off. After practicing each skill separately, give the students practice in using these skills successively.

GROUP II: FRIENDSHIP-MAKING SKILLS
SKILL 17: Joining In

STEPS	TRAINER NOTES
1. Decide if you want to join in.	Students should decide whether they really want to participate or whether they only want to disrupt the group.
2. Decide what to say.	Suggest possible things to say: "Can one more person play?" "Would it be okay with you if I played, too?"
3. Choose a good time.	Discuss how to choose a good time (during a break in the activity or before the activity has begun).
4. Say it in a friendly way.	Discuss the body language and nonverbal communicators that show a friendly attitude.

SUGGESTED CONTENT FOR MODELING DISPLAYS

A. *School:* Ask to join a group game at recess.

B. *Home:* Ask to join a game with parents or brothers and sisters.

C. *Peer group:* Ask to join an activity at a club or in the neighborhood.

COMMENTS

This skill is very useful for students who have difficulty deciding what to do in social play situations. This skill gives them the opportunity to join peers in an ongoing activity.

GROUP II: FRIENDSHIP-MAKING SKILLS
SKILL 18: **Playing a Game**

STEPS	TRAINER NOTES
1. Be sure you know the rules.	Discuss what to do if students don't know the rules (ask someone to explain them).
2. Decide who starts the game.	Discuss methods of deciding who begins the game (for example, roll the dice or offer to let the other person go first).
3. Remember to wait your turn.	Suggest that students repeat to themselves, "I can wait until it's my turn."
4. When the game is over, say something nice to the other person.	Discuss and practice appropriate ways of handling winning (tell the person he/she played a good game) and losing (congratulate the other person).

SUGGESTED CONTENT FOR MODELING DISPLAYS

A. *School:* Play a board game with a classmate or a group game at recess.

B. *Home:* Play a game with your parents, brother, or sister.

C. *Peer group:* Play a group game with friends in the neighborhood.

COMMENTS

It may be helpful to coach students in how to play a variety of games (e.g., classroom board games and group games played at recess or in the neighborhood) so that they will feel confident in playing the games. Posting lists of classroom games and recess games with which the students are familiar may also encourage them to play such acceptable games. Good skills to teach following this one are Skill 49 (Dealing with Losing) and Skill 50 (Showing Sportsmanship).

GROUP II: FRIENDSHIP-MAKING SKILLS
SKILL 19: Asking a Favor

STEPS	TRAINER NOTES
1. Decide if you want or need to ask a favor.	Discuss how to evaluate whether the favor is necessary.
2. Plan what you want to say.	Suggest things to say: "Could you help me with this?" "I can't see if I sit over there; would you mind making room for me?" "I'm having trouble getting my work done; would you please not talk?" Giving reasons for needing the favor may increase the chances that the person will help the student.
3. Ask the favor in a friendly way.	Discuss the body language and nonverbal communicators that show a friendly attitude.
4. Remember to thank the person.	Students should be taught Skill 3 (Saying Thank You).

SUGGESTED CONTENT FOR MODELING DISPLAYS

A. *School:* You would like to join a group and someone must move over to make room for you, or someone is making a noise that interferes with your work or bothers you.

B. *Home:* The television is too loud for you to do your homework.

C. *Peer group:* A friend is going to a movie and you'd like to go along, or you would like to borrow something of a friend's.

COMMENTS

The definition of a *favor*, as used in this skill, is anything a student needs help with, varying from problems with other people to school and other informational problems. It may be necessary to discuss what to do or say if the person can't do the favor for the student.

GROUP II: FRIENDSHIP-MAKING SKILLS
Skill 20: Offering Help to a Classmate

STEPS	TRAINER NOTES
1. Decide if the person may need and want your help.	Discuss how to determine if another student needs help (How does he/she look? What is he/she doing or saying?).
2. Think of what you may do to help.	Observing the person can help the student decide whether to offer physical help or verbal guidance.
3. Decide how to ask if you may help.	Discuss a variety of ways to offer help.
4. Ask yourself, "Is this a good time to offer help?"	Remind students to be sure that they are not supposed to be doing something else.
5. Ask the person in a friendly way if you may help.	Discuss the body language and nonverbal communicators that show a friendly attitude. Emphasize not feeling hurt or offended if the person says no or asks someone else for help.
6. Help the person.	Discuss the importance of following through with help.

SUGGESTED CONTENT FOR MODELING DISPLAYS

A. *School:* A classmate drops his/her books or is having difficulty with a project.

B. *Peer group:* A friend is having difficulty painting his/her bicycle or completing a chore (e.g., carrying heavy boxes).

COMMENTS

A discussion of how people feel when helping someone or being helped should be included.

GROUP II: FRIENDSHIP-MAKING SKILLS
SKILL 21: Giving a Compliment

STEPS	TRAINER NOTES
1. Decide what you want to tell the other person.	Discuss the types of things students may want to compliment someone on (appearance, behavior, an achievement).
2. Decide how you want to say it.	Give examples of compliments.
3. Choose a good time and place.	Discuss how to choose a good time (when the student and the other person aren't busy, and perhaps when a lot of other people aren't around).
4. Give the compliment in a friendly way.	Emphasize giving the compliment in a sincere manner. Discuss the body language and facial expression associated with sincerity.

SUGGESTED CONTENT FOR MODELING DISPLAYS

A. *School:* A classmate has done really well on an assignment or has worked very hard on a project.

B. *Home:* Your mom or dad makes a good dinner.

C. *Peer group:* You like what someone is wearing.

COMMENTS

Emphasis should be placed on sincerely complimenting someone. This skill may appear mechanical and insincere when students first begin using it. Once they have sufficient practice with Giving a Compliment, the skill will be used in a more natural manner. Discuss the way both the giver and recipient of the compliment would feel (e.g., embarrassed, pleased).

GROUP II: FRIENDSHIP-MAKING SKILLS
Skill 22: Accepting a Compliment

STEPS	TRAINER NOTES
1. Decide if someone has given you a compliment.	Discuss ways students can tell whether someone has given them a compliment—for instance, how the person looked and sounded when he/she made the comment.
2. Say "Thank you."	Students should be taught Skill 3 (Saying Thank You).
3. Say something else if you want to.	Give an example: "Yes, I tried hard." Suggest using Skill 15 (Beginning a Conversation).

SUGGESTED CONTENT FOR MODELING DISPLAYS

A. *School:* The teacher compliments you on work well done.

B. *Home:* Your parents compliment you on how well you did your chores.

C. *Peer group:* A friend compliments you on the way you look.

COMMENTS

This skill is important since children are frequently embarrassed when given a compliment. Children with low self-esteem may also become defensive when given a compliment, acting as if they don't believe what the person is saying. Such a child may interpret the compliment as harrassment.

GROUP II: FRIENDSHIP-MAKING SKILLS
SKILL 23: Suggesting an Activity

STEPS	TRAINER NOTES
1. Decide on an activity you want to suggest.	Discuss a variety of appropriate activities to suggest in various settings (playground, during free time in the classroom, etc.).
2. Decide what you will say.	Give an example: "How would you like to _____?"
3. Choose a good time.	Discuss how to choose a good time (when others aren't involved with another activity).
4. Say it in a friendly way.	Discuss the body language and nonverbal communicators that show a friendly attitude.

SUGGESTED CONTENT FOR MODELING DISPLAYS

A. *School:* Suggest a group game during recess.

B. *Home:* Suggest an evening out with your parents (e.g., going to a movie).

C. *Peer group:* Suggest a game or an activity to a friend.

COMMENTS

Children may need to have experience with a variety of activities and games in order to be successful in suggesting activities. It may be helpful to coach students in how to play a variety of games. The activity needs to be appropriate to the setting (for example, the classroom versus the playground or neighborhood) and to the number of students involved (group versus individual). Discuss what to say if someone says no to a suggested activity. (Students should ask, "What would you like to do?" or go ask someone else to play.)

GROUP II: FRIENDSHIP-MAKING SKILLS
SKILL 24: Sharing

STEPS	TRAINER NOTES
1. Decide if you want to share something.	Talk about how the other person might feel if the student does or doesn't share.
2. Decide whom you want to share with.	If the student can only share with one person, discuss how others around may feel left out.
3. Choose a good time and place.	Discuss how to choose a good time (when another person needs or would enjoy using something of the student's).
4. Offer to share in a friendly and sincere way.	Discuss the body language and facial expression associated with sincerity.

SUGGESTED CONTENT FOR MODELING DISPLAYS

A. *School:* Offer to share your materials (crayons, pencils, paper) with a classmate.

B. *Home:* Offer to share a treat with a friend, brother, or sister.

C. *Peer group:* Offer to share a game or toys with a friend.

GROUP II: FRIENDSHIP-MAKING SKILLS
SKILL 25: Apologizing

STEPS	TRAINER NOTES
1. Decide if you need to apologize for something you did.	Discuss how we sometimes do things for which we are later sorry. Apologizing is something we can do to let the other person know we are sorry. It also often makes us feel better.
2. Think about your choices:	
a. Say it out loud to the person.	Discuss when it is best to use verbal or written ways to apologize.
b. Write the person a note.	
3. Choose a good time and place.	Discuss how to choose a good time (apologize soon after the problem). The student may want to be alone with the person for a verbal apology.
4. Carry out your best choice in a sincere way.	Discuss the body language and facial expression associated with sincerity.

SUGGESTED CONTENT FOR MODELING DISPLAYS

A. *School:* You are late for a class.

B. *Home:* You accidentally break something.

C. *Peer group:* You said something cruel because you were angry, or you had planned to do something with a friend but you have to go somewhere with your parents instead.

COMMENTS

It may be beneficial to discuss how difficult it might be to apologize. Discussion of how a person might feel before apologizing (e.g., anxious, afraid) as well as how a person might feel receiving the apology (e.g., relieved, less upset or angry) may make students more willing to try.

GROUP III: SKILLS FOR DEALING WITH FEELINGS
Skill 26: Knowing Your Feelings

STEPS	TRAINER NOTES
1. Think of how your body feels.	Discuss the cues students' bodies may give them (for example, blushing, tight muscles, queasy stomach, or "jumpy" stomach).
2. Decide what you could call the feeling.	Discuss feelings such as frustration, fear, embarrassment, and their associated physical reactions.
3. Say to yourself, "I feel _____."	

SUGGESTED CONTENT FOR MODELING DISPLAYS

A. *School:* You are frustrated with a difficult assignment.

B. *Home:* You are angry because your parents forgot to do something they had promised to do.

C. *Peer group:* You are disappointed because a friend promised to go a movie with you, but he/she can't go.

COMMENTS

Additional activities specific to identifying and labeling feelings may need to be carried out. These might include generating a list of "feeling" words to be displayed in the classroom, along with pictures of persons expressing those feelings ("body talk").

GROUP III: SKILLS FOR DEALING WITH FEELINGS
SKILL 27: Expressing Your Feelings

STEPS	TRAINER NOTES
1. Stop and think of how you feel.	A list of feelings should be displayed in the classroom.
2. Decide what it is you are feeling.	Discuss how students can identify their feelings and what made them feel that way.
3. Think about your choices:	
a. Say to the person "I feel _____."	Consider when and where the student may be able to talk about the feeilng.
b. Walk away for now.	Discuss alternative activities.
4. Act out your best choice.	If the student is still angry after following these steps, he/she should wait until he/she isn't so angry before acting on the best choice. If one choice doesn't work, the student should try another one.

SUGGESTED CONTENT FOR MODELING DISPLAYS

A. *School:* You want to answer in class, but you're afraid your answer will be wrong.

B. *Home:* Your parents won't allow you to watch a movie on television that many of your friends are going to watch.

C. *Peer group:* Someone calls you a name or ignores you.

COMMENTS

The teacher can model this behavior throughout the school year by expressing his/her feelings to the class in the appropriate manner.

GROUP III: SKILLS FOR DEALING WITH FEELINGS
SKILL 28: Recognizing Another's Feelings

STEPS	TRAINER NOTES
1. Watch the person.	Discuss paying attention to the way the person looks (posture and facial expression), what the person does and says, and how he/she says it.
2. Name what you think the person is feeling.	A list of "feeling words" should be displayed in the classroom for reference.
3. Decide whether or not to ask the person if he/she is feeling that way.	If the person seems very angry or upset, it may be best for the student to wait until the person has calmed down.

SUGGESTED CONTENT FOR MODELING DISPLAYS

A. *School:* After assignments are handed back, a student starts to cry.

B. *Home:* Your dad or mom is slamming doors and muttering to himself/herself.

C. *Peer group:* A friend hasn't been chosen for a game, or a classmate just watches a game instead of asking to join.

COMMENTS

This skill should precede Skill 29 (Showing Understanding of Another's Feelings).

GROUP III: SKILLS FOR DEALING WITH FEELINGS
SKILL 29: Showing Understanding of Another's Feelings

STEPS	TRAINER NOTES
1. Name what you think the person is feeling.	Discuss how the student might feel if he/she were in that situation.
2. Think about your choices: a. Ask the person if he/she feels this way.	Discuss how the student should base his/her choice on how well he/she knows the other person and the cues the person is giving.
b. Ask the person if you can help.	
c. Leave the person alone.	If the person seems very angry or upset, it may be best to leave the person alone for now and then make another choice when the person is less upset.
3. Act out your best choice.	If one choice doesn't work, the student should try another one.

SUGGESTED CONTENT FOR MODELING DISPLAYS

A. *School:* A classmate is crying because someone teased him/her.

B. *Home:* Your brother or sister won't talk to anyone after having a talk with a parent.

C. *Peer group:* A friend throws a board game after losing.

COMMENTS

Skill 28 (Recognizing Another's Feelings) should be taught prior to this skill.

GROUP III: SKILLS FOR DEALING WITH FEELINGS
Skill 30: Expressing Concern for Another

STEPS	TRAINER NOTES
1. Decide if someone is having a problem.	Discuss ways to determine if someone is having a problem (What is the person doing? How does he/she look?) Discuss how it might feel to be in that position.
2. Think about your choices:	
a. Say "Can I help you?"	Emphasize sincerity.
b. Do something nice for the person.	Suggest that the student share something with the person or ask the person to join in an activity.
3. Act out your best choice.	If one choice doesn't work, the student should try another one.

SUGGESTED CONTENT FOR MODELING DISPLAYS

A. *School:* A classmate is struggling with a difficult assignment.

B. *Home:* A parent is having difficulty with an activity.

C. *Peer group:* A friend has hurt himself/herself.

GROUP III: SKILLS FOR DEALING WITH FEELINGS
SKILL 31: Dealing With Your Anger

STEPS	TRAINER NOTES
1. Stop and count to 10.	Discuss the importance of allowing oneself time to cool off and think.
2. Think about your choices:	
a. Tell the person in words why you are angry.	Discuss how to tell the person in a way that won't anger him/her too.
b. Walk away for now.	Students may need to ask the teacher if they can leave the room and run an errand for him/her, or leave the classroom for 2 to 3 minutes.
c. Do a relaxation exercise.	Students should be taught Skill 56 (Relaxing).
3. Act out your best choice.	If one choice doesn't work, the student should try another one.

SUGGESTED CONTENT FOR MODELING DISPLAYS

A. *School:* You don't think the teacher has been fair to you, you are angry at yourself for forgetting your homework, or you are having a day where everything seems to go wrong.

B. *Home:* Your parents won't let you have a friend over or won't let you leave the house.

C. *Peer group:* A friend talks about you behind your back.

COMMENTS

For a child who directs anger toward himself/herself, additional choices may need to be included. Such choices may include: "Write about how you feel" or "Decide how you can change to keep this from happening again." Skills such as Problem Solving (Skill 41) can also assist many children who have difficulty dealing with their anger at themselves.

GROUP III: SKILLS FOR DEALING WITH FEELINGS
Skill 32: Dealing with Another's Anger

STEPS	TRAINER NOTES
1. Listen to what the person has to say.	Discuss the importance of not interrupting or becoming defensive. If needed, the student should say to himself/herself, "I can stay calm."
2. Think about your choices:	Discuss the possible consequences of each choice.
a. Keep listening.	
b. Ask why he/she is angry.	
c. Give him/her an idea to fix the problem.	
d. Walk away for now.	If the student begins to feel angry too, he/she should walk away until he/she calms down.
3. Act out your best choice.	If one choice doesn't work, the student should try another one.

SUGGESTED CONTENT FOR MODELING DISPLAYS

A. *School:* The teacher is angry at you for not doing well on a test.

B. *Home:* Your parents are angry because you didn't clean your room.

C. *Peer group:* Another student is angry at you because you didn't choose him/her to play a game.

GROUP III: SKILLS FOR DEALING WITH FEELINGS
SKILL 33: Expressing Affection

STEPS	TRAINER NOTES
1. Decide if you have good feelings about the other person.	Discuss these feelings.
2. Decide if you think the other person would like to know you feel this way.	Discuss possible consequences of telling the person (for example, the person may become embarrassed, or it may make the person feel good).
3. Decide what you will say.	
4. Choose a good time and place.	Discuss how to choose a good time (being alone may make it easier to express affection).
5. Tell the person in a friendly way.	Discuss the body language and nonverbal communicators that show a friendly attitude.

SUGGESTED CONTENT FOR MODELING DISPLAYS

A. *School:* Thank a teacher for something he/she has done.

B. *Home:* Tell your parents that you love them.

C. *Peer group:* Tell friends that you like them and want to continue being friends.

COMMENTS

This skill may be difficult for many adults to carry out, and therefore students may have had this skill modeled for them quite infrequently. It is important for the teacher to provide this type of modeling for the students.

GROUP III: SKILLS FOR DEALING WITH FEELINGS
Skill 34: Dealing with Fear

STEPS	TRAINER NOTES
1. Decide if you are feeling afraid.	Discuss bodily cues of fear (e.g., sweaty hands or nausea).
2. Decide what you are afraid of.	Discuss real threats versus imagined ones. Students should ask themselves if the fear is a real threat to their physical safety. They may need to check this out with another person.
3. Think about your choices:	
a. Talk to someone about it.	Discuss choosing someone who can reassure you (teacher or parent).
b. Do a relaxation exercise.	Students should be taught Skill 56 (Relaxing).
c. Try doing what you are afraid of anyway.	
4. Act out your best choice.	If one choice doesn't work, the student should try another one.

SUGGESTED CONTENT FOR MODELING DISPLAYS

A. *School:* You are afraid to take a test, or you are afraid to go out to recess because someone said he/she would beat you up.

B. *Home:* You are home alone at night.

C. *Peer group:* Someone in the neighborhood keeps teasing you.

COMMENTS

Students should be encouraged to evaluate realistic versus unrealistic fears. When fears are realistic ones, the alternative of talking to someone about them would be the suggested choice. Students may also need to problem-solve ways to deal with realistic fears (see Skill 41: Problem Solving).

GROUP III: SKILLS FOR DEALING WITH FEELINGS
SKILL 35: Rewarding Yourself

STEPS	TRAINER NOTES
1. Decide if you did a good job.	Discuss ways to evaluate one's own performance.
2. Say to yourself, "I did a good job."	
3. Decide how else you will reward yourself.	Give examples of other self-rewards (ask if you can take a break or do something you enjoy). Discuss these choices.
4. Do it.	Point out that students should reward themselves as soon after their performance as possible.

SUGGESTED CONTENT FOR MODELING DISPLAYS

A. *School:* You completed all of your assignments.

B. *Home:* You cleaned your room.

C. *Peer group:* You helped a friend do his/her chores.

COMMENTS

Emphasize that a person doesn't always have to depend on others to reward his/her actions.

GROUP IV: SKILL ALTERNATIVES TO AGGRESSION
Skill 36: Using Self-control

STEPS	TRAINER NOTES
1. Stop and count to 10.	Discuss the importance of allowing oneself time to cool off and think.
2. Think of how your body feels.	Discuss how bodily cues may signal losing control (e.g., hands become sweaty; you feel hot).
3. Think about your choices:	
a. Walk away for now.	Students should ask to leave the room for a few minutes, if necessary, until they regain self-control.
b. Do a relaxation exercise.	Students should be taught Skill 56 (Relaxing).
c. Write about how you feel.	
d. Talk to someone about it.	Discuss choosing someone who would understand.
4. Act out your best choice.	If one choice doesn't work, the student should try another one.

SUGGESTED CONTENT FOR MODELING DISPLAYS

A. *School:* You are behind in your schoolwork.

B. *Home:* Your parents won't let you do what you want to do.

C. *Peer group:* A friend borrows something of yours and breaks it.

COMMENTS

This skill is to be used when the student is too angry or upset to identify what he/she is feeling and needs to control himself/herself first, rather than deal with the problem directly.

GROUP IV: SKILL ALTERNATIVES TO AGGRESSION
Skill 37: Asking Permission

STEPS	TRAINER NOTES
1. Decide what you want to do.	Remind students to be sure this activity won't be harmful to themselves or another person.
2. Decide whom to ask.	This will usually be parents or teachers.
3. Decide what you will say.	
4. Choose the right time and place.	Discuss how to choose a good time (when the person isn't involved with another activity). The student may want to ask privately.
5. Ask in a friendly way.	Discuss the body language and nonverbal communicators that show a friendly attitude.

SUGGESTED CONTENT FOR MODELING DISPLAYS

A. *School:* Ask the teacher for a special privilege.

B. *Home:* Ask your parents if you may go to a friend's house or if you may participate in a school activity.

C. *Peer group:* Ask a friend if you may borrow a toy.

COMMENTS

We hope that the students' use of the skills presented in this curriculum will be successful the majority of the time. With this skill, however, many times permission may not be granted (e.g., parents can't afford it, friend's house is too far away). Therefore, to prepare for instances in which permission is not given (the skill does not work for the student), the skills of Rewarding Yourself (Skill 35) and/or Accepting No (Skill 54) should be taught immediately after instruction of this skill.

GROUP IV: SKILL ALTERNATIVES TO AGGRESSION
SKILL 38: Responding to Teasing

STEPS	TRAINER NOTES
1. Stop and count to five.	Discuss how this can prevent students from losing control.
2. Think about your choices:	
a. Ignore the teasing.	Point out that ignoring for a short time doesn't always work; the student may need to ignore for a long time. Discuss ways to ignore (e.g., walk away).
b. Say how you feel, in a friendly way.	Give an example of an "I feel" statement: "I feel _____when _____."
c. Give a reason for the person to stop.	Suggest some possible reasons: The student will tell the teacher or another adult, the student is feeling uncomfortable, etc. Emphasize saying it in a friendly way.
3. Act out your best choice.	If one choice doesn't work, the student should try another one.

SUGGESTED CONTENT FOR MODELING DISPLAYS

A. *School:* Someone is poking you or making faces at you in class.

B. *Home:* Your brother or sister laughs at you.

C. *Peer group:* Someone calls you a name or teases you about your hair or clothes.

COMMENTS

The students may need practice in making appropriate, nonthreatening "I feel" statements.

GROUP IV: SKILL ALTERNATIVES TO AGGRESSION
SKILL 39: Avoiding Trouble

STEPS	TRAINER NOTES
1. Stop and think of what the consequences of an action might be.	It is helpful to list and discuss the possible consequences of particular actions with the students.
2. Decide if you want to stay out of trouble.	Discuss how to decide if it is important to avoid these consequences.
3. Decide what to tell the other person.	
4. Tell the person.	Discuss how to say no in a friendly but firm way.

SUGGESTED CONTENT FOR MODELING DISPLAYS

A. *School:* Another student wants you to help him/her cheat on a test.

B. *Home:* Your bother or sister wants you to take money from your parents.

C. *Peer group:* A friend wants you to tease another friend.

GROUP IV: SKILL ALTERNATIVES TO AGGRESSION
Skill 40: Staying Out of Fights

STEPS	TRAINER NOTES
1. Stop and count to 10.	Discuss how this can help the student to calm down.
2. Decide what the problem is.	Discuss the consequences of fighting, and whether fighting can solve a problem.
3. Think about your choices:	List a variety of alternatives.
a. Walk away for now.	Students should ask to leave the room for a few minutes, if necessary.
b. Talk to the person in a friendly way.	Discuss how to read the behavior of the other person (i.e., is he/she calm enough to talk with) and evaluate one's own degree of calmness and readiness to talk about the problem. Discuss ways to state the problem in a nonoffensive manner.
c. Ask someone for help in solving the problem.	Discuss who can be of the most help: a teacher, parent, or friend.
4. Act out your best choice.	If one choice doesn't work, the student should try another one.

SUGGESTED CONTENT FOR MODELING DISPLAYS

A. *School:* Someone says that you did poorly on your schoolwork.

B. *Home:* Your brother or sister tattles on you.

C. *Peer group:* Someone doesn't play fairly in a game or calls you a name.

GROUP IV: SKILL ALTERNATIVES TO AGGRESSION
SKILL 41: Problem Solving

STEPS	TRAINER NOTES
1. Stop and say, "I have to calm down."	Discuss additional ways to calm down (e.g., take three deep breaths, count to 10).
2. Decide what the problem is.	Discuss how students should reflect on why they are upset.
3. Think about different ways to solve the problem.	List and discuss a variety of alternatives and the consequences of each.
4. Choose one way.	Discuss how to weigh alternatives to pick the best.
5. Do it.	
6. Ask yourself, "How did this work?"	If one alternative doesn't work, the student should try another.

SUGGESTED CONTENT FOR MODELING DISPLAYS

A. *School:* You don't understand an assignment, or you forgot your lunch money.

B. *Home:* You broke a window at your house.

C. *Peer group:* You lost something you borrowed from a friend.

COMMENTS

As problems arise in the classroom, it may be beneficial if the teacher leads the class in a discussion of the alternatives to deal with the problem and the possible consequences of each alternative. By listing and discussing these alternatives and consequences, the students can choose the best one for them. Using this problem-solving technique when classroom problems arise will promote the students' ability to use this skill and will also teach them when the skill can be used. This is a good prerequisite skill for Skill 42 (Accepting Consequences).

GROUP IV: SKILL ALTERNATIVES TO AGGRESSION
Skill 42: Accepting Consequences

STEPS	TRAINER NOTES
1. Decide if you were wrong.	Discuss that it is okay to be wrong . . . it's not the end of the world.
2. If you were wrong, say to yourself, "I have to accept the consequences."	Discuss the possible consequences of particular actions.
3. Say to the person, "Yes, I did _____" (describe what you did).	Discuss how to describe the behavior without making excuses.
4. Say something else:	
a. How you will avoid this behavior the next time.	Point out that this should be said in a friendly manner.
b. Apologize.	Emphasize sincerity.

SUGGESTED CONTENT FOR MODELING DISPLAYS

A. *School:* You forgot your homework assignment.

B. *Home:* Your parents tell you that you can't go to a movie because you didn't do your chores.

C. *Peer group:* You lost the money your friend asked you to keep for him/her.

COMMENTS

Since this skill involves some problem solving, it is suggested that this skill be taught after Skill 41 (Problem Solving).

GROUP IV: SKILL ALTERNATIVES TO AGGRESSION
Skill 43: Dealing with an Accusation

STEPS	TRAINER NOTES
1. Stop and say, "I have to calm down."	Discuss additional ways to calm down (e.g., take three deep breaths, count to 10).
2. Think about what the person has accused you of.	
3. Ask yourself, "Is the person right?"	If the student decides that the person is correct, Skill 42 (Accepting Consequences) can be used.
4. Think about your choices:	
a. Explain, in a friendly way, that you didn't do it.	Discuss the body language and nonverbal communicators that show a friendly attitude.
b. Apologize.	Emphasize sincerity.
c. Offer to make up for what happened.	Discuss how to make amends (earning the money to pay for a lost or broken item, giving the person something of one's own, or giving back a stolen item to the person.
5. Act out your best choice.	If one choice doesn't work, the student should try another one.

SUGGESTED CONTENT FOR MODELING DISPLAYS

A. *School:* A teacher has accused you of cheating.

B. *Home:* Your parents accuse you of breaking something.

C. *Peer group:* A friend accuses you of taking something that wasn't yours.

GROUP IV: SKILL ALTERNATIVES TO AGGRESSION
SKILL 44: Negotiating

STEPS	TRAINER NOTES
1. Decide if you and the other person disagree.	Discuss signs of disagreement (Is the student getting angry? Is the other person getting angry?).
2. Tell how you feel about the problem.	Discuss the importance of saying this in a friendly way so the other person does not become more angry.
3. Ask the person how he/she feels about the problem.	
4. Listen to the answer.	Discuss the importance of not interrupting.
5. Suggest or ask for a compromise.	Discuss how to decide on something that will satisfy both the student and the other person.

SUGGESTED CONTENT FOR MODELING DISPLAYS

A. *School:* Your teacher gives you work that you feel you can't do.

B. *Home:* Your parents want you to baby-sit, but you need to do your homework.

C. *Peer group:* Your friend wants to play one game, but you want to play another.

COMMENTS

This skill may be difficult for the very young child and is considered to be more appropriate for students in fourth and fifth grades.

GROUP V: SKILLS FOR DEALING WITH STRESS
SKILL 45: Dealing with Boredom

STEPS	TRAINER NOTES
1. Decide if you are feeling bored.	Discuss how to recognize signs of boredom (e.g., you don't know what to do, you feel jittery inside).
2. Think of things you like to do.	Students should generate and discuss personal lists of acceptable activities.
3. Decide on one thing to do.	
4. Do it.	
5. Say to yourself, "Good for me. I chose something to do."	Discuss ways of rewarding oneself.

SUGGESTED CONTENT FOR MODELING DISPLAYS

A. *School:* There are no playground games you are interested in.

B. *Home:* It's a Saturday and no one is around.

C. *Peer group:* You and your friends can't think of anything to do.

COMMENTS

This skill, similar to Skill 12 (Deciding on Something to Do), is geared for use outside of the academic learning setting. It is suggested that the students generate a list of acceptable activities they may engage in on the playground, at home, and in the neighborhood, and that they include these lists in their prosocial skills folder. Self-reward (Step 5) is a skill (Skill 35) that may provide the student with necessary reinforcement until the skill can be reinforced by the teacher or parent.

GROUP V: SKILLS FOR DEALING WITH STRESS
Skill 46: Deciding What Caused a Problem

STEPS	TRAINER NOTES
1. Decide what the problem is.	Discuss how students can recognize a problem (by the way they feel inside, by what someone has said to them, or by how someone acted toward them).
2. Think about what may have caused the problem.	Discuss how to evaluate possible causes of a problem (one's own behavior, someone else's behavior, or no one's fault).
3. Decide what most likely caused the problem.	Discuss how to determine the most likely cause.
4. Check it out.	Ask someone, either the other person or an impartial judge.

SUGGESTED CONTENT FOR MODELING DISPLAYS

A. *School:* The teacher seems angry with you.

B. *Home:* Your parents have an argument about you.

C. *Peer group:* You feel angry at a friend, but don't know why, or you feel that someone doesn't like you.

COMMENTS

This skill is intended to help students distinguish between the problems that they are responsible for and those that are due to factors outside of their control.

GROUP V: SKILLS FOR DEALING WITH STRESS
SKILL 47: Making a Complaint

STEPS	TRAINER NOTES
1. Decide what the problem is.	Discuss how students can recognize a problem (by the way they feel inside, by what someone said to them, or by how someone acted toward them).
2. Decide whom to tell.	Students should decide with whom they are having the problem. Talking about the problem with the person should help solve it.
3. Choose a good time and place.	Discuss how to choose a good time (when the person isn't involved with something else or when the person is alone).
4. Tell the person your problem in a friendly way.	Tell students to wait until they are no longer angry or upset before talking about the problem. Discuss the body language and nonverbal communicators that show a friendly attitude.

SUGGESTED CONTENT FOR MODELING DISPLAYS

A. *School:* The teacher gives you an assignment that seems too difficult for you.

B. *Home:* You feel your parents were unfair because they wouldn't let you go to a movie with a friend.

C. *Peer group:* A friend usually chooses what the two of you will do.

GROUP V: SKILLS FOR DEALING WITH STRESS
Skill 48: Answering a Complaint

STEPS	TRAINER NOTES
1. Listen to the complaint.	Discuss proper body language while listening (ways to show that you aren't defensive).
2. Ask in a friendly way about anything you don't understand.	Discuss the body language and nonverbal communicators that show a friendly attitude.
3. Decide if the complaint is justified.	
4. Think about your choices:	
a. Apologize.	Emphasize sincerity.
b. Explain your behavior.	Discuss that even if a student did not intend to cause a problem, his/her behavior still might have caused a problem for someone else.
c. Suggest what to do now.	
d. Correct a mistaken impression.	Discuss how to respond to an unjustified complaint by explaining why it is wrong.
5. Act out your best choice.	If one choice doesn't work, the student should try another one.

SUGGESTED CONTENT FOR MODELING DISPLAYS

A. *School:* The teacher complains that you are too loud.

B. *Home:* Your parents complain that you haven't helped at home.

C. *Peer group:* A friend complains that you were teasing him/her.

GROUP V: SKILLS FOR DEALING WITH STRESS
Skill 49: Dealing with Losing

STEPS	TRAINER NOTES
1. Say to yourself, "Somebody has to lose. It's okay that I didn't win."	Memorizing this statement will act as an impulse-control technique for the student.
2. Think about your choices:	
a. Ask to help someone.	Offer help to the teacher or your parents.
b. Do an activity you like to do.	Students should generate and discuss personal lists of acceptable activities.
c. Do a relaxation exercise.	Students should be taught Skill 56 (Relaxing).
3. Act out your best choice.	If one choice doesn't work, the student should try another one.

SUGGESTED CONTENT FOR MODELING DISPLAYS

A. *School:* You lose a contest or a raffle.

B. *Home:* You lose at a game against your brother or sister.

C. *Peer group:* Your team loses at basketball (or some other game).

COMMENTS

This is a good prerequisite skill for Skill 50 (Showing Sportsmanship).

GROUP V: SKILLS FOR DEALING WITH STRESS
SKILL 50: Showing Sportsmanship

STEPS	TRAINER NOTES
1. Decide how you and the other person played the game.	Discuss evaluating one's own level of skill and an opponent's.
2. Think of what you can honestly tell the other person or group:	Emphasize sincerity in what the student chooses to say.
a. "Congratulations."	The student may also want to shake the person's hand.
b. "You played a good game."	
c. "You're getting a lot better at this game."	
3. Act out your best choice.	Discuss the body language and nonverbal communicators that show a friendly, sincere attitude.
4. Help the other person put the game or materials away.	

SUGGESTED CONTENT FOR MODELING DISPLAYS

A. *School:* Your team loses at a group game during recess, or your team wins.

B. *Home:* You lose at a game with your brother or sister, or you win.

C. *Peer group:* You lose at a game with a friend, or you win.

COMMENTS

Students should be taught Skill 49 (Dealing with Losing) before this one.

GROUP V: SKILLS FOR DEALING WITH STRESS
Skill 51: Dealing with Being Left Out

STEPS	TRAINER NOTES
1. Decide what has happened to cause you to feel left out.	Discuss possible reasons why a student may be ignored by peers.
2. Think about your choices:	
a. Ask to join in.	Students should be taught Skill 17 (Joining In).
b. Choose someone else to play with.	
c. Do an activity you enjoy.	Students should generate and discuss personal lists of acceptable activities.
3. Act out your best choice.	If one choice doesn't work, the student should try another one.

SUGGESTED CONTENT FOR MODELING DISPLAYS

A. *School:* You are left out of a group game at recess.

B. *Home:* Your brother or sister is leaving you out of an activity with his/her friends.

Peer group: A group of friends are going to a movie or a birthday party, but you weren't invited.

COMMENTS

It may be important to discuss the types of feelings that might result from being left out (feeling angry, hurt, or frustrated). When discussing this skill, the teacher might emphasize that it is important to deal with being left out through these skill steps, rather than to continue to feel angry or hurt.

GROUP V: SKILLS FOR DEALING WITH STRESS
Skill 52: Dealing with Embarrassment

STEPS	TRAINER NOTES
1. Decide what happened to cause you to feel embarrassed.	Discuss how students can recognize signs of embarrassment (e.g., face feels flushed).
2. Think of what you can do to feel less embarrassed.	Discuss the possible consequences of each choice.
a. Ignore it.	
b. Decide what to do next time.	
c. Say to yourself, "It's over. People will forget it."	
3. Act out your best choice.	If one choice doesn't work, the student should try another one.

SUGGESTED CONTENT FOR MODELING DISPLAYS

A. *School:* You give the wrong answer to a question in class.

B. *Home:* You drop and break something belonging to your parents.

C. *Peer group:* You fall down on the playground or make some other mistake when playing a game.

COMMENTS

Prior to teaching this skill, it is helpful to review Skill 26 (Knowing Your Feelings).

GROUP V: SKILLS FOR DEALING WITH STRESS
Skill 53: Reacting to Failure

STEPS	TRAINER NOTES
1. Decide if you have failed.	Discuss the difference between failing and not doing as well as hoped.
2. Think about why you failed.	Discuss reasons for failure (the student didn't try as hard as he/she could have, he/she wasn't ready to do this, it was a matter of chance).
3. Think about what you could do next time.	Suggest practicing more, trying harder, or asking for help.
4. Make your plan to do this.	This plan may be in written form such as a contingency contract.

SUGGESTED CONTENT FOR MODELING DISPLAYS

A. *School:* You failed a test.

B. *Home:* You failed to complete your chores at home.

C. *Peer group:* You failed to get someone to join in the activity you wanted to do.

GROUP V: SKILLS FOR DEALING WITH STRESS
SKILL 54: Accepting No

STEPS	TRAINER NOTES
1. Decide why you were told no.	Discuss the possible reasons for being told no in a particular situation.
2. Think about your choices:	Discuss the possible consequences of each choice.
a. Do something else.	Students should generate and discuss personal lists of acceptable activities.
b. Say how you feel, in a friendly way.	Practice "I feel" statements with the students. Discuss the body language and nonverbal communicators that show a friendly attitude.
c. Write about how you feel.	
3. Act out your best choice.	If one choice doesn't work, the student should try another one.

SUGGESTED CONTENT FOR MODELING DISPLAYS

A. *School:* The teacher says that you can't do an activity.

B. *Home:* Your parents say that you can't stay up late.

C. *Peer group:* A friend tells you he/she won't come over to your house.

COMMENTS

The choice "Write about how you feel" may not be appropriate for the very young child or the special education student who may not have such writing skills. Ask these students to generate other choices instead.

GROUP V: SKILLS FOR DEALING WITH STRESS
SKILL 55: Saying No

STEPS	TRAINER NOTES
1. Decide whether or not you want to do what is being asked.	Discuss situations when saying no is appropriate.
2. Think about why you don't want to do this.	Discuss reasons for saying no (the student may get into trouble or he/she has something else he/she wants to do).
3. Tell the person no in a friendly way.	Discuss the body language and nonverbal communicators that show a friendly attitude.
4. Give your reason why you won't do what the person asked.	Remind students that this, too, should be said in a friendly way.

SUGGESTED CONTENT FOR MODELING DISPLAYS

A. *School:* A friend wants you to run away from school with him/her.

B. *Home:* Your brother or sister wants you to play a game, but you want to watch your favorite television program.

C. *Peer group:* A friend wants you to play when you have work to do, or he/she wants you to go to a movie after school, but you'd rather play baseball.

GROUP V: SKILLS FOR DEALING WITH STRESS
SKILL 56: Relaxing

STEPS	TRAINER NOTES
1. Decide if you need to relax.	Discuss how to recognize bodily cues of tension (e.g., feeling tense or jittery inside or feeling one's stomach churning).
2. Take three slow, deep breaths.	
3. Tighten one part of your body; count to three; relax.	Instruct students about which parts of their bodies to tighten/relax.
4. Continue this for each part of your body.	Steps 3 and 4 will take much practice.
5. Ask yourself how you feel.	Discuss how the students feel physically before and after tightening muscles.

SUGGESTED CONTENT FOR MODELING DISPLAYS

A. *School:* You feel nervous before a test.

B. *Home:* Your grandparents are coming and you're excited.

C. *Peer group:* You are angry or upset with a friend, but you don't know why.

COMMENTS

Students may need a great deal of training in relaxation before they will be able to use this skill effectively. A useful source for this purpose is chapter 7.

GROUP V: SKILLS FOR DEALING WITH STRESS
Skill 57: Dealing with Group Pressure

STEPS	TRAINER NOTES
1. Listen to what others want you to do.	Discuss possible reasons why the group may want the student to participate in particular actions.
2. Think about what might happen.	Discuss possible consequences of particular actions (someone may be hurt or the student may get into trouble).
3. Decide what you want to do.	Discuss how difficult it is to resist pressure to do something from a group of friends.
4. If you decide not to go along with the group, say to them, "No, I can't because _____" (give the reason).	Discuss how giving a reason for not going along may help the group to think about what they want to do.
5. Suggest something else to do.	Students should generate and discuss a list of acceptable group activities.

SUGGESTED CONTENT FOR MODELING DISPLAYS

A. *Peer group:* The group is teasing someone or planning on taking something that belongs to someone else, and they want you to go along with them.

GROUP V: SKILLS FOR DEALING WITH STRESS
Skill 58: Dealing with Wanting Something That Isn't Mine

STEPS	TRAINER NOTES
1. Say to yourself, "I want this, but I can't just take it."	Discuss how hard it may be to want something and not take it.
2. Say "It belongs to _____."	Discuss how the other person might feel if the item were gone.
3. Think about your choices:	
a. I could ask to borrow it.	Discuss other alternatives depending upon the possibilities for your
b. I could earn the money to buy it.	students to get what they want.
c. I could ask the person to trade.	
d. I could do something else I like to do.	Students should generate and discuss personal lists of acceptable activities.
4. Act out your best choice.	If one choice doesn't work, the student should try another one.
5. Say, "Good for me. I didn't take it!"	Discuss ways of rewarding oneself.

SUGGESTED CONTENT FOR MODELING DISPLAYS

A. *School:* You see a notebook you'd really like to have.

B. *Home:* Your parents left money on the table.

C. *Peer group:* A friend has a game you would like to have, or he/she has candy in his/her coat hanging in his/her locker.

COMMENTS

Step 5 of this skill will be a crucial step for many children. Because observers may not know that the student actually wanted to take something but succeeded in controlling himself/herself, outside reinforcement is unlikely to be given. Therefore, the student must learn to give himself/herself this needed reinforcement.

GROUP V: SKILLS FOR DEALING WITH STRESS
Skill 59: Making a Decision

STEPS	TRAINER NOTES
1. Think about the problem.	Discuss how students may face conflicting desires or responsibilities at odds with desires.
2. Decide on your choices.	Have students make a list of the alternatives.
3. Think of the possible consequences for each choice.	Have students make a list of the consequences of each alternative and then discuss them.
4. Make the best decision.	Discuss how to evaluate competing alternatives to make the best choice.

SUGGESTED CONTENT FOR MODELING DISPLAYS

A. *School:* Decide what group to play with.

B. *Home:* Decide how to spend your money.

C. *Peer group:* Decide whether to go to a movie or stay home and study for a test.

GROUP V: SKILLS FOR DEALING WITH STRESS
SKILL 60: Being Honest

STEPS	TRAINER NOTES
1. Decide what might happen if you are honest.	Discuss politeness versus honesty. (Students should not be honest just to hurt someone, such as saying that they don't like a person's clothes, for example.) Also discuss how others may respect the student or trust the student more in the future if he/she is honest now.
2. Decide what might happen if you aren't honest.	Discuss how punishing consequences are usually less severe if a person is honest in the beginning.
3. Think of how to say what you have to say.	Give examples: "I'm sorry, but I did _____." "Yes, I did it, but I didn't mean to."
4. Say it.	Emphasize sincerity.
5. Say to yourself, "Good for me. I told the truth."	Discuss ways of rewarding oneself.

SUGGESTED CONTENT FOR MODELING DISPLAYS

A. *School:* You tore up your homework assignment or lost your reading book.

B. *Home:* You broke a window playing baseball.

C. *Peer group:* You borrowed someone's bike without asking permission.

COMMENTS

Self-reward (Step 5) is a skill (Skill 35) that may provide the student with necessary reinforcement until the skill can be reinforced by the teacher or parent.

Chapter 4

Situational Perception Training

The diverse, course-length interventions that collectively constitute the Prepare Curriculum are designed to teach a broad array of prosocial competencies. Included is an extended series of interpersonal skills, anger control, moral reasoning, problem solving, empathy, stress management, cooperation, prosocial model building, and group facilitation techniques. Yet, armed with these several enhanced capacities, the trainee may nevertheless remain incompetent because competency is the ability to use given skills or knowledge correctly *at the proper time and place.* Skilled prosocial ability, in this conceptualization of competency, has a behavioral component (what did the individual do?) and a situational component (where, when, and with whom was it done?). Because both components determine the success or effectiveness of the individual's skill use, both may be sources of the skill's failure and both can be appropriate targets of training. The intervention offered in the present chapter is designed to provide skill in this social diagnostic task (i.e., the ability to select which Prepare competencies will be used when, with which co-actors, and in which settings).

Theory and Research

Situational Perception Training rests on a basic assumption about human behavior that has become a central belief in contemporary psychology in recent decades: the belief that behavior is determined not only by characteristics, traits, or the personality of the individual, but also by qualities of the situation or setting in which the behavior occurs. This person-plus-situation interactionism had its early roots in the seminal works of Lewin (1935, 1936) and Murray (1938). In Lewin's well-known formula, $B = f(p,e)$, not only was behavior considered a function of both the person and the environment, but also the environment that was most influential in this regard was considered subjective in nature (i.e., the environment-as-perceived, also termed the *phenomenal field* or the *psychological situation*). Murray (1938) also described human behavior as a result of both needs (the person variable) and environmental press or need-satisfying potential (the situation variable).

Research support for this person × situation view of human behavior began to emerge even at this early point in interactionist thinking. In 1928, Hartshorne and May reported their now well-known studies of "deceit," a type of behavior originally assumed to be determined by enduring qualities and consistencies within the person and not substantially influenced by such environmental considerations as where, when, and with whom the behavior occurs. In these studies, later largely replicated by Burton (1963) and Nelson, Grinder, and Mutterer (1969), children were placed in a series of situations in which cheating behavior was possible, and their reactions across situations were examined. Results clearly supported an interactionist view. Cheating was a function of both the individual youngster and qualities of particular situations. In later years, such joint person-plus-situation determinism has been shown to be operative for other types of behaviors relevant to the goals of the Prepare Curriculum, including aggression on the one hand (Campbell, 1986; Cordilia, 1986; Forgas, 1986; Gibbs, 1986; Page & Moss, 1976; Raush, 1965, 1972) and an array of prosocial behaviors on the other (Leming, 1978; Zimmerman, 1983).

Others followed Lewin (1935) and Murray (1938). Angyal's (1941) phenomenological theory emphasized the inseparability of organism and environment and the subjectivity of environment in shaping human behavior. The social learning theorists, starting with Rotter (1954), Mischel (1968), and Bandura (1969), promoted similarly strong emphasis on situational determinants, although in this instance the objective environment (e.g., stimulus control, response contingencies) was given central importance. In addition to the phenomenologists and social learning theorists, a third interactionism-promoting view emerged, variously called *ecological psychology* and *environmental psychology*. Roger Barker and his research group's studies of the "stream of behavior" in a variety of field settings were the pioneering works in this context (Barker, 1968; Barker & Gump, 1964; Barker & Wright, 1954). These studies involved both an effort to examine the effects of diverse real-world "behavior settings" on the ability to predict individual behavior and an initial search for answers to the central methodological questions that have made interactionism, since its inception, a difficult position to concretize. Specifically, Barker's work sought to clarify how situational influences are optimally defined, classified, and measured. His investigations and those of Moos examining the influence of institutional environments on behavior (Insel & Moos, 1974; Moos, 1968, 1973; Moos & Houts, 1968) went beyond the important but broad generalizations of the early interactionist theorists and began pointing to specific situational characteristics that seemed potent as behavior change influences.

Price and Bouffard (1974) extended this effort further, demonstrating in their study of "behavioral appropriateness and situational constraints" how an array of common situations and settings (e.g., class, date, bus, own room, church, job interview, sidewalk, etc.) constrained, influenced the occurrence of, or were judged to fit or not fit a similarly lengthy array of common behaviors (e.g., run, talk, kiss, write, eat, sleep, read, fight, etc.) and how, reciprocally, these behaviors were variously judged appropriate or inappropriate to the situations represented. This diversity of situational characteristics will be discussed later in the chapter.

Having now set the stage for the person × situation viewpoint, we will readdress the relevance of interactionist thinking in the context of the Prepare Curriculum. Our perspective is articulated well by Morrison and Bellack (1981) in their paper "The Role of Social Perception in Social Skill." They comment that

> adequate social performance not only requires a repertoire of response skills, but knowledge about when and how these responses should be applied. Application of this knowledge, in turn, depends upon the ability to accurately "read" the social environment, determine the particular norms and conventions operating at the moment, and to understand the messages being sent and the particular emotions and intentions guiding the behavior of the interpersonal partner. . . . The literature on social perception . . . has important implications for social skills training. In the past, such training has primarily focused on response capability. Information about when and where to apply new responses has only been provided as an incidental part of treatment. (pp. 70, 76)

Forgas (1979) offers a similar view:

> The ecology of interaction episodes also plays an important role in . . . social skills therapy. Social skills therapy in essence seeks to develop skills in patients which enable them to perform effectively in the differently situated interaction episodes available in their milieu. . . . At each stage of the learning process, clients need to understand how ecological settings function as signifiers for social rule systems. Knowing how to engage in friendly conversation is by itself not enough: the client also has to know that such an episode is more likely to be compatible with some settings (e.g., pubs) than with others (e.g., lifts).
> Social skills training programmes, despite their growing popularity in recent years, are still largely based on an intra-individual "skill"

model, to the relative neglect of situational and ecological factors in interaction, which are only taken into account on an ad hoc basis.... Knowing how to decode, use and manipulate ecological cues in the interpretation and definition of social episodes is a major part of effective social skills. (p. 163)

Chapter 3 of this book, "Interpersonal Skills Training," presents in detail our own approach to social skills training, Structured Learning. It is an approach we have been actively developing, evaluating, and refining since the early 1970s, yet we too have not fully considered the ecological imperatives promoted above. Situational Perception Training corrects that problem by offering an intervention we believe can optimally be employed not only in conjunction with our own and other social skills training approaches, but also in tandem with the several additional psychoeducational interventions that constitute the Prepare Curriculum.

The phenomenologists, ecologists, and social learning theorists each have championed, in an interactionist context, the crucial behavior-influencing role of the psychological and objective environments. Social skills training programs have largely ignored this thrust, to the probable detriment of their effectiveness. We believe that the process of competent situational responsiveness begins with accurate perception of outcome-relevant situational characteristics. Thus, in order to develop a useful intervention, certain questions must be satisfactorily addressed. First, how does the social perception process typically fail? What are the characteristic misperceptions often made, especially by the types of youngsters for whom Prepare is intended, and what perceiver qualities appear to be associated with such misperceptions? Second, what dimensions, qualities, or characteristics of situations optimally need to be perceived accurately in order to increase the likelihood of effective (in-context) behavior?

Having addressed concerns associated with social perception and misperception, as well as the identification of accuracy-enhancing situational characteristics, we will turn directly to the means for Situational Perception Training. In doing so, we will describe both the techniques for effectively conducting such training and an extended pool of relevant situations to be employed as training materials.

Social Misperception

Social misperception can take several forms. As Morrison and Bellack (1981) comment, social perception is a complex process, and perception deficits could result from a number of different problems. For example, an individual may reach inaccurate conclusions about the environment because he/she: (a) fails to listen to the interpersonal partner, (b) fails to look, (c) fails to integrate what he/she has seen and heard, (d) does not know the meaning of what has been seen and heard, or (e) looks or listens for cues which are not relevant at the moment. (p. 76)

Trower, Bryant, and Argyle (1978) provide further elaboration:

Research has shown that there is great scope for misperceiving, particularly in unfamiliar settings, and mistaking cues in this way can lead to rapid breakdown in communication. . . . There are several forms of failure: (a) low level of discrimination and accuracy; (b) systematic errors, e.g., perceiving others as more hostile than they are; (c) inaccurate stereotypes, or over-use of them; (d) errors of attribution, e.g., attributing too much to a person, too little to a situation; (e) halo effects, e.g., perceiving people as consistently good or bad. (p. 10)

Numerous antecedents and concomitants of situational misperception have been identified or suggested. They include both transient and enduring qualities of the perceiver. Specifically, situational misperception has been shown to be caused by or associated with such perceiver demographic characteristics as age (Magnusson, 1981), sex (Magnusson, 1981), socioeconomic status (Forgas, Brown, & Menyhart, 1979), and education (Forgas et al., 1979), as well as with perceiver affective states (Feshbach & Singer, 1957), especially anxiety (Forgas, 1985). Other factors influencing perception include the affective state of the person(s) being perceived (Morrison & Bellack, 1981), including perceiver cognitive expectations (Forgas, 1979), particularly as they may function as self-fulfilling prophecies (Jones & Panitch, 1971), and perceiver self-confidence, involvement in the target situation, and dogmatism (Forgas, 1985). Finally, the role relationship between the perceiver and the perceived (Forgas, 1979), as well as past failure experiences (Mischel, Ebbeson, & Zeiss, 1973), the threat level (Magnusson, 1981), and unfamiliarity with or ambiguity of the situation being perceived, may have an impact.

It is clear from this array that the many types and levels of situational misperceptions enumerated earlier may have multiple demographic, affective, cognitive, and interpersonal antecedents. Training individuals in the ability to perceive more accurately the montage of situations constituting their interpersonal worlds is thus a difficult and challenging task. We believe this task begins with the identification of situational characteristics likely to be misperceived (i.e., those that may be ambiguous, confusing, threatening, conflict-associated, or in other important ways characteristic of the difficult settings and events youths often face—and face poorly).

Situational Characteristics

Unlike the 50-year-long personality testing effort to identify salient characteristics of individuals, the identification and measurement of situational characteristics is a relatively new and much less well-developed thrust in psychology, a thrust emerging from the interaction-ist view of human behavior discussed earlier. Some writers have sought to characterize situations in terms of their broad features. Avedon (1981) points to the situation's purpose, procedures for action, rules, number of participants, participant roles, interaction patterns, and results. Argyle (1981) suggests situational goal structure, repertoire of elements, rules, sequences of behavior, concepts, environmental setting, roles, skills, and difficulties. Jessor (1981) speaks of situational depth, texture, enduringness, developmental change, and content. Bennett and Bennett (1981) suggest that situations are optimally characterized in terms of

1. The container—the fixed external enclosure (e.g., building, room, mall, auto) in which the interaction occurs;
2. The props—physical objects such as furniture, clothing, or paintings in the enclosure;
3. The modifiers—qualities of light, sound, color, texture, odor, temperature, and humidity that may influence the affective character of the interaction;
4. Duration—the objective time during which the interaction occurs and the anticipated time it will require;
5. The actors—the persons involved in, peripheral to, or witness-ing the interaction;
6. Progression—the events that actually precede and are expected to follow the interaction.

Forgas (1985), in contrast, describes situations not in terms of features of the situation per se, but on the basis of the feelings a given situation generates in the main actors—namely, anxiety or self-confi-dence, intimacy, involvement, pleasantness, and formality.

Some writers have sought to focus on more specific situational features. Argyle (1981) places particular emphasis on explicating the rules governing diverse situations:

1. Maintaining communication (e.g., rules about turn taking, use of shared language);
2. Preventing withdrawal (e.g., rules about equity, division of rewards);
3. Preventing aggression (e.g., rules about restraint, conflict management);
4. Coordinating behavior (e.g., rules about driving, eating together, public behavior);
5. Achieving cooperation (e.g., rules about tandem effort toward shared goals).

Graham, Argyle, and Furnham (1981) have placed a similarly narrow focus on situational goals. Across diverse situations and respondents, they found that participants in situations may have any of the following purposes:

1. To be accepted by others;
2. To convey information;
3. To look after others;
4. To take charge;
5. To enjoy a social activity;
6. To reduce own anxiety;
7. To maintain self-esteem;
8. To sustain social relationships;
9. To be looked after;
10. To promote the physical well-being of others;
11. To eat or drink;
12. To engage in sexual activity;
13. To make a favorable impression;
14. To seek help, advice, or reassurance;
15. To persuade or influence others;
16. To obtain information or solve a problem;
17. To reduce other's anxiety;
18. To promote one's own physical well-being;
19. To let others take charge;
20. To be accepting or welcoming of others;
21. To make new friends or get to know others better.

Magnusson (1981) offers perhaps the best of both approaches— broad dimensions plus concrete features—in his characterization of situations in terms of the following aspects:

1. Complexity,
2. Clarity,
3. Strength,
4. Promotion versus restriction,
5. Tasks,
6. Rules,
7. Roles,
8. Physical settings,
9. Other persons,
10. Goals,
11. Perceived control,
12. Expectancies,
13. Needs and motivations,
14. Affective tones or emotions.

Situational Perception Training requires that trainees be confronted with an array of difficult situations and, by means of a discussional, problem-solving group process, do the following: (1) identify situational characteristics (e.g., rules, roles, goals, expectancies) relevant to reducing the situational difficulty, conflict, or ambiguity represented; (2) generate alternative means for carrying out such difficulty reduction; (3) select from among these means; and (4) evaluate likely alternative outcomes. Thus attention to specific situational dimensions and characteristics enables the trainee's perceptual and problem-solving effort to go forward in a situation-specific, differentiated manner rather than in a global, undifferentiated way. Trainees are led via problem-solving activities to perceive the situation more accurately and to plan for its solution more effectively.

Problematic Situations

What kinds of situations are frequently conflictual, uncomfortable, or ambiguous for many individuals? Research conducted by Richardson and Tasto (1976) and Stratton and Moore (1977) reveals seven clusters of difficult situations: (1) assertiveness situations; (2) performing in public; (3) conflict; (4) intimate situations; (5) meeting strangers; (6) dealing with people in authority; and (7) anticipating or experiencing fear of disapproval, criticism, or making mistakes. With regard to each of these seven categories of commonly misperceived situations, to which responses frequently are poor, we believe it is useful to describe the behavior of the perceiver (i.e., the individual entering into and needing to decode the situation) as being potentially *cross-cultural* in nature. To be sure, this term is typically reserved for encounters between persons of different nations, geographical entities, ethnic backgrounds, and so forth. However, we believe that the cross-cultural misperceptions, miscommunications, misunderstandings, and faulty interpretations described here are every bit as operative. They may even be more subtle and, thus, even more resistant to accurate identification, decoding, and correction in the situations identified above, in which the individual is required to behave assertively in a family, peer, business, or school context, or to perform before an audience, meet strangers, deal with authority figures, and so forth.

In all of these contexts, no less than in traditional cross-cultural settings, meanings can differ, values can conflict, causes and intentions can be inferred incorrectly, messages can be misheard, gestures can be interpreted erroneously and, in general, the perceiver and the perceived can be functioning in all major respects as if they were from different cultural groups. The youth facing his peers, his family, his school class, his employer, the principal, the police, the parole officer, or unknown strangers may be doing so with assumptions, expectations, and beliefs subtly or grossly different from those held by the situation's other actors. For these reasons, we believe a training technology that is well-established in cross-cultural contexts can find a valuable place, albeit in modified form, as the key set of procedures constituting our Situational Perception Training. We refer specifically to the Culture Assimilator, also known as the Intercultural Sensitizer. This approach was initiated in 1971 by Fiedler, Mitchell, and Triandis. Albert (1983) makes the following comments about the Culture Assimilator:

> Triandis (1972) has termed the manner in which individuals from a given group characteristically perceive their social environment the "subjective culture" of that group.... When persons with different subjective cultures interact, their assumptions about, and interpretations of, particular behaviors may differ markedly. These assumptions and interpretations can be viewed in terms of attributions a person makes. Attributions are inferences about the causes of behavior. For example, a compliment can be seen as an attempt to manipulate, help can be interpreted as an attempt to demean, a gift can be seen as a bribe, and so on. Discrepancies in attributions may result in misunderstandings, low interpersonal attraction, rejection, and even conflict. Such discrepancies are more likely to occur when two individuals

belong to different cultures because of the differences in norms, roles, attitudes, and values between the two cultures. One of the major aims of intercultural training is to help individuals understand the perspectives of persons from another culture and to teach them about the other's subjective culture. (pp. 187–188).

With these attributional/misattributional assumptions and attribution-correcting training goals as a rationale, the Culture Assimilator consists of a number of situations, episodes, or "critical incidents" depicting interactions between persons from two cultures, followed by alternative attributions or explanations of their behavior. Each incident presents "typical interaction situations in which misunderstandings are likely to occur" (Albert, 1983, p. 190). The alternative attributions presented (usually four) are all plausible interpretations of the situation, three of them fitting best the assumptions of the learner's culture, the fourth being a typical attribution of the other (target) culture. Using a programmed learning format, learners are asked to read the incident and the alternative attributions and to select the one attribution they believe members of the other culture typically choose. After each choice, learners receive culturally relevant, misperception-correcting feedback. The following examples of Culture Assimilator critical incidents, alternative attributions, and corrective feedback illustrate this approach.

The Rock Concert

Judy is a 15-year-old U.S. high school student spending a month in Mexico as part of an international living program. She lives with a middle-class Mexican family and has become a good friend of the 14-year-old daughter, Rosa, and, through her, her circle of girlfriends. Judy finds life in Mexico interesting because of the novelty of the situation but feels a little frustrated at the restricted range of activities she is permitted to indulge in compared with her life back home. Whenever she suggests they do something a little different or daring the others seem very uncomfortable and refuse to discuss it. She was thus excited to learn that a popular American rock group was to play in the city next week and suggested to Rosa and her friends that they should all go. Although they admitted they would like to go, the others looked

Note. "The Rock Concert" and "The Joys of City Driving" have been reprinted from *Intercultural Interactions: A Practical Guide* (pp. 82, 105–106; 75, 101), by R. W. Brislin, K. Cushner, C. Cherrie, and M. Yong. Copyright © 1986 by Sage Publications. Reprinted by permission.

very apprehensive and said they could never get permission to attend such an event. Judy then proposed that they should pretend to visit someone else and sneak off to the concert. The group refused even to consider the idea, and Judy concluded exasperatedly that they were a very unadventurous lot.

What is the source of the Mexican girls' reluctance to consider Judy's proposal?

1. They are much more conscious of conforming to social norms than Judy.
2. They resent Judy (a foreigner) trying to tell them what to do.
3. They do not really want to go to the rock concert and are just making excuses so as not to offend Judy.
4. They are scared of what might happen at the concert but do not wish to admit their fears.

Rationales for the Alternative Explanations

1. This is the most probable explanation. In Latin cultures the socialization of children is strictly controlled (especially for girls), and they learn early the value and necessity to conform to social norms. Behavior that might be viewed in more individualistic (and less conforming) societies as simply adventurous or explorative is regarded in conformist societies with apprehension and as potentially disruptive of the close, interdependent social network. Rebelliousness or delinquency amongst the young is thus rare in such societies. The Mexican girls are thus much more conscious than Judy of the need to strictly adhere to social norms and expected behavior, and they fear dire consequences and shame if they do not. Sojourners should be aware of the social pressures to conform in such cultures and should not place hosts in situations where they are asked to go against social norms.

2. There is little indication that this is the case. They seem to accept Judy as part of their group and while they may not be willing to take up her suggestions they do not resent them. There is a more probable explanation.

3. This seems unlikely. They are probably as interested in rock music as Judy, and would probably not see the need to fabricate excuses to Judy if they were not. There is a better explanation.

4. They are not afraid so much by what might happen at the concert as the consequences of what might happen if it is found out that they did attend. There is a more probable explanation. (Brislin et al., 1986, pp. 82, 105–106)

The Joys of City Driving

Tito Santos, a Filipino exchange student, had recently arrived at a large university community in the United States. He came from a rather wealthy background and had many conveniences at home such as servants, a large home, car, and swimming pool. One day as he was riding to a nearby shopping area, he asked his friend, Bob, if he could drive home as he missed driving his car at home. Seeing that Tito had an international license, Bob saw nothing wrong with that. On the way home they were busily chatting as they were nearing a busy intersection where many cars were already stopped at the red light. Tito expertly maneuvered between the rows of cars already there. Bob appeared alarmed, but as the light had just changed and they sped off, he said nothing. However at the next intersection where the light was also red, but no cars were coming from the opposite direction, Tito just continued through without even slowing down. Bob began yelling at Tito and asked him to stop and let him drive his own car.

What best explains this situation?

1. Filipinos are all reckless drivers.
2. Tito wanted to show his friend how daring he was.
3. Tito was used to driving where the rules are different.
4. Tito actually did not know how to drive but had wanted to learn and had tricked his friend into using this as a driving lesson.

Rationales for the Alternative Explanations

1. This is a stereotypical answer that simplifies and ignores too many other relevant factors. It would be unwise to make such an explicit and overgeneralized attribution. Please choose again.

2. Although most young men like to show off once in a while, Bob was alarmed rather than impressed. We should also note that Tito was actually oblivious to those alarming factors. This does not satisfactorily explain his behavior. Please choose again.

3. This is the best answer. In many countries, although there are traffic rules and regulations, there are also certain unwritten or unspoken rules of thumb. In some places as long as you can make it through an intersection safely, this is still very acceptable, even though it means going against the lights. This behavior seems very natural to Tito, although it violates the rules that Bob follows. Although the red light stimulated a "stop" response in Bob, it merely stimulated a "look to see if it's clear" response in Tito. Sojourners often bring with them

a myriad of unconscious customs and habits that can be stimulated by events in the host culture. When sojourning in a foreign place one should remember that behavior that is acceptable in one's own country may not be acceptable in another, even given similar situations.

4. This is incorrect. The scenario states that Tito already had his license. Although Tito's driving habits may have indicated to Bob that Tito was not a good driver, there is a better explanation. (Brislin et al., 1986, pp. 75, 101)

Training Procedures

The construction of a Culture Assimilator begins, Albert (1983) suggests, with the generation and construction of episodes. Fiedler et al. (1971) propose that, ideally, these situations are those that the learner "finds conflictual, puzzling, or which he is likely to misinterpret" (p. 191). For the modified "Subcultural" Assimilator represented in Situational Perception Training, we have already both generated and obtained from others a large pool of such critical incidents descriptive of problematic situations common in the lives of adolescents and younger children. These conflictual, ambiguous, or otherwise challenging situations appear at the end of the chapter.

In the typical development of a Culture Assimilator, over 100 of which exist (Brislin, 1986; Brislin et al. 1986), the next construction steps are the elicitation and selection of attributions. As Albert (1983) states, "once a large number of episodes depicting potentially problematic interactions are constructed, the researcher or practitioner will seek to identify the different cultural interpretations given to each episode" (p. 192). It is here that we depart from the typical procedure. In the usual construction sequence, alternative attributions or interpretations are generated by the researchers, the practitioners, or panels of persons hired from the two cultures represented in the incident. By means of a culling and piloting procedure, a final set of four alternative interpretations is selected for each incident. These alternatives are later presented to trainees, along with the incident description and instructions to choose the best alternative interpretation, as the heart of the intercultural sensitivity training. We wish to take an alternative route. Rather than present a fait accompli— incident plus interpretation—to trainees, we wish trainees to generate, evaluate, and select from *their own* array of alternative interpretations and perceptions of the given incident. We believe that a process of requiring a group of youngsters to examine relevant critical situations, generate alternative perceptions of the situations and means for their management, evaluate these alternatives, and select among them is, in itself, an effective training technique. This set of procedures constitutes our operational definition of Situational Perception Training.

Procedurally, Situational Perception Training also draws substantially for its methods on three other Prepare courses—namely, Problem-solving Training (chapter 2), Moral Reasoning Training (chapter 6), and Interpersonal Skills Training (chapter 3). From Problem-solving Training comes expertise in the ability to generate, evaluate, and choose among alternative solutions to problem situations. From Moral Reasoning Training come the dilemma discussion techniques necessary to enable a group to collectively, thoroughly, and productively conduct the type of problem-solving discussions outlined above. From Interpersonal Skills Training comes the pool of concrete interactional abilities, a selection of which typically includes the solution to the conflictual incident posed. Thus Situational Perception Training begins with the presentation of a conflictual, ambiguous, problematic situation. Via active group discussion, youngsters engage in increasingly skilled problem-solving centered on their perceptions and misperceptions of the meanings, attributions, rules, roles, and alternative resolutions embodied in the problematic situation. As a result of this active process, they are, we believe, more likely to achieve accurate perceptions of, and solutions for, the presented situation, usually in the form of a sequence of appropriate interpersonal skills.

The following example illustrates a Situational Perception Training session involving youth who have previously undergone the requisite training in problem-solving and interpersonal skills.

> Trainer: OK, let's go over the situation. John, would you please read it?
>
> John: OK. "One of your friends, Bill, really likes a girl named Debbie. But they are not going steady. You think she is pretty nice yourself. You went out with her Saturday night, and you both had a real good time. Someone must have told Bill because he comes running up to you on the street and says, 'You dirty, cheating shit. I just found out about you and Debbie. I'm going to knock your ugly face in.' What do you do and say now?"
>
> Trainer: Thank you, John. Now what do we do first?
>
> William: Ask questions. Stop, think, and ask questions.

Trainer:	Stop, think, and ask questions. That's very good. OK. Yes, Robert?
Robert:	It would be good to know where and when this happened, and if anyone else was there.
Larry:	How long has this guy been my friend, and are we really tight? I ain't going to fight over a girl with a tight friend.
John:	Maybe this guy Bill does think he and the girl, Debbie, are going steady, but she don't. Maybe that's why Bill thinks his friend should stay away and is pissed off at him.
William:	Before I knew what to do, I'd have to hear how my friend said, what does it say here, "I'm going to knock your ugly face in." If the girl was there, he could just be saying it for her benefit. Or, if she wasn't, it could be just big-shot kidding around. Or he could really mean it, and I better get ready to duke it out. It all depends how he said it.
Trainer:	William, could you explain more about "how he said it?" How would you know?
William:	It ain't hard. There's mean talk, jive talk, messing around talk. I know them when I hear them.
Trainer:	So, we'd want to gather information about where, when, what kind of friends you and Bill are, his expectations of Debbie—going steady or not—and how he put it to you. Anything else? What else would it be useful to know?
John:	Where I live, a guy don't put down a friend in front of a broad, especially one they both like, unless he's ready to fight. That's the way it is. If she was there, he and I would fight.
Tom:	It's a threat, but sometimes people say something they don't really mean.
Trainer:	Don't really mean?
Tom:	Yeah. They say it, maybe because they're angry, but don't really mean "knock your face in."
Trainer:	So we need, in situations like this, to try to figure out what the other person *really* means. I think

that's what William meant when he said he'd have to hear *how* Bill threatened and what Larry meant when he asked how good a friend Bill was. Any other information we need up front? The question in the beginning was what would you do and say? And you've identified a lot of things about the situation that would help make your decision, like who is there, where it is, what does Bill expect, how good friends are you and he, what's the tone of his threat, does it sound real, what are the unwritten rules of your neighborhood. Anything else, and let's try to talk one at a time. What about your own goals? How would you want a situation like this to work out?

Tom: I would like us to remain friends and to get the problem solved without any violence.

Trainer: OK. Good.

Robert: Me too, but I wouldn't back down. I'd also want to hear from Debbie, like what she wanted, or who, and was she the one who told Bill that we went out.

William: We need to ask questions. Are you jealous, and why are you confronting me? Why did you just come up and try and threaten me? Why did you threaten me?

John: Why is my best friend mad at me?

Trainer: OK. Why is my best friend mad at me? You are sure using good ideas and questions to figure out the situation, to figure out what's going on. Let's assume you got your answer and pretty much figured out what's happening. Say it was just you and him, on the street. He really sounded mad and looked really ready to punch you in the face. You've been good friends a long time, but he's jealous and pissed as hell. John says he'd fight maybe. But are there other solutions? Are there skills you could try first?

William: Dealing with someone else's anger?

Trainer: OK. Good. Give me at least two more.

Larry: Dealing with fear. You can handle yourself without falling apart. You know what I mean?

Robert: All right, keeping out of fights. Also making a decision. You might make the right decision.

Trainer: OK. Any others?

Larry: Negotiate.

Trainer: What would be the consequence of negotiating?

Larry: You can come to a compromise.

William: Convincing others. You can avoid a fight with a friend, and also you can talk the problem out.

Trainer: Avoid a fight and you can talk it out. Any others?

William: Asking questions.

Trainer: OK. And what would be the consequence of that?

William: To find out what's wrong.

Trainer: That's really great. You guys came up with seven alternatives, seven different skills you could use in this situation. Dealing with someone else's anger. Dealing with fear. Keeping out of fights. Making a decision. Negotiating. Convincing others. And asking questions. Sure are lots of good choices, good solutions. You all seem to have top choices, but I want you to pick one that is your best choice. The one that you'd use first. OK? Your number one choice.

William: Asking questions. I'd start by asking questions and find out why he's so upset. Then deal with his anger. Now it's time to deal with his anger.

Larry: I got one more skill, apologize. Yeah . . . tell him that you apologize if you hurt his feelings because you didn't know what was going on at the time.

Trainer: So that's your first choice?

Larry: But he's got to meet you halfway. That's why I said negotiate before.

William: First comes the questions, then dealing with anger. No, the opposite. First calm him down, then find out why he's pissed. Then decide what to do, and then apologize and compromise. I think that's the solution.

Trainer: That really makes sense to me. Dealing with his anger. Yes, its a good way to start . . . by dealing with his anger first. Then if you don't ask questions, you may not know enough about what the situation is and how he sees it. Then you have to make a decision: compromise, apologize, or both. Sounds like one pretty good set of solutions to me.

Training Situations

Successful Situational Perception Training will require, in the first place, interesting and relevant stimulus situations for youth to discuss and decode.* We have compiled, and provide below, an extended series of situations we believe possess such qualities. They are drawn from diverse investigations of social competence, interpersonal skills training, and related research domains and are appropriate for either elementary- or secondary-level youth.

The trainer, alone or in collaboration with trainees, may select for discussion from this pool of stimulus situations those most likely to be interesting, relevant, and involving for the participating youth. By employing these materials in a problem-solving (see chapter 2) and dilemma discussion (see chapter 6) format, the trainer can help participants develop their abilities to perceive accurately and respond satisfactorily to real-life situations.

1. Let's pretend we're outside at recess. You're playing tag, but all of a sudden you notice that I'm standing by myself. You come over to talk to me, and you see that I've been crying and there are tears in my eyes. What do you do and say?

2. Let's pretend that I'm playing with some of my friends after lunch. We're building a really neat house. You come in the schoolroom and see us. Pretend that you really want to play blocks with us. What do you do and say?

3. Let's pretend that we're in the lunchroom carrying our trays of food. I'm walking right beside you. I want to sit by my other friend. I accidentally bump you, and you drop your whole tray on the floor. I look back at you. What do you do and say?

4. Let's pretend that the teacher has told the whole class to get in line for lunch. Then I come and cut in front of you. Let's pretend that I say, "I'm standing here now." What do you do and say?

---

*Situations 1–15 are from *Scoring System for Child Role Plays*, by K. A. Dodge, C. L. McClasky, and E. Feldman, 1985, unpublished manuscript, Indiana University, Bloomington. Adapted by permission. Other situations have been adapted from the following sources: 16–45 from Keller, Goldstein, and Wynn (1987); 46–67 from Freedman (1974); 68–77 from Hummel (1980); 78–88 from Healy (1985); 89–102 from Greenleaf (1978); and 103–182 from Goldstein and Glick (1987).

5. Let's pretend that I and some other kids have a new video game that we're playing with. You can see that it looks like a lot of fun. We are taking turns playing with it. You ask, "Can I have a turn?" Let's pretend that I say, "No. You have to wait until I say you can play." What do you do and say?

6. Let's pretend that I'm a girl in your class. You have some free time and want to talk to someone. You see me sitting at my desk. Let's pretend that you decide to talk to me. What do you do and say?

7. Let's pretend that you're drawing with your crayons during free time. You are making a fire engine (or butterfly). I am coloring too, but some of my crayons are lost. Let's pretend that I ask you, "Can I use your red crayon?" What do you do and say?

8. Let's pretend that we're in class now. The teacher is handing back arithmetic papers. When the teacher gives you your paper, you smile because you got all of the answers correct. Then you notice that I missed six problems and I am almost ready to cry. What do you do and say?

9. Let's pretend that some boys in your class have started a club. It's a real fun club, and we do some neat things. I'm in the club. Let's pretend that you wish that you could join the club too. One day you see me walking down the hall on my way to a club meeting. What do you do and say?

10. Let's pretend that, when you get ready to go to school, your mother tells you that you can't leave unless you put on your rubber boots and your ugly black raincoat. When you get to school, all the other kids have on shorts and tennis shoes. When I see you, I start laughing. What do you do and say?

11. Let's pretend that your teacher has given you an assignment to write a report about reptiles. You don't even know what a reptile is or even how to spell the word. You notice me going right to the encyclopedia to start my report. You come over to see what's going on. You are really upset because you think you are going to get a bad grade. What do you do and say?

12. Let's pretend that I brought my new soccer ball (or Barbie doll) to school. I let you play with it. Let's pretend that I said you could use it for the whole recess. Halfway through recess I come over to you and say, "I want my ball/doll back right now." What do you do and say?

13. Let's pretend that we are in gym class. The teacher is having us run some races. I am a really fast runner and end up winning almost every race. At the end of class, the teacher says I will get to race against kids from other schools. You walk with me back to class. What do you do and say?

14. Let's pretend that you and I are playing checkers during free time. I have three kings, and you don't have any. I am almost ready to jump your last man. What do you do and say?

15. Let's pretend that the whole class is working on a big picture to hang in the hall. The teacher is going to choose one person to be in charge and decide what we're going to draw on the picture. You would really like to be the person in charge. The teacher says to me "[Name,] I'm going to let you be in charge. What shall we draw?" What do you do and say?

16. The student who is sitting next to you in math class is having trouble understanding the assignment. What would you do and say?

17. Two students in your class got into a dumb argument with each other, and now it looks like they are about to get into a fight neither of them wants. What would you do and say?

18. Your teacher has asked if there is anyone in your class who would help her move some boxes. What would you do and say?

19. You're trying to do your schoolwork, but the student sitting next to you keeps elbowing you and trying to get your attention. You know that you'll get into trouble if you start talking to him. What would you do and say?

20. You're working on a science project in your classroom. You only have 10 more minutes to work on it, and you still have a lot to do. You notice suddenly that it's snowing outside and you're excited because it's the first snowfall of the winter. You can't wait to go outside and play in the snow. What would you do and say?

21. Your mother is taking your temperature because she thinks you may be running a fever. Your little brother comes in and starts acting silly. You know you shouldn't laugh because the thermometer might fall out of your mouth. What would you do and say?

22. A friend has just told you that his brand new sneakers have been stolen. What would you do and say?

23. A new student in your class really looks sad. He tells you he is very homesick. What would you do and say?

24. A student in your class has just told the class that his mother died of cancer last night. What would you do and say?

25. A student in your class is angry with you because he feels that you have cut in front of him in the lunch line at school. What would you do and say?

26. Your teacher is angry with you because you have not followed his directions for cleaning up your desk. What would you do and say?

27. It is 8:30 p.m., and you have just arrived home. Your mother is

very angry because you were supposed to be home not later than 6:00. What would you do and say?

28. You got a haircut, and now your hair is much too short. Your classmates start making fun of you. What would you do and say?

29. You failed an easy spelling test, and your classmates start teasing you about it. What would you do and say?

30. You can't walk across the balance beam in gym class. All of the children start laughing at you. What would you do and say?

31. Another student has just come up to you and demanded that you give him some money. What would you do and say?

32. Another student has just bumped into you and made you spill your drink and drop your tray of food on the floor. What would you do and say?

33. Another student has just told you that you are a stupid ass because of the color of your skin. What would you do and say?

34. You are accused by a store owner of shoplifting a new pair of pants from his store. What would you do and say?

35. You are accused by your teacher of having set off a fire alarm. What would you do and say?

36. Your friends accuse you of always being selfish and thinking about yourself first. What would you do and say?

37. You share a room at home with your sister, who is always using your things without asking you. What would you do and say?

38. Your teacher keeps giving you work that is too easy. It's the same work over and over again, and you are really bored. What would you do and say?

39. You're trying to do your boardwork, but two students are blocking your view. What would you do and say?

40. You have just received the results of your reading exam and have found out that you did not pass. What would you do and say?

41. You wanted to do at least 20 pushups in a row but could only do 13. What would you do and say?

42. You have just been told that you will not be promoted to the next grade level. What would you do and say?

43. Several members of your class tell you that they're going to steal cigarettes from a locker and they want you to be the lookout. What would you do and say?

44. Your brother's friends pull over in a car you think they may have stolen. They ask you to get in and go for a ride. What would you do and say?

45. The members of your class want to win the classroom deco-

rating contest for the holidays, and they are all on your case because you really have not been doing your job very well. What would you do and say?

46. You're out on the street with a good friend on a hot, muggy summer night, and he says, "Whew, am I thirsty! I could really use a cold beer. Listen, I know a guy who sells it to anyone who comes, right off his front porch, and he doesn't even check ID's. How about our going over that way and getting some booze?" What would you do and say?

47. You've been going steady with a girl named Mary for about 3 months. It used to be a lot of fun to be with her, but lately it's been sort of a drag. There are some other girls you'd like to go out with now. You decide to break up with Mary, but you know she'll be very upset and angry with you. She may even tell lies about you to the other girls, and that could hurt your chances with them. How will you go about breaking up with her gently? What will you say to her?

48. Your father has been hassling you for months about getting home by midnight. Sometimes that's a problem because none of your friends has to be home before 1:00 a.m. and you feel like an idiot always leaving places early. One night you walk in at 1:30 a.m., and your father is sitting in the living room, looking mad. He says, "Where the hell have you been? Do you have any idea what time it is? Or don't you kids know how to tell time anymore?" What do you do and say now?

49. You're playing basketball in the schoolyard, and some guy you don't know well is standing on the sidelines. He starts agitating you, calling you names, and making fun of the way you play. He says, "Hey, look at him. He can't dribble. He can't shoot!" What do you do and say now?

50. One of your friends does some drug dealing on the street. Once in a while, he even gives you some pills or something for free. Now he says to you, "Listen, man, I've got to deliver some stuff on the south side, but I can't do it myself. How about it—will you take this stuff down there for me? I'll give you some new stuff to try plus 25 dollars besides for your time. Will you help me out?" What do you do and say now?

51. It's 1:30 a.m., and you're walking along a street near your home. You're on your way home from your friend's house, and you know it's after curfew in your town. You weren't doing anything wrong. You just lost track of time. You see a patrol car cruising along the street, and you feel scared because you know you can get into trouble for breaking curfew. Sure enough, the car stops next to you, the police officer gets

out, and says, "You there, put your hands on the car. Stand with your feet apart." What do you do and say now?

52. You're walking home through the schoolyard one day, and a boy you don't know very well calls you over to him. He smiles and says, "Hey man, I've got 5 dollars. Your ma doing anything tonight?" What do you do or say now?

53. You're looking around a discount department store with a friend. You're in the sporting goods section. You see that the glass case where they keep the handguns is open and the guns are just lying there where you can reach in and grab them. There's nobody in sight, no customers and no employees. Your friend says, "Quick, man, let's get some." What do you do and say now?

54. One of your friends really likes a girl named Debbie, but they're not going steady. You think she's pretty nice yourself. You went out with her Saturday night, and you both had a real good time. Someone must have told your friend because he comes running up to you on the street and says, "You dirty cheating shit! Bill just told me about you and Debbie. I'm gonna knock your ugly face in!" What do you do and say now?

55. Your friend calls on a Sunday night to ask if you want to get together with her and some other friends. You tell her you've been grounded because you got home after curfew the weekend before. She says, "So what's the big deal? Just sneak out the back door and meet me in the next block. Your mother will never know you're gone." What do you do and say now?

56. You're sitting at home watching television one weekday night. Your mother was there with you before, but she's out now. There's a knock at the door. You answer it. A police officer is standing there and calls you by name. What do you do and say now?

57. You're walking along a side street with a friend, and he stops in front of a late model Camaro. He looks inside, and then he says excitedly, "Look, man, the keys are still in it! Let's see what she can do. Come on, let's go!" What do you do and say now?

58. You have a part-time job as a stock clerk in a discount store, and one of your friends has been after you to steal a battery for his car. You figure it couldn't be too difficult because lots of times you're alone in the stock room and there's nobody who could see you. Your friend knows this too. Tonight he says, "Come on, man, tonight would be a perfect night, with your boss going home early. There won't be anyone in that back room. How about it?" What do you do and say now?

59. You have a friend who's a few years older than yourself. He's

been in trouble with the law a lot, and he's even been to prison, but he's out now. You really like him a lot and respect him, and you wish he would like and respect you, too, because he's a popular man in the neighborhood. He comes to your house one night and tells you that he and another man are going to hold up a gas station out in the country. He says, "You want to come along? We think you could be a big help to us." What do you do and say now?

60. You're looking for a job, and as you pass the local McDonald's, you notice a sign in the window that says "Part-time Help Wanted." You go in and ask for the manager. She comes to the counter. What do you do and say now?

61. You're at a party, and all the people there are smoking grass. You used to do a lot of smoking yourself, but now you're on probation because you got busted. Everyone knows you used to smoke. Your boyfriend offers you a joint. What do you do and say now?

62. You met a girl, and you asked her if she'd like to see the show Saturday night. She says, "I'd like to, but my father won't let me go out with boys who are on parole." What do you do and say now?

63. What if a girl had agreed to go out with you, but when you went to pick her up Saturday night, her father met you on the porch and said, "Sandra is not going out with you tonight or any other night! She's a good girl, and I don't want to ruin her reputation by having her seen with a boy who's done time." What do you do and say now?

64. You're in a job interview, and you really want the job because the pay is good and the hours aren't bad. The interviewer seems interested in you until he finds out that you are on parole. Now he says, "We have a policy of not hiring anyone who's on parole. We've had too many problems with you boys in the past. Sorry." What do you do and say now?

65. It's early afternoon, and ever since you woke up this morning, you've been in a bad mood. You feel empty, tired, a little angry, and a little sad, all at the same time. What can you do to get youself out of this bad mood?

66. Your parents never seem to like your friends. They say they're dirty, or that they have no manners, or that they'll get you into trouble. Kim, a new friend, has just left your house after her first visit over to your place. After she's gone, your mother gets on her case and calls her a good-for-nothing and forbids you to see her again. How will you go about handling this problem? What will you do and say?

67. The boy you've been going out with just broke up with you. He says that you're OK, but he'd like to go out with other girls too. You

still like him, and you're hurt that he doesn't want to go out with you and continue to be your guy. You're in a terrible, bad mood. You feel really down. How will you go about solving this problem?

68. Two boys are in the hallway. The first boy is carrying some books. The other boy knocks the books out of his arms. They smash the first boy's foot. Other kids are looking on and laughing as the two boys argue. If you were the first boy, what would you think, say, and do in that situation?

69. Two boys are in the gym, and they are trying to get a kickball game started. Both boys want the same boy, Bill, to be on their team. The first boy wants to get the game started. The other boy is acting real fresh and is trying to boss the situation. If you were the first boy, what would you think, say, and do in that situation?

70. Two boys are arguing over where they should play a basketball game. The first boy wants to play in the lot right by the school. The other boy wants to go across town and play. They are arguing and being fresh with each other. If you were the first boy, what would you think, say, and do in that situation?

71. One boy has brought in a special, handmade model of a bicycle. A second boy knocks the bike on the floor. The two boys are arguing over what they should do. What would you think, say, and do if you were the first person in that situation?

72. Two girls are arguing over who should represent their class in the special events show in the media center. You are the first girl, and you think you can do it really well. The other girl is giving you a hard time and says she should represent the class in the special event. What would you think, say, and do in that situation?

73. Two boys are arguing over who should get which basketball. There's one rubber one that's in tough shape, and there's a real good leather one. You are the first boy, and you want the best basketball. You get into a hot argument with the other kid over who gets the best one. What would you think, say, and do in that situation?

74. A girl comes into a classroom late, and her teacher sees her and tells her that she's going to have to stay after school and make up the time. The girl is getting angry about having to stay after school to make up the time. If you were the girl, what would you think, say, and do in that situation?

75. A boy is sitting doing his work, and his teacher says he has to get all these tough math problems finished before he can go and watch a special movie. She's looking at him real sternly and saying he's got to get this stuff done, but the kid doesn't think he can get it done. He

thinks he's going to miss the movie. If you were the boy, what would you think, say, and do in that situation?

76. You are the president of the class, and you think you should have a say about where your class goes on its special trip. But the teacher says that it's his decision and that it doesn't matter if you're president of the class. He tells you to be quiet. What would you think, say, and do?

77. There was a special project in your classroom, and you agreed to help clean it up if the teacher let you do it. But the mess is really worse than you thought, and there's a lot to clean up before you can get a chance to go to gym class. You don't want to miss gym class. The teacher looks at you and says you have to get it done. What would you think, say, and do?

78. You and your friend are waiting in line to see a movie. You have been waiting for over an hour when two other kids try to get in front of you. They give you an excuse, saying that they had been in line but that they had to leave it in order to make a phone call. You know that this is not the truth.

Female Peer: Uh . . . excuse me! We were standing in line before. We just had to leave in order to make a phone call, so we're just going to get back in line right here, OK?

What would you think, say, and do?

79. You've just entered math class and seated yourself as you wait for the class to begin. You know that the teacher usually collects the homework before the class begins, so you look in your notebook to get your papers out in order to pass them in. Although you look through all your notebooks, you can't find your homework. You plan to go up to the teacher after class in order to explain what happened. However, at the end of class, the teacher calls you up to her desk.

Teacher: Miss Jones, come up here immediately. I'd like to talk with you. Miss Jones, I have looked through the homework papers, and I see that you did not hand yours in. Now I don't want to hear some flimsy excuse like you've lost it. This has happened before. I'll bet you never did it!

What would you think, say, and do?

80. You've had a hard day at school, and you go home to listen to some of your favorite rock music in order to relax. You put on the record. You're really enjoying the music, and you start to feel better.

You're thinking about the homework that you're going to do that evening when your father opens your bedroom door without knocking and yells at you.

Father: Shut down that darn music! It's breaking my eardrums! And why aren't you studying? Remember, you got two C's on your last report card, and you're not going to improve your grades by listening to rock music.

What would you think, say, and do?

81. You are walking down the hallway, and you see another student who is in your class. He sometimes has a difficult time doing the homework, and he has asked you, on several occasions, to help him. You agreed even though you could have used the time for your own studying, but the only time he ever wants to talk to you is when he needs your help. You say hello to him as you're walking down the hallway.

Female Peer: Hi Bob! How's it going?

Male Peer: I can't talk to you now, Mary. I've got important things to do.

What would you think, say, or do?

82. You are in social studies class, and you are happy because it is Friday and you and several other students are going on a weekend camping trip. The teacher walks in and begins to talk.

Teacher: OK. I'd like to make an announcement before we begin class today. I know I had previously told you that we would have the exam next Wednesday. Well, I've changed my mind. We're going to have it on Monday. And I don't want to hear any complaining! You all have a long weekend ahead of you. If a whole weekend isn't enough time to prepare for the test, then that's your problem!

What would you think, say, or do?

83. You come home after having spent some time at an ice cream shop. You and your friends sometimes hang out there after school and play pinball. It's really only a place where young people can get together and have a good time, but your parents think otherwise.

Father: All right! Where have you been? Have you been hanging out at that lousy ice cream shop?

Mother: Now, you know perfectly well that we don't want you going there. We feel that it's just a hangout for young punks! We've said this before, and we're not going to say it again; we want you to stay away from that place.

What would you think, say, and do?

84. You are sitting in science class and working on a class assignment. The teacher leaves the class for a few minutes, and some of the students begin fooling around by making noise and throwing paper airplanes. You really want to finish the work, so you ignore the students who are fooling around and continue to do your work and finish. The teacher walks in.

Teacher: All right! Enough is enough! I'm going to assign this entire class detention! I leave the class for 5 minutes and you all begin acting like kindergarten children! I imagine that none of you has even touched the work I assigned. Well, I'm going to put a stop to all this nonsense once and for all!

What would you think, say, and do?

85. You have been invited to a party, and you're really looking forward to it. After school, you go home in order to get ready for the party, which is going to be held that night. When you enter your house, your mother says she wants you to baby-sit.

Mother: Oh, I've been waiting for you. Your father and I have been invited over to the Carter's tonight. That means we'll need you to baby-sit with little Richie.

What would you think, say, and do?

86. You are sitting in English class. You know that the teacher has talked to the principal because you cut class and failed the midsemester exam. You also know that both the teacher and the principal telephoned your parents in order to talk to them. You're wondering what's going on. The bell rings, and the rest of the students go out of the room, leaving you alone with the teacher. What would you think, say, and do?

87. You are leaving school, and you see two students talking to a friend of yours. You can see that they are giving your friend a hard time. They are threatening to beat him up if he doesn't give them the answers to the homework that they were assigned.

> Male Peer: All right! We're going to ask you one more time. We want the answers to those homework problems or you've had it!

What would you think, say, and do?

88. You and a new friend go out after school for ice cream sodas. You really like him, but you also know that your parents dislike him even though they hardly know him. You go home and enter the kitchen. Both of your parents are there waiting for you.

> Mother: All right. Where have you been? Have you been hanging out with that new, so-called friend of yours?
>
> Father: Now, you know very well that we don't want you hanging around with him. We've heard some very bad things about him. We've told you this before, but this is final! We do not want you seeing him!

What would you think, say, and do?

89. You are sitting in class, about to begin an assignment at your desk. The person next to you just broke her pencil as she was about to write. You have an extra pencil in your desk. What would you do? What would you say?

90. You are sitting in class, and your friend is at the desk next to you. The teacher has just given the class an assignment. You notice that your friend is looking at his book and getting very upset. He is having some kind of trouble with the assignment. What would you say to him?

91. You are sitting on the bus after school. Your friend gets on and sits next to you. You are surprised to see him because you know that he is usually at basketball practice after school. He looks upset and doesn't talk to you. What would you say to him?

92. You are in science class, about to begin working on a project that involves getting together a lot of materials. You were lucky and found everything you needed. You notice that another student was not so lucky and is looking all over for a piece of equipment. What would you do? What would you say?

93. You are in the hallway while changing classes, and a friend comes up to talk with you. He tells you how a person accidentally tripped over his stick while playing floor hockey in gym. Because this person tripped, he wants to fight your friend after school. Your friend tells you that he does not want to fight over a simple accident. What would you do? What would you say to him?

94. You are in class, and a substitute teacher walks in instead of

your regular teacher. The class is making a lot of noise and is giving the sub a hard time. The sub can't seem to find any plans on the teacher's desk. You know that the class is supposed to have a test today and that if you don't have the test the whole class may get a zero. What would you say? What would you do?

95. You are in the hallway after school, and only a few kids are still hanging around. You see someone you know across the hall who is being blocked by two other guys so he can't move away from his locker. You hear him say, "C'mon, guys, I told you I didn't have any money!" What would you do? What would you say?

96. You are in shop class. You have been building a lamp, and you are almost done with it. You will not need the whole class period to finish it. You notice someone else having trouble with her project, which is very similar to yours. What would you say? What would you do?

97. You are talking with a friend as you both leave math class about the test you're going to have in just 3 days. Your friend is very worried because he doesn't think he can pass the test. He tells you that if he doesn't pass the test, his parents may make him stay home from the concert you're both planning to see that weekend. What would you say? What would you do?

98. You had to stay after school to take a make-up exam. There are not many people left in the school when you finish. As you walk past the gym, you notice one of the teachers is alone in the gym pushing large tables around to get ready for the dance. What would you say? What would you do?

99. It is between classes. You notice a student whose foot is in a cast walking with crutches up the stairs. She has several books under her arm. You also notice that she is carrying her lock so you figure that she is on her way to gym class. She's making it up the stairs all right, but she's moving very slowly and with difficulty. What would you do? What would you say?

100. You had a substitute teacher for the last period of the day. The class gave him a hard time, and he told several students to stay after class. One of the students who has to stay after didn't fool around at all. You saw him working hard all period. The sub just made a mistake. But now the student is upset and angry. What would you say? What would you do?

101. It is the end of the day, and, as usual, everyone is trying to get out of the building without delay. You notice a student, whom you know pretty well, hanging around the hallways. He comes up to you and tells

you that he thinks some guys are going to hassle him once he gets outside. He tells you he doesn't want any trouble—he just wants to get home OK. What would you say? What would you do?

102. It is between classes, and you notice a new student trying to get his combination lock unlocked. He turns the knob and pulls on it, but the lock just doesn't open. He is getting upset. The next class will begin soon. What would you do? What would you say?

103. The parole board has just held you another 6 months. You think you should be able to go home because you haven't broken any of the rules. What would you do?

104. You are always doing the hardest work in the kitchen. None of the other workers is helping you out. What would you do?

105. You just bought a pair of sneakers and left the store, and now you realize the clerk didn't give you the correct change. What would you do?

106. One of the residents assigned to your unit is very upset. He has just been held at the parole board. What would you do?

107. A resident who is a friend of yours tells you that he has just received a letter from his girlfriend, and she has broken up with him. What would you do?

108. A resident you know in another unit is upset because her parents, who promised to visit her for the last 3 weeks, have not shown up. What would you do?

109. You are scheduled to appear before the commissioners at the parole board, which will decide whether you will stay longer in the facility. You will have to speak to the commissioners about this. What would you do?

110. You have been caught smoking a joint, and you know that you will have to speak about it to your counselor, who is coming in on the next shift. What would you do?

111. You have to go talk to a staff person, your teacher, to discuss an earlier incident in which you had been disrespectful and had cursed at her. What would you do?

112. You have to go to the facility nurse and tell her you think that you may have VD. What would you do?

113. A staff member is angry with you because you have not followed her directions for cleaning up your unit office. What would you do?

114. Your counselor is angry because your unit has continued to be in last place on the Unit-of-the-Week contest for the last 5 weeks. What would you do?

115. Another resident has just come up to you and demanded that you give her cigarettes. What would you do?

116. You just found out who stole your sneakers. What would you do?

117. A resident has just been told that his parents are here for their visit, but he has been assigned to work in the kitchen. What would you do?

118. A new resident has just been admitted to the program. It is the first time he has ever been away from home. What would you do?

119. You are walking down the street, and you notice a woman standing beside her car, which has a flat tire. What would you do?

120. Your teacher accuses you of being lazy and always refusing to do your work. What would you do?

121. Three residents have just asked you to go AWOL with them. You really don't like it in the facility, but you want to do well in the program. What would you do?

122. You've just been released home, and it's your first week in school. Some of your old friends have decided that they are going to skip the day and not go to school. The have just asked you to come with them. What would you do?

123. You have been in the program for about 45 days. Your parents have just arrived for their first visit. You are really excited about seeing them. What would you do?

124. Your counselor has just helped you to work out a very serious problem. What would you do?

125. You have really made a lot of progress in your reading, and it's time for you to be released from the program. You must say goodbye to your reading teacher. What would you do?

126. Your boyfriend has just told you on the telephone that he loves you. What would you do?

127. You have just received the results of your GED exam and have found out that you did not pass. What would you do?

128. You spent 3 weeks trying to help your little brother learn how to ride a bicycle, but he still has not learned. What would you do?

129. In woodshop, you have been working on building a bookcase, but it just won't come out right. What would you do?

130. You are having lunch at the facility, and you just took the first bite of your sandwich. Something tastes really spoiled. What would you do?

131. You are restricted for being disrespectful. You feel the staff provoked you and that the restriction is unfair. What would you do?

132. You are not getting along with the other residents in your unit, and you want to be transferred to another unit. What would you do?

133. A resident who is a good friend of yours tells you that he has just learned that his girlfriend is pregnant. What would you do?

134. Today there was a new admission to your unit, and she doesn't know anyone. What would you do?

135. Your counselor has just told you that you will have to talk with the resident who accused you of stealing his sneakers. What would you do?

136. You have to telephone your mother this afternoon and tell her that, because you got into a fight, the parole board may hold you for several months. What would you do?

137. You and another resident have had a physical confrontation, and staff members tell you that you must sit down with him after lunch and work it out. What would you do?

138. You have an appointment tomorrow to talk to your school's football coach about trying out for the team. He is known to be a very tough guy. What would you do?

139. A resident in your unit has just gotten heavily sanctioned. He says that you started the fight with him last week that made this happen and he's very angry with you. What would you do?

140. Some of the members of your unit are angry because, while playing basketball, you fouled an opposing player, he scored, and your unit lost the game. What would you do?

141. The cook who is serving the food is angry with you because he just heard you tell another resident how bad it tastes. What would you do?

142. A resident threatens you and the rest of your unit that he will get even with whoever took his stuff. What would you do?

143. Another resident tells you that she has rights to the chair you are sitting in at the unit office. What would you do?

144. You lost your privileges because someone told your counselor that you were smoking cigarettes in the bathroom, and you just found out who told. What would you do?

145. A resident to whom you lent a pack of cigarettes is now refusing to pay you back. What would you do?

146. Your mother's boyfriend is drunk and getting a little nasty. It looks as though he's getting up to come over and hit you. What would you do?

147. Two unit members got into a dumb argument, and now it

looks like they are about to get into a fight neither of them wants. What would you do and say?

148. Your teacher has asked whether there is anyone in your class who would help her move some boxes. What would you do and say?

149. Your mother has to go to work, your older sister is still sleeping, and there is no one else but you to watch your little brother. What would you do and say?

150. A friend of yours wants to go to the movies but doesn't have enough money. What would you do and say?

151. You are accused by your counselor of always getting other residents to do your dirty work for you. What would you do and say?

152. A resident in your unit has accused you of being a homosexual. What would you do and say?

153. Your mother accuses you of taking 10 dollars from her wallet. What would you do and say?

154. A neighbor at home accuses you of being just like your father, a no-good bum. What would you do and say?

155. You are at a party in a friend's house and some of the other kids ask you to help search for any liquor in the house. What would you do and say?

156. You know that four members of your unit were smoking marijuana last night. During group counseling, your counselor asks you what you know about the incident. What would you do and say?

157. The cooks at the facility have just made you a cake for your birthday. What would you do and say?

158. You are on an emergency home leave because your grandmother, who has spent the most time raising you, is very sick. You are visiting her in the hospital. What would you do and say?

159. Your little brother, who is 10 years old, is getting high every day. You really care for him a lot. What would you do and say?

160. You are leaving the facility after a year and have to say goodbye to another resident, who has become the best friend you ever had. What would you do and say?

161. Your basketball team just lost the championship game. What would you do and say?

162. You were hoping to get your ceramics project completed by the time you left on your release, but now you realize that you are not going to finish it on time. What would you do and say?

163. Your counselor always seems to have time to talk to the other residents in your unit but never seems to have time to talk with you. What would you do and say?

164. On your home visits, your mother always wants you in by 10:30 p.m., but you don't want to come home that early. What would you do and say?

165. On your home visit, you learn that your brother has just failed his GED exam. What would you do and say?

166. Your closest friend has just told you she found out today that her parents are getting separated. What would you do and say?

167. You have a job interview with the facility vocational specialist today at 2:00 p.m. What would you do and say?

168. You are sitting outside the facility director's office, waiting to see her about your escape attempt last night. What would you do and say?

169. Your teacher is angry with you because you were disruptive during class. What would you do and say?

170. Another resident in your unit is angry with you because he lent you his leather coat for your home visit and you have come back from the visit without it. What would you do and say?

171. A new resident, just admitted to the facility, comes up to you and calls you a punk and a sucker. What would you do and say?

172. You have just come to bat in a baseball game, and the other team's pitcher calls you a chickenshit. What would you do and say?

173. You are on a field trip. A staff member is pretty busy doing different things, and she complains to you that now she also has to do the cooking. What would you do and say?

174. Another resident in your unit is sitting alone on his bed, looking very sad. What would you do and say?

175. The facility cook has just accused you of taking food from the kitchen. What would you do and say?

176. You are walking down the street, and a police officer stops you and accuses you of burglarizing a house. What would you do and say?

177. You are on a home visit, and an old friend of yours has just asked you to join me and another old friend in snatching a purse from an old lady who is walking down the street. What would you do and say?

178. Two other unit members and I have just come to you and asked you to join us tonight in beating up a new resident whom no one seems to like. What would you do and say?

179. It is your first week home after being released from the facility. You have not seen your best and oldest friend for a year, and now you

spot him walking toward you on the street. What would you do and say?

180. Your mother has just given you a new coat you like very much for your birthday. What would you do and say?

181. You are alone. You have applied for a job at a factory downtown, and you really wanted it a lot, but you just found out someone else got it. What would you do and say?

182. You spent a lot of time helping your friend solve a problem she is having, but she has just told you that your ideas didn't work and that the problem is as bad as ever. What would you do and say?

Chapter 5

Anger Control Training

The ability to function in an effective and satisfying manner in one's interpersonal world is a matter of competence in knowing both what to do and what not to do in diverse circumstances.* The Prepare Curriculum courses presented thus far each seek to enhance or accelerate various prosocial behaviors: problem solving, interpersonal skills, and accurate situational perception. The present chapter provides a complementary offering to help teach youth means for decelerating anger arousal, a major precursor of antisocial, aggressive behavior.

Theory and Research

To best understand the origins of this component of the Prepare Curriculum, we begin this chapter in what at first may seem to be a setting quite distant from the study of anger and its management—the experimental psychology laboratory of the Russian psychologist Luria. In an extended series of investigations, Luria (1961) explored the manner in which in the course of normal development children come to regulate much of their external behavior by means of internal speech. Little and Kendall (1979) succinctly describe this unfolding pattern:

> The process of development of verbal control of behavior thus seems to follow a standard developmental sequence. First, the initiation of motor behavior comes under control of adult verbal cues, and then the inhibition of responses is controlled by the speech of adults. Self-control emerges as the child learns to respond to his own verbal cues, first to initiate responses and then to inhibit them.
>
> The 3- or 4-year-old child normally can follow rather complicated instructions given by an adult, and it is at this age that the child is said to begin to regulate his own behavior on the basis of verbal self-instructions. . . . Between the ages of 4 1/2 and 5 1/2, the child's self-verbalizations shift from overt to covert (primarily internal) speech. (p. 101)

---

*An earlier version of this chapter first appeared in *Aggression Replacement Training: A Comprehensive Intervention for Aggressive Youth* (pp. 67–95), by A. P. Goldstein and B. G. Glick, 1987, Champaign, IL: Research Press.

In addition to Luria's seminal research, a number of other investigators have examined and confirmed this verbal mediation process (Allport, 1924; Bem, 1967; Mussen, 1963; Vygotsky, 1962). But, as with all normative developmental processes, there are children in whom the expected sequence fails to occur, occurs only in part, or occurs in distorted or incomplete form. If the studies cited lead to the conclusion that "there is considerable evidence to support the belief that self-control develops largely as a function of a child's development of [internal] language mechanisms" (Little & Kendall, 1979, p. 104), what of the youngsters in whom this sequence fails to fully or correctly unfold? As we shall see, it is precisely such youngsters who—deficient in the ability to regulate overt behavior by internal speech—display the arrays of behavior associated with such terms as *hyperactivity, impulsivity, poor self-control, acting out,* and the like. However, as we shall also see, such impulsive behavior in these very same poorly self-controlled youngsters may be reduced by externally imposed interventions that very closely replicate the normal developmental sequence described by Luria.

Donald Meichenbaum and his research group have been especially active in this domain. Their initial investigations sought to establish further the relationship between impulsivity and poor verbal control of overt behavior. Meichenbaum and Goodman (1969), using what has become a standard measure for determining impulsivity/reflectivity, Kagan's (1966) Matching Familiar Figures Test, found that those youngsters who respond on the Kagan test quickly and make many errors (the impulsives) indeed exercise diminished verbal control over their overt behavior as compared with youngsters who take their time and make fewer errors (the reflectives). But just what do reflective and impulsive youngsters say to themselves, and how does their self-directed speech differ? To answer such questions, Meichenbaum and Goodman (1971) observed and recorded the play behavior and private speech of 16 4-year-olds matched for age, intelligence, and socioeconomic status, half of whom were reflective and half impulsive on the Kagan measure. Results indicated that

> the private speech of cognitively impulsive preschoolers was largely comprised of the most immature, self-stimulatory content. In comparison, reflective preschoolers manifested significantly more outer-directed and self-regulatory speech and significantly more inaudible mutterings. . . . The results of our observational studies suggested that cognitively reflective preschoolers use their private speech in a more mature, more instrumental, self-guiding fashion than impulsive preschoolers. (p. 28)

Other investigators concerned with self-directed speech in impulsive children reported concurring results (Dickie, 1973; Kleinman, 1974), and Camp (1977) extended the finding to a different category of youngsters often deficient in the developmental sequence described by Luria. Camp found that "aggressive boys fail to employ verbal mediational activity in many situations where it would be appropriate, and when it does occur, covert mediational activity may fail to achieve functional control over behavior" (p. 151).

The nature of the normative developmental sequence described by Luria and found wanting in impulsive youngsters by Meichenbaum and others led Meichenbaum (1977) to seek to duplicate the sequence as a remedial intervention for youngsters deficient in such self-regulatory skills. As he comments,

> Could we systematically train hyperactive, impulsive youngsters to alter their problem-solving styles, to think before they act, in short, to talk to themselves differently? Could we, in light of the specific mediational deficits observed, teach the children how to (a) comprehend the task, (b) spontaneously produce mediators and strategies, and (c) use such mediators to guide, monitor, and control their performances? This was the challenge that sparked the development of self-instructional training. (p. 31)

Self-instructional Training for the Impulsive Youngster

In research on self-instructional training, the typical sequence of instructional procedures is as follows:

1. The therapist models task performance and self-instructs out loud while the child observes;
2. The child performs the task, instructing herself out loud as she does so;
3. The therapist models task performance and whispers self-instructions while the child observes;
4. The child performs the task, instructing herself in a whisper as she does so.
5. The therapist performs the task using covert self-instructions, with pauses and behavioral signs of thinking such as raising his eyes toward the ceiling or stroking his chin;
6. The child performs the task using covert self-instructions.

Meichenbaum and Goodman's (1971) initial use of these procedures yielded decreased impulsivity and enhanced reflectiveness (i.e., increased response time and decreased error rate) in samples of hyperactive youngsters in comparison with those in appropriate control conditions. Children indeed could learn, as the investigators put it, "to stop, look, and listen." This early research also showed that observing a model utilize covert self-instructions was not sufficient to obtain the desired outcome; the youngster had to covertly self-instruct also.

Other investigators reported essentially confirming results vis-à-vis impulsiveness and hyperactivity (Bornstein & Quevillon, 1976; Camp, Blom, Hebert, & VanDoorninck, 1977; Douglas, Parry, Marton, & Garson, 1976; Palkes, Stewart, & Kahana, 1968) and began extending the apparent utility of self-instructional training to other, often related, types of problem behaviors. These include problematic classroom behaviors (Monahan & O'Leary, 1971; Robin, Armel, & O'Leary, 1975), tolerance for resisting temptation (Hartig & Kanfer, 1973), pain (Turk, 1976), anxiety (Meichenbaum, Gilmore, & Fedoravicius, 1971), and, as we shall examine in detail shortly, anger and aggression.

Beyond confirming effectiveness, a number of these studies provide valuable information regarding conditions under which self-instructional training effects may be maximized. Bender (1976), for example, showed enhanced reduction in impulsivity when the child's covert self-instructions included explicit strategies rather than just general instructions. Kendall (1977), proceeding further in this direction toward concrete instructions, recommended that the content of self-instructions used by impulsive youngsters optimally should consist of the following:

1. Problem definition—for example, "Let's see, what am I supposed to do?"
2. Problem approach—for example, "Well, I should look this over and try to figure out how to get to the center of the maze."
3. Focusing of attention—for example, "I better look ahead so I don't get trapped."
4. Coping statements—for example, "Oh, that path isn't right. If I go that way I'll get stuck. I'll just go back here and try another way."
5. Self-reinforcement—for example, "Hey, not bad. I really did a good job."

As is true for all psychological and educational interventions, not all tests of the efficacy of self-instructional training have yielded results confirming its value. Nonconfirming investigations include those of Heath (1978), Higa (1973), Weinreich (1975), and Williams and

Heath (1978), Higa (1973), Weinreich (1975), and Williams and Akamatsu (1978). As is pointed out in our closing remarks in chapter 14, and as these several nonconfirming studies concretely highlight, all interventions—including self-instructional training—are optimally offered *prescriptively*. Self-instructional training appears to yield its hoped-for effects with some youngsters but not with others, and under some conditions but not under others. In a seminal discussion of this perspective entitled "Outcome Inconsistency and Moderator Variables," Kendall and Braswell (1985) marshaled evidence from a large number of investigations to indicate that the effectiveness of self-instructional training is influenced by the youngster's age, sex, socioeconomic status, cognitive level, attributional style, and apparent motivation. The importance of these and other prescriptive moderator variables upon performance in the context of self-instructional training has also been emphasized by Copeland (1981, 1982); Pressley (1979); Braswell, Kendall, and Urbain (1982); and Kopel and Arkowitz (1975).

Self-instructional Training for the Aggressive Youngster

In 1975, Novaco sought to apply the self-instructional training approach to the management of anger. By way of definition, he comments that

> the arousal of anger is here viewed as an affective stress reaction. That is, anger arousal is a response to perceived environmental demands— most commonly, aversive psychosocial events. . . . Anger is thought to consist of a combination of physiological arousal and cognitive labeling of that arousal as anger. . . . Anger arousal results from particular appraisals of aversive events. External circumstances provoke anger only as mediated by their meaning to the individual. (Novaco, 1979, pp. 252–253)

It is important to note the central role of affective arousal in forming this definition of anger. Novaco's attempt to apply self-instructional training to the management of anger was based not only upon the general success of such training in altering self-regulatory processes, but also upon a separate series of studies consistently showing the marked influence (increases and decreases) of covert self-verbalization upon a variety of arousal states. Rimm and Litvak (1969), for example, found that affectively loaded implicit self-statements increased both respiration rate and depth. Schwartz (1971), using similar procedures, found increased heart rate to result, and May and Johnson (1973) reported similar findings plus an effect of inner speech on skin conductance. Russell and Brandsma (1974) also found such skin conductance changes.

These findings, viewed in the context of the work of Luria, Meichenbaum, and others, led Novaco (1975) to conclude that "a basic premise is that anger is fomented, maintained, and influenced by the self-statements that are made in provocation situations" (p. 17). The intervention he constructed and examined for its anger control value consisted of three stages. In the first, *cognitive preparation*, the trainee is taught about the cognitive, physiological, and behavioral aspects of anger; its positive and negative functions; and especially its antecedents. During the second stage, *skill acquisition*, trainees learn alternative coping skills to utilize in response to provocations. It is here that special emphasis is placed upon self-instruction. The third phase, *application training*, makes use of imaginal and role-play inductions of anger and homework assignments to facilitate practice of the coping skills acquired—particularly skill in self-instruction. To operationalize this three-stage intervention, Novaco (1975) construed the process of self-instructing to control anger as necessarily responsive to all phases of the provocation sequence: (1) preparation for provocation, (2) impact and confrontation, (3) coping with arousal, and (4) reflecting on the provocation. Table 5 provides examples of the self-statements relevant to each phase that were rehearsed by Novaco's subjects in his evaluation of self-instruction for anger management.

Novaco's (1975) initial research subjects were 34 persons who were both self-identified and externally assessed as having serious anger control problems. Four treatment conditions were established: self-instructional training plus relaxation training, each of these two conditions separately, and an attention-control condition. The effect of these interventions was measured by self-report and physiological indices, subject response to role-played provocations, and anger diary ratings. Results indicated that across these outcome criteria the combined treatment, and to a lesser extent the self-instructional treatment alone, led to significant decreases in anger and significantly improved anger management. Novaco was able later to replicate this success both in a clinical case study (Novaco, 1977) and in a group comparison study involving probation officers (Novaco, 1978).

Atrops (1978); Crain (1977); and Schrader, Long, Panzer, Gillet, and Kornbath (1977) have each reported successful use of Novaco's self-instructional training with chronically angry adolescent or adult offenders. This result is buttressed substantially by numerous other investigations demonstrating a decrease in anger or aggression as a

Table 5
Examples of Self-statements Rehearsed in
Self-instructional Training for Anger Management

Preparing for provocation

This is going to upset me, but I know how to deal with it.

What is it that I have to do?

I can work out a plan to handle this.

I can manage the situation. I know how to regulate my anger.

If I find myself getting upset, I'll know what to do.

There won't be any need for an argument.

Try not to take this too seriously.

This could be a testy situation, but I believe in myself.

Time for a few deep breaths of relaxation. Feel comfortable, relaxed, and at ease.

Easy does it. Remember to keep your sense of humor.

Impact and confrontation

Stay calm. Just continue to relax.

As long as I keep my cool, I'm in control.

Just roll with the punches; don't get bent out of shape.

Think of what you want to get out of this.

You don't need to prove yourself.

There is no point in getting mad.

Don't make more out of this than you have to.

I'm not going to let him get to me.

Look for the positives. Don't assume the worst or jump to conclusions.

It's really a shame she has to act like this.

For someone to be that irritable, he must be awfully unhappy.

If I start to get mad, I'll just be banging my head against the wall, so I might as well just relax.

There is no need to doubt myself. What he says doesn't matter.

I'm on top of this situation and it's under control.

Coping with arousal

My muscles are starting to feel tight. Time to relax and slow things down.

Getting upset won't help.

It's just not worth it to get so angry.

I'll let him make a fool of himself.

Note. From *Anger Control: The Development and Evaluation of an Experimental Treatment* (pp. 95–96), by R. W. Novaco, Lexington, MA: D.C. Heath. Reprinted by permission.

Table 5 *(continued)*

I have a right to be annoyed, but let's keep the lid on.

Time to take a deep breath.

Let's take the issue point by point.

My anger is a signal of what I need to do. Time to instruct myself.

I'm not going to get pushed around, but I'm not going haywire either.

Try to reason it out. Treat each other with respect.

Let's try a cooperative approach. Maybe we are both right.

Negatives lead to more negatives. Work constructively.

He'd probably like me to get really angry. Well I'm going to disappoint him.

I can't expect people to act the way I want them to.

Take it easy; don't get pushy.

Reflecting on the provocation

   a. When conflict is unresolved

Forget about the aggravation. Thinking about it only makes you upset.

These are difficult situations, and they take time to straighten out.

Try to shake it off. Don't let it interfere with your job.

I'll get better at this as I get more practice.

Remember relaxation. It's a lot better than anger.

Can you laugh about it? It's probably not so serious.

Don't take it personally.

Take a deep breath.

   b. When conflict is resolved or coping is successful

I handled that one pretty well. It worked!

That wasn't as hard as I thought.

It could have been a lot worse.

I could have gotten more upset than it was worth.

I actually got through that without getting angry.

My pride can sure get me into trouble, but when I don't take things too seriously, I'm better off.

I guess I've been getting upset for too long when it wasn't even necessary.

I'm doing better at this all the time.

---

result of self-statements whose contents were a more benign, cognitive reinterpretation of the provoking experiences (Green & Murray, 1973; Kaufman & Feshbach, 1963; Mallick & McCandless, 1966; McCullough,

Huntsinger, & Nay, 1977; Moon & Eisler, 1983; Schlichter & Horan, 1981; Snyder & White, 1979; Stein & Davis, 1982), although, as we noted with respect to the self-instructional training of impulsive youngsters, there are exceptions to successful use with high-anger individuals (Coats, 1979; Urbain & Kendall, 1981).

Just as Meichenbaum needed to view the remediation of impulsivity in the light of Luria's insights about the normal development of self-regulation, and as Novaco needed Meichenbaum's impulsivity research results in order to extend self-instructional training to chronically angry individuals, the final psychologist in the lineage of Anger Control Training whose work we will summarize built upon the substantial foundation provided by Novaco. Eva Feindler and her research group have contributed greatly to the development of anger control training, with both important research findings and substantial refinements in technique (Feindler, 1979; Feindler & Fremouw, 1983; Feindler, Latini, Nape, Romano, & Doyle, 1980; Feindler, Marriott, & Iwata, 1984). This series of investigations provides consistent additional support for the anger control potency of the cognitive preparation/skill acquisition/application training sequence examined earlier by Novaco, especially for the self-instructional components. In addition, these investigations provide refinement of the Novaco three-stage sequence into a chain in which clients learn (1) *cues*—the physiological and kinesthetic sensations that signal level of anger arousal to the individual; (2) *triggers*—the external events and internal appraisals that serve as provocations to anger arousal; (3) *reminders*—the self-instructional statements that may function to reduce anger arousal (e.g., the statements in Table 5); (4) *reducers*—techniques that in combination with reminders may reduce anger arousal (e.g., deep breathing, backward counting, pleasant imagery, and consideration of long-term consequences); and (5) *self-evaluation*—the opportunity to self-reinforce and/or self-correct depending on how well or poorly the preceding steps have been implemented. Finally, in addition to the empirical evidence provided and procedural refinements created and examined, Feindler and Fremouw (1983) sound a welcome prescriptive note:

> Further delineation is needed on individual subject variables that may predict appropriateness for self-control treatment or account for differential responses to treatment. Variables such as age, length of residential treatment, nature of aggressive acts, attributional style, cognitive ability, level of social skills, family stability, and degree of peer involvement in antisocial acts may all help to predict adolescent responsiveness to treatment. (p. 482)

In our own work on Anger Control Training as one of three constituent procedures of Aggression Replacement Training (Goldstein & Glick, 1987), we thus stood on a series of broad and creative shoulders—those of Luria, Meichenbaum, Novaco, Feindler, and others. With our own relevant research findings, we hope we have provided worthy additions to this ongoing progression of research and development (Goldstein & Glick, 1987; Goldstein, Glick, Irwin, McCartney, & Rubama, in press; Reiner, 1985).

Training Procedures

The goal of the Anger Control Training program described in this section is to teach adolescents and younger children (1) to understand what causes them to feel angry and act aggressively and (2) to master techniques they can use to reduce their anger and aggression.* Many youngsters believe that in many situations they have no choice: The only way for them to respond is with aggression. Although they may perceive situations in this way, it is the goal of Anger Control Training to give them the skills necessary to make a choice. By learning what causes them to become angry and by learning how to use a series of anger reduction techniques, participating trainees will become more able to stop their almost "automatic" aggressive responses long enough to consider constructive alternatives, such as those that constitute several of the other Prepare Curriculum courses.

Conducting the Anger Control Training Group

The Anger Control Training program described in this chapter is comprised of 10 weekly sessions of 1 hour each. Many schools and agencies will devote more than a week to each Anger Control Training topic, thus converting the program to a one- or two-semester course. Others run the program as described here for 10 weeks or one semester and then provide more widely spaced booster sessions on a scheduled or as-needed basis during a second semester. Anger Control Training requires active participation by trainees, both during the training

---

*The remainder of this chapter is generally based on *The Art of Self-control,* by E. L. Feindler, 1981, unpublished manuscript, Adelphi University, Garden City, NY. Prepare Curriculum trainers will also benefit considerably from reading *Adolescent Anger Control: Cognitive-behavioral Techniques,* by E. L. Feindler and R. B. Ecton, 1987, New York: Pergamon.

sessions themselves and in completing assigned homework between sessions. Anger Control Training is an active process for the trainer as well. The trainer is required to model the proper use of the anger reduction techniques that are the core of the program, guide the role playing as trainees practice the program's subskills, and provide feedback about how successful this practice has been in matching the trainer's modeling. The following guidelines more fully describe this training sequence.

Modeling

All modeling begins with the trainer's describing the particular anger control technique or chain of techniques that will be demonstrated and a conflict situation in which the techniques(s) may be used. If there are two trainers available, they should both participate in the modeling, with one trainer being the *main actor* who demonstrates the technique(s) and the other being the *co-actor* who represents the person who provokes the main actor. When two trainers are not available, a group member may serve as the co-actor. In such cases, it is important to rehearse briefly with the co-actor in order to provide a realistic example of provocation in a conflict situation.

Once the conflict situation has been briefly described, the two actors then act out the scene, with the main actor *carefully and clearly using the anger control technique(s)*. Following the completion of the scene, the trainer summarizes the technique(s) used and briefly discusses them with the trainees. The following are some general guidelines for modeling:

1. At least two examples should be used for each demonstration;
2. Scenes that are relevant to the trainees' real-life situations should be selected;
3. All scenes should result in positive outcomes, never in aggressive acts;
4. The main actor should be portrayed as being reasonably similar to the people in the Anger Control Training group in age, socioeconomic background, verbal ability, and other salient characteristics.

Role Playing

Following each modeling presentation, trainees are asked to take part in role plays in which they practice the just-modeled anger control technique or chain of techniques in situations they have recently encountered or expect to encounter in the near future. The Hassle Log (Figure 5) is an ideal source for such situations. This form, completed weekly by trainees, describes current conflicts and the manner in which such conflicts were resolved. Once a trainee describes the conflict situation from his Hassle Log, he becomes the main actor in the role play and chooses a second trainee (the co-actor) to play the part of the other person in the conflict. The trainer then asks for enough information (time, place, etc.) from the main actor to set the stage for the role play. The scene is then played out with the main actor's applying the anger control technique(s) as accurately as possible.

In Anger Control Training, trainees learn a number of anger reduction techniques, some of which may prove more useful than others. One trainee may need only one technique to control anger, whereas others may need two, three, or more techniques in combination. The trainer is encouraged to help trainees try out in the role plays all of the different techniques so that each person can identify which are most useful. As the program progresses and the role plays call for anger reducers, the main actor should use any or all of the anger reduction techniques that are helpful and/or necessary to achieve greater self-control and anger reduction.

Some general role-playing guidelines for trainers are as follows:

1. Just before beginning, remind the trainees of their parts: The main actor must use the anger control technique(s), and the co-actor should try to stay in the role described in the scene;
2. Instruct the observing group members to pay attention to whether the anger control technique(s) are being used properly by the main actor;
3. If the role play is clearly departing from the anger control technique(s) to be practiced, stop the role play, give whatever instructions are needed, and then restart the role play;
4. Continue role playing until each trainee has had the opportunity to be the main actor and practice using the technique(s) already, or about to be, encountered.

Performance Feedback

After each role play, there should be a brief feedback period that points out to the main actor how well she used the technique(s) being practiced. This also provides the main actor with a chance to see how the use of the anger control technique(s) affected the co-actor, as well as provides the encouragement to try the technique(s) outside of the

Figure 5
Hassle Log

Name _____ Date _____

Morning _____ Afternoon _____ Evening _____

Where were you?

Classroom	_____	Bathroom	_____	Off grounds	_____
Dorm	_____	Team office	_____	Halls	_____
Gym	_____	Dining room	_____	On a job	_____
Recreation room	_____	Outside/on grounds	_____	Other	_____

What happened?

Somebody teased me. _____

Somebody took something of mine. _____

Somebody told me to do something. _____

Somebody was doing something I didn't like. _____

I did something wrong. _____

Somebody started fighting with me. _____

Other: _____

Who was that somebody:

Another student _____ Another adult _____ Other _____

Teacher _____ Staff member _____

What did you do?

Hit back	_____	Told adult	_____
Ran away	_____	Walked away calmly	_____
Yelled	_____	Talked it out	_____
Cried	_____	Told peer	_____
Broke something	_____	Ignored it	_____
Was restrained	_____	Used Anger Control	_____

How did you handle yourself?

1	2	3	4	5
Poorly	Not so well	OK	Good	Great

How angry were you?

	Really	Moderately	Mildly angry but	Not angry
Burning _____	angry _____	angry _____	still OK _____	at all _____

training sessions. The feedback should be sequenced in the following manner: (1) The co-actor is asked to react; (2) the observers are asked to comment on how well the technique was used; and (3) the trainers comment on how well the technique was used and provide reinforcement as appropriate (praise, approval, encouragement). As recommended earlier in conjunction with the use of reinforcement following role playing in Interpersonal Skills Training (see chapter 3), we recommend several guidelines for providing effective reinforcement:

1. Provide reinforcement only after role plays in which the technique was used properly;
2. Provide reinforcement to the co-actor for help and cooperation;
3. Provide a degree of reinforcement that matches the quality of the role play;
4. Provide no reinforcement when the role play departs significantly from using the specific technique;
5. Provide reinforcement for a trainee's improvement over previous role plays in the use of the techniques.

After the feedback is provided, give the main actor an opportunity to make comments on both the role play and the feedback just received.

Program Sessions

We now wish to describe the procedures that constitute a 10-session Anger Control Training program. Table 6 offers a general overview of session goals and activities.

Week 1: Introduction

Explaining Program Goals
In the first session, it is necessary to introduce the program, "sell it" to the trainees, and get their commitment to participate. The basic introduction involves talking with the trainees about how being angry and aggressive can at times lead to trouble with authorities (police, school), with peers, and with others, as well as how such behavior causes them to feel about themselves. The following suggestions will help the trainer convince trainees that learning to achieve greater control of their anger is a worthwhile goal.

The trainer can give examples of admired people who have excellent self-control—for example, Bruce Lee and Sugar Ray Leonard. These people would not/could not be successful by being out of control.

Table 6
General Overview of Anger Control Training

Week 1: Introduction
1. Explain the goals of Anger Control Training and "sell it" to the youngsters.
2. Explain the rules for participating and the training procedures.
3. Give initial assessments of the *A-B-C*s of aggressive behavior: (*A*) What led up to it? (*B*) What did you do? (*C*) What were the consequences?
4. Review goals, procedures, and *A-B-C*s; give out binders.

Week 2: Cues and Anger Reducers 1, 2, and 3
1. Review first session.
2. Introduce the Hassle Log.
3. Discuss how to know when you are angry (cues).
4. Discuss what to do when you know you are angry.
   - Anger reducer 1: Deep breathing
   - Anger reducer 2: Backward counting
   - Anger reducer 3: Pleasant imagery
5. Role play: Cues + anger reducers.
6. Review Hassle Log, cues, and anger reducers 1, 2 and 3.

Week 3: Triggers
1. Review second session.
2. Discuss understanding what makes you angry (triggers).
   - External triggers
   - Internal triggers
3. Role play: Triggers + cues + anger reducer(s).
4. Review triggers, cues, and anger reducers 1, 2, and 3.

Week 4: Reminders (Anger Reducer 4)
1. Review third session.
2. Introduce reminders.
3. Model using reminders.
4. Role play: Triggers + cues + reminders + anger reducer(s).
5. Review reminders.

Week 5: Self-evaluation
1. Review fourth session.
2. Introduce self-evaluation.
   - Self-rewarding
   - Self-coaching
3. Role play: Triggers + cues + reminders + anger reducer(s) + self-evaluation.
4. Review self-evaluation.

Table 6 *(continued)*

Week 6: Thinking Ahead (Anger Reducer 5)
1. Review fifth session.
2. Introduce thinking ahead.
   - Short- and long-term consequences
   - Most and least serious consequences
   - Internal, external, and social consequences
3. Role play: "If–then" thinking ahead.
4. Role play: Triggers + cues + reminders + anger reducer(s) + self-evaluation.
5. Review thinking ahead.

Week 7: The Angry Behavior Cycle
1. Review sixth session.
2. Introduce the Angry Behavior Cycle.
   - Identifying your own anger-provoking behavior
   - Changing your own anger-provoking behavior
3. Role play: Triggers + cues + reminders + anger reducer(s) + self-evaluation.
4. Review the Angry Behavior Cycle

Week 8: Rehearsal of Full Sequence
1. Review seventh session.
2. Introduce using new behaviors (skills) in place of aggression.
3. Role play: Triggers + cues + reminders + anger reducer(s) + interpersonal skill + self-evaluation.

Week 9: Rehearsal of Full Sequence
1. Review Hassle Logs.
2. Role play: Triggers + cues + reminders + anger reducer(s) + interpersonal skill + self-evaluation.

Week 10: Overall Review
1. Review Hassle Logs.
2. Recap anger control techniques.
3. Role play: Triggers + cues + reminders + anger reducer(s) + interpersonal skill + self-evaluation.
4. Reinforce and encourage to continue.

These examples help make the point that having more self-control *does not* mean that the trainees will be pushed around or be "wimps."

After providing the examples, the trainer explains how greater self-control means greater personal power. Trainees are *more powerful* when they are in control of their reactions to others despite the attempts of others to provoke them. By being aggressive, they allow others to control them.

Explaining rules and procedures

As with all Prepare classes, relevant rules and course procedures need to be structured at the outset. It should be stressed that each trainee is expected to participate actively, cooperatively, and with respect for the other trainees. Homework will be given and used as the material for the next session; therefore, completion of the homework is required for the success of the program. The homework will require each trainee to complete a Hassle Log each week (see Figure 5). Different techniques for anger reduction will be taught by (1) explanations and demonstrations by the trainer and (2) practice in the form of role playing by trainees. Trainees will get to role play the anger control techniques in the situations they describe in their Hassle Logs so that the next time that situation or a similar one occurs, they will have the choice of doing something other than getting angry.

Giving initial assessments of the A-B-Cs

The trainer should explain to the group how each conflict situation has three steps: A—What triggered the problem? What led up to it? B—What did you do (the actual response to A)? and C—What were the consequences to you and to the other person? Then the trainer gives examples of how she has handled some conflicts, being sure to point out the A, B, and C steps. Finally, trainees give examples, and the trainer helps them identify the A, B, and C steps operating in the situation.

Reviewing

A brief review of the reasons for developing greater self-control, the rules and procedures of the group, and the A–B–Cs ends the meeting.

Week 2: Cues and Anger Reducers 1, 2, and 3

Reviewing the first session

Trainees should be reminded that they increase their personal power by having control over their reactions to others. Again, providing examples of popular sports figures who demonstrate exceptional self-control that leads to success is helpful. The trainer should review the rules and procedures, emphasizing that this program will involve learning anger control techniques by watching them being demonstrated and then practicing them. Then the trainer goes over the A–B–C model of conflicts, reminding the group of the three steps in each conflict. The trainer gives an example and asks a few trainees for examples that occurred in the past week.

Introducing the Hassle Log

The trainer shows the group an example of the Hassle Log (and asks someone different to read each item. Then he explains the importance of the log: (1) It provides an accurate picture of conflicts that occur during the week; (2) it helps trainees learn about what makes them angry and how they handle these situations (so that they can work to change those that they handle poorly, that cause them trouble, and that leave them feeling bad about themselves); and (3) it provides material for role playing in future sessions (using situations that really happen makes practicing the anger control techniques much more effective than using "made-up" situations). At this point, the trainer gives an example of a conflict and how to fill out the Hassle Log for it. The Hassle Log should be filled out for situations that trainees handle well in addition to those in which they become angry or aggressive. The trainer makes sure each trainee understands how to complete the Hassle Log by having each of them fill out a log in the session for a recent hassle. Then the trainer checks the logs and corrects any misunderstanding of the instructions. Trainees receive a stack of Hassle Logs and are instructed to fill one out as soon as possible after an incident.

Discussing cues

People have individual physical signs that let them know they are angry (e.g., muscle tension, a knot in the stomach, clenched fists, grinding teeth, or a pounding heart). The trainer should give some examples of the signs that let her know when she is angry and explain that individuals must know they are angry before they can use self-control to reduce their anger. Next, the trainees try to identify their own and each other's warning signs by role playing short conflict situations. The trainer gives feedback on how well each trainee could identify the warning signs or cues.

Discussing anger reducers 1, 2, and 3

Now that the trainees have begun to be able to identify their anger warning signs (cues), they can start to make use of anger reduction techniques to increase their self-control and personal power when they notice themselves getting angry. Any or all of the three anger reducers can be a first step in a chain of new behaviors giving the trainees greater self-control and the time needed to decide how to respond most effectively. The key sequence here is that noticing the cues leads to use of an anger reducer. As the trainer presents each of the three anger reducers, he models its use, has the trainees role play the sequence "cues + anger reducer," and then gives feedback on the role plays.

Anger reducer 1: Deep breathing. Taking a few slow, deep breaths can help in making a more controlled response in a pressure situation. Examples from sports of taking a few deep breaths can be presented (e.g., in basketball—before taking important foul shots—and in boxing). Trainees are reminded about their signs of being angry and how deep breathing can reduce tension by relieving physical symptoms of tension. Then the trainer models, has trainees role play, and gives feedback on the sequence of "cues + deep breathing."

Anger reducer 2: Backward counting. A second method of reducing one's level of anger arousal is to count silently backward (at an even pace) from 20 to 1 when faced with a provocative situation. Trainees should be instructed to turn away from the provoking person or situation, if appropriate, while counting. Counting backward is also a way of gaining time to think about how to respond most effectively. The trainer models, helps trainees role play, and gives feedback on the sequence of "cues + backward counting."

Anger reducer 3: Pleasant imagery. A third way of reducing tension in an anger-arousing situation is to imagine a peaceful scene that has a calming effect (e.g., "You are lying on the beach. The sun is warm, and there is a slight breeze."). The trainees are encouraged to think of scenes they find relaxing. Then the trainer models, helps the trainees role play, and gives feedback on the sequence of "cues + pleasant imagery."

Reviewing

The trainer reviews the Hassle Log and reminds the group of the importance of completing it. Each member's warning signs of anger (cues) and the three anger reducers are reviewed. Homework is given in which the trainees will attempt to use each of the three anger reducers during one situation in the coming week in which they notice that they are getting angry. Trainees note on their Hassle Logs for that situation which anger reducer they used.

Week 3: Triggers

Reviewing the second session

The trainer reviews the cues and anger reducers taught in Session 2 by going over the completed Hassle Logs for those situations in which trainees used one of the three anger reducers assigned in the homework from the last session. Reinforcement is provided for those trainees who successfully used the reducers following the identification of the warning signs (cues) of being angry. The trainer checks to be sure the Hassle Logs are filled out properly.

Discussing triggers

The trainer reviews the idea that each conflict situation has an *A* (trigger), a *B* (behavior), and a *C* (consequence). In this session, the focus will be on the *A* step, or trigger. The goal is to help trainees identify things that trigger, or arouse, their anger. Both external and internal triggers will be described.

External triggers are things done by one person that make another person angry. External triggers may be something others say to a trainee (e.g., being told what to do or being called a name) or they may be nonverbal (e.g., a push or an obscene gesture). The trainer helps trainees identify one or more external triggers (verbal or nonverbal) that led to their becoming angry or aggressive during the last few weeks. Almost always, it takes more than just an external trigger to lead to anger arousal and aggressive behavior: What youngsters think or say to themselves (*internal triggers*) when faced with an external trigger is of crucial importance in whether or not they become angry. Youngsters will often say things to themselves such as "That SOB is making fun of me," "He's making me look like a wimp," or "I'm going to tear that guy's head off." These self-statements are the internal triggers that often combine with external triggers to lead to aggressive behavior. Helping trainees identify their internal triggers sets the stage for the next session, in which they will learn how to replace internal triggers that make them angry with positive self-statements, or reminders, that reduce their anger in conflict situations.

Role playing

The trainer models, helps the trainees role play, and gives feedback on the following chain: "triggers (external and internal) + cues + anger reducer(s) (any or all of 1, 2, and 3)." For these role plays and all others, situations from the Hassle Logs are used. In this session's role playing, the emphasis is on identifying the internal triggers. Examples of situations that have been used for this role play include (1) sports situations in which someone is deliberately tripped or fouled, (2) getting into trouble for something one didn't do, and (3) feeling lied to by a peer or adult.

Reviewing

The trainer reviews the chain of events taught so far, including the idea of internal and external triggers, the cues for recognizing anger, and the use of anger reducers 1, 2, and 3.

Week 4: Reminders (Anger Reducer 4)

Reviewing the third session

The trainer briefly reviews the definitions of internal and external triggers by going through the completed Hassle Logs with the group and having them identify the internal and external triggers for one hassle for each of the trainees.

Introducing reminders

Reminders are statements that can be used to help increase success in provocative situations of all types. They are, in a sense, the opposite of internal triggers. Internal triggers are self-statements that increase anger arousal. Reminders are self-instructional statements intended to lower such arousal. Some examples of reminders that can be used during such situations in sports are (1) "Bend your knees and follow through" when making a foul shot in a basketball game and (2) "Watch out for his left" or "Jab and then hook" when boxing. Trainees should suggest several reminders of this type that they do use or could use. These reminders can be written on the board. Some possible reminders for conflict situations include "Take it easy," "Cool it," "Slow down," "Chill out," "Ignore it," and "Take a deep breath."

Modeling using reminders

The trainer should model the use of appropriate reminders to increase self-control and personal power in conflict situations as opposed to using internal triggers (e.g., "Cool it" versus "I'll kill him"). At first, it is useful for trainees to say the reminders out loud, but over time and with practice, the goal is to be able to "say" them silently—that is, to think them. This goal can be accomplished by gradually decreasing the frequency of saying a reminder out loud and increasing the frequency of saying a reminder silently. The trainer explains that a reminder should be used at the right time (not too early and not too late) and emphasizes that trainees must make a choice to use a reminder in a conflict situation.

Role playing
The trainer models the chain "triggers + cues + reminders + anger reducer(s)." Then trainees role play conflict situations from their Hassle Logs in which the main actor (1) identifies the external and internal triggers, (2) identifies the cues of anger, and (3) uses reminders and anger reducers 1, 2, and 3 (any or all). If the main actor is having trouble using the reminders, it may be helpful for the trainer to say examples of them quietly at the proper time. Focus in the role play should be on going from "out loud" reminders to silent ones. The trainer gives feedback on the role plays, particularly on the use of the reminders and anger reducers.

Reviewing
The trainer summarizes the use of reminders, their timing, and the rationale for their use. Then trainees are given index cards and asked to select and write down three reminders that they feel they might use in the coming week. As homework, trainees are instructed to use each of these reminders during hassles that arise during the week and to note in the Hassle Log for that situation the reminder they used.

Week 5: Self-evaluation

Reviewing the fourth session
The trainer reviews reminders by having each trainee relate a hassle from the past week in which she used a reminder from the ones written down in the last session and assigned as homework. The group is reminded about the *A–B–C* model, and each trainee is asked about the consequences to self and others of having used the reminder. Again, "out loud" and silent reminders are distinguished. The outcome of using the reminder is evaluated: Did the reminder work? If not, what went wrong?

Introducing self-evaluation
Self-evaluation is a way for trainees to (1) judge for themselves how well they have handled a conflict, (2) reward themselves for handling it well (self-rewarding), or (3) help themselves find out how they could have handled it better (self-coaching). Basically, self-evaluation uses a

set of reminders that can be used *after* a conflict situation. The trainer should present some statements that trainees can use to reward themselves (e.g., "I really kept cool" or "I was really in control") and to coach themselves when they have failed to remain in control in a conflict situation (e.g., "I need to pay more attention to my cues"). Then each trainee should generate a list of self-rewarding and self-coaching statements to use in the situations from the Hassle Logs. These statements are gone over individually and as a group.

Role playing

The trainer models the chain "triggers + cues + reminders + anger reducer(s) + self-evaluation." The reminders technique (anger reducer 4) is so important that it should always be included in the role-playing chain in addition to any or all of the other anger reducers taught so far. In this modeling, both self-rewarding and self-coaching self-evaluation statements are emphasized. Next, the trainer conducts role plays from Hassle Log situations in which the main actor carries out all of the following steps: (1) identifies external and internal triggers; (2) identifies cues of anger; (3) uses reminders plus anger reducer(s) 1, 2, and 3 (any or all); and (4) evaluates his performance, either rewarding or coaching himself. The trainer provides feedback on the role play with an emphasis on self-evaluation.

Reviewing

The two types of self-evaluation are reviewed. Then the trainer assigns homework requiring trainees to list on their Hassle Logs self-evaluation statements following conflicts (resolved or unresolved) that occur in the coming week.

Week 6: Thinking Ahead (Anger Reducer 5)

Reviewing the fifth session

The trainer reviews self-evaluation by going over the Hassle Logs for the self-rewarding and self-coaching statements written down as the homework assigned last session.

Introducing thinking ahead

Thinking ahead is another way of controlling anger in a conflict situation by judging the likely future consequences for current behavior. The trainer refers to the *A–B–C* model and explains that thinking ahead helps a trainee figure out what the *C* (consequence) will probably be before she decides what to do. The sentence "If I do this now, then this will probably happen later" is a good way to illustrate consequential thinking.

The trainer should distinguish between short- and long-term consequences, encouraging trainees to consider the long-term results over the short-term ones (e.g., short term—"If I slug him now, he'll shut up"; long term—"If I slug him now, my probation will probably get extended 3 months"). Trainees are asked to list short- and long-term consequences of specific aggressive acts they have engaged in during the last 2 months.

Next, trainees talk about the most and least serious consequences of being aggressive. Trainees are encouraged to list a series of consequences that might follow from an aggressive act they have engaged in during the last 2 months.

Finally, the trainer explains the difference between the internal and external consequences of being aggressive (e.g., external—going back to court, having to spend another 3 months in an institutional facility; internal—feeling terrible about yourself, losing self-respect). The trainer also talks about social consequences like losing friends or being excluded from a group. Group members each list negative external, internal, and social consequences of being aggressive and enumerate the positive consequences of using self-control.

Role playing: "If–then" thinking ahead

Using situations from the Hassle Logs, the trainer models, helps trainees role play, and gives feedback on the "if (I act aggressively), then (this will probably be the consequence)" thinking ahead procedure. Negative consequences are emphasized as additional reminders not to act aggressively.

Role playing anger control chain

The trainer models the chain "triggers + cues + reminders + anger reducer(s) + self-evaluation." Then she conducts role plays from the Hassle Log situations in which the main actor follows all of the above steps and uses any or all of anger reducers 1, 2, 3, and now 5 (thinking ahead). The trainer gives feedback on the role plays.

Reviewing

The reasons to use thinking ahead, the different types of consequences to aggression, and the "if–then" statements are reviewed. Then the trainer assigns as homework to use thinking ahead in two conflict situations in the coming week and to write the "if–then" statement on the Hassle Log for that situation.

Week 7: The Angry Behavior Cycle

Reviewing the sixth session
The trainer reviews thinking ahead by going over with the group the completed Hassle Logs, in which the trainees wrote down, as part of their homework, the "if–then" statements used in conflict situations in the past week.

Introducing the Angry Behavior Cycle
Until this point in the program, the focus has been on what to do when someone else makes one angry. Naturally, there are things that everyone does that can make other people angry and lead to conflicts. This session focuses on what trainees do to make other people angry.

The trainer should give some examples of things that he does that are very likely to make others angry (e.g., calling someone a name, making fun of a person's appearance). Trainees then think about and list three things they do that make other people angry at them. If the trainer feels the group can handle some confrontation, trainees can respectfully tell another group member what that person does to make them angry.

The trainer gets an agreement from each trainee to try to change these problematic behaviors in the coming week, perhaps by using the thinking ahead procedure ("If I do this, then this person may get angry and the situation may get out of hand"). Changing even one behavior may prevent some conflicts and lead to trainees' being better liked or having more friends.

Role playing
This role play is designed to allow practice of all the anger control techniques taught so far. The trainer models the full chain of "triggers + cues + reminders + anger reducer(s) + self-evaluation." Then the trainer conducts role plays of this chain, encouraging the main actor to use any or all of anger reducers 1, 2, 3, and 5 in addition to all the other steps. She then gives feedback on the role plays.

Reviewing
The trainer reviews the behaviors that each trainee has identified as often making other people angry. Trainees are reminded of their

agreement to try in the coming week to change at least one of the three behaviors they identified as being part of their Angry Behavior Cycle.

Week 8: Rehearsal of Full Sequence

Reviewing the seventh session
The trainer reviews the Angry Behavior Cycle—the idea that, in addition to getting angry at what other people do, we do things that make other people angry. He goes over with the trainees their attempts at changing their own anger-provoking behavior (the procedures they agreed to try in the last session).

Introducing using new behaviors
So far, Anger Control Training has worked to teach the trainees what *not* to do (be aggressive) and how *not* to do it (the anger control techniques). Although these are important accomplishments, trainees also need to learn what *to* do in place of being aggressive. In other words, they need to know how to meet the demands of provocative life situations constructively and in a satisfying manner without needing to resort to aggression. During the weeks that have passed since the beginning of the program, trainees may simultaneously participate in Interpersonal Skills Training (see chapter 3), in which they learn a series of new skills to use in getting along better with others and in handling life situations in an effective way. The last 3 weeks of Anger Control Training is the time to help the trainees practice putting together the anger control techniques and the new skills learned in Interpersonal Skills Training. In this way, trainees will have considerable practice in knowing what not to do in conflict situations and in being able to behave in a constructive, satisfying, and nonaggressive way instead. The trainer explains to the group that this week and the next 2 weeks will be spent doing role plays that use all the anger control techniques and add some of the skills they have learned in Interpersonal Skills Training.

Role playing
The trainer conducts role plays from situations in trainees' Hassle Logs that follow the entire sequence: "triggers + cues + reminders + anger reducer(s) + interpersonal skill + self-evaluation." Then she gives feedback on the role plays, focusing on how well all the steps were put together.

Week 9: Rehearsal of Full Sequence

Reviewing the Hassle Logs
The trainer goes over the completed Hassle Logs to reinforce how well the trainees are using all of the anger control techniques and beginning to add the use of the interpersonal skills.

Role playing
Role playing and feedback are continued using the entire series of steps: "triggers + cues + reminders + anger reducer(s) + interpersonal skill + self-evaluation."

Week 10: Overall Review

Reviewing the Hassle Logs
The trainer goes over the completed Hassle Logs to continue reinforcing trainees' new ways of handling conflict situations. It may be helpful to bring to this session some Hassle Logs for each trainee from very early in the program to compare against those filled out for this last week.

Recapping anger control techniques
All of the anger control techniques taught in the program should be briefly recapped: (1) increasing personal power through self-control; (2) the A–B–C model; (3) cues of being angry; (4) internal and external triggers; (5) anger reducers 1, 2, and 3; (6) using reminders; (7) self-evaluation; (8) thinking ahead; and (9) the Angry Behavior Cycle.

Role playing
The trainer conducts role plays and gives feedback using the full chain: "triggers + cues + reminders + anger reducer(s) + interpersonal skill + self-evaluation."

Reinforcing and encouraging continuation
If appropriate, the trainer lets the group know that they have learned how to control their anger, increase their personal power, be better liked and respected, and stay out of future trouble caused by aggression. Each of them now has a choice to make: to use or not use what has been learned. There may of course be times in which trainees have no choice but to defend themselves with aggression. There are, however, many situations in which they do have a choice; it's up to them to make the decision.

Chapter 6

Moral Reasoning Training

Throughout history adults have been involved in teaching children what is the "right" or "wrong" action to take in a particular situation.* Adults have also tried to teach children why one "ought" to behave in a certain manner. Unfortunately, with changing values and rules for appropriate behavior in today's complex society, youth are faced with many values-relevant but ambiguous situations. They are confronted with questions regarding what values are worthwhile, how to apply the values they do hold, and how to behave when two values conflict with each other. Moral Reasoning Training is designed to help youth deal with these difficult situations.

Theory and Research

Although its historical roots are diverse and include the thinking and investigative energy of numerous developmental, educational, social, and experimental psychologists, educators, and philosophers, the Moral Reasoning Training method presented in this chapter is largely the product of its primary contemporary developer and proponent, Lawrence Kohlberg.

Critical Assumptions

Primarily using Piaget's cognitive-developmental approach to moral development (Lickona, 1976; Piaget, 1932) and moral philosophy as the foundation for his theory, Kohlberg postulated that investigations of moral reasoning should encompass those situations "in which conflicting interests and values lie, and [where] morality involves reasoning and problem-solving abilities which can be used to resolve these conflicts" (cited in Edelman & Goldstein, 1981, p. 286). Specifying precisely what these reasoning and problem-solving abilities involve has been a major focus of Kohlberg's work for many years. From this

---

*An earlier version of this chapter first appeared in *Aggression Replacement Training: A Comprehensive Intervention for Aggressive Youth*, by A. P. Goldstein and B. Glick, 1987, Champaign, IL: Research Press.

research, Kohlberg (1971a) was able to delineate three criteria that could be used to determine whether an act or decision involved a moral component: *prescriptivity*, meaning that the ethical demands of the decision can be recognized by everyone; *universality*, meaning that the decision originates from an internal sense of duty; and *primacy*, describing the notion that nonmoral considerations are evaluated after moral ones have been examined. Although Kohlberg maintains that these criteria provide some insight into the meaning of morality, it is not until the concept of justice is incorporated that its essence unfolds.

In fact, Kohlberg argues that morality can be conceptualized primarily as the "principle of justice," which he describes as the basic understanding and acceptance of the value and equality of all human beings and as a reciprocity in all human interactions (Edelman & Goldstein, 1981). Specifically, Kohlberg (1969) states that

> justice is not a rule or a set of rules; it is a moral principle. By a moral principle we mean a mode of choosing which is universal, a rule choosing which we want all people to adopt in all situations. . . . There are exceptions to rules, then, but no exception to principles. . . . There is only one principled basis for resolving claims: justice or equality. . . . A moral principle is not only a rule of action but a reason for action. As a reason for action, justice is called respect for persons. (pp. 69–70)

The importance of "justice" in Kohlberg's theory is further reflected in his description of the structure of the six stages of moral reasoning (see Table 7) and their contents (see Table 8). It becomes apparent from these tables that a "sense of justice" becomes progressively more integrated and increasingly complex for individuals as stage level progresses.

It is important to note that Kohlberg does not believe that an individual reasons at only one stage in all situations. Rather, he sees people as reasoning primarily at one stage and secondarily at adjacent stages, either one stage below or above the predominant stage (Kohlberg, 1969). It is within this formulation that Kohlberg explains an individual's variability in responses to the Moral Judgment Interview (a method he developed to assess levels of moral development). This interview involves the presentation of a series of stories, all of which incorporate a moral dilemma that can be resolved by a number of alternative actions. Generally, the dilemma involves a conflict between behaving by conforming to authority figures or legal-social rules and responding in accordance with the welfare or needs of others (Arbuth-

Table 7
Kohlberg's Six Stages of Moral Development

I. Preconventional Level
At this level, the child is responsive to cultural rules and labels of good and bad and right or wrong, but interprets these labels in terms of either the physical or the hedonistic consequences of action (punishment, reward, exchange of favors) or in terms of the physical power of those who enunciate the rules and labels. The level comprises the following two stages:

Stage 1: Punishment and Obedience Orientation
The physical consequences of an action determine its goodness or badness regardless of the human meaning or value of the consequences. Avoidance of punishment and unquestioning deference to power are valued in their own right, not in terms of respect for an underlying moral order supported by punishment and authority (the latter being Stage 4).

Stage 2: Instrumental Relativist Orientation
Right action consists of that which instrumentally satisfies one's own needs and, occasionally, the needs of others. Human relations are viewed in terms similar to those of the marketplace. Elements of fairness, or reciprocity, and equal sharing are present, but they are always interpreted in a physical, pragmatic way. Reciprocity is a matter of "you scratch my back and I'll scratch yours," not of loyalty, gratitude, or justice.

II. Conventional Level
At this level, maintaining the expectations of the individual's family, group, or nation is perceived as valuable in its own right, regardless of immediate and obvious consequences. The attitude is one not only of conformity to personal expectations and social order, but of loyalty to it, of actively maintaining, supporting, and justifying the order and of identifying with the persons or groups involved in it. This level comprises the following two stages:

Stage 3: Interpersonal Concordance, or "Good Boy–Nice Girl" Orientation
Good behavior is that which pleases or helps others and is approved by them. There is much conformity to stereotypical images of what is majority or "natural" behavior. Behavior is frequently judged by intention: "He means well" becomes important for the first time. One earns approval by being "nice."

Note. From "Stages of Moral Development as a Basis for Moral Education," by L. Kohlberg. In *Moral Education: Interdisciplinary Approaches* (pp. 86–88), edited by C. M. Beck, B. S. Crittendon, and E. V. Sullivan, 1971, Toronto: University of Toronto Press. Reprinted by permission.

Table 7 *(continued)*

Stage 4: "Law and Order" Orientation
There is orientation toward authority, fixed rules, and the maintenance of
the social order. Right behavior consists of doing one's duty, showing
respect for authority, and maintaining the given social order for its own
sake.

III. Postconventional, Autonomous, or Principled Level
At this level, there is a clear effort to define moral values and principles
that have validity and application apart from the authority of the groups or
persons holding these principles and apart from the individual's own identification with these groups. This level again has two stages:

Stage 5: Social-Contract Legalistic Orientation
Generally, this stage has utilitarian overtones. Right action tends to be
defined in terms of general individual rights and in terms of standards that
have been critically examined and agreed upon by the whole society.
There is a clear awareness of the relativism of personal values and opinions and a corresponding emphasis on procedural rules for teaching consensus. Aside from what is constitutionally and democratically agreed
upon, the right is a matter of personal "values" and "opinion." The result is
an emphasis upon the "legal point of view," but with an emphasis upon
the possibility of changing law in terms of rational considerations of social
utility (rather than freezing it in terms of Stage 4 "law and order"). Outside
the legal realm, free agreement and contract are the binding elements of
obligation. This is the "official" morality of the United States government
and Constitution.

Stage 6: Universal Ethical-Principle Orientation
Right is defined by the decision of conscience in accord with self-chosen
ethical principles appealing to logical comprehensiveness, universality, and
consistency. These principles are abstract and ethical; they are not concrete
moral rules like the Ten Commandments. At heart, these are universal
principles of justice, the reciprocity and equality of human rights, and respect
for the dignity of human beings as individual persons.

---

not & Faust, 1981). The participant is asked to determine which action
the character in the story should take and why. Through a series of
probe questions, it is believed that the participant's decision-making
processes concerning the resolution of these dilemmas as they relate
to specific moral issues (e.g., value of human life, laws and rules,
punishment and justice, truth and contract, property rights) can be
ascertained. In addition, Kohlberg maintains that this technique can be
used to investigate the major hypotheses underlying his theory. It is a

Table 8
The Content of the Moral Reasoning Stages

Stage	What Is Right	Reasons for Doing Right	Social Perspective
		Level I—Preconventional	
Stage 1—Heteronomous morality	Avoidance of breaking rules backed by punishment; obedience for its own sake; avoidance of physical damage to persons and property.	Avoidance of punishment and the superior power of authority.	*Egocentric point of view.* Doesn't consider the interests of others or recognize that they differ from one's own. Doesn't relate two points of view. Actions are considered physically rather than in terms of psychological interests of others. Confusion of authority's perspective with one's own.
Stage 2—Individualism, instrumental purpose, and exchange	Following rules only when it is to someone's immediate interest; acting to meet one's own interests and needs and letting others do the same. Right is also what is fair, an equal exchange, a deal, an agreement.	Serving one's own needs or interests in a world where one recognizes that other people have their interests, too.	*Concrete individualistic perspective.* Aware that everybody has his own interest to pursue and that these interests conflict, so that right is relative (in the concrete individualistic sense).

Note: From "Moral Stages and Moralization: The Cognitive-developmental Approach," by L. Kohlberg. In *Moral Development and Behavior: Theory, Research, and Social Issues* (pp. 34–35), edited by T. Lickona, 1976, New York: Holt, Rinehart, & Winston. Reprinted by permission.

Table 8 (*continued*)

Stage	What Is Right	Reasons for Doing Right	Social Perspective
		Level II—Conventional	
Stage 3—Mutual inter-personal expecta-tions, relationships, and interpersonal conformity	Living up to what is expected by the people one is close to or what others generally expect of people in one's role as son, daugh-ter, brother, sister, or friend, etc. "Being good" is impor-tant and means having good motives and showing con-cern about others. It also means keeping mutual rela-tionships, such as trust, loyalty, respect, and gratitude.	The need to be a good per-son in one's own eyes and those of others. Caring for others. Belief in the Golden Rule. Desire to maintain rules and authority that sup-port stereotypical good behavior.	*Perspective of the individual in relationships with other individuals.* Aware of shared feelings, agreements, and expectations that take pri-macy over individual inter-ests. Relates points of view through the concrete Golden Rule, putting oneself in the other guy's shoes. Does not yet consider generalized system perspective.
Stage 4—Social system and conscience	Fulfilling the actual duties to which one has agreed. Laws are to be upheld except in extreme cases where they conflict with other fixed social duties. Right is also defined as contributing to society, the group, or institution.	Keeping the institution going as a whole; avoiding the breakdown in the system that would occur "if every-one did it", or obeying the imperative of conscience to meet one's defined obliga-tions. (Easily confused with Stage 3 belief in rules and authority.)	*Differentiates societal point of view from interpersonal agreement or motives.* Takes the point of view of the sys-tem that defines roles and rules. Considers individual relations in terms of place in the system.

Level III—Postconventional, or Principled

Stage 5—Social contract or utility and individual rights	Being aware that people hold a variety of values and opinions and that most values and rules are relative to the group. These relative rules should usually be upheld, however, in the interest of impartiality and because they are the social contract. Some nonrelative values and rights like life and liberty, however, must be upheld in any society and regardless of majority opinion.	A sense of obligation to law because of one's social contract to make and abide by laws for the welfare of all and for the protection of all people's rights. A feeling of contractual commitment, freely entered upon, to family, friendship, trust, and work obligations. Concern that laws and duties be based on rational calculation of overall utility, "the greatest good for the greatest number."	*Prior-to-society perspective.* Perspective of a rational individual aware of values and rights prior to social attachments and contracts. Integrates perspectives by formal mechanisms of agreement, contract objective impartiality, and due process. Considers moral and legal points of view; recognizes that they sometimes conflict and finds it difficult to integrate them.

281

Table 8 *(continued)*

Stage	What is Right	Reasons for Doing Right	Social Perspective
Stage 6—Universal ethical principles	Following self-chosen ethical principles. Particular laws or social agreements are usually valid because they rest on such principles. When laws violate these principles, one acts in accordance with the principle. Principles are universal principles of justice: The equality of human rights and respect for the dignity of human beings as individual persons.	The belief as a rational person in the validity of universal moral principles and a sense of personal commitment to them.	*Perspective of a moral point of view from which social arrangements derive.* Perspective is that of any rational individual recognizing the nature of morality or the fact that persons are ends in themselves and must be treated as such.

theory that rests upon a cognitive-developmental framework concerned with thinking about rules, laws, and principles (Arbuthnot & Faust, 1981), one that clearly differentiates between the content and structure of moral reasoning, with the former reflecting *what* one is thinking (i.e., opinions, what one actually states in the reasoning process) and the latter referring to *how* one thinks (i.e., the thinking process that determines what one says) (Arbuthnot & Faust, 1981). This suggests that, although the content of an individual's response to a moral dilemma may vary, the structure or reasoning process generally remains constant at a particular point in time. Furthermore, this idea implies that, whereas similarities may exist in the content of the responses of, for example, Stage 1 and Stage 2 persons, the reasoning processes underlying the responses will be different.

Also basic to the cognitive-developmental approach is the notion of developmental stages. Kohlberg's hypothesis of distinct stages of moral development suggests that, over the lifespan, there are qualitatively different ways of thinking and reasoning about moral issues. These qualitative changes are believed to emerge from transformations in the child's thought structure (Arbuthnot & Faust, 1981) and can be observed in the reasoning process. Implicit is the belief that these stages form an invariant sequence, with later stages representing more complex and abstract ways of reasoning (Kohlberg, 1973).

Evolving from the invariant sequence notion is the idea of hierarchical integrations, which has been described as a process in which the structures of an earlier stage serve as the building blocks for the structures of the next stage (Arbuthnot & Faust, 1981). Although each successive stage represents a transformation of the preceding stage, the notion of hierarchical integrations entails that each successive stage is more differentiated (i.e., more complex and more specialized) and more integrated (i.e., structured parts are better organized) than the prior stage.

As with the concept of hierarchical integrations, each stage is also believed to represent a structured whole, meaning that every stage reflects an organized system of thought (Kohlberg, 1973). Kohlberg's theory also posits that the "highest stage" represents the theoretically "ideal" endpoint of development. Finally, the theory postulates that progression to more advanced stages is induced by cognitive conflict (Kohlberg, 1969).

It is the latter assumption that is particularly relevant to any intervention designed to enhance an individual's level of moral reasoning. Kohlberg (1969), Turiel (1974), and Piaget (1932) maintain that through the child's interpersonal interactions with adults and peers he is increasingly exposed to situations of value conflict that ultimately lead to cognitive conflict. Resolution of this conflict requires that the child experiment with alternative ways of reasoning that are typically representative of the next higher stage of moral judgment. This result suggests that environmental stimulation may promote, within certain limits, the development of moral reasoning (Arbuthnot & Faust, 1981).

In addition, the literature suggests that critical periods exist in which the child must actively explore other means of dealing with her environment in order to prevent fixation at more developmentally immature levels (Kohlberg, 1969; Piaget, 1932; Turiel, 1974). For example, Kohlberg and Kramer's (1969) research indicates that, for Americans, one such critical or transitional period occurs between the ages of 10 and 13. It is during this period that a child typically moves from a preconventional to a conventional level of moral reasoning. Furthermore, they suggest that it is important for children to exhibit at least some conventional moral reasoning during this period in order to prevent fixation at a preconventional level. These ideas—that environmental stimulation can enhance moral reasoning and that critical transitional periods exist in the developmental sequence—suggest that the success of an intervention designed to promote moral reasoning may lie, in part, in the "readiness" of the individual to progress to higher stages of moral judgment.

The core postulates comprising Kohlberg's theory have received extensive critical scrutiny. Much of this research has yielded supportive evidence. Over the course of a longitudinal investigation of American boys between the ages of 10 and 16 from low- and middle-income families, Kramer (1968) and Kohlberg and Kramer (1969) found that moral reasoning did progress sequentially through stages. The longitudinal data also reveal that, although the time period between testing was 4 years, potentially allowing the participants to move through more than one stage during that interval, only 10 percent of the boys evidenced changes beyond one stage. The results also indicated that relatively few participants reached the highest stages of moral development and that the rate of development varied for different individuals. Similar results have also been found by Turiel (1966) in an investigation of individuals' reasoning at Kohlberg's Stages 2, 3, or 4, and by Lee (1971). Using 5- to 8-year-old children, Kuhn (1976) also found progression to the subsequent stage at a 1-year follow-up.

Kohlberg's (Kohlberg & Kramer, 1969; Kohlberg & Turiel, 1971; Turiel, Edwards, & Kohlberg, 1977) cross-cultural research, which included the countries of Mexico, Turkey, India, Taiwan, Israel, and Canada, provided support for the invariant sequence hypothesis. For instance, the results of studies involving 10-, 13-, and 16-year-old urban, middle-class boys of the United States, Mexico, and Taiwan and a comparable age group of boys in villages in Turkey and the Yucatan indicated that the predicted age-related changes occurred (when the changes occurred at all) regardless of country. Based on these studies, Kohlberg and his collaborators concluded that the invariant sequence hypothesis was culturally universal, even though rates of development and highest stage attained remained variable (lower for comparable groups in Turkey and the Yucatan). They also maintained that these results support the notion that all individuals reason about similar moral values (i.e., life, love, laws, contract, and punishment) regardless of culture or subculture. These conclusions have aroused extensive and diverse criticism in the literature. Although these objections will be addressed in detail later, at this point it is important to note that some of the criticisms are directed toward methodological flaws, particularly in the scoring techniques developed and utilized by the Kohlberg group in these studies. Since that time, scoring methods have been revised and used in at least one reported replication study (Nisan & Kohlberg, 1978). In this study, the predicted sequence was found both for longitudinal and for cross-sectional data.

Further support for the invariant sequence hypothesis is provided by studies that have suggested that moral judgment is significantly correlated with age (Grinder, 1964; Stuart, 1967; Whiteman & Kosier, 1964). Specifically, Colby, Kohlberg, and Gibbs (1979) found that, whereas at age 10 approximately 63 percent of the child's statements reflect Stage 1 reasoning, by age 24 to 26 only 5 percent of the statements reflect this stage. The results also indicated that there is an increase in percentage of Stage 3 reasoning with age and that Stage 4 reasoning emerges at approximately age 13 to 14 and also increases with age. Other researchers have found similar distributions of stage responses (Arbuthnot, 1973, 1975; Arbuthnot & Faust, 1981; Faust & Arbuthnot, 1978; Haan, Smith, & Block, 1968; Kohlberg & Kramer, 1969). In studying these percentages, it is important to recognize that individual differences exist, with some of this variation being accounted for by such factors as socioeconomic status, intelligence, and education. Thus the percentages presented are most appropriately viewed as rough estimations of the relationship between age and moral reasoning stage.

Related to the invariant sequence hypothesis is the question of the possibility of regression in moral stages. At this time, there is considerable debate among researchers on this question. A number of investigators have observed a regression in moral reasoning, particularly among college students (Haan, Smith, & Block, 1968; Holstein, 1976; Kohlberg & Kramer, 1969; Kramer, 1968; Turiel, 1974). In studying this phenomenon, Kohlberg and Kramer (1969) noted that it generally appears between late high school and the early years of college among middle-class students whose moral reasoning scores during high school were quite advanced in comparison to those of their age-related peers. Turiel (1974) and Kohlberg and Kramer (1969) argue that, theoretically, what appears to be a regression really reflects a transitional period during which the individual experiments with alternative ways of reasoning about moral issues and that ultimately leads to the enhancement of the moral structure. They maintain that the structure does not regress, even though the content of the individual's response may resemble that of a Stage 2 reasoner.

In support of this contention, Kohlberg and Kramer (1969) report that all of their participants who had evidenced stage regression had returned to at least a mixture of Stage 4 and Stage 5 reasoning and had in some cases reached dominant Stage 5 reasoning. These results, in conjunction with the Nisan and Kohlberg (1978) finding cited previously and those results indicating positive correlations between age and moral reasoning, suggest that the invariant sequence hypothesis is still tenable in spite of the observed regressions in college students. However, the results of studies in the area of stage regression strongly imply that individuals are capable of lower stage reasoning even after progressing to higher stages. It is important to note that this idea is clearly reflected in some of Kohlberg's other theoretical hypotheses and in the empirical investigations evolving from them. For example, although the structural whole hypothesis has been supported to some extent, most of the research evidence indicates that individuals reason at more than one stage at specific points in time (Arbuthnot & Faust, 1981; Kohlberg, 1973). In fact, the results suggest that, generally, 50 percent of the individual's reasoning reflects the dominant stage, with the remaining statements representing reasoning at adjacent stages (either a lower or higher stage).

Many studies have shown that individuals understand reasoning at or below their own stage but not more than one stage above their own (Rest, 1979; Rest, Turiel, & Kohlberg, 1969; Turiel, 1966). Rest (1979), for instance, asked adolescents to rewrite a number of moral statements in their own words and then to rank order them in terms of preference. The results indicated that participants correctly rewrote statements up to and representative of their own stage of reasoning but not beyond that stage. However, although they were capable of comprehending reasoning below their own stage, participants typically gave these responses low preference ratings and preferred statements that reflected reasoning one stage higher than their present reasoning skills. Statements two stages beyond present reasoning ability were also given low preference scores. The fact that lower stage reasoning continues to be understood but not preferred has important implications for both the development of measures of moral reasoning and interventions designed to advance moral reasoning levels.

A number of investigators have criticized Kohlberg's work on methodological, theoretical, and philosophical grounds. Most of these objections have evolved from the assumption of the universal applicability of the invariant sequence hypothesis, which Kohlberg claims has received support from both his 17-year longitudinal study and his cross-cultural work. Throughout these investigations, however, Kohlberg and his colleagues utilized the *aspect scoring system* for determining the participant's modal reasoning stage. Kurtines and Grief (1974) have criticized this scoring system on the basis of a lack of standardization of administration and scoring methods, which they claim has resulted in a lack of support for the validity and reliability of the Moral Judgment Interview. They also maintain that Kohlberg's failure to provide information concerning the interrater reliabilities emerging from his longitudinal research, his failure to specify the number of dilemmas used, and the lack of a published scoring manual have made it difficult for researchers outside of his immediate group to investigate the theory.

As mentioned previously, when Kohlberg and other researchers found data dissonant to the invariant sequence hypothesis, they proceeded to modify the original scoring system. What emerged was a new scoring system called *issue scoring*. Although the consistently high reliability coefficients reported imply that the Kohlberg issue-scoring procedure has some utility for assessing moral reasoning, it has been suggested that other measures may be more appropriate to use in short-term intervention research. Some support for this contention has been provided by Carroll and Nelson (1979), Carroll and Rest (1981), Rest (1979), and Enright (1980), who have proposed or developed measures of moral reasoning designed to incorporate a number of intervention-related considerations. Although it is not within the scope of this discussion to address these measures, the interested reader is referred to the aforementioned sources for a detailed discussion of their rationales and empirical bases. It is important, however, to reiterate that, even though reliabilities are adequate for the revised scoring system, the fact remains that many of Kohlberg's theoretical conclusions were based upon studies utilizing the old scoring method. Thus any interpretation based upon these studies must be advanced with caution; attention should be directed toward reanalyzing the original work using the new scoring procedure.

Thus far, our discussion has centered upon criticisms of Kohlberg's unstandardized administration protocol and scoring technique and the utility of his assessment procedure for research other than longitudinal developmental studies. Other criticisms have been voiced in the literature. In relation to Kohlberg's cross-cultural studies, for example, critics have commented on his failure to specify subject characteristics, sample sizes, or the methods used to establish the moral stages in different cultures (Kurtines & Grief, 1974); his failure to sample an adequate number of diverse cultures to support his claim of universality (Fraenkel, 1976; Simpson, 1974); and his failure to determine whether the values captured by the Moral Judgment Interview are deemed important within the particular culture investigated (this criticism is basic to the universal moral values assumption) (Simpson, 1974). He has been criticized for his failure to provide sufficient empirical evidence that a Stage 6 (postconventional reasoning level) even exists within the cultures studied (Simpson, 1974). Finally, not related solely to the cross-cultural research are philosophical objections to Kohlberg's description of the Stage 6 "ideal" moral individual (Peters, 1978; Simpson, 1974). Additional criticisms of Kohlberg's theory have emerged from the moral relativists (Raths, Harmin, & Simon, 1966), who maintain that moral principles are subjective, that values are not universal, and that Kohlberg's position of the "moral superiority" of the Stage 6 reasoner is an elitist point of view.

It is apparent that many of these criticisms call into question a number of Kohlberg's basic theoretical premises. Recently, supporters of the Kohlberg approach have made concerted efforts to respond to these criticisms. Concerning objections involving methodological and assessment issues, efforts have been made to specify more rigorously subject characteristics, sample sizes, and administration and scoring protocols, and, as previously mentioned, to develop new measures that tap broader aspects of moral reasoning. Specification of these procedures has enhanced opportunities for replication efforts.

The moderation of the criticisms concerning the existence of Stage 6 reasoning and descriptions of the Stage 6 reasoner as the "ideal" moral individual cannot be so briefly summarized because, in contrast to the former objections, which represent methodological problems, the latter two involve theoretical considerations. In fact, attempts to resolve these objections have emerged primarily from philosophical sources. Edelman and Goldstein (1981) describe the Stage 6 individual as "someone who, in a totally rational and impartial way, considers and reasons through the conflicting interests and values of different individuals on the basis of an abstract respect for the universal equal rights of all people" (p. 308).

Thus not only is there little empirical support for the existence of the Stage 6 individual (Cortese, 1984; Edelman & Goldstein, 1981; Snarey, 1985), even if reasoning of this form does occur, it does not necessarily represent an "ideal" way to think. Although objections to Kohlberg's lack of consideration of "moral habits and moral feelings" have primarily revolved around the Stage 6 individual, the criticism is valid for all six of the moral reasoning stages. Consequently, in line with Wilson's (1973) and Edelman and Goldstein's (1981) suggestion, an adequate definition of morality must incorporate its cognitive, affective, and behavioral components.

Wilson (1973), unlike Kohlberg, is one of the few investigators in the area of morality who has considered all three of these components. Briefly, he suggests that morality is comprised of the following aspects:

1. Concern and respect for other people as equals and consideration of the needs of others, as well as oneself. One attains these values by having the concept of a person which involves the recognition of the similarities and differences among human beings (cognitive component), claiming the concept as a moral principle by determining if the individual believes this is an important concept to use (cognitive component), by rule-supported feelings by determining if the person has any feelings of respect and consideration attached to human beings (affective component) and by helping others as a means of reflecting these feelings (behavioral component).

2. Awareness of feelings in oneself and others by determining if the individual has the concept of emotion (cognitive component) and the ability to identify and label emotions in oneself and others (affective and cognitive component).

3. Assessing the individual's knowledge of relevant hard facts (i.e., physical health, safety, laws) and the sources of these facts (Does the person have the knowledge to make moral decisions?).

4. Determination of the individual's ability to use the above components to make decisions in various moral situations (cognitive component).

5. Assessment of the person's ability to translate the moral decision into overt behavior (behavioral component). (pp. 41–44)

It is apparent that, although Wilson's definition encompasses the three major aspects of morality, its complexity and vagueness make it difficult to utilize in investigations of moral reasoning. To fill this gap, Edelman and Goldstein (1981) have offered another definition of morality, using Wilson's component analysis as its foundation:

> Morality involves those skills, values and abilities that comprise (1) thinking or reasoning (problem solving, decision making) in a rational way, while (2) showing an awareness of, and consideration for the needs, interests and feelings of others as well as oneself, and (3) behaving constructively, i.e., in ways that benefit both self and others, in the problematic or conflictual social-interpersonal situations which one encounters in one's daily interactions with other people. Morality, then, involves cognitive (thinking), affective (feeling), and behavioral (doing) aspects which are necessarily interrelated. (p. 259)

It must be noted that this definition does not in any way negate Kohlberg's conception of morality. Rather, this definition serves to include, yet transcend, Kohlberg's original ideas. In addition, it attempts to moderate those criticisms emerging from Kohlberg's belief in the "ideal" Stage 6 reasoning individual by incorporating the affective dimensions of morality.

Intervention Research

Since the 1920s, researchers within the moral reasoning domain have extended their work into the intervention realm. This move was prompted by the belief that the traditional institutions—family, religion, and the schools—were no longer successful in preparing children for the moral conflicts that confronted them (Arbuthnot & Faust, 1981; Edelman & Goldstein, 1981). Many researchers claim that these institutions promote rule-oriented reasoning (equating morality with conformity to conventions), rather than reasoning based on principles of justice (Arbuthnot & Faust, 1981; Edelman & Goldstein, 1981). Thus, when the rules of society change, the individual's rule-oriented reasoning no longer helps him to resolve moral conflicts, and a "moral crisis" may ensue. A moral crisis is characterized by an increased frequency of antisocial behavior and value confusion and a discrepancy between one's behavior and verbalized values. It emerges not only from questioning what values are worthwhile, but also from questioning how to apply values in specific situations or when values conflict with each

other (Arbuthnot & Faust, 1981; Edelman & Goldstein, 1981). Consequently, techniques were developed with the primary goal of enhancing
moral reasoning and the secondary goal of reducing antisocial behavior.
Most of the procedures were designed to be utilized within school
settings. Historically, the more prominent programs have included
Values Clarification (Kirschenbaum, 1975; Raths, Harmin, & Simon,
1966; Simon, Howe, & Kirschenbaum, 1972; Simon & Olds, 1976),
certain applications of role playing (Arbuthnot, 1975; Matefy & Acksen,
1976; Tracy & Cross, 1973), and Moral Education (Blatt & Kohlberg,
1975; Grimes, 1974; Stanley, 1976; Sullivan, 1980). Our decision to
include Kohlberg's Moral Education as part of the Prepare Curriculum's
Moral Reasoning Training, rather than the alternatives listed, is securely
based on substantial evidence that participation in Moral Education
procedures can indeed effectively increase the participant's level of
moral reasoning and, as we shall see, in a number of instances also
cause changes in overt prosocial behaviors (Arbuthnot & Gordon, 1983;
Blasi, 1980; Edelman & Goldstein, 1981; Gibbs, Arnold, Ahlborn, &
Cheesman, 1984; Zimmerman, 1983).

The practical application of Kohlberg's theory involves classroom
discussions of moral dilemmas in which cognitively stimulating dilemmas are used to promote debate and discussions among students. Since
classrooms are likely to be comprised of students reasoning at diverse
stages, Kohlberg maintained that the moral discussions engaged in
would induce cognitive conflict in an individual functioning at the
lower stages and would provide role-taking opportunities that, over
time, would result in a transition to the next higher stage of moral
reasoning—at least for those students initially reasoning at the lower
stages. Although these teacher-led moral discussions are believed to
prevent fixation at a particular moral reasoning stage in those students
who lag behind their peers, supporters of Moral Education do not claim
that it promotes the moral development of students who are progressing
satisfactorily. Nevertheless, these higher stage reasoners are a crucial
part of the Moral Education program since during discussions they
present statements that induce the cognitive conflict believed to be
necessary for moral growth. Although the presence of higher stage
reasoners is an absolute necessity for the inducement of cognitive
conflict, Edelman and Goldstein (1981) suggest that the potency of the
cognitive conflict can be enhanced by considering such factors as the
relevance the moral dilemma has for the individual, the extent to which
the dilemma is presented in a context that promotes the mutual

exchange of conflicting opinions, and the extent to which these opinions and underlying reasons reflect reasoning one stage higher than that of the lower reasoning individual.

Thus it is apparent that Moral Education involves at least three conditions that are believed to enhance moral reasoning: role-taking opportunities through reciprocal social interaction, cognitive conflict regarding genuine moral dilemmas, and exposure to the next higher stage of reasoning (Edelman & Goldstein, 1981). These three basic principles, in conjunction with the notion that the teacher's role is that of promoting self-discovery of higher stage reasoning and not moral indoctrination, form the basis for the specific procedures employed in Moral Education programs. After groups of from 8 to 15 individuals who reason at two or three consecutive moral reasoning stages are established, the teacher presents dilemmas that can induce cognitive conflict and that are relevant to the students. The trainer provides a rationale for Moral Education and describes what the group will be like, what her role is, and what the format will be for group participation (Arbuthnot & Faust, 1981). A four-step process ensues in which group members are asked to confront a moral dilemma, state a tentative position, examine the reasoning, and reflect on an individual position. Kohlberg and his collaborators maintain that these procedures, employed by a trainer who is able to establish a nonjudgmental climate, are the conditions necessary to promote moral development.

In fact, the research evidence suggests that moral dilemma discussion groups can successfully enhance moral reasoning. The results of a study involving sixth graders (11- to 12-year-olds) and tenth graders (15- to 16-year-olds) in which the experimenter led moral discussion groups (18 weekly 45-minute sessions) indicated that students in the experimental classrooms showed significantly more upward change in moral reasoning (one-third stage increase) as compared with various control group classrooms (Blatt & Kohlberg, 1975). In addition, participants in the experimental condition maintained the change at a 1-year follow-up. The changes observed were generally in the direction of the next higher stage, implying that true learning, rather than rote learning of phrases, had occurred. Similarly, the results of a study by Colby, Kohlberg, Fenton, Speicher-Dubin, and Lieberman (1977) indicated that students in a moral discussion group led by teachers in the context of a social studies class showed a significant upward change in moral reasoning as compared with students in control classrooms where no moral discussions were held. In addition, Colby et al. (1977) found that more change in moral reasoning occurred for students who were in the process of stage transition, who were in classrooms that included students with diverse levels of moral reasoning, and who had teachers skilled in promoting reasoning at adjacent stages and who used a greater number of discussion periods. In a series of studies reported by Sullivan (1980), Moral Education programs were again found to enhance moral reasoning. The results of a study using elementary-level children indicated that, whereas both the experimental group (twice-weekly participation in a minicourse in ethics in which moral dilemma discussions were held for 1 academic year) and the control group (no participation in the ethics class) showed movement primarily from Stage 1 to Stage 3 reasoning on posttesting, only the experimental group evidenced some Stage 4 reasoning and had completely abandoned the use of Stage 1 reasoning. This developmental pattern was also evident at a 1-year follow-up.

In an earlier study using secondary-level children, Beck, Sullivan, and Taylor (1972) found that there were no differences between the experimental and control groups in moral reasoning on posttests. However, a 1-year follow-up indicated that students in the experimental group evidenced more postconventional reasoning than did those in the control group. The authors maintain that the 1-year interval between posttesting and follow-up provided opportunities for students to use their newly learned reasoning skills and thus to consolidate Stage 5 reasoning. In another study using high school students, results were less supportive (Sullivan & Beck, 1975). No differences in moral reasoning enhancement were found for the experimental and control groups. The discrepancy between the results of the last two studies can perhaps be found in an examination of the teaching methods employed. In the latter study, an ethics textbook, reflecting more the interests of the teachers than those of the students, was used, whereas in the former study a textbook was not employed. The authors argue that the use of a textbook created a more structured environment, which restricted the type of moral discussions that could evolve. These results suggest that the relevance of the moral dilemmas used has significant effects on the success of a Moral Education program.

Other studies using direct moral discussion of real-life situations have yielded positive results. Rundle (1977), using a fifth-grade classroom in which moral issues were taught by the experimenter and a teacher within the context of classroom democracy, found that, after 29 hours of instruction, students in the experimental classroom (who discussed and modified classroom rules using democratic procedures) showed significantly more change (one-half stage) than students in either the classroom with no moral discussion or the one with moral discussion using hypothetical moral dilemmas. This again suggests that the efficacy of Moral Education programs is in part a function of the relevance of the dilemmas discussed. In addition, Rundle (1977) found that children in the experimental group performed significantly better on a cooperation task (brick-building) than did those in the two control groups. It is important to recognize, however, that the group participating in moral discussion using hypothetical dilemmas was led by a teacher who had not received training in Moral Education procedures. Thus the group differences may have resulted from differential levels of experience with Moral Education procedures rather than from exposure to real versus hypothetical dilemmas.

The work of Grimes (1974) indicated that moral discussion groups involving fifth- and sixth-grade children and their mothers can also lead to enhanced moral reasoning. Specifically, the results indicated that such group discussions between mothers trained in Moral Education prior to the initiation of the study and their children led to more change (between one-third and one whole stage) than was revealed in groups in which children, without their mothers, discussed hypothetical moral dilemmas (one-third stage increase) or in groups that did not discuss moral dilemmas at all (no change). The authors maintain that the presence of the mother increased the frequency of moral dilemma discussions in the home. Stanley (1976) found similar results in a study involving parents and their adolescent children. Not only did the parent-adolescent group show moral growth after the 10-week intervention (one-third stage increase), but a 1-year follow-up revealed that participants had continued to hold weekly family meetings involving family fairness discussions. In contrast, the parent-only group, as well as the control group, showed no significant pre- to posttest gains.

Also relevant to our decision to include Moral Reasoning Training as part of the Prepare Curriculum is the substantial evidence that such procedures reliably increase moral reasoning level in juvenile delinquent populations (Arbuthnot & Gordon, 1983; Fleetwood & Parish, 1976; Gibbs et al., 1984; Goldstein & Glick, 1987; Rosenkoetter, Landman, & Mazak, 1980). Although not all such Moral Education interventions have yielded enhanced moral reasoning (Schmidlin, 1977; Wright & Dixon, 1977), such attempts appear worthwhile given their overall efficacy with delinquents and the moral reasoning deficiency typically displayed by juvenile delinquents when compared to nondelinquents (see the next section). We strongly concur with Arbuthnot and Gordon (1983) that the necessary technology is in place, and that "the task for the correctional education may be seen, then, not as one of conversion or rehabilitation, but one of development, or habilitation, of a moral reasoning framework which the offender, for whatever reason in his or her developmental history, has not yet acquired" (p. 133).

A number of conclusions can be drawn from the results of these studies employing Moral Education procedures: (1) moral dilemma discussion groups can lead to significantly more moral growth (one-third to one whole stage increase over one academic semester) than in various control groups; (2) this change occurs when a range of reasoning stages are represented in the classroom; (3) the teacher must help the student probe his reasoning in an environment that promotes openness and trust; (4) the moral discussion must create divided opinions and controversy among the students; (5) the most effective Moral Education interventions occur with discussion of real dilemmas in the context of a "real" group (e.g., the classroom, the family); and (6) delinquent individuals characteristically function at lower levels of moral reasoning than do nondelinquent cohorts but can increase their levels of such reasoning ability as a result of participation in Moral Education groups.

What of the relationship between moral reasoning and overt behavior? Research concerned with this question has been considerable and of two types: that seeking connections between level of moral reasoning and antisocial behavior and that seeking similar connections with prosocial behavior.

Moral Reasoning and Antisocial Behavior

Although the study of moral behavior has been undertaken primarily in controlled laboratory settings and has usually involved the use of nondelinquent populations, research evidence suggests that—with exceptions—a relationship exists between moral judgment and unsocialized behavior. These studies consistently yield positive correlations between aggressive behavior/delinquency and preconventional levels of moral reasoning. Specifically, Freudlich and Kohlberg (see Kohlberg, 1973) found that, whereas 23 percent of working-class nondelinquent adolescents reasoned at preconventional stages (usually characteristic of children under age 10), 83 percent of delinquent adolescents reasoned at Stages 1 or 2. Similar results were found by Fodor (1972) in an investigation involving 14- to 17-year-old delinquent males (violations ranged from petty larceny to attempted homicide). When compared with nondelinquents, delinquents were found to score significantly lower on Kohlberg's Moral Judgment Interview. A study by

Campagna and Harter (1975) also indicated that sociopathic males evidenced significantly more preconventional reasoning than did a matched sample of nonsociopathic males. Hudgins and Prentice (1973) similarly found that 14- to 16-year-old nondelinquent males scored significantly higher (conventional level) on Kohlberg's moral dilemmas than did a matched sample of delinquent males (preconventional level). Blasi (1980) has carefully examined the relevant research in this domain and concluded that, in 10 of the 15 pertinent studies, evidence indicates that delinquent individuals characteristically utilize developmentally lower levels of moral reasoning than do matched nondelinquents. Thus, although certainly not always the case, the thrust of relevant evidence indicates the two preconventional stages to be the typical level of moral reasoning among juvenile delinquents.

Moral Reasoning and Prosocial Behavior

In general, and again with not insignificant exceptions, the literature suggests that a positive relationship exists between stage level and such prosocial behaviors as honesty, as measured by cheating behavior (Harris, Mussen, & Rutherford, 1976; Kohlberg & Turiel, 1971; Krebs, 1967; Schwartz, Feldman, Brown, & Heingartner, 1969); altruism, as reflected in helping people in distress and in generosity (McNamee, 1977; Ugurel-Semin, 1952); nonviolence, as measured by refusal to inflict pain on other people (Kohlberg & Turiel, 1971); and conformity behavior (Fodor, 1972; Saltzstein, Diamond, & Belenky, 1972).

There is considerable debate concerning the validity of using these behaviors to draw conclusions about the relationship between moral reasoning and "moral behavior." In studies of honesty, for example, the evidence suggests that more conventional than postconventional reasoners cheated on tasks when there were no explicit authoritative or group sanctions preventing it. Kohlberg and Turiel (1971) maintain that, because the postconventional reasoners define the situation as one that involves mutual trust and equality of opportunity, they are less likely to cheat. In contrast, the conventional reasoners maintained that there was no reason to resist cheating since the authority figure (i.e., the experimenter) did not disapprove of this behavior. Thus it seems that one of the consequences of a rule-oriented morality is that behavior is in part controlled by the prevailing rules of the situation (Arbuthnot & Faust, 1981).

Postconventional reasoners are believed to behave according to principles, not rules. Therefore, when conventional rules for behavior are no longer present in a situation, conventional reasoners' behavior is more likely to break down than is that of individuals reasoning at the principled level. These ideas were partially confirmed in a study by Harris, Mussen, and Rutherford (1976) in which fifth-grade boys were administered a resistance-to-temptation task based on the duplicating technique (participants are asked to score their own tests after they have been scored by the experimenter) used by Hartshorne and May (1928). The results indicated that honesty was positively, although not significantly, correlated with moral reasoning scores. In contrast, the Krebs (1967) study yielded significant positive correlations between moral reasoning and resistance to temptation as measured by a structured game in which it was easy to cheat. Although drawing conclusions from "box scores" of results across studies on any given topic is not without its own weaknesses, it is nevertheless useful to note that, according to Blasi (1980), of the 17 studies seeking to identify a possible relationship between moral reasoning level and honesty, 7 support such an association, 7 do not, and 3 report equivocal results.

McNamee (1977) conducted an experiment concerning altruism in which the participant could decide to help or not help a confederate drug user. Compliance with the experimenter's expectation was defined as the participant's willingness to help the confederate. The results indicated that, whereas all participants reasoning at Stage 6 offered the confederate assistance, only 68 percent of Stage 5 reasoners, 38 percent of Stage 4 reasoners, and 28 percent of Stage 3 reasoners offered some kind of assistance (either a referral or personal assistance). These results indicate that behavioral choice differs for higher and lower stage reasoners. The results of a study by Ugurel-Semin (1952) provide further support for the relationship between moral reasoning and altruistic behavior. Specifically, the results indicated that, for 4- to 16-year-old children in Istanbul, increases in moral judgment stage are associated with increasingly more mature justifications for their altruistic behavior. But as with the moral reasoning/honesty relationship, the connection between level of moral reasoning and altruistic behavior—all relevant evidence considered—is equivocal. Of 19 relevant studies, 11 confirm the relationship, 4 do not, and 4 are mixed in their findings (Blasi, 1980).

The results of a study by Kohlberg and Turiel (1971) on nonviolence again provide support for a positive relationship between moral reasoning and moral behavior. The investigators administered the Moral Judgment Interview to participants in Milgram's (1965) study of obedience to authority, in which one participant was told by the researcher to administer increasingly painful shocks to another participant. ("Victims" in this experiment did not actually receive the shocks but, in confederacy with the experimenter, reacted in a way audible to the other participant.) Although 75 percent of the Stage 6 reasoners refused to continue shocking the other participant, stating that the researcher did not have a right to inflict pain on another person, only 13 percent of the lower stage reasoners (including Stage 5) discontinued administering the shock. Although Stage 5 reasoners often felt uncomfortable with the experiment, they continued to administer shock because both they and the victim had made a commitment to the researcher to participate in the study. In contrast, the Stage 3 and Stage 4 participants continued shocking the victim because of the experimenter's definition of the situation. Thus it is apparent that, even though similar decisions may be elicited by people reasoning at different stages, the reasoning process underlying these behavioral choices differs for individuals functioning at different levels of moral development. And, finally, in a study examining the relationship between moral reasoning and conformity behavior, Saltzstein et al. (1972) found that significantly more Stage 3 reasoners conformed to group opinion than did those participants reasoning at Stage 4 or Stage 5. Yet again, as was the case for honesty and altruism, behaviors indicative of nonviolence and those reflective of resistance to conforming to group pressure are not consistent in the direction or the degree of their correlation with level of moral reasoning.

In summary, the results of the studies presented indicate that relationships may exist between moral reasoning stage and both antisocial and prosocial behavior but that the magnitude and reliability of such relationships appear to depend in part on the particular prosocial or antisocial behavior examined. As Blasi (1980) notes,

> The body of research reviewed here seems to offer considerable support for the hypothesis that moral reasoning and moral action are statistically related. This statement, however, should be qualified as soon as one looks at the findings in more detail. Empirical support, in fact, varies from area to area. It is strongest for the hypothesis that moral reasoning differs between delinquents and nondelinquents and that at higher stages of moral reasoning, there is greater resistance to the pressure of conforming one's judgment to others' views. The support is clear but less strong for the hypothesis that higher moral stage individuals tend to be more honest and more altruistic. Finally, there is little support for the expectation that individuals of the postconventional level resist more than others the social pressure to conform in their moral actions. (p. 37)

Discrepancies between Word and Deed in
Real-life Situations

The primary criticisms emerging from the use of such behaviors as cheating, altruism, and conformity to study the relationship between moral reasoning level and moral behavior have emerged within the Kohlberg group. Kohlberg (1969, 1973) and Turiel (1980) argue that these behaviors cannot always be viewed as representative of moral behavior because they do not take into consideration the individual's intentions and they do not reflect true moral dilemma situations. For example, Kohlberg (1969) argues that the invalidity of experiments utilizing honesty stems from the fact that they do not reflect true moral dilemmas. According to Kohlberg, a true moral dilemma involves a situation requiring the individual to choose between two courses of action in which "strong emotional reactions are activated." Kohlberg does not believe that cheating situations often evoke these emotions. Damon (1980) supports a similar view. He maintains that tests of cheating and lying, for instance, are trivial and do not capture an individual's true moral concerns.

Studies investigating the idea that people may reason and behave differently when confronted with a hypothetical versus a real-life moral dilemma have yielded inconsistent findings. Blasi's (1980) review of evidence bearing upon this question revealed six studies that reported a significant positive relationship between moral reasoning and real-life behaviors, three investigations that yielded negative data, and three reporting mixed results. For example, in the McNamee (1977) study discussed earlier, no discrepancy was found between reasoning in concrete versus hypothetical moral conflicts. However, in a study by Gerson and Damon (1975) using 4- to 10-year-old children, there was considerable discrepancy between the stage of reasoning used in hypothetical versus concrete situations. The results indicated that lower levels of reasoning were employed in concrete situations of generosity (actual distribution of candy bars) as compared to hypothetical situations (hypothetical distribution of money). Similarly, Kohlberg, Kauffman, Scharf, and Hickey (1975) found that prisoners use lower stage reasoning when responding to specific prison dilemmas than they do for standard hypothetical dilemmas.

The fact that individuals do not reason at only one stage makes these discrepant findings somewhat more interpretable. Nevertheless, these results also imply that situational and other extraneous variables may be operative in the reasoning process and may affect an individual's ultimate behavioral choice. This idea has received considerable support in the literature. For example, based upon a study indicating that significantly more preconventional (70 percent) and conventional (55 percent) reasoners than postconventional reasoners (15 percent) cheated, Kohlberg (1973) concluded that factors beyond moral judgment influence the translation of moral reasoning into moral action. This conclusion was based upon the fact that 15 percent of the principled reasoners still cheated, even though stage descriptions would suggest that they would not behave in this manner.

One factor believed to affect moral action is ego strength, defined as *attentional-will factors* (sense of will or purpose) (Grim, Kohlberg, & White, 1968). Kohlberg (1971b) suggests that ego strength may lead to impulse control and the ability to delay gratification. Specifically, Kohlberg maintains that the mediational effects of ego strength factors may cause people "to differentially follow the moral judgments that they themselves make in the situation" (p. 381). Related to this factor is the question of the role of affect in moral behavior (Rothman, 1980). Although little research has investigated the mediating role of affect, Ruma and Mosher (1967) found a positive relationship between the level of moral judgment of delinquents and the guilt they experienced about their behavior. Self-interest (Gerson & Damon, 1975) may be another variable accounting for a considerable percentage of the variance, in that it elicits different levels of personal investment in particular situations. The ability to role-take, perspective-take, or empathize may provide yet another link in the reasoning/behavior chain.

A host of situational factors have also been found to mediate moral behavior. These factors include the use of hypothetical versus concrete, real dilemmas (Gerson & Damon, 1975; Haan, 1975; Keasey, 1977; Straughan, 1975); demand characteristics of the situation or experiment (Adair & Schachter, 1972; Orne, 1962); and the parameters (type and variety) of the moral conflict within a particular situation (Damon, 1980). It has been suggested that situational factors are particularly potent in concrete situations of moral decision making since the individual often has considerable personal investment in the outcome of the dilemma (Rothman, 1980). Other factors proposed to account for the discrepancy between moral reasoning stage and moral behavior are age (increased consistency of moral behavior with increasing age) (Saltzstein et al., 1972; Turiel & Rothman, 1972) and the confusion between moral behavior and socially conventional behavior (Turiel, 1980). Concerning the latter point, Turiel (1980) argues that a distinction must be made between moral issues, involving consideration of justice, and conventional concerns, involving issues related to the expectations of others in society (e.g., mode of dress, forms of address).

He maintains that it is unreasonable to assume that one's conception of socially conventional issues should be related to one's conception of moral issues.

Thus, just as behavioral choices may vary for different individuals reasoning at the same stage, one person may behave differently across two situations even though her reasoning is the same. Nevertheless, although these factors are believed to influence the reasoning/behavior relationship, the degree of impact of each variable, alone or in combination, is as yet unknown. Furthermore, despite this impact, most researchers in the area of moral development continue to maintain that level of moral reasoning is the most influential factor and, in fact, the only distinctively moral factor having an impact upon moral behavior (Kohlberg, 1973). Support for this contention awaits future research.

From this discussion, two conclusions can be drawn concerning the relationship between moral reasoning and moral behavior. First, it can be stated that advanced moral reasoning is a necessary but not sufficient condition for consistent moral behavior (Arbuthnot & Faust, 1981). In other words, although one can observe consistency between an individual's maturity of moral reasoning and maturity of behavior, one cannot always predict behavior in real-life situations from knowledge of the individual's reasoning stage. As Hoffman (1970) maintains, it seems reasonable to assume "that both specificity and generality can be found in moral behavior as in any other trait. Individuals do vary between their general predispositions toward honesty and dishonesty, but their actual behavior in moral conflict situations is not an all-or-none matter" (p. 344). Second, the discrepancy between moral reasoning and moral behavior in real-life situations can be accounted for by mediating factors such as situational variables, concrete versus hypothetical moral dilemmas, ego strength, affect, role-taking ability, age, and the distinction between moral and socially conventional behavior. Research endeavors must, therefore, continue to address the question of the role these mediating variables play in the moral reasoning/moral behavior chain.

It should be apparent from this discussion that the application of procedures in Moral Reasoning Training to reduce aggressive behavior involves the consideration of a myriad of factors. Although these techniques have proven to be effective for increasing moral reasoning stage, there is at present only a modest amount of evidence indicating that these effects are transferred to moral behavior in real-life situations. Such efforts (and the enhanced levels of moral reasoning consequent to their implementation) may have their greatest impact upon overt behavior when account is taken of the array of artifactual and moderator variables already discussed and when the intervention is employed as a contributing component in a larger intervention package, all of whose components are designed to interact synergistically. As Zimmerman (1986) has commented,

> It is maintained that it is necessary to possess both anger inhibition skills and alternative behaviors to aggression when eliciting prosocial behaviors. However, if youngsters possess the ability to respond in a prosocial manner and if they have the skills necessary to inhibit or decrease impulsive anger and aggression, the question that remains is whether the delinquent youngster will choose to use these skills. To increase the probability that the youngster will make this choice, it is argued that one must intervene on a cognitive-moral level. In other words, youngsters must also understand *why* they are engaging in a certain behavior. Moral Education is designed to impact on this level and ... this method has proven to be effective in enhancing the sociomoral reasoning of aggressive youth. As with other techniques implemented in isolation, however, Moral Education does not consistently yield changes in actual behavior. Indeed, prosocial values by themselves may not be sufficient for the elicitation of prosocial behavior. This discrepancy may in part emerge because the youngsters did not have in their behavioral repertoires alternative prosocial behaviors or the skills needed to successfully inhibit antisocial behavior. (p. 80)

In the case of our Aggression Replacement Training intervention (Goldstein & Glick, 1987), the synergism of the training components appeared to increase the likelihood that prosocial behavior would occur by (1) explicitly teaching such behavior (Interpersonal Skills Training component—see chapter 3); (2) enhancing trainee ability to thwart competing anger arousal responses (Anger Control Training component—see chapter 5); and (3) maximizing the chance that the individual will choose to enact his newly learned prosocial skills because the consequent heightened level of moral reasoning permits, encourages, or even impels an enhanced sense of fairness, justice, and concern for others (Moral Reasoning Training component). It is in this and similar Prepare course combinations, therefore, that we urge the Moral Reasoning Training procedures we describe next be used.

Training Procedures

Moral Reasoning Training through dilemma discussion groups is a method designed to teach adolescents and younger children how to think about moral issues, how to deal with moral situations that do not have clear-cut situations, and how to use principles of fairness and justice in their interactions with others.* Dilemma discussion groups attempt to achieve two major goals: (1) increasing the moral reasoning stage of the trainees and (2) helping the trainees use newly learned and more advanced reasoning skills in the real world.

In general, these goals are achieved through peer group discussions of different kinds of stimulating moral dilemmas and the reasoning underlying various behavioral choices in these moral situations. Thus trainees are exposed to different ways of thinking about moral issues. In these discussions, trainees are asked to explain the thinking leading to the different stages of moral reasoning (i.e., different rationales underlying behavioral choices made by trainees operating at different levels of moral reasoning). Exposure to advanced reasoning stages (usually one stage higher than the youngster's own reasoning stage) creates confusion, called *cognitive conflict* or *disequilibrium,* that may contribute to the trainee's attainment of a higher level of moral reasoning as a means of resolving the conflict. Exposure to more advanced reasoning stages also provides trainees with the opportunity to take on the role of another person (i.e., to put oneself in someone else's shoes). In sum, there are at least three basic principles involved in enhancing moral reasoning development that form the basis for the specific procedures used in dilemma discussion groups: (1) exposure to the next higher stage of moral reasoning, (2) inducement of confusion over genuine moral dilemmas, and (3) opportunity to take on the role of another person. Dilemma discussion groups can be applied to many moral issues, including the values of life, property, law, truth, affiliation, authority, contract, conscience, and punishment.

It is important to note what dilemma discussion groups are not. First, this method does not involve "indoctrination" or the teaching of any specific values or beliefs. The trainer should never attempt to force trainees to accept her own personal values. Rather, this method is aimed at self-discovery and helping adolescents develop the effective problem-solving skills needed to arrive at their own solutions to moral conflicts they may be faced with in life. Although trainers do not

*These training procedures are generally based on *Teaching Moral Reasoning: Theory and Practice,* by J. A. Arbuthnot and A. Faust, 1981, New York: Harper & Row; and *Social Intelligence: Measuring the Development of Sociomoral Reflection,* by J. C. Gibbs, K. E. Widaman, and A. Colby, 1982, Englewood Cliffs, NJ: Prentice-Hall. The creative contribution of Deborah Zimmerman and Ben Taylor to the development of this training format is both very substantial and very much appreciated.

mandate what is good, they do attempt to encourage discussions from which trainees can discover for themselves what is good.

Second, it is important to stress that dilemma discussion groups do not simply provide opportunities to clarify values. In these groups, trainees are asked to defend the reasoning underlying their positions in relation to how consistent their rationales are with principles of fairness and justice. Since these rationales will vary, the trainer should not view one behavioral choice or reason as the only way to think effectively about a moral situation. In contrast, one aim of this method is to help adolescents develop flexible reasoning processes that can be adapted to the demands of their lives and the situations in which they find themselves.

Third, it is important to note that dilemma discussion groups are not a form of dynamic or behavioral therapy in which emotional conflicts are uncovered or specific behaviors are changed. Rather, these groups always remain focused on the discussion of moral issues by using specific, sequential procedures. This is not meant to imply that personally relevant moral issues cannot be discussed. It simply means that discussions should always focus on the examination of moral reasoning in relation to moral issues. Finally, dilemma discussion groups cannot be led successfully by all people. The next section addresses the knowledge and skills trainers need to run effective dilemma discussion groups.

Preparing for Moral Reasoning Training

The assessment of moral reasoning stage and the structuring of group discussions are the major activities of the moral reasoning trainer. As such, the trainer must lead, listen, and observe. Typically, one trainer finds it difficult to do all of these tasks successfully at the same time. Thus it is highly recommended that each group be run by a team of two trainers—a trainer and a co-trainer.

Selecting Trainers
The running of effective dilemma discussion groups involves these trainer attributes:

1. Knowledge of the main features of moral development theory and moral discussion group techniques: background, assumptions, procedures, and goals;
2. Knowledge of moral reasoning stage assessment (this involves the use of abstract reasoning abilities);
3. Ability to reason at least one stage above that of group members (+ 1 stage reasoning);

4. Ability to use a nondirective teaching style (i.e., to provide only a moderate amount of group structure);
5. Ability to maintain a "devil's advocate" position without leaving youngsters with the impression that there are specific ways to behave in moral situations or right/wrong answers to the dilemma being discussed;
6. Ability to orient both group members and supporting staff to dilemma discussion groups (i.e., to create the proper attitude);
7. Ability to create experiences that will promote the self-discovery of higher stage reasoning (i.e., to structure, initiate, and sustain group discussion);
8. Ability to deal effectively with group management problems.

Preparing Trainers

In an ideal situation, trainer preparation is maximized when potential leaders can both read relevant materials and participate in a dilemma discussion workshop. In this workshop, one or two experienced trainers demonstrate how moral stage assessments are made and how to conduct effective dilemma discussions. After this demonstration, beginning trainers practice by co-training several groups with an experienced trainer, thus gaining several opportunities to do what they have observed and to obtain feedback regarding their performance prior to running their own groups. To enhance the preparation process, trainers should first review the following theoretical notions, each of which is central to Moral Reasoning Training.

Theoretical review

Morality. The concept of morality cannot be easily defined. For the purpose of training, it may be best to think about morality in terms of key words such as *principles, justice, fairness, equality,* and *respect.* It is also useful to think about morality in terms of what processes it involves. In this way, morality may be seen as involving

1. Thinking or reasoning (problem solving, decision making) in a rational way;
2. Showing an awareness of, and consideration for, the needs, interests, and feelings of others as well as oneself;
3. Behaving constructively (i.e., in ways that benefit both self and others.

These abilities are expressed in problematic or conflictual social-interpersonal situations. Morality, then, involves necessarily related cognitive (thinking), affective (feeling), and behavioral (doing) aspects.

Content versus structure of thought. The basis for dilemma discussion groups can be found in cognitive-developmental theory. This theory focuses on cognition, particularly on the way people over the course of their development think or reason about laws, rules, and principles. The content of moral cognitions involves what one is thinking or actually saying (i.e., opinions). In contrast, the structure of moral reasoning involves how one is thinking, or the process of thinking (i.e., what underlies one's words). This distinction implies that, whereas the content of an individual's reasoning may vary from situation to situation, the structure remains relatively constant over different moral dilemmas for a person at a given level of moral reasoning. For example, the structure of moral reasoning will be fairly similar for a person whether he is reasoning about the value of life or property. It also implies that, although the content may be similar between lower and more advanced reasoners, the reasoning process will be different.

Moral situations. A moral situation involves a conflict in which at least two conflicting interests or values are evident. These situations often involve, but are not limited to, conflicts between responding to legal/societal norms or responding to the needs of others (e.g., stealing in order to save someone's life).

Moral issues. The concept of moral issues or moral norms relates to the distinction that has already been made between content and structure of thought. Moral issues relate to the content of the individual's moral reasoning rather than to how the person reasons (structure). More specifically, moral issues involve "the values the person is reasoning about" (Arbuthnot & Faust, 1981, p. 68). These moral issues include life, property, truth, affiliation, authority, law, contract, conscience, and punishment.

Moral stages. The cognitive-developmental theory of moral reasoning proposes six stages of moral development (see Table 7). These six stages represent qualitatively different ways of thinking and reasoning about moral issues and emerge over an individual's lifespan. Movement through these stages is said to occur in a predictable and invariant sequence (i.e., movement from Stage 1 to Stage 2 to Stage 3, etc.), with later stages representing more complex and abstract ways of reasoning about moral issues. The theory also suggests that the moral structures of the earlier stage serve as the foundation for the development of the moral structures of the next stage (hierarchical integration). In addition, each stage is believed to reflect an organized way of thinking about moral issues (structured whole).

However, although movement through the stages occurs in an invariable sequence and hierarchical order, the theory also maintains that an individual does not reason at only one stage in all situations. Rather, people are seen as reasoning primarily at one stage (dominant stage) and secondarily at adjacent stages, one stage either below or above the predominant stage. This idea of primary and secondary stage reasoning has important implications for those running dilemma discussion groups because it suggests that trainers likely will see some variability in an individual's responses across different moral dilemmas (e.g., Stage 1 reasoning on one moral dilemma and Stage 2 on another). A corollary of this idea is that people can understand reasoning at or below their own stage but usually cannot understand reasoning that is more than one stage above their own reasoning stage. As will become more apparent as the discussion proceeds, this is why efforts are made to create debates between adjacent stage reasoners (e.g., Stage 1 reasoners debating Stage 2 reasoners) in dilemma discussion groups. Finally, the theory proposes that the qualitative changes that emerge in moral development reflect changes in the individual's thought structure (reasoning process changes). This moral advancement is induced by cognitive conflict.

Cognitive conflict. The concept of cognitive conflict is crucial to the understanding of how dilemma discussion groups work. Cognitive-developmental theory proposes that, through the child's interactions with others, she is increasingly exposed to situations in which moral values conflict and appropriate rules for behavior are unclear. Repeated exposure to these "value-conflictual" situations leads to cognitive conflict. In an effort to resolve this unclear and value-conflictual state, children experiment with alternative ways of reasoning. These alternative ways of reasoning are usually reflective of the next higher stage of moral judgment. Dilemma discussion groups create cognitive conflict for group members through discussions of value-conflictual situations; these discussions expose youngsters both to the limitations of their current reasoning process and to alternative ways of thinking about and dealing with the situations.

Assessment of moral reasoning stage

Characteristics of the stages. In order to run effective dilemma discussion groups, it is important to know something about moral reasoning stage identification because, as will be discussed in detail later, this identification forms the basis for structuring the actual group discussions. As such, it is one of the major activities of the moral reasoning trainer. Although the precise identification of all moral reasoning statements requires extensive training and practice, the beginning trainer can develop basic assessment skills with some practice and time.

The first step in becoming an effective assessor of moral reasoning is to become familiar with the characteristics of each of the moral reasoning stages (see Table 8). At this time, it will be helpful to discuss the most commonly seen stages in more detail. The discussion will focus primarily on the major characteristics of the first four moral reasoning stages in terms of both their moral and social perspective features. Before this topic is addressed, however, some clarification of the term *social perspective* is needed. Social perspective refers to a person's perception "of the relationship of self to others, or the self to society's rules and regulations [and]... involves one's thinking about human relationships and their place in society" (Arbuthnot & Faust, 1981, p. 121). An assessment of the social perspective reflected in a statement can be more easily achieved than a direct assessment of an individual's moral reasoning stage because social perspective is often more clearly presented in the response. It can, therefore, provide good clues regarding the moral stage reflected by the particular statement.

As Table 8 indicates, the major orientation of the *Stage 1* reasoner is that of punishment and obedience. Adolescents at this stage determine what is right or wrong by focusing on the punishment, external threat, or physical consequences of a behavior (e.g., going to jail). They are not concerned with the emotional or psychological hurt their behavior may cause others. Behavior is seen as unacceptable if it leads to one's own punishment or if it results in physical harm to a high-status person or that person's belongings. Acceptable behavior is that which adheres to concrete, externally defined rules and avoids punishment, leads to reward, complies with power, or serves one's own interests when there are no external rules against it. As such, morality is seen as a number of clearly defined rules established by powerful people. These rules are not seen as having any relation to society. Indeed, the adolescent at this stage has no understanding of society, although he may have some conception of family. In addition, moral reasoning at this stage typically lacks any true sense of fairness and justice. Morality is, in effect, understood as an "eye for an eye, a tooth for a tooth." The value of life is often determined by the importance of the person, and one obeys simply to avoid punishment, not because it is for the social group's welfare. In sum, morality is determined by and learned from others, not oneself. The social perspective of youths at this stage is highly egocentric and narrow. Although there is an awareness of oneself and of an outside world, there is no recognition that other people may have feelings and thoughts different from one's own. The concept of mutuality does not exist; people act only in self-interest. Other people are seen only in terms of their ability to provide punishment or rewards; therefore, moral decisions tend to be based on concrete, physicalistic concerns.

The major orientation of the *Stage 2* reasoner, as indicated in Table 8, is that of instrumental relativism (i.e., individualism, instrumental purpose, and exchange). Youths at this stage determine what is right by doing what meets their own needs or perhaps those of another person and by focusing on making equitable and fair exchanges or deals. In other words, while making sure that their own needs are maximized, Stage 2 reasoners allow other people to satisfy their needs as well. To do this, adolescents must be able to recognize that other people may have needs different from their own. Acceptable behavior for everyone, therefore, includes those actions that allow one to acquire wanted materials, status, services, or help. Although there is a "market-place" quality to Stage 2 moral reasoning, it represents an advance over Stage 1 reasoning in that it is more internally defined (i.e., choices may allow one to meet personal needs) and there is less of a focus on the consequences of a behavior or physicalistic qualities. Youths at this stage also have developed a sense of the organization of social groups. This awareness of social organization is quite self-focused, however, in that it is determined by the exchange of egocentric interests between people (e.g., "You scratch my back and I'll scratch yours"). The intentions of others are not really considered to be important. As such, a good choice is evaluated in terms of whether it leads to a positive outcome for the person making the choice (i.e., the instrumental value of the behavior), rather than being determined by a sense of commitment and respect. Personal rights are highly determined by ownership: A person can do what she wants with her own belongings and with her life even if these choices are in conflict with the rights or needs of others. Rights are, therefore, determined by each individual rather than by a group or societal consensus.

As already alluded to, the social perspective of the Stage 2 reasoner involves the recognition that one's personal views may differ from other people's positions and that these other people may also perceive situations differently from one another. Youths at this stage also recognize that people depend on each other to respond in an agreed-upon way. Although mutuality is considered, it is typically understood in terms of one other or at most a few people. In addition, if a few people's viewpoints are being considered, their ideas will tend to be looked on as being separate rather than as related or as part of a group. In other words, relationships are generally seen in dyadic terms, with moral reasoning reflecting individual rather than group concerns. These individual concerns are self-oriented; issues involving the group good and the good of the larger society are not considered. In sum, Stage 2 reasoning is primarily characterized by the idea that one will meet the needs of others only when doing so also meets one's own needs.

As Table 8 indicates, the major orientation of the *Stage 3* reasoner is that of interpersonal concordance, or a "good boy/nice girl" position (i.e., mutual interpersonal expectations, relationships, and interpersonal conformity). Individuals at this stage determine what is right by following the "Golden Rule" principle of doing unto others what you would want them to do unto you. Acceptable behavior involves being nice, loyal, and trustworthy; having good intentions; conforming to group expectations; doing what will lead to approval; and behaving within role expectations. Stage 3 reasoners feel it is important to be concerned about others because they would want others to be concerned about them in a similar situation. As such, Stage 3 reasoners are concerned about establishing and maintaining good relationships with the people in their group network. This requires that the individual possess some sensitivity to the rights, feelings, and viewpoints of others, as well as an understanding of reciprocity and mutuality.

Stage 3 reasoners have developed the capacity for reciprocal perspective-taking—that is, the ability to view an action from another person's point of view. This capacity allows the Stage 3 reasoner to attend more closely to the intentions of others and the meaning of another's behavior. Thus the particular actions enacted become secondary to the person's motivation. By focusing on intentions rather than actions, Stage 3 reasoners are able to excuse typically unacceptable behavior (e.g., to condone stealing something in order to save a loved one's life). For the Stage 3 reasoner, moral conflict is often resolved by looking for and using previously and fairly established group rules. The expectation is that others will recognize one's own needs if one follows group rules. Although this requires the individual to perspective-take and to subordinate personal needs for the good of the social group and, as such, represents an advance over Stage 2 reasoning, the morality of people at Stage 3 continues to be somewhat self-oriented.

This egocentrism takes the form of seeking to gain approval from legitimate authority figures: The goodness of a behavior thus is determined by whether it results in approval. As such, a rather conventional, stereotyped morality is evident in that what is good continues to be defined externally. Concerns about society beyond the immediate social group have not yet emerged. It may already be apparent that the social perspective of the Stage 3 reasoner involves an understanding of the "group good" and the ability to perspective-take. Genuine concern is evident in Stage 3 reasoners' interest in others. Relationships and group membership are important simply for the sake of these relationships and not because one needs another person to achieve a desired goal. Indeed, relationships are perceived as a mutual sharing between two or more people. The desire for mutuality necessitates that the Stage 3 reasoner consider the thoughts and feelings of other group members and place his individual needs behind those of the relationship or group (i.e., be self-sacrificing). In other words, individuals will attempt to make choices that please everyone involved (i.e., will behave as a "good person" would).

The major orientation of the *Stage 4* reasoner, indicated on Table 8, involves considerations about law and order, the social system, and conscience. Appropriate behavior for the Stage 4 reasoner is determined by the desire to maintain order and law in the larger society and by meeting one's obligations to society in an effort to prevent social disorder or to maintain self-respect and a good conscience. In effect, the individual behaves in a manner that facilitates the functioning of the entire society. The Stage 4 reasoner often uses a legal position to determine what is acceptable or unacceptable. However, unlike the Stage 1 reasoner, who may uphold law out of fear of punishment, or the Stage 3 reasoner, who is obedient because of the desire to conform to being good, the Stage 4 reasoner obeys because laws are made by society and must be upheld out of respect and fairness to all members of society. Just as rights are earned by society's members, laws are rules designed by elected members of society to assure that everyone's rights are maintained. As such, laws assure that society will function in an orderly, peaceful manner.

It is apparent that this orientation reflects an advance over Stage 3 reasoning in a number of ways. First, the Stage 4 reasoner recognizes that, to guarantee equality, fairness, and order, society's rules must encompass all social groups rather than just certain segments of the society. Second, individuals at Stage 4 also realize that loyalty, the intention to do the right thing, and small group relationships (Stage 3) are not enough to guarantee that laws and rights are upheld. Rather, Stage 4 reasoners maintain that strict standardization of the law is needed to maintain equality and order. The rigidity evident in the reasoning process of the early Stage 4 individual emerges in response to the belief that if subjective feelings and favoritism enter into the running of society chaos will ensue.

As the Stage 4 individual develops, however, she begins to question the underlying principles used in establishing laws. Contradictions between legal laws and moral laws and the injustice of some legal laws become increasingly evident to the more advanced Stage 4 reasoner. This awareness marks the movement to the next stage of reasoning. (*Stage 5* reasoning, which emphasizes law but involves a realization that most values are relative and a belief in some nonrelative values that must be upheld in any society, and *Stage 6* reasoning, which emphasizes universal principles of justice, equality, and dignity over law, will not be addressed in detail in this chapter. Judgments at these two levels are attained by relatively few individuals and, as such, are not likely to be evident in dilemma discussion groups with youth.) The social perspective of the Stage 4 individual is characterized by the realization that all people, including oneself, are needed for the successful functioning of the larger society. It is this focus on the "social good" that differentiates Stage 4 from Stage 3 reasoners, whose focus is on the "group good." Although dyadic or small group relationships are still seen as important, the social perspective evolves to encompass the meaning and impact these relationships, and people in general, have on the entire society. People are seen not only as sharing a relationship but as sharing a society.

Eliciting information about moral reasoning stage. Once a trainer is familiar with the characteristics of each stage, the second step in becoming an effective assessor of moral reasoning involves learning how to get the kind of information needed to make accurate stage assessments. Specifically, the trainer needs information that reveals the underlying reasons for a behavioral choice. Simple statements like "I'd steal the drug" will not give the trainer the rationale used to make the decision. When this situation occurs, the trainer must be prepared to ask questions that will reveal the *why* behind the action. Two key guidelines should always be followed when asking for elaborations of responses:

1. Ask open-ended questions (ones that encourage explanation rather than simply a "yes" or "no") designed to reveal the reasons underlying the behavioral choice (e.g., "Could you tell me more about your reasons for making that choice?"; "In what way do you think that is the best action to take?"; "I'm not sure I understand your reasoning for that choice").

2. Listen actively and closely to the meaning of the youngster's statements and either mentally or verbally paraphrase or rephrase the statement to ensure complete comprehension of the response presented. If your paraphrase is inaccurate, ask the trainee for clarification with another open-ended question. An example of paraphrasing follows:

> Bill: John shouldn't report his friend to the police because friendship is based on mutual trust and respect. To report him to the police would be breaking an important rule of friendship.
>
> Trainer: The value of friendship is important to you. To report John would be like violating the rules of relationships. Does that capture what you were saying, Bill?

Paraphrasing requires some practice and should be done with friends, family, or colleagues before a trainer actually runs a dilemma discussion group.

It is also helpful to know what to avoid when evaluating moral reasoning stages. The following list briefly describes conditions to avoid when identifying moral stage during group discussions:

1. Regardless of the trainee's response, do not express negative judgments. Instead, encourage further elaboration of the response when necessary (e.g., "I'd like to be able to fully understand your ideas"; "Tell me a little more about that").

2. Do not pretend to agree with the trainee's ideas as a means of encouraging more discussion. Express interest, not agreement.

3. Avoid asking too many questions since this tends to elicit defensiveness from the trainee. Using open-ended questions, rather than closed questions (questions requiring yes/no answers or short responses), often prevents this from occurring. Avoid asking *why* questions repeatedly since they, too, tend to elicit defensiveness.

Practice exercises. Once a trainer is armed with the basic skills needed to be an effective moral reasoning assessor, practice in assessment is the next step. Two sets of practice exercises with answer keys follow. Referring to Tables 7 and 8 and to the earlier discussion in this chapter of the stages will help with the exercises. Although these exercises provide initial practice, it is important to reiterate that expertise in this area requires a great deal of practice and time. The reader is, therefore, referred to Gibbs, Widaman, and Colby (1982), in which additional practice exercises are presented.

Exercise I—Heinz Dilemma*

In Europe, a woman was near death from a special kind of cancer. There was one drug that the doctors thought might save her. It was a form of radium that a druggist in the same town had recently discovered. The drug was expensive to make, but the druggist wanted people to pay 10 times what the drug cost him to make.

The sick woman's husband, Heinz, went to everyone he knew to borrow the money, but he could only get together about half of what the druggist wanted. Heinz told the druggist that his wife was dying and asked him to sell the drug cheaper or let him pay later. But the druggist said, "No. I discovered the drug and I'm going to make money from it." So the only way Heinz could get the drug would be to break into the druggist's store and steal it. *What should Heinz do?*

Assess what stage of moral reasoning the following responses reflect:

1. Heinz should steal the drug because it isn't really bad to take it. And his wife might be a really important person.

2. It's wrong to steal someone's property because there are laws that protect property. In this case he wouldn't really be wrong, though, because a human life is at stake. Life has important value that overrides things like property. And it's his wife's life. He has taken a vow to protect her and has a responsibility as her husband to save her. He should expect to pay the druggist back and maybe go to jail for a while.

3. No, he shouldn't steal it. He couldn't be blamed if she died. It was the druggist who was mean and selfish. He should obey the law because if people just made selfish decisions all the time, there would be chaos.

4. No, he shouldn't steal it. He might not care for his wife anyway. And he could always find a new one. What good would it do to save her if he was in jail, anyway! And the druggist is just trying to make some money. After all, that's what people are in business for.

5. Heinz probably doesn't really want to steal the drug, but it's all right in this case because he needs it badly to save his wife's life. And he needs her and wants her to live. And the druggist deserves to have it stolen for trying to rip off his customers.

---

*Exercises I and II are from John C. Gibbs, Keith Widaman, and A. Colby, *Social Intelligence: Measuring the Development of Sociomoral Reflection,* © 1982, pp. 193–200. Reprinted by permission of Prentice-Hall, Englewood Cliffs, NJ.

6. The law forbids stealing from another person. But at the same time, the law was not designed with circumstances such as these in mind. Heinz would be justified in taking the drug but would have to make real and social compensations for it. The law here is not doing a good job in protecting basic human rights. The value of life is far more important than the value of private property. So Heinz should feel no guilt in his act.

7. He should steal the drug. He was only doing what a good and loyal husband would do. He should care enough about her to want to do it and should feel guilty if he didn't. And while it isn't nice to take someone else's property, the druggist was being heartless and cruel.

8. No, he shouldn't take it. He'd be taking property of the druggist and probably harm his store. He'd get caught and be punished. And besides, some really important person might need the drug badly.

9. No, even though the druggist morally had no right to charge that much, legally he does. Heinz doesn't have a legal right to take someone else's legal property. We all have to respect the rights we guarantee by law to others. If not, society would break down.

10. He shouldn't steal it because he should think about his life and future, so he should not get involved with his wife's death.

11. He shouldn't steal it because he would be taking other people's things.

12. It isn't really right to steal even though the community probably wouldn't blame him for the theft. However, he has agreed to live by the standards of the community. So he must weigh whether such individual acts would ultimately result in the greatest good for all. By breaking into another's legal property, Heinz would be violating principles of trust which are part of the contract he has made with the community.

13. I guess he should steal it because it would benefit his wife, and he was acting out of good conscience. But he still broke the law and should therefore be punished.

14. He shouldn't steal the drug because taking things from others is really mean. If Heinz took the drug it would not be right because the drug is the druggist's pride and joy, because he found something that can save lives.

15. No, because it's not yours and kids could be put in a detention home and adults could be put in jail.

Using the same dilemma, now determine the stage of the response to the question, *What should the judge do?*

16. Heinz shouldn't be sent to jail because he saved a life. It is better to steal than to let someone die. The judge should help Heinz, put him on probation, and warn him never to break the law again but to ask for help from the authorities.

17. He should be sent to jail because if the judge goes easy on him, then he'd have to go easy on everyone else and no one would get placed in jail.

18. Heinz should not be put in jail because the justice that would be served would be that of the individual. Individual rights rather than society's right would be served. If the judge feels that Heinz was forced to steal, the judge should be able to see the unfairness of the country's legal system and try to change it.

19. Heinz should be sent to jail because sooner or later everyone would feel justified to steal. Everybody would steal and say it was needed for this or that, and the morals of society would soon break down.

20. He shouldn't be sent to jail because he was trying to be good and he's nice.

Exercise I Answer Key

1. Stage 1	6. Stage 5	11. Stage 1	16. Stage 3
2. Stage 4	7. Stage 3	12. Stage 5	17. Stage 2
3. Stage 3	8. Stage 1	13. Stage 3	18. Stage 5
4. Stage 2	9. Stage 4	14. Stage 3	19. Stage 4
5. Stage 2	10. Stage 2	15. Stage 1	20. Stage 1

Exercise II—The Broken Promise

In this exercise, try to stage the responses without the benefit of referring to a specific moral dilemma.[1]

1. Keeping a promise to a friend is important because it's important to be able to place your trust in others. But if someone told me something that they were doing, I wouldn't tell because it's none of my business to tell on him.

2. Letting one's children keep earned money is important because if the parents take the money, then the children will get mad at their parents and it might end up in an argument or fight.

3. Keeping promises to one's children is important because children have to mind their parents and it's stupid to tell your children that they could go and then turn around and say no.

4. Helping one's parents is very important because if you love your mother and you want to do what she wants you to do, then do it.

5. Keeping a promise to a friend is very important because it's important to keep a promise to a friend, also to anybody else one knows, not necessarily friends only, because our words reflect the kind of a person we are.

6. Letting one's children keep earned money is very important because it not only lets the children have fun, but they may have worked hard for the money and to hand it over to parents isn't fair. Not unless the parents were in poverty. Then you should help them out.

7. Keeping a promise to a friend is important because being loyal to a friend is important. You should regard their trust in you very highly because much is based on trust.

8. Letting one's children keep earned money is important because the children should learn values, and the action of a parent reflects very highly on the children. By earning the money the children have shown responsibility, and, if this money is taken away, so will the meaning of earning the money.

9. Helping one's parents is very important because, even though it was Judy's money and her mother wasn't being fair when she changed

---

[1]Some responses in this exercise are transitional responses, in which a dominant level of reasoning is evident along with some reasoning at a higher level—for example, primary reasoning at Stage 3 with some Stage 4 reasoning indicated.

her mind, you should still respect what someone says and still trust them and not hold a grudge just for one mistake.

10. Letting one's children keep earned money is important because otherwise you will be stealing your children's money.

Exercise II Answer Key

1. Stage 3; Stage 3/4[2]   4. Stage 2; Stage 2/3   7. Stage 3
2. Stage 1   5. Stage 4   8. Stage 4
3. Stage 1   6. Stage 2; Stage 2/3   9. Stage 1; Stage 1/2
                                                   10. Stage 1

Group Organization

Number of trainees and trainers
Dilemma discussion groups are ideally run with groups large enough to provide a diversity sufficient to arouse cognitive conflict. In our Aggression Replacement Training projects (Goldstein & Glick, 1987), using 12 participating youth appeared to meet these criteria. As mentioned earlier, ideally, a trainer and a co-trainer should lead the discussion groups.

Number of sessions
As with several of the other courses that constitute the Prepare Curriculum, participation appears valuable to trainees whether a brief (e.g., 10 sessions) sequence of meetings is held (Goldstein & Glick, 1987) or whether courses last two full semesters or more (Keller, Goldstein, & Wynn, 1987).

Length and spacing of sessions
Dilemma discussion classes are held for about 1 hour. However, since the length of the class often depends on how verbal the trainees are, how interesting the dilemma is, and school class scheduling practices, sessions can range from 45 to 60 minutes. This variability raises a question: How many dilemmas should be discussed in each class?

---

[2]The representation *Stage 3/4* denotes a transitional response in which the primary moral reasoning process is at Stage 3 with some Stage 4 reasoning evident. The same principle holds true for numbers 4, 6, and 9.

During an hour-long class, a complete discussion of at least one and often two dilemmas will occur (a thorough discussion of one dilemma can take from 20 to 30 minutes). Discussion groups should be spaced a few days apart to encourage thinking about the dilemmas.

Conducting Dilemma Discussion Groups

There are six general steps involved in running dilemma discussion groups.

Step 1: Form small groups of trainees at two to three consecutive stages of moral reasoning.

Step 2: Choose and prepare moral dilemma situations that will induce cognitive conflict and that are relevant to the trainees.

Step 3: Create the proper set by explaining to the trainees the rationale for dilemma discussion groups, what they will be doing, what the trainer's role is in the group, and what guidelines will be followed in the group discussion.

Step 4: Begin the discussion by presenting the dilemma and getting initial opinions and rationales from the trainees. Then create a debate between the lowest reasoners and those one stage higher (noted as + 1 stage).

Step 5: Guide discussion through all the stages represented by group members (e.g., start with a debate between Stage 1 and Stage 2 reasoners, then structure a debate between Stage 2 and Stage 3 reasoners, and so on if more than three levels of reasoning are represented), creating cognitive conflict for as many trainees as possible. Then present a + 1 stage argument for the group to discuss (e.g., if the highest stage represented in the group is Stage 3, then present a Stage 4 argument).

Step 6: End discussion following the debate of the highest stage argument or when all the major issues and important differences of opinion have been addressed.

Before these six steps are discussed in detail, however, it will be helpful to define some of the terms that will be used throughout the remainder of this chapter. In dilemma discussion groups, cognitive conflict can be generated in two ways:

1. "+ 1 SC"

   This type of conflict is read as "plus one stage conflict." It occurs when group members hold different positions on a dilemma (e.g., some trainees say "steal the drug" while others say "do not steal") *and* when these different behavioral choices are based on reasoning one stage apart (e.g., "pro" stealing Stage 1s and "con" stealing Stage 2s). This type of conflict means that trainees at the lower stage are exposed to reasoning one stage above their own (+ 1 reasoning). The exposure to + 1 SC elicits the awareness that one's own reasoning is not fully adequate and thus generates disequilibrium—the sense that one's view of the world has been shaken up.

2. "Non-PC"

This type of conflict is read as "nonpreferred conflict." It is not as desirable as + 1 SC because it does not create as much disequilibrium and does not provide exposure to + 1 stage reasoning. As such, Non-PC is less likely to enhance moral reasoning. Non-PC occurs when group members maintain different positions on a dilemma, but these positions are based on reasoning at the same stages (e.g., everyone is at Stage 1) or two or more stages apart (e.g., some trainees reason at Stage 1 whereas the rest reason at Stage 3).

Whenever possible, it is better to create a + 1 SC discussion (detailed in the following section on preferred circumstances, Steps 4 and 5). If this is not possible (if statements are not provided that allow the trainer to structure a + 1 SC discussion or if the trainer is unable to assess reasoning stage accurately), the next best alternative is to structure a Non-PC discussion (detailed in the following section on nonpreferred circumstances, Steps 4 and 5). With this terminology in mind, the discussion will now focus on describing each of the six steps involved in running dilemma discussion groups.

Step 1: Forming Groups Based on
Initial Assessment of Stages

The first step in conducting dilemma discussion groups involves the formation of groups based on an initial assessment of moral reasoning stages. Before describing the conditions needed to form an ideal group, it is important to stress that dilemma discussion groups can be conducted even if the ideal conditions do not exist because of institutional restrictions (e.g., preformed classrooms or counseling groups) or because a range of different stages of reasoning is simply not available. In these cases, the trainer simply takes a more active role in the moral discussion process. For example, if only one moral reasoning stage is represented in the group, the trainer will always need to provide the + 1 reasoning arguments. In fact, in most dilemma discussion groups involving antisocial adolescents, the trainer will almost always be in the position of having to provide a + 1 stage argument, at least for some portion of the time. Thus groups can be formed even if only one stage is represented. It simply means that the trainer will need to work under Non-PC conditions. If possible, however, it is best to form an *ideal* group.

To form an ideal group, three conditions should be met:

1. A range of consecutive moral reasoning stages must be represented by the trainees (e.g., Stages 1 and 2 or Stages 1, 2, and 3). Meeting this condition means that almost all group members (all but the highest stage reasoners) will be exposed to + 1 stage reasoning. It also increases the chance that trainees will present different opinions. Finally, meeting this condition keeps the discussion manageable in that the trainer does not have to be concerned about structuring debates across too many different stages. This would not only be difficult but would also be of little benefit to most of the trainees (remember that Stage 1 reasoners, for example, are unlikely to understand the reasoning of Stage 4 individuals because it is too advanced for them).

2. The number of trainees reasoning at a particular moral stage should be almost equally represented in the group (e.g., four Stage 2s, four Stage 3s, and four Stage 4s). Meeting this condition decreases the chances for peer rejection because it guarantees that there will be more than one group member at a particular stage. It is often difficult for one trainee to present an argument that the rest of the group is likely to disagree with because they are at a different stage.

3. Relatively small groups should be established, consisting of about 6 to 12 people (groups have, however, ranged from 20 to 30 individuals). Keeping the groups small increases the chance that everyone will have an opportunity to participate and decreases group management problems. A final note regarding group composition is that the ages of the trainees should not vary too widely.

In order to meet the first two of these conditions, the trainer must be familiar with the procedures used for determining moral reasoning stage, previously described in the section on assessment of moral reasoning stage. To review briefly, these procedures involve (1) familiarizing yourself with the characteristics of each of the six moral reasoning stages, particularly Stages 1 through 4; and (2) either administering a test to identify moral reasoning stage (e.g., the Sociomoral Reflections Measure of Gibbs et al., 1982, or the Moral Judgment Interviews of Arbuthnot & Faust, 1981) or conducting informal interviews about solutions to moral dilemmas, as described earlier. Following the assessment of moral reasoning stage, trainees should be assigned to groups based on the three conditions previously described.

Step 2: Choosing and Preparing Dilemmas

Choosing dilemmas

The second step in conducting dilemma discussion groups involves the selection of dilemmas for debate. A total of 17 stimulating dilemmas have been preselected for use when running dilemma discussion groups and are included at the end of this chapter. However, if the trainer opts to choose or develop his own dilemmas, three major goals need to be achieved:

1. Select dilemmas that will generate cognitive conflict for as many trainees as possible;
2. Select dilemmas that will create interesting and productive discussion;
3. Select dilemmas that clearly deal with moral issues (e.g., issues of life, property, affiliation, etc.).

When running groups with trainees who reason at two or three consecutive stages, it is at times difficult to select dilemmas because the issues that create disequilibrium for one stage of reasoners may not create cognitive conflict for trainees reasoning at another stage. Nevertheless, different stages ideally need to be represented in the group. To avoid this potential problem, several guidelines can be followed in choosing dilemmas for discussion.

1. Select or construct dilemmas that generate several issues and questions but that are open-ended so that the dilemma can be elaborated if issues at certain stages are not automatically raised or if no counterarguments from higher stage reasoners are provided. A lack of extensive, precise details helps maintain the open-ended quality of a dilemma so that, when higher stage counterarguments are not generated spontaneously, elaborations can be added to create these higher stage arguments or new issues can emerge.

Example: Suppose that in response to the Heinz dilemma a Stage 2 reasoner argues that Heinz should steal the drug because he needs his wife. If a Stage 3 reasoner does not spontaneously produce a counterargument, the trainer might elaborate the dilemma by adding information that may change the position of the Stage 2 and not the Stage 3 reasoner. Specifically, the trainer might change the sick person from a wife to a friend or stranger. This kind of elaboration is likely to create the material needed for the development of a counterargument, which is necessary for the structuring of a debate.

2. Choose dilemmas involving genuine moral conflict—situations in which at least two people have differing claims (e.g., Heinz wants to save his wife's life and the druggist wants to earn money) and in which one behavioral alternative or another must be chosen.

3. Select dilemmas that trainees will be able to understand, given their intellectual abilities.

4. Select dilemmas that will most likely lead to different action alternatives for trainees reasoning at different stages. With experience and some knowledge of group members, the trainer's ability to anticipate probable responses correctly will increase.

5. Choose interesting dilemmas by considering their relevance to the youngsters, the probability that the moral situation will actually occur in real life, the novelty of the issue, and the ability of the dilemma to stimulate challenging questions, disagreement, and cognitive conflict. It is important to stress that not all relevant issues are moral issues. For instance, many relevant dilemmas deal with controversial or personal rather than moral issues (e.g., premarital sex). It is recommended that controversial and personal issues not be selected for discussion unless it appears that the group needs to discuss these issues to maintain sustained interest in the program. If controversial issues are introduced into the group, it is best to wait until trainees have met for a period of time.

Preparing dilemmas

After selecting a number of dilemmas to be discussed, the trainer, as in any teaching effort, must prepare the dilemmas prior to the beginning of each group. This preparation is designed to accomplish three goals:

1. To make the dilemmas useful in assessing the trainee's moral reasoning stage;
2. To stimulate debates at different stages;
3. To generate counterarguments at different stages, if necessary.

This preparation is particularly important for the inexperienced trainer because it is very difficult to elaborate a dilemma or develop a counterargument when one is on the spot. In order to prepare dilemmas adequately, the trainer should follow three general guidelines. The first guideline is to try to anticipate how trainees at a particular stage will respond to the dilemma by referring to the characteristics of each stage (see Tables 7 and 8). For example, using the Heinz dilemma, one might anticipate that Stage 1 reasoners will be concerned about the consequences of their actions. On the one hand, Heinz might not want to steal for his wife because he would end up in jail. On the other hand, maybe he would steal the drug because his wife would be angry if he did not. Stage 2 reasoners will be concerned about self-interests. In this view, Heinz might steal the drug because he needs his wife around to raise the children. However, he might not steal the drug because his wife never did anything for him. The trainer should be concerned with anticipating how the trainees will reason at a particular stage rather than with what behavioral alternative will be selected. This type of preparation will make it far easier to assess the actual responses made in the group when that time arrives.

The second guideline to attend to involves preparing elaborations of dilemmas for those instances when it is necessary to generate disagreements between trainees at different stages (see the previously described example). Third, it is important to prepare a counterargument for each of the stages represented in the group, as well as an argument that is one stage above the highest stage represented in the group. In addition, the trainer should be prepared to argue for at least two behavioral alternatives at each stage. Preparations of this kind are helpful in situations in which arguments at certain stages are not verbalized automatically and elaborations of the dilemma do not promote active discussion of counterpositions.

For the Heinz dilemma, stage preparations might include the following:

Stage 1: Steal—His wife may be an important person.
Not Steal—He will be put in jail for it.
Stage 2: Steal—He needs her to clean and take care of the children.
Not steal—He does not like her anymore.
Stage 3: Steal—Nobody wants to see someone die.
Not steal—If he went to jail he would not be around to take care of his family as a good husband would.
Stage 4: Steal—He would be saving the life of a human being. The value of life is more important in this instance than property.
Not steal—We have a contract with society to protect the rights of others (in this instance, property rights).

During an hour-long class, a complete discussion of at least one dilemma and the introduction and gathering of initial opinions on a second dilemma should occur. With less verbal trainees, it is often possible to discuss two different dilemmas completely in one session. Given that this situation is a possibility, the trainer must prepare three dilemmas for each class (i.e., anticipate stage responses, create elaborations, and develop counterarguments). It is certainly acceptable not to complete a discussion in one session. In fact, it is sometimes desirable to leave the discussion incomplete in order to encourage trainees to think about the dilemma after the class. This additional time between classes can lead to further thoughts that were not initially recognized and can facilitate advancements in moral reasoning. Discussion of the dilemma can be resumed in the next class if desired by the trainees.

Prior to the first dilemma discussion group, the trainer and co-trainer should also determine what responsibilities each will have during the group. For example, one trainer may decide to take primary responsibility for asking the questions needed to get stage responses while the other person records and assesses the level of the responses. Since the latter person has assessed the responses, she may then decide to take on the primary responsibility of structuring the initial discussion while the other trainer handles later debates. These rules should not be rigidly adhered to since the aim is to create a flexible, open, and nonjudgmental atmosphere. This division of labor is suggested only to prevent the new trainer from being overwhelmed with the many demands of these groups. So, even if the trainer has decided to assess responses during a particular class, she can feel free to ask questions, guide the discussion, or perform any of the other tasks as well.

Step 3: Creating the Proper Set

With Step 3, the trainer is at last in the class getting ready to start the initial dilemma discussion group session. The group has been formed (Step 1), and the dilemmas have been selected and prepared (Step 2). Creating the proper set (or appropriate expectations) marks the beginning of the actual class and is the first task the trainer undertakes in the initial meeting. It is a crucial step because it establishes the foundation for the structure of the subsequent group meetings. There are four general goals that need to be accomplished during this phase of the initial session. The first goal involves explaining the rationale for and purpose of dilemma discussion groups and some of the theory on which the group is based. The following ideas should be included in the presentation:

1. The group will meet to discuss situations in which people have conflicting claims;
2. The goal of the discussion group is to enhance everyone's ability to think or reason about these conflictual situations;
3. Although people may think they know how to resolve these situations, almost everyone can develop further by experimenting with different ways of thinking about conflictual situations and so can be better prepared when actually faced with a real conflictual problem;
4. As people mature, they develop different ways of thinking about these situations;
5. Discussion of conflictual situations seems to increase a person's ability to think about and solve these problems when they really happen.

In this discussion, the level of the presentation should be adjusted to suit the intellectual abilities of the trainees, to include all the major ideas about the rationale underlying dilemma discussion groups, and to limit the amount of time spent discussing the rationale (i.e., the explanation should not be a formal academic presentation). In addition, when introducing the class to trainees, the word *moral* should be dropped since it can sometimes elicit confusion and defensiveness (this reaction is why the class is referred to as a dilemma discussion group rather than as a Moral Reasoning Training group). Adjusting the level of the presentation to the trainees is applicable to all of the goals in Step 3.

The second goal is to discuss the trainees' role in the group and group procedures by explaining the format of the meetings. The following ideas should be included in the presentation:

1. Conflictual situations involving dilemmas will be presented by the trainer to all trainees.
2. These situations are not like math problems because there is never just one right answer in a situation.
3. After presentation of the situation, all trainees will have a chance to share their opinions and solutions.
4. Trainees' different viewpoints will then be discussed with one another. Group members will be expected to do most of the talking, which may be hard initially but will likely become easier with time. The discussions will be something like a debate; to help everyone be actively involved, the group will be sitting in a circle.

The third goal is to explain the trainer's role in the group:

1. There will be no evaluations of whether trainees' answers are right or wrong because there are no right or wrong answers;
2. The trainer's role is not to present the right solution to the situation because there is none and because this is a time for trainees to use and develop their own ways to think and reason about these problems;
3. Although most of the talking will be done by trainees, the trainer's role is to help everyone focus on a few ideas at a time and to help the group talk in an orderly manner about the ideas brought up;
4. Although the trainer will not express personal ideas and solutions (this tends to interfere with the quality of the discussion), at times the trainer will play "devil's advocate" when important ideas have been missed;
5. The trainer will make sure that all trainees have a chance to share their opinions, if desired, and that respect for one another is always maintained;
6. The trainer will help trainees share their ideas clearly.

The fourth goal involves explaining ethical rules for group behavior and involvement:

1. Respect others' ideas: It is important that trainees feel safe to share openly their ideas. Respecting others' ideas does not mean always agreeing with them; it is fine to disagree because that is the best way to learn from one another. However, it is not OK to disagree by talking about unrelated issues, by not allowing someone to express an opinion, or by using personal insults. Trainees who disagree with others should stay on the subject, give everyone an equal chance to answer, argue in a fair way, and listen to what others have to say.

2. Respect trainees' freedom of belief: No one should feel she has to agree with any of the positions argued by anyone else, including the trainer. There are no punishments for disagreements—everyone should listen to one another and keep an open mind.

3. Respect trainees' freedom of choice to determine when to share their solution to each dilemma.

4. Respect the confidentiality of all responses made during the class unless doing so is in some way dangerous to the individual or to others.

Sample introductory statement

A sample introductory statement to create the proper set follows: "I imagine you're wondering what this class is all about. In this class, we'll be talking about ways to resolve conflict situations—situations where there is more than one way to think and act. Together, we will be discussing and thinking about how you choose which way is fairer. We're really going to be focusing on how come you came up with that solution to the problem, not just what your solution is. In other words, we'll be talking about the reasons you have for coming up with that solution. I know that everybody probably thinks he knows how to solve problems involving conflicts, but almost everybody can benefit by thinking about and experimenting with different ways to handle these situations. We feel that, if you experiment with different ways to think about these situations now, you'll be better prepared to handle them in the future. You know that as people get older they naturally develop different ways of thinking about these situations. These classes often speed up this natural process by helping people develop new and better ways to think about the situations now. *Better* here does not mean right or wrong. There are no right or wrong answers in these situations. However, there are better or worse solutions in the sense of helping you learn how to get along better with people. For example, you can learn how to make better decisions so you won't be hassled by teachers, parents, and peers as much. Also, if you respond to these people differently, they are likely to act differently with you. So the goal of the group is to increase your ability to think about conflict situations so you might be able to avoid hassles in the future.

"We are going to start these classes by having somebody, either one of us [the trainers] or a group member, read a conflict situation out loud. Remember, these situations aren't like math problems because there's never one right answer. After reading the situation, everyone here will have a chance to share opinions and solutions. In fact, that's going to be your major job in the group. That is, your job will be to discuss with one another your differences of opinion. In other words, unlike lots of other classes you've been in, you're expected to do most of the talking. This may be hard at first, but with time I hope it will become easier. The discussions will be something like a debate, and to help everyone be involved we'll be sitting in a circle.

"Though your job is to do most of the talking in here, our job will be to help everyone focus on a few ideas at a time, to help the group talk in an orderly way about the ideas you bring up, to help everyone share ideas in an understandable way, and to help make sure that everyone who wants to will have a chance to share ideas. Sometimes we might take on a devil's advocate position when we think an important idea has been missed. By *devil's advocate,* I mean that we might take a position different from the group's to add to the discussion. However, we wouldn't be giving you the right solution to the situation for two reasons. One, because there isn't a right solution and, two, because this is a time for you to be developing and experimenting with your own ways to think about these problems. For the same reasons, we won't be sharing our personal opinions about how to think about the problems. Remember, you're not getting a grade in here, so we're not going to be judging your answers.

"A couple of other points. Though we want this to be a place that's open, flexible, and safe for everyone to share ideas, there will be some rules that we're going to follow very strictly. One rule is that all group members will be expected to respect other members' ideas. Our job is to make sure that respect is maintained. This doesn't mean that you can't disagree with one another. In fact, it's fine to disagree because that's the best way to learn from each other. But it's not OK to disagree by insulting others, changing the subject, or not letting someone express an opinion if it's different from your own. It's OK to disagree by giving everyone a fair chance to answer, arguing in a fair way, staying on the subject, and listening to one another. In other words, we don't want you to feel you have to agree with anyone else in the group, including us. Just keep an open mind. There are no punishments for disagreements. I also want to mention that we expect all group members to respect one another's privacy. This means that, if personal things are discussed in here, they shouldn't be discussed with others unless that person wants you to. Respecting one another's privacy doesn't mean that you can't continue to discuss the conflict problem outside the group. In fact, feel free to do this; it can often be helpful.

"Does anyone have any questions about what I just said? [Answer questions.] OK, then let's get started since that's the best way to understand all this."

Foundation for later steps
Some kind of an introductory statement *must* be presented in the initial meeting. Unless any confusion about these points emerges in later sessions, Step 3 does not need to be repeated during later classes. Thus the importance of addressing these issues early in the training cannot be overstated. It is ethically important because trainees have the right to know what is involved in the activity they are undertaking. Further-

more, it is useful because trainees often demonstrate greater interest when procedures are explained.

The procedures the trainer will follow when conducting Steps 4, 5, and 6 depend on what type of circumstances or conflicts unfold in the group. As noted earlier, two ways of generating cognitive conflict can emerge in dilemma discussion groups: + 1 SC, or preferred circumstances (when trainees at a lower stage are exposed to reasoning one stage above their own), and Non-PC, or nonpreferred circumstances (when trainees have different solutions to a dilemma but these positions are based on reasoning at the same stage or at two or more stages apart). Although preferred circumstances may evolve naturally, in work with antisocial youth the trainer is more likely to be in the position of having to create + 1 SC or work under Non-PC. Since the different procedures followed under these two circumstances can be confusing, the discussion will initially focus on conducting Steps 4, 5, and 6 under preferred circumstances (+ 1 SC). Subsequently, procedures to follow for conducting Steps 4, 5, and 6 under nonpreferred circumstances will be addressed. In each of these separate discussions, general issues will be discussed first; then specific procedures for each situation will be described.

Preferred Circumstances
Step 4: Initiating Discussion
In the first group meeting, the trainer will initially spend some time creating a proper set (Step 3 is not repeated in subsequent sessions unless necessary). This should not take longer than 10 to 15 minutes. Immediately following this introduction, the trainer will initiate a discussion of a dilemma. The overall goal when initiating discussion is to set up a debate between group members who have expressed the lowest reasoning stage on a dilemma and disagreeing trainees reasoning one stage above the lowest stage.

A discussion begins when the trainer reads a dilemma to the group (if desired, one of the trainees can be selected to read the dilemma). It is often helpful to provide written copies of the dilemma for trainees to follow while someone reads it out loud. The trainer should then make sure the dilemma is fully understood by (1) either summarizing it herself or asking group members to summarize the main points (these points and the characters and their roles can even be written on the board), (2) encouraging questions, and (3) clarifying misperceptions about the dilemma. Following this summarizing process, the trainer should provide a few minutes for trainees to think about the dilemma and formulate a solution to the dilemma problem (e.g., "In a minute, everyone will have a chance to give an opinion on the problem, but let's take a few minutes to think quietly about it first"). If desired, the trainer can have trainees write down their responses. It is important to reiterate that in these dilemmas a moral problem is presented in which trainees must decide between two behavioral choices (e.g., stealing versus not stealing). The trainees should also be thinking about why they have chosen a particular behavioral alternative.

After the thinking period, the trainer should go around the circle, having each trainee express an opinion about the dilemma and give reasons for choosing a particular solution (if desired, the different values presented by trainees can be written on the board to aid retention and focus discussion). It is often helpful to start with a verbal trainee or one who appears to want to speak. Inform trainees that they can "pass" if they want to and that they can express their opinions later if desired. The trainer will need to recall these initial statements for the subsequent discussion. As such, it is often helpful to take short summary notes of the initial opinions of trainees. This is easily accomplished by rephrasing out loud the trainee's response, and, if the paraphrase is accurate, recording the major idea in the response. If the major meaning of the statement is not accurately rephrased, the trainer should continue to ask "probe" questions. Probe questions are designed to get at the reasoning underlying the solution (e.g., "How come you think that is the fairest solution?"). The trainer should ask probe questions until he either understands the meaning of the response and, if possible, the stage of the response or until the trainee begins to perceive the questioning as threatening.

After getting everyone's initial opinion of the dilemma, the trainer's next task depends on what type of conflict has been presented. Under preferred circumstances, the following conditions will be evident:

1. Trainees will maintain different positions (behavioral alternatives) on a dilemma, which are based on different moral reasoning stages;
2. Trainees reasoning at different stages will have argued for different solutions;
3. The trainer has successfully identified the moral reasoning stage for most of the trainees' responses.

Under these circumstances, the trainer would first structure a debate between trainees reasoning at the two lowest stages who have different positions. Trainees reasoning at other stages would not initially be included in the discussion (they would, however, be asked to listen to the debate). When initiating the discussion, the trainer simply brings the attention of the group to the differing viewpoints (both solution and reasoning) by concisely restating the positions and by asking trainees at the lowest stage to debate their differences with the + 1 stage reasoners. The trainer can choose any of the trainees to begin the discussion by repeating or elaborating a response (it is helpful to pick someone who has presented a clear and complete argument). Subsequently, a + 1 stage reasoner with a different solution is asked to respond.

For example, the trainer may initiate a discussion of the Heinz dilemma by saying, "I've heard several different viewpoints about this situation. We'll start with two of these positions. Dave, Lee, and Steve don't think Heinz should steal the drug because he'll end up in jail [Stage 1 response]. On the other hand, Tom, Joe, and Fred think Heinz should steal the drug because he needs his wife around to take care of the children [Stage 2 response]. Dave, how about sharing your opinion again, and then, Tom, you explain to Dave and the others how come you disagree with them. The rest of you can feel free to jump in and support Dave or Tom or add any other ideas."

In summary, initiating a discussion under preferred circumstances involves getting initial opinions, determining that the opinions differ across solution and stage for a subset of the group, and setting up a discussion between lowest and + 1 stage reasoners who hold opposite opinions. It is also important to note that the process for initiating a discussion (i.e., read and summarize the dilemma, go around the circle to get opinions, set up the initial discussion) is repeated every time a new dilemma is introduced into the group. Indeed, following the initial session, it is how the trainer will begin every other session unless a dilemma from the prior session is being carried over into the subsequent one.

Preferred Circumstances
Step 5: Guiding Discussion
After an initial discussion between the lowest and + 1 stage reasoners has been structured, the trainer is now ready to move on to Step 5, guiding the discussion. The following comments apply not only to the initial discussion but to all subsequent debates. To guide a dilemma discussion effectively, the trainer must be able to get as many trainees as possible to experience + 1 SC. The experience of + 1 SC is achieved by (1) exposing trainees to + 1 stage reasoning and (2) exposing

trainees to additional factors that promote disequilibrium. The major factor needed to elicit disequilibrium involves helping lower stage reasoners realize that their reasoning does not completely help to resolve the dilemma. In other words, it is absolutely essential that during the + 1 SC discussion trainees become aware that their reasoning is inadequate to resolve the dilemma. This fact clearly does not imply that they are inferior people; therefore, this inadequacy should be explained in a way that does not elicit defensiveness. It is this awareness of inadequacy that creates disequilibrium, which in combination with + 1 stage reasoning stimulates moral development. Therefore, the overall goal when guiding the initial discussion and all subsequent discussions is to have the lower stage reasoners realize the inadequacies and limitations of their reasoning.

In the previous section, it was stated that the presence of + 1 stage reasoning is a condition for structuring + 1 SC. This means that, when the trainer moves to guide the discussion under preferred circumstances, she already knows that + 1 stage reasoning is evident. The question now becomes one of determining how to maximize opportunities for lower stage reasoners to become aware of the inadequacy of their reasoning. There are at least three ways that the awareness of inadequate reasoning or disequilibrium can emerge:

1. Lower stage reasoners may come to realize that + 1 stage reasoners are able to resolve specific aspects of the dilemma that they themselves are unable to resolve and that initially appeared to be unresolvable;
2. The + 1 stage reasoners may directly point out the limitations, flaws, or contradictions of the lower stage reasoners' rationale, or the + 1 stage reasoners may ask questions that the lower stage reasoners cannot answer;
3. General exposure to + 1 stage reasoning, even without discussion, can create disequilibrium.

Ideally, at least one of these three circumstances will emerge over the course of the + 1 SC discussion without the assistance of the trainer. However, even under the best of circumstances the + 1 stage reasoners will be able to accomplish this goal without the trainer's assistance only about 50 percent of the time.

When lower stage reasoners do not recognize the limitations of their reasoning and the greater adequacy of + 1 stage reasoning, the trainer should first attempt to determine the cause of the difficulty. The second step depends on what has been identified as the cause of the problem. The problem may be due to negative attitudes toward participation, defensiveness, closed-mindedness, or the lack of clarity of the + 1 stage reasoners' arguments. If the + 1 stage reasoners present a clear argument and the lower stage reasoners continue to reject the higher stage position, the trainer might first ask the lower stage reasoners to explain why they have dismissed the higher stage response. If they have rejected the argument because it is beyond their understanding, then perhaps some error in assessment has been made and the trainer will need to make the appropriate adjustments to continue to guide the debate (e.g., altering assessment of stages and restructuring the debate). If they have rejected the argument because of defensiveness or closed-mindedness, the trainer might intervene by asking trainees to try to think about these problems without letting their emotions interfere with their reasoning. Trainees should try to understand, but not necessarily accept, the differing opinion before rejecting it. It can be helpful to ask the lower stage reasoners to rephrase another's opinion to enhance active listening. The trainer can also simply encourage trainees to think about the arguments over the week before making a final decision. Of course, the trainer should not continue to challenge the position of lower stage reasoners to an irritating level since this will only increase defensiveness. If these interventions fail, the trainer simply goes on to other trainees and continues to guide the discussion by either structuring another debate or having a general discussion of the major issues presented.

If lack of clarity of the + 1 argument is behind the rejection, the trainer should first have other + 1 stage reasoners try to present the argument in a more precise manner. If this is unsuccessful, the trainer should next try to clarify the + 1 argument by rephrasing the position to help the + 1 reasoners continue the discussion. If this intervention fails, it will be necessary for the trainer to play devil's advocate by arguing for the prior + 1 position or a new + 1 position. The following methods can be helpful to the trainer when playing the devil's advocate role to create awareness of inadequacy (i.e., disequilibrium):

1. Point out the contradictions or flaws in the lower stage argument by asking questions and/or suggesting hypothetical situations. Of course, what contradiction is pointed out depends on the response (opinion and reasoning stage) given.

Example: Using the Heinz dilemma, suppose a trainee states that everyone, including Heinz, should look out for himself. The trainer might ask the trainee what Heinz should do if he (the trainee) needed the drug to live and it was in Heinz's best interest not to steal it. More than likely, the trainee will say Heinz should steal the drug to save his life. The trainer might then respond to this contradiction and the flaws in the argument by saying, "In one situation, you said that Heinz should look out for himself, but then you said if it were your life at stake, Heinz should steal the drug. It sounds as though you said two different things. What do you think?" If the trainee does not see the contradiction, the trainer might make a more direct statement: "Are you saying that you would not want Heinz to steal the drug because it is not in his best interest even though you might die without the drug and that is not in your best interest?"

2. Present unresolvable questions to the trainee. What questions you propose again depends on the opinion and reasoning stage of the trainee.

Example: Using the Heinz dilemma, suppose an argument is presented in which the solution is based on how much Heinz likes his wife or the druggist. The trainer could then propose that both the wife and the druggist are equally liked and ask, "Now how would you decide which choice to make?"

3. Point out the injustice of the decision from the perspective of another person in the dilemma (imaginary role playing), or ask trainees to imagine that an equal probability exists that they could be any person in the dilemma and, on that basis, to try to arrive at a fair solution. These role-playing techniques are effective in creating awareness of inadequacy because by taking another's perspective, the trainees can more easily recognize the injustice of a solution.

Example: In imaginary role playing, the trainer might say, "Tom, you said that Heinz should not steal the drug for his wife. Now pretend you are Heinz's wife. How would you feel about your husband's refusal to steal the drug because he does not want to go to jail when you will die without it?" In ideal role taking, the trainer might say, "Everybody pretend there is an equal chance you might be Heinz, his wife, the druggist, or the judge. Now try to solve the situation fairly."

4. Add hypothetical information to the dilemma or point out any overlooked details that might increase awareness of inadequacy. What information or details are specified will again depend on the response of the trainee.

Example: Suppose a trainee states that Heinz should not steal the drug because he would be put in jail. The trainer might point out that judges often consider the motive of the person when deciding what sentence they will give.

5. Clarify how + 1 reasoning can solve problems that lower stage reasoning cannot resolve. What clarification is used will depend on the solution and reasoning stage of the response.

Example: Consider once again the situation of what Heinz should do if he likes his wife and the druggist equally. The trainer might explain that, whereas both people are equally liked, being married involves a special kind of commitment, a vow, and responsibilities different from those someone has toward a friend. So in Heinz's position it might be fairer to uphold his vow as a husband because this decision would be based on both contract and friendship. By doing this, the trainer demonstrates how Stage 3 reasoning can be used to resolve a situation that Stage 2 reasoners may have found to be unresolvable.

6. Present a dilemma that is somewhat similar to the one being discussed but that differs in such a way that the reasoning used in the first dilemma would not be adequate for resolving the second dilemma. Then demonstrate the use of + 1 reasoning for the new situation.

Example: Using the Heinz dilemma as the first situation, the trainer might say, "Suppose there are two men, Tom and Dick, who work in a laboratory. It so happens that both of them are very close to discovering a cure for cancer. In fact, Tom has half the information that is needed to discover the cure, and Dick has the other half. Tom wants to collaborate with Dick so that together they can discover the cure. Dick does not want to collaborate with Tom because he wants all the credit for himself. Now Tom has to decide whether to steal this information from Dick. In the Heinz dilemma, some of you argued that Heinz should steal because that is what a good person would do (Stage 3 reasoner). Does your decision apply in this situation as well?" This analogous situation will often result in Stage 3 reasoners realizing that their solution is inadequate. The trainer might then explain that Tom could resolve the dilemma by using rules made by society that involve property rights of all people, including scientists. In this case, the rules involve respecting Dick's right to publish or share his information when he wants to (+ 1 stage reasoning).

It is important to note that these six methods for playing devil's advocate are not mutually exclusive and can be used simultaneously if the opportunity arises. The discussion should continue until the lower stage reasoners have realized that their arguments cannot resolve the dilemma and that the + 1 stage argument is more adequate or until all major issues have been discussed and it is obvious that the lower stage reasoners will not change their rationale. The initial discussion usually takes from 10 to 20 minutes. It is important to keep in mind that, if the trainer is unsure of how long to let the discussion continue, it is always better to end somewhat sooner than later. This decreases the chance that group members who are not involved in the debate will become bored or that defensiveness or hostility will emerge between the debaters.

Following the initial discussion, the trainer encourages a debate between the previous + 1 reasoners and trainees arguing from the next highest stage and suggesting an opposite behavioral solution (e.g., if the initial Heinz discussion is between Stage 1s against stealing and Stage 2s in favor of it, the next debate will be between Stage 2s in favor of stealing and Stage 3s against this action). Using the Heinz dilemma, the trainer might introduce the second discussion by saying, "The important differences in opinion between those who think Heinz should not steal the drug because of the negative consequences and those who think Heinz should steal the drug because of needing his wife to help around the house have just been discussed. Some other ideas were mentioned before that we need to get back to. Joe, Bruce, and Barry said that Heinz should not steal the drug but gave a reason we have not talked about yet. If I remember it right, all three of you said that you have to consider how the druggist would feel having someone steal his property. Did I remember it correctly? Joe, could you explain to the people who feel that Heinz should steal the drug why you think you have a fairer way of dealing with the problem?"

During the second discussion, the trainer's task again involves encouraging trainees to debate their differences, ensuring continued attention on the topic, ensuring respectful treatment among trainees, and, if necessary, taking on the role of devil's advocate by using any of the aforementioned methods. In this debate, the previous + 1 stage reasoners are provided with opportunities to discover the limitations of their reasoning and the greater adequacy of higher stage reasoning. The trainer ends this debate when lower stage reasoners recognize the inadequacy of their reasoning or when all major issues have been discussed. Once again, the trainer reviews what was argued and initiates a debate between the most recent + 1 stage reasoners and those at the next highest stage (e.g., if Stage 2s and Stage 3s have just debated, the Stage 3s and Stage 4s will debate next). For example, the trainer might say, "If I remember correctly, the three of you said.... Can you explain to the people who have just argued why you think you have a fairer solution?" Continue using these procedures until trainees at the next to the highest stage have debated those at the highest stage. In this way, the trainer proceeds, stage by stage, from the lowest to the highest stage argument presented in the group. When the highest stage argument presented by any trainee is reached, the trainer then presents a + 1 and opposing argument in order to point out to the highest stage reasoners the inadequacy of their argument. If available, the trainer should use a previously prepared argument (e.g., if the highest stage argument presented in the group is a pro-stealing Stage 4 position, the trainer would present a previously prepared Stage 5 position against stealing). The procedures for guiding a discussion under preferred circumstances are repeated for all sessions regardless of whether the session is the first or a subsequent meeting.

Preferred Circumstances
Step 6: Ending Discussion
In the sixth and final step of one moral discussion, the major task required of the trainer involves determining when it is appropriate to end the discussion. Under preferred circumstances, the discussion of a particular dilemma is stopped when the group debate has progressed sequentially up the stages and the trainer's + 1 stage argument has been discussed. In addition, the discussion is stopped when all trainees have had the chance to address all relevant issues regarding the dilemma. It is hoped that all trainees have experienced disequilibrium through exposure to + 1 stage reasoning and have realized that their current reasoning stage is inadequate.

It is important to stress that a discussion should not be stopped simply when interest decreases slightly, particularly if the group has not yet sequentially progressed up the stages, including the trainer's + 1 stage argument, or if the group has not completed discussing all the relevant issues in the dilemma. When interest decreases, the trainer should point out a missed issue or ask a stimulating question to again activate the discussion. A discussion should be stopped either when it is no longer productive (i.e., when interventions to stimulate discussion are repeatedly ineffectual) or when progression through the stages or discussion of major disagreements has been achieved. The trainer should also remember that to maintain interest it is always better to end a discussion somewhat early rather than too late.

The trainer can end the discussion of a particular dilemma by summarizing the major issues addressed in the debates and by relating the discussion to situations the trainees may have experienced or may experience in the future. Dilemma discussion meetings can be ended by following any one of several procedures. One method involves having trainees write down the single best argument they heard during the discussion and then read it out loud. A second procedure involves having trainees tell the person sitting next to them something helpful that person had said during the discussion. And finally, the trainer could ask several trainees to say something about what was better during the current week's discussion than the prior week's debate. When the discussion of one dilemma has ended, the trainer either stops the meeting or initiates discussion of the next dilemma. In the latter case, the same procedures are followed except that it is of course unnecessary to repeat Steps 1 through 3.

As previously mentioned, it is always preferable to try to create + 1 SC and thereby work under preferred circumstances. Since this is not always possible, it is important that the trainer develop the skills necessary to work under Non-PC, or nonpreferred circumstances. The next several sections address the methods that can be used when working under Non-PC.

Nonpreferred Circumstances
Step 4: Initiating Discussion

Initiating discussion under Non-PC begins just as it does under preferred circumstances. To review, each session begins with the reading of a dilemma, followed by a summary of the major points of the dilemma and a thinking period for formulating a solution. The trainer then goes around the circle, getting opinions and rationales about the dilemma, rephrasing statements and writing down their gist, or asking probe questions prior to evaluating the reasoning level evidenced by the statements. If a + 1 SC condition is not evident, the trainer proceeds by using Non-PC techniques. Whenever possible, the technique used to resolve the problem should be designed to try to elicit a + 1 SC situation. The four types of Non-PC situations and techniques to use in them follow.

Type 1

In this type of Non-PC situation, all group members agree on the solution to the dilemma, but the solutions represent different stages (e.g., everyone states that Heinz should steal but for reasons that are indicative of different stages of reasoning). In this situation, the trainer should present one of the prepared elaborations, particularly one that will lead to different solutions on the part of specific stage reasoners (e.g., Stage 1 reasoners will maintain their position while Stage 2 reasoners will change their opinion).

It is important to note that what elaborations are used will depend on what solutions have been offered and what stages are represented. In other words, the trainer needs to be able to anticipate what effect the elaboration will have on different stage reasoning. For example, if Stage 1 reasoners say Heinz should steal the drug because his wife is an important person and Stage 2 reasoners say Heinz should steal it because he needs his wife around to take care of the children, one might elaborate the dilemma by adding the information that Heinz does not love his wife anymore and that he has a girlfriend whom he wants to marry. With this elaboration, Stage 2 reasoners will likely change their position because, if Heinz's wife died, he would be free to marry his girlfriend, who would then take care of the children. Stage 1 reasoners would not be likely to change their position, so the elaboration would be useful because it would create + 1 SC in this case. However, this elaboration would be unlikely to affect Stage 3 or Stage 4 reasoners because the issues raised by the elaboration would not be very relevant to them. As such, a different elaboration would need to be developed. This variation in responsiveness is why it is important to prepare for group discussions by anticipating responses and preparing potentially useful elaborations.

If elaborations do not yield the desired + 1 SC, the trainer can present an opposing position (+ 1 SC) to begin the discussion. This argument should be directed toward trainees presenting the lower stage arguments.

Type 2

A Type 2 Non-PC situation occurs when opinions given on a dilemma do not divide evenly along stage lines (e.g., some of the Stage 1 and Stage 2 reasoners select one solution, whereas other Stage 1 and Stage 2 reasoners choose another position).

In this situation, two different paths can be taken. One path involves having trainees who disagree within the same stage debate their differences (e.g., Stage 1s for and against stealing) and then having the Stage 2 trainees with opposing views debate their differences among themselves. If it is possible to structure + 1 SC after this debate, proceed along those lines.

The second path involves having trainees one stage apart and holding different opinions discuss their differences (e.g., first have pro-stealing Stage 1s versus Stage 2s against stealing, then have Stage 1s against stealing versus pro-stealing Stage 2s). Two situations of + 1 SC will automatically develop when using this alternative. A general group discussion can then follow these two initial debates.

Type 3

When the trainer cannot accurately assess initial responses for stage, a Type 3 situation exists. In this situation, any two groups of trainees with differing opinions should discuss their differences, thus creating Non-PC. Further discussion may enable the trainer to carry out stage identification so that + 1 SC can then be structured at an appropriate time. If stage identification is still not possible, Non-PC structure can still be helpful. This situation frequently occurs for the beginning trainer and, as such, will be discussed in more detail in the section on guiding the discussion.

Type 4

Type 4 Non-PC situations occur when few or no trainees participate in the discussion. The type of intervention depends on the reasons underlying the problem. If the trainees cannot state initial opinions because the dilemma is puzzling, the trainer should encourage discussion of the questions or clarify the confusion. Typically, confusion is related to conflicts between different values (e.g., life versus law). The group can discuss which values should be considered more important and which are less important. Then the discussion of the dilemma can be stopped or elaborations can be provided to help structure a + 1 debate. If this is not possible, the trainer should either conduct a general discussion of the major issues or assume the devil's advocate role.

If trainees are inhibited or too frightened to speak in the group, the trainer should provide both gentle and sensitive encouragement to facilitate participation or should again explain the role of group members (i.e., that they should be doing most of the talking). If encouragement is unsuccessful, the trainer can implement a different format for starting the discussion. For example, trainees can be asked to write down, rather than verbalize, their initial opinions (without names). The papers can be given either to the trainer or to other members to read. The discussion can then systematically address all of the major arguments presented. Another method involves breaking the larger group into smaller groups of three or four members. Each group then develops a position on a dilemma, which they present together when the larger group again meets (presenting as a group is often less threatening to trainees). If the problem is due to boredom, other interventions may be used. These are presented in chapter 13, along with means for resolving other group management problems.

Role playing in nonpreferred circumstances

These four situations cover the major Non-PC conditions the trainer is likely to encounter. It is important to stress that, as with the assessment of stages, expertise at identifying how to structure a discussion emerges over time and with practice. So the trainer should not become discouraged if she misses a structuring opportunity when first learning the procedures involved.

Before moving on to Step 5, we should mention one other solution for use in a Non-PC situation. This solution involves the use of role playing. The best way to describe the use of role playing is through an example. Using the Heinz dilemma, the trainer could assign different roles to several of the group members. One trainee could play the role of Heinz, another the druggist, still another the wife, and, if desired, the judge could be brought into the situation. Having trainees act out different roles can sometimes lead to changes in opinion or reasoning, particularly when they are assigned to roles that require them to take on the perspective of a person they had not previously considered and to role play a + 1 stage argument. For example, one might assign a Stage 1 reasoner who has decided that Heinz should not steal the drug because he would end up in jail to the role of the wife. In this role, the trainee might be able to begin to understand the wife's position of not wanting to die and may, as a result, begin to think about the dilemma differently. When using role playing, it is important to remember that the role play itself is not likely to produce changes in reasoning stage since it simply focuses on what the trainee would do. This means that, following the role play, a group discussion of the issues that emerged during the role play should be conducted (i.e., the discussion focuses on the *why* issues). The discussion may elicit different initial opinions, allowing a + 1 SC debate to be structured. It is also important to note that role playing can also be used under preferred circumstances. Indeed, it can sometimes be a nice change in format from the typical procedure and can help to maintain interest in the group.

Nonpreferred Circumstances
Step 5: Guiding Discussion

Many of the suggestions described for initiating discussion under Non-PC and for guiding discussion under preferred circumstances (i.e., creating disequilibrium, especially by taking the devil's advocate role) are also relevant when the trainer is actually guiding a Non-PC discussion. When + 1 SC is not initially evident, the trainer should attempt to create it by following one of the procedures described in the preceding section. The discussion can then follow the guidelines for preferred circumstances. There are, however, several situations in which the trainer may be unable to achieve this goal. These circumstances and the methods used to deal with them when guiding the discussion will now be addressed.

When initial arguments do not create + 1 SC and when trainees at different stages present the same behavioral choice (Type 1 situation), or when trainees at the same stage offer different behavioral choices (Type 2 situation), the trainer intervenes by structuring a Non-PC discussion as described in the section on initiating discussion under nonpreferred circumstances. Briefly, the trainer could have trainees systematically discuss the major differences of opinion, could provide elaborations of the dilemma to generate conflict across the stages, or could introduce major points that participants have missed. A devil's advocate position could also be adopted. Again, if a + 1 SC condition emerges as a result of these interventions, the trainer should try to structure the appropriate debate. And finally, if possible, the trainer could structure two different + 1 SC debates as described under the Type 2 situation. After the discussion, the trainer should provide a + 1 stage argument relative to the highest stage represented in the group. The stage of this argument should be changed if it appears to be too low or high for the highest stage reasoners.

When the trainer is unable to identify the stages and cannot structure + 1 SC (Type 3 situation), Non-PC can be structured in two ways. One way is to rank order the initial responses in terms of their seeming complexity or sophistication. Then the trainer can ask trainees with the least complex rationale to debate those with the next simplest and opposing view. For example, a statement like "Heinz should not steal the drug because it is not nice" is much simpler than the response "Heinz should steal the drug because he has an obligation to his wife to help and protect her." These two groups of trainees can debate each other. The trainer then proceeds systematically up this rank-ordered hierarchy of responses until all the major issues have been raised and all trainees with different viewpoints have had a chance to discuss their opinions (this mirrors guiding the discussion under preferred circumstances except that the trainer is not aware of the precise stage). The discussion should focus on two or three opposing positions at a time so as to avoid confusion.

When all the major issues in the group have been discussed, the trainer should then point out any important ideas that were missed or present a + 1 stage argument (i.e., the trainer can place himself in the role of devil's advocate by using any of the methods described in the section on guiding the discussion under preferred circumstances). What + 1 stage argument is presented is based on the most complex argument provided by the group. Knowing what argument is most complex will naturally involve some guesswork since the trainer may still be unable to identify accurately the stages represented in the group. The trainer should closely observe the reactions of trainees to determine if the guess is accurate. If the + 1 argument induces conflict for those presenting the most complex argument, it is likely to have been a correct estimation of stage. The guess is probably inaccurate if the argument is not understood at all or if it is unstimulating for the assumed highest stage reasoners. It is important to note that, if over the course of the discussion the trainer can accurately identify stages, he should attempt to structure a + 1 SC debate instead of continuing with the Non-PC debate.

The second and less preferred method for guiding discussion when the trainer cannot identify stages involves having any two groups of trainees with differing opinions debate each other. Again, the trainer tries to structure + 1 SC if the opportunity arises.

Nonpreferred Circumstances
Step 6: Ending Discussion

Under nonpreferred circumstances, the trainer stops discussion when all important differing positions have been addressed, when trainees have had the chance to discuss any additional issues they see as important, and when the trainer has specified and encouraged discussion of any missed points and/or has proposed and discussed an estimated + 1 stage argument. The trainer can end the discussion of a particular dilemma or the entire dilemma discussion group meeting by following any one of the procedures previously described in the section on ending discussions in preferred circumstances.

As mentioned before, it is important that a discussion not be stopped simply when interest decreases slightly, particularly if the group has not yet progressed sequentially up the stages, including the trainer's + 1 stage argument, or if the group has not completed discussing all the relevant issues in the dilemma. When interest decreases, the trainer should point out a missed issue or ask a stimulating question to activate the discussion. A discussion should be stopped either when it is no longer productive (i.e., when interventions to stimulate discussion are repeatedly ineffectual) or when progression through the stages or discussion of major disagreements has been achieved. The trainer should also remember that to maintain interest it is always better to end a discussion somewhat early rather than too late. When the discussion of one dilemma has ended, the trainer either stops the meeting or initiates discussion of the next dilemma. The same procedures are followed as with the first dilemma except that it is of course unnecessary to repeat Steps 1 through 3.

Changes following the First Group Discussion

The behavior of trainees at times changes over the course of the program. As the group progresses, trainees sometimes begin to take on more and more responsibility for keeping the discussion active. The trainer should of course encourage this type of behavior and provide less guidance to trainees. For example, after a couple of meetings, older trainees rarely need to have it repeatedly explained that after reading the dilemma everyone will have a chance to share opinions about the situation. Toward the end of the dilemma discussion program, it is also possible to have trainees bring in their own moral dilemma situations. If this is done, however, the trainer should make sure that the situations actually deal with moral conflicts and issues. To guarantee this, the trainer should ask trainees to submit their dilemmas a couple of weeks before they are actually to be used. This will give the trainer enough time to review the dilemma and prepare it for discussion. Although these types of changes can be made over the course of the program, the trainer must always maintain the role of assessing stages, initiating discussions, structuring and guiding debates, and managing group behavior problems.

Transfer of Training: Homework Assignments

To facilitate opportunities for trainees to use what they have learned in the dilemma discussion group in real-life settings (i.e., to encourage transfer of training), the trainer can assign homework. In the area of moral reasoning, homework assignments simply involve handing out a dilemma at the end of one class and asking trainees to think about it and write down their opinions and rationales in preparation for the next week's class. As part of this assignment, trainees could be instructed to ask several different people (e.g., parents, teachers, employers, peers) what their positions and reasoning are on the dilemma. Trainees are asked to use, but not necessarily agree with, this input in their own thinking about the dilemma. Some dilemmas are particularly appropriate to use as homework assignments. For example, in a shoplifting dilemma, trainees could be instructed to go out and ask a store manager how she would feel if she learned a customer witnessed a shoplifting incident but did not report it to her. Since the ultimate goal of dilemma discussion groups is to prepare trainees for real-life conflict situations, it is strongly recommended that homework assignments be used whenever possible.

Alternative Format for Dilemma Discussion Groups

As mentioned previously, it takes some time and practice to assess moral reasoning stages. This process is complicated further because the trainer is responsible not only for making stage assessments, but for initiating, guiding, and ending discussions, and for managing group behavior problems. Because this is a lot for a new trainer to do, even with two trainers in the room, an alternative method has been established. In this method, there is less emphasis on specific stage assessment during the group. Although this procedure facilitates the development of group cohesion and permits general discussion during the debate, it is not the preferred format because it is less likely to create disequilibrium and the corresponding awareness of the inadequacy of lower stage reasoning to resolve the dilemma (i.e., there is the risk that there will be no exposure to + 1 stage reasoning). Therefore, this method should be used only if the trainer is having difficulty assessing stage responses or if there is continually little variation in the reasoning stages of trainees (e.g., the dominant reasoning stage of the entire group is Stage 2). The sequential steps when using this format are as follows:

1. As in the preferred format, perform Steps 1 and 2 (i.e., forming groups and choosing and preparing dilemmas) prior to beginning the moral discussion group (of course, less attention needs to be directed toward stage assessment).

2. In the initial session, perform Step 3 (i.e., creating the proper set). This step does not need to be repeated in subsequent sessions unless questions arise.

3. Hand out copies of the moral dilemma.

4. Read the dilemma out loud or have a trainee read it.

5. Summarize the major points of the dilemma or have a trainee summarize them. Clarify any misperceptions or answer any questions that emerge about the dilemma.

6. Get initial opinions (both solutions and reasoning) from the trainees by going around the circle. If necessary, when getting the

initial opinions ask probe questions or rephrase responses to assure accurate understanding of the statement and, if at all possible, to assess reasoning stage. It is not necessary to elaborate on the dilemma or initiate a debate with the trainees at this time. This step should take no more than 15 to 20 minutes.

7. After gathering the initial opinions, ask for a hand vote from the trainees regarding their behavioral choice (e.g., steal versus not steal).

8. Divide the larger group into two smaller groups. This division is based on which behavioral alternative has been selected (i.e., one group would be comprised of all trainees who voted to steal; the other group would be comprised of all trainees who voted against stealing). If the larger group cannot be divided into two fairly equal-sized groups, attempt to elaborate the dilemma in such a way as to get a more even split.

9. Separate the two smaller groups by having each group go to opposite sides of the room. One trainer should be with one of the groups, and the co-trainer should be with the other group. A trainer is needed for both of the small groups in order to guide the discussion.

10. Help each group develop a *best* reason for their position by having the trainees discuss and debate among themselves the reasons underlying their decision. To do this, follow many of the same procedures used in guiding discussion under preferred and nonpreferred circumstances. This step should take about 10 to 15 minutes.

11. As part of the small group discussion, have each group elect a spokesperson who will subsequently present the group's decision.

12. Have the elected spokesperson of each group present the group decision and rationale to the other group. Summarize the major ideas and reasoning presented by the spokesperson on a blackboard or large piece of paper. Any ideas that were discussed during the smaller group discussion but are overlooked during the spokesperson's presentation can be raised by any group member or the trainers.

13. Following the spokesperson's presentation, guide the two groups in a debate. At this time, any group member is free to contribute to the discussion. Again, follow the procedures already described for guiding group discussion. It is also important to remember to focus the debate on a couple of issues at a time to prevent chaos and to increase the probability that trainees will come to realize the inadequacy of their reasoning. If necessary, adopt the devil's advocate role to facilitate the discussion.

14. Allow the two groups to debate each other either until the groups are converging on a solution and rationale or until all major

issues have been addressed and the discussion is no longer providing opportunities for exposure to the limitations of current reasoning. If the two groups are not converging on a decision and rationale, end the debate by following any one of the several procedures previously described.

15. If desired, assign homework.
16. Repeat Steps 3 through 15 in all subsequent sessions.

The Moral Dilemmas

In the remaining section of this chapter, we present a pool of moral dilemmas for use in Moral Reasoning Training.* In each instance, we provide the dilemma itself plus discussion questions to be employed by the trainers as needed to enhance the activity level and depth of group discussion.

---

*The problem situations in this section are collected in *Small-group Sociomoral Discussions: Problem Situations for Use with Antisocial Adolescents,* by J. C. Gibbs, 1988, unpublished manuscript, The Ohio State University, Columbus. Additional situations appropriate for use with adolescents appear in *Hypothetical Dilemmas for Use in Moral Discussions,* by M. Blatt, A. Colby, and B. Speicher, Cambridge, MA: Harvard University, Moral Education and Research Foundation.

Sam's Problem Situation

Sam and his friend Dave are shopping in a record store. Sam has driven them to the store. Dave picks up a record he really likes and slips it into his backpack. With a little sign for Sam to follow, Dave then walks out of the store. But Sam doesn't see Dave. Moments later, the security officer and the store owner come up to Sam. The store owner says to the officer, "That's one of the boys who was stealing records!" The security officer checks Sam's backpack but doesn't find the record. "OK, you're off the hook, but what's the name of the guy who was with you?" the officer asks Sam. "I'm almost broke because of shoplifting," the owner says. "I can't let him get away with it."

What should Sam say or do?

1. Should Sam keep quiet and refuse to tell the security officer Dave's name?
   should keep quiet/should tell/can't decide
2. From the store owner's point of view, should Sam:
   keep quiet/tell/can't decide
3. What if the store owner is a nice guy, who sometimes lets kids buy a record even if they don't have quite enough money for it? Then should Sam:
   keep quiet/tell/can't decide
4. What if the store owner is Sam's father? Then should Sam:
   keep quiet/tell/can't decide
5. Is it ever right to tell on someone?
   yes/no/can't decide
6. Who's to blame in this situation?
   Sam/Dave/the store owner/other/can't decide
7. How important is it not to shoplift?
   very important/important/not important
8. How important is it for store owners to prosecute shoplifters?
   very important/important/not important

Note. From *Small-group Sociomoral Discussions: Problem Situations for Use with Antisocial Adolescents,* by J. C. Gibbs, 1988, unpublished manuscript, The Ohio State University, Columbus. Adapted by permission.

Sharon's Problem Situation

Sharon and her friend Jill are shopping in a clothing store. Sharon has driven them to the store. Jill picks up a blouse she really likes and takes it into the dressing room to try on. When Jill comes out of the dressing room, Sharon sees that she is wearing the blouse under her coat. Jill then walks out of the store. Moments later, the security officer and the store owner come up to Sharon. The store owner says to the officer, "That's one of the girls who took the blouse!" The security officer checks Sharon's bag but doesn't find the blouse. "OK, you're off the hook, but what's the name of the girl who was with you?" the officer asks Sharon. "I'm almost broke because of shoplifting," the owner says. "I can't let her get away with it."

What should Sharon say or do?

1. Should Sharon keep quiet and refuse to tell the security officer Jill's name?
   should keep quiet/should tell/can't decide
2. From the store owner's point of view, should Sharon:
   keep quiet/tell/can't decide
3. What if the store owner is a nice guy, who sometimes lets kids buy an item even if they don't have quite enough money for it? Then should Sharon:
   keep quiet/tell/can't decide
4. What if the store owner is Sharon's father? Then should Sharon:
   keep quiet/tell/can't decide
5. Is it ever right to tell on someone?
   yes/no/can't decide
6. Who's to blame in this situation?
   Sharon/Jill/the store owner/other/can't decide
7. How important is it not to shoplift?
   very important/important/not important
8. How important is it for store owners to prosecute shoplifters?
   very important/important/not important

Note. From *Leading Dilemma Discussion: A Workshop,* by E. Fenton, 1980, unpublished manuscript, Carnegie-Mellon University, Pittsburgh. Adapted by permission.

Sarah's Problem Situation

Sarah works as a clerk in a grocery store. The store isn't too busy. George, a friend of Sarah's at school, comes over to her cash register and says, "Hey, I've only got a dollar with me. Ring up these cigarettes and a six-pack for a dollar, won't you? The manager's in the back of the store—he'll never know." Sarah likes George a lot, and George has done some favors for her. But Sarah also feels trusted by the manager.

What should Sarah say or do?

1. Should Sarah refuse George, or should Sarah say yes to George's suggestion?
   yes/no/can't decide
2. Was it right for George to put Sarah on the spot with his request?
   yes, right/no, not right/can't decide
3. What if Sarah feels that other employees at the store do this for their friends? Then what should Sarah do?
   should refuse/should say yes/can't decide
4. What if Sarah feels that the store is making a profit and wouldn't miss a little money? Then what should Sarah do?
   should refuse/should say yes/can't decide
5. What if the store owner is a good friend of Sarah's family? Then what should Sarah do?
   should refuse/should say yes/can't decide
6. What if *you* are the owner of the store where Sarah works? Then what should Sarah do?
   should refuse/should say yes/can't decide
7. How important is it to be honest at a store where you work?
   very important/important/not important
8. Let's say after Sarah says no, George just walks out of the store with the cigarettes and six-pack. Should Sarah tell the manager?
   yes, tell manager/no, keep quiet/can't decide

Note: From "A Comparison of Social Skills in Delinquent and Nondelinquent Adolescent Girls Using a Behavioral Role-playing Inventory," by L. R. Gaffney and R. M. McFall, 1981, *Journal of Consulting and Clinical Psychology, 49,* 959–967. Adapted by permission.

Jim's Problem Situation

Jim and Derek are high school friends. Jim, whose birthday is coming up, has mentioned to Derek how great it would be to have a tape deck to listen to music with while he goes about his job driving a van. Derek steals a tape deck from a car in the school parking lot and gives it to Jim for his birthday. Jim is appreciative, not realizing the present is stolen.

The next day, Jim sees Scott, another friend. Jim knows Scott has a tape deck and is good at electronics. Jim asks Scott to help him install the tape deck. "Sure," Scott says with a sigh.

"You look down, Scott. What's wrong?" Jim asks.

"Oh, I was ripped off last night," Scott says.

"Oh, boy. What did they get?" Jim asks.

"My tape deck," Scott says.

Scott starts describing the stolen tape deck. Just before it's time for Scott to arrive to help Jim install the tape deck, Jim realizes that the tape deck he got from Derek is the one stolen from Scott! Scott might even recognize the tape deck as his. Scott is at the door, ringing the doorbell.

What should Jim say or do?

1. Should Jim tell Scott that it's Scott's tape deck?
   yes, should tell/no, shouldn't tell/can't decide
2. Should Jim tell Scott that Derek took his tape deck?
   yes, should tell/no, shouldn't tell/can't decide
3. Would Jim be able to trust Derek not to steal from *him*?
   yes, could trust/no, couldn't trust/can't decide
4. Derek stole the tape deck for a good cause (Jim's birthday). Does that make it all right for Derek to steal the tape deck?
   yes, all right/no, not all right/can't decide
5. What if Derek didn't steal the tape deck from Scott's car? What if instead Derek stole the tape deck from a stranger's car? Then would it be all right for Derek to steal the tape deck for Jim's birthday?
   yes, all right/no, not all right/can't decide

Note. From *Leading Dilemma Discussion: A Workshop,* by E. Fenton, 1980, unpublished manuscript, Carnegie-Mellon University, Pittsburgh. Adapted by permission.

Larry's Problem Situation

Larry is walking along a sidestreet with his friend Jim. Jim stops in front of a beautiful new sports car. Jim looks inside and then says excitedly, "Look, the keys are still in this baby! Let's see what she can do. Come on, let's go!"

What should Larry say or do?

1. Should Larry try to persuade Jim not to steal the car?
   should persuade/should let steal/can't decide

2. What if Jim says to Larry that the keys were left in the car, that anyone that careless deserves to get ripped off? Then should Larry try to persuade Jim not to steal the car?
   should persuade/should let steal/can't decide

3. What if Jim says to Larry that the car's owner can probably get insurance money to cover at least most of the loss? Then should Larry try to persuade Jim not to steal the car?
   should persuade/should let steal/can't decide

4. What if Jim tells Larry that stealing a car is no big deal, that plenty of his friends do it all the time? Then what should Larry do?
   should persuade/should let steal/can't decide

5. What if Larry knows that Jim has a wife and child who will suffer if Jim is caught, loses his job, and goes to jail? Then should Larry persuade Jim not to steal the car?
   should persuade/should let steal/can't decide

6. What if Larry knows that the car is *your* car. Then should Larry:
   persuade/let steal/can't decide

7. In general, how important is it for people not to take things that belong to others?
   very important/important/not important

8. Let's say Larry does try to persuade Jim not to take the car, but Jim goes ahead and takes it anyway. Larry knows Jim's in bad shape from being high—he could have a serious accident and someone could get killed. Should Larry:
   contact police/not contact police/can't decide

Note. From "A Social-behavioral Analysis of Skill Deficits in Delinquent and Nondelinquent Boys," by B. J. Freedman, L. Rosenthal, C. P. Donahoe, Jr., D. G. Schlundt, and R. M. McFall, 1978, *Journal of Consulting and Clinical Psychology, 46,* 1448–1462. Adapted by permission.

Howard's Problem Situation

Howard is in school taking a math test. All at once, the teacher says, "I'm going to leave the room for a few minutes. You are on your honor not to cheat." After the teacher has gone, Ed, Howard's best friend, whispers to him, "Let me see your answers, Howard."

What should Howard say or do?

1. Should Howard let Ed copy his answers?
    yes, let cheat/no, shouldn't let cheat/can't decide
2. What if Ed whispers that cheating is no big deal, that he knows plenty of guys who cheat all the time? Then should Howard let Ed cheat?
    yes, let cheat/no, shouldn't let cheat/can't decide
3. What if Howard knows the reason Ed is flunking is that he doesn't study? Then should Howard let Ed cheat?
    yes, let cheat/no, shouldn't let cheat/can't decide
4. What if *you* are the teacher? Would you want Howard to let Ed cheat?
    yes, let cheat/no, shouldn't let cheat/can't decide
5. Is it possible to have as a really close friend someone who cheats whenever the opportunity arises?
    yes, possible/no, not possible/can't decide
6. What if Howard hardly knows Ed? Then should Howard let Ed cheat?
    yes, let cheat/no, don't let cheat/can't decide
7. In general, how important is it not to cheat?
    very important/important/not important
8. Is it right for teachers to punish cheaters?
    yes, right/no, not right/can't decide

Note. From *Small-group Sociomoral Discussions: Problem Situations for Use with Antisocial Adolescents,* by J. C. Gibbs, 1988, unpublished manuscript, The Ohio State University, Columbus. Adapted by permission.

Leon's Problem Situation

Just after Leon arrived at an institution for boys, he tried to escape. As a result, he was given extra time. It took Leon nearly 4 months to earn the trust of the staff again. He now feels it is stupid to try to go AWOL. However, Bob, a friend of Leon's, tells Leon he is planning to escape that night. "I've got it all figured out," Bob says. "I'll hit the youth leader on the head with a lead pipe and take his keys." He asks Leon to come along.

What should Leon say or do?

1. Should Leon tell the staff about Bob's plan?
   should tell/should keep quiet/can't decide
2. What if Bob is a pretty violent type of guy? Leon realizes that Bob might seriously injure, perhaps even kill, the youth leader. Then what should Leon do?
   should tell/should keep quiet/can't decide
3. What if the youth leader were mean and everyone hated him? Then should Leon:
   tell/keep quiet/can't decide
4. What if Bob were not guilty of the crime for which he was sent to the institution? Then should Leon:
   tell/keep quiet/can't decide
5. What if Bob is Leon's brother? Then what should Leon do?
   tell/keep quiet/can't decide
6. Is it ever right to "narc" on somebody?
   yes, sometimes right/no, never right/can't decide
7. Which is more important?
   a. not telling on your friend
   b. not letting other people get hurt
   c. telling what you know so you don't get in trouble

Note. From *Moral Dilemmas at Scioto Village,* by D. W. Meyers, 1982, unpublished manuscript, The Ohio Youth Commission, Columbus. Adapted by permission.

Dave's Problem Situation

Dave's friend Matt does some dealing on the street. Once in a while, Matt even gives Dave some smoke for free. Now Matt says to Dave, "Listen, man, I've got to deliver some stuff on the south side, but I can't do it myself. How 'bout it—will you take the stuff down there for me in your car? I'll give you some new stuff to try plus 25 dollars besides for just a half-hour's drive. Will you help me out?"

What should Dave say or do?

1. Should Dave agree to deliver the stuff for Matt?
   yes, should deliver/no, shouldn't deliver/can't decide
2. What if Dave knows that Matt will be in big trouble if the stuff isn't delivered? Then should Dave deliver?
   yes, should deliver/no, shouldn't deliver/can't decide
3. What if Dave knows that the stuff Matt wants him to deliver is laced? Should he agree to deliver it?
   yes, should deliver/no shouldn't deliver/can't decide
4. What if Dave knows that his sister, who lives on the south side, might take some of the laced stuff? Then should he agree to deliver it?
   yes, should deliver/no, shouldn't deliver/can't decide
5. Should Dave be taking the free stuff from Matt?
   yes, should take it/no, shouldn't take it/can't decide
6. What if Dave knows that the stuff he'd be delivering is all marijuana and hash, but no pills? Then should he deliver the stuff?
   yes, should deliver/no, shouldn't deliver/can't decide
7. How important is it to stay away from drugs?
   very important/important/not important

Note. From "A Social-behavioral Analysis of Skill Deficits in Delinquent and Nondelinquent Boys," by B.J. Freedman, L. Rosenthal, C. P. Donahoe, Jr., D. G. Schlundt, and R. M. McFall, 1978, *Journal of Consulting and Clinical Psychology, 46,* 1448–1462. Adapted by permission.

Joe's Problem Situation

Joe is a member of a gang of teenagers who live near an old school. The school is run-down and dirty. One night, the gang decides to have a rock-throwing contest to see who can break out the most windows in the school. Since the school is next to the railroad tracks, there is little chance that the boys will get caught. The rest of the gang doesn't know it, but Joe's father is the principal of the old school. Joe's father will be the one who will get into trouble for not making sure the school has better protection. But Joe and his father don't get along too well—Joe feels that his father is too bossy. The gang asks Joe to join in the rock throwing.

What should Joe say or do?

1. Should Joe join in the rock throwing at the windows?
   yes, should join/no, shouldn't join/can't decide
2. What about the fact that the gang will think Joe's chicken if he doesn't join them in breaking windows? Then should Joe join in the rock throwing?
   yes, should join/no, shouldn't join/can't decide
3. The school can probably get insurance money to pay for new windows. Does that make it all right to break the windows?
   yes, all right/no, not all right/can't decide
4. What if the school is new and clean, and the students enjoy being there? Then should Joe join in the rock throwing?
   yes, should join/no, shouldn't join/can't decide
5. What if Joe's father will lose his job if the windows are broken? Then should Joe join in the rock throwing?
   yes, should join/no, shouldn't join/can't decide
6. What if Joe and his father get along great? Then should Joe join in the rock throwing?
   yes, should join/no, shouldn't join/can't decide
7. How important is it to go along with what your friends are doing?
   very important/important/not important
8. In general, how important is it not to vandalize buildings or property?
   very important/important/not important

Note. From *Small-group Sociomoral Discussions: Problem Situations for Use with Antisocial Adolescents,* by J. C. Gibbs, 1988, unpublished manuscript, The Ohio State University, Columbus. Adapted by permission.

Ned's Problem Situation

Ned and Phil are roommates at a juvenile institution. They get along well and have become good friends. Phil has confided that he has been pretty depressed lately and has managed to get hold of some razor blades. Ned sees where Phil hides the blades. The cottage officer, having learned of the razor blades, searches the room but doesn't find them. So the cottage officer asks Ned where the razor blades are hidden.

What should Ned say or do?

1. Should Ned cover for Phil, saying he doesn't know anything about any razor blades?
   yes, should cover/no, should tell the officer/can't decide
2. What if Phil has told Ned he plans to cut his wrists with the razor blades that night? Then should Ned:
   cover for Phil/tell the officer/can't decide
3. Would Phil feel that Ned cares about him if Ned tells?
   yes, would feel Ned cares/no, would not feel Ned cares/ can't decide
4. What if Ned and Phil actually don't get along well and are *not* friends? What if Phil has been a real pest? Then should Ned:
   cover for Phil/tell the officer/can't decide
5. What if Phil has had the razor blades for a long time and, despite talk, has never used them? In other words, what if Ned is pretty sure Phil doesn't really mean to use them? Then should Ned cover for Phil?
   yes, should cover/no, should tell the officer/can't decide
6. What if Ned isn't Phil's roommate but does know about the razor blades and where they are? The officer suspects Ned knows something and asks him about the razor blades. Then should Ned:
   cover for Phil/tell the officer/can't decide
7. How important is it for a juvenile institution to have rules against contraband?
   very important/important/not important
8. How important is it to live even when you don't want to?
   very important/important/not important
9. Who might be affected (in addition to Phil himself) if Phil were to commit suicide?

Note. From *Dilemma Session Intervention with Adult Female Offenders: Behavioral and Attitudinal Correlates,* by H. H. Ahlborn, 1986, unpublished manuscript, The Ohio State University, Columbus. Adapted by permission.

John's Problem Situation

One night two hit men come to the restaurant where John works, looking for Willie. Willie isn't there. The hit men make John and everybody else in the restaurant go into the back room. They have guns, and they say they are going to kill Willie when he comes in. But for some reason Willie doesn't come in. The hit men finally leave, saying they'll find Willie and kill him.

John knows where Willie lives, so he goes to his house to warn him that he is in danger. Willie is a nice guy, and John doesn't want him to get hurt. John knocks on Willie's door. Willie answers. John explains the danger, but Willie doesn't seem to want to listen. Willie says he's not a coward and he isn't going to run. "If they want to kill me," Willie says, "then let them go ahead."

What should John say or do?

1. Should John leave Willie?
   yes, should leave/no, should stay/can't decide
2. What if John and Willie have been good friends for many years? Then should John leave Willie?
   yes, should leave/no, should stay/can't decide
3. What if Willie has a wife and several kids to look after? Then should John leave Willie?
   yes, should leave/no, should stay/can't decide
4. Should John tell the police about the hit men?
   yes, should tell police/no, shouldn't tell police/can't decide
5. What if Willie is the town bully and everybody hates him? Then should John leave Willie?
   yes, should leave/no, should stay/can't decide
6. What if Willie has cancer and will die soon anyway? Then should John leave Willie?
   yes, should leave/no, should stay/can't decide
7. How important is it to live even when you don't want to?
   very important/important/not important

Note. From *Leading Dilemma Discussion: A Workshop,* by E. Fenton, 1980, unpublished manuscript, Carnegie-Mellon University, Pittsburgh. Adapted by permission.

Reggie's Problem Situation

"Your father is late again," Reggie's mother tells Reggie one night as he sits down to dinner. Reggie knows why. He had passed his father's car on the way home from school. It was parked outside the Midtown Bar and Grill. Reggie's mother and father had argued many times about his father's stopping off at the bar on his way home from work. After their last argument, his father had promised he would never do it again. "I wonder why your father is so late?" Reggie's mother says.

What should Reggie say or do?

1. Should Reggie cover for his father by lying to his mother?
   yes, should cover/no, should tell truth/can't decide
2. Was it right for Reggie's mother to put Reggie on the spot by asking him a question about his father?
   yes, right/no, not right/can't decide
3. Suppose Reggie's mother said she would leave home if she ever catches his father stopping at the bar again. Then should Reggie:
   cover for him/tell the truth/can't decide
4. What if Reggie's father drinks a lot when he stops at the bar and then comes home and often beats up on Reggie's mother— sometimes even Reggie? Then should Reggie:
   cover for him/tell the truth/can't decide
5. Which is most important for Reggie's decision?
   a. what's best for himself
   b. what's best for his mom
   c. what's best for his dad
   d. what's best for the family
6. In general, how important is it to tell the truth?
   very important/important/not important

Note. From *Moral Dilemmas at Scioto Village,* by D. W. Meyers, 1982, unpublished manuscript, The Ohio Youth Commission, Columbus. Adapted by permission.

Jerry's Problem Situation

Jerry had just moved to a new school and was feeling pretty lonely until one day a guy named Bob came up and introduced himself. "Hi, Jerry. My name is Bob. I heard one of the teachers say you're new here. If you're not doing anything after school today, how about coming over to shoot some baskets?" Pretty soon Jerry and Bob were good friends.

One day, when Jerry was shooting baskets by himself, the basketball coach saw him and invited him to try out for the team. Jerry made the team and every day after school would practice with the rest of the team. After practice, they would always go out together to get something to eat and sit around and talk about stuff, and on weekends they would sometimes take trips together. As Jerry spent more time with the team, he saw less and less of Bob, his old friend.

One day, Jerry gets a call from Bob. "Say, I was wondering," says Bob, "If you're not too busy on Thursday, my family is having a little birthday party for me. Maybe you could come over for dinner that night." Jerry tells Bob he'll come to the party. But during practice on Thursday, everyone tells Jerry about the great place they're all going to go to after practice.

What should Jerry say or do?

1. Should Jerry go with the team?
   yes, go with team/no, go to Bob's party/can't decide
2. What if Jerry calls Bob from school and says he's sorry, but something has come up and he can't come over after all? Then would it be all right for Jerry to go with the team?
   yes, go with team/no, go to Bob's party/can't decide
3. What if Jerry considers that his teammates may be upset if he doesn't come and start to think he's not such a good friend? Then should Jerry go with the team?
   yes, go with team/no, go to Bob's party/can't decide
4. What if *before* Bob asks Jerry to come over, the teammates ask if Bob will be coming along on Thursday (and Bob says he thinks so), and *then* Bob asks Jerry? Then what should Jerry do?
   go with team/go to Bob's party/can't decide

Note. From *Peer Relations Interview,* By R. L. Selman, 1982, unpublished manuscript, Harvard University, Cambridge, MA. Adapted by permission.

5. What if Jerry thinks that, after all, Bob came along and helped Jerry when he was lonely? Then should Jerry go with the team? yes, go with team/no, go to Bob's party/can't decide

6. What if Jerry and Bob are not good friends, but instead hardly know each other? Then should Jerry go with the team? yes, go with team/no, go to Bob's party/can't decide

7. Which is more important: to have one close friend or to have a group of regular friends? one close friend/group of regular friends/can't decide

Charlene's Problem Situation

Charlene and Joanne have been good friends for some time. Now they are in high school, and Joanne is trying out for the cheerleading squad. Joanne is afraid that a new girl in school, Tina, will be chosen. After the tryouts, Tina comes over to Joanne and Charlene and asks to join them for a snack. Joanne notices that Charlene and Tina are doing most of the talking and that they're getting along well together.

After Tina leaves, Joanne asks Charlene to come over to her house on Saturday afternoon. She has something important she wants to talk over with her. Charlene promises to come, but later that day, Charlene gets a call from Tina asking her to go to a popular movie with her on Saturday afternoon, the last chance to see the movie.

What should Charlene say or do?

1. Should Charlene go to the movie with Tina?
   yes, go with Tina/no, go to Joanne's house/can't decide
2. What if Charlene calls Joanne and says she's sorry, but something has come up and she can't come over after all? Then would it be all right for Charlene to go to the movie with Tina?
   yes, go with Tina/no, go to Joanne's house/can't decide
3. What if Charlene knows that Joanne is only trying to keep her from seeing Tina? Then what should Charlene do?
   go with Tina/go to Joanne's house/can't decide
4. What if *before* Joanne asks Charlene to come over, Tina asks Charlene to go to the movies (and Charlene says she thinks she can go), and *then* Joanne asks Charlene? Then what should Charlene do?
   go with Tina/go to Joanne's house/can't decide
5. Let's say Joanne does go with Tina to the movies. Joanne feels hurt and decides to get even. Should she get even?
   yes, get even/no, shouldn't get even/can't decide
6. What if Charlene and Joanne are not good friends but instead hardly know each other? Then what should Charlene do?
   go with Tina/go to Joanne's house/can't decide

Note. From *The Growth of Interpersonal Understanding: Developmental and Clinical Analysis,* by R. L. Selman, 1980, New York: Academic Press. Adapted by permission.

Mark's Problem Situation

Mark has been going steady with a girl named Mary for about 3 months. It used to be a lot of fun to be with her, but lately it's been sort of a drag. There are some other girls Mark would like to go out with now. Mark sees Mary coming along the school hallway.

What should Mark say or do?

1. Should Mark not talk to Mary about breaking up so Mary's feelings aren't hurt?

   yes, shouldn't bring it up/no, should bring it up/can't decide

2. Should Mark make up an excuse, like being too busy to see Mary, as a way of breaking up?

   yes, excuse/no, no excuse/can't decide

3. Should Mark simply start going out with other girls so that Mary will get the message?

   yes/no/can't decide

4. How should Mark respond to Mary's feelings?

5. What if Mark and Mary have been living together for several years and have two small children? Then should Mark still break up with Mary?

   yes, break up/no, shouldn't break up/can't decide

6. Mark does break up with Mary—he avoids her and starts dating another girl. Mary feels very hurt and jealous and thinks about getting even somehow. Should Mary get even?

   yes, get even/no, shouldn't get even/can't decide

7. What if the tables were turned and Mary did that to *Mark*? Should Mark get even?

   yes, get even/no, shouldn't get even/can't decide

Note. From "A Social-behavioral Analysis of Skill Deficits in Delinquent and Nondelinquent Boys," by B. J. Freedman, L. Rosenthal, C. P. Donahoe, Jr., D. G. Schlundt, and R. M. McFall, 1978, *Journal of Consulting and Clinical Psychology, 46,* 1448–1462. Adapted by permission.

Bill's Problem Situation

Bill and Harry are friends. Harry likes a girl named Debbie. Harry and Debbie have dated, but they are not really involved. Bill thinks Debbie is pretty nice. On Saturday night, Bill and Debbie are at the same party. Harry isn't there, and Bill and Debbie have a really good time together. Debbie hints to Bill about getting together again some time.

What should Bill say or do?

1. Should Bill date Debbie?
   yes, should date/no, shouldn't date/can't decide
2. What if Bill and Harry are best friends? Then should Bill date Debbie?
   yes, should date/no, shouldn't date/can't decide
3. Is it right to start dating your friend's girlfriend?
   yes, right/no, not right/can't decide
4. What if Harry and Debbie are almost engaged? Then should Bill date Debbie?
   yes, should date/no, shouldn't date/can't decide
5. What if Harry and Debbie are only acquaintances? Then should Bill date Debbie?
   yes, should date/no, shouldn't date/can't decide
6. What if Debbie has told Bill she doesn't like Harry very much and just dates him to avoid hurting his feelings? Then should Bill date Debbie?
   yes, should date/no, shouldn't date/can't decide
7. What if Harry pleads with Debbie to stop seeing Bill? Then should Debbie stop seeing Bill?
   yes, should stop/no, should see Bill/can't decide
8. Harry feels very hurt and decides to get even with Bill and Debbie. Should he get even?
   yes, should get even/no, shouldn't get even/can't decide

Note. From "A Social-behavioral Analysis of Skill Deficits in Delinquent and Nondelinquent Boys," by B.J. Freedman, L. Rosenthal, C. P. Donahoe, Jr., D. G. Schlundt, and R. M. McFall, 1978, *Journal of Consulting and Clinical Psychology, 46,* 1448–1462. Adapted by permission.

Judy's Problem Situation

Judy is about to be released from an institution for women offenders. She has made a strong commitment to "go straight"—that is, not to use drugs, do anything that has to do with drugs, or be around those who use drugs. She plans to go live with her husband, Paul, and their children, but Paul has been a heavy drug user. She loves Paul very much, and she wants to be paroled to her home. Paul has promised that he will quit using drugs, but he has broken that promise before. Paul manages to get a call through to Judy and asks her about her release plans.

What should Judy say or do?

1. Should Judy give Paul another chance and go home?
   yes, should go to Paul/no, should stay away/can't decide
2. What if Paul is not her husband but instead just her "live-in," and they have no children. Then what should Judy do?
   go to Paul/stay away/can't decide
3. Let's say Judy goes home to Paul. One day someone comes to the house carrying 1,500 dollars and says that Paul told him to pick up some cocaine. Judy tells the man Paul isn't there. She realizes that Paul has broken his promise again. Although she considers that the 1,500 dollars could do a lot for her and the children, she packs up, takes the kids, and goes to her mother's house. Should Judy have done that?
   yes, should go to mother's house/no, should stay with Paul/ can't decide
4. A police officer comes to Judy's mother's house and inquires about Paul. Judy denies knowing anything about Paul's dealing. Should Judy have done that?
   yes, should deny it/no, should tell the truth/can't decide
5. Judy's last baby was born addicted, and that has made her aware of how dangerous the drugs Paul deals in are. How important is it to avoid getting involved in drugs?
   very important/important/not important

Note. From *Dilemma Session Intervention with Adult Female Offenders: Behavioral and Attitudinal Correlates,* by H. H. Ahlborn, 1986, unpublished manuscript, The Ohio State University, Columbus. Adapted by permission.

Chapter 7

Stress Management Training

Having lived through childhood and adolescence, most adults know by experience that neither age is a period of singularly carefree development. Yet, not unlike the purported recollections of mothers regarding the pains of childbirth, most adults apparently underestimate markedly the pains and stresses that often characterize the daily lives of many children and adolescents. Johnson (1986) describes well many of the more frequent stresses of childhood:

> Children are exposed in varying degrees and in different ways to a wide range of situations that require coping and adaptation. Most experience the arrival of new brothers and sisters, the accompanying changes in family routines, and the frequent feelings of jealousy that result from having to share parental attention with a new family member. All must deal with separation issues associated with entering school for the first time. Many change from one school to another, move to a new home or perhaps a new community, and are faced with leaving behind old friendships, attempting to develop new ones, and adjusting to new and unfamiliar surroundings. Many children are exposed to stress resulting from conflict between their parents, and increasing numbers of children are forced to cope with all the feelings and life changes that come with parental separation or divorce. A smaller but still significant number experience the serious illness or death of a parent or other family member. And some are themselves faced with serious illnesses or major physical disabilities and the stress of repeated hospitalizations and intrusive medical procedures that these conditions sometimes require. This is to say nothing of those seemingly trivial (to adults) but more frequently occurring stressors that some children experience, such as being made fun of by others, not being asked to a birthday party, being the last person selected for the team at recess—all of which may be experienced as stressful when they occur.
>
> It is clear that for many childhood is far from being the trouble-free time we sometimes reminisce about when burdened by the demands of adult life. For some it is a time marked by extremely stressful events and life transitions that would severely tax the coping and adaptational abilities of even the most resilient child. (p. 15)

The Coddington Life Events Record (Coddington, 1972a, 1972b) formalizes and extends this inventory of significant stresses of childhood and adolescence. Table 9, compiled by Heisel, Ream, Raitz, Rappaport, and Coddington (1973), lists the events that constitute this measure and, for four age levels, the stressfulness of the given event (in terms of "Life Change Units") perceived by respondents.

Clearly, the stresses of childhood and adolescence are many and varied. Not only may the same stressful event have an impact with different potency depending upon the age of the youngster, but youth of different ages differ substantially in the events they perceive as stressful. Magnusson (1982) reports a study in which 12- to 18-year-olds were asked to report the three most anxiety-provoking situations they could think of and to describe why each situation made them anxious. The responses of the preadolescents centered on the physical properties of the situation, external bodily consequences, and possible external sanctions. Older teenagers, in contrast, referred much more to psychological consequences as the basis for anxiety in each situation (e.g., anticipated shame, guilt, separation, or lack of personal integrity). Stress during childhood and adolescence, therefore, is not only substantial in its impact and diverse in its origins, but it may also be seen as having both situational and developmental roots. Its developmental nature deserves special emphasis, especially in the interventionist context of this chapter, since the successful intervener will seek to anticipate client changes before they occur, intervene early in the sequence of stress-damaging events, and respect the fact that positive changes in the individual may be as much a result of continuing developmental forces as of the intervener's programmatic efforts.

Features associated with the situation, the stressor, and the youth himself may vary; in addition, what is experienced as stressful changes as society itself changes. J. Kagan (1972) notes that

> contemporary middle-class American fifteen-year-olds are waging war against feelings of isolation, commitment to action and belief, loyalty to others, and capacity for love. Earlier generations grappled with the themes of social status, financial security, and petting. It is not clear what issues future generations will engage and subdue. It is usually the case that each era is marked by one or two social problems of enormous priority.... Racial strife, density of population, and, more important, lack of transcendental ideology continue to loom as the potential catastrophes of the future. (p. 104)

As with stress itself, the effects on youngsters of the diverse and substantial stresses we have enumerated are themselves quite varied

Table 9

Events and Life Change Units for the Coddington Life Events Record for Use with Four Age Groups

	Life Change Units			
Life events	Preschool	Elementary	Junior high	Senior high
Beginning nursery school, first grade, or high school	42	46	45	42
Change to a different school	33	46	52	56
Birth or adoption of brother or sister	50	50	50	50
Brother or sister leaving home	39	36	33	37
Hospitalization of brother or sister	37	41	44	41
Death of brother or sister	59	68	71	68
Change of father's occupation requiring increased absence from home	36	45	42	38
Loss of job by parent	23	38	48	46
Marital separation of parents	74	78	77	69
Divorce of parents	78	84	84	77
Hospitalization of parent (serious illness)	51	55	54	55
Death of parent	89	91	94	87
Death of grandparent	30	38	35	36
Marriage of parent to stepparent	62	65	63	63
Jail sentence of parent for 30 days or less	34	44	50	53
Jail sentence of parent for 1 year or more	67	67	76	75
Addition of third adult to family	39	41	34	34
Change in parent's financial status	21	29	40	45
Mother beginning work	47	44	36	26

Note. From "The Significance of Life Events as Contributing Factors in the Diseases of Children," by J. S. Heisel, S. Ream, R. Raitz, M. Rappaport, and R. D. Coddington, 1973, *Journal of Pediatrics, 83,* p. 121. Reprinted by permission.

Table 9 *(continued)*

Life events	Life Change Units			
	Preschool	Elementary	Junior high	Senior high
Decrease in number of arguments between parents	21	25	29	27
Increase in number of arguments between parents	44	51	48	46
Decrease in number of arguments with parents	22	27	29	26
Increase in number of arguments with parents	39	47	46	47
Discovery of being an adopted child	33	52	70	64
Acquiring a visible deformity	52	69	83	81
Having a visible congenital deformity	39	60	70	62
Hospitalization of yourself (child)	59	62	59	58
Change in acceptance by peers	38	51	68	67
Outstanding personal achievement	23	39	45	46
Death of a close friend (child's friend)	38	53	65	63
Failure of a year in school		57	62	56
Suspension from school		46	54	50
Pregnancy of an unwed teen-age sister		36	60	64
Becoming involved with drugs or alcohol		61	70	76
Becoming a member of church/synagogue		25	28	31
Not making an extracurricular activity you wanted to be involved in (i.e., athletic team, band)			49	55
Breaking up with your boyfriend/girlfriend			47	53
Beginning to date			55	51
Fathering an unwed pregnancy			76	77
Unwed pregnancy			95	92
Being accepted to a college of your choice				43
Getting married				101

370

and influential. Some of these consequences are physiological and immediate, including rapid, pounding, uneven heartbeat; rapid, shallow, uneven breathing; muscle clenching; restlessness; perspiration; frequent urination; poor coordination; dry mouth; fatigue; headache; backache; shoulder, neck, and back tension; lack of appetite; and stomach distress. Other physiological effects are less immediate, with studies demonstrating significant relationships between life stresses experienced by the child or adolescent and accidental injury (Coddington & Trovell, 1980; Padilla, Rohsenow, & Bergman, 1976), infections (Meyer & Haggerty, 1962), rheumatoid arthritis (Heisel et al., 1973), recurrent pain (Green, Young, Swisher, & Miller, 1985), respiratory illness (Boyce et al., 1973), cancer (Jacobs & Charles, 1980), diabetes (Brand, Johnson, & Johnson, 1986), and morbidity (Beautrais, Fergusson, & Shannon, 1982). Stress has been demonstrated to have equally potent and diverse psychological consequences, including problems with school adjustment (Sterling, Cowen, Weissberg, Lotyczewski, & Boike, 1985), school performance (Fontana & Dovidio, 1984), delinquency (Vaux & Ruggiero, 1983), drug use (Bruns & Geist, 1984; Gad & Johnson, 1980), depression (Barrera, 1981), suicide (Cohen-Sandler, Berman, & King, 1982), anorexia nervosa (Coddington, 1972a, 1972b; Schwartz & Johnson, 1985), and general indices of maladjustment (Cowen, Weissberg, & Guare, 1984).

Thus it is clear that, as has been found consistently with adults, stressful life experiences have major negative consequences for the physical and psychological well-being of both children and adolescents. Essentially all systems of physiological and psychological functioning are demonstrably vulnerable to its impact. Clearly, enhancing the youth's ability to manage, cope with, or reduce the impact of life stresses is a valuable psychoeducational goal.

Stress Management

The child's or adolescent's response to stress has correctly been described as both cognitive and physiological (Cameron & Meichenbaum, 1982; Stoyva & Anderson, 1982). Cognitively, the individual appraises the stressors impinging upon her and plans an appropriate response. As Cameron and Meichenbaum (1982) note in this regard, "Efforts to cope may well be misguided to the extent that the 'true' nature of things is misconstrued ... given a reasonable appraisal, effective coping presupposes an adequate repertoire of responses or skills for dealing with the ongoing demands of life" (p. 698). Thus, in their view, an adequate cognitive response to stress requires both an accurate appraisal of the stressful situation and an adequate repertoire of relevant skills. These are the training goals, respectively, of the Situational Perception Training and Interpersonal Skills Training courses of the Prepare Curriculum (see chapters 4 and 3, respectively). Since we deal with these training sequences in detail elsewhere in this volume, we will not do so here save to underscore their direct relevance to Stress Management Training. Our concern here, instead, will be exclusively upon the physiological component of the stress response. We will present in detail a series of physical and mental activities whose shared goal is the control and reduction of the hormonal, chemical, cardiovascular, digestive, muscular, and related physical/physiological manifestations of the stress response and, consequently, the enhancement of the youngster's ability to induce in himself a state of relaxation. Mason (1980) sets the stage well for our presentation of these specific stress management techniques:

> Stress reduction reverses the adverse effects of stress.... You can elicit the feeling of deep relaxation and calm associated with the physiological state of relaxation. Your breathing becomes deep and slow. Your heart rate decreases, and the blood flow to the extremities increases. Muscles relax and return to their normal resting state. Hormonal equilibrium is established, and the overall metabolism is slowed. If you can elicit one characteristic of the relaxation response, then you can break into the chain of physiological changes that occur when you relax. Deep breathing will probably slow your heart rate, and generalize to an overall state of relaxation. Increased blood flow to the extremities, achieved through autogenics, will aid in muscular relaxation. Muscular relaxation, achieved through progressive relaxation, will contribute to increased blood flow to the extremities. Focusing the mind in meditation can slow the heart rate.... The various exercise techniques focus on different physiological responses, but they all elicit the relaxation response. (pp. 8–9)

As the following diverse stress management activities are described, both trainers and users of these techniques should bear in mind that it is very much an individual matter as to which techniques work best, in which sequence, for any particular person. Although these are potent procedures, each user must be an experimenter, trying them out and finding the specific procedure or sequence of procedures that is most effective.

Progressive Relaxation Training

In 1938, Jacobson published his pioneering work *Progressive Relaxation,* the basis for the stress management approach we wish to describe first. He reported his observation that an individual's response to stress is often accompanied by a measurable tightening of muscle fibers. Such muscle tension, he proposed, could be reduced by use of his progressive relaxation exercises, which involved systematically tensing and relaxing all major muscle groups while simultaneously paying close attention to the sensations of tension and relaxation. Jacobson (1938) also demonstrated that tightening a muscle before relaxing it helps it relax more deeply and helps the individual to differentiate more skillfully between even subtle levels of tension and relaxation. Progressive relaxation, though shortened and improved since Jacobson introduced it (Bernstein & Borkovec, 1973; Wolpe, 1958), has found an established place in the battery of stress management techniques in use today.

The progressive relaxation sequence, also recently labeled the *isometric squeeze exercise* (Smith, 1985), consists of having the user sequentially tense and then relax 10 major muscle groups. Each group is tensed (squeezed) and relaxed twice before focus is directed toward the next muscle group. The specific procedures constituting progressive relaxation are reflected in the following steps.

Phase One: Tension-relaxation Cycles

The first component of relaxation training seeks both to enable the individual to interrupt the tension build-up process as early as possible and to maximize her awareness of the "feel" of relaxation by introducing procedures that actively contrast relaxation with its opposite (tension). Thus relaxation training begins with having the individual engage, in cyclical sequence, in tension-enhancing and relaxation-enhancing behaviors. To do so in the most effective manner, a series of steps are usually employed.

Step 1. The user is asked to avoid use of nonprescription drugs, alcohol, drinks containing caffeine, and tobacco products in the 2 or 3 hours before the planned use of progressive relaxation training. When ready to begin, the user first selects an appropriate time and place, one in which he will be undisturbed in a quiet atmosphere for approximately a half hour. Steps are then taken to get comfortable (i.e., loosening clothing, dimming lights, finding a comfortable chair and position in it, and so forth).

Step 2. The essence of relaxation training, largely reflected in this step, is perhaps best communicated by quoting our exact instructions to users when implementing this step:

> Let your eyes close gently, do not shut them tight. You are now ready to begin. Start with the hands. Tense them by making tight fists with both hands and hold the tensed position as you slowly recite T–E–N–S–E. Say one letter about every two seconds so that you are tensing the muscles for about ten seconds. After approximately ten seconds of tension, relax the hands quickly and let them continue to relax while you slowly recite R–E–L–A–X–R–E–L–A–X. Again, say one letter every two seconds so that you are relaxing for about twenty seconds. This is one tension-relaxation cycle. Repeat the cycle again, still with your hands. For each muscle group do two cycles (i.e., Tense-Relax, Tense-Relax) and then move on to the next muscle group. (Goldstein & Rosenbaum, 1982, p. 17)

Step 3. The user is then instructed in conducting two tension-relaxation cycles for the musculature in her arms, shoulders, neck, forehead, eyes and nose, mouth, chest and back, abdomen, and legs and feet. Phase One in its entirety, therefore, consists of 20 tension-relaxation cycles (i.e., 2 each for 10 muscle groups). Further instructions to users from the trainer or on a self-instructional basis during this step are as follows:

> As you do each of these exercises, let your mind relax as well as your body. Focus your attention within your body. As you tense and relax each muscle group, focus on the bad feelings of tension within that part of your body and then on the good feelings of relaxation in that part. Notice what it feels like when those muscles are tense, so that you will recognize tension when it occurs naturally. (Goldstein & Rosenbaum, 1982, p. 17)

Phase Two: Relaxation Only

The goal of Phase Two is to move the individual toward deeper levels of relaxation. The tension-sensitizing aspects of the training are deleted, and the individual is instructed to concentrate on getting each muscle group more and more deeply relaxed. This phase seeks to establish a level of concentration on relaxation that will enable the final phase, deep relaxation, to occur:

> In [the first phase] you went through two tension-relaxation cycles for each muscle group and you should now be feeling very relaxed. Think of tense muscles as stretched rubber bands. You have now relaxed

those rubber bands about halfway. There is still much more relaxation to be done. In [the second phase] there is no tension, only relaxation. Beginning with your hands, concentrate on each muscle group and focus on getting them more and more deeply relaxed. Remember, do not tense the muscles, just think about letting them relax further and further. Spend about thirty seconds thinking about relaxing on each group. (Goldstein & Rosenbaum, 1982, p. 18)

Phase Three: Deep Relaxation
As above, an exact quotation of our instructions to users describes the essence of this phase:

Just let your entire body relax as you focus on a pleasant scene. It sometimes helps to imagine yourself lying on the beach on a warm sunny day, or drifting peacefully on a raft in a pool, or lying under a shady tree in the cool grass on a warm day. Find and imagine a scene that makes you feel good and imagine it as you relax. Let the rubber bands unwind all the way. Sink deeply into your chair or bed. Breathe deeply, slowly, evenly. Tune out the outside world completely. Continue this final phase for about three minutes or so, then gradually open your eyes. You should feel refreshed and very relaxed. (Goldstein & Rosenbaum, 1982, p. 20)

Most users, after approximately 2 weeks of daily practice of this three-phase process, are able to drop the first phase and commence with the relaxation-only phase. In turn, a week or two of practice at this level typically enables the individual to commence directly with Phase Three, perhaps in response to the self-command "Relax."

A great deal of research has sought to examine the effectiveness of relaxation training with both adults and children experiencing a wide array of tension-associated problems. Its effectiveness has been demonstrated in applications to insomnia (Borkovec, Grayson, O'Brien, & Weerts, 1979; Pendleton & Tasto, 1976), essential hypertension (Taylor, Farquhar, Nelson, & Agras, 1977), tension headache and migraine (Luther, 1971; Warner & Lance, 1975), test-taking anxiety (Delprato & Dekraker, 1976; Russell & Sipich, 1974), public-speaking anxiety (Goldfried & Trier, 1974; Weissberg, 1975), self-injurious behavior (Steen & Zuriff, 1977), and general tension and anxiety (Borkovec, Grayson, & Cooper, 1978; Sherman & Plummer, 1973).

Yogaform Stretching
This stress management intervention centers upon use of the focused stretch. The user gently and slowly stretches and unstretches the same

10 muscle groups as were tensed and relaxed in progressive relaxation training. In contrast to the active-then-passive quality of the latter approach, yogaform stretching requires continuous smooth movement. Following the same low-stimulation, high-comfort preparatory steps noted earlier, instructions for this activity proceed as follows:

> For each yogaform exercise, take about 20 seconds to stretch the indicated muscle group. When a muscle is stretched, hold the stretch and attend to the pleasant sensation for a few seconds. Then take about 20 seconds to unstretch. Take your time. Try to move as slowly, smoothly, and gently as possible. Keep your mind focused on what you are doing. As before, do each exercise twice. For each exercise done on the right side of the body, repeat on the left side. When you are finished, scan your body for any sources of residual tension. Repeat stretches for areas that are still tense. (Smith, 1985, p. 85)

These are the general instructions given to the user. Below is an example of specific yogaform stretching instructions for one muscle group, the hand:

Hand Stretch*

We'll begin with the right hand.

Slowly, smoothly, and gently open your fingers and easily stretch them back and apart.

PAUSE

Try not to stretch so it hurts.

PAUSE

Just enough to feel a good stretch.

PAUSE

Take your time.

PAUSE

Stretch every muscle completely.

PAUSE

Then hold the stretch.

---

*This exercise and others appearing on pp. 380–386, 388–391, 392–395, and 397–400 are from *Relaxation Dynamics: Nine World Approaches to Self-relaxation,* by J. C. Smith, 1985, Champaign, IL: Research Press. Reprinted by permission.

PAUSE

And slowly, smoothly, and gently release the stretch.

PAUSE

Let your fingers very slowly return to their original relaxed position.

PAUSE

Notice the sensations as the muscles unstretch.

PAUSE

Take your time, there is no need to hurry.

PAUSE

Now let's try that again.
Without hurrying, very easily and gently open the fingers of your right hand.

PAUSE

Open them wide apart so you can feel a good complete stretch.

PAUSE

Let each finger open more and more.

PAUSE

Notice the sensations of stretching.

PAUSE

Then hold the stretch.

PAUSE

Then slowly, smoothly, and gently release the stretch.

PAUSE

Let your movement be smooth.

PAUSE

Take your time.

PAUSE

Easily return your fingers to their original position.

PAUSE

We are now ready to move to the other hand.

PAUSE

Slowly, smoothly, and gently open the fingers.

PAUSE

Move them farther and farther apart.

PAUSE

Make sure your right hand remains relaxed.

PAUSE

Open them more and more so you feel a good complete stretch.

PAUSE

Then hold the stretch.

PAUSE

And gently and easily release your fingers.

PAUSE

Let your fingers gently and smoothly return to their resting position.

PAUSE

There is no need to hurry.

PAUSE

Move at a pace that feels comfortable for you.

PAUSE

And let's try that once again.

PAUSE

Very easily and gently open the fingers.

PAUSE

Notice how it feels as your fingers stretch farther apart.

PAUSE

Let the movement be smooth and graceful.

PAUSE

Each finger farther and farther apart.

PAUSE

And hold the stretch.

PAUSE

And gently and easily release the stretch.

PAUSE

Let the fingers gently return.

PAUSE

Try not to hurry or rush.

PAUSE

Notice the pleasant feelings of relaxation. (Smith, 1985, pp. 89–92)

Breathing Exercises

Deep, regular diaphragmatic breathing is a core stress management activity. As Smith (1985) notes,

> The way we breathe accurately reflects our tension and relaxation. We breathe quickly and choppily when angry, momentarily hold our breath when afraid, gasp when shocked, and choke when in despair. In contrast, we sigh deeply when relieved. When we are deeply relaxed our breathing is full, even, and unhurried. (p. 113)

There are many variations of breathing exercises designed to reduce stress and induce relaxation. Mason (1980) describes three-part breathing, one-to-eight-count breathing, five-to-one-count breathing, alternative-nostril breathing, and more. Smith (1985) details arm swing breathing, body arch breathing, stomach squeeze breathing, active diaphragmatic breathing, focused breathing, inhaling-through-nose/exhaling-through-lips breathing, and still more. All of these exercises are variations on the basic deep-breathing exercise theme. Each is designed to encourage relaxed, full, and rhythmic breathing and to increase the person's ability to detect and differentiate between relaxed and tense breathing. They are, as Smith (1985) notes, each designed to help the individual "breathe deeply and diaphragmatically, evenly, and slowly—the opposite of how we breathe under stress" (p. 115). The variations in these several exercises are all tuned to this goal. Those that incorporate attending to one's breathing pattern do so because such focusing appears to foster more relaxed breathing. Those that involve arm or torso stretching do so because such movement opens the diaphragm and chest fully. And breathing purposefully through the nose or lips facilitates an even breathing rhythm. The following excerpts from Smith (1985) illustrate more fully a sampling of these exercises.

Integrative Breathing

In this exercise sequence we are going to relax by breathing in a way that is full and even and unhurried.

Before we begin, make sure you are seated upright in a comfortable position.

PAUSE

Rest your hands comfortably in your lap.

PAUSE

Make sure your feet are placed flat on the floor.

PAUSE

Now gently close your eyes and let yourself settle into a position that is comfortable.

PAUSE

For the next few minutes let your body become more and more quiet.

PAUSE

Let yourself begin to settle down and relax as you remain still.

PAUSE 30 SECONDS

What is your breathing like?

PAUSE

Is it shallow or full?

PAUSE

Even or jerky?

PAUSE

Rushed or unhurried?

PAUSE

Deep Breathing

Now take a deep breath. And when you are ready, slowly and evenly exhale.

PAUSE 5 SECONDS

Let yourself breathe in a way that is comfortable.

PAUSE

Slow, easy, and rhythmical.

PAUSE

Take your time. Try not to force yourself to breathe in any particular way.

PAUSE

Let your stomach and chest slowly fill and empty with air.

PAUSE

Keep breathing this way.

PAUSE

Slowly in and slowly out.

PAUSE 15 SECONDS

Arm Swing Breathing

Now let your arms hang by your sides.

PAUSE 5 SECONDS

This time as you breathe in, circle your arms behind you in whatever way feels best. And when you are ready to breathe out, gently and easily circle your arms around to your front and let them cross your chest as if you were hugging a big pillow. Try breathing this way for a while.

PAUSE 5 SECONDS

Continue breathing this way... breathing in while gently circling your arms to your back... and pausing... and breathing out while circling your arms to your front.

PAUSE 5 SECONDS

Breathe gently and easily at an unhurried pace. Take your time.

PAUSE 5 SECONDS

Go easily.

PAUSE 5 SECONDS

Let each breath be full and complete.

PAUSE 5 SECONDS

And let yourself breathe without strain and without effort.

PAUSE 5 SECONDS

Without hurrying and without rushing.

PAUSE 5 SECONDS

Now let your arms hang by your sides.

PAUSE 5 SECONDS

Body Arch Breathing

This time, as you inhale, gently arch and stretch your back and let your head tilt back slightly. Let your lungs fill completely with air. And when you are ready, exhale and relax and return to a comfortable upright position. Gently tilt your head forward.

PAUSE 5 SECONDS

For a few seconds, continue breathing this way, gently and easily. Arch your back as you gently breathe in. And sit up as you breathe out. Do this gently and easily.

PAUSE 15 SECONDS (Smith, 1985, pp. 120–122)

Stomach Squeeze Breathing

Now sit up in your chair and open your hands and fingers and place them over your stomach.

PAUSE

Spread your fingers comfortably apart so they cover your entire stomach, with your thumbs touching the bottom part of your chest.

PAUSE 5 SECONDS

Now, very easily, take a full breath, filling your stomach and chest completely. And when you are ready to exhale, firmly press in with your hands and fingers, squeezing in.

And when you are ready to inhale, gradually release your fingers, and let your stomach relax and breathe in as if your stomach were filling with air.

PAUSE

Breathe easily and completely.

PAUSE 5 SECONDS

Now continue breathing this way, squeezing your stomach as you are breathing out, and relaxing your fingers as you are breathing in.

PAUSE

Do not force yourself to breathe at a hurried pace.

PAUSE

Take your time.
Breathe very gently and very easily.

PAUSE 5 SECONDS

Notice what it feels like to breathe completely and fully.

PAUSE 5 SECONDS

At your own pace, continue breathing evenly in and evenly out. Do not hurry. Take your time.

PAUSE 5 SECONDS

Notice the even flow of air as it rushes in and out of your lungs.

PAUSE 10 SECONDS

Now, when you are ready, exhale completely, and relax your fingers.

PAUSE

Active Diaphragmatic Breathing

This time, let your fingers remain relaxed over your stomach. As you breathe in, let the air come in on its own, as if it were filling your stomach.

Feel the stomach filling, like a large, soft balloon filling completely.

And when you are ready to exhale, this time do not press in with your fingers. Relax, and let the air flow out on its own, gently and slowly. When you have breathed out, pull your stomach in toward your backbone, not using your fingers. Squeeze out any remaining air.

PAUSE

Continue breathing this way for a little while, breathing completely and deeply.

PAUSE 5 SECONDS

Fill and empty your stomach and chest.

PAUSE 5 SECONDS

Take it easy, do not force yourself to breathe in a way that feels uncomfortable.

PAUSE 5 SECONDS

Breathe without strain.

PAUSE 5 SECONDS

Easily and completely.

PAUSE 5 SECONDS

Notice how it feels as breathing helps you become more and more relaxed.

PAUSE 15 SECONDS

And now, when you are ready, rest your hands in your lap. Let yourself breathe deeply and easily, without strain and without effort.

PAUSE

Now attend to the flow of air in and out of your nose.

PAUSE

How does it feel as the air rushes in and out?

PAUSE 5 SECONDS

Inhaling through Nose

This time, as you breathe in, imagine you are sniffing a very delicate flower. Let the flow of breath into your nose be as smooth and gentle as possible, so you barely rustle a petal. Take a full breath.

PAUSE

And relax, letting yourself breathe out naturally, without effort.

PAUSE 5 SECONDS

Continue breathing this way, breathing in and out quietly and evenly at your own pace.

PAUSE 5 SECONDS

Notice the inner calm that comes with breathing in a way that is slow, full, and even.

PAUSE 5 SECONDS

Notice the relaxing and refreshing rush of air as it quietly moves in and out of your lungs.

PAUSE 5 SECONDS

See how far you can follow the inward flow of air.

PAUSE 5 SECONDS

Can you feel it move past your nostrils?

PAUSE 5 SECONDS

Can you feel the air in the passages of your nose?

PAUSE 5 SECONDS

Can you feel the air flowing into your body?

PAUSE 10 SECONDS

Take your time. Breathe easily and fully.

PAUSE 10 SECONDS

Let yourself become more and more quiet, more and more relaxed.

PAUSE 10 SECONDS

Exhaling through Lips

Now take a slow deep breath and pause.

And breathe out slowly through your lips, as if you were blowing at a candle flame just enough to make it flicker, but not go out. Continue breathing out, emptying all the air from your stomach and chest.

PAUSE

Then breathe in through your nose.

PAUSE

Continue breathing this way, making the stream of air that passes through your lips as you exhale as smooth and gentle as possible.

PAUSE 5 SECONDS

Let the tension flow out with every breath.

PAUSE 5 SECONDS

Let the gentle movement of air dissolve any feelings of tension you might have.

PAUSE 10 SECONDS

Notice the easy flow of air as it relaxes and refreshes you.

PAUSE 10 SECONDS

Let each breath fill you with feelings of peaceful relaxation.

PAUSE 10 SECONDS

Notice the inner calm that comes with breathing in a way that is slow and full and even. (Smith, 1985, pp. 124–127)

Physical Exercise

Moving, playing, walking, running, and similar activities are very commonly used stress management procedures. As Girdano and Everly (1979) comment,

> The primary stress response is the fight or flight response. This reaction has helped ensure our survival and continues to do so; no amount of relaxation training can ever diminish the intensity of this innate reflex. Stress is physical, intended to enable a physical response to a physical threat; however, any threat—physical or symbolic—can bring about this response. Once the stimulation of the event penetrates the psychological defenses, the body prepares for action. Increased hormonal secretion, cardiovascular activity, and energy supply signify a state of stress, a state of extreme readiness to act as soon as the voluntary control centers decide the form of the action, which in our social situation is often no "action" at all. Usually the threat is not real, but holds only symbolic significance. Our lives are not in danger, only our egos. Physical action is not warranted and must be subdued, but for the body organs it is too late: what took only minutes to start will take hours to undo. The stress products are flowing through the system and will activate various organs until they are reabsorbed back into storage or gradually used by the body. And while this gradual process is taking place, the body organs suffer.
>
> The solution, very simply, is to use the physical stress arousal for its intended purpose—physical movement. In our cultured society, which does not include killing a saber-toothed tiger nor allow us to physically abuse our neighbor, the most efficient use of the physical arousal is physical exercise. The increased energy intended for fight or flight can be used simply in running or swimming or riding a bike. Thus, one can accelerate the dissipation of the stress products, and if the activity is vigorous enough, it can cause a rebound or overshoot after exercise into a state of deep relaxation. (p. 25)

There are hundreds of planned and spontaneous means for engaging in stress-reducing physical exercise. These include organized team and individual sports; the popular aerobic exercise, weight-training, and jogging activities of recent years; walking; one or another calisthenics program; swimming; bike riding; the various cooperation-enhancing or group-centered activities examined in chapters 10 and 11; or an exercise program intentionally designed to reduce chronic muscle tension (e.g., Mason's [1980] sequence of shoulder rolls, neck rotation, arm shakes, leg shakes, scalp tapping, scalp massage, eye stretches, and other activities). No matter which physical activities are selected, they should ideally involve at least moderate or greater activity levels, regularity of use (four or five times per week), and a half- to a full hour's duration.

The stress management activities examined thus far—progressive relaxation, yogaform stretching, breathing exercises, and physical exercise—all require some degree of physical movement or effort. The remaining techniques we wish to consider are more accurately described as mental activities, each in its own way an emphasis on focusing, centering, imagery, or contemplation.

Somatic Focusing

Somatic focusing, a more descriptive term for this activity than its more usual label, *autogenic training,* involves an attempt to induce specific physical sensations that are typically associated with relaxation. Mason (1980) offers the following comments:

> By inducing any of the characteristics of the relaxation response, such as warmth and heaviness, you can break into the chain of physiological changes that occur when you are relaxed.... The warmth that you strive for [in somatic focusing] is your perception of increased blood flow throughout the body, especially to the extremities (unlike the stress response which constricts blood flow to these areas). The heaviness is your perception of the skeletal muscles relaxing (unlike the tensing of the stress response). If you can teach yourself to elicit warmth and heaviness at your command then the other physiological changes that occur when you relax will follow. (pp. 21–22)

Mason (1980) stresses that a prerequisite for the success of the somatic focusing process is at least some movement toward a concomitant state of relaxation. In his words, it is "passive concentration" on a bodily state (e.g., warmth, heaviness) that facilitates the state's sensory occurrence. Smith's (1985) instruction to users is illustrative:

> First, let's demonstrate [passive concentration's] opposite, active thinking. Let your right hand drop to your side. Now, actively and effortfully try to make your hand feel warm and heavy. Work at it. Exert as much effort as you can trying to actively and deliberately will your hands to feel warm and heavy.

Now, simply relax. Let your hand fall limply by your side. Without trying to accomplish anything, simply let the phrase "My hand is warm and heavy" repeat in your mind. Let the words repeat on their own, like an echo. All you have to do is quietly observe the repeating words. Don't try to achieve warmth and heaviness. Just quietly let the words go over and over in your mind. While thinking the words warm and heavy, you might want to imagine your hand in warm sand, or in the sun, or in a warm bath. Pick an image that feels comfortable, and simply dwell upon it. (p. 134)

Smith (1985) continues with instructions (later usable as self-instructions) to elicit deeper relaxation by focusing on warmth and heaviness situations:

Warmth and Heaviness

Now attend again to your hands and fingers.

PAUSE 5 SECONDS

With every flow of breath, let yourself think words and images related to warmth and heaviness.

PAUSE

It is not important that you actually feel sensations of warmth and heaviness. Simply let thoughts related to warmth and heaviness float through your mind, like echoes.

PAUSE 10 SECONDS

Think the phrase "My hands and arms are heavy and warm . . . warmth is flowing into my hands and arms."

PAUSE

What pictures or images come to mind that go with warmth and heaviness? You might want to imagine your hands and arms in warm, soothing water, or in the sand. You might want to imagine a warm, relaxing breeze caressing your skin. Let pictures and images come to mind that suggest warmth and heaviness.

PAUSE 10 SECONDS

"My hands and arms are heavy and warm . . . so heavy it begins to feel as if I could barely lift them . . . as if heavy bricks were resting on my hands, pulling them down."

PAUSE 10 SECONDS

"Warmth flows into the spaces between my fingers, into my hands and arms."

PAUSE

Imagine these words quietly and passively, like an echo.

PAUSE

"Warm and heavy, hands and arms are warm and heavy, as blood carries warmth to every muscle."

PAUSE

"My arms and hands are so heavy it feels as if it might be hard to lift them."

PAUSE

"As if heavy bricks were attached to each arm."

PAUSE 10 SECONDS

You might imagine the warm sun shining on your hands and arms.

PAUSE

Or warm water or air, or a soft warm blanket.

PAUSE 10 SECONDS

Let the warmth and heaviness flow up your arms with every breath into your shoulders, back, and neck. You might want to imagine the warm sun, or warm water or air, bringing relaxation to your shoulders, back, and neck.

PAUSE 10 SECONDS

Think "My back is warm and heavy."

PAUSE 10 SECONDS

"My shoulders are warm and heavy."

PAUSE 10 SECONDS

"My neck is warm and heavy."

PAUSE 10 SECONDS

"It feels pleasant as my muscles relax and become warm and heavy, as if the sun were shining down on them, or they were covered by warm water or air."

PAUSE 10 SECONDS

If your mind is distracted, that's OK . . . easily and gently return to thinking "warm and heavy," passively and quietly, as if you were listening to words echo in your mind.

PAUSE 10 SECONDS

Let warmth and heaviness flow into the muscles of your face, dissolving any tension that may be there.

PAUSE 10 SECONDS

Let the flow of blood bring feelings of warmth and heaviness to your face, smoothing out the tension, bringing deeper and deeper relaxation.

PAUSE 10 SECONDS

Let yourself think "warm and heavy" as your face becomes more relaxed.

PAUSE

"My eyelids are comfortably warm and heavy. . . almost as if they were glued shut."

PAUSE

"I can feel the heavy weight of my eyelids beginning to build as they become so relaxed."

PAUSE

"It would take some effort to open my eyelids . . . it feels so good just to let them stay shut . . . warm and heavy."

PAUSE 10 SECONDS

Let the warmth and heaviness flow into your trunk and stomach, flowing deeply inside. Let go of any tension with every breath as you think, "I am warm and heavy, warm and heavy."

PAUSE 10 SECONDS

Let warmth and heaviness flow into your legs and feet. Focus on your legs and feet. Notice the pleasant sensations as warmth and heaviness flow with every breath.

PAUSE

Think silently to yourself "My legs and feet are becoming heavy and warm . . . warmth is flowing into my feet . . . my legs are warm and heavy. . . my feet are warm and heavy. . . warmth and heaviness is sinking into my legs and feet as they become more and more relaxed."

PAUSE

Your legs and feet feel more and more warm and heavy... so heavy that you can feel gravity pulling them down ... so heavy that it feels as if it would take some effort to lift them ... warm and heavy... as if heavy weights were resting on each leg ... heavy bricks pulling down.

PAUSE 10 SECONDS

Now, for the next minute or so, let your entire body feel pleasantly warm and heavy. Let waves of pleasant relaxation dissolve any tension you may have. Let every muscle sink and become more completely relaxed ... warm heavy.

PAUSE 1 MINUTE

Now, gently let go of what you are attending to.

PAUSE 5 SECONDS

Gently open your eyes.

PAUSE 5 SECONDS

Take a deep breath.

PAUSE 5 SECONDS

And stretch.

PAUSE 5 SECONDS

And this completes your beginning somatic focusing exercise sequence. (Smith, 1985, pp. 144–147)

Though our illustrative emphasis has been on the relaxation-associated sensations of warmth and muscular heaviness, somatic focusing appears to succeed equally well with a host of other bodily target areas and sensations. Smith (1985) in this context describes sequences for effective relaxation-enhancing focus on the solar plexis, spine, heart, throat, and eyes.

Thematic Imagery

Stress reduction may be a likely consequence not only of the types of internally oriented attention represented by somatic focusing, but also of diverse types of externally oriented attention. Thematic imagery, also called *visualization* (Mason, 1980), is this type of approach. This activity can in part be thought of as pleasurable daydreaming or as directed contemplation of a stress-reducing topic, place, event, behavior, or theme. Smith (1985) suggests a series of commonly used relaxation-associated themes as useful for such purposes.

1. *Escape.* Imagery whose content involves a pleasurable time, different place, a new enjoyable activity. In short, as Smith (1985) puts it, "a quick mental vacation from life's pressures and demands."

2. *Reminiscence.* A return in imagination to a past relaxation-engendering event, place, time, or relationship.

3. *Mastery.* Mental images of meeting and mastering a challenge—academic, vocational, habit change, interpersonal, or other.

4. *Expression.* Contemplating a creative act or experience, dancing, singing, writing poetry, etc.

5. *Intuition.* A more passive, take-it-as-it-comes imagery on a daily theme, anticipated event, or past experience. In a sense, this activity consists of starting purposefully down any given imaginal path and then letting one's mind wander wherever it flows.

6. *Sensation.* Re-creation in imagination of especially pleasant sensations (e.g., lying on a quiet beach, floating on a raft in a lake, enjoying particular fragrances or tastes).

Smith's (1985) thematic imagery instructions concretely illustrate this activity:

Sensation Exercise

In this exercise we are going to relax by letting our minds dwell on a relaxing scene or setting.

PAUSE

Make sure you are seated upright in a comfortable position.

PAUSE

Are your feet flat on the floor?

PAUSE

Are your hands resting comfortably in your lap?

PAUSE

Now gently close your eyes and let yourself settle into a position that is comfortable.

PAUSE

For the next minute or so let your body become more and more quiet.

PAUSE 1 MINUTE

Let yourself begin to settle down and relax as you remain still.

PAUSE

And now attend to your body.

PAUSE

Let your breathing be calm and even.

PAUSE

Let every outgoing breath carry away any tension you might feel.

PAUSE

Let yourself feel more and more comfortably relaxed.

PAUSE

And now quietly ask yourself "What scene or setting is most relaxing to me at the moment?"

PAUSE 10 SECONDS

You might want to picture a quiet beach, or a grassy plain, or a cool mountain top, or a peaceful pond.

PAUSE 10 SECONDS

Whatever scene or setting is most relaxing to you, let it come to you in whatever way it wishes.

PAUSE 10 SECONDS

And now, quietly let your mind dwell on this scene for the next few seconds.

PAUSE 15 SECONDS

Let the scene become as vivid and real as possible.

PAUSE 10 SECONDS

How does it look?

PAUSE 10 SECONDS

Can you see the sky?

PAUSE

Can you feel the wind brushing against your skin?

PAUSE

Can you smell the gentle, cool air?

PAUSE

Can you feel the warm sunlight or perhaps the cool night air?

PAUSE

Involve all of your senses.

PAUSE

What do you see?

PAUSE

What do you hear?

PAUSE

What is touching your skin?

PAUSE

Can you taste or smell anything?

PAUSE

And let the scene grow in whatever way is most relaxing to you.

PAUSE 10 SECONDS

Perhaps words come to your mind that describe the scene.

PAUSE

If words or phrases come, simply let them repeat over and over like echoes.

PAUSE

Try not to force these words to change or make sense. Simply let them repeat over and over, very peacefully and quietly.

PAUSE

There is nothing for you to do except to quietly attend to your relaxing scene.

PAUSE

Let it change and evolve on its own.

PAUSE 15 SECONDS

If your mind wanders or is distracted, that's OK.

PAUSE

Quietly and gently return to your relaxing scene.

PAUSE 10 SECONDS

If you find yourself engaged in thinking about something or trying to figure something out, that's OK.

PAUSE

Quietly and gently return to your relaxing scene.

PAUSE 15 SECONDS

Let yourself sink deeper and deeper into a pleasant state of relaxation.

PAUSE

From time to time let yourself quietly repeat whatever words or pictures suggest deeper, more complete, and more satisfying relaxation.

PAUSE

You might think the words "I am sinking deeper and deeper," or "I am letting go more and more," or "There is nothing for me to do but let go," or "I am more fully aware."

PAUSE

Let the deepening suggestions come to you in whatever way feels most satisfying and relaxing.

PAUSE 10 SECONDS

Again and again, every time your mind wanders or is distracted, gently return to your pleasant, relaxing scene.

PAUSE

And now, continue attending to your scene for about 10 minutes. See where it leads you. See how it deepens. See how it grows and becomes more relaxing for the next 10 minutes.

PAUSE 10 MINUTES

And now, very gently let go of what you are attending to.

PAUSE 5 SECONDS

When you are ready, gently open your eyes.

PAUSE 5 SECONDS

Take a deep breath.

PAUSE 5 SECONDS

And stretch.

PAUSE 5 SECONDS

This completes the thematic imagery exercise. (Smith, 1985, pp. 167–170)

Meditation

Meditation is a stress management method, or group of methods, whose central feature is the calm directing of attention toward a simple stimulus. Unlike thematic imagery or contemplation, in which images are pursued for their relaxation-engendering qualities, "meditation on a stimulus is done with complete indifference, expecting nothing, desiring nothing, you simply attend and nothing else" (Smith, 1985, p. 183). The meditator requires but three things: a quiet environment, a passive attitude reflected in a willingness to let go of self-consciousness and self-appraisal, and an object to focus upon, such as a word (*one* is a frequent choice), sound (*om* is a frequent choice), physical object, or even one's own breathing. The meditator's sole task, in the transcendental version of meditation, is to repeat mentally his mantra (word or sound) while sitting in a quiet place, concentrating completely on the mantra, letting distractions pass over and through consciousness. Mason (1980) suggests that meditations should last approximately 20 minutes and should be done once or twice daily, usually before a meal and when the meditator is not likely to fall asleep.

Girdano and Everly (1979) instruct further:

> Breathe softly, but now do not concentrate on your breathing. Repeat one of the mantras aloud. Say it over and over. Each time say it softer until it becomes just a mental thought with no muscular action involved. Pace yourself, gradually lengthening the interval between thoughts of the mantra. Allow the mantra to repeat itself in your mind. Do not force it, just let it flow. Gradually the mantra will fade, your mind will remain quiet. The quiet will occasionally be broken by sporadic thoughts. Let them come, experience them, go with them until you feel like you are controlling them to some preconceived outcome. At that point they become daydreams and usually involve ego arousal. At that point, stop the thought process and go back to the mantra.
>
> Remember, meditation is a feeling, a state of mind. It is not a technique, it is not saying the mantra. Sit quietly for 10 to 15 minutes and meditate. *Keep your movements to a minimum,* but if you are uncomfortable, move; if you are worried about time, look at a clock or the discomfort and anxiety will prevent the full attainment of the meditative state.
>
> *When you finish meditating,* do not be in too much of a hurry to get up. Open your eyes, stretch a little. Contract your muscles and reactivate yourself slowly. Having at least temporarily altered your emotional reactivity, continue your day with renewed inner capacity for meeting the day's challenges. (p. 178)

And Carrington (1978) adds the following:

> When meditating never force thoughts out of your mind. All kinds of thoughts may drift through your mind while you are meditating. Treat these thoughts just as you would treat clouds drifting across the sky. You don't push the clouds away—but you don't hold onto them either. You just watch them come and go. It's the same with thoughts during meditation. You just watch them, and then when it feels comfortable to do so, go back. (p. 25)

A number of variations have emerged over the thousands of years of using meditation. We have focused on mantra-repeating meditation. Other variations are visual focal-point meditation (candle meditation, spot-staring meditation), Zen breath counting, Shovasana (breath counting in a reclining position), symbolic meditation (focus on a higher order concept), open focus meditation (no focus chosen, focusing on and then letting go of all stimuli impinging on awareness), and meditation on a repetitive movement.

Smith's (1985) explicit instructions are again useful to our understanding of this activity.

Centered Focus Meditation

In this exercise we are going to relax by meditating on a mantra.

PAUSE

First, make sure you are seated upright in a comfortable position.

PAUSE 5 SECONDS

Are your feet flat on the floor?

PAUSE 5 SECONDS

Are your hands resting comfortably in your lap?

PAUSE 5 SECONDS

Now gently close your eyes, completely or part way.

PAUSE 5 SECONDS

How are you breathing?

PAUSE 5 SECONDS

Let your breathing become more calm and even and full.

PAUSE 5 SECONDS

Let yourself breathe in a manner that feels unhurried and relaxed.

PAUSE 10 SECONDS

There is nothing for you to do but attend to the gentle flow of breath, in and out.

PAUSE 10 SECONDS

Let each outgoing breath carry out the tensions of the day.

PAUSE 10 SECONDS

Let each incoming breath bring feelings of refreshing energy.

PAUSE 10 SECONDS

Now slowly let your mantra come to mind.

PAUSE

Let it come to you in whatever way it wishes.

PAUSE

Let it repeat, easily and effortlessly, like an echo, or clouds floating across the sky.

PAUSE 5 SECONDS

There is nothing for you to do but quietly attend to your mantra.

PAUSE 15 SECONDS

Every time your mind wanders or is distracted, that's OK. Gently and easily return to the mantra, again and again.

PAUSE 10 SECONDS

Let your mantra repeat effortlessly on its own for the next few minutes.

PAUSE 15 SECONDS

Now... slowly and easily let go of the mantra.

PAUSE 5 SECONDS

Gently and easily open your eyes. Do this very slowly, you have plenty of time.

PAUSE 10 SECONDS

And take a deep breath and stretch. This completes centered focus meditation.

Open Focus Meditation

In this exercise we are going to relax by attending to and noting all stimuli that come to mind.

PAUSE

First, make sure you are seated upright in a comfortable position.

PAUSE 5 SECONDS

Are your feet flat on the floor?

PAUSE 5 SECONDS

Are your hands resting comfortably in your lap?

PAUSE 5 SECONDS

Now gently close your eyes, completely or part way.

PAUSE 5 SECONDS

How are you breathing?

PAUSE 5 SECONDS

Let your breathing become more calm and even and full.

PAUSE 5 SECONDS

Let yourself breathe in a manner that feels unhurried and relaxed.

PAUSE 10 SECONDS

There is nothing for you to do but attend to the gentle flow of breath, in and out.

PAUSE 10 SECONDS

Let each outgoing breath carry out the tensions of the day.

PAUSE 10 SECONDS

Let each incoming breath bring feelings of refreshing energy.

PAUSE 10 SECONDS

Now easily attend to every stimulus that comes to mind.

PAUSE 5 SECONDS

Every time you hear, think, or feel something, quietly acknowledge what you experience.

PAUSE 5 SECONDS

And let go of what you have noted, and return to attending to whatever stimulus drifts into consciousness. (Smith, 1985, pp. 193–195)

Applications for Children and Adolescents

In this chapter, we have asserted that the stresses experienced by the typical child and adolescent are both diverse and substantial, as are the physiological and psychological consequences. We have described a series of physical and mental activities explicitly designed to reduce the several physiological manifestations of a high stress level and to induce high levels of relaxation. These stress management activities have historically been utilized primarily with adults, but we see no reason that their apparent effectiveness would not also extend robustly to adolescents and children. Some semantic "stepping-down" of instructions and requirements may be needed. In some instances, a decrease in activity complexity and an increase in the relevance of activity content may be useful. With such modifications in place, it is our view that progressive relaxation training, yogaform stretching, breathing exercises, physical exercise, somatic focusing, thematic imagery, and meditation can each be utilized effectively to reduce substantially the physiological and psychological concomitants of stress in adolescents and children.

Chapter 8

Empathy Training

Certain constructs in psychology and education are often so broadly and loosely employed, and so diversely operationalized, that the result is a confused and confusing construct carrying many varied and at times even conflicting definitions. *Anxiety* is such a construct, *dependency* is a second example, and *empathy* is most assuredly a third.

History and Rationale

We have been able to identify 18 definitions of empathy (Goldstein & Michaels, 1985), starting with Lipps' (1907/1926) view of empathy in the context of esthetic appreciation. Katz (1963) summarizes this view:

> An observer is stimulated by the sight of an object [painting, sculpture] and responds by imitating the object. The process is automatic and swift, and soon the observer feels himself into the object, loses consciousness of himself, and experiences the object as if his own identity had disappeared and he had become the object himself. (p. 85)

Others soon came to extend the essence of this "feeling into" definition derived from the domain of esthetics to more interpersonal realms. Thus there is Buber's (1948) notion of "gliding with one's feelings into the dynamic structure [of others]" (p. 97) and Koestler's (1949) view of empathy as "the experience of partial identity between the subject's mental processes and those of another" (p. 360). As sociology and social psychology became more overtly concerned with this domain, empathy came to be defined even more explicitly in role-taking and perspective-taking terms. Mead, in 1934, suggested that "empathy is the capacity to take the role of the others and to adopt alternative perspectives vis à vis oneself" (p. 27). Dymond, in 1949, saw empathy as "the imaginative transposing of oneself into the thinking, feeling and acting of another and so structuring the world as he does" (p. 127). And Coutu, in 1951, proposed that "empathy is the process by which a person momentarily pretends to himself that he is another person, projects himself into the perceptual field of the other person, imaginatively puts himself in the other person's place, in order that he may get an insight into the other person's probable behavior in a given situation" (p. 18).

Starting with the early 1960s, and largely continuing to the present time, two paths emerged in efforts to define empathy. One was the effort to define the construct operationally, in order that it might be better studied empirically and taught as a skill to others. The second was the move away from an essentially global perspective-taking definition toward a components view of empathy, one in which stages of an empathic process are identified and examined. Unfortunately, these two paths—operationalization for research and training purposes and a components perspective for purposes of fuller understanding of the meaning of empathy—proceeded separately. This chapter seeks to join together these divergent efforts toward both a clearer and more functional gestalt.

In 1957, when Carl Rogers underscored psychotherapist empathy as one of three therapeutic conditions "necessary and sufficient" for the occurrence of positive patient change, he defined empathy non-operationally (or meta-operationally) as an attitude that could be expressed by the therapist in any one of a wide number of ways. Not only could "the therapist's experiencing of an accurate understanding of the client's private world as if it were his or her own" (Rogers, 1957, p. 96) be communicated by means of such nondirective therapy, but it also could be at the procedural heart of other approaches (i.e., free association, suggestion, etc.).

In their energetic effort to examine experimentally the nature and consequences of therapist empathy, Rogers' students lost sight of his original attitudinal definition. They equated the *communication* of empathy with empathy in toto and defined empathic communication operationally by means of a well-anchored, five-point Scale for Empathic Understanding in Interpersonal Processes (Carkhuff, 1969b—see Table 10, pp. 408–409). This scale became so popular as a research instrument (producing literally hundreds of dissertations, theses, and other studies) that, in the field of clinical psychology, this particular operationalization of empathy *became* Empathy for many, many researchers. The *communication* of the role-taking perspective, which evolved through the empathy definitions put forth by Lipps, Buber, Koestler, Mead, Dymond, Coutu, and Rogers, but which was now conveniently and popularly operationalized by Truax and Carkhuff (1967), emerged in the thinking of many as what constituted the real nature of the construct.

Others, working independently, saw matters differently. For them, empathic communication was the final component, albeit an important one, in a multistage process, all of whose components combined to define empathy. As Katz (1963) notes, Theodore Reik (1949), for example, described empathy as a four-phase process:

> 1. *Identification.* Partly through an instinctive, imitative activity and partly through a relaxation of our conscious controls, we allow ourselves to become absorbed in contemplating the other person and his experiences.
>
> 2. *Incorporation.* By this term we mean the act of taking the experience of the other person into ourselves. It is hard to distinguish this phase from the initial act of feeling oneself into the other person. . . . These are two sides of the same process. When we identify, we project our being into others; when we incorporate, we introject the other person into ourselves.
>
> 3. *Reverberation.* What we have taken into ourselves now echos upon some part of our own experience and awakens a new appreciation. . . . We allow for an interplay between two sets of experiences, the internalized feelings of others and our own experience and fantasy.
>
> 4. *Detachment.* In this phase of empathic understanding, we withdraw from our subjective involvement and use the methods of reason and scrutiny. We break our identification and deliberately move away to gain the social and psychic distance necessary for objective analysis. (p. 41)

In a closely analogous manner, Keefe (1976) has defined empathy as a process consisting of perceptual, reverberatory, cognitive analysis, and communication components. The first phase of the empathic process begins, according to Keefe, as the observer perceives the feeling state and thoughts of the other by means of the overt behavioral cues displayed by the other. In the second phase, the observer's perceptions generate both cognitive and affective responses in herself. Here, in a manner consistent with Reik's notion of reverberation, the observer seeks to avoid stereotyping, value judgments, the formulation of hypotheses, or other forms of cognitive analysis. Instead, she seeks to hold such cognitive processes in abeyance while allowing and encouraging a largely unfettered, "as-if" experiencing of the other's affective world. Next, in the detachment and decoding phase of cognitive analysis, the observer seeks to distinguish among, sort out, and label her own feelings and those she perceives as being experienced by the other person. As noted earlier, communication operationally constitutes the whole of empathy for some, but in the fourth phase or component of Keefe's definition of empathy, the observer communicates accurate feedback to the other regarding the other's affect. Keefe (1976) nicely summarizes this four-component sequence:

> The foregoing four empathic behaviors—perceiving accurately the client's gestalt, allowing a direct feeling response to arise, holding qualifying or distorting cognitive processes in abeyance, and separating his own feelings from those shared with the client—all characterize the worker's receptivity to the client. But accurate reception must be complemented by accurate feedback. (pp. 12–13)

Thus we see that two major contemporary definitions of empathy have evolved: empathy defined as a communication process and empathy defined as a considerably more complex, multiphasic process, in which communication is merely one component. The communication process has been the operational definition for empathy not only in the hundreds of psychotherapy studies alluded to earlier, but also in most of the major empathy training programs developed and offered in recent years. As will be seen later, we have followed Keefe's (1976) definition of empathy in our Prepare Curriculum Empathy Training approach and have placed emphasis on explicit instruction in empathy components.

Our presentation thus far has sought to define and describe empathy as a process constituted of four sequentially related components. Though much still remains to be clarified, enough now appears to be understood about what empathy is—and enough has been demonstrated regarding its prosocial potency in significant interpersonal relationships—for the issue of means for its enhancement to be appropriately raised. Why have we included Empathy Training in the Prepare Curriculum? What do the major empathy training methods consist of and how much do they actually differ operationally? How can we unite our components perspective on empathy with available training techniques to yield recommendations for optimal training methods for each phase of the empathy process? These are among the questions we will seek to explore.

But first, why train empathy? Empathy, first of all, has a consistently positive association with a broad range of other prosocial behaviors. Cooperation, sociability, interpersonal competence, and, at times, altruism each covary with the individual's empathic ability (Batson, 1987; Batson & Coke, 1981; Brehm, Powell, & Coke, 1984; Eisenberg & Miller, 1987; Howard & Barnett, 1981; Knudson & Kagen, 1982; Krebs, 1975; Levin & Hoffman, 1975; Toi & Batson, 1982). This degree of association is a core set of findings in the context of the Prepare Curriculum's goal to promote prosocial behavior.

Empathy also has a consistently negative association with aggressive behavior (Chandler, Greenspan, & Barenboim, 1974; Feshbach, 1978; Iannotti, 1978; Miller & Eisenberg, 1988; Reed, 1981; Selman, 1980). The more we tune in to the other person, experience her emotional and/or cognitive world, and take her perspective, the less likely or able we are to inflict harm or injury on the other. Those interested in promoting aggression, whether via gang conflict or military warfare, capitalize on the reciprocal of this finding—that is, the more we can dehumanize others (label them pejoratively, ignore their perspectives)—the better able we are to aggress against them.

In addition to enhancing prosocial behavior and inhibiting anti-social behavior on the part of the empathy trainee, heightened levels of empathy may have very important consequences for the significant others who constitute this individual's interpersonal world. Research on counseling, education, and parenting clearly demonstrates the beneficial effects of empathic experiences on others. With high levels of empathy directed toward them, clients in a counseling context often improve more (Blackwood, 1975; Gladstein, 1977; Goldstein & Michaels, 1985; Lambert, DeJulio, & Stein, 1978; Mitchell, Bozarth, & Krauft, 1977); students in an educational context often achieve more and enjoy their schooling experiences more fully (Aspy & Roebuck, 1977; Kieran, 1979; Morgan, 1979; Rogers, 1983; Truax & Tatum, 1966; Wagner, 1969); and children exhibit more prosocial behavior, less conflict, and higher self-esteem (Bell & Bell, 1982; Eisenberg-Berg & Geisheker, 1979; Letourneau, 1981; Miller, 1976). It is not a far leap from these contexts to the diverse dyadic and group settings that constitute the interpersonal world of the youth for whom Prepare is designed. In family, friendship, school, work, and play contexts, trainees impinge upon others. With enhanced levels of empathy, such influence is all the more likely to be beneficial. There exists at least initial empirical support for this assertion in the peer and friendship development literature (Cohen, 1983; Epstein, 1983; Epstein & Karweit, 1983; Guralnick, 1981; Strain, 1981).

Current Training Methods

Four major training approaches have been developed in the past several years to enhance the empathy level of psychotherapists, counselors, and/or persons not in helper roles (i.e., couples, parents, teachers, adolescents, etc.). These include the didactic-experiential approach (Carkhuff, 1969a, 1969b); the interpersonal living laboratory (Egan,

1976); psychological skills training, including Relationship Enhancement (Guerney, 1977), microtraining (Ivey & Authier, 1971), and our own Structured Learning Approach (Goldstein, 1973); and programmed self-instruction (Bullmer, 1972). Other empathy training approaches do exist and will be briefly mentioned later in the chapter; however, the major "packages" indicated are, in essence, "empathy training today." They are, therefore, the source materials we must rely upon in building toward an effective empathy training sequence for Prepare Curriculum youth. Because we are deeply concerned with "empathy training tomorrow," we will seek to evaluate these packages critically and chart directions for the future of such training. We believe this future approach will produce far more reliable and enduring empathy enhancement than even the better of the present methods.

Didactic-experiential Training

In the mid-1960s, the research team of Truax and Carkhuff introduced the didactic-experiential approach to the training of a small cluster of purportedly facilitative helper behaviors that constituted the heart of the Rogerian approach to the helping process (Truax & Carkhuff, 1967; Truax, Carkhuff, & Douds, 1964). Chief among these training goals was a high level of helper empathy. Truax et al. (1964) held that traditionally didactic and traditionally experiential approaches each had much to offer but that neither alone was sufficient for the task at hand:

> The didactic orientation emphasizes passing down an accumulated store of knowledge in the traditional learning setting. Clearly, the flow is downward. That is, for the student the experience is one of accepting and incorporating a set of "established" premises, from which he may deduce certain modes of doing things in therapy. In contrast, while the experiential approach nurtures, elicits and even predicts behavioral change on the part of the supervisee, it focuses upon instituting certain attitudinal conditions. The belief is that growth, born of the trainee's own experience, will follow. In generalizing from experience, the flow is upward. Thus, the didactic orientation is largely deductive and the experiential orientation is largely inductive.
>
> The approach set forth... incorporates both the didactic and the experiential: the therapist supervisor brings to bear his knowledge of therapy accumulated from his own experience and the experiences and work of others in the context of a therapeutic relationship which provides for the trainee the conditions which... are essential for psychotherapeutic personality change. (p. 242)

Implementation and evaluation of this training philosophy became an active pursuit of this research team, and, in 1967, Truax and Carkhuff presented a detailed operational statement of the training orientation reflected above. The didactic-experiential training approach, circa 1967, contained several constituent procedures. Sequentially, it began with didactic input-seeking to provide trainees with a base of relevant knowledge. It then proceeded to a series of experiences (some didactic, some experiential, some an admixture of both) further reflecting the overriding training philosophy. Concretely, its procedures involved the following components:

1. *Reading list.* Extensive readings from a diverse range of psychotherapy theorists and practitioners were provided.

2. *Audiotape library.* To supplement the readings, trainees listened to 25 hours of individual and group psychotherapy sessions of various orientations.

3. *Discrimination practice.* Trainees were given copies of a version of the Scale for Empathic Understanding in Interpersonal Processes (see Table 10) and asked to rate specific excerpts from the audiotaped sessions of experienced therapists.

4. *Reflection of feeling.* A series of audiotaped patient statements was presented to trainees who, first privately and then out loud as called upon during group supervision, were required to provide interchangeable responses indicative of Level 3 empathy, as described on the Scale for Empathic Understanding in Interpersonal Processes.

5. *Live role play.* Trainees paired off and, alternately in the roles of helper and helpee, sought to respond with high levels of empathy when in the helper role. This experience provided opportunity for role-played empathic responses for larger units of time than had been available for responses to audiotaped excerpts.

6. *Feedback.* Live role-play responses were audiotaped, brought to group supervisory sessions, and rated by group members on the Scale for Empathic Understanding in Interpersonal Processes, thus providing feedback to the responding trainee and further modeling and empathy discrimination training to all other members of the training group.

7. *Therapeutic interviews.* Trainees met with actual clients first for single interviews and then for an extended series of interviews of a psychotherapeutic nature.

8. *Feedback.* As with the role-played experiences, the therapy interviews were audiotaped and utilized for feedback purposes in group supervision.

Table 10
Empathic Understanding in Interpersonal Processes:
A Scale for Measurement

Level 1

The verbal and behavioral expressions of the helper either do not attend to or detract significantly from the verbal and behavioral expressions of the helpee(s) in that they communicate significantly less of the helpee's feelings and experiences than the helpee has communicated himself.

EXAMPLE: The helper communicates no awareness of even the most obvious, expressed surface feelings of the helpee. The helper may be bored or disinterested or simply operating from a preconceived frame of reference which totally excludes that of the helpee(s).

In summary, the helper does everything but express that he is listening, understanding, or being sensitive to even the most obvious feelings of the helpee in such a way as to detract significantly from the communications of the helpee.

Level 2

While the helper responds to the expressed feelings of the helpee(s), he does so in such a way that he subtracts noticeable affect from the communications of the helpee.

EXAMPLE: The helper may communicate some awareness of obvious, surface feelings of the helpee, but his communications drain off a level of the affect and distort the level of meaning. The helper may communicate his own ideas of what may be going on, but these are not congruent with the expressions of the helpee.

In summary, the helper tends to respond to other than what the helpee is expressing or indicating.

Level 3

The expressions of the helper in response to the expressions of the helpee(s) are essentially interchangeable with those of the helpee in that they express essentially the same affect and meaning.

EXAMPLE: The helper responds with accurate understanding of the surface feelings of the helpee but may not respond to or may misinterpret the deeper feelings.

Note: From *Helping and Human Relations for Lay and Professional Helpers: Vol. 2. Practice and Research* (pp. 315–317), by R. R. Carkhuff, 1969, Amherst, MA: HRD. Reprinted by permission.

Table 10 *(continued)*

In summary, the helper is responding so as to neither subtract from nor add to the expressions of the helpee. He does not respond accurately to how that person really feels beneath the surface feelings; but he indicates a willingness and openness to do so. Level 3 constitutes the minimal level of facilitative interpersonal functioning.

Level 4

The responses of the helper add noticeably to the expressions of the helpee(s) in such a way as to express feelings a level deeper than the helpee was able to express himself.

EXAMPLE: The helper communicates his understanding of the expressions of the helpee at a level deeper than they were expressed and thus enables the helpee to experience and/or express feelings he was unable to express previously.

In summary, the helper's responses add deeper feeling and meaning to the expressions of the helpee.

Level 5

The helper's responses add significantly to the feeling and meaning of the expressions of the helpee(s) in such a way as to accurately express feelings levels below what the helpee himself was able to express or, in the event of ongoing, deep self-exploration on the helpee's part, to be fully with him in his deepest moments.

EXAMPLE: The helper responds with accuracy to all of the helpee's deeper as well as surface feelings. He is "tuned in" on the helpee's wave length. The helper and the helpee might proceed together to explore previously unexplored areas of human existence.

In summary, the helper is responding with a full awareness of who the other person is and with a comprehensive and accurate empathic understanding of that individual's deepest feelings.

---

9. *Quasi-group psychotherapy.* In parallel with all of the foregoing, and as one major reflection of the experiential thrust of this method, all trainees met regularly in a group-therapy-like experience designed, among other goals, to enhance trainees' awareness of their own affective functioning.

A second formulation of the didactic-experiential approach appeared in 1969 (Carkhuff, 1969a, 1969b). Its format moves discernably and importantly in the direction of a components view of empathy, a perspective also at the heart of the present chapter. The 1969 formulation by Carkhuff of the didactic-experiential approach, with its dual emphases on separate training for the discrimination of empathy and the communication of empathy, is a significant step in the direction of such a components strategy.

Carkhuff (1969b) comments as follows:

> There is substantial evidence to support the proposition that a high level of discrimination, insufficient in and of itself for a high level of communication, is nevertheless critical to a high level of communication. Since a high level of communication is the basic goal of training . . . it is meaningful to focus upon discrimination as a first stage of effective communication in the helping process. (p. 167)

The first phase of the training effort, therefore, is didactic-experiential empathy discrimination training. For the purpose of building an initial knowledge base, trainees begin with discussions regarding the nature of empathy, its functions, and its consequences. In tandem with this didactic beginning, the program provides an in-depth exposure to a wide variety of audiotaped counseling and psychotherapy sessions. In-session and homework assignments not only involve tape listening but also require trainees to rate taped helper responses on the Scale for Empathic Understanding in Interpersonal Processes (see Table 10). The procedure involved goes beyond rating per se. Trainees record their ratings and their reasons for them and discuss these estimations in group feedback sessions with supervisors and peers.

Carkhuff (1969b) summarizes the discrimination training phase in the following manner:

> We have found it most effective to begin with the dimension of empathy. Empathy is the key ingredient of helping. Its explicit communication, particularly during early phases of helping, is critical. Without an empathic understanding of the helpee's world and his difficulties as he sees them there is no basis for helping. In focussing upon training in the discrimination of the level of communication of empathic understanding in interpersonal processes, then, we first emphasize the critical nature of this necessary ingredient. We study its functions and effects as well as its qualification and modifications. Finally, we study those scales relevant to the assessment of the level of empathic understanding and apply them to taped material. (p. 173)

Moving on to the second component of empathy represented in this formulation, this approach follows the essentially didactic series of empathy discrimination-enhancing experiences with intensive training in the effective communication of empathic understanding—a jointly didactic and experiential undertaking. The experiential facet finds overt expression primarily via the empathic, warm, genuine relationship that trainers functioning at high levels of these facilitative conditions are purportedly able to offer trainees. According to Carkhuff (1969a), this training context provides "the trainee with the experience of having his own communications understood in depth with a fineness of discrimination that extends his communications and allows him to understand himself at ever deeper levels" (p. 200). It is important to note that the opportunity to interact with one or more such facilitative trainers also provides a significant empathy modeling experience for trainees.

The didactic component of this approach to empathy communication training involves (1) responding to taped materials; (2) role playing; and (3) participating as helper in interviews with actual clients, plus receiving feedback on these communication efforts. In carrying forward these audiotaped, role-played, and real-client interactions, the trainee is urged to utilize the following communication guidelines, which stress that the helper will find she is most effective in communicating an empathic understanding when she

1. Concentrates with intensity upon the helpee's expressions, both verbal and nonverbal;
2. Concentrates upon responses that are interchangeable with those of the helpee;
3. Formulates her responses in language that is most attuned to the helpee;
4. Responds in a feeling tone similar to that communicated by the helpee;
5. Is most responsive;
6. Moves tentatively toward expanding and clarifying the helpee's experiences at higher levels after having established an interchangeable base of communication;
7. Concentrates upon what is not being expressed by the helpee;
8. Employs the helpee's behavior as the best guideline to assess the effectiveness of her response.

The didactic-experiential approach to empathy training has been widely utilized since its initiation and also has been the focus of numerous studies seeking to evaluate its efficacy. With relatively few exceptions (e.g., Spadone, 1974), these several investigations have yielded results supporting the value of the didactic-experiential training program as an effective means for enhancing empathy (Avery, Rider, & Haynes-Clements, 1981; Bath, 1976; Beale, Payton, & Zachary, 1978; Becker & Zarit, 1978; Berenson, 1971; Bierman, Carkhuff, & Santilli, 1972; Carlson, 1974; Deshaies, 1974; Gustafson, 1975; Housley & Magnus, 1974; Isquick, 1978; LaMonica, Carew, Winder, Haase, & Blanchard, 1976; Pierce, Carkhuff, & Berenson, 1967).

Although it thus appears probable, even highly probable, that the didactic-experiential approach to empathy training as operationalized above is an effective program for empathy training, it is not without its drawbacks. Chief among these, as is also true to varying degrees for the other training packages yet to be described, are unanswered questions regarding the contribution of each of the packages' separate methods to the training outcome. Almost all of the evaluation research cited above compares the didactic-experiential package as a whole to either other packages or control groups. Of the several separate training processes that constitute the didactic-experiential package, do all or just a few contribute to the apparently effective outcome, and, if just a few, which ones? The program is long, involved, and expensive in terms of time and other resources. If all of its constituent processes contribute appreciably to outcome, fine; if not (as seems quite likely), further potency-identifying research seems necessary. We recommend in this context a research approach described by Kazdin (1980) as a *dismantling treatment strategy:*

> The dismantling treatment strategy refers to analyzing the components of a given treatment. . . . Once a treatment package has been shown to "work," research may begin to analyze the precise influence of specific components. The purpose of dismantling treatment research is to understand the basis for behavior change. To dismantle a given technique, individual treatment components are eliminated or isolated from treatment. Comparisons usually are made across groups that receive the treatment package or the package minus the specific components. (p. 84)

Notwithstanding the apparent need for a dismantling research strategy vis-à-vis the didactic-experiential training package, it is clear that the approach, both conceptually and operationally, stands as a major contribution to the domain of empathy training, especially in its communication aspects. To at least some significant extent, most of the remaining empathy training packages have been influenced, whether directly or implicitly, by the didactic-experiential approach and its ramifications.

Interpersonal Living Laboratory

The interpersonal living laboratory, developed by Gerard Egan in 1976, represents an effort to bring together, for purposes of the training of empathy and a host of other human relations skills, the essence of two contemporary movements in the United States. The first—known variously as the encounter group, sensitivity group, T-group, or human relations group movement—was an effort to employ the opportunities inherent in the small group structure when designed for purposes of interpersonal exploration, experimentation, and learning. The second and newer movement, still largely taking shape at the time Egan (1976) published his *Interpersonal Living: A Skills/Contract Approach to Human Relations Training in Groups,* is the psychological skills training movement, a now widely popular utilization of social learning and related instructional techniques for the purposeful teaching of discrete interpersonal and other behaviors. By bringing these two streams together in a manner quite different from that of Carkhuff (1969a, 1969b), Egan achieved what we may characterize fairly as an experiential-didactic training package approach to empathy training. The essence of this approach is the simultaneous didactic instruction of trainees in a spectrum of interpersonal skills and provision of a group experience in which the newly learned skills may be experimented with (tried, provided with feedback, modified) in a semiprotective human context—hence, an interpersonal living laboratory.

Group members (trainees), who typically are adults or adolescents wishing to become more sensitive or empathic in their daily lives, contractually commit themselves to certain types of behaviors and goals as a condition of participation in an interpersonal living laboratory group. According to Egan (1976), goals include

> 1. *Exploration.* You will use your time in the group, first of all, to examine your own interpersonal style [in the operational sense of the psychological skills that constitute the individual, didactic training].
> 2. *Experimentation.* You will also use your time to alter your interpersonal style in ways you deem appropriate. One mode of altering will be to check out and strengthen basic interpersonal skills. Your work in the group should help you to consolidate and develop your interpersonal strengths while beginning to work at eliminating or coming to grips with your weaknesses. (p. 24)

These interpersonal learning goals are to be achieved, according to Egan (1976), by the contractually stipulated effort each trainee is expected to put forth toward establishing and developing relationships with other laboratory group members:

Your first and overriding means of achieving these goals is to participate actively in the process of establishing and developing relationships with your fellow group members. This process demands that

a. In everything you do, throughout the training and in all of the exercises, you are attempting to establish and develop a relationship with every other member of your group.

b. As you move through the process of attempting to establish and develop these relationships, you observe at first hand your own interpersonal style.

c. At the same time, you receive feedback from your fellow group members on your style, including your strengths and your weaknesses.

d. You have the opportunity to experiment with "new" behavior— that is, to attempt to alter dimensions of your interpersonal style in order to become, in your own eyes, more interpersonally effective. (pp. 24–25)

In order to facilitate a group culture promoting member movement towards these goals, group leaders seek to help create a variety of group characteristics. The successful interpersonal living laboratory group is a psychologically safe and semiprotected environment in which experiential learning and a climate of experimentation are fostered. Its focus is "here and now" on within-group interpersonal relations. Its leaders are part facilitator, part member. It is a place where risk taking becomes possible and interpersonal growth may result. Many of these characteristics also describe the traditional sensitivity, encounter, or T-group. As noted earlier, what is different about the interpersonal living laboratory is its conjoint attention to didactic instruction in the array of interpersonal skills to be tried out and developed in the living laboratory of the small group.

Thus, concurrent with the establishment and development of the interpersonal living laboratory group, trainees participate in individual interpersonal living skills training and commit themselves to such skill training via stipulation of such commitment in the group participation contract. For each of the several skills constituting this effort, trainees (1) learn the theory underlying skill usage; (2) study a host of relevant examples; (3) practice the skill through a series of written exercises; (4) practice further in dyadic, face-to-face contexts; and (5) utilize the skill in the experimental-exploratory senses described above within the setting of the interpersonal living laboratory group. The skills thus taught (i.e., the interpersonal living laboratory skill curriculum or, as Egan [1976] puts it, *core interpersonal skills*) consist of

a. *Self-presentation skills.* Included here are the skills of appropriate self-disclosure, concreteness, and expression of feeling.
b. *Response skills.* Included here are the skills of attending and listening, the communication of empathic understanding, and the behavioral communication of genuineness and respect. Training in these two groups of skills will take place through the subgroupings made from your basic training group.
c. *Challenge skills.* You will be trained in a set of advanced skills, including skills of higher-level empathic understanding, confrontation, and immediacy (direct "you-me" talk). Much of this training will take place in the larger group.
d. *Group-specific skills.* You will be trained in how to use both self-presentation and response skills in the larger group. Initiating is more difficult in a group than in one-to-one dialogue. (Egan, 1976, p. 25)

As this skills listing suggests, two levels of accurate empathic responding are taught as part of this training program. The first, *Primary-level Accurate Empathy,* is equivalent in its process to Level 3, the level of interchangeable responding, in the Carkhuff (1969a, 1969b) system (see Table 10). The second, *Advanced Accurate Empathy,* analogous to Carkhuff's Levels 4 and 5, is defined by Egan (1976) as communicating "to the other person an understanding of not only what he actually says but also what he *implies,* what he hints at, what he fears to state more clearly" (p. 29).

We now wish to illustrate, in concrete terms, the materials and exercises utilized by interpersonal living laboratory trainees in learning these two levels of empathic communication.

Primary-level Accurate Empathy (AE I)
Egan (1976) defines this first level of empathy as

a communication to the other person that you understand what he says *explicitly* about himself. In AE I, you don't try to dig down into what the other person is only half-saying, or implying, or stating implicitly. You don't try to interpret what he is saying, but you do try to get inside his skin and get in touch with *his* experiencing. (p. 109)

The following exercises, excerpted from Egan (1976), are designed to build sequentially and systematically toward trainee competence in empathy, as thus defined. Exercises as they appear here have, in most cases, been abbreviated for the sake of space.

Exercise 27*
The Communication of Understanding of Feelings
(One Feeling)

These are the kinds of statements you might hear in your group. Picture yourself listening to the speaker. This exercise should give you some experience of responding directly to the feelings of another.

Directions

Read the statement, pause for a moment, and then write down the description of the speaker's feelings that comes to mind immediately. Then reread the statements and check yourself for accuracy. The second time, see if you can come up with a better response to each statement. Feel free to use not only individual words but phrases as well.

Note that in the next few exercises you will use the somewhat artificial formula "you feel (word or words indicating feelings) because (words indicating the content, experiences, and/or behaviors underlying feelings)." This formula will get you used to identifying both feelings and content. Later on you will be asked to do it in your own way, using your own language.

1. This is a hell of a mess! Everybody here's ready to talk but nobody is ready to listen. Are we all so self-centered that we can't take time to listen to one another?

    a. Your immediate response: "You feel _____ ."

    b. Your response on reflection: "You feel _____ ."

2. You and I have been fighting each other for weeks—not listening to each other, pushing our own agendas, being competitive. I think today we did what we feared the most. We talked to each other. And you know, it's been very good talking to you, or with you, rather than at you.

    a. Your immediate response: "You feel _____ ."

    b. Your response on reflection: "You feel _____ ." (p. 112)

---

*Exercises 27–34 and 40–41, as well as the quotations on pp. 424–426, are from *Interpersonal Living: A Skills/Contract Approach to Human-relations Training in Groups,* by G. Egan. Copyright © 1976 by Wadsworth Publishing Company, Inc. Reprinted by permission of Brooks/Cole Publishing Company, Pacific Grove, CA 93950.

Exercise 28
The Communication of the Understanding of Content

This exercise is the next step. You are asked not just to identify but also to communicate understanding of the experiences and/or behaviors that underlie the speaker's feelings.

In order to enable you to focus on just the content, the stems below will provide the "feeling" words or phrases. You supply merely the "because" part of the response. The stimulus phrases are the same as those for Exercise 27. You are still responding to those . . . statements.

"You feel angry because _____ ."

"You feel at peace because _____ ."

"You feel very pleasantly surprised because _____ ."

"You feel safe enough to risk yourself because _____ ." (p. 114)

Exercise 29
The Communication of the Understanding of Feelings
(More Than One Distinct Feeling)

When people speak to one another, they don't limit themselves to the expression of just one emotion. Often conflicting or contrasting emotions are expressed, even in a relatively short statement. For example: I love him a lot, but sometimes he really drives me up a wall!

The purpose of this exercise is to help you communicate primary-level accurate empathy—first with respect to feelings—to someone who expressed two different emotional states.

Read the following statements. Imagine that the person is speaking directly to you. In this exercise, limit yourself to responding to the two distinct emotions you see being expressed (in the next exercise you will be asked to deal with content). For the present, use the formula "You feel both . . . and. . . ."

1. George, I keep telling myself not to move too quickly with you. You are so quiet, and when you do talk you usually start with a statement about how nervous you are. It's obvious to me that right now you're pretty fidgety and probably wish that I hadn't said anything to you. It's like a checkmate; if I move I lose, and if I don't move nothing will happen between us, and I'd lose.

"You feel both _____ and _____ ."

2. Elaine, in the two weeks we've been together here my response to you has been very positive. It's a little hard to say this to you. My tendency is to get to know the men first in a social situation, since I

feel more comfortable and accepted initially by men than by other women. I like you, though, and want to trust that feeling instead of waiting to see if you'll somehow "prove yourself."

"You feel both _____ and _____ ." (p. 115)

Exercise 30
The Communication of the Understanding of Content
(More Than One Distinct Feeling)

This exercise concludes the previous exercise and asks you to hook up distinct feelings with content. Distinct experiences and/or behaviors give rise to the distinct feelings.

Once you have shared your responses to Exercise 29, you have already identified the distinct emotions expressed by the speakers in the statement. Now that you have correctly identified the emotions, tie each emotion in with content, as in the example below. Continue to use the formula "You feel ... because ... and/but you also feel ... because. . . . " The first one is an example.

1. You feel cautious with George because you want to respect his pace, but you also feel on edge because you're afraid that nothing is going to happen in your relationship.

Now continue to respond to the [other] statements [in Exercise 29].

Exercise 31
The Full Communication of AE I: Both Feeling and Content

This exercise is designed to achieve two goals: First, you are asked to "put it all together" and respond completely with accurate empathy— that is, to respond to both feelings and content. Second, you are asked to begin to use your own language —your own verbal style—instead of the formula "You feel ... because. . . . " By now this formula should have begun to outlive its usefulness. Genuineness demands that you respond to others naturally, using your own style.

Directions

Read the following statements. Try to imagine that the person is speaking directly to you. You have two tasks:

      a. Respond with accurate empathy (primary-level), using the formula "You feel ... because. . . ."

b. Next write a response that includes understanding of both feelings and content but is cast in your own language and style. Make this second response as natural as possible. The first is an example.

Group Member A: I had a hard time coming back here today. I felt that I shared myself pretty extensively last week, even to the point of letting myself get angry. This morning I was wondering what kind of excuse I could make up for not being here.

a. You're feeling awkward about being in the group tonight because—given last week—you aren't sure how I, or the others, will receive you.

b. It's not easy being here tonight. You've been asking yourself how you're going to be received. In fact, you're so uneasy that you almost didn't come.

1. John, why do you have to compare me to Jane and Sue? I do that so much myself—always trying to measure up to someone else's standards. It's something I'm really trying to break myself of. And then you come along and compare me, too.

a. _____ .

b. _____ .

2. Gary, you seem to have everything so together. You're good at all of these skills, and you even seem strong when you're talking about your vulnerabilities. Or, at least, when you're talking about some weak point I allow myself to hear only how you are on top of it, how you have it under control. And then I just take another long look at my own inadequacies.

a. _____ .

b. _____ . (p. 118)

Exercise 32
The Full Communication of AE I: Contrasting Emotions

This exercise is an expansion of the previous exercise. Therefore, it also has two goals. You are asked to "put it together" again and respond with full primary-level accurate empathy. This time, however, the speaker will express two distinct or contrasting emotions. We don't lead simple emotional lives. We very often feel two sets of emotions in our transactions with others (for example, approach and avoidance). Accuracy demands that we be able to identify and respond to both, for responding to only one distorts the picture. Second, you are again asked to cast your response into your own language and verbal style.

Read the following statements. Try to imagine that the person is speaking directly to you. Then:

a. Respond with AE I, using the formula "You feel . . . because. . . .," keeping in mind that the speaker will express more than one emotional state.

b. Second, write a response that expresses your understanding in your own language and verbal style. The first is an example.

Group Member A: I've never experienced anything quite like this before. I can speak my mind in this group. I can be utterly myself, and even see myself in a kind of mirror through the feedback I get. I get encouraged to be more assertive because that's what I want and need; but people here aren't afraid to tell me that when I become more assertive I also become more controlling. I wonder why then, I still act a bit defensive here. Almost in spite of myself, everything I do here still says "Be careful of me."

a. You feel a great deal of satisfaction here because you can entrust yourself more fully than ever to us, and yet you feel uneasy because the trust isn't complete. And you find yourself still instinctively on guard.

b. You trust people here: you trust the direct way they deal with you, and you like that very much. But something is still making you cautious, and this need to be cautious seems to be making you uneasy.

1. I always thought that doing exercises in groups would be very phony, but certainly can't say that about the exercise we just did. I'm still not sure that the physical touch part is really "me," but maybe it would do me good to be freer in the ways I express myself. If exercises can help me be more myself or what I want to be, well, maybe they're all right—at least some of them.

a. _____ .

b. _____ .

2. I don't know what to do with you! You look so sincere, and I believe you're sincere. I think you actually have my interests at heart. You talk to me here. You make me look at myself—my fears of getting close to others, my use of boredom as a defense. But the way you do it! You keep after me. You make the same point over and over again. Sometimes I want to run out of here screaming!

a. _____ .

b. _____ . (pp. 120–121)

Exercise 33
The Practice of Primary-level Accurate
Empathy in Everyday Life

If responding with accurate empathy is to become part of your natural communication style, you will have to practice it outside the formal training sessions. If accurate empathy is relegated exclusively to officially designated helping sessions, it may never prove genuine. Actually, practicing accurate empathy is a relatively simple process.

1. Begin to observe conversations between people from the viewpoint of the communication of accurate empathic understanding. Does a person generally take the time to communicate this kind of understanding to another person? Try to discover whether, in everyday life, the communication of accurate empathic understanding (primary-level) is frequent or rare. As you listen to conversations, keep a behavioral count of these interactions (without changing your own interpersonal style or interfering with the conversations of others).

2. Try to observe how often you use the communication of accurate empathic understanding as part of your communication style. In the beginning, don't try to increase the number of times you use accurate empathy in day-to-day conversations. Merely observe your usual behavior.

3. Increase the number of times you use accurate empathy in day-to-day conversations. Again, without being phony or overly preoccupied with the project, try to keep some kind of behavioral count. Use accurate empathy more frequently, but do so genuinely. You will soon discover that there are a great number of opportunities for using accurate empathy genuinely.

4. Observe the impact your use of primary-level accurate empathy has upon others. Don't use others for your own experimentation, but, once you increase your use of genuine accurate empathy, try to observe what it does for the communication process. (pp. 123–124)

Exercise 34
The Identification of Common Mistakes in Phase I

The following exercise deals with some of the common mistakes people make when responding·to another person. These faults or mistakes consist, in effect, of poor execution of primary-level accurate empathy. Before you do the exercise itself, let's review briefly what some of these common mistakes are:

- responses that imply condescension or manipulation
- unsolicited advice-giving

- premature use of advanced-level accurate empathy
- responses that indicate rejection or disrespect
- premature confrontation
- patronizing or placating responses
- inaccurate primary-level empathy
- longwindedness
- cliches
- incomplete or inadequate responses (such as "uh-huh")
- responses that ignore what the person said
- use of closed, inappropriate, or irrelevant questions
- use of inappropriate warmth or sympathy
- judgmental remarks
- pairing or side-taking
- premature or unfounded use of immediacy
- defensive responses

This list is certainly not exhaustive. Can you think of other mistakes? Some of these errors are demonstrated in the exercise that follows. You are asked to identify them.

However important it is to understand a person from his own frame of reference, there is still a tendency not to do so—to do many other things instead. One function of this exercise is to make you aware of the many different ways in which it is possible to fail to communicate basic empathic understanding to others.

Directions

Below are a number of statements made by various group members, followed by a number of possible responses.

    a. First, if the response is good—that is, if it is primary-level accurate empathy—give it a plus (+) sign. However, if it is an inadequate or poor response, give it a minus (−) sign.

    b. Second, if for any reason you give the response a minus (−), indicate briefly why it is poor or inadequate (disrespect, premature confrontation, defensiveness, judgmentalness, condescension, and so on). A response may be poor for more than one reason. Make your reasons as specific as possible.

Study the example below and then move immediately to the exercise.

Example

Group Member A: I have high expectations of this group. I think we've developed a pretty good level of trust among ourselves, and I'd like to start taking greater risks. The longer I'm here the more desire I have to learn as much as possible about myself. I want you to help me do this, and I want to do the same for you.

a. (−) Hey, I wish you wouldn't speak for me. I'm not at all sure that my expectations are the same as yours. I think you're being pretty idealistic.

Reason: *defensive, judgmental, accusatory.*

b. (+) Your enthusiasm is growing. There are a lot of resources here, and you'd like to take advantage of them.

Reason: *(none because it is a plus).*

c. (−) Do you think we're ready to do this sort of thing?

Reason: *inappropriate, closed question, vague.*

d. (−) Now, John, you've always been a good member, very eager; I appreciate your eagerness very much, but *festina lente,* as the Romans said—"make haste slowly."

Reason: *condescending, parental, advice-giving.*

e. (+) Your enthusiasm's infectious, John—at least for me. I think that I, coward that I am, am ready for a bit more risk, myself.

Reason: *(none because it is a plus).*

1. I didn't feel right barging in on Paul and Marie's conversation, so I waited until I thought they were finished. I keep thinking that people will get angry if I interrupt. It may be the wrong way to be, but I don't interrupt people outside the group, and it's hard for me to think that it's okay here.

a. ( ) It seems that you're afraid of being rejected if you interrupt. And rejection really hurts you, because you don't see yourself as a worthwhile person.

Reason: _____

b. ( ) I think that's pretty unfair of you, since you don't give Paul and Marie much credit.

Reason: _____

c. ( ) Peter, you know the contract here. What you call "barging in" is merely "owning" one of the interactions. I know you're timid, but I think you should push in anyway.

Reason: _____

d. ( ) Direct "owning" of another conversation just doesn't seem right to you—so it's really hard for you to move in.
Reason: _____

2. I think my skill level has improved significantly within the last two or three weeks. I'm able to express my feelings much more openly and honestly, and feeling more confident has helped me to become less defensive.

a. ( ) You feel half-finished because you haven't been able to lick your defensiveness completely.
Reason: _____

b. ( ) Yeah. I can see that.
Reason: _____

c. ( ) How have you managed to become less defensive?
Reason: _____

d. ( ) I know your skills are improving, but I can't say that I see you as less defensive.
Reason: _____ (pp. 131–133)

Advanced Accurate Empathy (AE II)
Once the trainee has shown mastery of primary-level accurate empathy and its initial skills, training advances to deeper levels of accurate empathic communication. As Egan (1976) notes, such communications may take several forms:

Expressing What Is Only Implied
The most basic form of advanced accurate empathy is to give expression to what the other person only implies as he communicates ideas to the group.

Group Member D: I've gotten in touch with resources for relating here that I never realized I had. At least in any full way. I see that I'm caring, that I can talk concretely, that I'm unafraid to reveal myself to others who give me half a chance. I'm not trying to blow my own horn. I'm just saying that these discoveries are important to me.

Group Member E: These resources are very real, and their discovery has been—well, exciting for you.

Group Member F: I hear a note of determination. Now that you've gotten in touch with these resources, you're going to make them a part of your interpersonal life. And that's even more exciting than doing well in the group.

The Summary

You can also communicate advanced accurate empathy by bringing together and summarizing what the other has presented in bits and pieces during the group experience. This summarizing helps the other person focus on his interpersonal behavior in a new way. He sees himself from a different frame of reference.

> Group Member B: Let me see if I can put some of this together. Different things seem to keep you from making contact with different people here. George and Jim are too strong, too assertive, and their strength makes you keep your distance. On the other hand, you're afraid that Sarah might become dependent on you—for this is her tendency anyway. You and Mary haven't been able to find any "common ground." You want to establish a closer relationship with me, but you hesitate because you're not sure that I want any kind of relationship. I don't think that I'm misrepresenting what you yourself have said in your interactions here, but I'd like you to check me out on it.

> Group Member A: Oh boy! I really hadn't realized that in one way or another I was saying "No!" to everyone here. (p. 163)

Identifying Themes

AE II includes the identification of behavioral and emotional themes as group members go about the business of exploring their interpersonal styles and establishing relationships. For instance, without saying so explicitly, a group member may intimate through what he reveals about himself and through the way he behaves in the group that he tends to be a dependent person.

> Group Member B: I've been thinking of some of the things you've said here, Ned, and trying to hook these up with the ways I see you acting here. You're hesitant to challenge anyone, especially the "strong" members in the group. You say things like "I've been quiet because other people haven't given me the kind of feedback I need." You've asked me outside the group for feedback on how you are coming across. The message I tend to get out of much of this from you is "I'm not my own person. I depend on others quite a bit. I don't value myself; I wait to see how others value me first." Perhaps

this is too strong. I'd like to find out how you're reacting to what I'm saying.

Ned: What you're saying is very painful for me to hear. It's even more painful because of the truth in it. (pp. 163–164)

Helping Another Draw Conclusions from Premises

Still another way of conceptualizing advanced accurate empathy is to help another person draw his own conclusions from the premises that he himself lays down.

Group Member E: I know I'm quiet here, but I don't believe that's any reason for people to pick on me, to make me feel like a second-class citizen. I've got resources. I can say a lot of the things that others say, but they move in first.

Group Member F: The logic of what you're saying seems to be: one, I don't want to appear to be a second-class citizen: two, I have what it takes to be an active member: three, I'm going to begin to take my rightful place in this group. I'm not sure whether I'm saying too much.

"Drawing a conclusion" will often deal with how the other person wants to behave within the group (or in interpersonal relations generally.) If the "conclusion" you help your fellow group member draw is not in his premises, your empathy will be seen as an attempt to make him behave in ways that are acceptable to you. Again, accuracy is extremely important, as are tact and timing. (pp. 164–165)

To develop competence in these diverse expressions of Advanced Accurate Empathy, the following exercises are utilized:

Exercise 40
Advanced Accurate Empathy: An Exercise in Self-Exploration

One way of making sure that you are careful in using confrontational skills is to use them on yourself first. The purpose of this exercise is to make you think about some of your interpersonal style and behavior at two different levels (roughly corresponding to AE I and AE II). Self-understanding and being in touch with your own feelings and emotions should (at least logically) precede being in touch with deeper dimensions of the interactional style of others.

Directions

1. Read the examples given below.

2. Choose some situation or issue or relationship having to do with your interpersonal style that you would like to take a deeper look into. Choose something that you will be willing to share with your fellow group members.

3. Briefly describe the issue (as is done in the examples).

4. As in the examples below,

   a. Write a statement that reflects a primary-level accurate empathic understanding of the issue you have chosen. This statement should reflect understanding of both your feelings and the behaviors/experiences underlying these feelings.

   b. Write a statement that reflects your advanced accurate empathic understanding of this issue. This understanding should go deeper into the issue.

Example 1

Issue: I'm concerned about the quality of my "being with" others in interpersonal and social situations.

   a. I enjoy being with people. I meet people easily, and I'm generally well received and well liked. I make others feel at home. I'm outgoing and, to a degree, uninhibited when I'm with others—I'm humorous, I try to understand the world of others, I show an interest in what they are doing. I also try to be careful with others; that is, I try not to be "too much" (AE I).

   b. When I'm with people, even though I am outgoing, I'm not "all there." I don't tend to share myself deeply with others. Therefore there is something almost superficial (perhaps this is too strong a word) about my "being with" others. In my deepest moments, I am alone with myself. Perhaps I haven't learned to share my deeper self with anyone. I may even be afraid to do so (AE II).

Exercise 41
Advanced Accurate Empathy:
Understanding Others More Deeply

Before trying to use advanced accurate empathy "on the spot" in your group, you can, through this exercise, prepare yourself at a leisurely pace for such empathy. This exercise should help you look before you leap into advanced accurate empathy.

Directions
This exercise is the same as the previous one, except that your attention is now directed toward your fellow group members instead of yourself.

1. Read the examples given below.

2. Consider each of your fellow group members one at a time. Choose some dimension of each one's interpersonal style that you would like to explore at both the AE-I and the AE-II level. Remember, you are trying to understand the person more deeply, not "psych him out."

3. Briefly describe the issue for each (see the examples).

4. As in the examples below,

   a. For each, write a statement that reflects a primary-level accurate empathic understanding of the issue you have chosen (feelings and content). Write the statement as if you were speaking directly to the person.

   b. For each, write a second statement that reflects your advanced accurate empathic understanding of this issue. Write the statement as if you were speaking directly to the person.

Example 1
Issue: John is both satisfied and dissatisfied with the strengths in interpersonal relating he manifests in the group.

   a. John, you come across in the group as very self-assured. Most of the group members seem to enjoy interacting with you, and they do so frequently. You are understanding. You reveal how you feel about each of the group members without "dumping" your emotions on them. At one level, you seem to enjoy your position in the group. You get a great deal of respect and even admiration, and you find something satisfying in this (AE I).

   b. John, even though you share yourself a great deal, by telling others how you are reacting to them as the group moves along, you don't speak much about your own interpersonal style. It may be that you are hesitant to do so, or that others box you in by putting you on a pedestal. Whatever the case, I sometimes see you wince slightly when you get positive feedback. I'm beginning to suspect that you feel you aren't allowed to share your vulnerabilities here, and that you're beginning to resent it (AE II). (pp. 167–192)

We have provided extensive examples of the diverse materials and creative exercises that constitute the empathy training components of the interpersonal learning laboratory approach. While this creative, systematically sequenced, and apparently comprehensive training package appears to be very useful, it has (unlike the other packages to be examined) given rise to very little empirical research evaluating its training impact. It most deservedly warrants such scrutiny.

Psychological Skills Training

As noted in chapter 3, in the early 1970s there began to emerge in the United States the development of a new style of psychological intervention. It had its historical beginning in both education and psychology. Education's contribution was diverse but expressed itself in the spirit of various efforts to teach nonacademic, personological qualities. These efforts included Character Education (Bain & Clark, 1966; Hill, 1965; Trevitt, 1964), Moral Education (Kohlberg, 1964, 1969, 1971a, 1971b, 1973, 1976) and Affective Education (Miller, 1976). This belief in the value of didactic, instructional techniques for the purposive teaching of personal attributes also found concrete expression in the hundreds of highly diverse personal development courses taught in America's over 2,000 community colleges as well as in the several hundred self-instructional, self-help books so popular in the United States today. These several historical and contemporary educational strands, each reflecting both processes and contents targeted toward personal change or personal growth, interwove with complementary themes long present in psychology. In particular, there has been an enduring and pervasive concern in American psychology with the theoretical bases, empirical context, and applied implications of the learning process. Psychology's deep interest in learning and its more recent attention to social learning combined in the early 1970s with the educational perspectives and technologies mentioned above. The result was the beginning of the psychoeducational training movement.

This movement has been known by several names: psychological education, psychological skills training, interpersonal skills training, social skills training, and more. At least two dozen programmatic expressions of this orientation have been formulated and implemented. In the present context, we wish to present and examine the following three psychoeducational skills training programs, which have devoted the greatest attention to the training of empathy. Though these approaches developed largely independently from one another, their shared philosophy and overlapping procedures justifiably enable us to view them as a constellation of empathy training methods.

Relationship Enhancement

Relationship Enhancement is the product of the sustained and creative efforts of Bernard Guerney and his research group. Guerney (1977) helps orient us to his approach with this statement of purpose:

> Relationship Enhancement (RE) therapy and programs are educational services designed to enhance the relationship between intimates, especially between family members. RE programs can be conducted with individuals, with dyads, or with larger groups. The purpose of the programs is to increase the psychological and emotional satisfactions that can be derived from such intimate relationships and, in addition, to thereby increase the psychological and emotional well-being of the individual participants. (p. 1)

And further:

> The purpose of RE programs is to give the participants skills that will allow them to be empathic when they want to be and to try to encourage them to try to use these skills at a variety of times and in a variety of situations. (p. 19)

The curriculum or training objective of this approach consists of four sets of skills: (1) the expressive; (2) the empathic responder; (3) mode switching (i.e., skill in the ability to switch between expressive and responsive modes); and (4) facilitator skills, which concern the ability to teach the first three skills to others. Guerney (1977) concretizes this empathic skill as follows:

The Empathic Responder Mode*

This mode might be explained to clients as follows.

Eliminating fear and creating an atmosphere of respectful acceptance is the function of the empathic responder. Even when you totally disagree, it is still possible to show respect, appreciation, and understanding of another person. In effect, the empathic responder says to the expresser: "I will respect and value you as a person, regardless of what your feelings and wishes may be, and whether I disagree with them or not. I appreciate the opportunity to assist you in your efforts to understand your wishes and feelings because I want you to communicate them to me more and more openly, honestly, directly, and

---

*This description of the Empathic Responder Mode is from *Relationship Enhancement: Skill Training Programs for Therapy, Problem-prevention, and Enrichment* (pp. 26–29), by B. G. Guerney, 1977, San Francisco: Jossey-Bass. Reprinted by permission.

specifically. Such communication affords me the opportunity to understand you better and work more realistically toward enhancing our relationship." The more you can convey such an attitude to your partner, the more your partner will be able to do likewise in response to your communication of your own needs and feelings.

In the empathic responder mode, the attitude that you adopt is the most important thing. You must strive to put yourself in a receptive frame of mind. Your attitude must be: "Nobody can help seeing things the way they see them, and nobody can help feeling the way they feel." You must say to yourself:

"If my partner's perceptions are wrong, or if I think that these faulty perceptions have given rise to feelings that need not be there, or that should be different than they are, I will soon have my turn to say so. I can very shortly be the expresser and express my perceptions and the feelings I wish that my partner would be able to experience if only my partner perceived the situation as I do. But while my partner is expressing his own outlook, I can best help my partner, myself, and our relationship by completely understanding how my partner does perceive the situation and how he does feel. It is on this basis that we can best proceed to enhance our relationship in an enduring way. I can do this best by temporarily setting aside my own perceptions, and my own reactions, and my own feelings. If I do have strong feelings, I will not have to put them aside for more than a moment. In a moment I can take the role of expresser myself.

"I must strive to put myself in my partner's shoes and to try with all the energy and heart I can muster to see the world through my partner's eyes at this moment in time. I must try to understand exactly how my partner is perceiving the situation and exactly what my partner's feelings are about the situation.

"Because I can never be sure that I have fully grasped another's views or feelings, I must check out my understanding with my partner. Moreover, my feedback to my partner must do much more than establish the accuracy of my understanding. In the tone and in the manner of my feedback, I must also try to convey my sincere interest in my partner's viewpoint. I must try by the tone and manner of my statement to convey that I accept unconditionally my partner's right to express honestly his or her own unique feelings and view of the world."

The word *empathy* epitomizes what you are trying to do. By empathy we mean putting yourself inside the skin of another person and being able to share the world that he sees and feels. The highest level of empathic understanding is reached when you have put together what has been said and the manner in which it has been said in a way that goes beyond the words used. You can then articulate your partner's views and feelings in a way that expresses them even more accurately and fully than he has been able to do himself. You must then communicate this deep level of understanding to your partner in a warm and accepting manner. We don't mean that you will have detected something that will come as a surprise to your partner, but rather that you've focused his feelings in a clearer way than he has been able to do as he struggled to understand and express them himself.

When you are responding only with empathy, as we wish you to do, there are many things that you will not be doing:

1. You cannot be asking your partner questions. For example, you cannot be asking: "What makes you think that? How do you feel about that? How long have you felt this way? Do you always feel this way? and What do I do to make you feel that way?" Questions have the effect of diverting your partner's attention from his or her own stream of communication by seeking information that your partner has not freely chosen to give. To ask such questions would violate the expresser's right to maintain complete direction over the flow of the communication, to explore what he wants to explore, and to say what he thinks needs to be said in the way, and in the order he prefers. Often your attempt to clarify your partner's views and feelings should be stated in a questioning tone of voice. It is appropriate to be tentative in your empathic reflections of your partner's views; but not appropriate, as the empathic responder, to seek new information. If you feel the need for such information in order to later express your own needs and views, then when you become the expresser you should tell your partner the information you wish to have.

2. You cannot present your own opinion, perception, and viewpoint about what your partner is saying. We will make it easy for you to switch from being a responder to being an expresser whenever you have a strong urge to present your own viewpoint or feelings, but while you are the responder you do not express your own feelings.

3. You must not interpret things for the speaker. That is, you must not add your own reasoning as to causality, make connections between different events, or between events and feelings, in a way that presents things in a different perspective from that in which your partner seems to be viewing the situation.

4. You must not make suggestions about how your partner might alter the situation in a favorable way or solve a problem.

5. Above all, you must avoid making judgments about what your partner has said. Your own evaluation of the validity of your partner's viewpoint, or the correctness, effectiveness, or morality of your partner's statements must not enter into your empathic statements.

When your partner takes the risk of an honest expression of needs and feelings and meets with your acceptance, there is an increase in his expectation that he can afford to be open and honest with you about his needs and feelings. Each time you provide accepting understanding, you will have increased the probability that your partner will communicate more openly, directly, and honestly with you in future communications. Conversely, each time you fail to be empathic, and instead say something that denies the importance or relevance of any speaker's communications, you raise your partner's expectation of future rejections and diminish the probability that your partner will communicate with you in an open and constructive manner. Even a rejecting tone or manner will have this undesirable effect. It is the accumulated weight of thousands of such exchanges—some, of course, having much more impact than others —that will determine whether communication proceeds to become better, remains stagnant, or deteriorates.

It is almost impossible to train a person to speak openly, honestly, and constructively of his innermost interpersonal wishes, needs, and feelings, unless he has acquired faith that such expressions will meet with acceptance rather than with coolness or rejection. Until he has a measure of such faith, he will hardly be aware himself of what these needs and wishes are, in the midst of a dialog, let alone be capable of communicating them. Therefore, in the early phases of your training we will put more emphasis on helping each of you to acquire good empathic responding skills and later on we will put more emphasis on helping you acquire good expressive skills. However, both skills will be taught from the start of the program. (Guerney, 1977, pp. 26–29)

The psychoeducational procedures by which the foregoing contents are taught to Relationship Enhancement trainees are collectively describable as social learning techniques. Following opening introductions and early rapport- and trust-building efforts, the nature of the program and its procedures, contents, and goals are explained to the participating couples, parent-child dyads, families, or other trainees. Such structuring importantly includes presentation, elaboration, discussion, and personalization of the description of empathy presented above. Incorrect skill use in the context of one or another type of communication conflict is demonstrated by the trainer, as is the correct use of empathic responding in the context of the same conflicts. These modeling portrayals are discussed in depth by the participants, who are encouraged to respond with similar skill levels both within group interactions and outside the group, in practice, and in homework activities. Ancillary to these training procedures are such trainer-initiated techniques as the use of graded expectations vis-à-vis skill improvement, social reinforcement for effective skill use, attention to nonverbal expressive accompaniments to verbal behavior, presentation of relevant factual data, and major attention to discriminating appropriate and productive from inappropriate and progress-retarding trainer responses. The Relationship Enhancement approach has taken several programmatic forms: Conjugal Relationship Enhancement, Filial Therapy, Parent-Adolescent Relationship Development, and Pupil Relationship Enhancement.

These diverse operationalizations of the Relationship Enhancement approach to training empathy and related skills have received substantial, rigorous research scrutiny (Collins, 1971; Coufal, 1975; Ginsberg, 1977; Guerney, 1964, 1977; Harrell & Guerney, 1976; Hatch & Guerney, 1975; Preston & Guerney, 1982; Stover & Guerney, 1967; Vogelsong, 1974, 1975; Wieman, 1973). The collective impact of these several evaluative investigations supports the effectiveness of the Relationship Enhancement approach in general and its specific training procedures in particular. As noted earlier, we will revisit most of the same training interventions again as we discuss related empathy skills training approaches.

Microtraining: Enriching Intimacy Program

Since their initial publications in the late 1960s, Alan Ivey and his research team (see Ivey & Authier, 1971) have energetically pursued the development of a skills orientation to behavior change. This approach has found concrete expression in counseling, teaching, and training contexts in series of programs variously termed *microcounseling, microteaching,* and *microtraining.* The "micro" quality of these programmatic interventions is the use of social learning techniques to teach highly discrete, segmented behavioral skills.

One microtraining subprogram, Enriching Intimacy, focuses substantially on empathy training and thus is the target of our attention here. In this program (as in all microtraining), the skills to be taught are first operationalized in especially concrete, at times even minute, behavioral form. As Ivey and Authier (1971) comment,

> The Enriching Intimacy (E.I.) program [proceeds by] teaching via a microtraining format specific behaviors . . . demonstrated to be aspects of empathy, genuineness and warmth. The program is divided into four stages: (1) teaching the behavioral components of respect, (2) teaching the behavioral components of empathy, (3) teaching the behavioral components of genuineness, and (4) an integrative group phase. . . . Within each skill learning phase, model tapes, five-minute practice sessions with role playing which are simultaneously video-taped, and immediate feedback during the review sessions are all part of the [micro]training program. Additionally, operational definitions of each behavioral component are discussed, and for the most part the skills are focused on singly. (p. 266)

With this procedural overview as context, how then is empathy operationalized?

> The behavioral components [of empathy] . . . consist of many of the behavioral components of respect [attending behavior, minimal encouragement to talk, open questions, paraphrasing], but for the most part, the use of the skills, especially the nonverbal skills, is intensified. Thus, eye contact may be more intense; facial expression may be showing more than interest, perhaps even concern; and seating distance may be closer, perhaps even with touching occurring. The main difference [from the respect portion of training] with regard to verbal skills is their focus on feelings. The format for the empathy training portion is similar to that of the respect portion of training with two major exceptions. The first exception is that there is a large emphasis given to identification of feelings, and a feeling word list is used for this purpose. Once the trainees have expanded their feeling word vocabulary, they listen to audiotapes of clients' statements of personal concern in an attempt to identify as accurately as possible the feelings the client is expressing. The second exception, related to the above, involves the trainees' viewing silent videotapes as a way of helping them become more aware of the nonverbal components of feelings. Other than these two exceptions, though, the training involves the trainees' focusing on one skill at a time, following the traditional microtraining format. (Ivey & Authier, 1971, pp. 267–268).

As is the case for Relationship Enhancement, microtraining, and its Enriching Intimacy operationalization, has been examined in some depth in research on comparative training outcomes and has acquitted itself well (Authier & Gustafson, 1973, 1975; Gustafson, 1975; Gustafson & Authier, 1976; Ivey & Authier, 1971). Clearly, we should encourage both further study and use of the microtraining package and its constituent training components for empathy training purposes.

Structured Learning

A third skills-oriented approach to empathy training that has found substantial use in recent years is Structured Learning, developed by our own research group (Goldstein, 1973, 1981; Goldstein & Goedhart, 1973; Goldstein & Sorcher, 1974; Goldstein, Sprafkin, & Gershaw, 1976; Goldstein, Sprafkin, Gershaw, & Klein, 1980, 1983). As presented in detail in chapter 3, "Interpersonal Skills Training," the Structured Learning method consists of most of the same psychoeducational-social learning procedures that essentially constitute Relationship Enhancement and microtraining. These procedures, in the sequence utilized, consist of:

1. *Modeling.* Small groups of trainees are shown a series of specific and detailed displays (audiotape, videotape, film, or live) of a person (the model) performing the empathic or other skill behaviors constituting the group's training goal.

2. *Role playing.* Trainees are then provided with extended opportunity and encouragement to rehearse the specific behaviors comprising the target skill (e.g., empathy), which they have seen or heard the model perform. The role playing is enacted in a manner as relevant as possible to each trainee's intended real-life use of the target skill.

3. *Performance feedback.* Following each role play, the trainee actor is provided with re-coaching and prompting as needed for improved performance and positive feedback, approval, or reward as her role-played enactment of the skill becomes more and more similar to that of the model.

4. *Transfer training.* The three processes just outlined are implemented in such a manner as to maximize the likelihood that what the trainee learns in the training context will be available as equally skilled behavior in real-world settings (e.g., home, school, work, etc.).

This series of procedures has been demonstrated to be an effective means for training empathy in parents (Guzzetta, 1974), counselors (Cominsky, 1981), aggressive adolescents (Berlin, 1976; Trief, 1977), undergraduates (Shaw, 1978), teachers (Gilstad, 1978), nurses (Goldstein, Cohen, Blake, & Walsh, 1971; Goldstein & Goedhart, 1973), ministers (Perry, 1975), mental hospital attendants (Sutton, 1970), mental hospital patients (Goldstein et al., 1976), and home aides (Robinson, 1973).

Each of the five training packages presented to this point has received considerable research scrutiny, and each has received considerable positive support, at least as far as skill acquisition, as opposed to skill transfer and maintenance, is concerned. Most of this research scrutiny has been in the form of comparisons of a total package against one or more of its constituent procedures and/or control groups; rarely have comparisons been made of one training package against another. When training packages have been compared, the result usually has been that both are equally potent and both are superior to controls. We believe this experimental outcome has resulted because the training packages, regardless of their differing names, are in actuality quite similar operationally. Almost all contain some form of instructions or structuring, modeling, role playing or behavioral rehearsal, and performance feedback. Thus it is appropriate to generalize about these training packages as a collective. The combined outcome research examining their efficacy for skill acquisition is indeed impressive. Later in this chapter, we will recommend the set of approaches collectively represented by these training packages as the optimal means for training the communication component of the empathic process.

Programmed Self-instruction

Although not yet as common as trainer-led group or individual empathy training, a number of programmed self-instructional approaches toward this goal have emerged in recent years (Bullmer, 1972; Keenan, 1976; Kozma, 1974; Laughlin, 1978; Saltmarsh, 1973). Bullmer's (1972) *The Art of Empathy* has proven to be the more widely used of these alternatives and thus will serve as an illustrative example. Just as the psychoeducational skills training approaches described above essentially concern themselves with teaching but a single phase of what we and Keefe (1976) view as the four-phase empathic process (i.e., communication), the programmed self-instructional approaches are for the most part means for training the initial, perceptual phase of empathy plus some elements of the discrimination phase. Such is the case for Bullmer's (1972) approach.

Bullmer's (1972) aspiration is captured by his introductory commentary:

> Empathy means many things to many people, but most properly it is defined as a process whereby one person perceives accurately another person's feelings and the meaning of these feelings and then communicates with sensitivity this understanding to the other person. This definition makes clear the important role played by accurate interpersonal perception in the empathic process. No matter how well phrased or sensitive a response may seem, a true state of empathy between

individuals cannot exist unless the responses are based on accurate percepts. In other words, people who are considered to be highly empathic are both empathic perceivers and empathic responders. (p. vi)

Bullmer's (1972) approach was designed to facilitate the development of empathic perception, not empathic response. Program materials are sequential in nature, with each unit building on the last to teach a single principle, concept, or idea at a time. Specifically, the self-instructional sequence proceeds through a series of programmed exercises in which an attempt is made to move the trainee through awareness of interpersonal perceptual processes, sources of error therein, antecedents and correlates of affective states (e.g., needs, desires, motives), "hidden meanings" reflected by diverse emotions, and the utilization of the foregoing in seeking to perceive accurately the emotions of another individual. Substantively, the sequenced lessons consist of explanations of relevant concepts, programmed exercises, and graduated proficiency tests. Since Bullmer's materials are a configuration of sequentially arranged informational bits, they do not readily lend themselves to illustrative excerpting. Therefore, we refer the reader directly to Bullmer (1975) for further details. Although this orientation toward empathy training has not yet received extensive evaluation, the relevant research that has been conducted has indeed proven promising (Bullmer, 1972, 1975; Keenan, 1976; Saltmarsh, 1973). This initial evidence combines with the marked inexpensiveness of this approach to warrant further examination.

Other Empathy Training Approaches

We have described and illustrated what we view as the major approaches to empathy training. Many, many other procedures and packages of procedures have been utilized for such purposes. Although their sheer number may surprise the reader, their broad diversity should not, given the equally broad diversity of conceptual definitions of empathy. The vast majority of these approaches, it should be noted, seek to enhance only a single component of the empathic process—usually communication—occasionally discrimination, rarely perception, and never affective reverberation.

Some of these additional empathy training programs are training packages, such as Danish and Hauer's (1973) Helping Skills Program and N. Kagan's (1972) Interpersonal Process Recall. Others rely on a single, usually social learning, procedure. Modeling is chief among these, and its record of positive contribution to the learning of empathy is substantial and reliable (Albert, 1974; Berenson, 1971; Bierman et al., 1972; Dalton & Sundblad, 1976; Fraser & Vitro, 1975; Gulanick & Schmeck, 1977; Hodge, 1976; Isquick, 1978; Josephson, 1979; Layton, 1978; Lehman, 1972; Perry, 1970; Ronnestad, 1977; Rosen, 1978; Uhlemann, Lea, & Stone, 1976). Role playing or behavioral rehearsal fares less well when used as a sole instructional procedure (Pruden, 1976; Wentink, 1975). Sensitivity groups, T-groups, or encounter groups, implemented without the companion interpersonal skills training employed by Egan (1976), appear to yield positive results, but the supportive evidence is largely anecdotal (Deshaies, 1974; McAuliffe, 1974).

As noted above, empathy training has occurred via many other methods. These include short term empathy communication training (Law, 1978); action training (Howard, 1975); modified, theme-centered interactional training (Larabee, 1980); clinical pastoral training (Strunk & Reed, 1960); flexibility training (Berenson, 1971); dyadic programmed instruction (Berenson, 1971); CUE: communication, understanding, empathy (Hundleby & Zingle, 1975); psychodramatic doubling (Kipper & Ben-Ely, 1979); interview skills training programs (Fine, 1980); videotape focused feedback (Morrison, 1974); role-play reversal (Miller, 1980); sequential refocusing (Moore, 1978); desensitization reappraisal plus communications skill training (McLean, 1979); controlled regression (Lichtenberg, Bornstein, & Silver, 1984); and storytelling, game activities, and other age-graded, prescriptive techniques for use with children (Feshbach, 1982).

What may be concluded about empathy training today? We have examined a small number of rather widely used training packages and have noted a few single-technique methods, as well as a number of largely innovative but not widely studied or implemented procedures. The operational diversity of the latter, we hold, follows logically from the equally diverse manner in which empathy has been defined. Both these lesser used methods, as well as the more frequently used training packages, have most typically been means for empathy *communication* training. We continue to assert that the development of empathy (and its training) requires attention to more than just certain classes of overt verbal behavior by the trainee (i.e., empathic communication). Speaking with an empathic tongue is not enough. In our view, doing so fails to capture the full (i.e., components) meaning of empathy, teaches form but not complete substance, provides the skeleton without the flesh, and yields a too-often mechanical caricature of the prosocial attitude that Rogers originally envisioned. More importantly, the singular focus on empathic communication alone, with general indifference to teaching the prerequisite perceptual, reverberatory, and cognitive analytic skills, may account in large part for the far too frequent failure of newly acquired skills—including empathy—to transfer and maintain in trainees' real-world settings. From the belief that empathy is a four-stage process follows the companion position that empathy training most effectively entails a components-specific training program, one in which each component of empathy is taught by means of that method or methods optimal for, or prescriptive for, the given component. In the section that follows, we seek to concretize this empathy components training perspective.

Empathy Components Training

It is our proposal that the training of empathy is optimally operationalized via a six-stage training program, as described below.

Readiness Training

An optimal empathy training program, in our view, commences with training activities designed to maximize the likelihood that the trainee is fully prepared to understand, acquire, and utilize the four component skills that constitute empathy per se. Such preparatory training would ideally take two complementary forms. The first concerns efforts to help the trainee acquire a series of what might be termed *empathy-preparatory skills* (i.e., abilities that make it possible to acquire empathy skills). Frank (1977) has developed and evaluated just such a readiness program. In it, trainees were successfully taught (1) imagination skills, which significantly increased accurate identification of implied meanings; (2) behavioral observation skills, which significantly increased accurate predictions of the other person's overt behavior; and (3) flexibility skills for shifting from the first to second skill area, which significantly increased the use of differentiated levels of social reasoning.

The likelihood that training in the perceptual, affective reverberation, cognitive analysis, and communication stages will proceed effectively may be enhanced not only by the augmentation or enhancement of propaedeutic skills, such as those offered by Frank (1977). Such training may also be potentiated by the reduction or elimination of what might be termed *empathy skill-acquisition inhibitors.* Bullmer's (1972) programmed self-instructional approach to training the perceptual component of empathy contains at least one such inhibition-reduction component (i.e., the effort to help trainees understand and ameliorate the influence of perceptual biases and certain types of implicit interpersonal theorizing). Pereira (1978) contributed a second such effort in his use of Interpersonal Process Recall (Kagan, 1972), not to teach aspects of empathy per se, but to reduce "affect-associated anxiety," making the trainee's approach to such affects more possible. Clearly, the potentiation of empathic skill development by means of training in readiness skills and the reduction of empathy inhibitors is a valuable path for future empirical efforts.

Perceptual Training
We have had rather little to say thus far about the initial, perceptual stage of the empathic process. As noted earlier, Keefe (1976) proposed that empathy commences with the perception of the other person, as the empathizer nonevaluatively observes and records an array of verbal and nonverbal behaviors, physical characteristics, environmental attributes, and other aspects of the ongoing interpersonal context. In agreement with this perspective, we thus propose that, in optimal empathy training, it is desirable that the readiness stage be followed by purposeful, effective perceptual training. The existing training technology for doing so is not large, but promising possibilities do exist. One is Situational Perception Training, as described in chapter 4. Another is the programmed, self-instructional approach developed by Bullmer (1972). As our earlier presentation of this approach sought to make clear, the thrust of Bullmer's (1972) materials is the training of more accurate, less distorted, less inferential, and more objective perception.

A third promising approach to enhancing perceptual accuracy in interpersonal contexts is described by Henry Smith, in his important works *Sensitivity to People* (Smith, 1966) and *Sensitivity Training* (Smith, 1973). As we have suggested be done for empathy, Smith takes a components perspective toward the target behavior of concern to him—namely, sensitivity. He does so to enhance training effectiveness, asserting as we do with regard to empathy that the components view is most appropriate when training is the aim:

> Should we take a general or components view of sensitivity? The answer depends, in part, on whether the purpose is to select sensitive people or to train them. If selection is the aim, then the general answer is to be favored. What we wish in selection is to place individuals on a single scale that ranges from the least to the most sensitive. If training is the aim, however, then a components view is very helpful. Viewing sensitivity as a general ability gives us no clues as to where to begin training, what to train for, or how to train. (Smith, 1973, p. 23)

To be sure, sensitivity, like empathy, in the real world of expression is conveyed as a gestalt, not as individual components. Although the components view may be in this sense artificial, it is in our view—and Smith's—heuristically superior for the purposes of training. As with programmed instruction, the pieces may be learned first and then combined sequentially with the whole. It is the first component of Smith's concept of sensitivity (i.e., "observational sensitivity") that is of most interest here. Observational sensitivity is identical to the perceptual accuracy component of empathy in Keefe's (1976) and our definition of the concept. As Smith (1973) points out,

> We define and shall use observational sensitivity in a specific way as the ability to look at and listen to another person and remember what he looked like and said. Observation is sometimes pictured as a quite passive affair; the eye is a motion-picture camera; the ear, a tape recorder. What we see a person do and hear him say is transcribed on the slate of our awareness. The records are then sorted, edited, and evaluated. No picture could be further from the truth, for we do not observe people; we perceive them. And we perceive what we want to perceive, what we expect to perceive, and what we have learned to perceive. Perceivers differ widely in their ability to discriminate what they see and hear from what they feel and infer about a person. It is an important task of training to develop the ability to make such discriminations. (p. 24).

Accordingly, Smith (1973) distinguishes between sensory impressions, the enhancement of which is the goal of perceptual accuracy training, and expressive impressions, which interfere with perceptual accuracy. The goal of Smith's observational sensitivity training—our perceptual accuracy training—is to increase trainee competence in recording sensory impressions (what the other person looked like, said, and did) and in discriminating them from inferential, derivative, interpretive expressive impressions (the other's feelings, beliefs, motivations, traits). In brief,

> To become a good observer, the trainee must learn to shift his attention from the subjective to the objective, from himself to the other person. . . . The goal of observational training should be to develop the trainee's ability to discriminate sensory from expressive qualities. The critical problem in observational training is not that we make poor observations that lead to faulty inferences; it is that we do not make observations or inferences at all. We do not merely see or hear a person, we perceive a quality in the person . . . We do not see a redhead and hear a loud voice; we perceive an "interesting," "intelligent," and

"level-headed" person or one who is "narrow-minded," "irritating," and "insincere." (Smith, 1973, pp. 78, 242)

How is this training goal to be sought? Smith (1973) proposes that an effective means for observational sensitivity training might be responsive to the apparent difficulties that individuals have in maintaining objectivity in anxiety-arousing interpersonal contexts: "*The* problem of observational training is to teach trainees to maintain the observer role in tense interpersonal situtions. It is then that the perception of sensory qualities fade and expressive qualities intensify" (p. 79).

Perhaps, then, participants in observational sensitivity training ought to be exposed to progressively more intense levels of interpersonal stress and even confrontation. This should be in conjunction with trainer efforts to have trainees keep their focus on the other and her objective qualities, not her inferred characteristics or the internal reactions of the trainee. Smith (1973) suggests that such a training effort might, for example, make use of the affect stimulation films developed by Kagan and Schauble (1969). In these filmed portrayals, the speaker addresses the viewer with progressively heightened negative affect-rejection, hostility, etc. The trainee's task in the face of such escalating affect is to continue to report what the person in the film looked like, said, and did. Smith (1973) suggests that interpersonal stress levels could be heightened yet further by use of simulated and then real-life, face-to-face implementations of this hierarchical training strategy. Although this proposal for effective observational sensitivity training has not yet received extensive empirical scrutiny, an initial examination of its value by Danish and Brodsky (1970) was clearly encouraging.

Affective Reverberation Training

An extended series of potentially useful procedures exists for purposes of affective reverberation training. These several procedures, described in detail in Goldstein and Michaels (1985), include meditation (Goleman, 1977; Lesh, 1970), structural integration or Rolfing (Keen, 1970; Rolf, 1977), Reichian therapy (Lowen, 1967; Reich, 1933/1949), bioenergetics (Lowen & Lowen, 1977), the Alexander Technique (Alexander, 1969), Feldenkrais' Awareness through Movement (Feldenkrais, 1981), dance therapy (Bernstein, 1975; Pesso, 1969), sensory awareness training (Brooks, 1974; Gunther, 1968), focusing (Gendlin, 1981, 1984), and the Laban-Bartenieff multi-level method (Bartenieff & Davis, 1972). All of these somatopsychic methods, oriented toward the enhancement of affective reverberation (and, in some instances, toward enhancing perceptual accuracy), have been at best on the fringes of scientific psychology. Yet that is precisely where some of psychology's most profound and most effective interventions began their existence: in the wisdom and experience of creative clinicians. Whether some or any of these techniques, and which ones, will prove on experimental scrutiny to be of substantial and reliable value for teaching the affective reverberation component of empathy is an empirical question whose pursuit seems especially worthwhile.

Cognitive Analysis Training

As stated earlier in our presentation of a components definition of empathy, following perception, which is the nonevaluative recording of the other's behavior (Stage 1), and affective reverberation, which is the trying-on or as-if experiencing of the other's affects (Stage 2), the observer steps back from the other's behavior and his own reverberatory experiencing to discern cognitively the nature of the other's affects and to label them. Training for high levels of competence in this cognitive analysis stage is currently best provided, we believe, by the Carkhuff (1969b) discrimination training procedures, which we examined and illustrated in detail earlier in this chapter. Such discrimination training rests on a reasonably firm foundation of supportive evaluation evidence, has been applied adaptively to diverse trainee populations, and has been shown to be a necessary prerequisite for adequate skill at the final, communicative stage of empathy.

Beyond Carkhuff's (1969a, 1969b) discrimination training method and materials, there exist additional techniques of potential value for cognitive analysis enhancement. Both some older research (Allport, 1924; Davitz, 1964; Guilford & Wilke, 1930; Jenness, 1932) and some more recent studies from our own research group (Berlin, 1974; Healy, 1975; Lopez, 1975) suggest that a combination of exposure to an array of facial expressions plus guided practice and feedback regarding the accuracy of judgments (i.e., cognitive analysis) about the affective labeling of the expressions provided is an effective technique for enhancing judgmental accuracy. Readers interested in pursuing further this ancillary means for the possible enhancement of the cognitive analysis phase of empathy will find ample experimental materials for doing so in the creative work put forth by the Ekman (Ekman & Friesen, 1975; Ekman, Friesen, & Tomkins, 1971) and Rosenthal (Rosenthal & De Paulo, 1979; Rosenthal, Hall, DiMatteo, Rogers, & Archer, 1979) research groups.

Communication Training

Earlier in this chapter, we described in considerable detail a number of existing and widely used empathy training packages, as well as an extended series of less frequently used techniques. When viewed collectively, these major and minor approaches to empathy training— almost all of which focus on the communication aspect of the process— consist largely of a small number of skills-development-oriented social learning techniques plus, in several instances, an experiential opportunity. The social learning methods thus utilized typically include instructions, modeling (an especially popular empathy-training technique), role playing or behavioral rehearsal, and some form of systematic feedback. The experiential component, when offered, typically has been a combination of supervised experience conducting actual counseling sessions and/or a group experience of a sensitivity-training type. There currently exists little empirical basis for evidentially discriminating among the major training packages available, and we are not convinced that the most productive research path to follow regarding the communication component of empathy would be comparisons between existing training packages. Ideally, as suggested earlier, the contribution, if any, of each procedure constituting a given training package first must be established by means of studies utilizing dismantling experimental designs. Until such research becomes available and helps us discern which procedures are in fact contributing positively to skill in empathic communication, or until such time as less valuable but still informative comparative studies of training packages are done, we are not in a position to discriminate in our training recommendation among the Carkhuff (1969a, 1969b), Egan (1976), Guerney (1977), Ivey and Authier (1971), and Goldstein (1973) training approaches.

Transfer and Maintenance Training

It has been substantially demonstrated in the context of psychotherapy that, in most cases, gains made by patients during the course of treatment fail to manifest themselves either outside the treatment setting (a failure of *transfer* or generalization over settings) or over time (a failure of *maintenance* or generalization over time) (Goldstein & Kanfer, 1979; Kazdin, 1980; Keeley, Shemberg, & Carbonell, 1976). These writers have held that such infrequency of transfer and maintenance of therapeutic gain is the most telling weakness of contemporary psychotherapy. The severe paucity of follow-up studies on the transfer and maintenance of empathic skill after training, and the essentially negative outcome of the few studies that do exist (e.g., Collingswood,

1971; Gantt, Billingsley, & Giordano, 1980; Guzzetta, 1974), lead us to believe that a similarly dismal postintervention picture also exists for empathy training. That is the bad news. The good news, however, is that an emerging array of techniques does exist whose explicit goal is the enhancement of transfer and maintenance. Furthermore, a fair amount of outcome evidence is already available demonstrating the efficacy of these techniques in a psychotherapeutic context and, in at least a few instances, in the context of empathy training (Bath, 1976; Collingswood, 1971; Guttman, 1970; Guzzetta, 1974; Rocks, Baker, & Guerney, 1982). These several contemporary approaches to the enhancement of transfer and maintenance are examined in detail in a separate chapter (see chapter 12) because of their major relevance to all the courses constituting the Prepare Curriculum, not just Empathy Training.

Empathy Training: A Prescriptive Summary

We have utilized a wide variety of research evidence and theoretical materials to propose a six-component view of empathy training. In summary, we believe optimal empathy training should attend to the components detailed in Table 11, first individually and then as a coherent gestalt.

For each of the foregoing components of the empathy training process, we have identified at least a few, and often several, potentially

Table 11
Empathy Training: A Components Approach

A. *Readiness Training*
   1. Acquisition of empathy preparation skills (Frank, 1977)
      a. Imagination skills to increase accurate identification of implied meanings.
      b. Behavioral observation skills to increase accurate prediction of others' overt behavior.
      c. Flexibility skills to increase differentiation ability in shifting from *a* to *b*.
   2. Elimination of empathy skill acquisition inhibitors
      a. Programmed self-instruction to understand one's perceptual biases (Bullmer, 1972).
      b. Interpersonal Process Recall to reduce affect-associated anxiety (Pereira, 1978).

Table 11 *(continued)*

B. *Perceptual Training*
   1. Situational Perception Training (chapter 4) to enhance accuracy of situational perception.
   2. Programmed self-instruction (Bullmer, 1972) to increase interpersonal perceptual accuracy and objectivity.
   3. Observational sensitivity training (Smith, 1973) to increase competence in recording sensory impressions and to discriminate them from inferential, interpretive impressions.
C. *Affective Reverberation Training*
   1. Meditation (Goleman, 1977; Lesh, 1970).
   2. Structural integration or Rolfing (Keene, 1970; Rolf, 1977).
   3. Reichian therapy (Lowen, 1967; Reich, 1933/1949).
   4. Bioenergetics (Lowen & Lowen, 1977).
   5. Alexander Technique (Alexander, 1969).
   6. Feldenkrais' Awareness through Movement (Feldenkrais, 1970, 1972, 1981).
   7. Dance therapy (Bernstein, 1975; Pesso, 1969)
   8. Sensory awareness training (Brooks, 1974; Gunther, 1968).
   9. Focusing (Gendlin, 1981, 1984).
   10. Laban-Bartenieff method (Bartenieff & Lewis, 1980).
D. *Cognitive Analysis Training*
   1. Discrimination training (Carkhuff, 1969a, 1969b) in utilizing perceptual (II) and reverberatory (III) information.
   2. Exposure (to facial expressions, for example) plus guided practice and feedback on affective-labeling accuracy (Allport, 1924; Davitz, 1964).
E. *Communication Training*
   1. Didactic-experiential Training (Carkhuff, 1969a, 1969b).
   2. Interpersonal Living Laboratory (Egan, 1976).
   3. Relationship Enhancement (Guerney, 1977).
   4. Microtraining: Enriching Intimacy Program (Ivey & Authier, 1971).
   5. Structured Learning Training (Goldstein, 1973).
F. *Transfer and Maintenance Training* (chapter 12).

---

viable specific training techniques. We earnestly hope that this presentation will help stimulate the research now necessary to sort through this array and yield a training technology consisting of optimal sets of techniques. We urge as a goal here not *the* set or the "one true (training) light" as far as training goes, but rather that *sets* of optimal techniques be utilized prescriptively with different types of trainees and trainers.

It is already the case that numerous investigators have raised prescriptive questions in their empathy training studies. Research has been directed toward the relevance for the training outcome of such trainee characteristics as the initial or "developmental" level of empathy brought to training (Bath, 1976; Birk, 1972; Geary, 1979; Uhlemann et al., 1976), age (Becker & Zarit, 1978), sex (Freely, 1977), cognitive level (Taylor, 1975), and such personality attributes as dogmatism (Relfalvy-Fodor, 1976), field dependence (Moore, 1980), and the array reflected by the Edwards Personal Preference Schedule (Burnham, 1976). In analogous empathy training studies, beginning prescriptive matches have been sought not by studying trainee characteristics, but by examining the prescriptive implications of the emotions being empathized with (Hayes, 1979; Lange, 1885/1922) or of qualities of the training techniques themselves (Burnham, 1976; Fauvre, 1979; Feshbach, 1978, 1981; Janaka, 1977). Such prescriptive leads appear to us to be especially valuable paths for future empathy training research to pursue.

Chapter 9

Recruiting Supportive Models

Our environments shape much of who we are and what we aspire to become. Our interpersonal, economic, and physical worlds in very many ways determine our daily behaviors, perceptions, decisions, and hopes. This widely accepted truism holds for better or worse. An environment characterized by interpersonal abuse, high crime rates, drug and alcohol abuse, high truancy and school dropout rates, high unemployment, and similar influences will tend to be strongly associated with juvenile delinquency, chronic aggression, poor school perform-ance, low levels of personal aspiration, and unhappy life outcomes. Environmental influences, however, can indeed be for the better. Even in the context of the array of negative influences enumerated above, positive forces may enter and prevail. In their aptly titled book *Vulnerable but Invincible,* Werner and Smith (1982) identify a series of discriminators that significantly differentiate between "resilient" youth and peers showing serious coping problems—both types of youth having grown up in environments characterized by problems in parental relationships, parent absence, parent mental illness, financial problems, serious illness during adolescence, teenage pregnancy, and numerous other life stresses.

One of the major discriminators between resilient and poorly coping youth that emerged in this study was the success of the former in identifying with, and relating on a sustained basis to, at least one supportive model. As Werner and Smith (1982) comment,

> The resilient youth . . . sought and received help from a great number of informal sources. . . . Peer friends (35%), including siblings and cousins; and older friends (30%), including older relatives and parents of boy and girlfriends, were the primary sources of support for the majority of resilient youth. Parents ranked next (25%), followed by ministers (11.5%), and teachers (11.5%). (p. 97)

Other investigators have similarly stressed the facilitating effects of exposure to, and identification with, a supportive model. Bandura (1982) stresses the value of family or friendship models in this regard for low-income youth. Ellis and Lane (1978), referring to similar populations, emphasize the frequent supportive modeling influence of parents, teachers, clergy, family friends, employers, and others. Pines (1979), in her examination of "superkids," stresses the crucial role played in positive psychological development of "a good relationship with at least one adult" (p. 58). Kauffman, Grunebaum, Cohler, and Gamer (1979) found that, among children of psychotic mothers, those with a close chum or extensive interaction with an adult other than a family member possessed the highest levels of social competence. Coates, Miller, and Ohlin (1978) found that, following incarceration, youth reporting new illegal acts were strongly influenced by antisocial peer models. Comparable youth not getting into post-release difficulties with criminal justice authorities

> seemed to develop an attachment to some adult in the community who was engaged in conventional activities and who subscribed to legal values and beliefs. These "successful" youths also appeared to have made new friends who were not involved in delinquent peer culture. (Hawkins & Fraser, 1983, p. 341)

Of special relevance to one of the primary types of youth for whom the Prepare Curriculum is designed is the fact that several investigators have reported the "protective effect" (Rutter & Giller, 1984) of a sustained, positive relationship with one prosocial figure among youth raised in environments associated with delinquency (Anthony & Cohler, 1987; Conway, 1957; Pringle & Bossio, 1960; Rutter, Quinton, & Liddle, 1983; Wolkind, 1971).

It is the purpose of this Prepare course to teach youth the skills necessary to identify, seek out, and establish and maintain a relationship with supportive models. Supportive models are persons skilled at offering youth help, nurturance, and problem-solving advice and who, by dint of their display of such supportive behavior, may also function as valuable prosocial models. Such persons can function as especially powerful environmental influences upon psychoeducationally skill-deficient youth.

Recent theory and research in the domain of social support and its consequences lend further weight to the apparent value for youth—even those in "high-risk" populations—of a relationship with a nurturant, helping, problem-solving, or otherwise prosocial model. Kahn and Quinn (1977) define *social support* as consisting of "the expression of positive *affect,* including liking, admiration, respect, and other kinds of positive evaluation; the expression of *affirmation,* including endorsement of an individual's perceptions, beliefs, values, attitudes or actions; or the provision of *aid,* including materials, information, time, and entitlements" (p.3). Gottlieb (1983) elaborates this definition further, viewing social support as possibly including emotional support, cognitive guidance, companionship, environmental action, and/or material aid and concrete services.

The positive mental and physical health consequences to recipients of social support, as thus defined, are substantial. Of direct relevance to our earlier focus on vulnerable but resilient youth growing up in stress-laden environments is the apparent stress-buffering potency of social support. As Gottlieb (1983) points out, "persons who experienced high levels of stress either in the company of 'significant others' or with the knowledge that they had access to supportive social ties did not develop the adverse health consequences experienced by those who were relatively isolated or who felt unsupported" (p. 21). This conclusion rests on an especially broad foundation of confirming research findings (Barrera, 1981; Cassell, 1974; Cobb, 1976; Sandler, 1980) and includes results showing less maladjustment with increasing social support in both young children (Sandler, 1980) and adolescents (Compas, Slavin, Wagner, & Vannatta, 1986) for whom the Prepare Curriculum is appropriate. Thus studies of both the interpersonal assets available to resilient youth, and of the consequences of actual and anticipated social support, confirm the belief that a supportive relationship with a prosocial, help-offering other can have both protective and ameliorative effects for high-risk adolescents and children.

Identification of Supportive Models

Since it is our goal to train such youth in the skills necessary to identify, reach out to, and build relationships with supportive models, our first task is to describe such helpers. Who are society's supportive models? By occupation, they may be anyone with whom a youth might come into at least moderately regular contact (e.g., parents, relatives, guidance counselors, teachers, peers, coaches, siblings, clergy, and others). In terms of characteristics, they optimally are stable, committed, accessible, experienced, well-informed, empathic, and good managers of stressful circumstances (Pancoast, 1980). Concerning model characteristics that enhance the likelihood that modeling will occur, research suggests further characteristics such as model warmth, nurturance, observability, power, and prestige (Perry & Furukawa, 1986). Having "been there" (Barth, 1983) in terms of having had experiences similar to those of the youth and having the same ethnic background (Cauce, Felner, & Primavera, 1982) are further recommended characteristics of supportive models. Finally, by overt behavior, such potential helpers are persons willing and able to provide the emotional sustenance, problem-solving, personal influence, or environmental actions that operationally constitute the act of helping. The specific behaviors defining these four categories of helper actions, according to Gottlieb (1978), are indicated in Table 12.

Table 12
Helping Behaviors

A. Emotionally Sustaining Behaviors
Talking (unfocused)
Provides reassurance
Provides encouragement
Listens
Reflects understanding
Reflects respect
Reflects concern
Reflects trust
Reflects intimacy
Provides companionship
Provides accompaniment in stressful situation
Provides extended period of care

B. Problem-solving Behaviors
Talking (focused)
Provides clarification
Provides suggestions
Provides directive
Provides information about source of stress
Provides referral
Monitors directive
Buffers S from source of stress
Models or provides testimony of own experience
Provides material aid or direct service
Distracts from problem focus

C. Indirect Personal Influence
Reflects unconditional access
Reflects readiness to act

D. Environmental Action
Intervenes in the environment to reduce source of stress

Beyond these several occupational, personality, and behavioral characteristics, youth may be encouraged to identify as likely supportive models either persons new to them or persons already known to them in another capacity but with potential for a restructured helping relationship (Gottlieb, 1983). It is crucial, of course, that the youth be encouraged to choose his own supportive model(s) rather than have such persons selected for him (Barth, 1983). Also, the youth should be aided, where possible, in distinguishing between potentially effective and ineffective supportive models (Rook & Dooley, 1985).

Resistance to Support

Potential supportive models, thus defined, may well exist in the youth's environment and be identified as such, but the youth may elect not to seek to relate to such persons. Help or support may be viewed by the youth as a mixed blessing, on the one hand reflecting the helpgiver's caring and concern, but on the other hand also signifying inferiority, failure, and dependency (Fisher & Nadler, 1979). Potential or actual help from others may also stimulate negative affect associated with a sense of indebtedness (Gergen, Ellsworth, Masloch, & Seipel, 1975), a need to reciprocate (Gross & Latane, 1974), or a restriction upon one's freedom (Brehm, 1966). When the offer of support, or actual support, is perceived in such ways by the recipient, she is less likely to ask for it, more likely to refuse it, and more likely to break off the relationship sooner with the helpgiver (Castro, 1974; Greenberg & Shapiro, 1971). Help or support is more likely to be accepted, and perhaps even sought, when sense of indebtedness, need to reciprocate, and restriction of freedom are low, when the aid is offered voluntarily; and when the helpgiver possesses the several qualities described earlier as positive characteristics of effective prosocial models (Fisher, Nadler, & Whitcher-Alagna, 1982).

Building Relationships with Supportive Models

Once the youth has identified a potential supportive model and has at least begun to deal with his resistance to the help-seeking process, his task is one of reaching out to and building a relationship with the target helper. Our recommended methods for doing so, and the heart of the process for recruiting supportive models, are individualized sequences of the interpersonal skills described in detail in chapter 3. Depending on the youth, helpgiver, and situational characteristics, the Prepare trainer and the youth (who has earlier, or simultaneously, taken the

Prepare course on Interpersonal Skills Training) should collaboratively select and arrange in order a tailored series of interpersonal skills designed to accomplish effectively the relationship-initiation and establishment process. Three hypothetical skill sequences for doing so are described here.

Skill Sequence 1

The first skill sequence we have constructed seeks to illustrate the process of initiating and building a positive relationship with a supportive model when no special problems arise. It assumes a cooperative model and a successful outcome. The skills chosen for this sequence and for the other skill sequences described have been selected from our original Structured Learning skills curriculum for adolescents (Goldstein, Sprafkin, Gershaw, & Klein, 1980); all are detailed in chapter 3 in the section on skills for adolescents. Parallel curricula have also been developed for elementary school children (see the section on skills for elementary-age children in chapter 3, as well as McGinnis & Goldstein, 1984) and for adults (Goldstein, Sprafkin, & Gershaw, 1976). Skills in these curricula can be used to create sequences appropriate for these latter two groups.

In this initial sequence, the youth, having identified the potential supportive model to whom she would like to relate, first determines concretely what she wishes to accomplish with that target person (Skill 45: Setting a Goal), collects any further information necessary about the model, determines the time and place to make an initial approach, and considers the most appropriate content of that approach (Skill 47: Gathering Information). After weighing this information (Skill 49: Making a Decision), she makes the initial contact (Skill 2: Starting a Conversation), speaks with the target person (Skill 3: Having a Conversation), and at the appropriate time requests specific assistance (Skill 9: Asking for Help). The supportive model responds affirmatively and offers suggestions for steps to be taken by the youth (Skill 12: Following Instructions), to which the youth responds with appreciation and a sharing of her feelings (Skill 16: Expressing Your Feelings). At parting, having done so well at initiating and building a beginning relationship with the supportive model, the youth justly praises herself and promises herself a special treat for a job well done (Skill 21: Rewarding Yourself).

Sequentially, the youth role plays this series of skill steps as follows:

Skill 45: Setting a Goal
   1. Figure out what goal you want to reach.

2. Find out all the information you can about how to reach your goal.
3. Think about the steps you will need to take to reach your goal.
4. Take the first step toward your goal.

Skill 47: Gathering Information
1. Decide what information you need.
2. Decide how you can get the information.
3. Do things to get the information.

Skill 49: Making a Decision
1. Think about the problem that requires you to make a decision.
2. Think about possible decisions you could make.
3. Gather accurate information about these possible decisions.
4. Reconsider your possible decisions using the information you have gathered.
5. Make the best decision.

Skill 2: Starting a Conversation
1. Greet the other person.
2. Make small talk.
3. Decide if the other person is listening.
4. Bring up the main topic.

Skill 3: Having a Conversation
1. Say what you want to say.
2. Ask the other person what he/she thinks.
3. Listen to what the other person says.
4. Say what you think.
5. Make a closing remark.

Skill 9: Asking for Help
1. Decide what the problem is.
2. Decide if you want help for the problem.
3. Think about different people who might help you and pick one.
4. Tell the person about the problem and ask that person to help you.

Skill 12: Following Instructions
1. Listen carefully while you are being told what to do.

2. Ask questions about anything you don't understand.
3. Decide if you want to follow the instructions, and let the other person know your decision.
4. Repeat the instructions to yourself.
5. Do what you have been asked to do.

Skill 16: Expressing Your Feelings
1. Tune in to what is going on in your body.
2. Decide what happened to make you feel that way.
3. Decide what you are feeling.
4. Think about the different ways to express your feeling and pick one.
5. Express your feeling.

Skill 21: Rewarding Yourself
1. Decide if you have done something that deserves a reward.
2. Decide what you could say to reward yourself.
3. Decide what you could do to reward yourself.
4. Reward yourself.

Skill Sequence 2

An alternative role-play scenario involves an effort on the part of a help-seeking youth that fails and requires "recycling," as it were. Here, a youth decides to approach a given potential supportive model (Skill 49: Making a Decision) and proceeds actually to do so (Skill 6: Introducing Yourself), but his initial overture elicits little interest and is rebuffed. The youth must then pull back a bit, consider the failure, and choose a new target figure (Skill 38: Responding to Failure). To minimize the likelihood of a second such lack of success, the youth decides to engage in additional preparatory rehearsal (Skill 41: Getting Ready for a Difficult Conversation). As a second part of this preparation effort, he also practices an empathic response to possible statements by the target person (Skill 17: Understanding the Feelings of Others). He introduces himself to a second potential model (Skill 6: Introducing Yourself), seeks to persuade this person to meet further at a future point (Skill 14: Convincing Others), and expresses appreciation when the helper agrees (Skill 5: Saying Thank You).

The skill steps constituting this second hypothetical skill sequence are as follows:

Skill 49: Making a Decision

1. Think about the problem that requires you to make a decision.
2. Think about possible decisions you could make.
3. Gather accurate information about these possible decisions.
4. Reconsider your possible decisions using the information you have gathered.
5. Make the best decision.

Skill 6: Introducing Yourself

1. Choose the right time and place to introduce yourself.
2. Greet the other person and tell your name.
3. Ask the other person his/her name if you need to.
4. Tell or ask the other person something to help start your conversation.

Skill 38: Responding to Failure

1. Decide if you have failed at something.
2. Think about why you failed.
3. Think about what you could do to keep from failing another time.
4. Decide if you want to try again.
5. Try again using your new idea.

Skill 41: Getting Ready for a Difficult Conversation

1. Think about how you will feel during the conversation.
2. Think about how the other person will feel.
3. Think about different ways you could say what you want to say.
4. Think about what the other person might say back to you.
5. Think about any other things that might happen during the conversation.
6. Choose the best approach you can think of and try it.

Skill 17: Understanding the Feelings of Others

1. Watch the other person.
2. Listen to what the person is saying.
3. Figure out what the person might be feeling.
4. Think about ways to show you understand what he/she is feeling.
5. Decide on the best way and do it.

Skill 6: Introducing Yourself
1. Choose the right time and place to introduce yourself.
2. Greet the other person and tell your name.
3. Ask the other person his/her name if you need to.
4. Tell or ask the other person something to help start your conversation.

Skill 14: Convincing Others
1. Decide if you want to convince someone about something.
2. Tell the other person your idea.
3. Ask the other person what he/she thinks about it.
4. Tell why you think your idea is a good one.
5. Ask the other person to think about what you said before making up his/her mind.

Skill 5: Saying Thank You
1. Decide if the other person said or did something that you want to thank him/her for.
2. Choose a good time and place to thank the other person.
3. Thank the other person in a friendly way.
4. Tell the other person why you are thanking him/her.

Skill Sequence 3

A youth's effort to recruit a supportive model may have to begin in a very different way from what we have just depicted. He may first have to recognize and deal effectively with the pressures and persuasions of antisocial models, especially his peers. In rapid and stressful succession, his peers may pressure him to behave in ways other than he planned (Skill 42: Dealing with Group Pressure), accuse him of one or another major shortcoming (Skill 40: Dealing with an Accusation), and overtly reject him when he refuses to yield to either their importuning or their insults (Skill 35: Dealing with Being Left Out). Freer then to approach the teacher, coach, uncle, or other potential supportive model, the youth may begin doing so by offering a compliment about the probable value to him of further association (Skill 8: Giving a Compliment), asking a question about its availability (Skill 4: Asking a Question), and listening openly (Skill 1: Listening) to the target person's response. If relationship-building progress is apparent, expression of appreciation (Skill 5: Saying Thank You) and praising one's own efforts (Skill 21: Rewarding Yourself) are appropriate responses.

The skill steps constituting this third scenario are the following:

Skill 42: Dealing with Group Pressure
1. Think about what the group wants you to do and why.
2. Decide what you want to do.
3. Decide how to tell the group what you want to do.
4. Tell the group what you have decided.

Skill 40: Dealing with an Accusation
1. Think about what the other person has accused you of.
2. Think about why the person might have accused you.
3. Think about ways to answer the person's accusation.
4. Choose the best way and do it.

Skill 35: Dealing with Being Left Out
1. Decide if you are being left out.
2. Think about why the other people might be leaving you out of something.
3. Decide how you could deal with the problem.
4. Choose the best way and do it.

Skill 8: Giving a Compliment
1. Decide what you want to compliment about the other person.
2. Decide how to give the compliment.
3. Choose the right time and place to say it.
4. Give the compliment.

Skill 4: Asking a Question
1. Decide what you'd like to know more about.
2. Decide whom to ask.
3. Think about different ways to ask your question and pick one way.
4. Pick the right time and place to ask your question.
5. Ask your question.

Skill 1: Listening
1. Look at the person who is talking.
2. Think about what is being said.
3. Wait your turn to talk.
4. Say what you want to say.

Skill 5: Saying Thank You
1. Decide if the other person said or did something that you want to thank him/her for.
2. Choose a good time and place to thank the other person.
3. Thank the other person in a friendly way.
4. Tell the other person why you are thanking him/her.

Skill 21: Rewarding Yourself
1. Decide if you have done something that deserves a reward.
2. Decide what you could say to reward yourself.
3. Decide what you could do to reward yourself.
4. Reward yourself.

It must be stressed that these three examples of support-recruiting interpersonal skill sequences are merely hypothetical illustrations. Which skills, in which order, make sense for any given youth must be a prescriptive, individualized decision made by the youth himself, perhaps in collaboration with his Prepare trainer and/or co-trainees.

Maintaining Relationships with Supportive Models

If successful in identifying a potential supportive model and in both initiating and establishing a supportive relationship with such a person, the youth's remaining recruitment task concerns the longer term maintenance of that relationship. One hopes that the model will initiate much of what will make such a relationship persist, but this Prepare course concerns the youth's own skills repertoire and initiatives. Are there steps the youth can take to enhance the likelihood of a long-term relationship? A series of investigations suggest there are.

Behavior modification techniques—especially including the presentation or withdrawal of reinforcement contingent, respectively, on appropriate or inappropriate behaviors—have a long and valuable history in educational practice, juvenile corrections, and the other arenas in which the Prepare Curriculum is relevant. But in its decades of usage in classrooms, residential centers, and the like, behavior modification has mostly involved the adult change agent (teacher, youth care worker, special educator, school psychologist) as the behavior modifier, and it has been the child's behavior that has been modified. In recent years, research has emerged that has successfully reversed this process by demonstrating that both children and adolescents can be trained to modify the behavior of their teachers, their parents, and other caretakers. Graubard, Rosenberg, and Miller (1971) taught a group of seven 12- to 15-year-old students from a class for children considered "incorrigible" skills in the effective use of reinforcement to modify their teacher's behavior. The rewards they were taught to dispense following positive, helpful teacher behaviors included smiling, sitting up straight, making eye contact, offering praise (e.g., "I like to work in a room where the teacher is nice to kids"), demonstratively showing understanding of and appreciation for work taught by the teacher, and similar behaviors. This effort to increase positive teacher behaviors was coupled with a companion effort to discourage negative teacher behaviors (e.g., saying, "It's hard for me to do good work when you're cross with me"). Results of this study clearly confirmed the behavior modification potency of students in this role. Over the 5-week measurement period, positive comments from the teacher to the participating students increased substantially, and negative comments correspondingly declined. In the same year that Graubard et al. (1971) reported their study on training adolescents to be effective behavior modifiers, Berberich (1971) reported similar findings with young children serving as shapers of teacher behavior, and Klein (1971) did likewise with college students.

Sherman and Cormier (1974) and Cantor and Gelfand (1977) subsequently replicated and extended these findings. Children indeed can be trained to be effective, skilled, and purposeful shapers of adult behavior. Cantor and Gelfand (1977) report that

> children can control the rate of adults' verbal and nonverbal helping as well as of other forms of positive attention directed toward the children.... When the children behaved in an animated, socially responsive manner, their adult partners rated them as more intelligent, skillful, and attractive than when the same children were only minimally responsive to the adults. (p. 236)

A final investigation in this context is worth examining. Its findings not only further confirm the results of earlier studies, which suggest that children can indeed modify others' behavior, but also speak directly to the maintenance over time of such help-increasing effects. In this instance, Stokes, Fowler, and Baer (1978) taught preschool children what constituted good work in school and then how to prompt and cue their teacher for positive evaluation when their work was of good quality. Participating children, both "normal" and "deviant," learned to ask, "Have I worked well?" "Have I been working carefully?" "How is this work?" or assert, "Look how careful I've been." Learning these initiations, as well as the timing and location of their usage, indeed led to a substantial increase in teacher praise. Furthermore, via generalization training for these behaviors, the children continued to recruit teacher reinforcement across new teachers and over time. In the words of Stokes et al. (1978), "These data... established that the children were able to contact, recruit, and cultivate a dormant, but readily available natural community of increased reinforcement" (p. 293). And, additionally, "Deviant children might benefit particularly from these special procedures because their 'deviant' label often follows them through their school days and so it might be advantageous for these children to have skills in their repertoires that could be used, if required, to modify interaction with their teachers in a positive way" (p. 287).

Children and adolescents, as we have said, are likely to benefit substantially from a continuing relationship with an adult or peer who can simultaneously serve as a source of help as needed and, by such acts, also function as a prosocial model. We have described the characteristics of potential supportive models in the effort to help Prepare Curriculum trainers assist youth in identifying such models in their own real-life environments.

Once identified, the recruitment task we have suggested and illustrated might optimally proceed by having the youth, with the aid of the trainer and/or other trainees, if desired, select and arrange in functional order a set of interpersonal skills. These should be skills that seem to be effective for that particular youth in reaching out to the identified model and building a positive relationship with that person. This individualized skill sequence, once selected, should be utilized by the youth in an Interpersonal Skills Training format (i.e., modeled by the trainer, role-played by the trainee, and reacted to by fellow trainees). Finally, to maintain the relationship gains thus accomplished, we recommend that participating youth learn contingency management techniques to provide skill in modifying and maintaining the help-giving behavior of their supportive models.

Chapter 10

Cooperation Training

Cooperating with others, under certain structured conditions, enhances the likelihood of future cooperation, as well as the frequency of several other types of prosocial behavior. In support of this assertion, this chapter presents two broad approaches designed to increase cooperative behavior. Each approach, in its own way, relies exclusively on cooperative activities toward this end. The first, *cooperative learning,* will be examined in light of its history, rationale, and principles. We will contrast this approach with alternative learning approaches, describe specific methods, and discuss research examining its effects upon cooperation and a host of related prosocial and achievement behaviors.

Cooperative gaming is the second promising route to enhanced cooperation. Games and sports in highly competitive Western societies are most typically anything but cooperative in their structure. However, cooperative games and cooperative versions of traditional sports do exist, are enjoyed, and can channel behavior in prosocial directions.

Cooperation Defined

Cooperation has been defined in the theoretical and research literature in four different, although related, ways. As Slavin (1983a) observes,

> It can refer to *cooperative behavior,* such as working with or helping others. It can refer to a *cooperative incentive structure* ... in which a group of two or more individuals are rewarded based on the performance of all group members. Cooperation often refers to *cooperative task structures,* in which a group of two or more individuals can or must work together but may or may not receive rewards based on the group's performance. Finally, it can refer to *cooperative motives,* the predisposition to act cooperatively or altruistically in a situation that allows individuals a choice between cooperative, competitive, or individualistic behavior. (p. 3)

All four of these complementary definitions are relevant to the Cooperation Training program described in this chapter. In our program, cooperative learning and gaming activities, whose central procedures fully reflect cooperative incentive and task structures, are

463

utilized in order to enhance both cooperative behavior potential and future motivation to cooperate. In operationalizing this complex definition, however, our emphasis will clearly be upon cooperative *behavior,* especially with regard to the goals of Cooperation Training. This overt, behavioral emphasis is consistent with the overall performance-enhancement thrust of the Prepare Curriculum. Thus a major goal of Cooperation Training may be stated as seeking to increase cooperative behavior "defined as working with others for mutual benefit" (Schofield, 1980, p. 161), or, as Sapon-Shevin (1986) illustrates, such cooperation-defining skills as "listening to one another, coordinating one's movements and energies with those of other children, and engaging in those social behaviors that will facilitate and prolong interacting with other children rather than driving them away" (p. 281). These are but a few of the prosocial behaviors that may define cooperation and its concomitants. Such behaviors exemplify our training goals. We now turn to cooperative learning, its rationale, constituent procedures, operational guidelines, and demonstrated effects.

Cooperative Learning

Cooperative learning is both a philosophy of teaching and a series of several different, but related, teaching methods. Across areas of academic content, most of these methods involve a heterogeneous group of youngsters working together on a shared task or project (e.g., a cooperative task structure) and the provision of grades or other rewards to the group as a whole based upon either the sum of individual improvement scores or the group's overall task performance (e.g., a cooperative incentive structure). Though the methods of cooperative learning are mostly a phenomenon of the 1970s, like so much that is prosocial in contemporary educational theory and practice, cooperative learning has its spiritual roots in the writings of John Dewey (1916/1952; 1938/1966). Schmuck (1985) describes well the sense of this philosophical underpinning:

> Dewey argued that if humans are to learn to live cooperatively, they must experience the living process of cooperation in schools. Life in the classroom should represent the democratic process in microcosm, and the heart of democratic living is cooperation in groups. (p. 2)

Dewey's views, and what eventually came to be seen as the cooperative learning movement, found wide support and implementation in the 1920s (e.g., Kilpatrick, 1925); receded in influence in the face of a strong, pro-competition backlash in the 1930s; regained both influence and empirical support via the work of Lewin (1943, 1947), Deutsch (1951, 1957), and their co-workers in the 1940s and 1950s; and came to fullest operational expression via the cooperative learning methods created in the 1970s. These contemporary cooperative learning approaches, in diverse ways, seek to express principles of cooperative incentive and task structures; task specialization; distributed or shared group leadership; heterogeneous group membership; positive interdependence among this membership; individual accountability; high levels of group autonomy; equal opportunity scoring based on improvement compared to self, not others; and between-group competition. The following approaches to cooperative learning illustrate these various principles.

Student Teams–Achievement Divisions

In Slavin's (1978) Student Teams–Achievement Divisions (STAD), four- or five-member learning teams are constituted. Youngsters assigned to each team ideally represent the heterogeneity of the larger class, school, or community (i.e., boys and girls; high-, average-, and low-performing students; students of different ethnic or racial backgrounds). The teacher regularly introduces new materials to be learned. In a peer-tutoring format, students study the materials together, take turns quizzing one another, discuss the materials as a group, or use other self-selected means to master the material. The teacher communicates to each team that studying of any given material is not completed until all teammates are sure they understand it. Quiz scores are transformed into team scores by the teacher, with each student's contribution to the team score being not the absolute level of her performance but, instead, the amount of improvement in that student's score over her past average score. Such use of individual improvement scores helps increase the likelihood that low-performing students will also contribute to the total team score and be viewed as fully accepted group members. In STAD, the team or teams with the highest scores, and the students who exceed their own past performance by the greatest amounts, are acknowledged in a weekly one-page class newsletter.

Teams–Games–Tournaments

The Teams–Games–Tournaments (TGT) approach to cooperative learning, developed by DeVries and Slavin (1978), employs the same team structure, instructional format, and worksheets as STAD. Instead of quizzes, however, students engage in cross-team academic games as the means for demonstrating their individual mastery of the given subject matter. These games are played in weekly tournaments in which students compete against members of other teams that are comparable in past performance. Slavin (1983a) captures the flavor of these games well:

> The competitions take place at tournament tables of three students. Thus a high performing student from the "Fantastic Four" might compete with a high performer from the "Pirates" and one from the "Superstars." Another table might have average performing students from the "Pirates," the "Masterminds," and the "Chiefs." . . . The students are not told which is the highest table, which is next, and so on, but they are told that their competition will always be fair. (p. 26)

To maintain a fair level of competition, students' table assignments are changed every week, with the high scorer at each table being moved to the next higher table and the low scorer at each table being moved to the next lower table. Since any given student's contribution to the total team score, as in STAD, is based on improvement over past performance, this equalizing of tournament competition maximizes all students' potential contributions to the team score. Also, as in STAD, a weekly class newsletter is employed to provide recognition of high-scoring teams and individual tournament winners.

Team Assisted Individualization

Team Assisted Individualization (TAI) was developed by Slavin, Leavey, and Madden (1982) for use when the members of a class are too heterogeneous to be taught the same material at the same rate. To date, TAI has been used primarily for the cooperative learning of mathematics. It is the only cooperative learning method to use individual instruction rather than class-paced learning. As in STAD and TGT, heterogeneous groups of four to five students are formed. Diagnostic testing of each student is carried out and, based upon the results of this assessment, a programmed mathematics unit is prescribed for each student. The student works at his own pace—reading instructions, working on successive skill sheets, taking "checkouts," and being tested. This progression occurs in self-selected teams of two students each. Team members exchange answer sheets and check each other's skill sheets and checkouts. Slavin et al. (1982) note that, in this cooperative approach, student test scores and the number of tests completed in a given week contribute to a team score which, if it exceeds present team performance standards, results in certificates being awarded to each team member for progress that week.

Jigsaw

In contrast to the individualization feature of TAI, Aronson, Blaney, Stephan, Sikes, and Snapp's (1978) Jigsaw approach was designed to maximize student interdependence. Interestingly, however, such interdependence is reflected in the approach's task structure, not its incentive structure. Students are assigned to heterogeneous six-member teams, and the academic material to be covered is broken down into five sections. For example, Aronson et al. describe a fifth-grade Jigsaw classroom in which biographies of great Americans were being studied. The teacher created five biographies that respectively described the famous figure's ancestors and how he came to America; his childhood and adolescence; his early adulthood, education, and employment; his middle years and their highlights; and events in society at large during this latter period. Each team member was assigned one of these sections to read and study in order to become expert (six team members for five sections were used to cover absentees). Members of different teams who had studied the same sections then met as "expert groups" to consider their section. Having thus become experts by study and discussion, students then returned to their own teams and took turns teaching their teammates about their sections. Students were encouraged to listen to, support, and show interest in one another's reports to the team. After the reports were completed, students were individually quizzed across all topics and received individual, not team, grades.

Jigsaw II

As in STAD and TGT, students in Slavin's (1980) Jigsaw II work in heterogeneous teams of four or five members. Unlike Jigsaw, in which team members are responsible for a unique section of the material, Jigsaw II requires all students to read the same chapter or story. Each student is, however, assigned a topic within this context in which to become expert. As in Jigsaw, the students from each group who are assigned the same topic meet in expert groups to discuss the topic and then return to their own teams to teach what they have learned. Individual quizzes are taken, and scores for individual improvement over previous performance are computed and used as the basis for determining an overall team score. As in STAD and TGT, a class newsletter provides public acknowledgment and recognition of high-scoring teams and individuals.

Learning Together

Learning Together (Johnson & Johnson, 1975) is the most group-oriented of the cooperative learning alternatives. Students work on assignment sheets in heterogeneous four- or five-member groups. The group members hand in for evaluation a single assignment sheet from all of them. As the method's title indicates, they then receive feedback as a group regarding how well they are "learning together." Reflecting a cooperative incentive structure, grades are based on the average achievement scores of individual members.

Group Investigation

Cooperative learning via the Group Investigation method (Sharon & Sharon, 1976) is a six-stage process initiated and conducted by the participating students themselves. Specifically, the process involves the following steps:

1. Identifying the topic and organizing into self-selected, two- to six-member groups.
2. Planning the learning task, in which the members choose subtopics for investigation.
3. Carrying out the investigation (i.e., gathering and evaluating relevant information, drawing conclusions, and so forth).
4. Preparing a final report, which requires the coordination and integration of the efforts of each team member.
5. Presenting the final report, as a group, to the class as a whole. This presentation may be a written document, exhibition, skit, etc.
6. Evaluating themselves in collaboration with the teacher.

These seven approaches to cooperative learning are the more frequently utilized and more thoroughly evaluated of those in existence, but they do not exhaust the alternatives. Other techniques exist and deserve further scrutiny by the serious educator/researcher (see Huber, Bogatzki, & Winter, 1982; Kagan, 1985; Lew & Bryant, 1981; Peterson & Janicki, 1979; Weigel, Wiser, & Cook, 1975; Wheeler & Ryan, 1973).

As noted earlier, the typical American classroom is far different from what we have described in this section. Rather than working together for group rewards (i.e., cooperative task and incentive structures), most classes are organized according to an individualistic task structure (e.g., students work alone) or a competitive incentive structure (e.g., curve marking). Slavin (1983a) describes the usual classroom situation accurately:

> With regard to task structure, most teachers use some combination of lectures, discussions, individual seatwork, small homogeneous groups working with the teacher, and individual tests. Students are rarely allowed, and even less often encouraged, to help one another with their work; in most schools, peer relationships during school hours are largely restricted to the playground and lunchroom. The almost universal incentive structure used is a grading system, in which students compete for a limited number of good grades. (p. 2)

The interpersonal consequences of the cooperative, competitive, and individualistic orientations can be dramatically different. Johnson and Johnson (1975) offer the schema presented in Table 13 to help categorize these consequences.

The typical classroom structure involving individualistic work for competitive rewards may be particularly damaging for the very types of low-performing youth for whom the Prepare Curriculum is of special relevance. Slavin (1985) comments in this regard that

> for many low-performing students, no amount of effort is likely to put them at the top of the class because they have already missed so much in past years. Thus, the competition for top score in the classroom is poorly matched. Because they have such a small chance of success, low performers may give up or try to disrupt the activity. They can hardly be expected to do otherwise ... low performing students ... may turn to delinquency or withdrawal as a means of maintaining self-esteem in the face of what they perceive as a hostile school environment. (p. 6)

A portion of low-performing students are also members of minority groups, and a number of studies demonstrate that Black and Chicano students appear to respond particularly well to cooperative learning experiences, perhaps because of compatible cultural group-oriented experiences (Beady & Slavin, 1981; Lucker, Rosenfield, Sikes, & Aronson, 1976; Slavin, 1977; Slavin & Oickle, 1981).

Thus cooperative learning does have value, especially for low-performing youth. Decisions for usage, however, must be based primarily on empirical evidence as to whether cooperative learning increases cooperative behavior and the use of other prosocial behaviors.

Table 13

Goal Structures and Interpersonal Processes

Cooperative	Competitive	Individualistic
High interaction	Low interaction	No interaction
Mutual liking	Mutual dislike	No interaction
Effective communication	No or misleading communication	No interaction
High trust	Low trust	No interaction
High mutual influence	Low mutual influence	No interaction
High acceptance and support	Low acceptance and support	No interaction
High use of other students' resources	No use of other students' resources	No interaction
High sharing and helping	Attempts to mislead and obstruct	No interaction
High emotional involvement of all	Emotional involvement of winners	No interaction
High coordination of effort	Low coordination of effort	No interaction
Division of labor possible	Division of labor not possible	No interaction
High divergent thinking	Low divergent thinking	No interaction
No self-other comparisons	High self-other comparisons	No interaction

Note. From David W. Johnson/Roger T. Johnson, *Learning Together and Alone,* © 1975, p. 27. Reprinted by permission of Prentice-Hall, Inc., Englewood Cliffs, New Jersey.

470

Research Evaluation

We began this chapter with the assertion that participation in cooperative learning activities enhances the participants' level of cooperative behavior. This assertion is supported solidly by empirical evidence. Hertz-Lazarowitz, Sharan, and Steinberg (1980) found both acquisition and transfer of cooperation effects in a study of elementary school children taking part in a Group Investigation cooperative learning program. Participating youngsters, when compared to appropriate control-group children, were more cooperative and altruistic in their behavior both during the training experience and when assigned to new groups. Sharan, Raviv, and Russell (1982) successfully replicated these transfer findings. In a third investigation, Hertz-Lazarowitz, Sapir, and Sharan (1981) found significantly less competitiveness in children participating in Group Investigation than in control-group youths. Johnson, Johnson, Johnson, and Anderson (1976), using their Learning Together approach, similarly reported substantial increases in participants' cooperative behavior, in comparison to that of youth learning competitively or individually. Ryan and Wheeler (1977) essentially replicated this result.

Jigsaw has yielded similarly enhanced levels of cooperation, not only in terms of overt cooperative behavior (Aronson et al., 1978), but also with regard to motivation for future cooperativeness (Blaney, Stephen, Rosenfield, Aronson, & Sikes, 1977). Kagan, Zahn, Widaman, Schwarzwald, and Tyrrell (1985) report similarly enhanced levels of cooperative behavior compared to behavior in traditional classroom structures in their cooperative learning investigations. However, at both the elementary and high school levels, their research showed that the effect held for minority students (Black, Mexican-American) but not for majority students (Caucasian).

In all, the evidence is clear, substantial, and almost uniformly positive that participation in cooperative learning programs indeed enhances subsequent cooperative behavior. Apparently, it also does much more. Such participation has also been demonstrated to increase a host of other prosocial and cognitive characteristics, including interpersonal attraction among students (Aronson et al., 1978; Edwards & DeVries, 1974; Slavin, 1978; Slavin et al., 1982); internal locus of control (DeVries, Edwards, & Wells, 1974b; Gonzales, 1979; Slavin, 1978); motivation on academic tasks (Hulten & DeVries, 1976; Johnson et al., 1976; Slavin, 1978); time on task (Janke, 1978; Slavin, 1977; Ziegler, 1981); self-esteem (Blaney et al., 1977; Geffner, 1978; Lazarowitz, Baird, Bowlden, & Hertz-Lazarowitz, 1982; Johnson, Johnson, &

Scott, 1978); quality of cross-ethnic interaction (DeVries, Edwards, & Slavin, 1978; Slavin, 1977, 1983b; Slavin & Oickle, 1981); quality of cross-handicapped interaction (Johnson & Johnson, 1975; Martino & Johnson, 1979; Rynders, Johnson, Johnson, & Schmidt, 1980); quality of student-teacher interaction (Johnson et al., 1978); attitudes toward heterogeneity of peers (Johnson et al., 1978); role taking (Bridgeman, 1981); peer norms supporting academic performance (Slavin, 1978); and, in an especially substantial number of investigations, academic achievement (Humphreys, Johnson, & Johnson, 1982; Johnson, Maruyama, Johnson, Nelson, & Skon, 1981; Slavin, 1983a). Cooperative learning is indeed an educational strategy and set of techniques of considerable potency. It appears to hold great value for the enhancement of a broad array of prosocial behaviors, including, but going beyond, cooperative behavior per se. It is therefore an important segment of the Prepare Curriculum.

Cooperative Gaming

Low-achieving youth, acting-out youth, withdrawn youth, delinquent youth, chronically aggressive youth, and those otherwise deficient in a broad array of prosocial behaviors are the target students for the Prepare Curriculum. A central question in the delivery of any curriculum concerns its prescriptive appropriateness for the particular types of students targeted. Do the content, format, and manner of delivery of a given curriculum fit the target youths' "channels of accessibility" (Hunt, 1971)?

Many of the youth identified above may accurately be described, in terms of their optimal channels of accessibility, as action-oriented and relatively nonverbal (Goldstein, 1971, 1973). They are no less expressive than other youth, but they often lean toward motor behavior as a preferred means of communication. Athletic activities, games, and related behaviors are concrete illustrations of such preferences, and it is our aspiration to be responsive to these channels of accessibility in furthering our goal of teaching cooperative behavior. Thus, in addition to the several cooperative learning approaches described earlier, we now wish to examine and promote the use of cooperative sports and games as an especially promising route to the enhancement of cooperative behavior in youth displaying chronic prosocial deficiencies.

Cooperative sports and games are activities in which the format, rules, and materials employed explicitly avoid competitive strategies and instead reflect a cooperative interactional philosophy (e.g., "working with others for mutual benefit"). The following practices are among the ways this philosophy may be operationalized:

1. Encouraging players to help one another toward activity goals;
2. Avoiding player eliminations (i.e., having all participants play);
3. Ensuring that any competition is against one's own past performance and not against other players;
4. Having players rotate across all positions and play for equal amounts of time;
5. Scoring collectively across teams or across all individual players if the activity does not involve teams (or otherwise structuring scoring so that all participants "win");
6. Changing team captains each game;
7. Having everyone on a team touch the ball/puck before a shot is taken;
8. Deemphasizing awards and trophies and emphasizing the instrinsic benefits of the sport or game.

Terry Orlick (1978), who in most creative senses is the father of the cooperative sports and games movement, communicates its spirit and aspiration:

> The main difference [from competitive games] is that in cooperative games everybody cooperates . . . everybody wins . . . and nobody loses. Children play with one another rather than against one another. These games eliminate the fear of failure and the feeling of failure. They also reaffirm a child's confidence in himself or herself as an acceptable and worthy person. In most games . . . this reaffirmation is left to chance or awarded to just one winner. In cooperative games it is designed into the games themselves. (pp. 3–4)

But Orlick (1978) also cautions that

> patience may be needed to learn this "new" form of play, particularly if the participants have never before played cooperatively. However, with appropriate challenges, enlightened supervision, repeated exposure, and players' constructive input on cooperative changes, the games will begin to take off on a positive note. (p. 4)

As is consistent with our purpose in promoting Cooperation Training as part of the Prepare Curriculum, Orlick (1978) stresses the manner in which cooperative play increases the likelihood of future cooperative behavior:

> Cooperation is directly related to communication, cohesiveness, trust, and the development of positive social-interaction skills. Through

cooperative ventures, children learn to share, to empathize with others, to be concerned with other's feelings, and to work to get along better. (pp. 6–7)

A substantial amount of empirical evidence supports Orlick's assertion. Cooperative play indeed enhances cooperation and a number of its prosocial concomitants. Bryant and Crockenberg (1974), DeVries and Edwards (1973), and Ryan and Wheeler (1977) each demonstrated the potency of cooperative games for the enhancement of such components of cooperation as mutual concern, attentiveness to and feelings of obligation for other students, and mutual liking. Hulten (1974); DeVries, Muse, and Wells (1971); and Spilerman (1971) successfully used cooperative games to produce a peer climate combining academic involvement and peer encouragement. In a study by DeVries, Edwards, and Wells (1974a), cooperative games increased divergent thinking, time on task, student preference for cooperative versus competitive activities, and student belief that peers had a substantial interest in one's academic success. Cook (1969) and DeVries and Edwards (1973) also successfully employed cooperative games to increase cooperative behavior between interracial groups. Finally, in Jacovino's (1980) evaluation of cooperative games, results showed a significant increase in cooperative behavior in a sample of low-performing adolescents very much like those for whom the Prepare Curriculum is intended. In all, cooperative gaming, much like cooperative learning, has been shown to yield reliable and substantial cooperation-enhancing and related prosocial effects in both elementary and secondary level students.

Having thus provided an empirical rationale for their use, we now turn to the cooperative activities themselves. Grouped according to three age levels—ages 3–7, 8–12, and adolescent—these activities are sufficient in number, variety, appropriateness to age level, and intrinsic interest to youth to form an excellent pool of activities from which Cooperation Training programs can be constituted and implemented. We urge those readers interested in organizing and conducting cooperation training to consult the major sources from which we chose these cooperative games and sports. These sources are as follows:*

The Cooperative Sports and Games Book, by T. Orlick, 1978. Pantheon, 201 East 50th Street, New York, NY 10022.

---

*The following descriptions have been adapted by permission from these five sources. Each selection has been identified by author and date of publication.

The Second Cooperative Sports and Games Book, by T. Orlick, 1982. Pantheon, 201 East 50th Street, New York, NY 10022.

For the Fun of It! Selected Cooperative Games for Children and Adults, by M. Harrison, 1975. Friends Peace Committee, 1515 Cherry Street, Philadelphia, PA 19102.

Playfair: Everybody's Guide to Noncompetitive Play, by M. Weinstein and J. Goodman, 1980. Impact Publishers, P. O. Box 1094, San Luis Obispo, CA 93406.

Sports Manual of Cooperative Recreation, by J. Deacove, 1978. Family Pastimes, R.R. 4, Perth, Ontario, Canada K7H 3C6.

Other valuable resources include *Games Manual of Noncompetitive Games* (Deacove, 1974), *The New Games Book* (Flugelman, 1976), *More New Games* (Flugelman, 1981), *A Manual on Nonviolence and Children* (Judson, 1984), and *Everybody Wins: Noncompetitive Games for Young Children* (Sobel, 1983).

Ages 3–7

Jack-in-the-Box Name Game

Children form a circle. The first person starts by standing up and saying her name: "I'm Cynthia." Then she introduces four people on her left, starting with the farthest person: "This is Joe, Susan, Pam, Bob." When each name is said, that person stands up and sits down quickly. There is a jack-in-the-box effect, with people standing and sitting one after the other. Then the person on Cynthia's right stands up and introduces himself and the four people to his left: "I'm Pat and this is Susan, Pam, Bob, and Cynthia," dropping one person introduced previously (in this case, Joe). Again, when each person's name is mentioned, that participant stands or sits quickly. By the time introductions get around the circle, the names will be more familiar and the smiles a little bigger. With younger children, fewer people can be introduced, maybe one or two. (Harrison, 1975)

Elbow-Nose

Children form a circle. The leader starts by turning to the person on the right and saying, "This is my elbow" while pointing to her nose. This second person then responds, "This is my nose" while pointing to his own elbow. Then the second person turns to the next person on the right (third person) and points to some part of the body while naming another part, to which the third person responds with the opposite, and so on. The pace needs to be quick and lively, otherwise the activity tends to drag. Good for small groups. (Harrison, 1975)

Cooperative Hide-and-Seek

This is a hide-and-seek game in reverse. Instead of having one player searching for everyone else, everyone else seeks out one player. All the players but one count to 100 with their eyes closed. While they do this, the single player finds a place to hide that is big enough to hold everyone in the game. (It might be a squeeze, but that's all right.) Then everyone searches for the hider. Each player who finds the hiding place tries to hide there, too, without being seen by the others. Finally, everyone will be squashed into the hiding place, just like sardines in a can. (Orlick, 1978)

Cooperative Pin-the-Tail-on-the-Donkey

In the traditional game, which is always a party favorite, it is the blindfolded player's mishaps that delight those watching. In the cooperative form of this game, all the players play together to direct the person who is blindfolded. The object is to get the donkey's tail pinned onto the right place. The onlookers shout "A little higher!" "No, no the other way!" etc., and, by playing together, everybody wins. (Orlick, 1978)

Puppet on a String

One player is the puppet on the ground, unable to move. Along comes the puppeteer, who brings the puppet to life with pretend strings. The puppeteer pulls the strings, and the puppet responds to every tug. Allow everyone a chance to be the puppeteer as well as to be the puppet. (Orlick, 1978)

Honk, Honk

Practically every teenager these days learns how to drive a car, but even the very young can drive in this activity. The players choose partners. One is the car, the other the driver. The "cars" get down on their hands and knees, and the "drivers" climb aboard! Off they go, honking their horns. (If the driver is too heavy for the car, tell her to keep both feet on the ground.) *Variations:* One player can be a puppeteer, the other the puppet. Or one player can be a mad scientist and the other a monster, to be directed by a master. (Orlick, 1978)

Cooperative Singing

Songs are sung by a group as they enact together the given lyrics. Examples include "The More We Get Together," "The Big Ship Sails," "Thread the Needle," and "Here We Come Walking." (Orlick, 1978)

Partner Gymnastics

Gymnastics include Partner Pull-up, Partner Back-up, Wring the Dishrag, and Hop-along. Each is a stunt or activity in which two children move in a synchronous, mutually helpful manner to get up, move, form certain positions, or carry out certain activities. (Orlick, 1978)

Nonelimination Simon Says

Two games begin simultaneously, each with its own leader. If a player follows when a leader says "Do this" with no "Simon says," that player transfers to the second game and joins in. *No* elimination, only movement back and forth between two parallel games. (Orlick, 1978)

Secret Message (Telephone)

Children sit in a group and whisper a message around the circle as fast as they can. The last person says the secret out loud to see how it compares with the original. This activity can work in both directions or use signs (wink, smile, hug) instead of the whispered message. (Orlick, 1978)

Tiptoe through the Tulips

Children paint a long, winding lane of flowers and leaves on paper and, as a group, tiptoe through the tulips. (Orlick, 1978)

Shoe Twister

Each child removes one shoe and puts it in a pile. Everyone then picks up someone else's shoe. While in a circle or otherwise, each child locates the shoe's owner and returns the shoe. (Orlick, 1978)

Blizzard

Two children are lost in a snowstorm. One is blindfolded; the other leads the "snow-blinded" through the blizzard (i.e., an obstacle course). This can include going through a snow tunnel (hoop), under an ice log (bench), over part of a frozen river (mat), etc. The child can also pretend to be leading a pilot to land in fog, etc. Once they reach safety, partners can switch roles. (Orlick, 1978)

Barnyard

Each child selects an animal name or picture from a hat (e.g., cow, wolf, snake). Then they scatter around the room. Children are blindfolded and must find other members of their animal group by making the sound of that animal only. (Orlick, 1978)

Blup-Blup Up-Up

Pairs of children try to keep a balloon up by hitting (with hands, water gun, blowing) in alternate turns. The score is the number of consecutive hits. A good game to introduce the idea of collective scoring. (Orlick, 1978)

Mile of Yarn

One child wraps yarn (or a strip of material) around his waist and passes the ball to next child, who does the same, and so on. When all are wrapped, they proceed progressively to unwrap in reverse order. (Orlick, 1978)

Magic Carpet

A group of approximately seven children take turns giving one another magic carpet rides on a gym mat. The rider can choose her riding position, speed, direction, etc. (Orlick, 1978)

Frozen Bean Bag (Help Your Friends)

All children move around the gym with bean bags on their heads. The pace of movement can be varied: slow, skip, walk, hop, etc. If the bean bag falls, that child freezes until another child puts a bean bag on the frozen player's head and thus unfreezes him. (Orlick, 1978)

Wagon Wheels

Approximately seven children face one another and join hands in a circle. The wheel then moves in a circular motion around the perimeter of the gym. Two or three children, the bottom of the wheel, have their backs touching the wall momentarily as the wheel spins. As the wheel picks up speed, the fun increases. (Orlick, 1978)

Choo-Choo Train

Two or more children in single file grab the hips or shoulders of the child in front. They move in unison like train cars—going up and down hills, ducking through a tunnel, etc. (Orlick, 1978)

Toesies

Partners lie stretched on the floor, feet to feet, and attempt to roll across the floor while keeping feet touching. (Orlick, 1978)

Little People's Big Sack

Sew sheets or sacks together so 8 to 20 children can crawl in and try to move the sack by collective crawling, rolling, hopping, etc. (Orlick, 1978)

Big Snake

Children stretch out on their stomachs in single file, holding the ankles of the person in front. The "snake" turns over, goes over "mountains," through "holes," etc. (Orlick, 1978)

Big Turtle

A group of seven or eight children get on their hands and knees under a large "turtle shell" (e.g., gym mat, blanket, etc.) and try to make the turtle move in one direction. Older children may try having the turtle move over an obstacle course (e.g., a bench) without losing its shell. (Orlick, 1978)

Numbers, Shapes, and Letters Together

With one or more partners, children are asked to form given shapes, numbers, or letters with their bodies. Everyone in the group must take part. Or the whole class can spell a "body sentence." (Orlick, 1978)

Partners

Children skip, hop, etc. alone. "Partners" is called. Children find a partner and freeze together, holding hands. One plays mirror (imitator) of the other; then the other does the same. Then they run again, "Partners" is called again, and they find a new partner. If there are "left-outs," you can cut magazine pictures in half, distribute the pieces, and have kids partner up with their "other halves." (Orlick, 1978)

Cooperative Musical Hoops

Two kids are in a hula hoop; music is playing. When the music stops, two pairs join up inside their two hula hoops and skip around the room as a group. This continues until as many kids as possible (usually eight) are fit into a set of stacked-up hoops. (Orlick, 1978)

Cooperative Musical Hugs

Music plays, and children skip around the room. When the music stops, each child hugs another. Next time, three kids hug together, etc., until at the end "all the children squish together in one massive musical hug." (Orlick, 1978)

Water Cup Pass

Players stand in a circle with paper cups in their teeth. One person's cup is filled with water. That person begins by pouring the water into the next person's cup without hands, and so on around the circle. A delightful game on a hot summer day. (Orlick, 1978)

Musical Laps

This is a cooperative version of Musical Chairs. The whole group forms a circle, all facing in one direction, close together, each with hands on the waist of the person ahead. When the music starts, everyone begins to walk forward. When the music stops, everyone sits down in the lap of the person to the rear. If the whole group succeeds in sitting in laps without anyone falling to the floor, the group wins. If people fall down, gravity wins. Works best with more than 10 people about the same size (a big man will have a hard time sitting in the lap of a 6-year-old!). (Harrison, 1975)

Clapping Game

One person goes out of the room. The rest of the group decides on an object for the person to find or an action for the person to do. The person returns to try to find the object while the group claps. The group will help the person complete the task by clapping louder and louder as the person approaches the object or act decided upon. If the person is far away from doing the activity or finding the object, the clapping is soft. *Variation:* This game can also be played with two people going out of the room and coming back to do something in tandem. Examples of things to have people do: hug each other, face each other with hands on shoulders, sit back to back. Think up your own variations! (Harrison, 1975)

Human Pretzel

Two people leave the room. The others hold hands in a circle and twist themselves over and under and through one another without dropping hands. The two people waiting outside come back in and are challenged to untangle the group. The Pretzel cooperates as the "untanglers" figure out who goes where. (Harrison, 1975)

Switchbacks (Variation on Musical Laps)

Everyone is in pairs, back to back. If there is an odd number of people, the free person sings or talks in monologue (or plays some kind of simple instrument, like a drum) while everyone moves around the room or field, back to back with a partner (elbows can be locked). When the singing stops, each person finds a new partner and the free person must find a partner. The current odd person is now the music-maker, and the game is repeated. If there is an even number of people, there is no free person, and someone is designated to be the caller while she participates. *Variation:* Each time the music stops, the music-maker can quickly indicate a different part of the body that is to be touched (head-to-head or big-toe-to-big-toe). (Harrison, 1975)

The Itch Name Game

First person says, "My name is Joan and I itch here" (scratching some part of the body—e.g., head). Second person says, "Her name is Joan and she itches there" (reaching out to scratch Joan on the head) "and my name is Jim and I itch here" (scratching). Third person says, "His name is Jim and he itches there, and my name is Marcia and I itch here" (scratching the other person and then herself). And so it continues around the circle amidst the giggles. A good name game. (Harrison, 1975)

Pass the Mask

With everyone sitting in a circle, one player turns to the next, looks right into his eyes, and makes a funny face. The second player passes on the face to the third, and so on around the circle. At the same time, the first player has turned to the person on the other side and made a different funny face, which is passed around in the other direction. Continue until both "masks" have reached the first player again, or until laughter has stopped the game. (Harrison, 1975)

Cooperative Snowpeople

Did you ever think of how the snowman feels, standing there all alone? Let's give him friends, and a family, too. The object is to build many snowpeople—an entire village of snowpeople. Build snowmoms and snowdads and even snowchildren. Don't forget to dress warmly. *Variation:* Try to roll the biggest snowball you ever saw. For this, the players will need the help of all their friends in order to push the ball when it starts to get very big. (Harrison, 1975)

Cooperative Murals

Needed: Very large piece of paper, finger or poster paints. Two or more players can color a picture together, or, better yet, many, many people can paint a mural. Get a very large piece of paper and start painting. No one has to be an experienced artist. *Variation:* Try having the players use their feet to paint the mural. Everyone takes off shoes and socks and really gets into painting. (Harrison, 1975)

Ages 8–12

Cooperative Bowling

All we've done here is convert conventional bowling into a cooperative game. The game is played and scored in the same fashion as regular bowling, except that, within each frame, each player throws only one ball, and the second person tries to increase the score. In the next frame, the second player goes first. The score is taken together. If a player gets a strike, her partner starts the next frame. *Variations:* Try bowling through your legs—or, better yet, through your partner's legs. Try it with the opposite hand. Try it blindfolded. Make up your own way. By playing around with the rules, the emphasis is taken off the score and placed where it belongs—on having fun. (Deacove, 1978)

Cooperative Billiards

Anyone who can play regular billiards can play this version of it. One player shoots until he misses a shot; then it is the next player's turn. But, unlike regular pool, in this version the players try to set up the next person for a good shot instead of trying to leave nothing to shoot at. They can set an objective, and when it is reached, everybody has won. This is a great way for young players to learn the game without pressure. (Deacove, 1978)

New Basketball

In this cooperative form of an old favorite, we try to eliminate the dominant "big man" who is so often present in a basketball game. That's why this version of the game has different rules:

- No dribbling; everyone must pass the ball.
- Each player must touch the ball before a shot is attempted. In this way, everyone is involved and no one stands around just watching.

- No shooting from beyond the foul line—this makes the game more team-oriented.
- Sometimes the players count the number of passes aloud as the ball goes from player to player.

Variations include the following:

1. Statues: This game helps the offensive team score and eliminates the emphasis on body contact. When the offense brings the ball up to and across half court, the defense must freeze wherever they are. Then the offensive team passes the ball from player to player and tries to score. The defense can pivot on one foot to try to prevent the score. The defense only resume moving when they reacquire the ball or after the offense gets a basket.

2. Sink it: In this version, one player attempts a shot. If successful, all the other players in turn try to make that same shot. If everyone makes the shot, the team as a whole gets an "S," the first letter in "sink it." Then the next player tries another shot. All the players keep shooting until they have spelled "sink it." (Deacove, 1978)

Collective Track Meets

No one is eliminated; rather, the focus is on the fastest collective time. Individual times are added or averaged. Sometimes partners are randomly paired; each runs a half track, and their combined times are averaged. You can use the same system for jumps, throws, lifting, hurdling, etc. (Deacove, 1978)

Three-sided Soccer

Three goals are set as a triangle. Regular rules apply except that teams rotate in the goals they shoot at while goalies remain at the same goal throughout. Each team defends one goal but can score at the other two. You can use several balls; no official scoring. (Deacove, 1978)

Incorporations

The game involves forming and reforming groups rapidly. The leader rings a bell and calls out a variety of group arrangements (e.g., 3 + 1, the letter "H," all players wearing the same color). (Weinstein & Goodman, 1980)

Tug of Peace

People sit in a circle with a thick rope inside the circle at their feet. The ends of the rope are tied together. Everyone pulls at the same time so that the entire group can stand up together. (Orlick, 1978)

Let's Build a Machine

People try to represent a machine, with each person portraying a moving part. The machine can be imaginary, allowing for creativity in the wheres and hows of moving parts. Or it can be a real machine (washing machine, sewing machine) in which the fun lies in trying to figure out how to represent the parts with people. This game is good in the physical contact as well as the cooperation category.

Note: "Machine" is good for the physically handicapped, who can use crutches, etc. A person confined to a wheelchair can be of central importance. (Harrison, 1975)

Kings of the Mountain

Try to make a snowball large enough for all players to get on. (Orlick, 1982)

Car and Driver

The game is played in pairs. One (the driver) stands directly behind the other (the car) with hands on shoulders. The car has eyes open first, then closed. The driver starts, stops, and turns using touch signals. The pair moves through and around obstacles. This can extend to buses (longer cars), with signals being passed from last person to first. (Orlick, 1982)

Reversing the Gauntlet

One person walks or skips between two lines of others, stops at will, and looks at another, who must say or do something to make the first person feel good—wink, hug, say "I like you," smile, etc. (Orlick, 1982)

Imaginary Ball Toss

Children are in a circle. They toss and catch an imaginary ball, which, as the game progresses, can be changed by the tosser into a bean bag, watermelon, live chicken, etc. (Weinstein & Goodman, 1980)

All on One Side

One team plays. The object is to move the team to the other side of the net as many times as possible. Each player volleys a balloon to another player and then scoots under the net to the other side. The last player hits the balloon over the net and scoots under. The process is then repeated. (Orlick, 1978)

Togeth-air Ball (Collective Score Volleyball)

This game is regular volleyball with an extra one-point score anytime anyone hits the ball or hits the ball over the net. This can be played "all touch," in which all members must touch the ball before hitting it over the net. You can also use two balls or have unlimited number hits per side. (Orlick, 1978)

Collective-score Blanketball

Two teams use a blanket to toss a beach ball back and forth over a volleyball net. Each time the ball is caught, the team scores one collective point. Every team member is part of every toss. You can use different sized balls, blankets, and even towels. (Orlick, 1978)

Ladder Travel

Several youths spread out along both sides of a sturdy ladder, bench, or plank and lift it up so it is held horizontally below their waists. One end is lowered so that the "traveler" can step or crawl on it. The ladder is brought back to horizontal, and the traveler walks or crawls it. (Orlick, 1978)

Human Supports

Two or more people hold a horizontal bar while another does a pull-up, pull-over or knee-hang. Everyone takes a turn holding and performing on the bar. (Orlick, 1978)

Nonverbal Birthday Line-up

Players are asked to line up according to month and day of birth—without any talking. (Orlick, 1978)

Cross-over Dodge Ball

This game is played like regular dodge ball, but if a player is hit she runs to the other team and continues play. (Orlick, 1978)

Esti-Win

Each runner estimates the time it will take him to run a given distance. The winner is the one who comes closest to the prediction. Another way of "winning" is to judge the amount of improvement over a past estimate. (Orlick, 1978)

Log Roll
Several players lie side by side on their stomachs on the floor, mat, grass, etc. A rider lies on her stomach perpendicular to and on the "logs" across their backs. All the logs begin rolling in same direction, giving the rider a ride. At the end, after the rider has gone over the last log, she then becomes a log and the first log becomes a rider. (Orlick, 1978)

Towering Tower
Children work together to build a single tower out of bean bags, cardboard boxes, hoops, etc. This can be done as part of a game in which a leader calls "Tower," and each child grabs a piece from supply and places it in the middle of the room to help build the tower. (Orlick, 1978)

Watermelon Split
This activity involves relay transportation of a watermelon by pairs of children. At the end, the melon is eaten. (Orlick, 1978)

Circle of Friends
Eight children kneel down in a tight circle, shoulder to shoulder. The person in the middle stiffens his body and falls in any direction; those in the circle gently push him in the other direction. (Orlick, 1978)

Long, Long, Long Jump
One child jumps, and a second child uses the place where the first landed as a jump-off place. Players can attempt to better their total collective distance on successive tries. (Orlick, 1978)

Nonelimination Musical Chairs
Chairs are systematically removed as music stops, but everyone is kept in the game via chair sharing. At the end, 20 kids can end up in one chair. (Orlick, 1978)

Beach-ball Balance
Two children have two or more balls between them. They use no hands, but they can use stomach-to-stomach, head-to-head, etc. (Orlick, 1978)

Knots
Twelve people are shoulder to shoulder in a circle. All put their hands in the center and grab another couple of hands. The group then tries to untangle. (Harrison, 1975)

Stand Up

The group sits in a circle with their backs to the center and arms linked. Then they try to stand up. (Orlick, 1978)

Adolescent

Basketball Adaptations

Use a lighter ball, bigger baskets, lower baskets, smaller court, or move the free-throw line closer. (Deacove, 1978)

Strike-outless Baseball

In this version, there is no pitching; the batter bats the ball off a stationary tee or hits a larger ball. The batter swings until she hits a fair ball. Other adaptations are as follows:

1. All bases count—Each time a player advances to a new base, the team gets a point.
2. All batters run—A group or entire team runs when the ball is hit. Large bases are used, and the more players that get to base, the more points scored.
3. All fielders touch—Every fielder must make contact with the ball after it is hit in order to stop the runner. Bases can be moved further apart, and the number of balls in play can be increased. (Deacove, 1978)

Track, Javelin, Shot Put

Individual scores are kept for running time or distance thrown. A person's best score (in six tries) is averaged with the other team members' best scores. The group's score is thus the collective average. (Deacove, 1978)

Blindfolded Soccer

Players on each team pair up. One of each pair is blindfolded and is the only one who can touch the ball. The other gives verbal instruction but can't contact the ball. There are no goalies and two balls. After a few goals, pairs change roles. (Orlick, 1978)

New Volleyball

1. Rotation ball—Players rotate from one side to the other, not just within teams.

2. Volley-volleyball—A team can score one to three points depending on the number of times its members hit the ball before it is hit over the net.

3. Infinity ball—Uses regular volleyball rules, but the score is the number of times the ball is hit over the net by the two teams combined. (Orlick, 1978)

Moonwalk

This exercise simulates what it is like to jump in weaker gravity. The middle one of three people stands with hands on hips. The two side partners hold the middle person's wrists and elbows. On the count of three, the middle person jumps with partners' support. (Weinstein & Goodman, 1980)

The Human Spring

Two people are 2 feet away from each other, face to face, palms out at chest level. Players lean forward simultaneously and let their hands meet to break the fall together. Then they push off and spring back to original position until they get a rhythm going. (Weinstein & Goodman, 1980)

Off Balance

Two people face each other, grasping hands or wrists. They lean backward until both are off balance so that if the partner weren't providing support, the other would fall. Players move around, balance, and re-balance. (Weinstein & Goodman, 1980)

Brussels Sprouts

This is a game of tag in which, if A tags B, both A and B are "it," then they tag C, who joins the chain, etc. until everyone is tagged. The game can be changed to Lima Beans, which is the same in slow motion. (Weinstein & Goodman)

Floating on the Ocean

One person relaxes backward into the arms of two partners, who support her and rock back and forth in wavelike motion. (Weinstein & Goodman, 1980)

Flying Back Stretch

Player A rests backwards on bent-over B as players C and D support A. (Weinstein & Goodman, 1980)

Octopus Massage

In turn, four people massage (rub, gently slap, stroke) a fifth one. (Weinstein & Goodman, 1980)

Back-to-back Dancing

Players find a partner, link arms back to back, and dance. Switch partners during dance. (Weinstein & Goodman, 1980)

Boss, I Can't Come to Work Today

Players pair up. Pair number one starts a sentence (e.g., "Boss, I can't come to work today"). Each pair in turn adds one or more words to the original sentence. The sentence can be expanded by giving ailments in alphabetical order. (Weinstein & Goodman, 1980)

Mutual Storytelling

One person starts a story; then others take over (starting with "I was present"). A group story/fantasy. (Weinstein & Goodman, 1980)

Stop and Go

All mill around. Anyone can yell "stop," and all freeze. Then anyone yells "go," and the group resumes walking. This activity introduces a sense of participant control. (Weinstein & Goodman)

Touch Blue

This activity is like Stop and Go, but participants shout "Touch blue" or "Touch a head." Participants do so, alternating with "Walk." Gives a sense of control. (Weinstein & Goodman, 1980)

Cooperative Darts, Billiards, Horseshoes, Bowling, Archery

Use collective scoring. (Deacove, 1978)

Cooperation begets cooperation. Cooperative learning and cooperative gaming are the two major, contemporary psychoeducational expressions of this phenomenon. Together they form Cooperation Training, a vital component of the Prepare Curriculum.

Chapter 11

Understanding and Using Groups

Group processes are an exceedingly important influence upon the daily lives of adolescents and many younger children. Groups often shape much of what the youngster thinks, feels, does, hopes, and avoids. Peer groups, family, schoolmates, teammates, and larger collectives each loom large as cognitive, emotional, and behavioral shapers. It is vital, then, that a course sequence on groups be included in the Prepare Curriculum. Its broad goal is to help youngsters better understand the group forces impinging upon them and, via such understanding, gain a measure of control over the contents and outcomes of their group interactions, thus, it is hoped, enhancing the likelihood of their prosocial utilization.

This chapter has two major sections, devoted respectively to *understanding* and *using* groups. The first section is essentially an essay on groups: their nature, dynamics, problems, and opportunities. Drawing on a variety of contemporary sources, we seek in this essay to provide the Prepare Curriculum trainer with an initial knowledge base about groups and their viscissitudes. Beyond such heightened understanding, it is our purpose in this essay to supply the trainer with materials for planning lectures to be used in introducing trainees to the group activities, games, and simulations that constitute, from their perspective, the heart of this course. Finally, it is our hope that the contents of this essay, and the additional readings its presentation may motivate the trainer to pursue, will form a basis for the prescriptive act of selecting which group activities to use with which youngsters in any given setting.

The second part of this chapter directs the reader to group activities, games, and simulations. These activities are drawn from the extensive series of such materials presented in the five volumes of the *Handbook of Structured Experiences for Human Relations Training,* compiled by Pfeiffer and Jones (1974). Other activities to be used by the trainer may be drawn from those presented earlier in our chapter on Cooperation Training (chapter 10). This broad pool of activities reflects, and provides trainees the opportunity to directly experience, the full range of major group dynamic processes, including getting acquainted, group development, leadership, self-disclosure, relationship formation, verbal and nonverbal communication, consensus seeking, conflict, exclusion, risk taking, decision making, feedback, use and abuse of power, movement toward group goals, intergroup competition, and more. Thus this chapter offers a conceptual context as well as a pool of experiential opportunities. Both seem to us to be necessary components in the effort to help youth better understand and use groups to prosocial advantage.

Group Dynamics

In order to understand the events and processes that constitute the birth and development of many types of groups, it is helpful to have a framework or schema that meaningfully organizes such numerous and diverse events and processes. Tuckman (Tuckman, 1965; Tuckman & Jensen, 1977) has offered just such a framework. His perspective on the stages of group development, summarized in Table 14, shows the approximate developmental sequence characterizing many different types of groups, organized for various age levels, for diverse purposes, and for use in several types of settings. In this sequence, groups organize and establish themselves; begin dealing with potential obstacles to meeting their group goals; solidify their structure, "groupness," and the roles and norms that will facilitate goal-relevant performance; perform their task; and adjourn. We will employ this five-stage sequence as a means of organizing both this descriptive essay as well as the group activities presented later in the chapter.

Forming

Why do groups form? Why do people need, seek, and appear to derive benefit from the company of others? An early answer (Edman, 1919; McDougall, 1908) spoke of the "herd instinct," an answer that has more recently reappeared in sociobiological writings about a "biologically rooted urge to affiliate" (Wilson, 1975). Like instinctual explanations of other behaviors, however, such speculations, however elaborate they may be, are essentially circular and untestable. An explanation of group behavior based on need satisfaction is rather more tenable. This is especially so when the formulation is sufficiently complex to include both need similarity and need complementarity among group members, as well as particular needs and need patterns demonstrated empirically to relate to the quality of the group experience and the quantity of the group product. Schutz's (1967) perspective on interpersonal needs as

Table 14
Five Stages of Group Development

Stage	Major processes	Characteristics
Forming	Development of attraction bonds; exchange of information; orientation towards others and situation	Tentative interactions; polite discourse; concern over ambiguity; silences
Storming	Dissatisfaction with others; competition among members; disagreement over procedures; conflict	Ideas are criticized; speakers are interrupted; attendance is poor; hostility
Norming	Development of group structure; increased cohesiveness and harmony; establishment of roles and relationships	Agreement on rules; consensus-seeking; increased supportiveness; we-feeling
Performing	Focus on achievement; high task orientation; emphasis on performance and productivity	Decision making; problem solving; increased cooperation; decreased emotionality
Adjourning	Termination of duties; reduction of dependency; task completion	Regret; increased emotionality; disintegration

Sources. Tuckman (1965); Tuckman and Jensen (1977). Reprinted from *An Introduction to Group Dynamics* (p. 20), by D. R. Forsyth, 1983, Monterey, CA: Brooks/Cole.

a prime influence on group process fits this description well. His work points to group formation and process as the result of the members' needs to express or receive inclusion (associate, belong, join), control (power, dominance, authority), and affection (cohesiveness, love, friendship). A related position on group formation as a function of interpersonal need emphasizes the role of need for affiliation as the central determinant of member behavior (Murray, 1938; Smart, 1965). The social comparisons theory of group formation takes a somewhat more cognitive direction. According to Festinger (1954) and Schachter (1959), people affiliate into dyads or groups when doing so provides useful information derived from comparing oneself, one's attitudes, or one's beliefs with those of others. This basis for group formation is especially attractive, it is held, when one's attitudes or beliefs are shaken and the act of communicating with and comparing oneself to others has potential for restoring equanimity or clarity, or at least for providing a sense of safety in numbers.

The social exchange view of group formation is rather more "economic-like" in its specifics. According to its proponents (Kelley & Thibaut, 1978; Thibaut & Kelley, 1959), individuals make group affiliation decisions based on their estimate of the interpersonal value of such participation. *Value* is defined in terms of both estimated rewards and potential costs. What are the primary rewards and costs of belonging to groups? Rewards may include social support, the group's process, or the group's activities themselves; the benefits of experiencing certain group member characteristics suggestive of likely success at group goals (e.g., authenticity, competence, sociability); and, especially, the group goals themselves. Costs of affiliation may be discomfort with the ambiguous or unfamiliar; the investment that may have to be made in time, energy, self-disclosure, or other resources; possible social rejection; inefficiency or ineffectiveness in progress toward the group's goal; and reactance (i.e., the loss of a sense of freedom, autonomy, or "choicefulness" as the group brings pressure to bear upon its members to conform, reach consensus, or behave in a synchronus manner).

Starting early in its formation and continuing throughout its life, the group develops a sense of cohesiveness. This centrally important quality of groups has been defined in terms of (1) the attraction members feel toward other group members and the group as a unit, (2) member motivation to participate in the group's activities and contribute to the group's goals, and (3) the coordination of member effort. Cohesiveness has sometimes been measured by questionnaire (e.g., Schachter, Ellertson, McBride, & Gregory, 1951). Among the questions often included in such measures are the following:

1. Do you want to remain a member of this group?
2. How often do you think this group should meet?
3. If it seems this group might discontinue, would you like the chance to persuade members to stay?

More typically, inter-member attraction (which emerged as the prime definition of cohesiveness) has been measured by sociometrics, a technique for estimating the social relationships among group members (Moreno, 1960). Members are asked to indicate whom they like most and least, with whom they would most like to work, and so forth. Responses are plotted on a sociogram, which not only reflects the level, spread, and content of inter-member attraction, but also reveals such cohesiveness-related selections as the group's stars, isolates, pairs, chains, rejections, and integration.

We have singled out cohesiveness as primary among the group processes characteristic of group development because cohesiveness has been shown to be an especially powerful influence upon the character and quality of group interaction, as well as a major determinant of the group's longevity and success at reaching its goals. The more cohesive the group, the more likely its members will

1. Be more open to influence by other group members,
2. Place greater value on the group's goals,
3. Be active participants in group discussion,
4. Be more equal participants in group discussion,
5. Be less susceptible to disruption as a group when a member terminates membership,
6. Be absent less often,
7. Remain in the group longer.

Cohesiveness is indeed a crucial foundation of group formation and development. It will tend to diminish the more there is disagreement within the group, the more the group makes unreasonable or excessive demands on its members, the more the leader or other members are overly dominating, the higher the degree of self-oriented behaviors, the more group membership limits the satisfactions members can receive outside the group, the more negatively membership is viewed by outsiders, and the more that conflict exists within the group.

Storming

Groups may experience conflict at any stage in their development. We wish here to focus on the growth and resolution of such conflict not only to better understand this significant group dynamic but also because the reduction or resolution of inter-member difficulties will quite often be a prerequisite to satisfactory progress toward the achievement of group goals. Forsyth (1983) proposes that group conflict characteristically moves through five phases. The first is *disagreement,* in which members discover that two or more group members are in conflict regarding a group task, an interpersonal matter, or other group-relevant concern. *Confrontation* is the second phase of a typical group conflict. Here the opposing factions openly debate the issues in contention. This phase is often characterized by attempts to convert or discredit one's opponent; increased or intensified commitment to one's own position; heightened tension among the disputants and within the group at large; and the formation of coalitions as previously neutral group members elect to, or are pressured to, choose sides. Flowing from such positional commitment, heightened tension, and polarization within the group, the third conflict phase, *escalation,* may ensue. Forsyth (1983) graphically describes this process:

> Many groups are caught up in a conflict spiral.... The final remnants of group unity are shattered as the combatants' exchanges become increasingly hostile; persuasive influence is dropped in favor of coercion, promises are replaced by threats, and in extreme cases verbal attacks become physically violent assaults. (p. 84)

If the group holds together and weathers the storm of disagreement, confrontation, and escalation, then the fourth phase of group conflict, *deescalation,* may occur. Group members tire of fighting, feel their efforts and energy are being wasted, become increasingly more rational, begin to accept a bit of the other side's perspective, and decide to reinvest their efforts in movement toward the group's original purposes and goals. Such deescalation will often not occur without the aid and intervention of third parties (such a conflict resolution strategy will be examined shortly). Finally, the last phase, *resolution,* occurs when the conflict is terminated. Conflict may end via compromise, in which both sides gain some and yield some until an agreement is reached; via withdrawal, in which one side essentially yields for the sake of peace and unity; via imposition, in which by sheer power of numbers or authority one viewpoint is made to prevail; or by conversion, in which the discussion, persuasion, and promises of one side cause the other side to be won over and change its position.

Conflict, of course, may never occur. Many groups organize, set their tasks, get down to business, perform competently, and reach their goals with no disagreement, minimal tension, or general absence of conflict. But when conflict does occur and the group members themselves are not able to resolve it, aid from others outside the group may be necessary. Such help may take several forms. Mediation is one possibility. Here a third party (an outsider or a neutral group member) seeks to help the disputants come to agreement. The mediator avoids offering answers or solutions but serves instead as a facilitator; a go-between; an aid to helping those in disagreement to express their views, listen openly to the other side, and move toward compromise or other solutions. When mediation fails, either because the disputants can't really hear each other or are themselves unable to suggest compromise solutions, the third party may do so. In this negotiator role, the third party proposes possible solutions, compromises, or other effective outcomes for the disputants to consider and agree upon. When negotiation too fails, or is not appropriate, the third party's role may be further escalated in directiveness and authority and become not that of a mediating go-between or a negotiating proposer of solutions but one of an arbitrating imposer of outcomes. Arbitration is a process in which both sides agree on a third-party decisionmaker who listens fully to the competing positions and then renders a binding decision upon the contending group members.

Although we believe that mediation, negotiation, and arbitration may each serve a valuable role in the reduction of group conflict, there is a fourth approach we particularly recommend. The alternative routes to group conflict resolution described above may work, but none of them contributes to the disputants' or the group's ability to ward off further conflicts or to resolve them when they do occur. Training the group members to be effective communicators in conflict situations does, however, have the potential to teach group members how to reduce conflict in the future. In such a training effort (Goldstein & Keller, 1987), group members are taught techniques for preparing for communication in the context of conflict, conducting such communication effectively, and avoiding obstacles to its success. An outline of this communications training program follows.

A Communication Training Program for Conflict Resolution
A. Preparing for communication
  1. Plan on dealing with one problem at a time, sequencing problems in order of significance if more than one exists.
  2. Choose the right time and place, emphasizing privacy and minimizing interruptions or distractions.
  3. Review your own position and hoped-for outcomes, as well as those of the other disputant, placing particular emphasis on possible mutually satisfying solutions.
B. Conducting constructive communication
  1. Acknowledge subjectivity not only in the other's position but also in one's own as a means of establishing a nondefensive climate for discussion.
  2. Be rational in stating your views, the reasons underlying them, and your hoped-for outcomes.

3. Be direct in putting forth what you need, feel, prefer, or expect, and minimize censoring or half-truths.

4. Make ongoing communication checks by asking questions, restating your understanding of the other's position, and asking that hard-to-understand content be repeated in order to be sure you and the other party are communicating accurately.

5. Focus on behavior and on actual actions that you and the other disputant have taken or might take (what, where, when, how often, how much) and do not focus on more difficult-to-change disputant qualities, such as motivations, beliefs, character, personality, or other nonobservable inner characteristics.

6. Reciprocate by showing willingness to acknowledge your own role in problem causation and by showing your own openness to change behavior toward the goal of problem solution.

7. Be empathic, by means described elsewhere in this book (see chapter 8); try to accurately perceive and overtly communicate your awareness of the other disputant's feelings relevant to the conflict in progress.

8. Pay attention to nonverbal behavior—it is central to an accurate understanding of the nature and intensity of the other disputant's views, feelings, and perhaps even willingness to continue engaging in the communication process.

C. Avoiding communication blocks

Communication in conflict situations may falter for a variety of reasons. Group members should become sensitive to—and actively avoid—the following behaviors:

1. Threats,
2. Commands,
3. Interruptions,
4. Sarcasm,
5. Put-downs,
6. Counterattacks,
7. Insults,
8. Teasing,
9. Yelling,
10. Overgeneralizations,
11. Unresponsiveness,
12. Exaggeration,
13. Speaking for the other person,
14. Lecturing,

15. Kitchen-sinking,
16. Building straw men,
17. Use of guilt arousal.

Communication training offered in accord with this schema has been shown to make a substantial contribution to the reduction of within-group conflict (Carkhuff, 1969a, 1969b; Guerney, 1964; Rose, 1977).

Intergroup conflict is a second broad class of group-relevant conflict. A considerable amount of research and theorizing has been put forth in this domain, especially with regard to conflict associated with inter-group competition. The work of Sherif and his research group (Sherif, Harvey, White, Hood, & Sherif, 1961) on conflict between camp groups of adolescents is the classic, initiating research on this topic. It inspired a great deal of subsequent research, focused mainly on the effects of such conflict and means to reduce it. Intergroup competition increases the level of cohesiveness within groups (Coser, 1956; Sherif & Sherif, 1953), an effect that is particularly pronounced within the group that wins the competition (Dion, 1973; Ryan & Kahan, 1970; Wilson & Miller, 1961). Intergroup competition tends to increase the rejection of the other group's members. Such rejection by each group of the other is heightened or moderated by how similar the two groups are, by whether they anticipate they will have to interact in the future, and by features of the competitive task itself (Brewer, 1979; Coser, 1956). Intergroup competition serves to establish and maintain boundaries between groups, as reflected in member tendencies to emphasize between-group differences and minimize between-group similarities (Cooper & Fazio, 1979; Coser, 1956). Intergroup competition often leads to significant misperception of the other group's behavior and intentions. The other group may be stereotyped, dehumanized, or seen as immoral or malevolent; one's own group may be idealized as being moral, overly powerful, or totally right in its views (Linville & Jones, 1980; Oskamp & Hartry, 1968; White, 1970, 1977).

These several negative effects of conflict between groups can be reduced, however. Contact between the competing groups helps considerably in this regard, especially if (1) the contact is between persons of equal status from each group, (2) the contact is in-depth and not superficial, (3) the social climate in which the contact takes place is friendly, (4) the behavior during the contact contradicts the earlier-formed stereotypes, and (5) the contact occurs within a reward structure that reinforces cooperation but not competition (Amir, 1976; Cook, 1972; Foley, 1976). Between-group hostility and the accompanying negative effects of intergroup competition will be reduced even more reliably when members of the two groups are brought together to deal with tasks or challenges that each is motivated to change but that can't be changed successfully by one group acting alone. The conflict-reducing effect of superordinate goals or common enemies is a finding psychologists have proposed as useful not only at the level of small group conflict (Sherif & Sherif, 1953) but also as it might apply to nations in conflict (Lindskold, 1978, 1979a, 1979b; Osgood, 1979).

Norming

As the group deals effectively with potential and emergent instances of inter-member conflict, and as inter-member attraction and groupwide cohesiveness build, the way becomes clearer for the group to establish its explicit and implicit norms or guidelines, to solidify its choice of leaders and leadership styles, to carve out and begin enacting individual roles for its members, and to settle on particular patterns of communication that members feel to be comfortable and effective. These group dynamics (norms, leadership, roles, and communication patterns) form the primary concerns of the present section.

Norms

Norms are the overtly stated or covertly assumed rules of action specifying which behaviors are appropriate (prescriptive norms) or not appropriate (proscriptive norms) for group members. Thus norms are evaluative standards implying or even directly stating that some member behaviors are better or more desirable than others. Norms often come into being not so much by means of prior discussion and overt choice as by gradual use and implicit adoption. They may come to be assumed and taken for granted by group members and may only become evident when they are violated. Normative behavior may be adopted initially because of positive feelings of group cohesion; because continuation of membership is desired; or in order to avoid pressure, rejection, or other group sanctions. Eventually, such behavior comes to be internalized or "owned" by group members. Norms are the organizers, shapers, and broad guidelines determining much of what does or does not occur in any given group, what the group expects and aspires to achieve, how it allocates its resources, how it will be led, and much more.

Leadership

The topic of effective leaders and leadership has been a central concern of group dynamics researchers. For decades, through the 1940s, the "Great Man" theory of leadership prevailed. This view essentially held that effective leaders are persons who are born with or have come to possess certain personality traits and who, by dint of such characteristics, can and do lead in a variety of settings and situations. The research task thus became one of leadership-associated trait identification and, in fact, leaders have been shown to be somewhat more achievement-oriented, adaptable, alert, ascendant, energetic, responsible, self-confident, and sociable than other group members (Bass, 1981; Forsyth, 1983; Gibb, 1969). Over time, however, the correlations between these traits and effective leadership behavior proved modest. Although such traits certainly contribute to the success of leadership attempts, their importance was eclipsed by the potency of the group situation itself. Carron (1980) comments with regard to this more modern, situational view of leader effectiveness that

> it is now generally accepted that there are no inherent traits or dispositions within an individual which contribute to ascendancy and maintenance of leadership [across diverse situations]. Instead, it is believed that the specific requirements of different situations dictate the particular leadership qualities which will be most effective. (pp. 126–127)

Such situational thinking about leadership led to two research tasks. The first was the identification of specific behaviors, not traits, characteristic of acts of leadership. The second was the prescriptive determination of which leadership behaviors were optimal for which group members in which situations. Successful leadership, in this perspective, becomes a matter of matching leadership behaviors with appropriate situations (members, tasks, goals, settings) for their use. The Ohio State Leadership Studies (Hemphill & Coons, 1957) identified the following behaviors as constituting what leaders actually do: initiation, membership, representation, integration, organization, domination, communication, recognition, and production. Consistent with the situational view of effective leadership, Chelladurai and Saleh (1978) applied the Ohio State results to coaching behavior in athletic contexts. Table 15 indicates how leader behavior is held to vary optimally by task demand.

Though their categories of leadership behavior vary somewhat, both studies yield two broad classes of effective leadership behavior—

Table 15
Leader Behavior Dimensions in Sport

Dimension	Description
Training behavior	Behavior aimed at improving the performance level of the athletes by emphasizing and facilitating hard and strenuous training, clarifying the relationships among the members
Autocratic behavior	Tendency of the coach to set himself (herself), apart from the athletes, and to make all decisions by himself (herself)
Democratic behavior	Behavior of the coach that allows greater participation by the athletes in deciding on group goals, practice methods, and game tactics and strategies
Social support behavior	Behavior of the coach indicating his (her) concern for individual athletes and their welfare and for positive group atmosphere
Rewarding behavior	Behavior of the coach that provides reinforcement for an athlete by recognizing and rewarding good performance

Note. From "Preferred Leadership in Sport," by P. Chelladurai and S. D. Saleh, 1978, Canadian Journal of Applied Sport Sciences, 3, p. 91. Reprinted by permission.

namely, those that are task-oriented and focus on performance and group goals and those that are relationship-oriented and hence more concerned with enhancing group cohesiveness and reducing group conflict. This view of group leadership behavior as consisting of two broad dimensions—task orientation and relationship orientation—has become quite popular in group dynamics theory and research, taking the several diverse expressions reflected in Table 16.

As the situational view of effective leadership proposes, research demonstrates that neither a task nor a relationship orientation is uniformly optimal. With some groups, under some circumstances, and when working towards certain goals, a task focus on work, production, performance, and solutions is appropriate. For other situations, support, relationships, conflict reduction, and similar emphases are appropriate.

Table 16

The Two Basic Dimensions of Leadership Behavior

Leadership dimensions	Alternative labels	Conceptual meaning	Sample behaviors
Consideration	Relationship orientation Socioemotional Supportive Employee centered Relations skilled Group maintenance	Degree to which the leader responds to group members in a warm and friendly fashion; involves mutual trust, openness, and willingness to explain decisions.	Listens to group members Easy to understand Is friendly and approachable Treats group members as equals Is willing to make changes
Initiating structure	Task orientation Goal oriented Work facilitative Production centered Administratively skilled Goal achiever	Extent to which leader organizes, directs, and defines the group's structure and goals; regulates group behavior, monitors communication, and reduces goal ambiguity.	Assigns tasks to members Makes attitudes clear to the group Is critical of poor work Sees to it that the group is working to capacity Coordinates activity

Sources. Halpin and Winer (1952); Lord (1977). Reprinted from *An Introduction to Group Dynamics* (p. 215), by D. R. Forsyth, 1983, Monterey, CA: Brooks/Cole.

Not surprisingly, there appear to be many group situations in which the most effective leadership behaviors reflect a balanced combination of task and relationship orientations.

Other category systems of leadership behavior exist. Lewin's research team (Lewin, Lippitt, & White, 1939; White & Lippitt, 1968) early on offered the dimensions of authoritarian, democratic, and laissez-faire leadership. Vroom and Yetton (1973) more recently suggested autocratic, consultative, and group leadership behavioral patterns. What is noteworthy about these, and other, leadership category systems is the uniformity in agreeing that, whatever the system, one must first take account of the "attributes of the group situation to consider in judging which type of leadership to use" (Forsyth, 1983, p. 235).

Roles

Leader is but one of many roles assumed by group members. As is the case for the leader, the way in which an individual in the group behaves at a given point in time is partly a matter of that individual's dispositions or traits, but it is even more so a result of the situational demands and opportunities operating within the group. Such situational determinants of members' roles include the leader's behavior, the behavior of other group members, the group's cohesiveness level, group tasks, group communication patterns, group goals, and other salient group characteristics. As it has for the role of leader, group dynamics thinking has gravitated toward categorizing member behavior in terms of task-oriented roles and relationship-oriented (socioemotional) roles, as detailed in Table 17.

Table 17
Task Roles and Socioemotional Roles in Groups

Role	Function
Task roles	
1. Initiator contributor	Recommends novel ideas about the problem at hand, new ways to approach the problem, or possible solutions not yet considered.
2. Information seeker	Emphasizes "getting the facts" by calling for background information from others.
3. Opinion seeker	Asks for more qualitative types of data, such as attitudes, values, and feelings.

Table 17 *(continued)*

Role	Function
4. Information giver	Provides data for forming decisions, including facts that derive from expertise.
5. Opinion giver	Provides opinions, values, and feelings.
6. Elaborator	Gives additional information—examples, rephrasings, implications—about points made by others.
7. Coordinator	Shows the relevance of each idea and its relationship to the overall problem.
8. Orienter	Refocuses discussion on the topic whenever necessary.
9. Evaluator-critic	Appraises the quality of the group's efforts in terms of logic, practicality, or method.
10. Energizer	Stimulates the group to continue working when discussion flags.
11. Procedural technician	Cares for operational details, such as the materials, machinery, and so on.
12. Recorder	Provides a secretarial function.
Socioemotional roles	
1. Encourager	Rewards others through agreement, warmth, and praise.
2. Harmonizer	Mediates conflicts among group members.
3. Compromiser	Shifts his or her own position on an issue in order to reduce conflict in the group.
4. Gatekeeper and expediter	Smooths communication by setting up procedures and ensuring equal participation from members.
5. Standard setter	Expresses, or calls for discussion of, standards for evaluating the quality of the group process.
6. Group observer and commentator	Informally points out the positive and negative aspects of the group's dynamics and calls for change if necessary.
7. Follower	Accepts the ideas offered by others and serves as an audience for the group.

Note. From "Functional Roles of Group Members," by K. D. Benne and P. Sheats, 1948, *Journal of Social Issues, 4,* p. 46. Reprinted by permission.

Communication Patterns

A final aspect of the norm-setting process occurring in groups is the establishment and maintenance of viable communication patterns or networks by means of which the group will conduct its task- and relationship-oriented business. The communication network(s) established in any given group reflect many qualities of the group but most especially its preferred leadership style and the nature of its goals. Figure 6 depicts three of the more common communication patterns.

Each letter in these networks represents a different group member, and each line represents a two-person communication linkage. Marked variability exists among these networks in the degree to which members are free to communicate with one another. Group member *B*, for example, is free to communicate with all other group members in the Comcon (or All-channel) network, with two other members (*A* and *C*) in the Circle network, and with only one other member (*C*) in the Wheel network. Differences also exist in member centrality—that is, in the number of linkages tied to members—and the number of linkages (distance) from them to each other member. In the Wheel network, member *C* is most central. Within the other two networks, all members are equally central or peripheral. Studies demonstrate that, in centralized networks like the Wheel, central position members (leader, teacher, boss) are more satisfied than are peripheral members. Most people, in fact, tend to prefer one or another decentralized network since it permits, and may even encourage, independence of action, autonomy, and self-direction (Shaw, 1964). Centralized networks organize more rapidly, are more stable in performance, and are most efficient for the performance of simple tasks. However, as task complexity grows, the decentralized networks prove superior (Shaw, 1964). This finding is one more example of the need to vary a group characteristic depending on the situation—in this instance, the group's task.

Figure 6
Communication Networks Relevant to Group Therapy Leadership

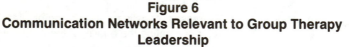

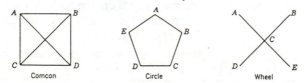

Note. From *Psychotherapy and the Psychology of Behavior Change* (p. 383), by A. P. Goldstein, K. Heller, and L. B. Sechrest, 1966, New York: Wiley. Reprinted by permission.

Performing

The tasks facing the youngster in peer, family, school, or other groups are numerous and varied. As such groups develop, deal with conflict, and establish participation norms and roles, they concomitantly seek to perform the tasks that motivated the group's formation in the first place. In this section, we will present the approaches group dynamicists have taken to categorize group tasks, examine means that have been identified for improving group performance on such tasks, and consider the implications for member performance of the use of power to wield influence. Finally, we will turn to such collective behaviors as deindividuation and groupthink in order to better understand the performance behavior of individuals in groups larger than those considered thus far.

Group Tasks

Forsyth (1983) points out that a group's specific tasks depend, in the first place, on the group's ultimate goals. Is the group organized to make decisions, solve problems, generate ideas, learn facts, create products? Tasks to be performed, according to Shaw (1981), are also determined by (1) the difficulty of the group's overall problem, (2) the number of acceptable solutions, (3) the intrinsic interest level of the task, (4) the amount of cooperation required of group members for successful task performance, (5) the intellectual and related demands presented, and (6) member familiarity with task components. Steiner (1972, 1976) has proposed a system of classifying tasks based on task divisibility, the type of performance desired, and the manner in which group member inputs contribute to group goals. This system is described by Forsyth (1983) in Table 18.

How well will the group perform its designated tasks? In part, the answer depends on task characteristics. On additive tasks, for example, it has been shown that the larger the group, the lower the quantity or quality of each individual's contribution to task performance. This so-called *Ringelmann effect* (Forsyth, 1983) has been explained by Latane, Williams, and Harkins (1979) as being due to "coordination losses" (e.g., pulling on a tug-of-war rope at different times) and "social loafing" (i.e., working less hard when one's own contribution to task performance will remain unknown by other group members). Conjunctive group tasks, as a second example, pose a different performance problem. Here, because all group members must contribute to task performance, the group as a whole performs at the level of its weakest member. As Forsyth (1983) notes, the speed of a group of mountain climbers, a

Table 18
A Summary of Steiner's Typology of Tasks

Question	Answer	Task type	Examples
Can the task be broken down into subcomponents or is division of the task inappropriate?	Subtasks can be identified	Divisible	Playing a football game, building a house, preparing a six-course meal
	No subtasks exist	Unitary	Pulling on a rope, reading a book, solving a math problem
Which is more important: quantity produced or quality of performance?	Quantity	Maximizing	Generating many ideas, lifting the greatest weight, scoring the most runs
	Quality	Optimizing	Generating the best idea, getting the right answer, solving a math problem
How are individual inputs related to the group's product?	Individual inputs are added together	Additive	Pulling a rope, stuffing envelopes, shoveling snow
	Group product is average of individual judgments	Compensatory	Averaging individuals' estimates of the number of beans in a jar, weight of an object, room temperature

508

Group selects the product from pool of individual members' judgments	Disjunctive	Questions involving "yes-no, either-or" answers such as math problems, puzzles, and choices between options
All group members must contribute to the product	Conjunctive	Climbing a mountain, eating a meal, relay races, soldiers marching in file
Group can decide how individual inputs relate to group	Discretionary	Deciding to shovel snow together, opting to vote on the best answer to a math problem, letting leader answer question

Sources. Steiner (1972, 1976). Reprinted from *An Introduction to Group Dynamics* (p. 151), by D. R. Forsyth, 1983, Monterey, CA: Brooks/Cole.

truck convoy, or a funeral procession is determined by its slowest member. However, conjunctive task performance can be improved if the task is divided and the weakest members are assigned to the least difficult subtasks.

Task performance is affected substantially by the group's task-relevant communication patterns. Deutsch and Krauss (1960), Harper and Askling (1980), Katz and Tushman (1979), and numerous other investigators have shown that, in comparison to unsuccessful groups, successful groups have a significantly higher rate and accuracy of communication.

The several techniques outlined earlier in this chapter for enhancing the quality of communication and the problem-solving methods examined in chapter 2 each hold considerable potential for contributing positively to task performance. However, task performance may be impeded when the group's climate and associated communication patterns become defensive. Forsyth (1983) comments as follows:

> Whenever members of a group feel personally threatened, they begin to behave defensively. Effort is shifted from the group tasks to defensive tactics, and individual efficiency drops as concern over evaluations, worry about others' intentions, counterattack planning, and defensive listening escalate. (p. 163)

Gibb (1961, 1973) proposes a number of ways in which groups engender such defensive, task-impeding communication and also highlights the features of a more supportive, communication-encouraging group climate (see Table 19).

Power

Thus far, we have proposed that performance in diverse groups is significantly influenced by the nature of the group's tasks, as well as by the rate and accuracy of members' task-relevant communication. However, task performance in group contexts is also a function of the relative power bases, levels, and tactics utilized by group leaders and group members. French and Raven (1959) proposed that an individual's power in a group context may derive from one or more of several sources (see Table 20). As is consistent with the situational view of group leadership presented earlier in this chapter, the effect and effectiveness of the five alternative bases for leader or member power or influence, as well as the effectiveness of whichever tactic(s) are employed to express them (see Table 21), are very much a function of characteristics of the particular group involved. Group cohesiveness;

Table 19

Characteristics of Defensive and Supportive Group Climates

Characteristic	Defensive climate	Supportive climate
1. Evaluation versus description	1. People in the group seem to be judging your actions.	1. People in the group are seen as trying to describe outcomes and information.
2. Control versus problem oriented	2. Others are seen as manipulative, attempting influence.	2. Others seem to be focused on the problem at hand.
3. Strategy versus spontaneity	3. Members seem to plan out their "moves," interactions, and comments.	3. Interaction seems to flow smoothly with little strategic control.
4. Neutrality versus empathy	4. People in the group seem to react to you with aloofness and disinterest.	4. People in the group seem to identify with your ideas and interests.
5. Superiority versus equality	5. Others seem condescending, acting as if they are better than you are.	5. Group members treat one another as equals.
6. Certainty versus provisionalism	6. Some people in the group seem to feel that their own ideas are undoubtedly correct.	6. People in the group are not committed to any one viewpoint, for they are keeping an open mind.

Sources. Gibb (1961, 1973). Reprinted from *An Introduction to Group Dynamics* (p. 164), by D. R. Forsyth, 1983, Monterey, CA: Brooks/Cole.

Table 20
Five Bases of Power

Label	Definition
1. Reward power	The powerholder's control over the positive and negative reinforcements desired by the target person.
2. Coercive power	The powerholder's ability to threaten and punish the target person.
3. Legitimate power	Power that stems from the target person's belief that the powerholder has a justifiable right to require and demand the performance of certain behaviors.
4. Referent power	Power that derives from the target person's identification with, attraction to, or respect for the powerholder.
5. Expert power	Power that exists when the target person believes that the powerholder possesses superior skills and abilities.

Source. J.R.P. French, Jr., & B. Raven (1959), "The Bases of Social Power," p. 160, in D. Cartwright (Ed.), *Studies in Social Power* (Ann Arbor: Institute for Social Research, The University of Michigan). Reprinted by permission.

the manner in which the group's leader has been selected, elected, or imposed; the group's size; and the group's task and any deadlines associated with its completion are among the several group qualities determining the impact of diversely based expressed power.

Falbo (1977) has shown that the power tactics described in Table 21 vary on two dimensions: rationality and directness. Bargaining, compromise, and persuasion are rational means for exerting influence on task performance; evasion, threat, and deceit are nonrational means. Threats, persistence, and fait accompli are direct power tactics; hinting and thought manipulation are more indirect. Research has shown that group leaders and members who are especially concerned with being accepted and liked by their fellow group members make heaviest use of rational and indirect influence tactics, rather than nonrational and direct means. In contrast, nonrational and indirect tactics are the power methods of choice for manipulative group members.

The foregoing discussion provides a sense of how power holders in groups seek to influence other group members. But what are the effects

Table 21
Examples and Definitions of Sixteen Power Tactics

Strategy	Definition	Example
Reason	Any statement about using reason or rational argument to influence others.	I argue logically. I tell all the reasons why my plan is best.
Expertise	Claiming to have superior knowledge or skills.	I tell them I have a lot of experience with such matters.
Compromise	Both agent and target give up part of their desired goals in order to obtain some of them.	More often than not we come to some sort of compromise, if there is a disagreement.
Bargaining	Explicit statement about reciprocating favors and making other two-way exchanges.	I tell her that I'll do something for her if she'll do something for me.
Persuasion	Simple statements about using persuasion, convincing, or coaxing.	I get my way by convincing others that my way is best.
Simple statement	Without supporting evidence or threats, a matter-of-fact statement of one's desires.	I simply tell him what I want.
Persistence	Continuing in one's influence attempts or repeating one's point.	I reiterate my point. I keep going despite all obstacles.
Assertion	Forcefully asserting one's way.	I voice my wishes loudly.
Thought manipulation	Making the target think that the agent's way is the target's own idea.	I usually try to get my way by making the other person feel that it is his idea.

Note. From "The Multidimensional Scaling of Power Strategies," by T. Falbo, 1977, *Journal of Personality and Social Psychology, 35,* p. 540. Reprinted by permission.

513

Table 21 *(continued)*

Strategy	Definition	Example
Fait accompli	Openly doing what one wants without avoiding the target.	I do what I want anyway.
Hinting	Not openly stating what one wants; indirect attempts at influencing others.	I drop hints. I subtly bring up a point.
Emotion-target	Agent attempts to alter emotions of target.	I try to put him in a good mood.
Threat	Stating that negative consequences will occur if the agent's plan is not accepted.	I'll tell him I will never speak to him again if he doesn't do what I want.
Deceit	Attempts to fool the target into agreeing by the use of flattering or lies.	I get my way by doing a good amount of fast talking and sometimes by telling some white lies.
Emotion-agent	Agent alters own facial expression.	I put on a sweet face. I try to look sincere.
Evasion	Doing what one wants by avoiding the person who would disapprove.	I got to read novels at work as long as the boss never saw me doing it.

of holding power on the power holder? First of all, researchers have found that, in experimental groups, people with power clearly tend to use it (Deutsch, 1973; Kipnis & Consentino, 1969). If successful in its use, they often feel self-satisfaction, overestimate their interpersonal influence, and assign themselves unrealistically positive self-evaluations (Kipnis, 1974). They may assume that they themselves are the major determinant of other people's behavior (Kipnis, Castell, Gergen, & Mauch, 1976), devalue those toward whom the influence attempt was directed (Zander, Cohen, & Stotland, 1959), and in other ways distance from and derogate the targets of their power tactics (Sampson, 1965;

Strickland, 1958). Powerful members of groups, in addition, will tend to protect the sources of their influence (Lawler & Thompson, 1979) and seek to expand upon it (McClelland, 1975).

Deindividuation and Groupthink

Deindividuation is the process of losing one's sense of individuality or separateness from others and becoming submerged in a group. A mob in a riot situation, an aroused audience at an athletic event or rock concert, a congregation at an emotional religious meeting, those listening to an impassioned speaker at a political rally, and the crowd assembled at a hostage event or watching a potential suicide unfold are all examples of large groups in which one can psychologically lose oneself and one's sense of self in the collective experience. Some have tried to explain this phenomenon in terms of "the convergence of people with compatible needs, desires, motivations, and emotions" (Forsyth, 1983, p. 311). In the last century, Le Bon (1895) held otherwise and put forth the view that deindividuated behavior in crowds and mobs was due to a process of contagion. He observed that riotous behavior, not unlike the spread of a physical disease, began at one point in the larger group and then involuntarily spread throughout it. Yet a third perspective seeking to explain deindividuation is the emergent-norm theory (Turner & Killian, 1972), in which a variety of group phenomena combine to foster the emergence of an array of arousal-associated and often antisocial behaviors. Forsyth (1983) correctly points out that all three explanations may fit a given instance of deindividuated collective behavior:

> The three perspectives on collective behavior—convergence, contagion, and emergent-norm theory—are in no sense incompatible with one another.... For example, consider the behavior of baiting crowds—groups of people who urge on a person threatening to jump from a building, bridge, or tower.... Applying the three theories, the convergence approach suggests that only a certain "type" of person would be likely to bait the victim to leap to his or her death. Those shouts could then spread to other bystanders through a process of contagion until the onlookers were infected by a norm of callousness and cynicism. (p. 315)

What is known about the deindividuation process? Zimbardo (1969) has described the conditions promoting it, the cognitive states reflecting it, and the overt behaviors characterizing it (see Table 22). A substantial amount of research evidence supports Zimbardo's observations regarding the causes, concomitants, and behavioral consequences of deindi-

Table 22
The Process of Deindividuation

Conditions of deindividuation →	The state of deindividuation →	Deindividuated behaviors
1. Anonymity	Loss of self-awareness	Behavior is emotional,
2. Responsibility	↓	impulsive, irrational, re-
3. Group membership	Loss of self-regulation	gressive, with high
4. Arousal	1. Low self-monitoring	intensity
5. Others (sensory overload, novel situations, drug usage, altered states of consciousness, and so on)	2. Failure to consider relevant norms	1. Not under stimulus control
	3. Little use of self-generated reinforcements	2. Counternormative
	4. Failure to formulate long-range plans	3. Pleasurable

Note. From "The Human Choice," by P.G. Zimbardo. Adapted by permission from the *1969 Nebraska Symposium on Motivation* (p. 293), edited by W.J. Arnold and D. Levine. Copyright © 1970 by the University of Nebraska Press, Lincoln. (Reprinted from Forsyth, 1983.)

viduation (Diener, 1976; Prentice-Dunn & Rogers, 1980; Singer, Brush, & Lublin, 1965; Zillman, Bryant, Cantor, & Day, 1975; Zimbardo, 1969).

A different, if related, influence of the group on individual member behavior has been termed *groupthink*. Forsyth (1983) defines this influence as

> a strong concurrence-seeking tendency that interferes with effective decision making.... At the core of the process is the tendency for group members to strive for solidarity and cohesiveness to such an extent that they carefully avoid any questions or topics that could lead to disputes. If members anticipate arguments over an issue, they never raise it. If they are unable to answer a question, they never ask it. If they can find shortcuts and reach simplistic solutions, they take them. Thus, as a result of an irrational emphasis on maintaining unanimity and cohesiveness, the group's decisions are ill-considered, impractical, and unrealistic. (p. 341)

Groupthink is not an uncommon phenomenon. It surfaces to varying degrees in groups that are highly cohesive, insulated, headed by a powerful leader, and under pressure to make important decisions (Janis, 1972, 1979). Gangs, certain committees, policy-making groups, industrial planning teams, and adolescent peer groups are all concrete examples of potential groupthink settings. Groupthink is more likely to occur when two sets of conditions are operating. The first is premature concurrence seeking or excessive in-group pressure early in the group's decision-making deliberations. Premature concurrence seeking occurs if certain factors exist: (1) high pressure to conform with norms that support compliance and rule out disagreement; (2) self-censorship of dissenting ideas; (3) "mindguards" diverting controversial information away from group consideration by "losing it, forgetting to mention it, or deeming it irrelevant and thus unworthy of the group's attentions" (Forsyth, 1983, p. 345); and (4) apparent unanimity, in which group members focus on their areas of agreement and deemphasize divergencies. The second set of conditions promoting groupthink involves illusions and misperceptions. These include illusions of invulnerability, illusions of morality, biased perceptions of the out-group, and collective rationalizing (Forsyth, 1983; Janis, 1972).

Correspondingly, groupthink can be reduced or eliminated by steps that limit premature concurrence seeking and that correct illusions and misperceptions. Premature concurrence seeking can be thwarted by promoting open inquiry and welcoming new ideas and perspectives; by moderating the directiveness of leader behavior; and by having the leader (1) delay stating her own beliefs until late in the group's discussion, (2) request that all pros and cons of an issue be presented and explored, (3) reward criticism and dissent, and (4) arrange for the group to meet without her on a number of occasions. Errors in perception can be corrected if (1) members acknowledge their own lack of knowledge on given topics and seek expert consultation, (2) an effort is made to understand the out-group's views and feelings, and (3) "second chance" meetings are held after the group reaches a tentative decision in order for residual doubts and questions to be raised and considered. Janis (1972) provides an interesting case study of the causes, development, and reduction of groupthink as it occurred with President Kennedy and his panel of advisors at the time of the Cuban Bay of Pigs invasion.

Adjourning

The peer group, family group, school group, or athletic group has established itself, dealt with areas of conflict, developed its norms of leader behavior and member roles, performed its task, and therefore reached its goal. It is thus time for the group to adjourn.

Group Activities

The group games, simulations, and activities listed in this section will provide participating youngsters with direct and clarifying experiences in the wide variety of group dynamics that constitute the growth and development of the many groups of which they will be a part. These activities, drawn from Pfeiffer and Jones' (1974) five-volume *Handbook of Structured Experiences for Human Relations Training,* are organized according to the same group-stages format devised by Tuckman (Tuckman, 1965; Tuckman & Jensen, 1977) and described in the first part of this chapter.

For each activity, we provide a title and goal statement, as offered by Pfeiffer and Jones, along with a citation directing the reader to the appropriate volume and pages of the *Handbook.* Full descriptions provided in this original source include discussion of materials, time requirements, physical setting, constituent procedures, and thematic variations.

Forming

1. Listening and Inferring: A Getting Acquainted Activity (Vol. 1, pp. 3–4)
   To facilitate the involvement of individuals in a newly formed group.
2. Who Am I? A Getting Acquainted Activity (Vol. 1, pp. 19–21)
   To allow participants to become acquainted quickly in a relatively nonthreatening way.
3. Who Am I? Variations: A Getting Acquainted Activity (Vol. 3, pp. 3–5)
   To allow participants to become acquainted quickly in a relatively nonthreatening way.
4. Group Conversation: Discussion Starters (Vol. 2, pp. 3–6)
   To develop a compatible climate and readiness for interaction in a group through sharing personal experience.
5. Verbal Activities within Groups: A Potpourri (Vol. 2, pp. 91–93)
   To provide a number of diverse activities useful as openers for groups that meet infrequently or as within-group interventions for groups that meet on a regular basis.
6. Getting Acquainted: A Potpourri (Vol. 4, pp. 3–4)
   An additional series of ice-breakers and facilitative activities for use in a variety of groups.
7. Group Development: A Graphic Analysis (Vol. 2, pp. 76–78)
   To compare members' perceptions of the developmental status of a group at a given time.

8. Graphics: Self-disclosure Activities (Vol. 1, pp. 88–89)
To generate self-disclosure data through often inhibition-reducing graphics activities.

Storming

9. Conflict Resolution: A Collection of Tasks (Vol. 1, pp. 70–71)
A variety of activities designed to generate data about, and provide experience in, how groups resolve conflict.
10. The In-group: Dynamics of Exclusion (Vol. 4, pp. 112–114)
To allow participants to experience excluding and being excluded and to examine processes by which social identity is conferred by the excluding group and accepted by the excluded member.
11. Discrimination: Simulation Activities (Vol. 3, pp. 62–63)
To explore interpersonal stereotyping and discrimination.
12. Model-building: An Intergroup Competition (Vol. 2, pp. 29–31)
To experience interpersonal and intergroup competition and the feelings and behaviors associated with winning and losing.
13. Towers: An Intergroup Competition (Vol. 3, pp. 17–21)
To experience intergroup competition and the feelings and behaviors associated with winning and losing.
14. Listening Triads: Building Communication Skills (Vol. 1, pp. 31–35)
To develop skills in active listening and study barriers to effective listening.
15. Rumor Clinic: A Communications Experiment (Vol. 2, pp. 12–15)
To illustrate distortions that may occur in transmission of information from an original source through several individuals to a final destination.
16. Ball Game: Controlling and Influencing Communication (Vol. 4, pp. 27–29)
To explore the dynamics of assuming leadership in a group and to increase awareness of the power held by the member of a group who is speaking at any given time.
17. Nonverbal Communication: A Collection of Activities (Vol. 1, pp. 101–103)
To explore channels of nonverbal communication and the manner in which they relate to verbal interaction.
18. Nonverbal Communication: A Collection of Activities (Vol. 2, pp. 94–96)

To explore channels of nonverbal communication and the manner in which they relate to verbal interaction.

19. Behavior Description Triads: Reading Body Language (Vol. 3, pp. 6–7)
To study the body language messages that accompany verbalization and alert group members to the variety of such signals they use to communicate.

Norming

20. Dyadic Encounter: A Program for Developing Relationships (Vol. 1, pp. 90–100)
To explore knowing and trusting another person through mutual self-disclosure and risk taking.

21. Process Observation: A Guide (Vol. 1, pp. 45–48)
To provide experiences for group members in observing process variables in group meetings.

22. Group Self-evaluations: A Collection of Instruments (Vol. 3, pp. 22–30)
To explore the norms that have developed in a group that has been meeting for a period of time and to help a group evaluate its own functioning.

23. Growth Group Values: A Clarification Exercise (Vol. 4, pp. 45–48)
To clarify group member values and explore values held in common within a group.

24. Group-on-Group: A Feedback Experience (Vol. 1, pp. 22–24)
To develop skills in process observation and in giving appropriate feedback to individual members.

25. Leveling: Giving and Receiving Adverse Feedback (Vol. 1, pp. 79–81)
To let participants compare their perceptions of how a group sees them with the actual feedback obtained from the group and to legitimize the act of giving negative feedback within a group.

26. Role Nominations: A Feedback Experience (Vol. 2, pp. 72–75)
To provide feedback to group members on the roles fellow members see them playing and to examine various types of roles in relation to group goals.

27. Nominations: Personal Instrumented Feedback (Vol. 3, pp. 33–40)

To analyze group climate and norms by studying member behavior, group composition, and members' expectations of one another.

28. Peer Perceptions: A Feedback Experience (Vol. 3, pp. 41–45)
To explore the degree to which each member is seen as similar and dissimilar to each other member.

29. The Gift of Happiness: Experiencing Positive Feedback (Vol. 4, pp. 15–17)
To experience giving and receiving positive feedback in a nonthreatening way and to promote a climate of trust within a group.

30. The Portrait Game: Individual Feedback (Vol. 4, pp. 24–26)
To allow participants to receive a composite feedback picture from the members of their group and to compare this to their individual perceptions of how the group experiences their behavior.

31. T–P Leadership Questionnaire: An Assessment of Style (Vol. 1, pp. 7–12)
To evaluate oneself in terms of task orientation versus relationship orientation.

32. Styles of Leadership: A Series of Role Plays (Vol. 5, pp. 19–33)
To explore the impact that leaders have on decision making in groups and to demonstrate the effects of hidden agendas.

33. Pins and Straws: Leadership Styles (Vol. 5, pp. 78–84)
To provide awareness of three leadership styles (autocratic, laissez-faire, and democratic) and the effects of these styles on the performance of subordinates.

Performing

34. Cash Register: Group Decision Making (Vol. 5, pp. 10–12)
To explore the impact that assumptions have on decision making and to demonstrate how decision making is improved by consensus seeking.

35. Top Problems: A Consensus-seeking Task (Vol. 1, pp. 49–55)
To compare the results of individual decision making with those of group decision making.

36. NORC: A Consensus-seeking Task (Vol. 2, pp. 18–23)
To discuss decision-making patterns in task groups.

37. Miniversity: Sharing Participants' Ideas (Vol. 2, pp. 7–9)
To provide for dissemination of information using group members as resources in task groups.

38. Line Up and Power Inversion: An Experiment (Vol. 3, pp. 46–48)
    To experience power inversion and to expand the individual's awareness of his influence on the group.
39. Cups: A Power Experience (Vol. 5, pp. 108–110)
    To increase awareness of the meanings of power and to experience giving, receiving, and not receiving power.
40. Stretching: Identifying and Taking Risks (Vol. 4, pp. 107–111)
    To help participants become aware of their risk-taking behavior and to encourage such behavior as a way of expanding participants' behavioral repertoires.

Chapter 12

Transfer and Maintenance

The courses that constitute the Prepare Curriculum are, in our view, a formidable array of demonstrated and potential means for enhancing the prosocial behavior of prosocially deficient youth. For more than half the courses presented, there already exists substantial evidence of resultant prosocial gain, an outcome we predict will be further advanced as these courses are increasingly utilized in appropriate combinations and sequences. But can these gains be generalized to settings and people other than those involved in the original training? And what of the durability or persistence over time of whatever gains do generalize? These are, respectively, questions of *transfer* and *maintenance,* the questions that the present chapter addresses. Historically, concern with transfer and maintenance of gains from psychological and psychoeducational interventions has passed through three phases: (1) intervention as inoculation, (2) train and hope, and (3) the development and use of transfer- and maintenance-enhancing procedures.

Intervention as Inoculation

Many traditional interventions—reflecting both a core belief in "personality change" as both the target and outcome in effective treatment and a their strong tendency to ignore environmental influences upon behavior—viewed successful intervention as a sort of psychological inoculation. The positive changes purported to have taken place within the individual's personality structure were supposed to arm her to deal effectively with problematic events wherever and whenever they might occur. That is, transfer and maintenance were viewed as automatically occurring processes, following by definition the within-intervention changes themselves. As Ford and Urban (1963) note in this regard, with reference to the prevailing psychoanalytic view on this matter,

> If the patient's behavior toward the therapist is modified, the changes are expected to transfer automatically to other situations. The conflicts involved in the neurosis all become directed toward the therapist during the "transference neurosis." They are not situation-specific. They are responses looking for an object to happen to. Thus, if they

are changed while they are occurring in relation to the therapist, they will be permanently changed, and can no longer attach themselves to any object in their old form. No special procedures are necessary to facilitate the transfer from the therapist to other situations if the therapist has successfully resolved the transference pattern of behavior. (p. 173)

Such purported automatic maintenance and transfer, diversely explained, also characterize the therapeutic positions of Adler (1924), Horney (1939), Rank (1945), Rogers (1951), and Sullivan (1953). In each instance, the view put forth is that, when the given therapy process results in positive intrapsychic changes in the patient, the patient is assumed to be able to "take these changes with him" and apply them where and when needed in the real-life environment. As Ford and Urban (1963) note, Rogers, like Freud,

assumes that changes in behaviors outside of the therapy interview will follow automatically upon changes in the self-evaluative thoughts and associated emotions during the therapy hour. Changes in the self-evaluative thoughts and their emotional concomitants result in reduced anxiety, improved discrimination among situational events and responses, more accurate symbolization of them, and greater confidence in one's own decisions. These provide the conditions from which more appropriate instrumental and interpersonal responses will naturally grow. (p. 435)

This intervention-as-inoculation perspective was thus quite widespread among diverse approaches to psychological change through the 1950s. Since transfer and maintenance were held to occur inexorably as a consequence of within-treatment gains, no call emerged for the development of purposeful means for their enhancement.

Train and Hope

In the 1960s and 1970s, it became increasingly clear, first on an intuitive basis and then based on a wealth of empirical follow-up evidence, that psychological inoculation was far more myth than reality. In fact, we held, much of what constituted traditional psychotherapy was anti-transfer and anti-maintenance in its design and impact:

If we wish to minimize the transfer of psychotherapy learning to extra-therapy situations, a number of things may be done. First, a single therapist should provide some rather distinctive personal cues, such as appearance, dress, and manner, that would mark him as a rather special person, different from others. Second, an unvarying and powerful stimulus pattern should provide a context for the therapy, thus ensuring that whatever responses may be developed would become very strongly attached to the unique therapy stimuli. For example, the therapist would use one office for every situation. The furniture in the office would be distinctive and it would not vary from session to session. There should be some stimuli which would identify the office as such and mark it off from other places; for example, diplomas on the wall, bookshelves, and filing cabinets. And, not to belabor the point unduly, the therapy would be conducted on the same day of every week, at the same time of day, and for some standard length of time, say 50 minutes.

Although the picture we have just drawn may seem exaggerated, we are convinced that it is substantially justified. It is evident to us that the field of psychotherapy can profit greatly from a more intent look at its practices and possibilities from the standpoint of the concept of transfer of training. (Goldstein, Heller, & Sechrest, 1966, p. 226)

Psychotherapy research as a viable enterprise was initiated in the 1950s and grew in both quantity and scope during the 1960s and 1970s. Much of the outcome research conducted at the time included systematic follow-up probes, which sought to ascertain whether gains evident at the termination of formal intervention had generalized across settings and/or time. Stokes and Baer (1977) described this phase as one in which transfer and maintenance were hoped for and noted but not pursued. They comment as follows:

Studies that are examples of Train and Hope across time are those in which there was a change from the intervention procedures, either to a less intensive but procedurally different program, or to no program or no specifically defined program. Data or anecdotal observations were reported concerning the maintenance of the original behavior change over the specified time intervening between the termination of the formal program and the postchecks. (p. 351)

The overwhelming result of these many investigations was that, much more often than not, transfer and maintenance of intervention gains did not occur. Treatment and training did not often serve as an inoculation; gains did not persist automatically; transfer and maintenance did not necessarily follow from the initial training and the hoped-for generalization of its effects (Goldstein & Kanfer, 1979; Hayes, Rincover, & Solnick, 1980; Karoly & Steffen, 1980; Kauffman, Nussen, & McGee, 1977; Kazdin, 1975; Keeley, Shemberg, & Carbonell, 1976). Marlatt and Gordon (1980) demonstrated, in fact, that relapse was a common follow-up outcome (especially with addictive disorders). However, highlighting the potency of the environment in determining whether transfer or maintenance occurs, results revealed that 76 percent of the relapse episodes could be accounted for by environmental demands requiring coping with social pressures, interpersonal conflict, and the negative emotional states the pressures and conflict subsequently engendered. If such be the case, these several writers chorused, then transfer and maintenance must be actively sought. In fact, the failure of inoculation thinking, as revealed by the evidence accumulated during the train-and-hope phase, indeed led to the third, current phase of concern with generalization—the energetic development, evaluation, and clinical use of a number of procedures explicitly designed to enhance transfer and maintenance of intervention gains.

The Development of
Transfer and Maintenance Enhancers

The early call by ourselves and others for the development of transfer and maintenance enhancers also made explicit the belief that the enhancement that might result would have its roots in the empirical literature on learning and its transfer in nonclinical contexts:

> A different assumption regarding response maintenance and transfer of therapeutic gains has in recent years begun to emerge in the psychotherapy research literature, especially that devoted to the outcome of behavior modification interventions. This assumption also rests on the belief that maintenance and transfer of therapeutic gain are not common events but, instead of positing that they should occur via an automatic process whose instigation lies within the procedures of the therapy itself, the position taken is that new maintenance-enhancing and transfer-enhancing techniques must be developed and purposefully and systematically incorporated into the ongoing treatment process. Thus, not satisfied that "behaviors usually extinguish when a program is withdrawn (Kazdin, 1975, p. 213)," or that "removal of the contingencies usually results in a decline of performance to or near baseline levels (Kazdin, 1975, p. 215)," a number of therapy practitioners and researchers are actively seeking to identify, evaluate, and incorporate into ongoing treatment a series of procedures explicitly designed to enhance the level of transfer which ensues. As we have stated elsewhere, the starting point in this search for effective gain maintenance and transfer-enhancers is clear: We need specific knowledge of the conditions under which learning or other changes that take place in therapy will be carried over into extra-therapy

situations. . . . We cannot assume that a behavior acquired in the therapy situation, however well learned, will carry over into other situations. Unquestionably the phenomena of therapy are orderly and lawful; they follow definite rules. We must, then, understand the rules that determine what responses will be generalized, or transferred, to other situations and what responses will not. As a first approximation to the rules obtaining in psychotherapy, we suggest the knowledge gained from study of transfer of other habits. (Goldstein et al., 1966, p. 244)

The effort to develop effective and reliable means for maximizing transfer and maintenance, although clearly still in progress, has been largely successful. A variety of useful techniques have been developed, evaluated, and incorporated into clinical practice. These several procedures, which collectively constitute the current technology of transfer and maintenance enhancement, are listed in Table 23 and are examined in detail in the remainder of this chapter.

Table 23
Transfer- and Maintenance-enhancing Procedures

Transfer

1. Sequential modification
2. Provision of general principles (general case programming)
3. Overlearning (maximizing response availability)
4. Stimulus variability (training sufficient exemplars, training loosely)
5. Identical elements (programming common stimuli)
6. Mediated generalization (self-recording, self-reinforcement, self-instruction)

Maintenance

1. Thin reinforcement (increase intermittency, unpredictability)
2. Delay reinforcement
3. Fade prompts
4. Provide booster sessions
5. Prepare for real-life nonreinforcement
   a. Teach self-reinforcement
   b. Teach relapse and failure management skills
   c. Use graduated homework assignments
6. Program reinforcement
7. Use natural reinforcers
   a. Observe real-life settings
   b. Identify easily reinforced behaviors
   c. Teach reinforcement recruitment
   d. Teach reinforcement recognition

Transfer-enhancing Procedures

Sequential modification

Sequential modification refers to the utilization of an intervention in one setting (e.g., school, agency), testing for transfer in a second setting (e.g., home, playground) and, if transfer is not found to occur, implementing the same intervention in that second (or third, fourth, etc.) setting. Epps, Thompson, and Lane (1985) comment as follows:

> Stokes and Baer (1977) refer to generalization as the occurrence of behavior under different, nontraining conditions without implementing the same behavior-change program in these conditions as was used in the original training environment. Technically, then, sequential modification is not really an example of programming for generalization because what was originally a nontreatment setting... becomes a treatment setting when the intervention is implemented there.... It is a frequently used technique that may help students demonstrate appropriate behavior under a variety of conditions. (p. 100)

We will not dwell at length on this approach to enhancing appropriate behaviors in real-world contexts since we agree that, formally, it is not a transfer-enhancing technique. It is identified here because both its frequency of use and its behavior-spread goals are identical to those sought by the transfer-enhancing techniques we will now consider.

Provision of general principles

Transfer of training may be facilitated by providing the trainee with the general mediating principles that govern satisfactory performance on both the original and transfer tasks. The trainee can be given the rules, strategies, or organizing principles that lead to successful performance. This general finding—that mediating principles for successful performance can enhance transfer to new tasks and contexts—has been reported in a number of domains of psychological research. These include studies of labeling, rules, advance organizers, learning sets, and deutero-learning. It is a robust finding indeed, with empirical support in both laboratory (Duncan, 1953, 1958; Goldbeck, Bernstein, Hellix, & Marx, 1957; Hendrickson & Schroeder, 1941; Ulmer, 1939) and clinical psychoeducational settings, the latter including the scripted roles in Kelly's (1955) fixed role therapy; directives in Haley's (1976) problem-solving therapy; strategies in Phillips' (1956) assertion-structured therapy; principles in MacGregor, Ritchie, Serrano, and Schuster's

(1964) multiple impact therapy; problem-solving skills in Steiner, Wyckoff, Marcus, Lariviere, Goldstine, and Schwebel's (1975) radical therapy; and in many of the self-regulatory, mediational interventions that lie at the heart of cognitive behavior therapy (Kanfer & Karoly, 1972; Kendall & Braswell, 1985).

Overlearning

Transfer of training has been shown to be enhanced by procedures that maximize overlearning or response availability. The likelihood that a response will be available is very clearly a function of its prior usage. We repeat and repeat foreign language phrases we are trying to learn, we insist that our child spend an hour per day in piano practice, and we devote considerable time practicing to make a golf swing smooth and "automatic." These are simply expressions of the response-availability notion—that is, the more we have practiced (especially correct) responses, the easier it will be to use them in other contexts or at later times. We need not rely solely on everyday experience. It has been well-established empirically that, other things being equal, the response that has been emitted most frequently in the past is more likely to be emitted on subsequent occasions. This finding is derived from studies of the frequency of evocation hypothesis and the spew hypothesis (Underwood & Schultz, 1960), preliminary response pretraining (Atwater, 1953; Cantor, 1955; Gagne & Foster, 1949), and overlearning (Mandler, 1954; Mandler & Heinemann, 1956). In all of these related research domains, real-life or laboratory-induced prior familiarization with given responses increased the likelihood of their occurrence on later trials. Mandler (1954) summarizes much of this research as it bears upon transfer by noting that "learning to make an old response to a new stimulus showed increasing positive transfer as the degree of original training was increased" (p. 412). Mandler's own studies of overlearning are especially relevant to our present theme because it is not sheer practice of attempts at prosocially effective behaviors that is of most benefit to transfer, it is practice of successful attempts.

Overlearning involves extending learning over more trials than are necessary merely to produce initial changes in the individual's behavior. In all too many instances of near-successful training, one or two successes at a given task are taken as evidence to move on to the next task or the next level of the original task. This is a training technique error if one wishes to maximize transfer via overlearning. Mandler's (1954) subjects were trained on the study task until they were able to perform it without error (0, 10, 30, 50, or 100 consecutive times). As noted earlier, transfer varied with the degree of original learning. To maximize transfer through the use of this principle, the guiding rule should not be *practice makes perfect* (implying that one simply practices until one gets it right and then moves on), but *practice of perfect* (implying numerous overlearning trials of correct responses after the initial success).

Stimulus variability

In the previous section, we addressed enhancement of transfer by means of practice and repetition—that is, by the sheer number of correct responses the trainee makes to a given stimulus. Transfer is also enhanced by the variability or range of stimuli to which the individual responds. For example, Duncan (1958) has shown that, on a paired-associates task, transfer is markedly enhanced by varied training. Training on even only two stimuli is better than training on a single stimulus. Other investigators have obtained similar results in concept attainment tasks, showing more rapid attainment when a variety of examples is presented (Callantine & Warren, 1955; Shore & Sechrest, 1961). As we noted several years ago in response to such studies, "The implication is clear that in order to maximize positive transfer, training should provide for some sampling of the population of stimuli to which the response must ultimately be given" (Goldstein et al., 1966, p. 220). As Kazdin (1975) comments,

> One way to program response maintenance and transfer of training is to develop the target behavior in a variety of situations and in the presence of several individuals. If the response is associated with a range of settings, individuals, and other cues, it is less likely to be lost when the situations change. (p. 211)

Epps et al. (1985) discuss stimulus variability for transfer enhancement purposes as it might operate in a special education context under the rubrics *train sufficient examples* and *train loosely.* They observe that

> generalization of new skills or behaviors can also be facilitated by training students under a wide variety of conditions. Manipulating the numbers of trainers, settings, and response classes involved in the intervention promotes generalization by exposing the student to a variety of situations. (p. 26)

Stimulus variability has only a modest history of use in clinical and psychoeducational contexts thus far—for example, multiple impact therapy by MacGregor et al. (1964); use of multiple therapists by

Dreikurs, Schulman, and Mosak (1952), Hayward, Peters, and Taylor (1952), and Whitaker, Malone, and Warkentin (1966); round-robin therapy (Holmes, 1971); and rotational group therapy (Frank, 1973; Slavin, 1967). In the clinical realm of anger management, Feindler and Ecton (1986) urge the employment of stimulus variability (varied task training) for transfer enhancement purposes through the use of diverse role-play stimulus situations. In their training for anger control (see chapter 5), they note that chronically aggressive youngsters respond to such provocations as the following:

1. Conflict over property, money, relationships, trust, teasing, drugs, sex, and pressure to conform, as well as family conflict over curfew, household responsibilities, money, friends, personal property, other restrictions, personal hygiene, and habits.

2. Conflict with authority figures such as teachers, counselors, probation officers, police officers, bus drivers, lifeguards, salespeople, and so forth (usually revolving around rule violation and punishment).

3. Conflict with unknown peers such as members of other groups whom the adolescent does not know (e.g., those in a class or a gang). These conflicts usually involve some sort of provocative act, such as stealing, teasing, or ignoring.

Identical elements

In perhaps the earliest experimental work dealing with transfer enhancement, Thorndike and Woodworth (1901) concluded that, when there was a facilitative effect of one habit on another, it was to the extent that, and because, habits shared identical elements. Ellis (1965) and Osgood (1953) have more recently emphasized the importance for transfer of similarity between characteristics of the training and application tasks. As Osgood (1953) notes, "the greater the similarity between practice and test stimuli, the greater the amount of positive transfer" (p. 213). This conclusion rests on a particularly solid base of experimental support, involving studies of both motor (Crafts, 1935; Duncan, 1953; Gagne, Baker, & Foster, 1950) and verbal (Osgood, 1949, 1953; Underwood, 1951; Young & Underwood, 1954) behaviors.

In the contexts of psychotherapy and psychoeducational training, the principle of identical elements could be implemented by procedures that function to increase the "real-lifeness" of the stimuli (people, behaviors, places, events, etc.) to which the therapist or trainer is helping the target person learn to respond with effective, satisfying behaviors. There exist two broad strategies for attaining such high levels of veridicality between in-therapy and extra-therapy stimuli. The first is to move the training or therapy out of the typical office setting and into the very interpersonal and physical context in which the person's real-life difficulties are being experienced. Such in vivo interventions are, in fact, a growing reality; the locus of at least some approaches has shifted to homes, planes, bars, elevators, and other problem sites (Sherman, 1979; Sherman & Levine, 1979). To be sure, the several marital and family therapies are all examples of use of identical elements in the interpersonal sense since the persons treated and the persons to whom they must apply their therapeutic learnings are one and the same.

The second broad approach to maximizing identical elements—or, as Epps et al. (1985) put it, *programming common stimuli*—is to remain in a training setting but to enhance its physical and/or interpersonal real-lifeness. We regularly follow this strategy in our prosocial skills training with aggressive adults and youth by creating role-play contexts (with each trainee's help) that appear like and feel like "the real thing" (Goldstein et al., 1986). Transitional living centers and the systematic use of *barbs* (Epps et al., 1985) or *red flags* (McGinnis & Goldstein, 1984) in classroom contexts are each examples of promoting transfer by maximizing identical elements.

Mediated generalization

The one certain commonality, which by definition is present in both training and application settings, is the individual target trainee. Mediated generalization—mediated by the trainee, not others—is an approach to transfer enhancement that relies upon instructing the trainee in a series of context-bridging, self-regulation competencies (Kanfer & Karoly, 1972; Neilans & Israel, 1981). Operationally, it consists of instructing the trainee in self-recording, self-reinforcement, self-punishment, and self-instruction. Epps et al. (1985), working in a special education setting, have structured these generalization-mediating steps as follows:

Self-recording

1. The teacher sets up the data collection system—that is, selects a target behavior, defines it in measurable terms, and decides on an appropriate recording technique;
2. The teacher tries out the data collection system;
3. The teacher teaches the trainee how to use the data collection system;
4. The teacher reinforces the trainee for taking accurate data.

Self-reinforcement
1. The teacher determines how many points a trainee has earned, and the trainee simply records these;
2. The teacher tells the trainee to decide how many points should be awarded for appropriate behavior;
3. The trainee practices self-reinforcement under teacher supervision;
4. The trainee employs self-reinforcement without teacher supervision.

Self-punishment
Self-punishment, operationalized in this example by response cost (taking away points), is taught in a manner directly parallel to that just described for self-reinforcement, in which the teacher employs the technique of fading.

Self-instruction
1. The teacher models the appropriate behavior while talking herself through the task out loud so that the trainee can hear;
2. The trainee performs the task with overt instructions from the teacher;
3. The trainee performs the task with overt self-instructions;
4. The trainee performs the task with covert self-instructions.

As the cognitive behavior modification therapies have grown in popularity in recent years, especially those relying heavily on self-instructional processes, self-mediated approaches to generalization have grown correspondingly in frequency of use.

Maintenance-enhancing Techniques
The persistence, durability, or maintenance of behaviors developed by means such as those presented in the Prepare Curriculum courses is primarily a matter of the manipulation of reinforcement both during the original training and in the post-intervention, real-world context. There are several specific means by which such maintenance-enhancing manipulation of reinforcement may proceed.

Thinning of reinforcement
A rich, continuous reinforcement schedule is optimal for the establishment of new behaviors. Maintenance of such behaviors will be enhanced if the reinforcement schedule is gradually thinned. Thinning of reinforcement will proceed best by moving from a continuous (all trials) schedule, to one or another form of intermittent schedule, to the level of sparse and infrequent reinforcement characteristic of the natural environment. In fact, the maintenance-enhancing goal of such a thinning

process is to make the trainer-offered reinforcement schedule indistinguishable from that typically offered in real-world contexts.

Delay of reinforcement

Resistance to extinction is also enhanced by delay of reinforcement. As Epps et al. (1985) note,

> During the early stages of an intervention, reinforcement should be immediate and continuously presented contingent on the desired response.... After the behavior becomes firmly established in the student's repertoire, it is important to introduce a delay in presenting the reinforcement. Delayed reinforcement is a closer approximation to reinforcement conditions in the natural environment. (p. 21)

Delay of reinforcement may be implemented, according to Sulzer-Azaroff and Mayer (1977) by (1) increasing the size or complexity of the response required before reinforcement is provided; (2) adding a time delay between the response and the delivery of reinforcement; and, (3) in token systems, increasing the time interval between receiving tokens and the opportunity to spend them and/or requiring more tokens in exchange for a given reinforcer.

Fading of prompts

Maintenance may be enhanced by the gradual removal of suggestions, reminders, prompts, or similar coaching or instruction. Fading of prompts is a means of moving away from artificial control (the trainer's) to more natural (self) control of desirable behaviors. As with all the enhancement techniques examined here, fading of prompts should be carefully planned and systematically implemented.

Booster sessions

Notwithstanding the importance of fading of prompts, it may be necessary periodically to reinstate instruction in the specifics of given appropriate behaviors in order for those behaviors to continue in the natural environment. Booster sessions between trainer and trainee, either on a preplanned schedule or as needed, have often proven quite valuable in this regard (Feindler & Ecton, 1986; Karoly & Steffen, 1980).

Preparation for natural environment nonreinforcement

Both trainer and trainee may take several energetic steps to maximize the likelihood that reinforcement for appropriate behaviors will occur in the natural environment. Nevertheless, on a number of occasions, reinforcement will not be forthcoming. Thus it is important for maintenance purposes that the trainee be prepared for this eventuality. As described in our earlier examination of mediated generalization, self-reinforcement is one means of responding in a maintenance-promoting manner when the desirable behaviors are performed correctly but are unrewarded by external sources. When the trainee performs the behaviors incorrectly or inappropriately in the natural environment, he will respond best to the environment's nonreinforcement if he has earlier learned skills and cognitive interpretations for dealing with relapse and failure experiences. Kendall and Braswell (1985) have proposed means for implementing this suggestion. A third way in which the trainee may be prepared for nonreinforcement in the natural environment, at least in the context of prosocial skills training and similar interventions, is the use of graduated homework assignments. In Interpersonal Skills Training (chapter 3), for example, skills role played successfully within group sessions are assigned as homework to be performed outside the group. The main actor's task is to perform the skills before the next session with the real-life parent, sibling, classmate, etc. portrayed by the co-actor in the role play. On occasion, it becomes clear as the homework is discussed that the real-life figure is too difficult a target, too harsh, too unresponsive, or simply too unlikely to provide reinforcement for competent skill use. When faced with this circumstance, with the newly learned skill still fragile and the potential homework environment looming as nonrewarding, we have recast the homework assignment toward two or three more benevolent and more responsive target figures. When the trainee finally does utilize the skill correctly with the originally skipped-over target figure and receives no contingent reinforcement, her string of previously reinforced trials help minimize the likelihood that the behavior will be extinguished.

Programming for reinforcement in the natural environment
The maintenance-enhancing techniques examined thus far are targeted toward the trainee himself—his reinforcement schedule, instruction, booster sessions, and preparation for nonreinforcing consequences. But maintenance of appropriate behaviors also may be enhanced by efforts directed toward others, especially those others in the trainee's natural environment who function as the main providers of the trainee's reinforcement. As Galassi and Galassi (1984) comment,

> Significant others can be trained to deliver the same or similar contingencies in the natural environment as occurred during treat-

ment. Parents, peers, and teachers can be taught to apply reinforcement for appropriate behavior.... Perhaps even better than individuals being taught new behaviors in a treatment setting by professionals and later having significant others trained to insure transfer to the natural environment, is training significant others initially to conduct the entire training process in the natural environment. (p. 12)

Patterson and Brodsky (1966); Nay (1979); Tharp and Wetzel (1969); and Walker, Hops, and Johnson (1975) are among the several investigators who have repeatedly demonstrated the efficacy of this now generally employed approach to maintenance enhancement.

Using natural reinforcers

A final and especially valuable approach to maintenance enhancement is the use of reinforcers that naturally and readily exist in the trainee's real-world environment. Stokes and Baer (1977) observe that

perhaps the most dependable of all generalization programming mechanisms is the one that hardly deserves the name: the transfer of behavioral control from the teacher-experimenter to stable, natural contingencies that can be trusted to operate in the environment to which the subject will return, or already occupies. To a considerable extent, this goal is accomplished by choosing behaviors to teach that normally will meet maintaining reinforcement after the teaching. (p. 353)

Galassi and Galassi (1984) offer the following similar comment:

We need to target those behaviors for changes that are most likely to be seen as acceptable, desirable, and positive by others. Ayllon and Azrin (1968) refer to this as the "Relevance of Behavior Rule." "Teach only those behaviors that will continue to be reinforced after training." (p. 10)

Alberto and Troutman (1982) suggest a four-step process that facilitates effective use of natural reinforcers: (1) observe which specific behaviors are regularly reinforced and how they are reinforced in the major settings that constitute the trainee's natural environment; (2) instruct the trainee in a selected number of such naturally reinforced behaviors (e.g., certain social skills, grooming behaviors); (3) teach the trainee how to recruit or request reinforcement (e.g., by tactfully asking peers or others for approval or recognition); and (4) teach the trainee how to recognize reinforcement when it is offered since its presence in certain gestures or facial expressions may be quite subtle for many trainees.

The call in the 1960s for a technology of transfer and maintenance enhancement has been vigorously and effectively answered. That technology, examined in this chapter, is substantial and still growing. Its full employment in the context of the Prepare Curriculum is most strongly recommended.

Chapter 13

Classroom Management

As we have indicated at a number of points earlier, the Prepare Curriculum is designed for a rather broad array of skill-deficient youth. Our intended trainees are both adolescent and younger, aggressive or withdrawn, antisocial or asocial, delinquent, just regularly "in trouble," or otherwise demonstrably deficient in the several prosocial behaviors that simultaneously constitute Prepare and—when well learned—augment the likelihood that one will lead an effective, satisfying, and socially responsible life. Many of the prosocial deficiencies we seek to remediate regularly manifest themselves in trainees' overt behavior during Prepare training itself: deficiencies in interpersonal skills, anger control, problem solving, use and understanding of group process, etc. Thus it is vital that, as part of our concern with Prepare Curriculum delivery, we attend directly to classroom management.

Problem Behaviors

What are the specific off-task or inappropriate behaviors that have emerged during Prepare classes? As described in detail in the following discussion, they seem largely to be manifestations of inactivity, hyperactivity, active resistance, or cognitive inadequacies and emotional disturbance.

Inactivity

Minimal participation involves trainees who seldom volunteer, provide only brief answers, and in general give the trainers a feeling that they are "pulling teeth" to keep the group at its various skills-training tasks.

A more extreme form of minimal participation is *apathy,* in which nearly everything the trainers do to direct, enliven, or activate the group is met with a lack of interest and spontaneity and little if any progress toward group goals.

While it is quite rare, *falling asleep* does occur from time to time. The sleepers need to be awakened, and the trainers might wisely inquire into the cause of the tiredness since boredom in the group, lack of sleep, and physical illness are all possible reasons, each requiring a different trainer response.

Hyperactivity

Digression is a repetitive, determined, and strongly motivated movement away from the purposes and procedures of the Prepare Curriculum. Here the trainees feel some emotion strongly, such as anger or anxiety or despair, and are determined to express it. Or the brief lecture given or the skill portrayed by the trainers or other trainees may set off associations with important recent experiences, which the trainees feel the need to present and discuss. Digression is also often characterized by "jumping out of role" in Prepare courses requiring role playing. Rather than merely wandering off track, in digression the trainees *drive* the train off its intended course.

Monopolizing involves subtle and not-so-subtle efforts by trainees to get more than a fair share of time during a Prepare session. Long monologues, unnecessary requests by the trainees to role play again, elaborate feedback, and attention-seeking efforts to "remain on stage" are examples of such monopolizing behavior.

Similar to monopolizing but more intrusive and insistent, *interruption* is literally breaking into the ongoing flow of a moral dilemma discussion, a stress management exercise, a cooperative game, a group leadership simulation, or a trainer's modeling display with comments, questions, suggestions, observations, or other statements. Interruptions may be overly assertive or angry, on the one hand, or they may take a more pseudo-benevolent guise of being offered as help to the trainer. In either event, such interruptions more often than not retard the group's progress toward its goals.

Excessive restlessness is a more extreme, more physical form of hyperactivity. The trainees may fidget while sitting; rock their chairs; get up and pace; or display other nonverbal, verbal, gestural, or postural signs of restlessness. Excessive restlessness will typically be accompanied by digression, monopolizing, or interrupting behavior.

Active Resistance

Trainees involved in *participation but not as instructed* are off target. They may be trying to role play, serve as co-actor, give accurate feedback, or engage in other tasks required in a given Prepare class, but their own personal agendas or misperceptions interfere, and they wander off course to irrelevant or semirelevant topics. As such, this problem behavior is related to digression, although digression is perhaps a more intense manifestation of off-task behavior.

Passive-aggressive isolation is not merely apathy, in which the trainees are simply uninterested in participating. Nor is it participation but not as instructed, in which trainees actively go off task and raise personal agendas. Passive-aggressive isolation is the purposeful, intentional withholding of appropriate participation, an active shutting down of involvement. It can be thought of as a largely nonverbal "crossing of one's arms" in order to display deliberate nonparticipation.

When displaying *negativism,* trainees signal more overtly, by word and deed, the wish to avoid participation in the Prepare class. They may openly refuse to be part of a game or simulation, do required exercises, listen to trainer instructions, or complete homework assignments. Or they may not come to sessions, come late to sessions, or walk out in the middle of a session.

Disruptiveness encompasses active resistance behaviors more extreme than negativism, such as openly and perhaps energetically ridiculing the trainers, other trainees, or aspects of the Prepare Curriculum. Or disruptiveness may be shown by gestures, movements, noises, or other distracting nonverbal behaviors characteristically symbolizing overt criticism and hostility.

Cognitive Inadequacies and Emotional Disturbance

Closely related at times to excessive restlessness, the *inability to pay attention* is often an apparent result of internal or external distractions, daydreaming, or other pressing agendas that command the trainees' attention. Inability to pay attention except for brief time spans may also be due to one or more forms of cognitive impairment.

Cognitive deficits due to developmental disability, intellectual inadequacy, impoverishment of experience, disease processes, or other sources may result in trainees' *inability to understand* aspects of the Prepare Curriculum. Failure to understand can, of course, also result from errors in the clarity and complexity of statements presented by the trainers.

Material presented in the Prepare class may be both attended to and understood by the trainees, but not remembered. *Inability to remember* may result not only in problems of skill transfer, but also in group management problems when what is forgotten includes rules and procedures for trainee participation, homework assignments, and so forth.

Bizarre behavior is not common, but when instances of it do occur they can be especially disruptive to group functioning. This type of group management problem may not only pull other trainees off task, but it may also frighten them or make them highly anxious. The range of bizarre behaviors possible is quite broad, including talking to oneself or inanimate objects, offering incoherent statements to the group, becoming angry for no apparent reason, hearing and responding to imaginary voices, and exhibiting peculiar mannerisms.

Our goal in seeking to reduce these behaviors is straightforward: to maximize the level of youth involvement, on-task time, and, thus, potential learning and to minimize time spent in distraction, aggression, or other off-task behaviors. In addition to potentiating curriculum learning, effective use of classroom management procedures can directly promote the later use of prosocial behavior via such processes as the provision of reinforcement following their utilization.

It is our belief that both trainee behaviors promoting classroom learning as well as behaviors inhibiting such progress can optimally be managed via skilled use of behavior modification techniques. As will be made clear throughout this chapter, this belief in the effectiveness of behavior modification technology rests upon a firm experimental foundation.

Beyond the repeated demonstration that "they work," behavior modification techniques are relatively easy to learn and utilize; may be teacher-, peer-, parent-, and/or self-administered; are generally cost-effective; yield typically unambiguous behavior-change results; have a long history of successful application (with aggressive youngsters in particular); and, for these several reasons, can maximize the opportunity in both available time and student accessibility for teachers to do most what teachers do best: teach!

That, as the expression goes, is the good news. Many persons see a darker, much less positive side to the use of behavior modification. Some of its constituent techniques are viewed as bribery and as likely to cause a contagion of disruptive behaviors as nondisruptive youngsters see their more aggressive peers receive rewards for reducing their levels of disruptiveness. All behavior modification techniques, critics further hold, are unfair, highly manipulative, mechanistic, overly simplistic, demanding of extra teacher effort, and, more generally, encouraging of a view of people as objects to be acted upon. We address these serious ethical and philosophical reservations and objections later in this chapter. At this point, however, it is appropriate to turn directly to the methodological substance of behavior modification. We wish to sketch briefly the historical development of behavior modification and to define and describe its major behavior-change procedures and the rules optimally governing their utilization, especially as regards aggression-reducing and prosocial-behavior-enhancing interventions that may be readily employed in classroom settings.

Behavior Modification Techniques

Behavior modification is a set of techniques, derived from formal learning theory, systematically applied in an effort to change observable behavior and rigorously evaluated by experimental research. Almost all of its constituent techniques derive from the basic premise developed by Skinner and his followers (Ferster & Skinner, 1957; Skinner, 1938, 1953) that behavior is largely determined by its environmental consequences. In a broadly operational sense, this premise has found expression in techniques that, by one means or another, contingently present or withdraw rewards or punishments (i.e., environmental consequences) to alter the behavior preceding these consequences. It is this contingent quality that has led to the use of the term *contingency management* to describe most of the activities in which the behavior modifier engages. Specifically, if one's goal is to increase the likelihood that a given (e.g., prosocial) behavior will occur, one follows instances of its occurrence with positive consequences—that is, by means of one or another technique for presenting a reward or removing an aversive event. In a directly analogous management of contingencies, if one's goal is to decrease the likelihood that a given (e.g., antisocial) behavior will occur, one follows instances of its occurrence with negative consequences—that is, by means of one or another behavior modification technique for presenting an aversive event or removing a rewarding event. To decrease the disruptiveness, aggression, or acting-out behavior of a given youngster and simultaneously to increase the chances that he will behave in a constructive, attentive, prosocial manner, the skilled behavior modifier will often use a combination of aversive or reward-withdrawing techniques (for the aggressive behaviors) and aversiveness-reducing or reward-providing techniques (for the constructive behaviors). A few definitions will help clarify further the substance of the contingency management process.

A *reinforcer* is an event that increases the subsequent frequency of any behavior it follows. When the presentation of an event following a behavior increases its frequency, the event is referred to as a *positive reinforcer.* Praise, special privileges, tokens or points exchangeable for toys, or snacks are a few examples of positive reinforcers. When the removal of an event following a behavior increases the subsequent frequency of the behavior, the event is referred to as a *negative reinforcer.* When a youngster ceases to behave in a disruptive manner following her teacher's yelling at her to do so, we may say that the youngster has negatively reinforced, and thus increased the future likelihood of, teacher yelling. When the presentation of an event following a behavior decreases its subsequent frequency, the event is referred to as a *punisher.* In the preceding example, the teacher's yelling, which was negatively reinforced by the student's decrease in disruptive behavior, functions as a punishment to the student to the extent that it decreases the likelihood of subsequent student disruptiveness. A second way of decreasing the probability of a given behavior is by removing positive reinforcers each time the behavior occurs. Ignoring the behavior or removing the reinforcer of attention (i.e., extinction), physically removing the person from important sources of reinforcement (i.e., time out), and removing the reinforcers from the person (i.e., response cost) are three means of contingently managing behavior by *removing positive reinforcers.* To repeat, these four groups of techniques—positive reinforcement, negative reinforcement, punishment, and the removal of positive reinforcers—constitute the core methods of contingency management, from which stem all the specific contingency management techniques described later in this chapter.

It will aid in understanding the relationship among these four procedures, as well as their characteristic implementation in classroom settings, to point out that they are all means for either presenting or removing positive reinforcers or presenting or removing aversive stimuli. The various procedures for presenting or removing positive reinforcement are by far the more common uses of contingency management in school contexts. We will examine these two sets of procedures first and in considerable depth. Procedures for the presentation of aversive stimuli (i.e., punishment) or for their removal (i.e., negative reinforcement) are appropriately employed less frequently in school and agency settings, and we will examine them more briefly following our consideration of positive reinforcement.

Early Applications

Though much of the basic thinking relevant to the contingency management approach to human behavior was available for a number of years (Mowrer & Mowrer, 1938; Skinner, 1938; Watson & Rayner, 1920), it was not until the 1950s that these methods began to find substantial, overt implementation in hospitals, clinics, schools, and other institutions in which one finds disturbed or disturbing youngsters.

Skinner's (1953) book *Science and Human Behavior* was a significant stimulus to this growth, as were a large number of investigations conducted during the 1950s and 1960s in the contexts just noted. All of these studies successfully demonstrated the behavior-change effectiveness of contingency management. Much of this research sought to alter the highly aggressive or otherwise severely deviant behavior of institutionalized emotionally disturbed, autistic, or developmentally disabled children and adolescents—and did so with considerable levels of success (Ayllon & Michael, 1959; Ferster & DeMeyer, 1962; Lovaas, Schaeffer, & Simmons, 1965; Wolf, Risley, & Mees, 1964). In outpatient clinic and laboratory settings, successful use of contingency management was reported with such diverse behaviors as delinquency (Patterson, Ray, & Shaw, 1968; Schwitzgebel, 1964), social withdrawal (Allen, Hart, Buell, Harris, & Wolf, 1964; Lovaas, Koegel, Simmons, & Long, 1973), fearfulness (Lazarus & Rachman, 1967; Patterson, 1965), hyperactivity (Allen, Kenke, Harris, Baer, & Reynolds, 1967; Hall, Lund, & Jackson, 1968), depression (Wahler & Pollio, 1968), anorexia (Bachrach, Erwin, & Mohr, 1965; Leitenberg, Agras, & Thomson, 1968), mutism (Sherman, 1965; Straughan, 1968), and dozens of other diverse deviant behaviors involving hundreds of youngsters. As is made explicit throughout this chapter, the general success of this orientation to behavior change has flowered further in the 1970s and 1980s, finding still wider application across many, many behaviors and settings. It is not surprising, given the breadth and depth of this successful demonstration of behavior-change effectiveness, that numerous studies evaluating the classroom application of contingency management have also been forthcoming. We will refer briefly to a number of these studies later, in the context of the particular contingency management technique to which they pertain.

Classroom Contingency Management Procedures

Classroom use of contingency management optimally begins with (1) selecting behavioral *goals;* (2) informing the class of the behavioral *rules* ideally followed in order to reach such goals; (3) observing and recording current (base rate) classroom *behavior;* and then (4) applying one or a combination of *behavior-change procedures* (the presentation or removal of positive reinforcement or the presentation or removal of aversive stimuli) in order to alter current undesirable behaviors in desirable goal directions. Let us examine each step in this process in detail.

Selecting Behavioral Goals

What will be the behavioral climate of the Prepare (or other) classroom? Which student behaviors will be defined by the teacher as truly disruptive and as impediments to learning and which will be tolerated and perhaps even welcomed as normative and maybe even facilitative of the learning process? Behavior-change goal selection should (1) concern itself with reducing those aggressive, disruptive, acting-out behaviors that interfere with the learning process; (2) be acutely responsive to normal developmental stages; and (3) be established to the extent possible in collaboration with the students themselves. Behavior modification should also be appropriately but not overly responsive to both teacher needs and the influence of overall school climate and policy on decisions about classroom decorum. Each teacher, we feel, must make his own decisions in this regard, but our position vis-à-vis behavioral goal setting is that it is better to err slightly on the side of permissiveness and underregulation than risk an overly conforming, perhaps rigid classroom climate that is likely to inhibit both aggression and enduring learning. Sarason, Glaser, and Fargo (1972) reflect this sentiment well in the following statement:

> Disruptive children can be managed, but if behavior modification is used to make children conform to a rigid idea of goodness or to squelch creativity or to force sterile compliance, the cost of an orderly classroom may be too high. Behavior modification is not intended to serve as a new type of tranquilizer. It is intended to serve as a means of facilitating efforts to bring about meaningful learning. (p. 13)

Teachers' decisions about behavioral goals for the classroom can meaningfully follow from thoughtful answers to such questions as the following:

1. What kind of student behavior interferes with the learning of the rest of the class, and what is perhaps annoying to you, but essentially harmless to the learner and his peers?
2. How much classroom freedom can be permitted without interfering with the rights of other students? On the other side of this coin, what are your responsibilities and the responsibilities of the students?
3. Should silence be maintained while children are working, or should reasonable communication among students be permitted, such as is encouraged in the "open classroom?"
4. Are your classroom regulations really for the benefit of the students or primarily for your own comfort and convenience?

5. Are you thinking about how the disruptive child can be helped to learn better, not just how his disruptive behavior can be decreased?

6. Have you been able to maintain an attitude of openness to new ideas and approaches which can benefit children even though they do not coincide with your personal biases?

7. Have you considered the attitudes and standards of the child and his family in setting standards for the child? Are your standards in conflict with theirs?

8. Have you discussed your goals for the class with the class?

9. Have you discussed your goals for the child with the child and his parents? (Sarason et al., 1972, p. 23)

These are not often easy questions to answer, but they reflect the fact that the teacher is primary among the several determiners of classroom behavior. Given this fact, we urge that such goals be selected in a careful, thoughtful, ethical manner in which conduciveness to learning is the central criterion.

Communicating Behavioral Rules

Having decided (with the class, one hopes) the behavioral directions in which the teacher wishes the class to head, particularly with regard to reducing aggressive and disruptive behaviors and increasing positive behaviors, the teacher should next clearly communicate to the students the rules and procedures they are to follow in order to attain these goals. A number of effective "rules for use of rules" have emerged in the contingency management literature (Greenwood, Hops, Delquadri, & Guild, 1974; Sarason et al., 1972; Walker, 1979), including the following:

1. Define and communicate rules for student behavior in clear, specific, and, especially, behavioral terms. As Walker (1979) notes, it is better (more concrete and behavioral) to say "Raise your hand before asking a question" than "Be considerate of others." Similarly, "Listen carefully to teacher instructions" or "Pay attention to the assignment and complete your work" are more likely to serve as rules that actually find expression in student behavior than the more ambiguous "Behave in class" or "Do what you are told."

2. It is more effective to tell students what to do, rather than what not to do. This accentuating of the positive would, for example, find expression in rules about taking turns, talking over disagreements,

or working quietly, rather than in rules directing students not to jump in, not to fight, or not to speak out.

3. Rules should be communicated in such a manner that students are aided in memorizing them. Depending on the age of the students and the complexity and difficulty of enacting the rules the teacher is presenting, such memorization aids may include keeping the rules short, keeping the rules few in number, repeating your presentation of the rules several times, and posting the rules in written form where they can readily be seen.

4. Rule adherence is likely to be more effective when students have had a substantial role in their development, modification, and implementation. This sense of participation may be brought about by explicit student involvement in rule development, thorough discussion of rules with the entire class, having selected students explain to the class the specific meaning of each rule, and student role play of the behaviors identified by the rule.

5. In addition to the foregoing, further effective rules for rules are that they be developed at the start of the school year before other less useful and less explicit rules emerge; that they be fair, reasonable, and within the students' capacity to follow; that all members of the class understand them; and that they be applied equally and evenly to all class members.

Observing and Recording Behavior

The teacher and the class have set behavioral goals to be worked toward and have defined the rules to be followed in getting there. The teacher's attention can now turn to the particular students displaying those aggressive, disruptive, rule-breaking, or goal-avoiding behaviors she wishes to modify. In doing so, the first task is to identify as concretely as possible the specific behaviors to be changed. Stated otherwise, the beginning stages of behavior modification include specification of desirable or appropriate behaviors (goal behaviors), behavioral means to reach these goals (rule behaviors), and behaviors to be altered (undesirable or inappropriate behaviors). This specification of undesirable behaviors ideally proceeds by means of systematic observation and recording. There are a number of purposes served by this process.

First, systematic observation and recording seek to identify not only which behaviors are undesirable, and thus possibly to be changed, but also the rate or frequency of such behaviors. This establishment of a *base rate* permits the teacher to determine later (against the base rate) whether the behavior is remaining constant, increasing in rate or frequency, or, as is hoped, actually decreasing. This *monitoring* of change in the behavior over time is, then, the second purpose of systematic observation and recording. Finally, because it is suggested that after the establishment of a base-rate level the teacher intervene with one or more contingency management procedures, the third purpose of observation and recording is to *evaluate* the success or failure of the completed intervention. At all three stages of this process—establishment of a base rate, monitoring, and evaluation of outcome—it is crucial that observation and recording be conducted in a systematic manner. Many authorities on classroom contingency management have commented that teacher guesses regarding the rate or frequency of a given student's aggressive, disruptive, or acting-out behavior are very often erroneously high. It is as if a small number of perhaps seriously disruptive behaviors by a student leads to a teacher's global impression of the student as a troublemaker or as chronically aggressive, an impression or label that often clouds the fact that most of the time that youngster is engaged in appropriate behaviors. Thus, for these reasons, it is crucial to obtain an accurate accounting of how often or how long the student engages in problematic behaviors.

Whom shall the observer be, especially given the obvious fact that the Prepare trainer often will have to strive to teach a full classroom of youngsters and not only those relative few who on occasion behave aggressively? The contingency management literature contains numerous examples not only of teachers as observer-recorders, but also of teacher aides, parents, peers, and the target youngsters themselves performing this task. Whoever serves in this capacity, the task is greatly facilitated by observing and recording by means prepared explicitly for such purposes. Recording sheets, special classroom behavior charts, wrist counters, and other similar means exist as aids to observer-recorders in systematically identifying and noting representative samples of the frequency or rate of student inappropriate behaviors (see Jackson, Della-Piana, & Sloane, 1975; Morris, 1976; Sarason et al., 1972; Walker, 1979). We refer the interested reader to these sources for such operational information and materials.

The following excerpt from Walker (1979) will help reiterate the all-important theme that, at all phases of the contingency management process, the teacher optimally will think and act in strictly behavioral terms. Commenting on the observation-recording process, Walker (1979) notes that

> pinpointing requires attention to the overt features of child behavior. Classroom behaviors that are capable of being pinpointed are characterized by being: (1) controllable, (2) repeatable, (3) containing

movement, (4) possessing a starting and ending point. Instances and noninstances of classroom behaviors that qualify as behavioral pinpoints are listed below:

Instances of Good Pinpoints
1. Argues
2. Steals
3. Does not comply with directions
4. Out of seat
5. Talks out
6. Has temper tantrums
7. Hits peers
8. Looks away from assigned tasks

Noninstances of Good Pinpoints
1. Hyperactive
2. Lazy
3. Belligerent
4. Angry
5. Hostile
6. Frustrated
7. Unmotivated (p. 55)

Applying Behavior-change Procedures

Identifying Positive Reinforcers
At this point in the contingency management sequence, the teacher is aware of goals, rules, and specific inappropriate behaviors. Our overall purpose is to substitute appropriate for inappropriate behaviors by means of skilled management of contingencies. As noted earlier, one major means for doing this is to present positive reinforcement to the trainee following and contingent upon the occurrence of an instance of appropriate behavior. Our earlier consideration of behavioral goals helped identify what constitutes appropriate behaviors. Before discussing optimal procedures for the actual presentation of positive reinforcers, however, we must first consider the process of identifying—both for a given youngster and for youngsters in general—just what events may in fact function as positive reinforcers.

Classroom contingency managers have worked successfully with four types of positive reinforcers: material, social, activity, and token. *Material reinforcers* (sometimes called *tangible reinforcers*) are actual goods or objects presented to the individual contingent upon enactment of appropriate behaviors. One especially important subcategory of material reinforcement, *primary reinforcement,* occurs when the contingent event presented satisfies a basic biological need. Food is one such primary reinforcer.

Social reinforcers—most often expressed in the form of attention, praise, or approval—are particularly powerful and are frequently used in the classroom. Both teacher lore and extensive experimental research testify to the potency of teacher-dispensed social reinforcement in influencing a broad array of personal, interpersonal, and academic student behaviors.

Activity reinforcers are those events the youngster freely chooses when an opportunity exists to engage in several different activities. Given freedom to choose, many youngsters will watch television rather than complete their homework. The parent wishing to use this activity reinforcer information will specify that the youngster may watch television for a given time period contingent upon the prior completion of the homework. Stated otherwise, the opportunity to perform a higher probability behavior (given free choice) can be used as a reinforcer for a lower probability behavior.

Token reinforcers, usually employed when more easily implemented social reinforcers prove insufficient, are symbolic items or currency (chips, stars, points, etc.) provided to the youngster contingent upon the performance of appropriate or desirable behaviors. Tokens thus obtained are exchangeable for a wide range of material or activity reinforcers. The system by which specific numbers of tokens are contingently gained or lost, and the procedures by which they may be exchanged for the backup material or activity reinforcers, is called a *token economy.*

In making decisions about which type of reinforcer to employ with a given youngster, the teacher should keep in mind that social reinforcement (e.g., teacher attention, praise, approval) is easiest to implement on a continuing basis and is most likely (for reasons discussed in chapter 12, dealing with transfer and maintenance) to lead to enduring behavior change. Thus it is probably the type of reinforcement the teacher will wish to utilize most frequently. Unfortunately, in the initial stages of a behavior-change effort—especially when aggressive, disruptive, and other inappropriate behaviors are probably being richly rewarded by the social reinforcement of teacher and peer attention as well as by tangible reinforcers—heavier teacher reliance on material and activity reinforcers for desirable behaviors will likely be more appropriate. Alternatively, a token reinforcement system may prove most effective as the initial reinforcement strategy. Youngsters' reinforcement preferences change over time, and teacher views of the appropriate reward value of desirable behaviors also change over time; both variable factors are easily reflected in token-level adjustments. For these and reasons related to ease of administration and effectiveness of outcome, the skilled contingency manager should be intimately acquainted with the full range of token-economy procedures (Ayllon & Azrin, 1968; Christophersen, Arnold, Hill, & Quilitch, 1972; Kazdin, 1975; Morris, 1976; Walker, Hops, & Fiegenbaum, 1976). Again, however, it is crucial to remember that, with few exceptions, it is desirable that reliance on material, activity, or token reinforcement eventually give way to reliance upon more "real-lifelike" social reinforcement. Table 24, excerpted from Safer and Allen (1976), lists specific examples of commonly used material (edible and nonedible), social, activity, and token reinforcers.

Given this wide though nonexhaustive array of potential reinforcers and the fact that almost any event may serve as a reinforcer for one individual but not another, how may the teacher or others decide which reinforcer(s) may be optimally utilized with a particular youngster at a given point in time? Most simply, the youngster can be asked straightforwardly which items he would like to earn. Often, however, this approach will not prove sufficient because youngsters are frequently not fully aware of the range of reinforcers available to them or, when aware, may discount in advance the possibility that the given reinforcer will actually be forthcoming in a particular instance. When this is the case, other identification procedures must be employed. Carr (1981) and others have reported three procedures that typically have been used for this purpose.

First, the teacher can often make an accurate determination of whether a given event is in fact functioning as a reinforcer by carefully *observing effects* on the youngster. The event probably is reinforcing if the youngster (1) asks that the event be repeated, (2) seems happy during the event's occurrence, (3) seems unhappy when the event ends, or (4) will work in order to earn the event. If one or more of these reactions are observed, the chances are good that the event is a positive reinforcer and that it can be contingently provided to strengthen appropriate, nonaggressive, or interactive behaviors.

Observing choices can also be helpful. As we noted earlier in connection with activity reinforcers, when a youngster is free to choose among several equally available activities, which one he chooses and how long he engages in the chosen activity are both readily observed clues to whether an event is reinforcing.

A small number of *questionnaires* exist that have been effectively utilized in identifying positive reinforcers. Tharp and Wetzel's (1969) Mediation-Reinforcer Incomplete Blank is one often used example. It consists of a series of incomplete sentences that the youngster must complete by specifying particular reinforcers: for example, "The thing I like to do best with my mother/father is _____ " or "I will do almost anything to get _____ ." Most of the items help specify not only the nature of the events the youngster perceives as positive reinforcers, but also who the mediators of such reinforcers are. This is highly important information in carrying out a contingency management effort. Going to a ball game may be a powerful reinforcer if one is accompanied by peers, a weak one if accompanied by one's teacher or mother. Praise from a respected teacher may be a potent reinforcing event, whereas the same praise delivered by a peer considered by the youngster to be ignorant vis-à-vis the behavior involved may be totally lacking in potency. The response format of this questionnaire also asks the youngster to indicate her sense of the potency of the reinforcer written in for each item. Thus this measure provides a self-report of *which* events are reinforcing for the youngster, when delivered or mediated by *whom,* as well as the youngster's perception of just *how* reinforcing each event is.

A rather different type of questionnairelike instrument for identifying positive reinforcers, especially appropriate for younger children and children with limited verbal abilities, is Homme, Csanyi, Gonzales, & Rechs' (1969) Reinforcing Event Menu. This measure is essentially a collection of pictures showing a variety of material and activity reinforcers, as well as pictures depicting a number of potential reinforcement mediators. It is the youngster's task to select from these pictures those reinforcers for which he would most like to work.

This process of identifying positive reinforcers for given youngsters completes the series of preparatory steps a teacher or other contingency manager must undertake prior to actually presenting such events contingently upon the occurrence of appropriate behaviors.

Presenting Positive Reinforcers

The basic principle of contingency management is that the presentation of a reinforcing event contingent upon the occurrence of a given behavior will function to increase the likelihood of the reoccurrence of that behavior. Research has demonstrated a substantial number of considerations that influence the success of this reinforcement effort

Table 24
Commonly Used Reinforcers

Edible	Nonedible	Social	Activity	Token (points)
Gum	Balloons	Attention	Gym time	(For general exchange)
Candy	Clothes	Public praise	Shop time	
M & M's	Scout uniform	Posting work in school or	Library time	
Popcorn	Shoes, etc.	at home	Driver's license	
Cracker Jacks	Toys (dolls, cars)	Approval	Movies	
Sodas	Sports-related items	Access to privilege areas	Concerts (folk, rock,	
Cakes	Baseball cards	(e.g., blackboard,	ballet)	
Pies	Baseball	lavatory, parent's office,	Field trips	
Ice cream	Sports equipment	den, T.V. room)	Hobbies	
(bars, etc.)	Records	Time off from school	Theater	
Hamburgers	Music equipment	Hours for out-of-house	Ballet	
Nuts (peanuts)	Car parts	Private areas	Sports teams	
Raisins	(also motorcycle,	Private times	Camping	
	etc., parts)	T.V. privileges	Travel	
	Motorcycle, minibike,	Program choice	Day trips	
	bicycle	Time watching	Overnight trips	
	Furnishings for room (T.V.,	Dinner out	Telephone	
	posters, black lights, dolls)	Dinnertime choice		
		Friend's privileges		
		In house, at dinner		
		Overnight		

554

Bedtime
Bath choices
Parties
Time with one parent
Special work
    Collecting papers
    Run recorders
    Carrying messages
Telephone privilege
Hair length
Clothing choice

Note. From *Hyperactive Children*, (pp. 154–155), by D.J. Safer and R.P. Allen, 1976, Baltimore: University Park Press. Reprinted by permission.

and that are thus optimally reflected in the actual presentation of reinforcers when one is seeking to increase appropriate behaviors.

Contingency

Although this rule for reinforcer presentation may be largely obvious at this point, it is a crucial one that is sometimes forgotten or inadequately implemented. The connection between the desirable behavior and the subsequent provision of reward should be made explicit to the youngster. As is true for all aspects of a contingency management effort, this description should be behaviorally specific—that is, it is the connection between particular behavioral acts and reinforcement that should be emphasized, not behaviorally ambiguous comments about "good behavior," "being a good boy," "being well-behaved," or the like.

Immediate reinforcement

Related to the communication of the behavioral reinforcement contingency is the fact that the more immediately the reinforcer follows the desirable behavior, the more likely is its effectiveness. Not only will rapid reinforcement augment the message that the immediately preceding behavior is desirable, but delayed reinforcer presentation increases the risk that a sequence will occur of A (desirable behavior), B (undesirable behavior), and C (reinforcement for A that in actuality reinforces B).

Consistent reinforcement

The effects of positive reinforcement on altering behavior are usually gradual, not dramatic, working slowly to strengthen behavior over a period of time. Thus it is important that positive reinforcement be presented consistently. Consistency here means not only that the teacher must be consistent, but also that the teacher must make certain, as best she can, that the reinforcement delivery efforts are matched by similar efforts from as many other important persons in the youngster's life as possible. Concretely, this means that, when the youngster enacts the behavior to be reinforced—in school in the presence of other teachers, at home in the presence of parents or siblings, or at play in the presence of peers—such reinforcement will ideally be forthcoming.

Frequency of reinforcement

When first trying to establish a new appropriate behavior, the teacher should seek to reinforce all or almost all instances of that behavior. This high frequency of reinforcement is necessary initially to establish the behavior in the individual's behavioral repertoire. Once it seems clear that the behavior has actually been acquired, it is appropriate for the teacher to thin the reinforcement schedule, decreasing the presentation of reinforcement so that only some of the youngster's desirable behaviors are followed by reinforcement. This thinner reinforcement by the teacher, known as *partial reinforcement,* is an important contribution to the continued likelihood of the appropriate behavior because such a reinforcement schedule closely parallels the sometimes-reinforced/sometimes-not reaction the youngster's appropriate behavior will elicit in other settings from other people. Partial reinforcement of the youngster's appropriate behaviors may be on a fixed time schedule (e.g., at the end of each class), on a fixed number of response schedule (e.g., every fifth instance of the appropriate behavior), or on variable time or number of response schedules. In any event, the basic strategy for reinforcement frequency remains a rich level for initial learning and partial reinforcement to sustain performance.

Amount of reinforcement

In our preceding discussion of frequency of reinforcement, we began to distinguish between learning (i.e., acquiring knowledge about how to perform new behaviors) and actual performance (i.e., overtly using these behaviors). The amount of reinforcement provided influences performance much more than learning. Youngsters will learn new appropriate behaviors just about as fast for a small reward as for a large reward, but they are more likely to perform the behaviors on a continuing basis when large rewards are involved. Yet rewards can be too large, causing a *satiation effect* in which the youngster loses interest in seeking the given reinforcement because it is "too much of a good thing." Or rewards can be too small: too little time on the playground, too few tokens, too thin a social reinforcement schedule. The optimal amount can be determined empirically. If a youngster has in the past worked energetically to obtain a particular reinforcer but gradually slacks off and seems to lose interest in obtaining it, a satiation effect has probably occurred, and the amount of reinforcement should be reduced. On the other hand, if a youngster seems unwilling to work for a reinforcer believed desirable, it can be given once or twice for free— that is, not contingent on a specific desirable behavior. If the youngster seems to enjoy the reinforcer and even wishes more of the same, the amount used may have been too little. The amount can be increased and made contingent; observations will then show whether it is yielding the desired behavior modification effect. If so, the amount of reinforcement offered is appropriate.

Variety of reinforcement

In the preceding discussion, we mentioned a reinforcement satiation effect due to an excessive amount of reinforcement. A parallel type of satiation of reinforcement occurs when the teacher uses the same approving phrase or other reward over and over again. Youngsters may perceive such reinforcement as taking on a mechanized quality, and they may thus lose interest in or decrease responsiveness to it. By varying the content of the reinforcer presented, the teacher can maintain its potency. Thus, instead of repeating "Nice job" four or five times, using a mix of comments ("I'm really proud of you," "You're certainly doing fine," or "Well done") is more likely to yield a sustained effect.

Pairing with praise

Our earlier statements about types of reinforcers emphasized that social reinforcement is most germane to enduring behavior change, though there are circumstances under which an emphasis upon material, activity, or token reinforcers is (at least initially) more appropriate. To aid in the desired movement toward social reinforcement, the teacher should seek to pair all presentations of material, activity, or token rewards with some expression of social reinforcement: an approving comment, a pat on the back, a wink, a smile, and so forth. A major benefit of this tactic is noted by Walker (1979):

> By virtue of being consistently paired with reinforcement delivery, praise can take on the reinforcing properties of the actual reinforcer(s) used. This is especially important since teacher praise is not always initially effective with many deviant children. By systematically increasing the incentive value of praise through pairing, the teacher is in a position to gradually reduce the frequency of [material, activity, or token] reinforcement and to substitute praise. After systematic pairing, the teacher's praise may be much more effective in maintaining the child's appropriate behavior. (p. 108)

Shaping new behaviors

Reinforcement cannot be presented contingently upon new behaviors when such behaviors are not part of the youngster's behavioral repertoire. A child cannot be rewarded at all for talking over disputes with other students at the proper frequency, amount, consistency, and so forth if he never does so. Yet the teacher is not doomed to perpetual waiting, reinforcers ready, for nonemergent desirable behaviors. In addition to attempting to teach appropriate behaviors directly via such Prepare courses as Interpersonal Skills Training (see chapter 3), the teacher can make use of *shaping* techniques. Approximations to desirable negotiating behaviors, for example—even remote approximations—can be positively reinforced. Looking at the other disputant, walking towards her, and discussing a topic irrelevant to the dispute are all reinforceable steps in the direction of the ultimately desired behaviors. By using a process of reinforcing behaviors successively closer to the final target behavior, coupled with successive withdrawal of such reinforcement for weaker approximations, the behavior-change process can proceed in a stepwise fashion in which youngsters' behaviors are systematically shaped into ever better approximations of the final target behavior.

These aforementioned rules for maximizing the effectiveness of the presentation of positive reinforcement are all essentially remedial in nature. They are efforts to substitute appropriate prosocial behaviors for aggressive, disruptive, antisocial, withdrawal, or asocial behaviors that have already begun to be displayed by specific youngsters. It is also worth noting, however, that the presentation of positive reinforcement may also be used for preventive purposes. Sarason et al. (1972) urge teachers to present positive reinforcement openly to specific youngsters in such a manner that the entire class is aware of it. As they comment,

> Positive reinforcements for productive activity for the whole group is a powerful preventive technique. It can eliminate or reduce the great majority of behavior problems in classrooms. Try to praise the children who are paying attention. Attend to those who are sitting in their seats, doing their work in a nondisruptive manner. "That's right, John, you're doing a good job." "You watched the board all the time I was presenting the problem. That's paying attention." ... These responses not only reinforce the child to whom they are directed, but they also help to provide the rest of the class with an explicit idea of what you mean by paying attention and working hard. Young children, especially ... learn to model their actions after the positive examples established and noted by the teacher. (p. 18)

We wish to close this discussion of procedures for the presentation of positive reinforcement by suggesting additional sources for the reader wishing to pursue the substantial experimental evidence that exists in support of this dimension of contingency management. Especially comprehensive reviews include those by Bandura (1969), Gambrill (1977), Kazdin (1977), O'Leary and O'Leary (1976, 1980), and Walker (1979). Individual studies that seem to be particularly instructive of methods and results involving these procedures as applied to youngsters displaying aggressive or disruptive behavior are those by Adams (1973); Becker, Madsen, Arnold, and Thomas (1967); Buys (1972); Hall, Panyan, Rabon, and Broden (1968); Kirschner and Levin (1975); Pinkston, Reese, LeBlanc, and Baer (1973); Sewell, McCoy, and Sewell (1973); and Ward and Baker (1968).

Removing Positive Reinforcers

The teacher's behavior modification goal with youngsters displaying aggressive behaviors is, in a general sense, twofold. Both sides of the behavioral coin—appropriate and inappropriate, prosocial and antisocial, desirable and undesirable—must be attended to. In a proper behavior-change effort, procedures are simultaneously or sequentially employed to reduce and eliminate the inappropriate, antisocial, or undesirable components of the youngster's behavioral repertoire and to increase the quality and frequency of appropriate, prosocial, or desirable components. This latter task is served primarily by the direct teaching of prosocial behaviors via Prepare courses and by the contingent presentation of positive reinforcement following their occurrence. Conversely, the contingent removal of positive reinforcement in response to aggressive, disruptive, or similar behaviors is the major behavior modification strategy for reducing or eliminating such behaviors. Therefore, in conjunction with the procedures discussed previously for presenting positive reinforcement, the teacher should also simultaneously or consecutively employ one or more of the following three techniques for removing positive reinforcement.

Extinction

Knowing when to use extinction. Extinction is the withdrawal or removal of positive reinforcement for aggressive or other undesirable behaviors that have been either deliberately or inadvertently reinforced in the past. This technique can be thought of prescriptively as the procedure of choice with milder forms of aggression (e.g., threats, swearing, or other forms of verbal aggression) or with low-amplitude physical aggression. More generally, extinction should be used when other individuals are not in any serious physical danger from the aggression being displayed. Determining when the use of extinction is appropriate is, of course, in part a function of each teacher's guiding classroom management philosophy and tolerance for deviance. Extinction is usually implemented by teachers and classroom peers seeking to ignore ongoing inappropriate behavior. Each teacher will have to decide individually the range of undesirable behaviors that can be safely ignored. Taking a rather conservative stance, Walker (1979) suggests that extinction "should be applied only to those inappropriate behaviors that are minimally disruptive to classroom atmosphere" (p. 40). Others are somewhat more liberal in its application (e.g., Carr, 1981). In any event, it is clear that the first step in applying extinction is knowing when to use it.

Providing positive reinforcement for appropriate behaviors. As noted earlier, attempts to reduce inappropriate behavior by reinforcement withdrawal should always be accompanied by tandem efforts to increase appropriate behaviors by reinforcement provision. This combination of efforts will succeed especially well when the appropriate and inappropriate behaviors involved are opposite from, or at least incompatible with, each other (e.g., reward in-seat behavior, ignore out-of-seat behavior; reward talking at a conversational level, ignore yelling).

Identifying the positive reinforcers maintaining inappropriate behaviors. The reinforcers maintaining inappropriate behaviors are the ones to be withheld. Using essentially the same observation and recording procedures described earlier in conjunction with the identification of positive reinforcers maintaining appropriate behaviors, the teacher should discern what the youngster is working for; what payoffs are involved; and what reinforcers are being sought or earned by aggression, disruptiveness, and similar behaviors. Very often, the answer will be attention. Laughing, looking, staring, yelling at, talking to, or turning toward are common teacher and peer reactions to a youngster's aggression. The withdrawal of such positive social reinforcement by ignoring the behaviors (by turning away and not yelling, talking, or laughing at the perpetrator) are the teacher and classmate behaviors that will effect extinction. Ignoring someone who would normally receive one's attention is itself a talent, as the next extinction rules illustrate.

Knowing how to ignore aggressive behaviors. Carr (1981) has suggested three useful guidelines for ignoring low-level aggressive behaviors. These are summarized as follows:

1. Do not comment to the child that you are ignoring him. Long (or even short) explanations provided to youngsters about why teachers,

peers, or others are going to avoid attending to given behaviors provide precisely the type of social reinforcement extinction is designed to withdraw. Such explanations are to be avoided. Ignoring behavior should simply occur with no forewarning, introduction, or prior explanation.

2. Do not look away suddenly when the child behaves aggressively. Jerking one's head away suddenly so as not to see the continuation of the aggressive behavior or other abrupt behaviors exhibited by the teacher may communicate the message "I really noticed and was impelled to action by your behavior," the exact opposite of an extinction message. As Carr recommends, "It is best to ignore the behavior by reacting to it in a matter of fact way by continuing natural ongoing activities" (p. 38).

3. Do protect the victims of aggression. If one youngster actually strikes another, the teacher must intervene. One may do so without subverting the extinction effort by providing the victim with attention, concern, and interest and by ignoring the perpetrator of the aggression.

Using extinction consistently. As is true for the provision of reinforcement, its removal must be consistent for intended effects to be forthcoming. Within a given classroom, this rule of consistency means both that the teacher and classmates must act in concert and that the teacher must be consistent across time. Within a given school, consistency means that, to the degree possible, all teachers having significant commerce with a given youngster must strive to ignore the same inappropriate behaviors. In addition, to avoid a type of "I can't act up here, but I can out there" discrimination being made by the youngster, parent conferences should be held to bring parents, siblings, and other significant real-world figures in the youngster's life into the extinction effort. As Karoly (1980) notes, when consistency of nonattending is not reached, the aggressive behavior will be intermittently or partially reinforced, a circumstance that we noted earlier would lead to its becoming highly resistant to extinction.

Using extinction for a long enough period of time. Aggressive behaviors often have a long history of positive reinforcement and, especially if much of that history is one of intermittent reinforcement, efforts to undo them have to be sustained. Teacher persistence in this regard will, however, usually succeed. Carr (1981) suggests that, within a week, clear reductions in aggressive behavior should be observable. There are, however, two types of events to keep in mind when judging the effectiveness of extinction efforts. The first is what is known as the *extinction burst.* When extinction is first introduced, it is not uncommon for the rate or intensity of the aggressive behavior to first increase sharply before it begins its more gradual decline toward a zero level. It is important that the teacher not get discouraged during this short detour in direction. Its meaning, in fact, is that the extinction is beginning to work. In addition, inappropriate behaviors that have been successfully extinguished will reappear occasionally for reasons that are difficult to determine. Like the extinction burst, this *spontaneous recovery* is transitory and will disappear if the teacher persists in the extinction effort.

The effectiveness of extinction in modifying inappropriate or undesirable behaviors in a classroom context has been demonstrated by many investigators, including Brown and Elliott (1965); Jones and Miller (1974); Madsen, Becker, and Thomas (1968); Wahler, Winkel, Peterson, and Morrison (1965); and Ward and Baker (1968).

Time out

In time out, a youngster who engages in aggressive or other inappropriate behaviors is physically removed from all sources of reinforcement for a specified time period. As with extinction, the purpose of time out is to reduce the (undesirable) behavior that immediately precedes it and on which its use is contingent. It differs from extinction in that extinction involves removing reinforcement from the person, whereas time out usually involves removing the person from the reinforcing situation.

In classroom practice, time out has typically taken three forms. *Isolation time out,* the most common form, requires that the youngster be physically removed from the classroom to a time-out room according to specific procedures described later in this section. *Exclusion time out* is somewhat less restrictive but also involves physically removing the youngster from sources of reinforcement. Here the youngster is required to go to a corner of the classroom and perhaps to sit in a "quiet chair" (Firestone, 1976), which is sometimes behind a screen. The youngster is not removed from the classroom, but is excluded from classroom activities for a specified time period. *Nonexclusion time out* (also called *contingent observation*), the least restrictive time-out variant, requires the youngster to sit and watch on the periphery of classroom activities, to observe the appropriate behaviors of other youngsters. It is a variant that, in a sense, combines time out with modeling opportunities. Its essence is to exclude the youngster from a participant role for a specified time period while leaving intact the opportunity to function as an observer. The implementation of time out in any of its forms optimally employs the procedures next described.

Knowing when to use time out. Extinction, it will be recalled, is the recommended procedure for those aggressive or otherwise undesirable behaviors that can be safely ignored. Behaviors potentially injurious to other youngsters require a more active teacher response, possibly time out. In the case of many youngsters at the upper junior high school and senior high school levels, physical removal by the teacher is often not wise, appropriate, or even possible. For such youngsters, procedures other than extinction or time out, discussed later in this chapter, have to be employed. Thus, to reflect both the potential injuriousness of the youngster's behavior and the youngster's age and associated physical status, time out is recommended as the technique of choice for youngsters ages 2 to 12 years who are displaying high rates of potentially dangerous aggressive behavior. It is also the procedure to utilize for less severe forms of aggression when the combination of extinction and positive reinforcement for other, more positive behaviors has been attempted and has failed.

Providing positive reinforcement for appropriate behaviors. As is the case for extinction, positive reinforcement for appropriate behaviors should accompany time out. When possible, the behaviors positively reinforced should be opposite to, or at least incompatible with, those for which the time-out procedure is instituted. Furthermore, there is an additional basis for recommending the combined use of these two techniques. As Carr (1981) observes,

> Although one important reason for using positive reinforcement is to strengthen nonaggressive behaviors to the point where they replace aggressive behaviors, there is a second reason for using reinforcement procedures. If extensive use of positive reinforcement is made, then time out will become all the more aversive since it would involve the temporary termination of a rich diversity of positive reinforcers. In this sense, then, the use of positive reinforcement helps to enhance the effectiveness of the time out procedure. (pp. 41–42)

Arranging an effective time-out setting. We will focus our description of the characteristics of an effective time-out setting on an isolation time-out arrangement because its general principles readily carry over to both exclusion and nonexclusion time-out environments. Essentially, two general principles are involved. The first concerns the youngster's health and safety. The time-out setting should be a small, well-lit, and well-ventilated room that provides a place for the youngster to sit. The second principle reflects the fact that the central quality of this procedure is time out from positive reinforcement. Time out must be a boring environment, with all reinforcers removed. There should be no attractive or distracting objects or opportunities: no toys, television, radio, books, posters, people, windows to look out, sound sources to overhear, or other obvious or not-so-obvious potential reinforcers. A barren isolation area is the optimal time-out environment.

Placing a youngster in time out. A number of actions may be taken by the teacher when initiating time out to increase the likelihood of its effectiveness. As with the immediate presentation of positive reinforcement contingent upon appropriate behaviors, time out is optimally instituted immediately following the aggressive or other behaviors one is seeking to modify. Having earlier explained to the target youngster the nature of time out, as well as when and why it will be used, the teacher should initiate the procedure in a more or less automatic manner following undesirable behavior—that is, in a manner that minimizes the social reinforcement of the aggression. Concretely, this means placing the youngster in time out without a lengthy explanation but with a brief, matter-of-fact description of the precipitating behaviors. This process is best conducted without anger by the teacher and, when possible, without having to use physical means for moving the youngster from the classroom to the time-out room. To minimize reinforcement of aggression during this process, it is also best if the distance between classroom and time-out room is small: The shorter the distance and the briefer the transportation time, the less opportunity exists for inadvertent social reinforcement by the teacher. In addition to these considerations, the effectiveness of time out is further enhanced by its consistent application, when appropriate, by the same teacher on other occasions as well as by other teachers. Immediacy, consistency, and various actions aimed at minimizing teacher presentation of reinforcement following inappropriate behavior thus function to augment the behavior-change effectiveness of time out.

Maintaining a youngster in time out. The skilled contingency manager must deal with two questions during a youngster's period in time out: "What is the youngster doing?" and "How long should time out last?" Answering the first question by teacher monitoring makes certain that the time-out experience is not in fact functioning as a pleasant, positively reinforcing one for a given youngster. For example, rather than serve as a removal from positive reinforcement, time out may in reality be a removal from an aversive situation (negative reinforcement) if the teacher institutes it at a time when a youngster is in an unpleasant situation from which she would prefer to escape or if time out helps her avoid such a situation. Similarly, if monitoring reveals that the youngster is singing or playing enjoyable games, the effectiveness of time out will be lessened. Unless the situation can be made essentially nonreinforcing, a different behavioral intervention may have to be used.

With regard to duration, most successful time-out implementations have been from 5 to 20 minutes long, with some clear preference for the shorter levels of this range. When experimenting to find the optimal duration for any given youngster, it is best, as White, Nielson, and Johnson (1972) have shown, to begin with a short duration (e.g., 3 to 5 minutes) and to lengthen the time until an effective span is identified rather than to shorten successively an initially lengthier span. This latter approach would, again, risk the danger of introducing an event experienced as positive reinforcement by the youngster when the intention was quite the opposite.

Releasing a youngster from time out. We noted earlier in connection with extinction that withdrawal of positive reinforcement not infrequently leads to initial instances of an extinction burst, in which more intense or more frequent aggressiveness appears before it begins to subside. This same pattern is evident with withdrawal from positive reinforcement—that is, time out. The first few times a youngster is placed in time out, what might be termed a *time-out burst* of heightened aggressiveness may occur. These outbursts will usually subside, especially if the teacher adds to the duration of the time-out span the same number of minutes that the outburst lasts.

Whether the release of the youngster from time out is on schedule or is delayed for the reasons just specified, it should be conducted in a matter-of-fact manner, and the youngster should be quickly returned to regular classroom activities. Lengthy teacher explanations or apologies at this point in time are, once again, tactically erroneous provisions of positive reinforcement that communicate to the youngster that acting out in the classroom will bring a short period of removal from reinforcement and then a (probably lengthier) period of undivided teacher attention.

The effectiveness of time out in substantially reducing or eliminating aggressive or disruptive behaviors has been demonstrated by Allison and Allison (1971); Bostow and Bailey (1969); Calhoun and Matherne (1975); Drabman and Spitalnik (1973); Patterson, Cobb, and Ray (1973); Patterson and Reid (1973); Vukelich and Hake (1971); Webster (1976); and White et al. (1972).

Response cost

Response cost involves the removal of previously acquired reinforcers contingent upon and in order to reduce future instances of the occurrence of inappropriate behaviors. The reinforcers previously acquired and to be removed contingently may have been earned, as when the use of response-cost procedures is a component of a token-reinforcement system, or they may have been simply provided, as is the case with a freestanding non-token-economy response-cost system. In either instance, reinforcers are removed (the cost) whenever previously targeted undesirable behaviors occur (the response). The two other means we have examined for the systematic removal of positive reinforcement, extinction and time out, have sometimes proven insufficient for delinquent or severely aggressive adolescents, even when combined with teacher praise or other reinforcement for appropriate behaviors. In a number of these instances, response-cost procedures—especially when combined with the provision of positive reinforcement (via a token-economy system) for Prepare-related and other desirable prosocial behaviors—have proven effective. Thus not only must a teacher's selection of the response-cost approach be a prescriptive function of the target youngster's characteristics, but the teacher must also combine response-cost usage with tandem procedures for providing positive reinforcement for appropriate behaviors.

We do not detail here the rules for the effective implementation of a token-economy system since they overlap considerably with rules delineated earlier in this chapter for the provision of nontoken positive reinforcers and may also be found in Christophersen et al. (1972), Ayllon and Azrin (1968), Kazdin (1975), Morris (1976), and Walker et al. (1976). We do wish to specify, however, those rules for removing token or nontoken reinforcement that constitute the essence of the response-cost procedure.

Defining inappropriate behaviors in specific terms. As with every other contingency management procedure, it is requisite that the teacher think, plan, and act "behaviorally." When specifying the inappropriate target behaviors whose occurrence will cost tokens, points, privileges, or other commodities or events, the teacher must delineate specific overt acts, not broader behavioral characterological categories. Thus "is aggressive" (a characterological observation) or "acts withdrawn" (a broad behavioral observation) are too vague, but "swears, makes threats, raises voice, raises hands, pushes classmates, sits by self, doesn't play with others" are all useful specifications.

Determining the cost of specific inappropriate responses. As is the case for the amount, level, or rate of positive reinforcement to be provided contingent upon desirable behaviors, the specific cost to be lost contingent upon undesirable behaviors must be determined—whether such cost is a finite number of tokens or points, a finite amount of time the television will be kept off, or another outcome. Cost setting is a crucial determinant of the success or failure of implementing this approach. For example, Carr (1981) notes that

> the magnitude of response cost must be carefully controlled. If fines are too large, bankruptcy will ensue and the child will be unable to purchase any back-up reinforcers. Further, if the child develops too large a deficit, he may adapt an attitude of "what do I have to lose?" and engage in considerable misbehavior. On the other hand, if the fines are too small, the child will be able to negate his loss easily by performing any of a variety of appropriate behaviors. (p. 52)

Yet other aspects of response-cost implementation will make demands on the teacher's skills as a creative economist. The relationship of points or other reinforcers available to earn to those that can be lost; the relationship of cost to the severity of the inappropriate behavior for which that cost is levied; and a host of similar marketing, pricing, and, ultimately, motivational considerations may come into play and thus require a substantial level of contingency management expertise on the part of the teacher. This is especially true if the teacher is not only the implementer of the response cost system, but also its originator, planner, and monitor.

Communicating contingencies. Once the teacher has decided upon the specific token, point, or privilege value of the appropriate and inappropriate behaviors relevant to the effective management of the classroom, it is necessary to communicate these values to the class. A readily visible reinforcer value list indicating earnings and losses should be drawn up and posted. Table 25 is a composite example of such a list, designed to be appropriate for use at the junior high school level.

Removing reinforcement. Class members must not only be able to know in advance what earnings and losses are contingent upon what desirable and undesirable behaviors, but must also have ongoing knowledge of their own earnings status. A good example of how this may be accomplished is provided by Walker (1979), who developed a simple, easily used delivery/feedback system that gives each youngster ongoing cumulative information indicating (1) when response cost or earnings have been applied; (2) to which specific behaviors response

Table 25
Behaviors That Earn and Lose Points

Behaviors That Earn Points	Points
1. Reading books	5 per page
2. Greeting people appropriately	100 per instance
3. Remaining in seat	100 per 15 minutes
4. Taking notes	250 per 15 minutes
5. Being on time for school	250 per day
6. Being quiet in lunch line	300 per instance
7. Being quiet in cafeteria	300 per instance
8. Displaying appropriate playground behavior	500 per 15 minutes
9. Doing completed homework	1000 per day
10. Getting an A/B/C/D grade	2000/1000/500/250 per grade
11. Talking out disagreements	1000 per instance

Behaviors That Lose Points	Points
1. Greeting people inappropriately	100 per instance
2. Being out of seat inappropriately	150 per instance
3. Being late for school	10 per minute
4. Being noisy in classroom	300 per instance
5. Being noisy in lunch line	300 per instance
6. Being noisy in cafeteria	300 per instance
7. Swearing	500 per instance
8. Cheating	1000 per instance
9. Having incomplete homework	1000 per instance
10. Getting an F grade	1000 per grade
11. Showing physical aggression	1000 per instance
12. Stealing	2500 per instance

Note. From A. P. Goldstein/S. J. Apter/B. Haroutunian, *School Violence,* © 1984, p. 62. Reprinted by permission of Prentice-Hall, Inc., Englewood Cliffs, New Jersey.

cost or earnings have been applied; and (3) how many points have been lost or earned as a result. To help implement the response-cost component of this system, each youngster was given a 4 × 6-inch card once each week. The card, whose content appears in Figure 7, was taped to the corner of each youngster's desk.

As the first step in implementing the delivery and feedback of response cost, both the use of the cards and the specific behaviors

Figure 7
Response-Cost Delivery/Feedback System

Behaviors[a]	Point Values	M	T	W	TH	F
Out of seat	2	o o				
Talks out	2	o	o o			
Nonattending	1	o o		o o		
Noncompliance	3		o			
Disturbing others	2	o				
Foul language	4		o			
Fighting	5					

Note. From *The Acting-out Child: Coping with Classroom Disruption* (p. 127), by H.M. Walker, 1979, Boston, MA: Allyn & Bacon. Reprinted by permission.

[a]The youngster whose appropriate behaviors are recorded here lost 11 points on Monday and 12 points on Tuesday.

involved in their use were explained and illustrated. During the week, whenever a given youngster engaged in one of the inappropriate behaviors, the teacher walked to the youngster's desk and, with a special marking pen, placed a dot in the box corresponding to the day of the week and to the particular inappropriate behavior to which the cost was being applied. Consistent with the effort to avoid providing social reinforcement while implementing this procedure, the teacher concurrently told the youngster which behavior(s) were involved and the number of points lost but engaged in no other dialogue with the youngster.

A delivery/feedback card such as the one illustrated in Figure 7 may be used as part of a response-cost system in which the youngster (1) is simply given a fixed number of points initially and noncontingently; (2) keeps or loses points as a function of behavior during a fixed time period; and (3) is given the opportunity to exchange points remaining for backup material or activity reinforcers at the end of that time period. Alternatively, such means for keeping a youngster posted on point status may also be part of a token-economy system in which points are earned (see Table 25) contingently for appropriate behaviors, not awarded initially on a noncontingent basis. When this earning requirement is in effect, a second delivery/feedback card (or the reverse side of the first card) may be used to keep an ongoing record of points earned each day in each appropriate behavior category.

As is true for the other major procedures for the removal of positive reinforcement (extinction and time out), optimal implementation of response-cost procedures requires that the teacher be (1) *consistent* in the application of procedures across students and across time for each student; (2) *immediate* in delivering contingent costs as soon as possible after the inappropriate behavior occurs; and (3) *impartial* and *inevitable* in ensuring that an instance of inappropriate behavior leads to an instance of response cost almost automatically, with an absolute minimum of special exceptions.

A number of investigations have independently demonstrated the behavior modification effectiveness of response-cost procedures. Among these are studies by Burchard and Barrera (1972); Christophersen et al. (1972); Kaufman and O'Leary (1972); O'Leary and Becker (1967); and O'Leary, Becker, Evans, and Saudargas (1969).

Presenting and Removing Aversive Stimuli

The two contingency management approaches examined in this section—namely, the presentation of aversive stimuli (i.e., punishment) and the removal of aversive stimuli (i.e., negative reinforcement)—are in our view generally less recommendable than the positive reinforcement presentation and removal procedures discussed in earlier sections. Our bases for this disinclination to recommend and utilize these procedures are explained in the following discussion.

Punishment

Punishment is the presentation of an aversive stimulus contingent upon the performance of a given behavior and is usually intended to decrease the likelihood of future occurrences of that behavior. Two of the major forms that punishment has taken in United States classrooms are verbal punishment (i.e., reprimands) and physical punishment (i.e., paddling, spanking, slapping, or other forms of corporal punishment). The effectiveness of these and other forms of punishment in altering targeted inappropriate behaviors, such as aggression, has been shown to be a function of several factors:

1. Likelihood of punishment,
2. Consistency of punishment,
3. Immediacy of punishment,
4. Duration of punishment,
5. Severity of punishment,
6. Possibility for escape or avoidance of punishment,
7. Availability of alternative routes to goal,
8. Level of instigation to aggression,
9. Level of reward for aggression,
10. Characteristics of the prohibiting agents.

Punishment is more likely to lead to behavior-change consequences the more certain its application, the more consistently and rapidly it is applied, the longer and more intense its quality, the less the likelihood it can be avoided, the more available are alternative means to goal satisfaction, the lower the level of instigation to aggression or reward for aggression, and the more potent as a contingency manager the prohibiting agent. Thus there are clearly several determinants of the impact of an aversive stimulus on a youngster's behavior. But let us assume an instance in which these determinants combine to yield a substantial impact. What, ideally, may we hope that the effect of punishment on aggression or other undesirable behavior will be? A reprimand or a paddling will not teach new behaviors. If the youngster is deficient in the ability to ask rather than take, request rather than command, and negotiate rather than strike out, all the teacher scolding, scowling, and spanking possible will not teach the youngster desirable alternative behaviors. Thus punishment, if used at all, must be combined with efforts to instruct the youngster in those behaviors in which she is deficient. When the youngster does possess alternative desirable behaviors, but in only approximate form, punishment may best be combined with shaping procedures. And, when high-quality appropriate behaviors are possessed by the youngster, but she is not displaying them, teacher use of punishment is optimally combined with any of the other procedures described earlier for the systematic presentation of positive reinforcement. In short, the application of punishment techniques should always be combined with a companion procedure for strengthening appropriate alternative behaviors, whether these behaviors are absent, weak, or merely unused.

Our urging this tandem focus on teaching desirable alternative behaviors stems in particular from the fact that most investigators report the main effect of punishment to be a *temporary* suppression of inappropriate behaviors. Although we appreciate the potential value of such a temporary suppression to the harried classroom teacher seeking a classroom environment in which teaching time can exceed discipline time, it is not uncommon for the teacher to have to punish the same youngsters over and over again for the same inappropriate behaviors.

To recapitulate, we have urged thus far in this section that, if punishment is used, its use be combined with one or another means for simultaneously teaching desirable behaviors. This recommendation is underscored by the common finding that, when punishment does succeed in altering behavior, such effects are often temporary.

In part because of this temporary effect, but more so for a series of even more consequential reasons, a number of contingency management researchers have assumed an antipunishment stance, seeing little place for punishment, especially in the contemporary classroom. This view corresponds to punishment research demonstrating such undesirable side effects as withdrawal from social contact, counteraggression toward the punisher, modeling of punishing behavior, disruption of social relationships, failure of effects to generalize, selective avoidance (refraining from inappropriate behaviors only when under surveillance), and stigmatizing labeling effects (Azrin & Holz, 1966; Bandura, 1973).

An alternative, propunishment view does exist. It is less widespread and more controversial, but it too seeks to make its case based upon empirical evidence. These investigators hold that there are numerous favorable effects of punishment: rapid and dependable reduction of inappropriate behaviors; the consequent opening up of new sources of positive reinforcement; the possibility of complete suppression of inappropriate behaviors; increased social and emotional behavior, imitation, and discrimination learning; and other potential positive outcomes (Axelrod & Apsche, 1982; Newsom, Favell, & Rincover, 1982; Van Houten, 1982).

The evidence is clearly not all in. Data on which punishers should appropriately be used with which youngsters under which circumstances are incomplete. At the present time, decisions regarding the classroom utilization of aversive stimuli to alter inappropriate behaviors must derive from partial data and each teacher's carefully considered ethical beliefs regarding the relative costs and benefits of employing punishment procedures. Our own weighing of relevant data and ethical considerations leads to our stance favoring the selective classroom utilization of verbal punishment techniques and our rejecting under all circumstances the use of physical punishment techniques.

Verbal reprimands. Though results are not wholly unmixed, the preponderance of research demonstrates that punishment in the form of teachers' verbal reprimands is an effective means for reducing disruptive classroom behavior (Jones & Miller, 1974), littering (Risley, 1977), object throwing (Sajwaj, Culver, Hall, & Lehr, 1972), physical aggression (Hall et al., 1971), and other acting-out behaviors (O'Leary, Kaufman, Kass, & Drabman, 1970). These and other relevant studies also indicate that, beyond overall effectiveness, reprimands are most potent when the teacher is physically close to the target youngster, clearly specifies in behavioral terms the inappropriate behavior being reprimanded, maintains eye contact with the youngster, uses a firm voice, and firmly grasps the youngster while delivering the reprimand. Finally, White et al. (1972) and Forehand, Roberts, Dolays, Hobbs, and Resick (1976) each compared reprimands to other commonly employed forms of punishment and found reprimands to be superior in effectiveness.

Our position favoring the selective use of teacher reprimands rests jointly on our understanding of the foregoing research findings and on our cost/benefit belief that such procedures have not only a high likelihood of being effective, but also a low likelihood of being injurious—especially when combined, as we and others have repeatedly urged, with one or another means for presenting positive reinforcement for appropriate behaviors. In this latter regard, both White (1975) and Thomas, Presland, Grant, and Glynn (1978) have independently shown that teachers deliver an average of one reprimand every 2 minutes in both elementary and junior high schools, a rate that substantially exceeds, at all grade levels beyond the second, their rate of offering praise to students for appropriate behaviors. Stated otherwise, in contemporary educational settings, teachers now reprimand students at very high rates, and far too infrequently are such reprimands accompanied by social reinforcement for desirable behaviors. We urge a change in both regards.

Physical punishment. Newsom et al. (1982) speculate that physically painful punishment that succeeds in altering inappropriate behaviors may be less injurious and more helpful in toto to the target youngster than nonphysically painful but perhaps less effective alternatives. We do not know of empirical evidence bearing on this conclusion and, given pause by their speculation, take a stance opposed to corporal punishment in school (or any other) settings. As Axelrod and Apsche (1982) urge, our guiding ethical principle is to promote "the implementation of the least drastic alternative which has a reasonable probability of success" (p. 16). Given the substantial number of demonstrations of effective procedures involving the presentation of positive reinforcers, the similarly strong results bearing on techniques for removing such reinforcement, the just-cited evidence vis-à-vis verbal punishment, and the paucity of research evaluating the effectiveness of corporal punishment, we see no place for such practices in the domain of effective classroom management.

Yet 43 of the 50 United States permit corporal punishment, and its schoolhouse and community advocates seem to be loud and numerous, especially as regards many of the types of youngsters for whom the Prepare Curriculum seems appropriate. Is it, as Hagebak (1979) darkly suggests, that physically punitive teachers should ask themselves "whether they tend to interpret classroom problems as a personal threat, whether they inflict punishment to protect their self-esteem, whether they retaliate rather than consider the causes of disruptive behavior objectively, and whether they derive sexual satisfaction from inflicting physical punishment" (p. 112)? Or, more parsimoniously, recalling our earlier definition of negative reinforcement, is teacher use and reuse of corporal punishment a simple function of the fact that it intermittently succeeds in reducing or eliminating the student disruptiveness, aggression, or other behavior experienced as aversive by the teacher?

Whatever the motivations and reinforcements that have sustained its use, corporal punishment—like all means of punishment—typically fails to yield sustained suppression of inappropriate behaviors; increases the likelihood that the youngster will behave aggressively in other settings (Hyman, 1978; Maurer, 1974; Welsh, 1978); and makes no contribution at all to the development of new, appropriate behaviors. We feel quite strongly that one's behavior as a classroom teacher must be ethically responsive to such accumulated empirical evidence. Ample research exists to conclude firmly that the science of behavior modification must replace the folklore advocating corporal punishment.

Negative reinforcement

Negative reinforcement is the final contingency management procedure we wish to consider, and our consideration of it will be brief. As defined earlier, negative reinforcement is the removal of aversive stimuli contingent upon the occurrence of desirable behaviors. Negative reinforcement has seldom been utilized as a behavior modification approach in a classroom context. The major exception to this rule is the manner in which youngsters may be contingently released from time out (an aversive environment), depending upon such desirable behaviors as quietness and calmness. Such release serves as negative reinforcement for these behaviors. Unfortunately, negative reinforcement often proves important in a classroom context in a less constructive way. Consider a teacher-student interaction in which the student behaves disruptively (shouts, swears, fights), the teacher responds with anger and physical punishment toward the youngster, and the punishment brings about a temporary suppression of the youngster's disruptiveness. The decrease in student disruptiveness may also be viewed as a decrease in aversive stimulation experienced by the teacher, which functions to negatively reinforce the immediately preceding teacher behavior (in this case, corporal punishment). The net effect of this sequence is to increase the future likelihood of teacher use of corporal punishment. Analogous sequences may occur and function to increase the likelihood of other ineffective, inappropriate, or intemperate teacher behaviors.

Other Behavior Modification Procedures

In addition to the various procedures we have examined for the presentation or removal of positive reinforcement or the use of aversive stimuli, there are a number of behavior modification procedures available for classroom use that do not rely upon the management of contingencies for their apparent effectiveness. In this section we briefly consider these procedures.

Overcorrection

Overcorrection is a behavior modification approach developed by Foxx and Azrin (1973) for those circumstances when extinction, time out, and response cost have either failed or cannot be utilized and when few alternative appropriate behaviors are available to reinforce. Overcorrection is a two-part procedure, having both restitutional and positive practice components. The restitutional aspect requires that the target individual return the behavioral setting (e.g., the classroom) to its status prior to disruption or better. Thus the objects broken by an angry youngster must be repaired, the classmates struck in anger apologized to, the papers scattered across the room picked up. Further, the positive practice component of overcorrection requires that the disruptive youngster then, in the specific examples just cited, be made to repair objects broken by others, apologize to classmates who witnessed the classmate being struck, or clean up the rest of the classroom (including areas not messed up by the target youngster). It is clear that the restitution and positive practice requirements may serve both a punitive and an instructional function.

Modeling

Modeling (also known as *imitation learning, vicarious learning,* and *observational learning*) is an especially powerful behavior modification procedure. Modeling may teach new behaviors or strengthen or weaken previously learned behaviors. Its effects have been demonstrated across a particularly wide array of target behaviors, including student aggression (Bandura, 1969; Goldstein, Sprafkin, Gershaw, & Klein, 1980; Perry & Furukawa, 1986; Sarason, 1968). Modeling procedures, facilitators, and consequences are examined in depth in chapter 3, our discussion of Interpersonal Skills Training.

Behavioral rehearsal

With deep roots in both psychodrama and more contemporaneous role-play activities, behavioral rehearsal has become an important behavior modification procedure. In it, appropriate alternative behaviors are enacted by the target individual in a safe, quasi-protected training environment prior to utilization in real-world contexts. Behavioral rehearsal, which is also described in detail in chapter 3, is often used in conjunction with modeling (which instructs *what* to rehearse) and feedback (regarding *how well* the behavior as rehearsed matches the model's). This technique has been used effectively with both individuals and groups to teach such alternatives to aggression as assertiveness (Galassi & Galassi, 1977), negotiation (Goldstein & Rosenbaum, 1982), self-control (Novaco, 1975), and a host of other prosocial behaviors (Goldstein et al., 1981).

Contingency contracting

A contingency contract is a written agreement between a teacher and student. It is a document each signs that specifies, in detailed behavioral terms, desirable student behaviors and their positive, teacher-provided consequences, as well as undesirable student behaviors and their contingent undesirable consequences. As Homme et al. (1969) specified in their initial description of this procedure, such contracts will more reliably lead to desirable student behaviors when the contract payoff is immediate; approximations to the desirable behavior are rewarded; the contract rewards accomplishment rather than obedience; accomplishment precedes reward; and the contract is fair, clear, honest, positive, and systematically implemented.

Procedural combinations

It is increasingly the accepted view in both education and psychology that interventions designed to modify overt behavior in personal, interpersonal, or academic realms are optimally designed and implemented prescriptively (Cronbach & Snow, 1969; Goldstein, 1978; Goldstein & Stein, 1976; Hunt & Sullivan, 1974). This differential, or tailored, intervention strategy proposes that the modification of behavior will proceed most effectively and efficiently when change methods used fit the type or intensity of the behaviors to which they are applied. For the most part, the state of prescriptive guidelines in education and psychology is still largely rudimentary, and only approximate prescriptions are currently possible. Such prescriptions, however, are clearly superior to trial-and-error application of interventions, which view all interventions as more or less equivalent, or to "one-true-light" prescriptions, in which one's favored approach is applied to all types and intensities of undesirable behavior. Thus, beginning steps though they may be, certain rudimentary prescriptive guidelines are available to help the teacher determine which procedure to use with which youngster. Because research support for these guidelines is as yet only modest, the reader should view these prescriptions only as suggestions.

Walker (1979) has proposed the following prescriptive hierarchy of interventions of increasing potency for particularly disruptive, acting-out, or aggressive youngsters. Each of the following interventions combines means for both the presentation and removal of positive reinforcement:

1. Teacher praise for appropriate behavior and brief time out for inappropriate behavior (Wasik, Senn, Welsh, & Cooper, 1968),
2. Teacher praise and token reinforcement for appropriate behavior and time out for inappropriate behavior (Walker, Mattson, & Buckley, 1971),
3. Teacher praise for appropriate behavior and response cost for inappropriate behavior (Walker et al., 1976),
4. Teacher praise and positive nonsocial reinforcement for appropriate behavior and response cost for inappropriate behavior (Walker, Street, Garrett, & Crossen, 1977).

Beyond these recommendations, we have three approximate prescriptions to offer. The first are our earlier "semiprescriptions" regarding the optimal utilization of extinction, time out, and response cost. The second is the view incorporating the ideas that Prepare-related prosocial modeling, behavioral rehearsal, and similar instructional measures are prescriptively most useful in teaching appropriate behaviors not yet in the individual's repertoire; that shaping is especially useful when the person is capable of approximations to appropriate behavior but not the behavior itself; and that presentations of positive reinforcement fit best when appropriate behaviors have been learned but for one reason or another are not being performed. Finally, it is generally appropriate to prescribe employment of the procedure or procedures that are least restrictive, least costly, and simplest to implement and that seem to hold a reasonable possibility of effective outcome.

Ethical Issues

Earlier in this chapter, we briefly alluded to a series of objections that have been raised, on ethical grounds, to the utilization of behavior modification procedures in school settings. At this point, having both described these procedures in detail and underscored their behavior-change potency, we wish to readdress these ethical concerns in greater depth. The substantial, often dramatic, effectiveness of behavior modification procedures by no means dictates that such procedures must be used. Criteria of acceptability that transcend effectiveness exist, criteria that—in addition to effectiveness—must unequivocally be met prior to the utilization of any behavioral or nonbehavioral procedure. Let us examine whether behavior modification procedures meet such criteria.

Manipulation

Webster's Encyclopedic Dictionary of the English Language (1973) defines manipulation as "the act of operating upon skillfully, for the purpose of giving a false appearance to" (p. 515). Unfortunately, what we perceive to be the all-too-frequent naive use of behavior modification techniques has provided evidence for a view of behavioral technology as the clever (some would say Machiavellian) but not very thorough or longlasting manipulation of superficial behavior. In fact, we would agree that, when behavior modification is used by uninformed adults in a cursory and not very thoughtful way to control the behavior of other adults or children, Webster's definition may indeed apply. There is, however, another perspective. With a small but significant change in the dictionary definition, we would grant that behavior modification is indeed manipulative. Were one to replace *false* in this definition with *changed*, we would clearly label behavior modification as manipulation. Furthermore, in this altered definition, the term *manipulation* is, in our view, very far from a term of disapproval. In our sense of the term, *all* educational, psychological, and psychoeducational interventions are, and optimally should be, manipulative: the behavioral, the psychodynamic, the humanistic, and all others. Where approaches differ is in how effective their efforts are and how open intervenors are—to both others and especially to themselves—to the notion that they are indeed "operating upon skillfully, for the purpose of giving a *changed* appearance to." Referring to therapeutic applications of behavior modification, O'Leary and Wilson (1975) have reflected this viewpoint well in the following observation:

> Behavior modification is often indicted for supposedly denying individual freedom and for being a mechanistic, manipulative, and impersonal approach which deliberately sets out to control behavior. On the other hand, purportedly more humanistic forms of therapy are applauded because they claim to promote individual "growth" or "self-actualization" without imposing any external control. What such a comparison overlooks is the now widely accepted truism that all forms of therapy involve control or social influence. Truax (1966), for example, has shown how even Carl Rogers' "nondirective" therapy results in the therapist unwittingly reinforcing particular types of client verbalizations which the therapist believes to be therapeutic. The issue is not whether clients' behavior should or should not be controlled; it unquestionably is. The important question then becomes whether the therapist is aware of this control and the behaviors it is used to develop. (pp. 28–29)

Precisely the same point may be made about the everyday behavior of the typical classroom teacher. By dint of presenting or withholding approval, smiles, stares, touching, scolding, praise, permission to engage in pleasurable activities, denial of opportunity for such activities, and literally dozens of other reinforcement-relevant teacher behaviors, the teacher functions as a highly active, highly influential, highly manipulative (in our revised definitional sense) modifier of students' behavior. Manipulation is present; its effective and efficient utilization often are not. We hope that the discussion of behavior modification procedures in the present chapter will serve as a small contribution to enhancing the effectiveness of such utilization.

Freedom of Choice

The technology of behavior modification has been criticized by some as resulting in a diminution of the target person's freedom of choice. Other people (i.e., the intervenors), it is held, act upon the person and, by the effective use of behavior modification procedures, choose the behaviors that person comes to utilize. In our view, this is the least cogent argument that has been brought to bear in criticizing the ethics of behavior modification. On the contrary, we would agree with those who have held that enhanced, not diminished, freedom of choice is the net consequence of behavioral interventions for target youngsters. What intervenors do choose, should choose, are the procedures for reaching goal behaviors—that is, the *how* of behavior modification. The goals themselves, or the *what* of this intervention, as well as the *why* and *when*, can often be selected not only by the teacher, school, and larger community, but also by the youngster. Participation by the target youngster in the selection of goal behaviors is not always possible and is sometimes inappropriate. But in a great many interventions, though probably not the majority, the behaviors pinpointed for modification will be a decision to which the youngster contributes substantially.

There is a second, equally significant way in which successful behavior modification produces enhanced freedom of choice. It does so by enlarging the target individual's behavioral repertoire. Prior to the successful application of, for example, positive reinforcement for negotiating differences with a fellow student and time out for physically brawling with peers, a given youngster may well be essentially choiceless when faced with a dispute. That is, the youngster's typical response—to lash out, punch, fight—may be that individual's *only* potential response. Negotiation of disputes, calling upon others, withdrawal, or other possible and less aggressive responses may never have been used by the youngster, or may have been used exceedingly rarely, and hence, for all practical purposes, may not be called upon. In essence, not knowing alternatives at all or very well, the youngster has no choice but to fight. When the behavioral intervention succeeds in increasing the likelihood of negotiation as a response by arming the youngster with this new alternative, the youngster is correspondingly armed with "choicefulness." Now she may fight or negotiate as *she* chooses and as *she* perceives the potential rewards and punishments of the existing alternatives. The decision to use reinforcement and time out is largely the teacher's; the decision to reward negotiation behavior is, it is hoped, jointly the teacher's and the youngster's; but the decision actually to negotiate a given dispute with a peer is and should be wholly the youngster's. Thus the heart of our view is that, by collaborating when possible in decisions about target behaviors to be modified and by allowing the student to decide unilaterally about the use or nonuse of newly learned (and heretofore unavailable, thus unchoosable) appropriate behaviors, those who employ behavior modification are indeed providing a choice-enhancing technology for the youngsters to whom it is directed.

Bribery

The accusation that those behavior modification procedures that present reinforcement for appropriate behaviors are equivalent to the use of bribery also seems erroneous to us. Bribery is defined as "a prize, gift, or other favor bestowed or promised to pervert the judgment or corrupt the conduct of a person" (*Webster's Encyclopedic Dictionary of the English Language,* 1973, p. 275). In behavior modification, reinforcement is used neither to pervert nor corrupt but, instead, to reward and broaden the person's repertoire of personally and socially useful behaviors. A reward for the prosocial differs greatly in an ethical sense from a reward for the antisocial.

Yet the objection is raised, even when the distinction between bribery and appropriate reward is acknowledged, that youngsters should not need an external reward for doing what society expects them to do. Instead, it is argued that negotiating disputes, paying attention, remaining in one's seat, conversing appropriately, not cursing, not fighting, and exhibiting other desirable classroom behaviors should be intrinsically rewarding. This view, we feel, is both hypocritical and factually incorrect. It is hypocritical because rewards are presented for appropriate behavior at all other levels of society. Not infrequently, such rewards are extended to teachers themselves for appropriate teaching behaviors; in addition, these same teachers consistently offer rewards (albeit in an unsystematic manner) to youngsters for other types of behavior, such as academic excellence. We also hold that it is factually incorrect that youngsters should not need an external reward for doing what society expects them to do because, simply put, some youngsters do. This generalization applies to many youngsters with special needs and most certainly includes the chronically aggressive, disruptive, withdrawn, or asocial youngsters who are the particular focus of the Prepare Curriculum.

Whose Needs Are Served?

A further ethical concern we wish to examine pertains to decisions about whose needs will take precedence when choices must be made about whether or not to employ behavior modification procedures in a given classroom and how to use such procedures when they are employed. Among the earliest applied uses of behavior modification were applications in mental hospitals to alter the behavior of long-term, adult psychiatric patients. Literally hundreds of research papers attest to the success of this effort. But which behaviors were altered? How was success defined? In far too large a percentage of these investigations, the "appropriate" patient behaviors successfully developed met the needs of the staff (the intervenors) at least as much as, and often more than, those of the patient. "Good patient" behaviors were rewarded—that is, behaviors such as patient compliance, passivity, and dependency, which led to an orderly and predictable ward, one relatively comfortable and manageable for the staff. Such a regime, which has come to be appropriately associated with the term *colonization effect* for its "robotizing" influence upon patients, ill-prepared such patients for the demands of community living when the deinstitutionalization movement (between 1965 and 1985) led to 400,000 patients' discharge from United States public mental hospitals.

This apparent digression into the adult mental health realm is relevant to the ethical question, "Whose needs will be served?" Will it be the school's at large? The teacher's? The youngster's? Although it would be naive to argue that schools have not utilized behavior modification as a powerful tool to teach "good student" behaviors (the analog of "good patient" behaviors, including compliance, passivity, and dependency), it would be equally foolish, in our view, to throw out the technology because some (perhaps even many) schools and teachers have misused it. If our goal is to be truly helpful to youngsters and to enhance their educational potential and not only to maintain an orderly and manageable classroom, teachers should and will make the decision to employ appropriate behavior modification procedures. They will apply them toward the development of appropriate behaviors that not only will contribute to a calm classroom climate but will also enhance the learning process.

Responsiveness to Research

Behavior modification has suffered from bad press and bad public relations. The specific procedures described in this chapter have been associated with Machiavellian fictional accounts (e.g., the film *A Clockwork Orange*) and identified with other existing procedures that seek to change behavior by means having nothing whatsoever in common with behavior modification (e.g., psychosurgery and sterilization). This negative public image is all the more surprising when one recognizes the vast and unique level of empirical support attesting to the real-world effectiveness of this approach. No other existing means for altering, influencing, or modifying human behavior in appropriate directions rests on as comparably broad and deep an empirical foundation. It is our belief that one of our highest ethical responsibilities is to be responsive to objective evidence, to offer our students what research repeatedly demonstrates to be effective, to try to overcome our own subjective biases, and to act in the welfare of others in ways that are most clearly indicated by cumulative scientific evidence. Meeting this ethical responsibility will, we feel, often mean greater utilization of behavior modification programs based on the thoughtful application of appropriate principles to the diverse manifestations of student aggression, withdrawal, and other learning-inhibiting behaviors. We must be careful in doing so not to oversell this approach, however empirically based or useful it appears to be. Although we have amply indicated that behavior modification programs are quite often able to document success in facilitating the learning of both traditional academic content and curricula like Prepare, as well as in directly enhancing appropriate behaviors in children and adults, much empirical work remains to be done. It is our hope that the creative researcher and thoughtful teacher will join each other in responding to this promising challenge.

Chapter 14

Future Directions

We have presented a 10-course curriculum designed to teach diverse prosocial behaviors and have suggested a variety of means for motivating its trainees, enhancing its delivery, and maximizing both its transfer to real-life settings and its durability over time. It is a curriculum developed for both adolescents and younger children who, in one or another major way, regularly manifest serious prosocial deficiencies. Both the antisocial, aggressive youngster and the asocial, withdrawn youth are prime curriculum targets, as are youth more moderately deficient in prosocial competencies. The Prepare Curriculum adapts well not only to diverse trainees, but also to a variety of trainers and settings. Components of this curriculum have been effectively offered by teachers, teacher aides, youth care workers, counselors, social workers, paraprofessionals, and others in such contexts as elementary and secondary schools, group homes, facilities for delinquent or emotionally disturbed youth, and other educational or clinical settings. We have sought in the curriculum's conceptualization and preparation to develop course domains that are relevant to the real-world needs of its target trainees, comprehensive in their coverage yet responsive to the need to remain open-ended and encouraging of additional course development, prescriptive in their optimal use, and complementary as they relate to one another. In order to help facilitate these several qualities, as well as the overarching goal of the enhancement of prosocial behavior, we wish in this final chapter to examine a series of issues, each of which bears importantly on the effective use, development, or extension of Prepare.

Enhancing Trainee Motivation

Many of the youth for whom the Prepare Curriculum is intended will not be highly motivated to attend its classes, learn its substance, or apply its lessons. For a variety of developmental and environmental reasons (e.g., absence of prosocial models, infrequent prosocial support, minimal prosocial opportunity), as well as for the reason that antisocial and asocial behavior is often richly and reliably rewarded, the desire to act prosocially, or to learn to do so, may be greatly diminished. It is quite likely, therefore, that, without substantial attention to the enhance-ment of trainee motivation, the Prepare training effort may fail. In the present section we offer a modest array of facts, and some speculation, about means for motivation enhancement.

Keller (1978) defines motivation as including "all factors which arouse, sustain, and direct behavior, and can be both toward or away from an activity" (p. 27). One category of trainee motivation, most central to the success of Prepare, we call *participation motivation*. It includes all facets of the trainee's desire (or lack of desire) to attend classes and participate therein as required for optimal course learning. To date, our efforts to maximize participation motivation have involved two broad categories of purported motivators: *extrinsic* and *intrinsic*. Extrinsic motivators are tangible things, activities, or arrangements offered to youth contingently upon adequate course participation. Pizza parties, special movies, T-shirts with a group logo, and points tradable for consumables or privileges are among the tangibles we have employed. Course arrangements that make participation special have also appar-ently served as valuable extrinsic motivators. These include having the Prepare classes meet at a special time (e.g., when what the participants will miss are activities or classes they don't especially enjoy), with special teachers serving as trainers, and at special places in the school building (perhaps typically off-limits places). Also motivationally important, particularly at the beginning of most Prepare courses, is for youth to have a substantial role in selecting particular contents to be learned. Elsewhere, we have called this effort *negotiating the curricu-lum* (Goldstein & Pentz, 1984). It provides the youth the opportunity to feed into the lesson selection process his preferences or needs (e.g., which interpersonal skill, which anger reducer, or which stress man-agement technique he feels can be used *now*). Extrinsic motivators, in our experience, are especially valuable in the early weeks of Prepare course instruction. As time and sessions roll by, however, it becomes increasingly important for motivational purposes that the inherent value of the course contents become apparent to participating youth. Stated otherwise, the major intrinsic motivator available to drive the Prepare engine is that the course lessons "work": They pay off in both class and the outside world. The several techniques described in our discussion of transfer and maintenance (chapter 12) will certainly help in this regard. So too will continued use by the trainer of curriculum negotiation, in which trainer and trainees collaboratively select some or all of the course contents to be taught from each class's pool of alternative lessons, activities, or skills. In the final analysis, not to attend or participate actively in Prepare courses when their contents are irrelevant to the real-world in which the trainees live is a wise and appropriate trainee decision. We have sought in developing Prepare to maximize its real-world relevance. We urge upon its trainers the challenging task of continuing this effort and thus seeking to enhance intrinsic motivation by maximizing in the delivery of Prepare its usefulness and relevance for participating trainees.

We have spoken thus far only about participation motivation. There are two other categories of trainee motivation relevant to the success or failure of Prepare. Both deserve the attention of researchers and practitioners concerned with the efficacy of psychoeducational interventions such as Prepare. The first, *achievement motivation,* already has a long history in the research and training literature. Developed initially from Murray's (1938) concept of need-achievement by McClelland and his research group (McClelland, 1953; McClelland, Atkinson, Clark, & Lowell, 1953) and the target of much theoretical interest—for example, Atkinson's (1958) expectancy-value theory, Weiner's (1974) attribution theory, Deci's (1975) cognitive evaluation theory, Beery's (1975) self-worth theory, and Eccles (1983) task value theory-achievement—motivation has also been the focus of a number of training programs. We will not detail these efforts here since they are elaborate and beyond our present scope, but each has considerable potential relevance to the youth for whom Prepare is intended and thus is deserving of careful scrutiny by those wishing to further advance the motivational underpinning of its successful implementation. We thus refer the interested reader to the achievement motivation training programs of Alschuler, Tabor, and McIntyre (1971) and Alschuler (1973); DeCharms (1968); Dweck (1986); and McClelland and Winters (1969).

Enhancing youth motivation to participate in Prepare and achieve mastery of its contents is, we believe, a difficult goal to accomplish. But even more difficult, in our view, is the enhancement of the third type of trainee motivation: *prosocial motivation.* How will we increase trainees' desire to use, in their daily lives, the many prosocial lessons of the Prepare Curriculum? As noted earlier, alternative behaviors of an asocial and (especially) antisocial nature are often immediately, richly, and reliably rewarded in our society. Why seek to cooperate when competition pays off, to negotiate when hitting yields reward, to empathize when indifference is less trouble? Stated otherwise, one major route to enhanced prosocial motivation lies well outside the scope of Prepare and concerns societal values and circumstances surrounding egocentric behaviors and their rewards versus the nonrewards often associated with allocentrism. Within the psychoeducational literature, however, what has been offered regarding the enhancement of prosocial motivation has focused mostly on the creation by the teacher of a prosocial classroom climate rather than on direct prosocial motivational instruction. As Brophy (1983) comments,

> Some of this socialization (such as rules for classroom conduct or for interpersonal behavior generally) is taught directly in the same way that academic content is taught. More of it, however, is communicated indirectly through modeling and other behavior that expresses teachers' beliefs, attitudes, and expectations concerning what is or is not right, just, interesting, desirable, et cetera. Consistent teacher communications on these issues will provide a direct or indirect press on students to adopt similar beliefs, attitudes, expectations, and associated behaviors. If anything, the potential for socialization effects in general and for self-fulfilling prophecy effects in particular is probably greater in the personal, social, and moral spheres than the area of academic achievement, where the possibilities open to students at a given time are limited by their intellectual abilities and present repertoires of academic knowledge and skill. (p. 183)

Staub (1979) similarly observes as follows:

> I would expect an environment in which there is reasonable structure (and effective control) that limits harmful interactions among children and encourages positive interactions, interdependence among members of the group so that cooperation and positive behavior in response to need occur naturally, a fair amount of autonomy that children are allowed so that they can learn and develop effective modes of interaction and conflict resolution, and basically democratic and just relationships between children and adults to contribute to prosocial orientation, high self-esteem, a sense of competence, role taking, and positive social behavior. (p. 254)

Although such speculations are valuable leads, the goal of enhanced prosocial motivation is so central to the entire purpose and intent of the Prepare Curriculum that we especially recommend further work in this domain. The Prepare Curriculum is, we believe, an important beginning in charting out the materials and methods of prosocial instruction. An equally energetic effort in the realm of prosocial motivation would seem to be a particularly worthwhile and valuable undertaking.

Curriculum Evaluation: Assessment of Competence

We believe strongly that remedial curricula like Prepare must be offered to trainees in an individualized, prescriptive manner. Results will be substantially enhanced, in our view, when youth participate only in those Prepare courses in whose contents they are substantially deficient. Such a prescriptive aspiration is, at first, a matter of adequate assessment. Adequate assessment is also central to the tracking of trainee progress through the given Prepare courses being taken so that instructional adjustments can be made and degree of competency enhancement can be evaluated. Finally, adequate assessment of trainee change is also vital for curriculum evaluation purposes so that we may discern which courses to retain, alter, delete, and improve. How shall such measurement of trainee proficiency/deficiency proceed? A comprehensive battery of appropriate assessment devices for the measurement of competence level in Prepare course domains is yet to be constructed. Our efforts in this task are progressing in two complementary directions. The first direction begins with the use of established inventories, checklists, and similar assessment devices. These recommended measures, detailed in Table 26, are relevant to those five Prepare courses that, in current or similar format, have been in existence for some time: Problem-solving Training (chapter 2), Interpersonal Skills Training (chapter 3), Anger Control Training (chapter 5), Moral Reasoning Training (chapter 6), and Stress Management Training (chapter 7).

In addition to utilization of such standardized measurement devices, several other approaches to the assessment of competence levels in these Prepare course domains have been used. These include behavioral observation of in vivo, naturalistic behavior or response to role-play test situations (Goldfried & Kent, 1972; Goldstein, 1981; Jacob, 1976; Patterson, 1974); self-monitoring (Arkowitz, 1977; Kanfer & Gaelick, 1986); structured interviews (Banaka, 1971; Matarazzo & Wiens, 1972; Shoubsmith, 1968); evaluations by significant others (Kane & Lawler, 1978; Weiss, Hops, & Patterson, 1973; Whitehill, Hersen, & Bellack, 1978); and community functioning indices (Goldstein, Glick, Irwin, McCartney, & Rubama, in press; Kirigin, Braukmann, Atwater, & Wolf, 1982). In our own utilization of these several measurement approaches to evaluate the effectiveness of Prepare Curriculum courses, we have followed certain measurement principles (Goldstein, 1981; Goldstein & Glick, 1987; Goldstein et al., in press). First, we have always utilized a *multimodal assessment battery.* That is, recognizing that there are

Table 26
Measures for Assessing Deficit in Established Prepare Courses

Course	Recommended measure
Interpersonal Skills Training	Child Behavior Checklist (Achenbach & Edelbrock, 1983)
	Classroom Adjustment Rating Scale (Lorion, Cowen, & Caldwell, 1975)
	Structured Learning Skill Checklist (Goldstein, Sprafkin, Gershaw, & Klein, 1980)
	Taxonomy of Problematic Social Situations for Children (Dodge & Murphy, 1984)
	Matson Evaluation of Social Skills with Youngsters (Matson, Rotatori, & Helsel, 1983)
	Adolescent Problem Inventory (Freedman, Rosenthal, Donahoe, Schlundt, & McFall, 1978)
	Problem Inventory for Adolescent Girls (Gaffney & McFall, 1981)
Anger Control Training	Children's Action Tendency Scale (Deluty, 1979)
Moral Reasoning Training	Sociomoral Reflections Measure (Gibbs, Widaman, & Colby, 1982)
	Measure of Moral Development (Carroll & Rest, 1981)
Problem-solving Training	The Optional Thinking Test (Platt & Spivack, 1977)
	The Awareness of Consequences Test (Platt & Spivack, 1977)
	Means-ends Stories (Platt & Spivack, 1977)
Stress Management Training	State-trait Anxiety Inventory for Children (Spielberger, 1976)
	Stress Inventory (Garmezy, 1981)
	The Adolescent Perceived Events Scale (Compas, Davis, Forsythe, & Wagner, 1986)
	Life Events Checklist (Johnson & McCutcheon, 1980)

errors of measurement associated with each of the assessment approaches noted above, we have typically included measures of each of these types in the belief that their method variance and other inherent distortions are not additive and may, in fact, cancel each other out to an appreciable degree. A second, related basis for our use of this array of measures lies in the value of assessing trainee change from *several vantage points*: self, peer, teacher, parent, etc. None is more "true" than the other; each contributes to our understanding of the Prepare courses' outcome efficacy. Our assessment batteries have always included both *proximal* and *distal measures*—that is, measures assessing the immediate, short-term effects of Prepare participation and those reflecting its more enduring consequences. Stated otherwise, we have sought to discern both *acquisition effects* as well as *transfer and maintenance* of change. We have typically used these diverse assessment devices in a *repeated measures format,* in which trainee competence level is measured before course participation to establish base-rate competency level, at two or more times during course participation to determine in-process change trends, immediately following the course, and at a later follow-up to evaluate maintenance of change effects.

A number of the Prepare courses seek to teach contents either not represented before in psychoeducational instruction or, if represented before, not typically assessed rigorously. Situational Perception Training (chapter 4) and Recruiting Supportive Models (chapter 9) are in the "brand new" category. Cooperation Training (chapter 10) and Understanding and Using Groups (chapter 11) rely heavily on existing games and simulations, but these activities are quite typically used clinically and impressionistically, their impact very rarely being evaluated rigorously. The final Prepare course we wish to include in our measurement recommendation is Empathy Training (chapter 8). Here a long history of psychometric attention exists, but it is confusing, contradictory, and largely inadequate, thus calling for new measurement approaches in much the same way as for the foregoing new or impressionistically measured Prepare courses. Until such time as standardized, validated assessment devices in these Prepare domains become available, the measurement approach we would recommend for evaluation of trainee competency is Curriculum-based Assessment (Deno, 1987; Fuchs 1987; Tindal, 1987; Wesson, 1987). This approach to (thus far primarily) the measurement of competence in academic skill subjects has been defined as

> any procedure that directly assesses student performance within the course content for the purpose of determining that student's instructional needs.... Materials used to assess progress are always drawn

directly from the course of study. Thus, in [Curriculum-based Assessment], reading level and reading ability are assessed by having the student read material from the school's own curriculum. (Tucker, 1985, p. 200)

In establishing a Curriculum-based Assessment program—for reading, math, or, we would suggest, Situational Perception Training, Cooperation Training, and so forth—the following steps, adapted from Blankenship (1985), are utilized:

1. List the skills presented in the course materials used,
2. Examine the list to see if all important skills are included,
3. Arrange the skills in logical sequence,
4. Prepare objectives for each listed skill,
5. Prepare or select test segments of course materials for each objective,
6. Plan an assessment administration procedure,
7. Administer the Curriculum-based Assessment immediately prior to beginning instruction on the topic,
8. Examine the precourse assessment results to determine which students have and have not already mastered the skills targeted for instruction,
9. Readminister the Curriculum-based Assessment at points during and immediately after instruction on the topic,
10. Examine the intermediate and post-course assessment results to determine which students have and have not mastered the skills instructed.

This relatively straightforward process of directly tracking trainee learning through the contents of instruction and providing reinstruction when needed has considerable appeal not only vis-à-vis the five less established Prepare courses, but also for the entire Prepare Curriculum. Our overall assessment recommendation, therefore, is that trainee competence in Prepare content domains be measured by a judiciously selected and implemented combination of the traditional assessment approaches and devices described earlier, combined with the individualized progressive tracking of Curriculum-based Assessment.

Curriculum Utilization:
Remediation and Prevention

Throughout this book, we have described Prepare as a body of courses intended largely for remedial use, to correct an array of prosocial deficiencies in diverse adolescents and younger children. Indeed, it is a remedial program, an effort to rehabilitate the prosocially deficient youth. But it is also a preventive curriculum, ideally to be used as habilitation too. Stated otherwise, it is our aspiration that Prepare also be employed for the initial teaching of its constituent skills in order that aggression, withdrawal, and similar behavioral reflections of prosocial deficiency be forestalled—and thus rarely appear in the repertoires of participating youth. It is true that, thus far in education and other human services, prevention is a theme more in spirit than in substance, more in hope than in accomplishment. Nevertheless, successful exceptions do exist, and some of these involve direct preventive use of Prepare Curriculum courses. Keller, Goldstein, and Wynn (1987), for example, describe a year-long implementation of what they termed Aggression Prevention Training with second-, fourth-, and sixth-grade children at an inner city elementary school. All participating youth were moderately aggressive or withdrawn, not yet in serious delinquency or emotional difficulty but, by such behaviors, showing early predictive precursors of such later problematic involvement (Loeber & Dishion, 1983). Over the course of a school year, these youngsters met in small groups for weekly sessions of Interpersonal Skills Training, Anger Control Training, and Moral Reasoning Training. Compared to control group youth, participating trainees showed prosocial skill enhancement clearly supportive of the view that psychoeducational interventions such as these can in practice serve in a potentially preventive manner.

Curriculum Enhancement:
A Systems Perspective

Our several descriptions throughout this book of aspects of the implementation of the Prepare Curriculum have been largely trainee-oriented (i.e., how to increase trainee motivation, decrease disruptiveness, increase transfer, and the like). We have omitted attention to an exceedingly important determinant of the probable success of such psychoeducational interventions—namely, the ecological context in which it is offered. Such a systems concern has become quite popular in recent years (Apter, 1982; Apter & Propper, 1986; Barth, 1983; Goldstein, Apter, & Haroutunian, 1984; Plas, 1987), but, as with preventive interventions, the implementation of a systems perspective is much more hope than reality.

There are at least two ecological means by which the impact of Prepare might be potentiated. The first involves offering appropriate

Prepare courses or parts thereof to significant persons in the real-world environments of adolescent or young child Prepare trainees. We have done so already, with apparent success, in offering a combination of Interpersonal Skills Training (focused on skills reciprocal to those being taught the adolescent trainees in this program) and Anger Control Training to parents and siblings of adjudicated juvenile delinquents (Goldstein et al., in press).

A second, more ambitious strategy for mobilizing the youth trainee's world toward the prosocial ends aspired to by Prepare is reflected in Table 27, modified from Haroutunian's (1986) systems consideration of school violence. The mode × level intervention strategy depicted in this table seeks to illustrate the notion that effective, systemwide interventions for prosocially deficient youth (in this instance, aggressive youth) may optimally occur simultaneously at several levels: with the youth, as well as with the teacher, school, and/or larger community. In addition, interventions may be of several complementary types: psychological, educational, administrative, legal, and physical. As a rough, initial hypothesis, we would assert that the greater the number of system levels and modes of intervention, the greater the likelihood of substantial, enduring prosocial change in participating youth. As we have commented elsewhere with regard to school violence and its reduction,

> When a teacher or student is beaten in school, corrective steps must focus not only upon the student involved, not only upon the teacher and his or her colleagues, not only upon the school and its curricula and organization, and not only upon the community or state in which the school is located, but simultaneously upon all of these levels of potential intervention. To reduce the likelihood that another beating will occur, or another window will be broken, or another fire started, and to increase the likelihood that prosocial, rather than antisocial, values and behaviors will be demonstrated and reinforced, our optimal interventions should occur concurrently at the student, teacher, school, and community levels. (Goldstein et al., 1984, p. viii)

Curriculum Expansion

It is our hope and expectation that the Prepare Curriculum will remain perpetually in transition, being implemented, evaluated, altered, and, when appropriate, expanded. There is nothing magical about the 10 course areas we have selected for development. Basing our decision on both our experience as psychoeducators and the relevant empirical

Table 27

A Mode × Level Systems Intervention Strategy for School Violence

Multi-level targets of intervention	Multi-modal interventions				
	Psychological	*Educational*	*Administrative*	*Legal*	*Physical*
Community	Programs for disturbed children	Prosocial television programs	Adopt-a-School programs	Gun control legislation	Near school, mobile home vandalism watch
School	Use of skilled conflict negotiators	Prescriptively tailored course sequences	Reduction of class size	Legal-rights handbook	Lighting, painting, paving programs
Teacher	Aggression management training	Enhanced knowledge of student ethnic milieu	Low teacher-pupil ratio	Compensation for aggression-related expenses	Personal alarm systems
Student	Counseling services	Prepare Curriculum	School transfer	Use of security personnel	Student murals, graffiti boards

Note. From "School Violence and Vandalism," by B. Haroutunian. In *Youth Violence* (p. 133), edited by S. J. Apter and A. P. Goldstein, 1986, New York: Pergamon. Reprinted by permission.

595

literature, we chose course domains of apparent value. But many others were considered, have not yet been developed by us, and should continue to be considered for such development efforts by creative psychoeducators subscribing to the philosophy on which Prepare rests. What are some of these further possible courses? We would propose the following, in no special order of preference:

1. Creativity Training,
2. Negotiation Training,
3. Parenting Training,
4. Family and Marital Relations,
5. Leadership Training,
6. Dealing with Authority Figures,
7. Making and Keeping Friends,
8. Confrontation Training,
9. Surviving and Thriving on the Street,
10. Advocacy Skills Training

Surely, there are many more domains ripe for psychoeducational instruction. We urge upon the reader this challenging and rewarding development effort and hope that future attempts to enhance and expand Prepare will go beyond courses, course contents, and the refinement and evaluation of current courses to include further concern for the many obstacles and opportunities involved in the delivery of a curriculum such as this, as is exemplified in our focus on motivation, classroom management, and transfer and maintenance.

References

Achenbach, T. M., & Edelbrock, C. (1983). *Manual for the Child Behavior Checklist and Revised Child Behavior Profile.* Burlington, VT: University of Vermont, Department of Psychiatry.

Adair, J. G., & Schachter, B. S. (1972). To cooperate or to look good? The subject's and experimenter's perceptions of each others' intentions. *Journal of Experimental Social Psychology, 8,* 74–85.

Adams, G. R. (1973). Classroom aggression: Determinants, controlling mechanisms, and guidelines for the implementation of a behavior modification program. *Psychology in the Schools, 10,* 155–168.

Adkins, W. R. (1970). Life skills: Structured counseling for the disadvantaged. *Personnel and Guidance Journal, 49,* 108–116.

Adler, A. (1924). *The practice and theory of individual psychology.* New York: Harcourt Brace Jovanovich.

Agras, W. S. (1967). Transfer during systematic desensitization therapy. *Behaviour Research and Therapy, 5,* 193–199.

Ahlborn, H. H. (1986). *Dilemma session intervention with adult female offenders: Behavioral and attitudinal correlates.* Unpublished manuscript, Ohio State University, Columbus.

Albert, R. D. (1983). The intercultural sensitizer or culture assimilator: A cognitive approach. In D. Landis & R. W. Brislin (Eds.), *Handbook of intercultural training* (Vol. 2). New York: Pergamon.

Albert, S. J. (1974). *The effects of videotaped modeling presentations, sex of the model and written materials in teaching affective attending responses to undergraduate students.* Unpublished doctoral dissertation, University of Virginia, Charlottesville.

Alberto, P. A., & Troutman, A. C. (1982). *Applied behavior analysis for teachers: Influencing student performance.* Columbus, OH: Charles E. Merrill.

Alexander, F. M. (1969). *The resurrection of the body.* New York: Dell.

Allen, K. E., Hart, B., Buell, J. S., Harris, F. R., & Wolf, M. M. (1964). Effects of social reinforcement on isolate behavior of a nursery school child. *Child Development, 35,* 511–518.

Allen, K. E., Kenke, L. B., Harris, F. R., Baer, D. M., & Reynolds, N. J. (1967). Control of hyperactivity by social reinforcement of attending behavior. *Journal of Educational Psychology, 58,* 231–237.

Allison, T. S., & Allison, S. L. (1971). Time-out from reinforcement: Effect on sibling aggression. *Psychological Record, 21,* 81–88.

Allport, F. H. (1924). *Social psychology.* New York: Houghton Mifflin.

Allport, G. W. (1961). *Pattern and growth in personality.* New York: Holt, Rinehart & Winston.

Alschuler, A. G. (1973). *Developing achievement motivation in adolescents.* Englewood Cliffs, NJ: Educational Technology.

Alschuler, A. G., Tabor, D., & McIntyre, J. (1971). *Teaching achievement motivation.* Middletown, CT: Educational Ventures.

Amir, Y. (1976). Contact hypothesis in ethnic relations. *Psychological Bulletin, 71,* 319–342.

Angyal, A. (1941). *Foundations for a science of personality.* Cambridge, MA: Harvard University Press.

Anthony, E. J., & Cohler, B. J. (1987). *The invulnerable child.* New York: Guilford.

Apter, S. J. (1982). *Troubled children/troubled systems.* New York: Pergamon.

Apter, S. J., & Propper, C. A. (1986). Ecological perspectives on youth violence. In S. J. Apter & A. P. Goldstein (Eds.), *Youth violence.* New York: Pergamon.

Arbuthnot, J. (1973). Relationships between maturity of moral judgment and measures of cognitive abilities. *Psychological Reports, 33,* 945–946.

Arbuthnot, J. (1975). Modification of moral judgment through role-playing. *Developmental Psychology, 11,* 319–324.

Arbuthnot, J., & Faust, A. (1981). *Teaching moral reasoning: Theory and practice.* New York: Harper & Row.

Arbuthnot, J., & Gordon, D. A. (1983). Moral reasoning development in correctional intervention. *Journal of Correctional Education, 34,* 133–138.

Argyle, M. (1981). The experimental study of the basic features of situations. In D. Magnusson (Ed.), *Toward a psychology of situations: An interactional perspective.* Hillsdale, NJ: Erlbaum.

Argyle, M., Trower, P., & Bryant, B. K. (1974). Explorations in the treatment of personality disorders and neuroses by social skill training. *British Journal of Medical Psychology, 47,* 63–72.

Arkowitz, H. (1977). Measurement and modification of minimal dating behavior. In M. Hersen, R. M. Eisler, & P. M. Miller (Eds.), *Progress in behavior modification* (Vol. 5). New York: Academic.

Aronson, E., Blaney, N., Stephan, C., Sikes, J., & Snapp, M. (1978). *The jigsaw classroom.* Beverly Hills, CA: Sage.

Asarnow, J. R., & Callan, J. W. (1985). Boys with peer adjustment problems: Social cognitive processes. *Journal of Consulting and Clinical Psychology, 53,* 80–87.

Aspy, D. N., & Roebuck, F. N. (1977). *Kids don't learn from people they don't like.* Amherst, MA: Human Resource Development Press.

Atkinson, J. W. (1958). *Motives in fantasy, action, and society.* Princeton, NJ: D. Van Nostrand.

Atrops, M. (1978). *Behavioral plus cognitive skills for coping with provocation in male offenders.* Unpublished doctoral dissertation, Fuller Theological Seminary, Pasadena, CA.

Atwater, S. K. (1953). Proactive inhibition and associative facilitation as affected by degree of prior learning. *Journal of Experimental Psychology, 46,* 400–404.

Authier, J., & Gustafson, K. (1973). *Enriching intimacy: A behavioral approach.* Unpublished manuscript, University of Nebraska Medical Center, Omaha.

Authier, J., & Gustafson, K. (1975). Application of supervised and nonsupervised microcounseling paradigms in the training of paraprofessionals. *Journal of Counseling Psychology, 22,* 74–78.

Avedon, E. (1981). The structural elements of games. In A. Furnham & M. Argyle (Eds.), *The psychology of social situations.* New York: Pergamon.

Avery, A. W., Rider, K., & Haynes-Clements, L. A. (1981). Communication skills training for adolescents: A five-month follow-up. *Adolescence, 16,* 289–298.

Axelrod, S., & Apsche, J. (Eds.). (1982). *The effects and side effects of punishment on human behavior.* New York: Academic.

Ayllon, T., & Azrin, N. H. (1968). *The token economy: A motivational system for therapy rehabilitation.* New York: Appleton-Century-Crofts.

Ayllon, T., & Michael, J. (1959). The psychiatric nurse as a behavioral engineer. *Journal of the Experimental Analysis of Behavior, 2,* 323–334.

Azrin, H. H., & Holz, W. C. (1966). Punishment. In W. K. Honig (Ed.), *Operant behavior: Areas of research and application.* New York: Appleton-Century-Crofts.

Bachrach, A. J., Erwin, W. J., & Mohr, J. D. (1965). The control of eating behavior in an anorexic by operant conditioning techniques. In L. P. Ullmann & L. Krasner (Eds.), *Case studies in behavior modification.* New York: Holt, Rinehart & Winston.

Bain, O., & Clark, S. (1966). *Character education: A handbook of teaching suggestions based on freedom's code for elementary teachers.* San Antonio, TX: The Children's Fund.

Banaka, W. H. (1971). *Training in depth interviewing.* New York: Harper & Row.

Bandura, A. (1969). *Principles of behavior modification.* New York: Holt, Rinehart & Winston.

Bandura, A. (1973). *Aggression: A social learning analysis.* Englewood Cliffs, NJ: Prentice-Hall.

Bandura, A. (1982). The psychology of chance encounters and life paths. *American Psychologist, 37,* 747–755.

Barker, R. G. (1968). *Ecological psychology.* Stanford, CA: Stanford University Press.

Barker, R. G., & Gump, P. (1964). *Big school, small school.* Stanford, CA: Stanford University Press.

Barker, R. G., & Wright, H. F. (1954). *Midwest and its children: The psychological ecology of an American town.* Evanston IL: Row-Peterson.

Barrera, M., Jr. (1981). Social support in the adjustment of pregnant adolescents. In B. H. Gottlieb (Ed.), *Social networks and social support.* Beverly Hills, CA: Sage.

Bartenieff, E., & Davis, M. (1973). Effort-shape analysis of movement: The unity of expression and function. In M. Davis (Ed.), *Research approaches to movement and personality.* New York: Arno.

Bartenieff, I., & Lewis, D. (1980). *Body movement: Coping with the environment.* New York: Gordon & Breach.

Barth, R. (1983). Social support networks for adolescents and their families. In J. Whittaker & J. Garbarino (Eds.), *Social support networks: Informal helping in the human services.* New York: Aldine.

Bash, M. A., & Camp, B. W. (1985a). *Think aloud: Increasing social and cognitive skills—A problem-solving program for children (Classroom Program Grades 3–4).* Champaign, IL: Research Press.

Bash, M. A., & Camp, B. W. (1985b). *Think aloud: Increasing social and cognitive skills—A problem-solving program for children (Classroom Program Grades 5–6).* Champaign, IL: Research Press.

Bass, M. (1981). *Stogdill's handbook of leadership.* New York: Free Press.

Bateson, G. (1941). The frustration-aggression hypothesis and culture. *Psychological Review, 48,* 350–355.

Bath, K. E. (1976). Comparison of brief empathy training. *Perceptual and Motor Skills, 43,* 925–926.

Batson, C. D. (1987). Prosocial motivation: Is it ever truly altruistic? In L. Berkowitz (Ed.), *Advances in experimental social psychology.* New York: Academic.

Batson, C. D., & Coke, J. S. (1981). Empathy: A source of altruistic motivation for helping? In J. P. Ruston & R. M. Sorrentino (Eds.), *Altruism and helping behavior: Social, personality, and developmental perspectives.* Hillsdale, NJ: Erlbaum.

Beady, C., & Slavin, R. E. (1981). Making success available to all students in desegregated schools. *Integrated Education, 18,* 28–31.

Beale, A. V., Payton, O. D., & Zachary, I. G. (1978). The effects of a communications course for health professionals on empathy discrimination. *Journal of Applied Rehabilitation Counseling, 9,* 46–49.

Beautrais, A. L., Fergusson, D. M., & Shannon, F. T. (1982). Life events and childhood morbidity: A prospective study. *Pediatrics, 70,* 935–940.

Beck, C. M., Sullivan, E. V., & Taylor, P. (1972). Stimulating transition to post-conventional morality: The Pickering High School study. *Interchange, 17,* 28–37.

Becker, F., & Zarit, S. H. (1978). Training older adults as peer counselors. *Educational Gerontology, 3,* 241–250.

Becker, W. C., Madsen, C. J., Arnold, C. R., & Thomas, D. R. (1967). The contingent use of teacher attention and praise in reducing classroom behavior problems. *Journal of Special Education, 1,* 287–307.

Beery, R. G. (1975). Fear of failure in student experience. *Personnel and Guidance Journal, 54,* 190–203.

Bell, L., & Bell, D. (1982, September). *Parental validation as a mediator in adolescent development.* Paper presented at the meeting of the American Psychological Association, Washington, DC.

Bem, S. L. (1967). Verbal self-control: The establishment of effective self-instruction. *Journal of Experimental Psychology, 74,* 485–491.

Bender, N. N. (1976). Self-verbalization versus tutor verbalization in modifying impulsivity. *Journal of Educational Psychology, 68,* 347–354.

Benne, K. D., & Sheats, P. (1948). Functional roles of group members. *Journal of Social Issues, 4,* 41–49.

Bennett, D. J., & Bennett, J. D. (1981). Making the scene. In A. Furnham & M. Argyle (Eds.), *The psychology of social situations.* New York: Pergamon.

Berberich, J. P. (1971). Do the child's responses shape the teaching behavior of adults? *Journal of Experimental Research in Personality, 5,* 92–97.

Berenson, D. (1971). The effects of systematic human relations training upon classroom performance of elementary school teachers. *Journal of Research and Development in Education, 4,* 70–85.

Berlin, R. (1974). *Training of hospital staff in accurate affective perception of fear-anxiety from vocal cues in the context of varying facial cues.* Unpublished master's thesis, Syracuse University, NY.

Berlin, R. (1976). *Teaching acting-out adolescents prosocial conflict resolution through structured learning training of empathy.* Unpublished doctoral dissertation, Syracuse University, NY.

Bernstein, D., & Borkovec, T. (1973). *Progressive relaxation training: A manual for the helping professions.* Champaign, IL: Research Press.

Bernstein, P. (1975). *Theory and methods in dance-movement therapy.* Dubuque, IA: Kendall/Hunt.

Bierman, R., Carkhuff, R. R., & Santilli, M. (1972). Efficacy of empathic communication training groups for inner city preschool teachers and family workers. *Journal of Applied Behavioral Science, 8,* 188–202.

Birk, J. M. (1972). Effects of counseling supervision methods and preference on empathic understanding. *Journal of Counseling Psychology, 19,* 542–546.

Blackwood, G. L., Jr. (1975). *Accurate empathy: Critique of a construct.* Unpublished manuscript, Vanderbilt University.

Blaney, N. T., Stephen, S., Rosenfield, D., Aronson, E., & Sikes, J. (1977). Interdependence in the classroom: A field study. *Journal of Educational Psychology, 69,* 121–128.

Blankenship, C. S. (1985). Using curriculum-based assessment data to make instructional decisions. *Exceptional Children, 52,* 233–238.

Blasi, A. (1980). Bridging moral cognitive and moral action: A critical review of the literature. *Psychological Bulletin, 88,* 1–45.

Blatt, M., Colby, A., & Speicher, B. (1974). *Hypothetical dilemmas for use in moral discussions.* Cambridge, MA: Harvard University, Moral Education and Research Foundation.

Blatt, M., & Kohlberg, L. (1975). The effects of classroom moral discussion upon children's level of moral judgment. *Journal of Moral Education, 4,* 129–161.

Blechman, E. A. (1974). The family contract game. *The Family Coordinator, 23,* 269–281.

Borkovec, T. D., Grayson, J. B., & Cooper, K. M. (1978). Treatment of general tension: Subjective and physiological effects of progressive relaxation. *Journal of Consulting and Clinical Psychology, 46,* 518–528.

Borkovec, T. D., Grayson, J. B., O'Brien, G. T., & Weerts, T. C. (1979). Relaxation treatment of pseudoinsomnia and idiopathic insomnia: An electroencephalographic evaluation. *Journal of Applied Behavior Analysis, 12,* 37–54.

Bornstein, P. H., & Quevillon, R. P. (1976). The effects of a self-instructional package on overactive preschool boys. *Journal of Applied Behavior Analysis, 9,* 179–188.

Bostow, D. E., & Bailey, J. S. (1969). Modification of severe disruptive and aggressive behavior using brief time out and reinforcement procedures. *Journal of Applied Behavior Analysis, 2,* 31–37.

Boyce, T. W., Jensen, E. W., Cassell, J. C., Collier, A. M., Smith, A. H., & Raimey, C. T. (1973). Influence of life events and family routines on childhood respiratory tract illness. *Pediatrics, 60,* 609–615.

Branca, M. C., D'Augelli, J. F., & Evans, K. L. (1975). *Development of a decision-making skills education program.* Unpublished manuscript, Pennsylvania State University, University Park.

Brand, A. H., Johnson, J. H., & Johnson, S. B. (1986). *The relationship between life stress and diabetic control in insulin-dependent diabetic children and adolescents.* Unpublished manuscript, University of Florida, Gainesville.

Braswell, L., Kendall, P. C., & Urbain, E. S. (1982). A multistudy analysis of the role of socioeconomic status (SES) in cognitive-behavioral treatments with children. *Journal of Abnormal Psychology, 10,* 443–449.

Brehm, J. W. (1966). *A theory of psychological reactance.* New York: Academic.

Brehm, S. S., Powell, L. K., & Coke, J. S. (1984). The effects of empathic instructions on donating behavior: Sex differences in young children. *Sex Roles, 10,* 405–416.

Brewer, M. B. (1979). The role of ethnocentrism in intergroup conflict. In W. G. Austin & S. Worchel (Eds.), *The social psychology of intergroup conflict.* Monterey, CA: Brooks/Cole.

Bridgeman, D. (1981). Enhanced role taking through cooperative interdependence: A field study. *Child Development, 52,* 1231–1238.

Brislin, R. W. (1986). A culture general assimilator. *International Journal of Intercultural Relations, 10,* 215–234.

Brislin, R. W., Cushner, K., Cherrie, C., & Yong, M. (1986). *Intercultural interactions: A practical guide.* Beverly Hills, CA: Sage.

Brooks, C. V. W. (1974). *Sensory awareness: The rediscovery of experiencing.* New York: Viking.

Brophy, J. E. (1983). Conceptualizing student motivation. *Educational Psychologist, 18,* 200–215.

Brown, P., & Elliott, R. (1965). Control of aggression in a nursery school class. *Journal of Experimental Child Psychology, 2,* 103–107.

Bruns, C., & Geist, C. S. (1984). Stressful life events and drug use among adolescents. *Journal of Human Stress, 9,* 135–139.

Bryant, B. K., & Crockenberg, S. B. (1974). Cooperative and competitive environments. *Catalogue of Selected Documents in Psychology, 4,* 53.

Buber, M. (1948). *Between man and man.* New York: Macmillan.

Bullmer, K. (1972). Improving accuracy of interpersonal perception through a direct teaching method. *Journal of Counseling Psychology, 19,* 37–41.

Bullmer, K. (1975). *The art of empathy: A manual for improving accuracy of interpersonal perception.* New York: Human Sciences.

Burchard, J. D., & Barrera, F. (1972). An analysis of time out and response cost in a programmed environment. *Journal of Applied Behavior Analysis, 5,* 271–282.

Burglass, M. E., & Duffy, M. G. (1974). *Thresholds: Teacher's manual.* Cambridge, MA: Correctional Solutions Foundation.

Burnham, T. L. (1976). *Personality and time as factors in the training of pre-service teachers in empathy skills.* Unpublished doctoral dissertation, University of Minnesota, Minneapolis.

Burton, R. V. (1963). Generality of honesty reconsidered. *Psychological Review, 70*, 481–499.

Buys, C. J. (1972). Effects of teacher reinforcement on elementary pupils' behavior and attitudes. *Psychology in the Schools, 9*, 278–288.

Calhoun, K. S., & Matherne, P. (1975). The effects of varying schedules of time-out on aggressive behavior of a retarded girl. *Journal of Behavior Therapy and Experimental Psychiatry, 6*, 139–143.

Callantine, M. F., & Warren, J. M. (1955). Learning sets in human concept formation. *Psychological Reports, 1*, 363–367.

Cameron, R., & Meichenbaum, D. (1982). The nature of effective coping and the treatment of stress related problems. In L. Goldberger & S. Breynitz (Eds.), *Handbook of stress.* New York: Free Press.

Camp, B. W. (1977). Verbal mediation in young aggressive boys. *Journal of Abnormal Psychology, 86*, 145–153.

Camp, B. W., & Bash, M. A. (1981). *Think aloud: Increasing social and cognitive skills—A problem-solving program for children (Primary Level).* Champaign, IL: Research Press.

Camp, B. W., & Bash, M. A. (1985). *Think aloud: Increasing social and cognitive skills—A problem-solving program for children (Primary Grades 1–2).* Champaign, IL: Research Press.

Camp, B. W., Blom, G., Hebert, F., & Van Doorninck, W. (1977). Verbal mediation in young aggressive boys. *Journal of Abnormal Psychology, 86*, 145–153.

Campagna, A. F., & Harter, S. (1975). Moral judgment in sociopathic and normal children. *Journal of Personality and Social Psychology, 31*, 199–205.

Campbell, A. (1986). Overview. In A. Campbell & J. J. Gibbs (Eds.), *Violent transactions.* New York: Basil Blackwell.

Cantor, J. H. (1955). Amount of pretraining as a factor in stimulus pre-differentiation and performance set. *Journal of Experimental Psychology, 50*, 180–184.

Cantor, N. J., & Gelfand, D. M. (1977). Effects of responsiveness and sex of children on adult's behavior. *Child Development, 48*, 232–238.

Carkhuff, R. R. (1969a). *Helping and human relations: A primer for lay and professional helpers: Vol. 1. Selection and training.* Amherst, MA: Human Resource Development.

Carkhuff, R. R. (1969b). *Helping and human relations: A primer for lay and professional helpers: Vol. 2. Practice and research.* Amherst, MA: Human Resource Development.

Carlson, K. W. (1974). Increasing verbal empathy as a function of feedback and instruction. *Counselor Education and Supervision, 12*, 208–213.

Carr, E. G. (1981). Contingency management. In A. P. Goldstein, E. G. Carr, W. Davidson, & P. Wehr (Eds.), *In response to aggression.* New York: Pergamon.

Carrington, P. (1978). *Clinically standardized meditation: Instructor's manual.* Kendall Park, NJ: Pace.

Carroll, J. L., & Nelson, E. A. (1979). *Explorations in the evaluation of the moral development of pre-adolescents.* Unpublished manuscript.

Carroll, J. L., & Rest, J. R. (1981). Development in moral judgment as indicated by rejection of lower-stage statements. *Journal of Research in Personality, 15,* 538–544.

Carron, A. V. (1980). *Social psychology of sport.* Ithaca, NY: Mouvement Publications.

Cartledge, G., & Milburn, J. F. (1980). *Teaching social skills to children.* New York: Pergamon.

Cassell, J. C. (1974). Psychosocial processes and stress: Theoretical formulations. *International Journal of Health Services, 4,* 471–482.

Castro, M. A. (1974). Reactions to receiving aid as a function of cost to the donor and opportunity to aid. *Journal of Applied Social Psychology, 4,* 194–209.

Cauce, A. M., Felner, R. D., & Primavera, J. (1982). Social support in high-risk adolescents: Structural components and adaptive impact. *American Journal of Community Psychology, 10,* 417–428.

Chandler, M., Greenspan, S., & Barenboim, C. (1974). Assessment and training of role-taking and referential communication skills in institutionalized emotionally disturbed children. *Developmental Psychology, 10,* 546–553.

Chelladurai, P., & Saleh, S. D. (1978). Preferred leadership in sport. *Canadian Journal of Applied Sport Sciences, 3,* 85–97.

Christophersen, E. R., Arnold, C. M., Hill, D. W., & Quilitch, H. R. (1972). The home point system: Token reinforcement procedures for application by parents of children with behavior problems. *Journal of Applied Behavior Analysis, 5,* 485–497.

Coates, R. B., Miller, A. D., & Ohlin, L. E. (1978). *Diversity in a youth correctional system: Handling delinquents in Massachusetts.* Cambridge, MA: Ballinger.

Coats, K. I. (1979). Cognitive self-instructional training approach for reducing disruptive behavior of young children. *Psychological Reports, 44,* 122–134.

Cobb, S. (1976). Social support as a moderator of life stress. *Psychosomatic Medicine, 38,* 300–314.

Coche, E., & Flick, A. (1975). Problem solving training groups for hospitalized psychiatric patients. *Journal of Psychology, 91,* 19–29.

Coddington, R. D. (1972a). The significance of life events as etiological factors in the diseases of children: A study of a normal population. *Journal of Psychosomatic Research, 16*, 205–213.

Coddington, R. D. (1972b). The significance of life events as etiological factors in the diseases of children: A survey of professional workers. *Journal of Psychosomatic Research, 16*, 7–18.

Coddington, R. D., & Trovell, J. R. (1980). The effect of emotional factors on football injury rates: A pilot study. *Journal of Human Stress, 6*, 3–5.

Cohen, J. (1983). The relationship between friendship selection and peer influence. In J. L. Epstein & N. Karweit (Eds.), *Friends in school*. New York: Academic.

Cohen-Sandler, R., Berman, A. L., & King, R. A. (1982). Life stress and symptomatology: Determinants of suicidal behavior in children. *Journal of the American Academy of Child Psychiatry, 21*, 178–186.

Colby, A., Kohlberg, L., Fenton, E., Speicher-Dubin, B., & Lieberman, M. (1977). Secondary school moral discussion programmes led by social studies teachers. *Journal of Moral Education, 6*, 90–111.

Colby, A., Kohlberg, L., & Gibbs, J. (1979, June). *The longitudinal study of moral judgment*. Paper presented at the meeting of the Society for Research in Child Development, San Francisco.

Collingswood, T. R. (1971). Retention and retraining of interpersonal communication skills. *Journal of Clinical Psychology, 27*, 294–296.

Collins, J. D. (1971). *The effects of the conjugal relationship modification method on marital communication and adjustment*. Unpublished doctoral dissertation, Pennsylvania State University, University Park.

Cominsky, I. (1981). *Transfer of training in counselor education programs: A study of the use of stimulus variability and the provision of general principles to enhance the transfer of the skill of reflection of feeling*. Unpublished doctoral dissertation, Syracuse University, NY.

Compas, B. E., Davis, G. E., Forsythe, C. J., & Wagner, B. M. (1986). *Assessment of major and daily life events during adolescence: The Adolescent Perceived Events Scale*. Unpublished manuscript, Burlington, VT.

Compas, B. E., Slavin, L. A., Wagner, B. M., & Vannatta, K. (1986). Relationship of life events and social support with psychological dysfunction among adolescents. *Journal of Youth and Adolescence, 15*, 205–211.

Conger, J. J., Miller, W. C., & Walsmith, C. R. (1975). Antecedents of delinquency: Personality, social class, and intelligence. In P. H. Mussen, J. J. Conger, & J. Kagan (Eds.), *Readings in child development and personality*. New York: Harper & Row.

Conway, E. S. (1957). *The institutional care of children: A case history*. Unpublished doctoral dissertation, University of London.

Cook, S. W. (1969). Motives in conceptual analysis of attitude-related behavior. In W. J. Arnold & D. Levine (Eds.), *1969 Nebraska Symposium on Motivation*. Lincoln: University of Nebraska Press.

Cooper, J., & Fazio, R. H. (1979). The formation and persistence of attitudes that support intergroup conflict. In W. G. Austin & S. Worchel (Eds.), *The social psychology of intergroup relations*. Monterey CA: Brooks/Cole.

Copeland, A. P. (1981). The relevance of subject variables in cognitive self-instructional programs for impulsive children. *Behavior Therapy, 12,* 520–529.

Copeland, A. P. (1982). Individual difference factors in children's self-management: Toward individualized treatments. In P. Karoly & F. H. Kanfer (Eds.), *Self-management and behavior change: From theory to practice*. New York: Pergamon.

Cordilia, A. T. (1986). Robbery arising out of a group drinking context. In A. Campbell & J. J. Gibbs (Eds.), *Violent transactions*. New York: Basil Blackwell.

Cortese, A. J. (1984). Standard scoring of moral reasoning: A critique. *Merrill-Palmer Quarterly, 30,* 227–246.

Coser, L. A. (1956). *The functions of social conflict*. Glencoe, IL: Free Press.

Coufal, J. D. (1975). *Preventive therapeutic programs for mothers and adolescent daughters: Skill training versus discussion methods*. Unpublished doctoral dissertation, Pennsylvania State University, University Park.

Coutu, W. (1951). Role-playing vs. role-taking: An appeal for clarification. *American Sociological Review, 16,* 180–184.

Covington, M. V., Crutchfield, R. S., & Daves, L. B. (1966). *The productive thinking program*. Berkeley, CA: Brazelton.

Cowen, E. L., Weissberg, R. P., & Guare, J. (1984). Differentiating attributes of children referred to a school mental program. *Journal of Abnormal Child Psychology, 12,* 397–410.

Crafts, L. W. (1935). Transfer as related to number of common elements. *Journal of General Psychology, 13,* 147–158.

Crain, D. (1977). *Awareness and the modification of anger problems*. Unpublished doctoral dissertation, University of California at Los Angeles.

Crawford, R. P. (1950). *How to get ideas*. Lincoln, NE: University Associates.

Crawford, R. P. (1954). *Techniques of creative thinking*. New York: Hawthorn.

Cronbach, L. J., & Snow, R. E. (1969). *Individual differences in learning ability as a function of instructional variables* (Office of Education Final Report). Stanford, CA: Stanford University.

Crutchfield, R. S., & Covington, M. V. (1964). Programmed instruction and creativity. *Programmed Instruction, 4,* 1–10.

Dalton, R., & Sundblad, L. (1976). Using principles of social learning in training for communication of empathy. *Journal of Counseling Psychology, 23,* 454–457.

Damon, W. (1980). Structural-developmental theory and the study of moral development. In M. Windmiller, H. Lambert, & E. Turiel (Eds.), *Moral development and socialization.* Boston: Allyn & Bacon.

Danish, S., & Brodsky, S. L. (1970). Training police in emotional control and awareness. *American Psychologist, 24,* 368–369.

Danish, S., & Hauer, A. (1973). *Helping skills: A basic training program.* New York: Behavioral Publications.

Davis, G. A. (1973). *Psychology of problem solving.* New York: Basic.

Davitz, D. (1964). *The communication of emotional meaning.* New York: McGraw-Hill.

Deacove, J. (1974). *Games manual of non-competitive games.* Perth, Ontario: Family Pastimes.

Deacove, J. (1978). *Sports manual of cooperative recreation.* Perth, Ontario: Family Pastimes.

DeCharms, R. (1968). *Personal causation.* New York: Academic.

Deci, E. L. (1975). *Intrinsic motivation.* New York: Plenum.

Delprato, D. J., & Dekraker, T. (1976). Metronome-conditioned hypnotic-relaxation in the treatment of test anxiety. *Behavior Therapy, 7,* 379–381.

Deluty, R. H. (1979). Children's Action Tendency Scale: A self-report measure of aggressiveness, assertiveness, and submissiveness in children. *Journal of Consulting and Clinical Psychology, 47,* 1068–1071.

Deno, S. L. (1987). Curriculum-based measurement. *Teaching Exceptional Children, 20,* 41–42.

Deshaies, G. (1974). *The effects of group sensitivity training and group didactic-experiential training on the accurate empathy of counselor trainees.* Unpublished doctoral dissertation, Boston University.

Deutsch, M. (1951). Social relations in the classroom and grading procedures. *Journal of Educational Research, 45,* 145–152.

Deutsch, M. (1957). *Conditions affecting cooperation: I. Factors related to the initiation of cooperation. II. Trust and cooperation.* Washington, DC: Office of Naval Research.

Deutsch, M. (1973). *The resolution of conflict.* New Haven, CT: Yale University Press.

Deutsch, M., & Krauss, R. M. (1960). The effect of threat upon interpersonal bargaining. *Journal of Abnormal and Social Psychology, 61,* 181–189.

DeVries, D. L., & Edwards, K. J. (1973). Learning games and student teams: Their effects on classroom processes. *American Educational Research Journal, 10,* 307–318.

DeVries, D. L., & Edwards, K. J. (1974, April). *Cooperation in the classroom: Towards a theory of alternative reward-task classroom structures.* Paper presented at the meeting of the American Educational Research Association, Chicago.

DeVries, D. L., Edwards, K. J., & Slavin, R. E. (1978). Biracial learning teams and race relations in the classroom: Four field experiments on Teams-Games-Tournaments. *Journal of Educational Psychology, 70,* 356–362.

DeVries, D. L., Edwards, K. J., & Wells, E. H. (1974a). *Team competition effects on classroom processes.* Baltimore: Johns Hopkins University, Center for Social Organization of Schools.

DeVries, D. L., Edwards, K. J., & Wells, E. H. (1974b). *Teams-Games-Tournaments in the social studies classroom: Effects on academic achievement, student attitudes, cognitive beliefs, and classroom climate.* Baltimore: Johns Hopkins University, Center for Social Organization of Schools.

DeVries, D. L., Muse, D., & Wells, E. H. (1971). *The effects on students of working in cooperative groups: An exploratory study.* Baltimore: Johns Hopkins University, Center for Social Organization of Schools.

DeVries, D. L., & Slavin, R. E. (1978). Teams-Games-Tournaments (TGT): Review of ten classroom experiments. *Journal of Research and Development in Education, 12,* 28–38.

Dewey, J. (1952). *Democracy and education.* New York: Free Press. (Original work published 1916)

Dewey, J. (1966). *Experience and education.* New York: Collier. (Original work published 1938)

Dickie, J. (1973). *Private speech: The effect of presence of others, task and intrapersonal variables.* Unpublished doctoral dissertation, Michigan State University, East Lansing.

Diener, E. (1976). Effects of prior destructive behavior, anonymity, and group presence on deindividuation and aggression. *Journal of Personality and Social Psychology, 33,* 497–507.

Dion, K. L. (1973). Cohesiveness as a determinant of ingroup-outgroup bias. *Journal of Personality and Social Psychology, 28,* 163–171.

Dodge, K. A., McClasky, C. L., & Feldman, E. (1985). *Scoring system for child role plays.* Unpublished manuscript, Indiana University, Bloomington.

Dodge, K. A., & Murphy, R. R. (1984). The assessment of social competence in adolescents. In P. Karoly & J. J. Steffen (Eds.), *Advances in child behavioral analysis and therapy* (Vol. 4). New York: Plenum.

Douglas, V. I., Parry, P., Marton, P., & Garson, C. (1976). Assessment of a cognitive training program for hyperactive children. *Journal of Abnormal Child Psychology, 4,* 389–410.

Drabman, R. S., & Spitalnik, R. (1973). Social isolation as a punishment procedure: A controlled study. *Journal of Experimental Child Psychology, 16,* 236–249.

Dreikurs, R., Grunwald, B. B., & Pepper, F. C. (1971). *Maintaining sanity in the classroom.* New York: Harper & Row.

Dreikurs, R., Schulman, B. H., & Mosak, H. (1952). Patient-therapist in multiple psychotherapy: Its advantages to the therapist. *Psychiatric Quarterly, 26,* 219–227.

Duncan, C. P. (1953). Transfer in motor learning as a function of degree of first-task learning and inner-task similarity. *Journal of Experimental Psychology, 45,* 1–11.

Duncan, C. P. (1958). Transfer after training with single versus multiple tasks. *Journal of Experimental Psychology, 55,* 63–72.

Durlak, J. A. (1983). Social problem-solving as a primary prevention strategy. In R. D. Felner, L. A. Jason, J. N. Moutsugu, & S. S. Farber (Eds.), *Preventive psychology.* New York: Pergamon.

Dweck, C. S. (1986). Motivational processes affecting learning. *American Psychologist, 41,* 1040–1048.

Dymond, R. F. (1949). A scale for the measurement of empathic ability. *Journal of Consulting Psychology, 13,* 127–133.

D'Zurilla, T. J., & Goldfried, M. R. (1971). Problem solving and behavior modification. *Journal of Abnormal Psychology, 78,* 107–126.

Eccles, J. (1983). Expectancies, values and academic behaviors. In J. T. Spence (Ed.), *Achievement and achievement motives.* San Francisco: W. H. Freeman.

Edelman, E. M., & Goldstein, A. P. (1981). Moral education. In A. P. Goldstein, E. G. Carr, W. S. Davidson, & P. Wehr (Eds.), *In response to aggression.* New York: Pergamon.

Edman, I. (1919). *Human traits and their social significance.* New York: Houghton Mifflin.

Edwards, K. J., & DeVries, D. L. (1974). *The effects of Teams-Games-Tournaments and two structural variations on classroom process, student attitudes, and student achievement.* Baltimore: Johns Hopkins University, Center for Social Organization of Schools.

Egan, G. (1976). *Interpersonal living: A skills/contract approach to human-relations training in groups.* Pacific Grove CA: Brooks/Cole.

Eisenberg, N., & Miller, P. A. (1987). The relation of empathy to prosocial and related behaviors. *Psychological Bulletin, 101,* 91–119.

Eisenberg-Berg, N., & Geisheker, E. (1979). Content of preachings and power of the model/preacher: The effect on children's generosity. *Developmental Psychology, 15,* 168–175.

Ekman, P., & Friesen, W. V. (1975). *Unmasking the face: A guide to recognizing emotions from facial clues.* Englewood Cliffs, NJ: Prentice-Hall.

Ekman, P., Friesen, W. V., & Tomkins, S. S. (1971). Facial Affect Scoring Technique (FAST): A first validity study. *Semiotics, 3,* 37–58.

Elardo, P. T., & Caldwell, B. M. (1979). The effects of an experimental social development program on children in middle childhood period. *Psychology in the Schools, 16,* 93–100.

Elardo, P. T., & Cooper, M. (1977). *AWARE: Activities for social development.* Reading, MA: Addison-Wesley.

Ellis, H. (1965). *The transfer of learning.* New York: Macmillan.

Ellis, R. A., & Lane, W. C. (1978). Structural supports for upward mobility. *American Sociological Review, 53,* 743–756.

Enright, R. D. (1980). An integration of social cognitive development and cognitive processing: Educational applications. *American Educational Research Journal, 17,* 21–41.

Epps, S., Thompson, B. J., & Lane, M. P. (1985). *Procedures for incorporating generalization programming into interventions for behaviorally disordered students.* Unpublished manuscript, Iowa State University, Ames.

Epstein, J. L. (1983). Friends among students in schools: Environmental and developmental factors. In J. L. Epstein & N. Karweit (Eds.), *Friends in school.* New York: Academic.

Epstein, J. L., & Karweit, N. (Eds.). (1983). *Friends in school.* New York: Academic.

Falbo, T. (1977). The multidimensional scaling of power strategies. *Journal of Personality and Social Psychology, 35,* 537–548.

Faust, D., & Arbuthnot, J. (1978). Relationship between moral and Piagetian reasoning and the effectiveness of moral education. *Developmental Psychology, 14,* 435–436.

Fauvre, M. (1979). *The development of empathy through children's literature.* Unpublished doctoral dissertation, University of California at Los Angeles.

Feffer, M. H., & Jahelka, M. (1968). Implications of decentering concept for the structuring of projective content. *Journal of Consulting and Clinical Psychology, 32,* 434–441.

Feindler, E. L. (1979). *Cognitive and behavioral approaches to anger control training in explosive adolescents.* Unpublished doctoral dissertation, West Virginia University, Morgantown.

Feindler, E. L., & Ecton, R. B. (1986). *Adolescent anger control: Cognitive-behavioral techniques.* New York: Pergamon.

Feindler, E. L., & Fremouw, W. J. (1983). Stress inoculation training for adolescent anger problems. In D. Meichenbaum & M. E. Jaremko (Eds.), *Stress reduction and prevention.* New York: Plenum.

Feindler, E. L., Latini, J., Nape, K., Romano, J., & Doyle, J. (1980, November). *Anger reduction methods for child-care workers at a residential delinquent facility.* Paper presented at the meeting of the Association for the Advancement of Behavior Therapy, New York.

Feindler, E. L., Marriott, S. A., & Iwata, M. (1984). Group anger control training for junior high school delinquents. *Cognitive Therapy and Research, 8,* 299–311.

Feldenkrais, M. (1970). *Body and mature behavior.* New York: International Universities Press.

Feldenkrais, M. (1972). *Awareness through movement.* New York: Harper & Row.

Feldenkrais, M. (1981). *The elusive obvious.* Cupertino, CA: Meta.

Fenton, E. (1980). *Leading dilemma discussion: A workshop.* Unpublished manuscript, Carnegie-Mellon University, Pittsburgh.

Ferster, C. B., & DeMeyer, M. K. (1962). A method for the experimental analysis of the behavior of autistic children. *American Journal of Orthopsychiatry, 32,* 89–98.

Ferster, C. B., & Skinner, B. F. (1957). *Schedules of reinforcement.* New York: Appleton-Century-Crofts.

Feshbach, N. D. (1978). Studies of empathic behavior in children. In B. A. Maher (Ed.), *Progress in experimental personality research* (Vol. 8). New York: Academic.

Feshbach, N. D. (1982). Empathy, empathy training and the regulation of aggression in elementary school children. In R. M. Kaplan, V. J. Konecni, & R. Novaco (Eds.), *Aggression in children and youth.* Alphen den Rijn, The Netherlands: Siuthogg/Noordhoff.

Feshbach, S., & Singer, R. P. (1957). The effects of personal and shared threat upon social prejudice. *Journal of Abnormal and Social Psychology, 54,* 411–416.

Festinger, L. (1954). A theory of social comparison processes. *Human Relations, 7,* 117–140.

Fiedler, F. E., Mitchell, T., & Triandis, H. C. (1971). The culture assimilator: An approach to cross-cultural training. *Journal of Applied Psychology, 55,* 95–102.

Fine, J. M. (1980). *The effects of an interviewing skills training program on law students' communication of empathy and respect.* Unpublished doctoral dissertation, Boston University.

Firestone, P. (1976). The effects and side effects of time out on an aggressive nursery school child. *Journal of Behavior Therapy and Experimental Psychiatry, 6,* 79–81.

Fischman, A. (1984). *Evaluation of the effectiveness of structured learning with abusive parents.* Unpublished master's thesis, Syracuse University, NY.

Fischman, A. (1985). *Skill transfer enhancement in structured learning of abusive parents.* Unpublished doctoral dissertation, Syracuse University, NY.

Fisher, J. D., & Nadler, A. (1979). The effect of similarity between donor and recipient on reactions to aid. *Journal of Applied Social Psychology, 4,* 230–243.

Fisher, J. D., Nadler, A., & Whitcher-Alagna, S. (1982). Recipient reactions to aid. *Psychological Bulletin, 91,* 27–54.

Fleetwood, R. S., & Parish, T. S. (1976). Relation between moral development test scores of juvenile delinquents and their inclusion in a moral dilemma discussion group. *Psychological Reports, 39,* 1075–1080.

Fleming, D. (1976). *Teaching negotiation skills to preadolescents.* Unpublished doctoral dissertation, Syracuse University, NY.

Fluegelman, A. (1976). *The new games book.* Garden City, NY: Dolphin.

Fluegelman, A. (1981). *More new games.* Garden City, NY: Dolphin.

Fodor, E. M. (1972). Delinquency and susceptibility to social influence among adolescents as a function of level of moral development. *Journal of Social Psychology, 86,* 257–260.

Foley, L. A. (1976). Personality and situational influences on changes in prejudice. *Journal of Personality and Social Psychology, 34,* 846–856.

Fontana, A., & Dovidio, J. F. (1984). The relationship between stressful life events and school related performances of Type A and Type B adolescents. *Journal of Human Stress, 10,* 50–54.

Ford, D. H., & Urban, H. B. (1963). *Systems of psychotherapy.* New York: Wiley.

Forehand, R., Roberts, M. W., Dolays, D. M., Hobbs, S. A., & Resick, P. A. (1976). An examination of disciplinary procedures with children. *Journal of Experimental Child Psychology, 21,* 109–120.

Forgas, J. P. (1979). *Social episodes: The study of interaction routines.* New York: Academic.

Forgas, J. P. (1985). *Interpersonal behavior.* New York: Pergamon.

Forgas, J. P. (1986). Cognitive representations of aggressive situations. In A. Campbell & J. J. Gibbs (Eds.), *Violent transactions.* New York: Basil Blackwell.

Forgas, J. P., Brown, L. B., & Menyhart, P. (1979). Dimension of aggression: The perception of aggressive episodes. *British Journal of Social and Clinical Psychology, 18,* 17–26.

Forsyth, D. R. (1983). *An introduction to group dynamics.* Monterey, CA: Brooks/Cole.

Foxx, R. M., & Azrin, N. H. (1973). Restitution: A method of eliminating aggressive-disruptive behavior for retarded and brain damaged patients. *Behaviour Research and Therapy, 10,* 15–27.

Fraenkel, J. R. (1976). The Kohlberg bandwagon: Some reservations. *Social Education, 40,* 216–222.

Frank, R. (1973). Rotating leadership in a group therapy setting. *Psychotherapy: Theory, Research and Practice, 10,* 337–338.

Frank, S. J. (1977). *The facilitation of empathy through training in imagination.* Unpublished doctoral dissertation, Yale University, New Haven, CT.

Fraser, J. A. H., & Vitro, F. T. (1975). The effects of empathy training on the empathic response levels and self-concepts of students in a teacher-training program. *Canadian Counselor, 10,* 25–28.

Freedman, B. (1974). *A social-behavioral analysis of skill deficits in delinquent and nondelinquent adolescent boys.* Unpublished doctoral dissertation, Syracuse University, NY.

Freedman, B. J., Rosenthal, L., Donahoe, C. P., Schlundt, D. G., & McFall, R. M. (1978). A social-behavioral analysis of skill deficits in delinquent and nondelinquent adolescent boys. *Journal of Consulting and Clinical Psychology, 46,* 1448–1462.

Freely, H. D. (1977). *Differential effects of Carkhuff model communciations skills training on selected sex-role types.* Unpublished doctoral dissertation, University of Kentucky, Lexington.

French, J. R. P., Jr., & Raven, B. (1959). *The bases of social power.* Ann Arbor, MI: University of Michigan, Institute for Social Research.

Fuchs, L. S. (1987). Program development. *Teaching Exceptional Children, 20,* 42–44.

Gad, M. T., & Johnson, J. H. (1980). Correlates of adolescent life stress as related to race, SES, and levels of perceived social support. *Journal of Clinical Child Psychology, 9,* 13–16.

Gaffney, L. R., & McFall, R. M. (1981). A comparison of social skills in delinquent and nondelinquent adolescent girls using a behavioral role-playing inventory. *Journal of Consulting and Clinical Psychology, 49,* 959–967.

Gagne, R. M., Baker, K. E., & Foster, H. (1950). On the relation between similarity and transfer of training in the learning of discriminative motor tasks. *Psychological Review, 57,* 67–79.

Gagne, R. M., & Foster, H. (1949). Transfer to a motor skill from practice on a pictured representation. *Journal of Experimental Psychology, 39,* 342–354.

Galassi, J. P., & Galassi, M. D. (1984). Promoting transfer and maintenance of counseling outcomes. In S. D. Brown & R. W. Lent (Eds.), *Handbook of counseling psychology*. New York: Wiley.

Galassi, M. D., & Galassi, J. P. (1977). *Assert yourself!* New York: Human Science.

Gambrill, E. D. (1977). *Behavior modification*. San Francisco: Jossey-Bass.

Gantt, S., Billingsley, D., & Giordano, J. A. (1980). Paraprofessional skill: Maintenance of empathic sensitivity after training. *Journal of Consulting Psychology, 27,* 374–379.

Garmezy, N. (1981). Children under stress: Perspectives on antecedents and correlates of vulnerability and resistance to psychopathology. In A. I. Rabin, J. Aranoff, A. M. Barclay, & R. A. Zucker (Eds.), *Further explorations in personality*. New York: Wiley.

Garrison, S. R., & Stolberg, A. L. (1983). Modification of anger in children by affective imagery training. *Journal of Abnormal Child Psychology, 11,* 115–130.

Geary, E. A. (1979). *A construct validity study of "developmental empathy" in counselor skills training programs.* Unpublished doctoral dissertation, Catholic University of America, Washington, DC.

Geffner, R. (1978). *The effects of interdependent learning on self-esteem, inter-ethnic relations, and intra-ethnic attitudes of elementary school children: A field experiment.* Unpublished doctoral dissertation, University of California at Santa Cruz.

Gendlin, E. (1981). *Focusing.* New York: Bantam.

Gendlin, E. (1984). The politics of giving therapy away: Listening and focusing. In D. Larson (Ed.), *Teaching psychological skills.* Monterey, CA: Brooks/ Cole.

Gergen, K. J., Ellsworth, P., Masloch, C., & Seipel, M. (1975). Obligation, donor resources, and reactions to aid in three nations. *Journal of Personality and Social Psychology, 3,* 390–400.

Gerson, R., & Damon, W. (1975, April). *Relations between moral behavior in a hypothetical-verbal context and in a practical, "real-life" setting.* Paper presented at the meeting of the Eastern Psychological Association, New York.

Gibb, C. A. (1969). Leadership. In G. Lindzey & E. Aronson (Eds.), *The handbook of social psychology* (Vol. 4). Reading, MA: Addison-Wesley.

Gibb, J. R. (1961). Defensive level and influence potential in small groups. In L. Petrullo & B. M. Bass (Eds.), *Leadership and interpersonal behavior.* New York: Holt, Rinehart & Winston.

Gibb, J. R. (1973). Defensive communication. In W. G. Bennis, D. E. Berlew, E. H. Schein, & F. I. Steele (Eds.), *Interpersonal dynamics.* Homewood, IL: Dorsey.

Gibbs, J. C. (1988). *Small group sociomoral discussions: Problem situations for use with antisocial adolescents or preadolescents.* Unpublished manuscript, Ohio State University, Columbus.

Gibbs, J. C., Arnold, K. D., Ahlborn, H. H., & Cheesman, F. L. (1984). Facilitation of sociomoral reasoning in delinquents. *Journal of Consulting and Clinical Psychology, 52,* 37–45.

Gibbs, J. C., Widaman, K. F., & Colby, A. (1982). *Social intelligence: Measuring the development of sociomoral reflection.* Englewood Cliffs, NJ: Prentice-Hall.

Gibbs, J. J. (1986). Alcohol consumption, cognition and context: Examining tavern violence. In A. Campbell & J. J. Gibbs (Eds.), *Violent transactions.* New York: Basil Blackwell.

Giebink, J. W., Stover, D. S., & Fahl, M. A. (1968). Teaching adaptive responses to frustration to emotionally disturbed boys. *Journal of Consulting and Clinical Psychology, 32,* 336–368.

Gilstad, R. (1978). *Acquisition and generalization of empathic response through self-administered and leader-directed structured learning training and the interaction between training method and conceptual level.* Unpublished doctoral dissertation, Syracuse University, NY.

Ginsberg, B. G. (1977). Parent-adolescent relationship program. In B. G. Guerney, Jr. (Ed.), *Relationship enhancement: Skill-training programs for therapy, problem prevention, and enrichment.* San Francisco: Jossey-Bass.

Girdano, D., & Everly, G. (1979). *Controlling stress and tension.* Englewood Cliffs, NJ: Prentice-Hall.

Gladstein, G. A. (1977). Is empathy important in counseling? *Personnel and Guidance Journal, 48,* 823–827.

Goldbeck, R. A., Bernstein, B. B., Hellix, W. A., & Marx, M. H. (1957). Application of the half-split technique to problem-solving tasks. *Journal of Experimental Psychology, 53,* 330–338.

Golden, R. (1975). *Teaching resistance-reducing behavior to high school students.* Unpublished doctoral dissertation, Syracuse University, NY.

Goldfried, M. R., & Davison, G. C. (1976). *Clinical behavior therapy.* New York: Holt, Rinehart & Winston.

Goldfried, M. R., & Kent, R. N. (1972). Traditional vs. behavioral personality assessment: A comparison of methodological and theoretical assumptions. *Psychological Bulletin, 77,* 409–420.

Goldfried, M. R., & Trier, C. S. (1974). Effectiveness of relaxation as an active coping skill. *Journal of Abnormal Psychology, 83,* 348–355.

Goldner, B. B. (1962). *The strategy of creative thinking.* Englewood Cliffs, NJ: Prentice-Hall.

Goldstein, A. P. (1971). *Psychotherapeutic attraction.* New York: Pergamon.

Goldstein, A. P. (1973). *Structured learning therapy: Toward a psychotherapy for the poor.* New York: Academic.

Goldstein, A. P. (Ed.). (1978). *Prescriptions for child mental health and education.* New York: Pergamon.

Goldstein, A. P. (1981). *Psychological skill training.* New York: Pergamon.

Goldstein, A. P. (1983). *Prevention and control of aggression.* New York: Pergamon.

Goldstein, A. P., Apter, S. J., & Haroutunian, B. (1984). *School violence.* Englewood Cliffs, NJ: Prentice-Hall.

Goldstein, A. P., Cohen, R., Blake, G., & Walsh, W. (1971). The effects of modeling and social class structuring in paraprofessional psychotherapist training. *Journal of Nervous and Mental Diseases, 153,* 47–56.

Goldstein, A. P., & Glick, B. (1987). *Aggression replacement training: A comprehensive intervention for aggressive youth.* Champaign, IL: Research Press.

Goldstein, A. P., Glick, B., Irwin, M. J., McCartney, C., & Rubama, I. (in press). *Reducing delinquency: Intervention in the community.* Champaign, IL: Research Press.

Goldstein, A. P., Glick, B., Reiner, S., Zimmerman, D., Coultry, T., & Gold, D. (1986). Aggression Replacement Training: A comprehensive intervention for juvenile delinquents. *Journal of Correctional Education, 37,* 120–126.

Goldstein, A. P., & Goedhart, A. (1973). The use of structured learning for empathy-enhancement in paraprofessional psychotherapist training. *Journal of Community Psychology, 1,* 168–173.

Goldstein, A. P., Heller, K., & Sechrest, L. B. (1966). *Psychotherapy and the psychology of behavior change.* New York: Wiley.

Goldstein, A. P., & Kanfer, F. H. (1979). *Maximizing treatment gains.* New York: Academic.

Goldstein, A. P., & Keller, H. (1987). *Aggressive behavior: Assessment and intervention.* New York: Pergamon.

Goldstein, A. P., Keller, H., & Erne, D. (1985). *Changing the abusive parent.* Champaign, IL: Research Press.

Goldstein, A. P., Lopez, M., & Greenleaf, D. M. (1979). Introduction. In A. P. Goldstein & F. H. Kanfer (Eds.), *Maximizing treatment gains.* New York: Academic.

Goldstein, A. P., & Michaels, G. Y. (1985). *Empathy: Development, training and consequences.* Hillsdale, NJ: Erlbaum.

Goldstein, A. P., Monti, P. J., Sardino, T. J., & Green, D. J. (1979). *Police crisis intervention.* New York: Pergamon.

Goldstein, A. P., & Pentz, M. A. (1984). Psychological skill training and the aggressive adolescent. *School Psychology Review, 13,* 311–323.

Goldstein, A. P., & Rosenbaum, A. (1982). *Aggress-less.* Englewood Cliffs, NJ: Prentice-Hall.

Goldstein, A. P., Sherman, M., Gershaw, N. J., Sprafkin, R. P., & Glick, B. (1978). Training aggressive adolescents in prosocial behavior. *Journal of Youth and Adolescence, 7,* 73–92.

Goldstein, A. P., & Simonson, N. (1971). Social psychological approaches to psychotherapy research. In A. E. Bergin & S. L. Garfield (Eds.), *Handbook of psychotherapy and behavior change.* New York: Wiley.

Goldstein, A. P., & Sorcher, M. (1973). Changing managerial behavior by applied learning techniques. *Training and Development Journal,* March, 36–39.

Goldstein, A. P., & Sorcher, M. (1974). *Changing supervisor behavior.* New York: Pergamon.

Goldstein, A. P., Sprafkin, R. P., & Gershaw, N. J. (1976). *Skillstreaming for community living.* New York: Pergamon.

Goldstein, A. P., Sprafkin, R. P., Gershaw, N. J., & Klein, P. (1980). *Skillstreaming the adolescent.* Champaign, IL: Research Press.

Goldstein, A. P., Sprafkin, R. P., Gershaw, N. J., & Klein, P. (1983). Structured learning: A psychoeducational approach for teaching social competencies. *Behavior Disorders, 8,* 161–170.

Goldstein, A. P., & Stein, N. (1976). *Prescriptive psychotherapies.* New York: Pergamon.

Goleman, D. (1977). *The varieties of the meditative experience.* New York: Dutton.

Gonzales, A. (1979, September). *Classroom cooperation and ethnic balance.* Paper presented at the meeting of the American Psychological Association, New York.

Gordon, W. J. (1961). *Synectics.* New York: Collier.

Gordon, W. J. (1971). *The metaphorical way.* Cambridge, MA: Porpoise.

Gottlieb, B. H. (1978). The development and application of a classification scheme of informal helping behaviors. *Canadian Journal of Behavioural Science, 10,* 105–110.

Gottlieb, B. H. (1983). *Social support strategies.* Beverly Hills, CA: Sage.

Graham, J. A., Argyle, M., & Furnham, A. (1981). The goal structure of situations. In A. Furnham & M. Argyle (Eds.), *The psychology of social situations.* New York: Pergamon.

Grant, J. E. (1987). *Problem solving intervention for aggressive adolescent males: A preliminary investigation.* Unpublished doctoral dissertation, Syracuse University, NY.

Graubard, P. S., Rosenberg, H., & Miller, M. B. (1971). Student applications of behavior modification to teachers and environments or ecological approaches to social deviancy. In E. A. Ramp & B. L. Hopkins (Eds.), *A new direction for education: Behavior analysis.* Lawrence, KS: Support and Development Center for Follow Through.

Green, R., & Murray, E. (1973). Instigation to aggression as a function of self-disclosure and threat to self-esteem. *Journal of Consulting and Clinical Psychology, 40,* 440–443.

Green, W. A., Young, L. E., Swisher, S. N., & Miller, G. (1985). Psychological factors and reticuloendothelial disease: Observations on a group of females with lymphomas and leukemias. *Psychosomatic Medicine, 18,* 284–303.

Greenberg, M. S., & Shapiro, S. P. (1971). Indebtedness: An adverse aspect of asking for and receiving help. *Sociometry, 34,* 290–301.

Greene, R. J., Hoffman, M. L., & Plunkett, J. W. (1987, September). *Experimentally induced empathy and its role in reducing aggression.* Paper presented at the meeting of the American Psychological Association, New York.

Greenleaf, D. O. (1978). *The use of structured learning therapy and transfer of training programming with disruptive adolescents in a school setting.* Unpublished master's thesis, Syracuse University, NY.

Greenwood, C. R., Hops, H., Delquadri, J., & Guild, J. (1974). Group contingencies for group consequences in classroom management: A further analysis. *Journal of Applied Behavior Analysis, 7,* 413–425.

Gresham, F. M. (1985). Conceptual issues in the assessment of social competence in children. In P. Strain, M. Guralnick, & H. Walber (Eds.), *Children's social behavior: Development, assessment, and modification.* New York: Academic.

Grim, P. F., Kohlberg, L., & White, S. H. (1968). Some relationships between conscience and attentional processes. *Journal of Personality and Social Psychology, 8,* 239–252.

Grimes, P. (1974). *Teaching moral reasoning to eleven year olds and their mothers: A means of promoting moral growth.* Unpublished doctoral dissertation, Boston University.

Grinder, R. E. (1964). Relations between cognitive dimensions of conscience in middle childhood. *Child Development, 35,* 881–891.

Gross, A. E., & Latane, J. G. (1974). Receiving help, giving help, and interpersonal attraction. *Journal of Applied Social Psychology, 4,* 210–223.

Gruber, R. P. (1971). Behavior therapy: Problems in generalization. *Behavior Therapy, 2,* 361–368.

Guerney, B. G. (1964). Filial therapy: Description and rationale. *Journal of Consulting Psychology, 28,* 304–310.

Guerney, B. G. (1977). *Relationship enhancement: Skill training programs for therapy, problem-prevention, and enrichment.* San Francisco: Jossey-Bass.

Guilford, J. F., & Wilke, M. (1930). A new model for the demonstration of facial expressions. *American Journal of Psychology, 42,* 436–439.

Gulanick, N., & Schmeck, R. R. (1977). Modeling, praise, and criticism in teaching empathic responding. *Counselor Education and Supervision,* June, 284–290.

Gunther, B. (1968). *Sense relaxation below your mind.* New York: Collier.

Guralnick, M. J. (1981). Peer influences on the development of communicative competence. In P. Strain (Ed.), *The utilization of classroom peers as behavior change agents.* New York: Plenum.

Gustafson, K. (1975). *An evaluation of enriching intimacy—A behavioral approach to the training of empathy, respect-warmth, and genuineness.* Unpublished doctoral dissertation, University of Massachusetts, Amherst.

Gustafson, K., & Authier, J. (1976). *Marathon versus weekly enriching intimacy relationship skills training for physician assistants.* Unpublished manuscript, University of Nebraska Medical Center, Omaha.

Guttman, E. S. (1970). Effects of short-term psychiatric treatment for boys in two California Youth Authority institutions. In D. C. Gibbons (Ed.), *Delinquent behavior.* Englewood Cliffs, NJ: Prentice-Hall.

Guzzetta, R. A. (1974). Acquisition and transfer of empathy by the parents of early adolescents through structured learning training. *Journal of Counseling Psychology, 23,* 449–453.

Haan, N. (1975). Hypothetical and actual moral reasoning in situations of civil disobedience. *Journal of Personality and Social Psychology, 32,* 255–270.

Haan, N., Smith, M. B., & Block, T. (1968). The moral reasoning of young adults. *Journal of Personality and Social Psychology, 10,* 183–201.

Hagebak, R. (1979). Disciplinary practices in Dallas. In D. G. Gil (Ed.), *Child abuse and violence.* New York: AMS.

Haley, J. (1976). *Problem solving therapy.* San Francisco: Jossey-Bass.

Hall, R. V., Axelrod, S., Foundopoulos, M., Shellman, J., Campbell, R. A., & Cranston, S. S. (1971). The effective use of punishment to modify behavior in the classroom. *Educational Technology, 11,* 24–26.

Hall, R. V., Lund, D., & Jackson, D. (1968). Effects of teacher attention on study behavior. *Journal of Applied Behavior Analysis, 1,* 1–12.

Hall, R. V., Panyan, M., Rabon, D., & Broden, M. (1968). Instructing beginning teachers in reinforcement procedures which improve classroom control. *Journal of Applied Behavior Analysis, 1,* 315–322.

Halpin, A. W., & Winer, J. B. (1952). *The leadership behavior of the airplane commander.* Columbus: Ohio State University Research Foundation.

Hare, M. A. (1976, March). *Teaching conflict resolution situations.* Paper presented at the meeting of the Eastern Community Association, Philadelphia.

Haroutunian, B. (1986). School violence and vandalism. In S. J. Apter & A. P. Goldstein (Eds.), *Youth violence.* New York: Pergamon.

Harper, N. L., & Askling, L. R. (1980). Group communication and quality of task solution in a media production organization. *Communication Monographs, 47,* 77–100.

Harrell, J., & Guerney, B. G. (1976). Training married couples in conflict negotiation skills. In D. Olson (Ed.), *Treating relationships.* Lake Mills, IA: Graphic.

Harris, S., Mussen, P. H., & Rutherford, E. (1976). Some cognitive, behavioral and personality correlates of maturity of moral development. *Journal of Genetic Psychology, 128,* 123–185.

Harrison, M. (1975). *For the fun of it! Selected cooperative games for children and adults.* Philadelphia: Friend's Peace Committee.

Hartig, M., & Kanfer, F. H. (1973). The role of verbal self-instruction in children's resistance to temptation. *Journal of Personality and Social Psychology, 25,* 259–267.

Hartshorne, H., & May, M. A. (1928). *Studies in the nature of character. Vol. 1. Studies in deceit.* New York: Macmillan.

Hatch, E. J., & Guerney, B. G. (1975). A pupil relationship enhancement program. *Personnel and Guidance Journal, 54,* 103–105.

Hawkins, J. D., & Fraser, M. W. (1983). Social support networks in delinquency prevention and treatment. In J. K. Wittaker & J. Garbarino (Eds.), *Social support networks.* New York: Aldine.

Hawley, R. C., & Hawley, I. L. (1975). *Developing human potential: A handbook of activities for personal and social growth.* Amherst, MA: Educational Research Associates.

Hayes, L. (1979). *A comparison of techniques for teaching empathic responding to counselor-directed hostility.* Unpublished doctoral dissertation, University of Tennessee, Knoxville.

Hayes, S. C., Rincover, A., & Solnick, J. V. (1980). The technical drift of applied behavior analysis. *Journal of Applied Behavior Analysis, 13,* 275–285.

Hayward, M. L., Peters, J. J., & Taylor, J. E. (1952). Some values of the use of multiple therapists in the treatment of psychoses. *Psychiatric Quarterly, 26,* 244–249.

Hazel, J. S., Schumaker, J. B., Sherman, J. A., & Sheldon-Wildgen, J. (1981). *ASSET: A social skills program for adolescents* (Video and Leader's Manual). Champaign, IL: Research Press.

Healy, J. A. (1975). *Training of hospital staff in accurate affective perception of anger from vocal cues in the context of varying social cues.* Unpublished master's thesis, Syracuse University, NY.

Healy, J. A. (1985). *Structured learning therapy and the promotion of the transfer of assertion through the employment of overlearning and stimulus variability.* Unpublished doctoral dissertation, Syracuse University, NY.

Heath, B. L. (1978). *Application of verbal self-instructional training procedures to classroom behavior management.* Unpublished doctoral dissertation, University of Minnesota, Minneapolis.

Heiman, H. (1973). Teaching interpersonal communications. *North Dakota Speech and Theatre Association Bulletin, 2,* 7–29.

Heisel, J. S., Ream, S., Raitz, R., Rappaport, M., & Coddington, R. D. (1973). The significance of life events as contributing factors in the diseases of children. *Behavioral Pediatrics, 83,* 119–123.

Hemphill, J. K., & Coons, A. E. (1957). Development of the Leader Behavior Description Questionnaire. In R. M. Stogdill & A. E. Coons (Eds.), *Leader behavior: Its description and measurement.* Columbus, OH: Ohio State University Press.

Hendrickson, G., & Schroeder, W. H. (1941). Transfer of training in learning to hit a submerged target. *Journal of Educational Psychology, 32,* 205–213.

Hertz-Lazarowitz, R., Sharan, S., & Sapir, C. (1981, April). *Academic and social effects of two cooperative learning methods in a desegregated classroom.* Paper presented at the meeting of the American Educational Research Association, New York.

Hertz-Lazarowitz, R., Sharan, S., & Steinberg, R. (1980). Classroom learning styles and cooperative behavior of elementary school children. *Journal of Educational Psychology, 72,* 99–106.

Higa, W. R. (1973). *Self-instructional versus direct training in modifying children's impulsive behavior.* Unpublished doctoral dissertation, University of Hawaii at Honolulu.

Hill, R. C. (1965). *Freedom's code: The historic American standards of character, conduct, and citizen responsibility.* San Antonio, TX: The Children's Fund.

Hodge, E. A. (1976). *Supervision of empathy training: Programmed vs. individual and peer vs. professional.* Unpublished doctoral dissertation, University of Cincinnati, OH.

Hoffman, M. L. (1970). Moral development. In P. Mussen (Ed.), *Carmichael's manual of child psychology.* New York: Wiley.

Holmes, D. S. (1971). Round robin therapy: A technique for implementing the effects of psychotherapy. *Journal of Consulting and Clinical Psychology, 37,* 324–331.

Holstein, C. B. (1976). Irreversible, stepwise sequence in the development of moral judgment: A longitudinal study of males and females. *Child Development, 47,* 51–61.

Holzworth, W. A. (1964). *Effects of selective reinforcement therapy in a miniature situation in nursery school children.* Unpublished master's thesis, University of Illinois at Urbana.

Homme, L., Csanyi, A. P., Gonzales, M. A., & Rechs, J. R. (1969). *How to use contingency contracting in the classroom.* Champaign, IL: Research Press.

Horney, K. (1939). *New ways in psychoanalyses.* New York: Norton.

Housley W. F., & Magnus, R. E. (1974). Increasing empathy for employment service counselors: A practicum. *Journal of Employment Counseling,* March, 28–31.

Howard, J. A., & Barnett, M. A. (1981). Arousal of empathy and subsequent generosity in young children. *Journal of Genetic Psychology, 138,* 307–308.

Howard, M. S. (1975). *The effectiveness of an action training model in improving the facilitative interpersonal functioning of nursing students with dying patients.* Unpublished doctoral dissertation, University of Maryland, College Park.

Huber, G., Bogatzki, W., & Winter, M. (1982). *Cooperation: Condition and goal of teaching and learning in classrooms.* Unpublished manuscript, University of Tübingen, West Germany.

Hudgins, W., & Prentice, N. M. (1973). Moral judgment in delinquent and nondelinquent adolescents and their mothers. *Journal of Abnormal Psychology, 82,* 145–152.

Hulten, B. H. (1974, April). *Games and teams: An effective combination in the classroom.* Paper presented at the meeting of the American Educational Research Association, Chicago.

Hulten, B. H., & DeVries, D. L. (1976). *Team competition and group practice: Effects on student achievement and attitudes.* Baltimore: Johns Hopkins University, Center for Social Organization of Schools.

Hummel, J. W. (1980). *Teaching preadolescents alternatives to aggression using structured learning training under different stimulus conditions.* Unpublished doctoral dissertation, Syracuse University, NY.

Humphreys, B., Johnson, R., & Johnson, D. W. (1982). Effects of cooperative, competitive, and individualistic learning on students' achievement in science class. *Journal of Research in Science Teaching, 19,* 351–356.

Hundleby, G., & Zingle, H. (1975). Communication of empathy. *Canadian Counselor, 9,* 148–154.

Hunt, D. E. (1971). *Matching models in education: The coordination of teaching methods with student characteristics.* Toronto: Ontario Institute for Studies in Education.

Hunt, D. E., & Sullivan, E. V. (1974). *Between psychology and education.* Hinsdale, IL: Dryden.

Hyman, I. A. (1978). Is the hickory stick out of tune? *Today's Education, 2,* 30–32.

Iannotti, R. J. (1978). Effect of role-taking experiences on role taking, empathy, altruism, and aggression. *Developmental Psychology, 14,* 119–124.

Insel, P. M., & Moos, R. H. (1974). Psychological environments: Expanding the scope of human ecology. *American Psychologist, 29,* 179–188.

Intagliata, J. (1976). *Increasing the responsiveness of alcoholics to group therapy: An interpersonal problem solving approach.* Unpublished doctoral dissertation, State University of New York at Buffalo.

Isquick, M. F. (1978). *Empathy, self-exploration, and attitudes in older people following empathy training.* Unpublished doctoral dissertation, California School of Professional Psychology, San Diego.

Ivey, A. E., & Authier, J. (1971). *Microcounseling.* Springfield, IL: Charles C. Thomas.

Jackson, D. A., Della-Piana, G. M., & Sloane, H. N. (1975). *How to establish a behavior observation system.* Englewood Cliffs, NJ: Educational Technology Publications.

Jacob, T. (1976). Family interaction in disturbed and normal families: A methodological and substantive review. *Psychological Bulletin, 82,* methodological and substantive review. *Psychological Bulletin, 82,* 33–65.

Jacobs, T. J., & Charles, E. (1980). Life events and the occurrence of cancer in children. *Psychosomatic Medicine, 42,* 11–24.

Jacobson, E. (1938). *Progressive relaxation.* Chicago: University of Chicago Press.

Jacovino, J. A. (1980). *The use of cooperatively structured games as a teaching strategy in a secondary school class to increase the group cooperation behaviors of its students.* Unpublished doctoral dissertation, University of Pennsylvania.

Jahoda, M. (1953). The meaning of psychological health. *Social Casework, 34,* 349–354.

Jahoda, M. (1958). *Current concepts of positive mental health.* New York: Basic.

Janaka, C. H. (1977). *Twelve, twenty-four, and thirty-six hours of Carkhuff empathy training with federally incarcerated youth offenders.* Unpublished doctoral dissertation, New Mexico State University, Las Cruces.

Janis, I. L. (1972). *Victims of groupthink.* Boston: Houghton Mifflin.

Janis, I. L. (1979, March). *Preventing groupthink in policy planning groups.* Paper presented at the meeting of the International Society of Political Psychology, Washington, DC.

Janke, R. (1978, April). *The Teams-Games-Tournaments (TGT) method and the behavioral adjustment and academic achievement of emotionally impaired adolescents.* Paper presented at the meeting of the American Educational Research Association, Toronto.

Jenness, A. F. (1932). *Experimental studies of response to social stimulation.* Unpublished doctoral dissertation, Syracuse University, NY.

Jennings, R. L. (1975). *The use of structured learning techniques to teach attraction-enhancing interviewee skills to residentially hospitalized, lower socioeconomic, emotionally disturbed children and adolescents: A psychotherapy analogue investigation.* Unpublished doctoral dissertation, University of Iowa, Iowa City.

Jessor, R. (1981). The perceived environment in psychological theory and research. In D. Magnusson (Ed.), *Toward a psychology of situations: An interactional perspective.* Hillsdale, NJ: Erlbaum.

Johnson, D. W., & Johnson, R. T. (1975). *Learning together and alone.* Englewood Cliffs, NJ: Prentice-Hall.

Johnson, D. W., Johnson, R. T., Johnson, J., & Anderson, D. (1976). Effects of cooperative versus individualized instruction on student prosocial behavior, attitudes toward learning, and achievement. *Journal of Educational Psychology, 68,* 446–452.

Johnson, D. W., Johnson, R. T., & Scott, L. (1978). The effects of cooperative and individualized instruction on student attitudes and achievement. *Journal of Social Psychology, 104,* 207–216.

Johnson, D. W., Maruyama, G., Johnson, R., Nelson, D., & Skon, L. (1981). Effects of cooperative, competitive, and individualistic goal structures on achievement: A meta-analysis. *Psychological Bulletin, 89,* 47–62.

Johnson, J. H. (1986). *Life events as stressors in childhood and adolescence.* Newbury Park, CA: Sage.

Johnson, J. H., & McCutcheon, S. (1980). Assessing events in older children and adolescents: Preliminary findings with the Life Events Checklist. In I. G. Sarason & C. D. Spielberger (Eds.), *Stress and anxiety* (Vol. 7). Washington, DC: Hemisphere.

Jones, F. H., & Miller, W. H. (1974). The effective use of negative attention for reducing group disruption in special elementary school classrooms. *The Psychological Record, 24,* 435–448.

Jones, M. (1953). *The therapeutic community.* New York: Basic.

Jones, S. C., & Panitch, D. (1971). The self-fulfilling prophecy and interpersonal attraction. *Journal of Experimental Social Psychology, 7,* 356–366.

Josephson, L. M. (1979). *The effect of modeling and interpersonal process recall on para-professional trainees.* Unpublished doctoral dissertation, University of Cincinnati, OH.

Judson, S. (1984). *A manual on nonviolence and children.* Philadelphia: New Society.

Kagan, J. (1966). Reflection-impulsivity: The generality and dynamics of conceptual tempo. *Journal of Abnormal Psychology, 71,* 17–24.

Kagan, J. (1972). A conception of early adolescence. In J. Kagan & R. Coles (Eds.), *Twelve to sixteen: Early adolescence.* New York: Norton.

Kagan, N. (1972). *Influencing human interaction.* East Lansing: Michigan State University Press.

Kagan, N., & Schouble, P. G. (1969). Affect simulation in interpersonal process recall. *Journal of Consulting Psychology, 16,* 309–313.

Kagan, S. (1985). Learning to cooperate. In R. Slavin, S. Sharan, S. Kagan, R. Hertz-Lazarowitz, C. Webb, & R. Schmuck (Eds.), *Learning to cooperate, cooperating to learn.* New York: Plenum.

Kagan, S., Zahn, G. L., Widaman, K. F., Schwarzwald, J., & Tyrrell, G. (1985). Classroom structural bias. In R. Slavin, S. Sharan, S. Kagan, R. Hertz-Lazarowitz, C. Webb, & R. Schmuck (Eds.), *Learning to cooperate, cooperating to learn.* New York: Plenum.

Kahn, R. L., & Quinn, R. P. (1977). *Mental health, social support, and metropolitan problems.* Unpublished manuscript, University of Michigan, Ann Arbor.

Kane, J. S., & Lawler, E. E. III. (1978). Methods of peer assessment. *Psychological Bulletin, 85,* 555–586.

Kanfer, F. H., & Gaelick, L. (1986). Self-management methods. In F. H. Kanfer & A. P. Goldstein (Eds.), *Helping people change.* New York: Pergamon.

Kanfer, F. H., & Karoly, P. (1972). Self-control: A behavioristic excursion into the lion's den. *Behavior Therapy, 3,* 398–416.

Karlins, M., & Schroder, H. M. (1967). Discovery learning, creativity and the inductive teaching program. *Psychological Reports, 20,* 867–876.

Karoly, P. (1980). Operant methods. In F. Kanfer & A. P. Goldstein (Eds.), *Helping people change.* New York: Pergamon.

Karoly, P., & Steffen, J. J. (Eds.). (1980). *Improving the long term effects of psychotherapy.* New York: Gardner.

Katz, R., & Tushman, M. (1979). Communication patterns, project performance, and task characteristics. *Organization Behavior and Group Performance, 23,* 139–162.

Katz, R. L. (1963). *Empathy: Its nature and uses.* New York: Free Press.

Kauffman, C., Grunebaum, H., Cohler, B. J., & Gamer, E. (1979). Superkids: Competent children of psychotic mothers. *American Journal of Psychiatry, 136,* 1398–1402.

Kauffman, J. M., Nussen, J. L., & McGee, C. S. (1977). Follow-up in classroom behavior modification: Survey and discussion. *Journal of School Psychology, 15,* 343–348.

Kaufman, H., & Feshbach, S. (1963). The influence of antiaggressive communications upon the response to provocation. *Journal of Personality, 31,* 428–444.

Kaufman, K. F., & O'Leary, K. D. (1972). Reward, cost, and self-evaluation procedures for disruptive adolescents in a psychiatric hospital school. *Journal of Applied Behavior Analysis, 5,* 293–310.

Kazdin, A. E. (1975). *Behavior modification in applied settings.* Homewood, IL: Dorsey.

Kazdin, A. E. (1977). *The token economy.* New York: Plenum.

Kazdin A. E. (1980). *Research design in clinical psychology.* New York: Harper & Row.

Keasey, C. B. (1977). Young children's attribution of intentionality to themselves and others. *Child Development, 48,* 261–264.

Keefe, T. (1976). Empathy: The critical skill. *Social Work, 21,* 10–14.

Keeley, S. M., Shemberg, K. M., & Carbonell, J. (1976). Operant clinical intervention: Behavior management or beyond? Where are the data? *Behavior Therapy, 7,* 292–305.

Keen, S. (1970, October). Sing the body electric. *Psychology Today, pp. 56–61.*

Keenan, R. C. (1976). *An investigation of the effects of four training approaches on the empathic communication skill levels of selected career soldiers and their spouses.* Unpublished doctoral dissertation, American University, Washington, DC.

Keller, H., Goldstein, A. P., & Wynn, R. (1987). *Aggression prevention training.* Unpublished manuscript, Syracuse University, NY.

Keller, J. M. (1978). Motivation and instructional design: A theoretical perspective. *Journal of Instructional Development, 2,* 26–34.

Kelley, H. H., & Thibaut, J. W. (1978). *Interpersonal relations: A theory of interdependence.* New York: Wiley.

Kelly, G. A. (1955). *The psychology of personal constructs.* New York: Norton.

Kendall, P. C. (1977). On the efficacious use of verbal self-instruction procedures with children. *Cognitive Therapy and Research, 1,* 331–341.

Kendall, P. C., & Braswell, L. (1985). *Cognitive-behavioral therapy for impulsive children.* New York: Guilford.

Kieran, S. S. (1979). *The development of a tentative model for analyzing and describing empathic understanding in teachers of young children.* Unpublished doctoral dissertation, Columbia University Teachers College, NY.

Kilpatrick, W. H. (1925). *Foundations of method.* New York: Columbia University Press.

Kipnis, D. (1974). *The powerholders.* Chicago: University of Chicago Press.

Kipnis, D., Castell, P. J., Gergen, M., & Mauch, D. (1976). Metamorphic effects of power. *Journal of Applied Psychology, 61,* 127–135.

Kipnis, D., & Consentino, J. (1969). Use of leadership powers in industry. *Journal of Applied Psychology, 53,* 460–466.

Kipper, D. A., & Ben-Ely, Z. (1979). The effectiveness of the psychodramatic double method, the reflection method, and lecturing in the training of empathy. *Journal of Clinical Psychology, 39,* 370–375.

Kirigin, K. A., Braukmann, C. J., Atwater, J. D., & Wolf, M. M. (1982). An evaluation of teaching family (Achievement Place) group homes for juvenile offenders. *Journal of Applied Behavior Analysis, 15,* 1–16.

Kirschenbaum, D. S., & Ordman, A. M. (1984). Preventive interventions for children: Cognitive behavioral perspectives. In A. W. Meyers & W. E. Craighead (Eds.), *Cognitive behavior therapy for children.* New York: Plenum.

Kirschenbaum, H. (1975). Recent research in values education. In J. R. Meyer, B. Burnham, & J. Chotvat (Eds.), *Values education: Theory, practice, problems, prospects.* Waterloo, Ontario: Wilfrid Laurier University Press.

Kirschner, N. M., & Levin, L. (1975). A direct school intervention program for the modification of aggressive behavior. *Psychology in the Schools, 12,* 202–208.

Klein, S. S. (1971). Student influence on teacher behavior. *Educational Research Journal, 8,* 403–421.

Kleinman, A. (1974). *The use of private speech in young children and its relation to social speech.* Unpublished doctoral dissertation, University of Chicago.

Knudson, K. H. M., & Kagan, S. (1982). Differential development of empathy and prosocial behavior. *Journal of Genetic Psychology, 140,* 249–251.

Koestler, A. (1949). The novelist deals with character. *Saturday Review of Literature, 32,* 7–8.

Kohlberg, L. (1964). Development of moral character and moral ideology. In M. L. Hoffman & L. W. Hoffman (Eds.), *Review of child development research* (Vol. 1). New York: Russell Sage Foundation.

Kohlberg, L. (1969). Stage and sequence: The cognitive-developmental approach to socialization. In D. A. Goslin (Ed.), *Handbook of socialization theory and research.* Chicago: Rand McNally.

Kohlberg L. (1971a). From is to ought: How to commit the naturalistic fallacy and get away with it in the study of moral development. In T. Meschal (Ed.), *Cognitive development and epistemology.* New York: Academic.

Kohlberg, L. (1971b). Stages of moral development as a basis for moral education. In C. M. Beck, B. S. Crittendon, & E. V. Sullivan (Eds.), *Moral education: Interdisciplinary approaches.* Toronto: University of Toronto Press.

Kohlberg, L. (Ed.). (1973). *Collected papers on moral development and moral education.* Cambridge, MA: Harvard University, Center for Moral Education.

Kohlberg, L. (1976). Moral stages and moralization: The cognitive-developmental approach. In T. Lickona (Ed.), *Moral development and behavior: Theory, research and social issues.* New York: Holt, Rinehart & Winston.

Kohlberg, L. (Ed.). (1973). *Collected papers on moral development and moral education.* Cambridge, MA: Harvard University, Center for Moral Education.

Kohlberg, L., & Kramer, R. S. (1969).' Continuities and discontinuities in childhood and adult moral development. *Human Development, 12,* 93–120.

Kohlberg, L., & Turiel, E. (1971). Moral development and moral education. In G. S. Lesser (Ed.), *Psychology and educational practice.* Chicago: Scott, Foresman.

Kopel, S., & Arkowitz, H. (1975). The role of attribution and self-perception in behavior change: Implications for behavior therapy. *Genetic Psychology Monographs, 92,* 175– 212.

Kozma, R. B. (1974, April). *Evaluation of a self-instructional mini-course on empathic responding.* Paper presented at the meeting of the American Educational Research Association, Chicago.

Kramer, R. (1968). *Changes in moral judgment response pattern during late adolescence and young adulthood: Retrogression in a developmental sequence.* Unpublished doctoral dissertation, University of Chicago.

Krebs, D. (1975). Empathy and altruism. *Journal of Personality and Social Psychology, 32,* 1134–1146.

Krebs, R. L. (1967). *Some relationships between attention and resistance to temptation.* Unpublished doctoral dissertation, University of Chicago.

Kuhn, D. (1976). Short-term longitudinal evidence for the sequentiality of Kohlberg's early stages of moral judgment. *Developmental Psychology, 12,* 162–166.

Kurtines, W., & Grief, E. B. (1974). The development of moral thought: Review and evaluation of Kohlberg's approach. *Psychological Bulletin, 81,* 453–470.

Lack, D. Z. (1975). *The effects of problem solving, structured learning and contingency management in training paraprofessional mental health personnel.* Unpublished doctoral dissertation, Syracuse University, NY.

Lambert, M. J., DeJulio, S. S., & Stein, D. M. (1978). Therapist interpersonal skills: Process, outcome, methodological considerations, and recommendations for future research. *Psychological Bulletin, 85,* 467–489.

LaMonica, E.L., Carew, D. K., Winder, A. E., Haase, A. B., & Blanchard, K. H. (1976). Empathy training as the major thrust of a staff development program. *Nursing Research, 25,* 447–451.

Lange, C. (1922). The emotions. In K. Dunlap (Ed.), *The emotions.* Baltimore: Williams & Wilkins. (Original work published 1885, I. Haupt, Trans.)

Larabee, D. H. (1980). *Effects of a modified, theme-centered interactional method on raising empathy in psychiatric nurses and patient care assistants.* Unpublished doctoral dissertation, University of Pittsburgh.

Larcen, S. W., Chinsky, J. M., Allen, G., Lochman, J., & Selinger, H. W. (1974, April). *Training children in social problem solving strategies.* Paper presented at the meeting of the Midwestern Psychological Association, Chicago.

Larcen, S. W., Spivack, G., & Shure, M. (1972, May). *Problem-solving thinking and adjustment among dependent-neglected preadolescents.* Paper presented at the meeting of the Eastern Psychological Association, Boston.

Latane, B., Williams, K., & Harkins, S. (1979). Many hands make light the work: The causes and consequences of social loafing. *Journal of Personality and Social Psychology, 37,* 822–832.

Laughlin, S. G. (1978). *Use of self-instruction in teaching empathic responding to social work students.* Unpublished doctoral dissertation, University of California at Berkeley.

Law, E. J. (1978). *Toward the teaching and measurement of empathy for staff nurses.* Unpublished doctoral dissertation, Brigham Young University, Provo, UT.

Lawler, E. J., & Thompson, M. E. (1979). Subordinate response to a leader's cooptation strategy as a function of type of coalition power. *Representative Research in Social Psychology, 9,* 69–80.

Layton, J. M. (1978). *The use of modeling to teach empathy to nursing students.* Unpublished doctoral dissertation, Michigan State University, East Lansing.

Lazarowitz, R., Baird, H., Bowlden, V., & Hertz-Lazarowitz, R. (1982). *Academic achievements, learning environment, and self-esteem of high school students in biology taught in cooperative-investigative small groups.* Unpublished manuscript, The Technion, Haifa, Israel.

Lazarus, A. A., & Rachman, S. (1967). The use of systematic desensitization in psychotherapy. *South African Medical Journal, 31,* 934–937.

Le Bon, G. (1895). *The crowd.* London: Ernest Benn.

Lee, L. C. (1971). The concomitant development of cognitive and moral modes of thought: A test of selected deductions from Piaget's theory. *Genetic Psychology Monographs, 83,* 93–146.

Lehman, J. D. (1972). *The effects of empathy training involving modeling, feedback, and reinforcement on the ability of high school students to respond emphathically in a tutoring session.* Unpublished doctoral dissertation, University of Tennessee, Knoxville.

Leitenberg, H., Agras, W. S., & Thomson, L. E. (1968). A sequential analysis of the effect of selective positive reinforcement in modifying anorexia nervosa. *Behaviour Research and Therapy, 6,* 211–218.

Leming, J. S. (1978). Intrapersonal variations in stage of moral reasoning among adolescents as a function of situational context. *Journal of Youth and Adolescence, 7,* 405–416.

Lesh, T. V. (1970). Zen meditation and the development of empathy in counselors. *Journal of Humanistic Psychology, 10,* 39–74.

Letourneau, C. (1981). Empathy and stress: How they affect parental aggression. *Journal of Social Work, 26,* 383–389.

Levin, L., & Hoffman, M. L. (1975). Empathy and cooperation in 4-year-olds. *Developmental Psychology, 11,* 533–534.

Lew, M., & Bryant, R. (1981, October). *The use of cooperative groups to improve spelling achievement for all children in the regular classroom.* Paper presented at the meeting of the Massachusetts Council for Exceptional Children, Boston.

Lewin, K. (1935). *A dynamic theory of personality: Selected papers.* New York: McGraw-Hill.

Lewin, K. (1936). *Principles of topological psychology.* New York: McGraw-Hill.

Lewin, K. (1943). Defining the field at a given time. *Psychological Review, 50,* 292–310.

Lewin, K. (1947). Frontiers in group dynamics. *Human Relations, 1,* 5–42.

Lewin, K., Lippit, R., & White, R. (1939). Patterns of aggressive behavior in experimentally created "social climates." *Journal of Social Psychology, 10,* 271–299.

Liberman, B. (1970). *The effect of modeling procedures on attraction and disclosure in a psychotherapy analogue.* Unpublished doctoral dissertation, Syracuse University, NY.

Lichtenberg, J., Bornstein, M., & Silver, D. (1984). *Empathy.* Hillsdale, NJ: Analytic.

Lickona, T. (1976). Critical issues in the study of moral development and behavior. In T. Lickona (Ed.). *Theory, research, and social issues.* New York: Holt, Rinehart & Winston.

Lindskold, S. (1978). Trust development, the GRIT proposal, and the effects of conciliatory acts on conflict and cooperation. *Psychological Bulletin, 85,* 772–793.

Lindskold, S. (1979a). Conciliation with simultaneous or sequential interaction. *Journal of Conflict Resolution, 23,* 704–714.

Lindskold, S. (1979b). Managing conflict through announced conciliatory initiatives backed with retaliatory capacity. In W. G. Austin & S. Worchel (Eds.), *The social psychology of intergroup conflict.* Monterey, CA: Brooks/ Cole.

Linville, P. W., & Jones, E. E. (1980). Polarized appraisals of out-group members. *Journal of Personality and Social Psychology, 38,* 689–703.

Lipps, T. (1907). Das Wissen von Fredmden Ichen. *Psychologischen Untersuchungen, 1,* 694–722.

Little, V. L., & Kendall, P. C. (1979). Cognitive-behavioral interventions with delinquents: Problem solving, role-taking, and self-control. In P. C. Kendall & S. D. Hollan (Eds.), *Cognitive-behavioral interventions.* New York: Academic.

Litwack, S. E. (1976). *The use of the helper therapy principle to increase therapeutic effectiveness and reduce therapeutic resistance: Structured learning therapy with resistant adolescents.* Unpublished doctoral dissertation, Syracuse University, NY.

Loeber, R., & Dishion, T. (1983). Early predictors of male delinquency: A review. *Psychological Bulletin, 94,* 68–99.

Lopez, M. A. (1975). *The influence of vocal and facial cue training on the identification of affect communicated via paralinquistic cues.* Unpublished master's thesis, Syracuse University, NY.

Lopez, M. A. (1977). *The effects of overlearning and prestructuring in structured learning therapy with geriatric patients.* Unpublished doctoral dissertation, Syracuse University, NY.

Lopez, M. A., Hoyer, W. I., Goldstein, A. P., Gershaw, N. J., & Sprafkin, R. P. (1982). Effects of overlearning and incentive on the acquisition and transfer of interpersonal skills with institutionalized elderly. *Journal of Gerontology, 35*(3), 403–408.

Lord, R. G. (1977). Functional leadership behavior: Measurement and relation to social power and leadership perceptions. *Administrative Science Quarterly, 22,* 114–133.

Lorion, R. P., Cowen, E. L., & Caldwell, R. A. (1975). Normative and parametric analyses of school maladjustment. *American Journal of Community Psychology, 3,* 291–301.

Lovaas, O. I., Koegel, R., Simmons, J. Q., & Long, J. S. (1973). Some generalization and follow-up measures on autistic children in behavior therapy. *Journal of Applied Behavior Analysis, 6,* 131–166.

Lovaas, O. I., Schaeffer, B., & Simmons, J. Q. (1965). Building social behavior in autistic children by use of electric shock. *Journal of Experimental Research in Personality, 1,* 99–109.

Lowen, A. (1967). *The betrayal of the body.* New York: Macmillan.

Lowen, A., & Lowen, L. (1977). *The way to vibrant health: A manual of bioenergetic exercises.* New York: Harper & Row.

Lucker, G. W., Rosenfield, D., Sikes, J., & Aronson, E. (1976). Performance in the interdependent classroom: A field study. *American Educational Research Journal, 13,* 115–123.

Luria, A. R. (1961). *The role of speech in the regulation of normal and abnormal behavior.* New York: Liveright.

Luther, E. R. (1971). Treatment of migraine headache by conditioned relaxation: A case study. *Behavior Therapy, 2,* 592–593.

MacGregor, R., Ritchie, A. M., Serrano, A. C., & Schuster, F. P. (1964). *Multiple impact theory with families.* New York: McGraw-Hill.

Madsen, C. J., Becker, W. C., & Thomas, D. R. (1968). Rules, praise, and ignoring: Elements of elementary classroom control. *Journal of Applied Behavior Analysis, 1,* 139–150.

Magnusson, D. (1981). Wanted: A psychology of situations. In D. Magnusson (Ed.), *Toward a psychology of situations: An interactional perspective.* Hillsdale, NJ: Erlbaum.

Magnusson, D. (1982). Situational determinants of stress: An interactional perspective. In L. Goldberger & S. Breznitz (Eds.), *Handbook of stress.* New York: Free Press.

Maher, C. A., & Zinns, J. E. (Eds.). (1987). *Psychoeducational intervention in the schools.* New York: Pergamon.

Mallick, S. K., & McCandless, B. R. (1966). A study of catharsis of aggression. *Journal of Personality and Social Psychology, 4,* 591–596.

Maltzman, I. (1960). On the training of originality. *Psychological Review, 67,* 229–242.

Mandler, G. (1954). Transfer of training as a function of degree of response overlearning. *Journal of Experimental Psychology, 47,* 411–417.

Mandler, G., & Heinemann, S. H. (1956). Effect of overlearning of a verbal response on transfer of training. *Journal of Experimental Psychology, 52,* 39–46.

Marlatt, G. A., & Gordon, J. R. (1980). Determinants of relapse: Implications for maintenance of behavior change. In P. O. Davidson & S. M. Davidson (Eds.), *Behavioral medicine: Changing health lifestyles.* New York: Brunner/Mazel.

Marsh, D. T. (1982). The development of interpersonal problem solving among elementary school children. *Journal of Genetic Psychology, 140,* 107–118.

Martino, L., & Johnson, D. W. (1979). The effects of cooperative vs. individualistic instruction of interaction between normal-progress and learning-disabled students. *Journal of Social Psychology, 107,* 177–183.

Mason, L. J. (1980). *Guide to stress reduction.* Los Angeles: Peace Press.

Matarazzo, J. D., & Wiens, A. N. (1972). *The interview: Research on its anatomy and structure.* Chicago: Aldine.

Matefy, R. E., & Acksen, B. A. (1976). The effect of role-playing discrepant positions on change in moral judgments and attitude. *The Journal of Genetic Psychology, 128,* 189–200.

Matson, J. L., Rotatori, A. F., & Helsel, W. J. (1983). Development of a rating scale to measure social skills in children: The Matson Evaluation of Social Skills with Youngsters (MESSY). *Behaviour Research and Therapy, 21,* 335–340.

Maurer, A. (1974). Corporal punishment. *American Psychologist, 29,* 614–626.

May, J. R., & Johnson, H. J. (1973). Physiological activity to internally elicited arousal and inhibitory thoughts. *Journal of Abnormal Psychology, 82,* 239–245.

McAuliffe, S. E. (1974). *The differential effect of three training models upon the acquisition and transfer of interpersonal communication skills.* Unpublished doctoral dissertation, University of Minnesota, Minneapolis.

McClelland, D. C. (Ed.). (1953). *Studies in motivation.* New York: Appleton-Century-Crofts.

McClelland, D. C. (1975). *Power: The inner experience.* New York: Irvington.

McClelland, D. C., Atkinson, J. W., Clark, R. W., & Lowell, E. L. (1953). *The achievement motive.* New York: Appleton-Century-Crofts.

McClelland, D. C., & Winters, D. G. (1969). *Motivation of economic achievement.* New York: Free Press.

McClure, L. F. (1975). *Social problem-solving training and assessment: An experimental investigation in an elementary school setting.* Unpublished doctoral dissertation, University of Connecticut, Storrs.

McCorkle, L., Elias, A., & Bixby, F. (1958). *The Highfields story: A unique experiment in the treatment of juvenile delinquency.* New York: Holt.

McCullough, J. P., Huntsinger, G. M., & Nay, W. R. (1977). Self-control treatment of aggression in a sixteen year old male. *Journal of Consulting Psychology, 45,* 322–331.

McDougall, W. (1908). *An introduction to social psychology.* London: Methuen.

McGinnis, E., & Goldstein, A. P. (1984). *Skillstreaming the elementary school child: A guide for teaching prosocial skills.* Champaign, IL: Research Press.

McLean, M. M. (1979). *The differential effects of three training programs on attained levels of facilitative conditions: Empathy, warmth and genuineness.* Unpublished doctoral dissertation, University of Toronto.

McNamee, S. (1977). Moral behavior, moral development and motivation. *Journal of Moral Education, 7,* 27–31.

Mead, G. H. (1934). *Mind, self and society.* Chicago: University of Chicago Press.

Mearns, H. (1958). *Creative power: The education of youth in the creative arts.* New York: Dover.

Meichenbaum, D. H. (1977). *Cognitive-behavior modification: An integrative approach.* New York: Plenum.

Meichenbaum, D. H., Gilmore, B., & Fedoravicius, A. (1971). Group insight vs. group desensitization in treating speech anxiety. *Journal of Consulting and Clinical Psychology, 36,* 410–421.

Meichenbaum, D. H., & Goodman, J. (1969). The developmental control by verbal operants. *Journal of Experimental Child Psychology, 7,* 533–565.

Meichenbaum, D. H., & Goodman, J. (1971). Training impulsive children to talk to themselves: A means of developing self-control. *Journal of Abnormal Psychology, 77,* 113–126.

Mesibov, G. B., & LaGreca, A. M. (1981). A social skills instructional module. *The Directive Teacher, 3,* 6–7.

Meyer, R. J., & Haggerty, R. J. (1962). Streptococcal infections in families. *Pediatrics, 29,* 539–549.

Milgram, S. (1965). Some conditions of obedience and disobedience to authority. *Human Relations, 18,* 57–76.

Miller, P. A., & Eisenberg, N. (1988). The relation of empathy to aggressive and externalizing/antisocial behavior. *Psychological Bulletin, 103,* 324–344.

Miller, R. L. (1980). *The impact of training upon the level of affective sensitivity (empathy) in fifth and sixth grade children.* Unpublished doctoral dissertation, Michigan State University, East Lansing.

Miller, T. (1976). The effects of core facilitative conditions in mother on adolescent self-esteem. *Journal of Social Psychology, 100,* 147–148.

Mischel, W. (1968). *Personality and assessment.* New York: Wiley.

Mischel, W., Ebbeson, E., & Zeiss, A. (1973). Selective attention to the self: Situational and dispositional determinants. *Journal of Personality and Social Psychology, 27,* 129–142.

Mitchell, K. M., Bozarth, J. D., & Krauft, C. C. (1977). A reappraisal of the therapeutic effectiveness of accurate empathy, nonpossessive warmth, and genuineness. In A. S. Gurman & A. M. Razin (Eds.), *Effective psychotherapy: A handbook of research.* New York: Pergamon.

Monahan, J., & O'Leary, K. D. (1971). Effects of self-instruction on rule-breaking behavior. *Psychological Reports, 29,* 1059–1066.

Montague, A. (1978). *Learning non-aggression.* New York: Oxford University Press.

Moon, J. R., & Eisler, R. M. (1983). Anger control: An experimental comparison of three behavioral treatments. *Behavior Therapy, 14,* 493–505.

Moore, D. D. (1978). *The relationship of selected familial, personality, and participant characteristics to empathy in middle childhood.* Unpublished doctoral dissertation, University of Maine, Orono.

Moore, J. E. (1980). *Facilitating children's social understanding through cognitive conflict and role playing.* Unpublished doctoral dissertation, University of Toronto.

Moos, R. H. (1968). Situational analysis of a therapeutic community milieu. *Journal of Abnormal Psychology, 73,* 49–61.

Moos, R. H. (1973). Conceptualizations of human environments. *American Psychologist, 28,* 652–665.

Moos, R. H., & Houts, P. S. (1968). Assessment of the social atmospheres of psychiatric wards. *Journal of Abnormal Psychology, 73,* 595–604.

Moreno, J. L. (1960). *The sociometry reader.* Glencoe, IL: Free Press.

Morgan, S. R. (1979). A model of the empathic process for teachers of emotionally disturbed children. *American Journal of Orthopsychiatry, 49,* 446–453.

Morris, R. J. (1976). *Behavior modification with children.* Cambridge, MA: Winthrop.

Morrison, J. L. (1974). *The effects of videotape focused feedback on levels of facilitative conditions.* Unpublished doctoral dissertation, University of North Dakota, Grand Forks.

Morrison, R. L., & Bellack, A. S. (1981). The role of social perception in social skills. *Behavior Therapy, 12,* 69–79.

Mowrer, O. H., & Mowrer, W. A. (1938). Enuresis: A method for its study and treatment. *American Journal of Orthopsychiatry, 8,* 436–447.

Murray, H. A. (1938). *Explorations in personality.* New York: Oxford University Press.

Mussen, P. H. (1963). *The psychological development of the child.* Englewood Cliffs, NJ: Prentice-Hall.

Mussen, P. H., Conger, J. J., Kagan, J., & Gerwitz, J. (1979). *Psychological development: A life span approach.* New York: Harper & Row.

Muuss, R. E. (1960). The relationship between "causal" orientation, anxiety, and insecurity in elementary school children. *Journal of Educational Psychology, 51,* 122–129.

Myers, R. E., & Torrance, E. P. (1965). *Can you imagine?* Boston: Ginn.

Nay, W. R. (1979). Parents as real-life reinforcers: The enhancement of parent-training effects across conditions other than training. In A. P. Goldstein & F. H. Kanfer (Eds.), *Maximizing treatment gains.* New York: Academic.

Neilans, T. H., & Israel, A. C. (1981). Towards maintenance and generalization of behavior change: Teaching children self-regulation and self-instructional skills. *Cognitive Therapy and Research, 5,* 189–195.

Nelson, E. A., Grinder, R. E., & Mutterer, M. L. (1969). Sources of variance in behavioural measures of honesty in temptation situations: Methodological analyses. *Developmental Psychology, 1,* 265–279.

Newsom, C., Favell, J. E., & Rincover, A. (1982). The side effects of punishment. In S. Axelrod & J. Apsche (Eds.), *The effects and side effects of punishment on human behavior.* New York: Academic.

Nisan, M., & Kohlberg, L. (1978). *University and cross-cultural variance in moral development: A longitudinal and cross-sectional study in Turkey.* Unpublished manuscript, Harvard University, Center for Moral Education.

Novaco, R. W. (1975). *Anger control: The development and evaluation of an experimental treatment.* Lexington, MA: Lexington.

Novaco, R. W. (1977). A stress inoculation approach to anger management in the training of law enforcement officers. *American Journal of Community Psychology, 5,* 327–346.

Novaco, R. W. (1978). Anger and coping with stress. In J. Foreyt & D. Rathjen (Eds.), *Cognitive behavior therapy: Therapy, research and practice.* New York: Plenum.

Novaco, R. W. (1979). The cognitive regulation of anger and stress. In P. C. Kendall & S. D. Hollon (Eds.), *Cognitive-behavioral interventions.* Orlando, FL: Academic.

Oden, S. (1980). A child's social isolation: Origins, prevention, intervention. In G. Cartledge & J. F. Milburn (Eds.), *Teaching social skills to children.* New York: Pergamon.

O'Leary, K. D., & Becker, W. C. (1967). Behavior modification of an adjustment class: A token reinforcement program. *Exceptional Children, 33,* 637–642.

O'Leary, K. D., Becker, W. C., Evans, M. B., & Saudargas, R. A. (1969). A token reinforcement program in a public school: A replication and systematic analyses. *Journal of Applied Behavior Analysis, 2,* 3–13.

O'Leary, K. D., Kaufman, K. F., Kass, R. E., & Drabman, R. S. (1970). The effects of loud and soft reprimands on the behavior of disruptive students. *Exceptional Children, 37,* 145–155.

O'Leary, K. D., & O'Leary, S. G. (1980). *Classroom management.* New York: Pergamon.

O'Leary, K. D., O'Leary, S. G., & Becker, W. C. (1967). Modification of a deviant sibling interaction pattern in the home. *Behaviour Research and Therapy, 5,* 113–120.

O'Leary, K. D., & Wilson, G. T. (1975). *Behavior therapy: Applications and outcome.* Englewood Cliffs, NJ: Prentice-Hall.

O'Leary, S. G., & O'Leary, K. D. (1976). Behavior modification in the school. In H. Leitenberg (Ed.), *Handbook of behavior modification and behavior therapy.* Englewood Cliffs, NJ: Prentice-Hall.

Orenstein, R. (1973). *Effect of teaching patients to focus on their feelings on level of experiencing in a subsequent interview.* Unpublished doctoral dissertation, Syracuse University, NY.

Orlick, T. (1978). *The cooperative sports and games book.* New York: Pantheon.

Orlick, T. (1982). *The second cooperative sports and games book.* New York: Pantheon.

Orne, M. T. (1962). On the social psychology of the psychological experiment: With particular reference to demand characteristics and their implications. *American Psychologist, 17,* 776–783.

Osborn, A. F. (1953). *Applied imagination.* New York: Scribner's.

Osgood, C. E. (1949). The similarity paradox in human leaning: A resolution. *Psychological Review, 56,* 132–143.

Osgood, C. E. (1953). *Method and theory in experimental psychology.* New York: Oxford University Press.

Osgood, C. E. (1979). GRIT for MBFR: A proposal for unfreezing force-level postures in Europe. *Peace Research Review, 8,* 77–92.

Oskamp, S., & Hartry, A. (1968). A factor-analytic study of the double standard in attitudes toward U.S. and Russian actions. *Behavioral Science, 13,* 178–188.

Padilla, E. R., Rohsenow, D. J., & Bergman, A. B. (1976). Predicting accident frequency in children. *Pediatrics, 58,* 223–226.

Page, R. A., & Moss, M. K. (1976). Environmental influences on aggression: The effects of darkness and proximity of victim. *Journal of Applied Social Psychology, 6,* 126–133.

Palkes, H., Stewart, M., & Kahana, B. (1968). Porteus Maze performance of hyperactive boys after training in self-directed verbal commands. *Child Development, 39,* 817–826.

Pancoast, D. L. (1980). Finding and enlisting neighbors to support families. In J. Garbarino & S. H. Stocking (Eds.), *Protecting children from abuse and neglect.* San Francisco: Jossey-Bass.

Papanek, V. J. (1969). Tree of life: Bionics. *Journal of Creative Behavior, 3,* 5–15.

Parnes, S. J. (1967a). *Creative behavior guidebook.* New York: Scribner's.

Parnes, S. J. (1967b). *Creative behavior workbook.* New York: Scribner's.

Patterson, G. R. (1965). A learning theory approach to the treatment of the school phobic child. In L. P. Ullmann & L. Krasner (Eds.), *Case studies in behavior modification.* New York: Holt, Rinehart & Winston.

Patterson, G. R. (1974). Interventions for boys with conduct problems: Multiple settings, treatments and criteria. *Journal of Consulting and Clinical Psychology, 42,* 471–481.

Patterson, G. R., & Anderson, D. (1964). Peers as social reinforcers. *Child Development, 35,* 951–960.

Patterson, G. R., & Brodsky, G. A. (1966). A behavior modification program for a child with multiple problem behaviors. *Journal of Child Psychiatry, 7,* 277–295.

Patterson, G. R., Cobb, J. A., & Ray, R. S. (1973). A social engineering technology for retraining the families of aggressive boys. In H. E. Adams & I. P. Unikel (Eds.), *Issues and trends in behavior therapy.* Springfield, IL: Charles C. Thomas.

Patterson, G. R., Ray, R. S., & Shaw, D. (1968). *Direct intervention in families of deviant children.* Unpublished manuscript, University of Oregon, Eugene.

Patterson, G. R., & Reid, J. B. (1973). Reciprocity and coercion: Two facets of social systems. In C. Neurenger & J. Meichael (Eds.), *Behavior modification in clinical psychology.* New York: Appleton-Century-Crofts.

Patterson, G. R., Reid, J. B., Jones, R. R., & Conger, R. E. (1975). *A social learning approach to family intervention* (Vol. 1). Eugene, OR: Castalia.

Pendleton, L. R., & Tasto, D. L. (1976). Effects of metronome-conditioned relaxation, metronome-induced relaxation, and progressive muscle relaxation on insomnia. *Behaviour Research and Therapy, 14,* 165–166.

Pereira, G. J. (1978). *Teaching empathy through skill building versus interpersonal anxiety reduction methods.* Unpublished doctoral dissertation, Catholic University of America, Washington, DC.

Perry, M. A. (1970). *Didactic instructions for and modeling of empathy.* Unpublished doctoral dissertation, Syracuse University, NY.

Perry, M. A. (1975). Modeling and instructions in training for counselor empathy. *Journal of Counseling Psychology, 22,* 173–179.

Perry, M. A., & Furukawa, M. J. (1986). Modeling methods. In F. K. Kanfer & A. P. Goldstein (Eds.), *Helping people change.* New York: Pergamon.

Pesso, A. (1969). *Movement in psychotherapy.* New York: New York University Press.

Peters, R. S. (1978). The place of Kohlberg's theory in moral education. *Journal of Moral Education, 7,* 147–157.

Peterson, P. L., & Janicki, T. C. (1979). Individual characteristics and children's learning in large-group and small-group approaches. *Journal of Educational Psychology, 71,* 677–687.

Pfeiffer, J. W., & Jones, J. E. (1974). *A handbook of structured experiences for human relations training* (Vols. 1–5). La Jolla, CA: University Associates.

640 The Prepare Curriculum

Phillips, E. L. (1956). *Psychotherapy: A modern theory and practice.* Englewood Cliffs, NJ: Prentice-Hall.

Piaget, J. (1932). *The moral judgment of the child.* London: Routledge & Kegan Paul.

Pierce, R., Carkhuff, R. R., & Berenson, B. G. (1967). The differential effects of high and low functioning counselors upon counselors-in-training. *Journal of Clinical Psychology, 23,* 212–215.

Pines, M. (1979, January). Superkids. *Psychology Today, pp. 53–63.*

Pinkston, E. M., Reese, N. M., LeBlanc, J. M., & Baer, D. M. (1973). Independent control of a preschool child's aggression and peer interaction by contingent teacher attention. *Journal of Applied Behavior Analysis, 6,* 115–124.

Plas, J. M. (1987). *Systems psychology in the schools.* New York: Pergamon.

Platt, J. J., Scura, W. C., & Hannon, J. R. (1973). Problem-solving thinking of youthful incarcerated heroin addicts. *Journal of Community Psychology, 1,* 278–281.

Platt, J. J., & Spivack, G. (1973, September). *Studies in problem-solving thinking of psychiatric patients.* Paper presented at the meeting of the American Psychological Association, Montreal.

Platt, J. J., & Spivack, G. (1975). *Manual for the means-ends problem-solving procedure.* Philadelphia: Hahnemann Community Mental Health Center.

Platt, J. J., & Spivack, G. (1977). *Workbook for training in interpersonal problem-solving thinking.* Philadelphia: Hahnemann Community Mental Health Center.

Platt, J. J., Spivack, G., Altman, N., Altman, D., & Peizer, S. B. (1974). Adolescent problem-solving thinking. *Journal of Consulting and Clinical Psychology, 42,* 787–793.

Prentice-Dunn, S., & Rogers, R. W. (1980). Effects of deindividuating situation cues and aggressive models on subjective deindividuation and aggression. *Journal of Personality and Social Psychology, 39,* 104–113.

Pressley, M. (1979). Increasing children's self-control through cognitive interventions. *Review of Educational Research, 49,* 319–370.

Preston, J. C., & Guerney, B. G. (1982). *Relationship enhancement skill training.* Unpublished manuscript, Pennsylvania State University, University Park.

Price, R. H., & Bouffard, D. L. (1974). Behavioral appropriateness and situational constraint as dimensions of social behavior. *Journal of Personality and Social Psychology, 30,* 579–586.

Prince, G. M. (1970). *The practice of creativity.* New York: Collier.

Pringle, M. L. K., & Bossio, V. (1960). Early prolonged separation and emotional adjustment. *Journal of Child Psychology and Psychiatry, 1,* 37–48.

Pruden, C. W. (1976). *The effects of role playing and trainee feedback in the development of selected facilitative skills.* Unpublished doctoral dissertation, University of Cincinnati, OH.

Raleigh, R. (1977). *Individual vs. group structured learning therapy for assertiveness training with senior and junior high school students.* Unpublished doctoral dissertation, Syracuse University, NY.

Rank, O. (1945). *Will therapy.* New York: Knopf.

Raths, L. E., Harmin, M., & Simon, S. B. (1966). *Values and teaching: Working with values in the classroom.* Columbus, OH: Charles E. Merrill.

Raush, H. L. (1965). Interaction sequences. *Journal of Personality and Social Psychology, 2,* 487–499.

Raush, H. L. (1972). Process and change. *Family Processes, 11,* 275–298.

Redl, F., & Wineman, D. (1957). *The aggressive child.* Glencoe, IL: Free Press.

Reed, N. H. (1981). *Psychopathic delinquency, empathy, and helping behavior.* Unpublished doctoral dissertation, Loyola University of Chicago.

Reich, W. (1949). *Character analysis.* New York: Farrar, Straus & Giroux. (Original work published 1933)

Reid, J. B., & Patterson, G. R. (1976). The modification of aggression and stealing behavior of boys in the home setting. In E. Ribes-Inesta & A. Bandura (Eds.), *Analysis of delinquency and aggression.* Hillsdale, NJ: Erlbaum.

Reik, T. (1949). *Listening with the third ear.* New York: Farrar, Straus & Giroux.

Reiner, S. (1985). *Interpersonal maturity level as a measure of differential responsiveness to Aggression Replacement Training.* Unpublished master's thesis, Syracuse University, NY.

Reissman, F. (1965). The helper therapy principle. *Social Work, 10,* 27–32.

Rest, J. R. (1979). *Development in judging moral issues.* Minneapolis: University of Minnesota Press.

Rest, J. R., Turiel, E., & Kohlberg, L. (1969). Level of moral development as a determinant of preference and comprehension of moral judgments made by others. *Journal of Personality, 37,* 225–252.

Relfalvy-Fodor, M. V. (1976). *Effects of supervisory style on the learning of empathy for trainees with high/low levels of dogmatism.* Unpublished doctoral dissertation, West Virginia University, Morgantown.

Richardson, F. C., & Tasto, D. L. (1976). Development and factor analysis of a social anxiety inventory. *Behavior Therapy, 7,* 453–462.

Rickards, T. (1974). *Problem solving through creative analysis.* Essex, England: Power Press.

Rimm, D. C., & Litvak, S. B. (1969). Self-verbalization and emotional arousal. *Journal of Abnormal Psychology, 74,* 181–187.

Risley, T. R. (1977). The social context of self-control. In R. Stuart (Ed.), *Behavioral self management*. New York: Brunner/Mazel.

Robin, A. L., Armel, S., & O'Leary, K. D. (1975). The effects of self-instruction on writing deficiencies. *Behavior Therapy, 6,* 178–187.

Robinson, R. (1973). *Evaluation of a structured learning empathy training program for lower socio-economic status home-aide trainees.* Unpublished master's thesis, Syracuse University, NY.

Rocks, T. G., Baker, S. B., & Guerney, B. G. (1982). *Effects of counselor-directed relationship enhancement training on underachieving, poorly communicating students and their teachers.* Unpublished manuscript, Pennsylvania State University, University Park.

Roff, M., Sell, S., & Golden, M. (1972). *Social adjustment and personality development in children.* Minneapolis: University of Minnesota Press.

Rogers, C. R. (1951). *Client-centered therapy: Its current practice, implications, and theory.* Boston: Houghton Mifflin.

Rogers, C. R. (1957). The necessary and sufficient conditions of therapeutic personality change. *Journal of Consulting Psychology, 21,* 95–103.

Rogers, C. R. (1983). *Freedom to learn.* Columbus, OH: Charles E. Merrill.

Rolf, I. (1977). *Rolfing: The integration of human structures.* Boulder, CO: The Rolf Institute.

Ronnestad, M. H. (1977). The effects of modeling, feedback, and experiential methods on counselor empathy. *Counselor Education and Supervision,* March, 194–201.

Rook, K. S., & Dooley, D. (1985). Applying social support research: Theoretical problems and future directions. *Journal of Social Issues, 41,* 5–28.

Rose, S. D. (1977). *Group therapy: A behavioral approach.* Englewood Cliffs, NJ: Prentice-Hall.

Rosen, J. (1978). *The efficacy of modeling and instructional techniques for counselor acquisition of non-verbal empathy skills.* Unpublished doctoral dissertation, Indiana University, Bloomington.

Rosenkoetter, L. D., Landman, S., & Mazak, S. G. (1980). Use of moral discussion as an intervention with delinquents. *Psychological Reports, 16,* 91–94.

Rosenthal, R., & DePaulo, B. M. (1979). Sex differences in accomodation in nonverbal communication. In R. Rosenthal (Ed.), *Skill in nonverbal communication.* Cambridge, England: Oelgeschlager, Gunn & Hain.

Rosenthal, R., Hall, J. A., DiMatteo, M. R., Rogers, P. L., & Archer, D. (1979). *Sensitivity to nonverbal communication: The PONS test.* Baltimore: Johns Hopkins University Press.

Ross, D. M., & Ross, S. A. (1973). Cognitive training for the EMR child: Situational problem solving and planning. *American Journal of Mental Deficiency, 78,* 20–26.

Rothman, G. R. (1980). The relationship between moral judgment and moral behavior. In M. Windmiller, N. Lambert, & E. Turiel (Eds.), *Moral development and socialization.* Boston: Allyn & Bacon.

Rotter, J. B. (1954). *Social learning and clinical psychology.* Englewood Cliffs, NJ: Prentice-Hall.

Rubin, K. H., & Krasnor, L. R. (1986). Social cognitive and social behavioral perspectives in problem solving. In M. Perlmutter (Ed.), *The Minnesota Symposium on Child Psychology: Vol. 18. Cognitive perspectives on children's social and behavioral development.* Hillsdale, NJ: Erlbaum.

Ruma, E. H., & Mosher, D. L. (1967). Relationship between moral judgment and guilt in delinquent boys. *Journal of Abnormal Psychology, 72,* 122–127.

Rundle, L. (1977). *The stimulation of moral development in the elementary school and the cognitive examination of social experience: A fifth grade study.* Unpublished doctoral dissertation, Boston University.

Russell, P. L., & Brandsma, J. M. (1974). A theoretical and empirical integration of the rational-emotive and classical conditioning theories. *Journal of Consulting and Clinical Psychology, 42,* 389–397.

Russell, R. K., & Sipich, J. F. (1974). Treatment of test anxiety by cue-controlled relaxation. *Behavior Therapy, 5,* 673–676.

Rutter, M., & Giller, H. (1984). *Juvenile delinquency: Trends and perspectives.* New York: Guilford.

Rutter, M., Quinton, D., & Liddle, C. (1983). Parenting in two generations: Looking backwards and looking forwards. In N. Madge (Ed.), *Families at risk.* London: Heinemann.

Ryan, A. H., & Kahn, A. (1970). Own-group bias: The effects of individual competence on group outcome. *Proceedings of the Iowa Academy of Science, 77,* 302–307.

Ryan, F. L., & Wheeler, R. (1977). The effects of cooperative and competitive background experiences of students on the play of a simulation game. *Journal of Educational Research, 70,* 295–299.

Rynders, J., Johnson, R., Johnson, D. W., & Schmidt, B. (1980). Producing positive interaction among Downs Syndrome and nonhandicapped teenagers through cooperative goal structuring. *American Journal of Mental Deficiency, 85,* 268–273.

Safer, D. J., & Allen, R. P. (1976). *Hyperactive children: Diagnosis and management.* Baltimore: University Park.

Sajwaj, T., Culver, P., Hall, C., & Lehr, L. (1972). Three simple punishment techniques for the control of classroom disruptions. In G. Semb (Ed.), *Behavior analysis and education.* Lawrence, KS: University of Kansas Press.

Saltmarsh, R. E. (1973). Development of empathic interview skills through programmed instruction. *Journal of Counseling Psychology, 20,* 375–377.

Saltzstein, H. D., Diamond, R. M., & Belenky, M. (1972). Moral judgment level and conformity behavior. *Developmental Psychology, 7,* 327–336.

Sampson, R. V. (1965). *Equality and power.* London: Heinemann.

Sandler, I. N. (1980). Social support resources, stress and the maladjustment of poor children. *American Journal of Community Psychology, 8,* 41–52.

Sapon-Shevin, M. (1986). Teaching cooperation. In G. Cartledge & J. F. Milburn (Eds.), *Teaching social skills to children.* New York: Pergamon.

Sarason, I. G. (1968). Verbal learning, modeling, and juvenile delinquency. *American Psychologist, 23,* 254–266.

Sarason, I. G., Glaser, E. M., & Fargo, G. A. (1972). *Reinforcing productive classroom behavior.* New York: Behavioral Publications.

Schachter, S. (1959). *The psychology of affiliation.* Stanford, CA: Stanford University Press.

Schachter, S., Ellertson, N., McBride, D., & Gregory, D. (1951). An experimental study of cohesiveness and productivity. *Human Relations, 4,* 229–238.

Schlichter, K. J., & Horan, J. J. (1981). Effects of stress inoculation on the anger and aggression management skills of institutionalized juvenile delinquents. *Cognitive Therapy and Research, 5,* 359–365.

Schmidlin, S. S. (1977). *Moral judgment and delinquency: The effect of institutionalization and peer pressure.* Unpublished doctoral dissertation, University of Florida, Gainesville.

Schmuck, R. (1985). Learning to cooperate, cooperating to learn: Basic concepts. In R. Slavin, S. Sharan, S. Kagan, R. Hertz-Lazarowitz, C. Webb, & R. Schmuck (Eds.), *Learning to cooperate, cooperating to learn.* New York: Plenum.

Schneiman, R. (1972). *An evaluation of structured learning and didactic learning as methods of training behavior modification skills to lower and middle socioeconomic level teacher-aides.* Unpublished doctoral dissertation, Syracuse University, NY.

Schofield, J. W. (1980). Cooperation as social exchange. Resource gaps and reciprocity in academic work. In S. Sharan, P. Hare, C. D. Webb, & R. Hertz-Lazarowitz (Eds.), *Cooperation in education.* Provo, UT: Brigham Young University Press.

Schrader, C., Long, J., Panzer, C., Gillet, D., & Kornbath, R. (1977, November). *An anger control package for adolescent drug abusers.* Paper presented at the meeting of the Association for the Advancement of Behavior Therapy, Atlanta.

Schutz, W. C. (1967). *FIRO.* New York: Holt, Rinehart & Winston.

Schwartz, G. E. (1971). Cardiac responses to self-induced thoughts. *Psychophysiology, 8,* 462–467.

Schwartz, S., & Johnson, J. H. (1985). *Psychopathology of childhood: A clinical-experimental approach.* New York: Pergamon.

Schwartz, S. H., Feldman, K. A., Brown, M. E., & Heingartner, A. (1969). Some personality correlates of conduct in two situations of moral conflict. *Journal of Personality, 37,* 41–57.

Schwitzgebel, R. (1964). *Street corner research: An experimental approach to the juvenile delinquent.* Cambridge: MA: Harvard University Press.

Selman, R. L. (1980). *The growth of interpersonal understanding: Developmental and clinical analyses.* New York: Academic.

Selman, R. L. (1982). *Peer relations interview.* Unpublished manuscript, Harvard University, Cambridge, MA.

Sewell, E., McCoy, J. F., & Sewell, W. R. (1973). Modification of antagonistic social behavior using positive reinforcement for other behavior. *The Psychological Record, 23,* 499–504.

Sharan, S., Raviv, S., & Russell, P. L. (1982). *Cooperative and traditional classroom learning and the cooperative behavior of seventh-grade pupils in mixed-ethnic classrooms.* Unpublished manuscript, University of Tel-Aviv, Israel.

Sharon, S., & Sharon, Y. (1976). *Small-group teaching.* Englewood Cliffs, NJ: Educational Technology.

Shaw, L. W. (1978). *A study of empathy training effectiveness: Comparing computer assisted instruction, structured learning training, and encounter training exercises.* Unpublished doctoral dissertation, Syracuse University, NY.

Shaw, M. E. (1964). Communication networks. In L. Berkowitz (Ed.), *Advances in experimental social psychology* (Vol. 1). New York: Academic.

Shaw, M. E. (1981). *Group dynamics: The psychology of small group behavior.* New York: McGraw-Hill.

Sherif, M., Harvey, O. J., White, B. J., Hood, W. R., & Sherif, C. W. (1961). *Intergroup conflict and cooperation: The Robbers Cave Experiment.* Norman, OK: Institute of Group Relations.

Sherif, M., & Sherif, C. W. (1953). *Groups in harmony and tension.* New York: Harper & Row.

Sherman, A. R. (1979). In vivo therapies for phobic reactions, instrumental behavior problems, and interpersonal communication problems. In A. P. Goldstein & F. H. Kanfer (Eds.), *Maximizing treatment gains.* New York: Academic.

Sherman, A. R., & Levine, M. P. (1979). In vivo therapies for compulsive habits, sexual difficulties, and severe adjustment problems. In A. P. Goldstein & F. H. Kanfer (Eds.), *Maximizing treatment gains.* New York: Academic.

Sherman, A. R., & Plummer, I. L. (1973). Training in relaxation as a behavioral self-management skill. *Behavior Therapy, 4,* 543–550.

Sherman, J. A. (1965). Use of reinforcement and imitation to reinstate verbal behavior in mute psychotics. *Journal of Abnormal Psychology, 70,* 155–164.

Sherman, T. M., & Cormier, W. H. (1974). An investigation of the influence of student behavior on teacher behavior. *Journal of Applied Behavior Analysis, 7,* 11–21.

Shore, E., & Sechrest, L. (1961). Concept attainment as a function of number of positive instances presented. *Journal of Educational Psychology, 52,* 303–307.

Shoubsmith, G. (1968). *Assessment through interviewing.* New York: Pergamon.

Shure, M. B., Newman, S., & Silver, S. (1973, May). *Problem-solving thinking among adjusted, impulsive and inhibited Head Start children.* Paper presented at the meeting of the Eastern Psychological Association, Washington, DC.

Shure, M. B., & Spivack, G. (1970). *Problem-solving capacity, social class and adjustment among nursery school children.* Paper presented at the meeting of the Eastern Psychological Association, Atlantic City.

Shure, M. B., & Spivack, G. (1972). Means-ends thinking, adjustment and social class among elementary school-aged children. *Journal of Consulting and Clinical Psychology, 38,* 348–353.

Shure, M. B., & Spivack, G. (1978). *Problem-solving techniques in childrearing.* San Francisco: Jossey-Bass.

Shure, M. B., Spivack, G., & Powell, L. (1972, May). *A problem-solving intervention program for disadvantaged preschool children.* Paper presented at the meeting of the Eastern Psychological Association, Boston.

Siegel, J. M., & Spivack, G. (1973). *Problem-solving therapy* (Research Rep. No. 23). Philadelphia: Hahnemann Medical College.

Simon, S. B., & Olds, S. W. (1976). *Helping your child learn right from wrong: A guide to values clarification.* New York: McGraw-Hill.

Simon, S. B., Howe, L. W., & Kirschenbaum, H. (1972). *Values clarification: A handbook of practical strategies for teachers and students.* New York: Dodd.

Simpson, E. L. (1974). Moral development research: A case of scientific cultural bias. *Human Development, 17,* 81–106.

Singer, J. E., Brush, C. A., & Lublin, S. C. (1965). Some aspects of deindividuation: Identification and conformity. *Journal of Experimental Social Psychology, 1,* 356–378.

Skinner, B. F. (1938). *The behavior of organisms: An experimental analysis.* New York: Appleton-Century-Crofts.

Skinner, B. F. (1953). *Science and human behavior.* New York: Macmillan.

Slavin, D. R. (1967). *Response transfer of conditional affective responses as a function of an experimental analogue of rotational psychotherapy.* Unpublished doctoral dissertation, Northwestern University, Chicago.

Slavin, R. E. (1977). *Student learning team techniques: Narrowing the achievement gap between the races.* Baltimore, MD: Johns Hopkins University, Center for Social Organization of Schools.

Slavin, R. E. (1978). Student teams and achievement divisions. *Journal of Research and Development in Education, 12,* 39–49.

Slavin, R. E. (1980). *Using student team learning* (rev. ed.). Baltimore, MD: Johns Hopkins University, Center for Social Organization of Schools.

Slavin, R. E. (1983a). *Cooperative learning.* New York: Longman.

Slavin, R. E. (1983b). When does cooperative learning increase student achievement? *Psychological Bulletin, 94,* 429–445.

Slavin, R. E. (1985). An introduction to cooperative learning research. In R. Slavin, S. Sharan, S. Kagan, R. Hertz-Lazarowitz, C. Webb, & R. Schmuck (Eds.), *Learning to cooperate, cooperating to learn.* New York: Plenum.

Slavin, R. E., Leavey, M., & Madden, N. A. (1982, April). *Effects of student teams and individualized instruction on student mathematics achievement, attitudes, and behaviors.* Paper presented at the meeting of the American Educational Research Association, New York.

Slavin, R. E., & Oickle, E. (1981). Effects of cooperative learning teams on student achievement and race relations: Treatment by race interactions. *Sociology of Education, 54,* 174–180.

Slavson, S. R. (1964). *A textbook in analytic group psychotherapy.* New York: International Universities Press.

Smart, R. (1965). Social group membership, leadership, and birth order. *Journal of Social Psychology, 67,* 221–225.

Smith, H. C. (1966). *Sensitivity to people.* New York: McGraw-Hill.

Smith, H. C. (1973). *Sensitivity training.* New York: McGraw-Hill.

Smith, J. C. (1985). *Relaxation dynamics: Nine world approaches to self-relaxation.* Champaign, IL: Research Press.

Snarey, J. R. (1985). Cross-cultural universality of social-moral development: A critical review of Kohlbergian research. *Psychological Bulletin, 97,* 202–232.

Snyder, J. J., & White, M. J. (1979). The use of cognitive self-instructions in treatment of behaviorally disturbed adolescents. *Behavior Therapy, 10,* 227–235.

Sobel, J. (1983). *Everybody wins: Noncompetitive games for young children.* New York: Walker.

Solomon, E. (1977). *Structured learning therapy with abusive parents: Training in self-control.* Unpublished doctoral dissertation, Syracuse University, NY.

Spadone, A. L. (1974). *An investigation of rated levels of accurate empathy as a function of training method.* Unpublished doctoral dissertation, University of Southern California, Los Angeles.

Spatz-Norton, C. (1985). *The effect of self-statements and structured learning training of empathy upon aggressive behavior and pro-social conflict resolution in aggressive elementary school aged males.* Unpublished master's thesis, Syracuse University, NY.

Spence, S. H. (1981). Differences in social skills performance between institutionalized juvenile male offenders and a comparable group of boys without offense records. *British Journal of Clinical Psychology, 20,* 163–171.

Spielberger, C. D. (1976). *Manual for the State-Trait Anxiety Inventory for Children.* Palo Alto, CA: Consulting Psychologist Press.

Spilerman, S. (1971). Raising academic motivation in lower class adolescents: A convergence of two research traditions. *Sociology of Education, 44,* 103–118.

Spivack, G., & Levine, M. (1973). *Self-regulation in acting-out and normal adolescents* (Report No. M-4531). Washington, DC: National Institute of Mental Health.

Spivack, G., Platt, J. J., & Shure, M. B. (1976). *The problem-solving approach to adjustment.* San Francisco: Jossey-Bass.

Spivack, G., & Shure, M. B. (1974). *Social adjustment of young children.* San Francisco: Jossey-Bass.

Spivack, G., & Shure, M. B. (1975, June). *Maternal childrearing and the interpersonal cognitive problem-solving ability of four-year-olds.* Paper presented at the meeting of the Society for Research in Child Development, Denver.

Stanley, S. (1976). *A curriculum to affect the moral atmosphere of the family and the moral development of adolescents.* Unpublished doctoral dissertation, Boston University.

Staub, E. (1979). *Positive social behavior and morality: Vol. 2. Socialization and development.* New York: Academic.

Steen, P. L., & Zuriff, G. E. (1977). The use of relaxation in the treatment of self-injurious behavior. *Journal of Behavior Therapy and Experimental Psychiatry, 8,* 447–448.

Stein, M., & Davis, J. K. (1982). *Therapies for adolescents: Current treatment for problem behaviors.* San Francisco: Jossey-Bass.

Stein, M. I. (1974). *Stimulating creativity.* New York: Academic.

Steiner, C., Wyckoff, H., Marcus, J., Lariviere, P., Goldstine, D., & Schwebel, R. (1975). *Readings in radical psychiatry.* New York: Grove.

Steiner, I. D. (1972). *Group process and productivity.* New York: Academic.

Steiner, I. D. (1976). Task-performing groups. In J. W. Thibaut, J. T. Spence, & R. C. Carson (Eds.), *Contemporary topics in social psychology.* Morristown, NJ: General Learning.

Stephens, T. M. (1976). *Directive teaching of children with learning and behavioral handicaps.* Columbus, OH: Merrill.

Sterling, S., Cowen, E. L., Weissberg, R. P., Lotyczewski, B. S., & Boike, M. (1985). Recent stressful life events and young children's school adjustment. *American Journal of Community Psychology, 13,* 87–99.

Stokes, T. F., & Baer, D. M. (1977). An implicit technology of generalization. *Journal of Applied Behavior Analysis, 10,* 349–367.

Stokes, T. F., Fowler, S. A., & Baer, D. M. (1978). Training preschool children to recruit natural communities of reinforcement. *Journal of Applied Behavior Analysis, 11,* 285–303.

Stone, G. L., Hinds, W. C., & Schmidt, G. W. (1975). Teaching mental health behaviors to elementary school children. *Professional Psychology, 6,* 36–40.

Stover, L., & Guerney, B. G. (1967). Efficacy of training procedures for mothers in filial therapy. *Psychotherapy: Theory, Research and Practice, 4,* 110–115.

Stoyva, J., & Anderson, C. (1982). A coping-rest model of relaxation and stress management. In L. Goldberger & S. Breznitz (Eds.), *Handbook of stress.* New York: Free Press.

Strain, P. (Ed.). (1981). *The utilization of classroom peers as behavior change agents.* New York: Plenum.

Stratton, T. T., & Moore, C. (1977). Application of the robust factor concept to the fear survey schedule. *Journal of Behavior Therapy and Experimental Psychology, 8,* 229–235.

Straughan, J. (1968). The application of operant conditioning to the treatment of elective mutism. In H. M. Sloane, Jr. & B. A. MacAulay (Eds.), *Operant procedures in remedial speech and language training.* Boston: Houghton Mifflin.

Straughan, R. R. (1975). Hypothetical moral situations. *Journal of Moral Education, 4,* 183–189.

Strickland, L. H. (1958). Surveillance and trust. *Journal of Personality, 26,* 206–215.

Strunk, O., & Reed, K. (1960). The learning of empathy: A pilot study. *Journal of Pastoral Care, 14,* 44–48.

Stuart, R. B. (1967). Decentration in the development of children's concepts of moral and causal judgment. *The Journal of Genetic Psychology, 111,* 59–68.

Sturm, D. (1980). *Therapist aggression tolerance and dependence tolerance under standardized conditions of hostility and dependency.* Unpublished master's thesis, Syracuse University, NY.

Suchman, J. R. (1961). Inquiry training: Building skills for autonomous discovery. *Merrill-Palmer Quarterly, 7,* 147–170.

Suchotliff, L. (1970). Relation of formal thought disorder to the communication deficit of schizophrenics. *Journal of Abnormal Psychology, 76,* 250–257.

Sullivan, E. V. (1980). Can values be taught? In M. Windmiller, N. Lambert, & E. Turiel (Eds.), *Moral development and socialization.* Boston: Allyn & Bacon.

Sullivan, E. V., & Beck, C. M. (1975). Moral education in a Canadian setting. *Phi Delta Kappan, 56,* 697–701.

Sullivan, H. S. (1953). *Conceptions of modern psychiatry.* New York: Norton.

Sulzer-Azaroff, B., & Mayer, G. R. (1977). *Applying behavior analysis procedures with children and youth.* New York: Holt, Rinehart & Winston.

Sutton, K. (1970). *Effects of modeled empathy and structured social class upon level of therapist displayed empathy.* Unpublished master's thesis, Syracuse University, NY.

Sutton-Simon, K. (1973). *The effects of two types of modeling and rehearsal procedures upon the adequacy of social behavior of hospitalized schizophrenics.* Unpublished doctoral dissertation, Syracuse University, NY.

Swanstrom, C. R. (1974). *An examination of structured learning therapy and the helper therapy principle in teaching a self-control strategy in school children with conduct problems.* Unpublished doctoral dissertation, Syracuse University, NY.

Synectics, Inc. (1968). *Making it strange: Teacher's manual.* New York: Harper.

Taylor, C. B., Farquhar, J. W., Nelson, E., & Agras, S. (1977). Relaxation therapy and high blood pressure. *Archives of General Psychiatry, 34,* 339–342.

Taylor, R. H. (1975). *A comparison of conceptual and behavioral formats for interpersonal training.* Unpublished doctoral dissertation, University of California at Los Angeles.

Tharp, R. G., & Wetzel, R. J. (1969). *Behavior modification in the natural environment.* New York: Academic.

Thibaut, J. W., & Kelley, H. H. (1959). *The social psychology of groups.* New York: Wiley.

Thomas, J. D., Presland, I. E., Grant, M. D., & Glynn, T. L. (1978). Natural rates of teacher approval and disapproval in grade-7 classrooms. *Journal of Applied Behavior Analysis, 11,* 91–94.

Thorndike, E. L., & Woodworth, R. S. (1901). The influence of improvement in one mental function upon the efficiency of other functions. *Psychological Review, 8,* 247–261.

Tindal, G. (1987). Graphic performance. *Teaching Exceptional Children, 20,* 44–46.

Toi, M., & Batson, C. D. (1982). More evidence that empathy is a source of altruistic motivation. *Journal of Personality and Social Psychology, 43,* 281–292.

Torrance, E. P. (1975). *Rewarding creative behavior.* Englewood Cliffs, NJ: Prentice-Hall.

Tracy, J. J., & Cross, H. J. (1973). Antecedents of shift in moral judgment. *Journal of Personality and Social Psychology, 26,* 238–244.

Trevitt, V. (1964). *The American heritage: Design for national character.* Santa Barbara, CA: McNally & Loftin.

Trief, P. (1977). *The reduction of egocentrism in acting-out adolescents by structured learning therapy.* Unpublished doctoral dissertation, Syracuse University, NY.

Trower, P. (1979). Fundamentals of interpersonal behavior: A social-psychological perspective. In A. S. Bellack & M. Hersen (Eds.), *Research and practice in social skills training.* New York: Plenum.

Trower, P., Bryant, B., & Argyle, M. (1978). *Social skills and mental health.* London: Methuen.

Truax, C. B. (1966). Some implications of behavior therapy for psychotherapy. *Journal of Counseling Psychology, 13,* 160–170.

Truax, C. B., & Carkhuff, R. R. (1967). *Toward effective counseling and psychotherapy: Training and practice.* Chicago: Aldine.

Truax, C. B., Carkhuff, R. R., & Douds, J. (1964). Toward an integration of the didactic and experiential approaches to training in counseling and psychotherapy. *Journal of Counseling Psychology, 11,* 240–247.

Truax, C. B., & Tatum, C. D. (1966). An extension from the effective psychotherapeutic model to constructive personality change in preschool children. *Childhood Education, 42,* 456–462.

Truax, C. B., Wargo, D. G., & Silber, L. D. (1966). Effects of group psychotherapy with high accurate empathy and nonpossessive warmth upon female institutionalized deliquents. *Journal of Abnormal Psychology, 71,* 267–274.

Tucker, J. A. (1985). Curriculum-based assessment: An introduction. *Exceptional Children, 52,* 199–204.

Tuckman, B. W. (1965). Developmental sequences in small groups. *Psychological Bulletin, 63,* 384–399.

Tuckman, B. W., & Jensen, M. A. (1977). Stages of small group development revisited. *Group and Organization, 2,* 419–427.

Turiel, E. (1966). An experimental test of the sequentiality of developmental stages in the child's moral judgments. *Journal of Personality and Social Psychology, 3,* 611–618.

Turiel, E. (1974). Conflict and transition in adolescent moral development. *Child Development, 45,* 14–29.

Turiel, E. (1980). The development of social-conventional and moral concepts. In M. Windmiller, N. Lambert, & E. Turiel (Eds.), *Moral development and socialization.* Boston: Allyn & Bacon.

Turiel, E., Edwards, C. P., & Kohlberg, L. (1977). *Moral development in Turkish children, adolescents, and young adults.* Cambridge, MA: Harvard University, Center for Moral Development.

Turiel, E., & Rothman, G. (1972). The influence of moral reasoning on behavior choices at different stages of moral development. *Child Development, 43,* 741–756.

Turk, D. (1976). *An expanded skills training approach for the treatment of experimentally induced pain.* Unpublished doctoral dissertation, University of Waterloo, Ontario.

Turner, R. H., & Killian, L. M. (1972). *Collective behavior.* Englewood Cliffs, NJ: Prentice-Hall.

Ugurel-Semin, R. (1952). Moral behavior and moral judgment of children. *Journal of Abnormal and Social Psychology, 47,* 463–475.

Uhlemann, M. R., Lea, G. W., & Stone, G. L. (1976). Effect of instructions and modeling on trainees low in interpersonal-communication skills. *Journal of Counseling Psychology, 23,* 509–513.

Ulmer, G. (1939). Teaching geometry to cultivate reflective thinking: An experimental study with 1,239 high school pupils. *Journal of Experimental Education, 8,* 18–25.

Underwood, B. J. (1951). Associative transfer in verbal learning as a function of response similarity and degree of first-list learning. *Journal of Experimental Psychology, 42,* 44–53.

Underwood, B. J., & Schultz, R. W. (1960). *Meaningfulness and verbal behavior.* New York: Lippincott.

Urbain, E. S., & Kendall, P. C. (1981). *Interpersonal problem-solving, social perspective-taking and behavioral contingencies: A comparison of group approaches with impulsive-aggressive children.* Unpublished manuscript, University of Minnesota, Minneapolis.

Van Houten, R. (1982). Punishment: From the animal laboratory to the applied setting. In S. Axelrod & J. Apsche (Eds.), *The effects and side effects of punishment on human behavior.* New York: Academic.

Vaux, A., & Ruggiero, M. (1983). Stressful life change and delinquent behavior. *American Journal of Community Psychology, 11,* 169–183.

Vogelsong, E. L. (1974). *Empathy training for preadolescents in public schools.* Unpublished manuscript, Pennsylvania State University, University Park.

Vogelsong, E. L. (1975). *Preventive therapeutic programs for mothers and adolescent daughters: A follow-up of relationship enhancement versus discussion and booster versus no-booster methods.* Unpublished doctoral dissertation, Pennsylvania State University, University Park.

Von Fange, E. K. (1959). *Professional creativity.* Englewood Cliffs, NJ: Prentice-Hall.

Vorrath, H., & Brendtro, L. K. (1974). *Positive peer culture.* Chicago: Aldine.

Vroom, V. H., & Yetton, P. W. (1973). *Leadership and decision making.* Pittsburgh: University of Pittsburgh Press.

Vukelich, R., & Hake, D. F. (1971). Reduction of dangerously aggressive behavior in a severely retarded resident through a combination of positive reinforcement procedures. *Journal of Applied Behavior Analysis, 4,* 215–225.

Vygotsky, L. S. (1962). *Thought and language.* Cambridge, MA: Massachusetts Institute of Technology Press.

Wagner, B. R., Breitmeyer, R. G., & Bottum, G. (1975). Administrative problem solving and the mental health professional. *Professional Psychology, 6,* 55–60.

Wagner, H. M. (1969). *A measurement of instructors' and students' perception of empathy, warmth, and genuineness in the instructors compared with the students' final examination scores.* Unpublished doctoral dissertation, University of Arkansas at Little Rock.

Wahler, R. G., & Pollio, H. R. (1968). Behavior and insight: A case study in behavior therapy. *Journal of Experimental Research in Personality, 3,* 45–56.

Wahler, R. G., Winkel, G. H., Peterson, R. F., & Morrison, D. C. (1965). Mothers as behavior therapists for their own children. *Behaviour Research and Therapy, 3,* 113–124.

Walker, H. M. (1979). *The acting-out child: Coping with classroom disruption.* Boston: Allyn & Bacon.

Walker, H. M., Hops, H., & Fiegenbaum, E. (1976). Deviant classroom behavior as a function of combinations of social and token reinforcement and cost contingency. *Behavior Therapy, 7,* 76–88.

Walker, H. M., Hops, H., & Johnson, S. M. (1975). Generalization and maintenance of classroom treatment effects. *Behavior Therapy, 6,* 188–200.

Walker, H. M., Mattson, R. H., & Buckley, N. K. (1971). The function analysis of behavior within an experimental classroom setting. In W. C. Becker (Ed.), *An empirical basis for change in education.* Chicago: Science Research Associates.

Walker, H. M., Street, A., Garrett, B., & Crossen, J. (1977). *Experiments with response cost in playground and classroom settings.* Eugene, OR: University of Oregon, Center for Research in the Behavioral Education of the Handicapped.

Ward, M. H., & Baker, B. L. (1968). Reinforcement therapy in the classroom. *Journal of Applied Behavior Analysis, 1,* 323–328.

Warner, G., & Lance, J. W. (1975). Relaxation therapy in migraine and chronic tension headache. *Medical Journal of Australia, 1,* 298–301.

Wasik, B., Senn, K., Welsh, R. H., & Cooper, B. R. (1968). Behavior modification with culturally deprived school children: Two case studies. *Journal of Applied Behavior Analysis, 2,* 171–179.

Watson, J. B., & Rayner, R. (1920). Conditioned emotional reactions. *Journal of Experimental Psychology, 3,* 1–114.

Webster, R. E. (1976). A time-out procedure in a public school setting. *Psychology in the Schools, 13,* 72–76.

Webster's Encyclopedic Dictionary of the English Language. (1973). Chicago: Consolidated.

Weigel, R. H., Wiser, P. L., & Cook, S. W. (1975). Impact of cooperative learning experiences on cross-ethnic relations and attitudes. *Journal of Social Issues, 31,* 219–245.

Weiner, G. (1974). A theory of motivation for some classroom experiences. *Journal of Educational Psychology, 71,* 3–25.

Weinreich, R. J. (1975). *Inducing reflective thinking in impulsive, emotionally disturbed children.* Unpublished master's thesis, Virginia Commonwealth University, Richmond.

Weinstein, E. A. (1969). The development of interpersonal competence. In D. A. Goslin (Ed.), *Handbook of socialization theory and research.* Chicago: Rand McNally.

Weinstein, M., & Goodman, J. (1980). *Playfair: Everybody's guide to noncompetitive play.* San Luis Obispo, CA: Impact.

Weiss, R. L., Hops, H., & Patterson, G. P. (1973). A framework for conceptualizing marital conflict: A technology for altering it, some data for evaluating it. In L. A. Hamerlynch, L. C. Handy, & E. J. Mash (Eds.), *Behavior change: Methodology, concepts, and practice.* Champaign, IL: Research Press.

Weissberg, M. (1975). Anxiety-inhibiting statements and relaxation combined in two cases of speech anxiety. *Journal of Behavior Therapy and Experimental Psychiatry, 6,* 163–154.

Weissberg, R. P., Gesten, E., Carnrike, C., Toro, P., Rapkin, B., Davidson, E., & Cowen, E. L. (1981). Social problem solving training: A competence building intervention with second- to fourth-grade children. *American Journal of Community Psychology, 9,* 411–423.

Welsh, R. S. (1978). Delinquency, corporal punishment and the schools. *Crime & Delinquency,* July, 336–354.

Wentink, E. (1975, July). *The effect of social perspective-taking training on role-taking ability and social interaction in preschool and elementary school children.* Paper presented at the meeting of the International Society for the Study of Behavioral Development, Guildford, Great Britain.

Werner, E. E., & Smith, R. S. (1982). *Vulnerable but invincible.* New York: McGraw-Hill.

Wesson, C. L. (1987). Increasing efficiency. *Teaching Exceptional Children, 20,* 46–47.

Wheeler, R. C., & Ryan, F. L. (1973). Effects of cooperative and competitive classroom environments on the attitudes and achievement of elementary school students engaged in social studies inquiry activities. *Journal of Educational Psychology, 65,* 402–407.

Whitaker, C. A., Malone, T. P., & Warkentin, J. (1966). Multiple therapy and psychotherapy. In F. Fromm-Reichmann & M. Morens (Eds.), *Progress in psychotherapy.* New York: Grune & Stratton.

White, G. D., Nielson, G., & Johnson, S. M. (1972). Time out duration and the suppression of deviant behavior in children. *Journal of Applied Behavior Analysis, 5,* 111–120.

White, M. A. (1975). Natural rates of teacher approval and disapproval in the classroom. *Journal of Applied Behavior Analysis, 8,* 367–372.

White, R. K. (1970). *Nobody wanted war: Misperception in Vietnam and other wars.* New York: Doubleday.

White, R. K. (1977). Misperception in the Arab-Israeli conflict. *Journal of Social Issues, 33,* 190–221.

White, R. K., & Lippitt, R. (1968). Leader behavior and member reaction in three "social climates." In D. Cartwright & A. Zander (Eds.), *Group dynamics: Research and theory.* New York: Harper & Row.

Whitehill, M. B., Hersen, M., & Bellack, A. S. (1978). *A conversation skills training program for socially isolated children.* Unpublished manuscript, University of Pittsburgh.

Whiteman, P. H., & Kosier, K. P. (1964). Development of children's moralistic judgments: Age, sex, I.Q. and certain personal-experiential variables. *Child Development, 35,* 843–850.

Whiting, C. S. (1958). *Creative thinking.* New York: Reinhold.

Whitman, T., Mercurio, J., & Caponigri, V. (1970). Development of social responses in two severely retarded children. *Journal of Applied Behavior Analysis, 3,* 133–138.

Wieman, R. J. (1973). *Conjugal relationship modification and reciprocal reinforcement: A comparison of treatments for marital discord.* Unpublished doctoral dissertation, Pennsylvania State University, University Park.

Williams, D. Y., & Akamatsu, T. J. (1978). Cognitive self-guidance training with juvenile delinquents. *Cognitive Therapy and Research, 2,* 285–288.

Williams, F. E. (1972). *A total creativity program for individualizing and humanizing the learning process.* Englewood Cliffs, NJ: Educational Technology Publications.

Wilson, E. O. (1975). *Sociobiology: The new synthesis.* Cambridge, MA: Belknap.

Wilson, J. (1973). *The assessment of morality.* Windsor, England: National Foundation of Educational Research.

Wilson, W., & Miller, N. (1961). Shifts in evaluations of participants following intergroup competition. *Journal of Abnormal and Social Psychology, 63,* 428–431.

Wolf, M., Risley, T., & Mees, H. (1964). Application of operant conditioning procedures to the behavior problems of an autistic child. *Behaviour Research and Therapy, 1,* 305–312.

Wolkind, S. (1971). *Children in care: A psychiatric study.* Unpublished M.D. thesis, University of London.

Wolpe, J. (1958). *Psychotherapy by reciprocal inhibition.* Stanford, CA: Stanford University Press.

Wright, W. E., & Dixon, M. C. (1977). Community prevention and treatment of juvenile delinquency: A review of evaluation studies. *Journal of Research in Crime and Delinquency, 14,* 35–67.

Young, R. K., & Underwood, B. J. (1954). Transfer in verbal materials with dissimilar stimuli and response similarity varied. *Journal of Experimental Psychology, 47,* 153–159.

Zander, A., Cohen, A. R., & Stotland, E. (1959). Power and relations among the professions. In D. Cartwright (Ed.), *Studies in social power.* Ann Arbor, MI: University of Michigan, Institute for Social Research.

Ziegler, S. (1981). The effectiveness of cooperative learning teams for increasing cross-ethnic friendship: Additional evidence. *Human Organization, 40,* 264–268.

Zillman, D., Bryant, J., Cantor, J. R., & Day, K. D. (1975). Irrelevance of mitigating circumstances in retaliatory behavior at high levels of excitation. *Journal of Research in Personality, 9,* 282–293.

Zimbardo, P. G. (1969). The human choice. In W. J. Arnold & D. Levine (Eds.), *1969 Nebraska Symposium on Motivation.* Lincoln: University of Nebraska Press.

Zimmerman, D. (1983). Moral education. In A. P. Goldstein (Ed.), *Prevention and control of aggression.* New York: Pergamon.

Zimmerman, D. (1986). *The enhancement of perspective-taking and moral reasoning via structured learning therapy and moral education.* Unpublished doctoral dissertation, Syracuse University, NY.

Zwicky, F. (1957). *Morphological astronomy.* Berlin: Springer-Verlag.

Zwicky, F. (1969). *Discovery, invention, research: Through the morphological approach.* New York: Macmillan.

Author Index

Subject Index

About the Author

Arnold P. Goldstein, Ph.D. (Pennsylvania State University, 1959), joined the clinical psychology section of Syracuse University's Psychology Department in 1963 and both taught there and directed its Psychotherapy Center until 1980. In 1981, he founded the Center for Research on Aggression, which he currently directs. He joined Syracuse University's Division of Special Education in 1985. Professor Goldstein has a career-long interest, as both researcher and practitioner, in difficult-to-reach clients. Since 1980, his main research and psychoeducational focus has been incarcerated juvenile offenders and child-abusing parents. He is the developer of Structured Learning, a psychoeducational program and curriculum designed to teach prosocial behaviors to chronically anti-social persons. Professor Goldstein's books include *Structured Learning Therapy: Toward a Psychotherapy for the Poor; Skill Training for Community Living; Skillstreaming the Adolescent; School Violence; Aggress-Less; Police Crisis Intervention; Hostage; Prevention and Control of Aggression; Aggression in Global Perspective; In Response to Aggression; Youth Violence; Aggression Replacement Training;* and *Aggressive Behavior: Assessment and Intervention.*